S0-ATV-942

THE PAPERS

of

JOHN C. CALHOUN

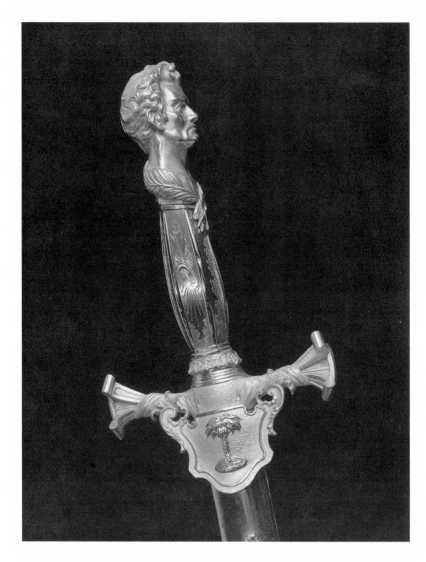

One of a number of ceremonial swords bearing Calhoun's likeness that were presented by the State of South Carolina to its citizens who were officers in the war with Mexico. (Bee Sword. Courtesy of South Carolina State Museum.)

THE PAPERS

of

JOHN C. CALHOUN

Volume XXV, 1847–1848

Edited by

Clyde N. Wilson

and Shirley Bright Cook

Alexander Moore, *Associate Editor*

University of South Carolina Press, 1999

Copyright © 1999 by the
University of South Carolina

*Publication of this book was made possible
by a grant from the National Historical Publications
and Records Commission.*

*International Standard Book Number: 1–57003–306–4
Library of Congress Catalog Card Number: 59–10351*

Manufactured in the United States of America

*This book is printed on acid-free paper that meets the ANSI/NISO
specifications for permanence as revised in 1992.*

CONTENTS

◫

PREFACE

॥

This volume coincides exactly with the first session of the 30th Congress of the Union and brings Calhoun within about seventeen months of the end of his life.

The collection of documents has been made as complete as many years of effort could secure. Jeffrey Rogers assisted in the preparation of the volume. Indispensable support has been provided by the National Historical Publications and Records Commission and the University South Caroliniana Society.

CLYDE N. WILSON

Columbia, February 1998

INTRODUCTION

◫

Calhoun has three primary concerns in 1848: the infatuation of some of his countrymen with war and imperial conquest; the evils of the noisy and aggressive but principleless party system; and the apparent determination of the Northern majority to deny the South the benefits of the Union and reduce it to a beleaguered and exploited minority.

For him all of these issues were but results of one fundamental problem—a people who had forgotten the virtues of their fathers that were necessary for the preservation of republican institutions. He told the Senate in arguing against escalation of the war against Mexico:

> The maxim of former times was, that power is always stealing from the many to the few; the price of liberty was perpetual vigilance. They were constantly looking out and watching for danger. Then, when any great question came up, the first inquiry was, how it could affect our free institutions—how it could affect our liberty. Not so now. Is it because there has been any decay of the spirit of liberty among the people? Not at all. I believe the love of liberty was never more ardent, but they have forgotten the tenure of liberty by which alone it is preserved.
>
> We think we may now indulge in everything with impunity, as if we held our charter of liberty by "right divine"—from Heaven itself. Under these impressions, we plunge into war, we contract heavy debts, we increase the patronage of the Executive, and we even talk of a crusade to force our institutions, our liberty, upon all people. There is no species of extravagance which our people imagine will endanger their liberty in any degree. But it is a great and fatal mistake.[1]

In the same vein, he wrote his daughter:

> Our people have undergone a great change. Their inclination is for conquest & empire, regardless of their institutions & liberty; or rather, they think they hold their liberty by a devine tenure, which no imprudence, or folly on their part, can defeat.[2]

[1] Speech on the War with Mexico (First Report), January 4, 1848, herein.
[2] To Anna Maria Calhoun Clemson, December 26, 1847, herein.

ix

Against Empire

Calhoun devoted his efforts during the early part of the 1848 Congressional session to combatting the James K. Polk administration's proposal to expand the Army and the war in order "to conquer a peace," despite the fact that Americans already occupied the enemy capital and had control of New Mexico and California, all the territory that could reasonably be desired. Of his speech of January 4 on his resolutions to this effect, a reporter wrote:

> The Senate chamber was crowded to overflowing to-day—and the audience was one of the most brilliant and imposing ever assembled within the walls. . . . Every avenue and alcove was occupied with ladies. . . . No man could have received a more marked compliment than this.[3]

Another paper reported: "Mr. Calhoun's speech is still the subject of conversation. All who heard it, are loud in their plaudits of his masterly effort. His clear views, carrying conviction . . . . render him the most gifted of our public men."[4]

Fortunately, in less than a month, a treaty arrived in Washington that was acceptable to the Senate except for the more rabid Democratic expansionists, and the administration's plans did not go forward.

On March 16 and 17 Calhoun made further speeches against the expansion of the Army. James K. Paulding, New York author and formerly Martin Van Buren's Secretary of the Navy, commented to Calhoun on these speeches that he admired "the grandeur of the position you now occupy" and that despite Calhoun's minority position, "your opinions have more influence over the People of the United States than probably those of all the majority combined."[5]

Because of the spread of the newly perfected magnetic telegraph, speeches and other doings in Washington could now reach papers in the West and be printed within a few days, a fact which no doubt intensified political participation and conflict.

Later in the session Calhoun spoke against the administration's request for support to occupy the troubled territory of Yucatan for

[3] Louisville, Ky., *Morning Courier*, January 11, 1848, p. 2, reprinting the Baltimore, Md., *American*.

[4] Baltimore, Md., *Sun*, January 13, 1848, p. 4. Of course, Calhoun was well aware that his stand on the war was unpopular in circles where he usually enjoyed support.

[5] From James K. Paulding, April 5, 1848, herein.

alleged security and humanitarian reasons. His speech of May 15 was an eloquent plea against foreign military involvement as a danger to republican institutions, prophetic and still startlingly relevant for later American history.

One of Calhoun's concerns in his anti-war efforts was the inevitable tendency of war, so evident in Europe and Latin America in the nineteenth century, to aggrandize executive power. This was related to his long campaign against the spoils system and the party organizations it supported and encouraged.

The Two-Party Game

Calhoun continued his long-running criticism and aloofness from the meaningless agitation of political organizations to nominate and elect a President, which he saw as only office-seeking and plundering accompanied by evasion of critical public issues and indifference to the long-range health of the Union. He refused to be drawn into the widespread popular and politicians' enthusiasm for the plain, honest military hero General Zachary Taylor, a man, like Andrew Jackson, of no known political beliefs.

To a confidant Calhoun described the ongoing Presidential contest as merely a scramble between "two miserable factions . . . without any fixed principle or rule of policy."[6] He had written earlier: "I keep aloof, standing independently on my own ground, seeking nothing either from the Govern[men]t or the people. I would not change my position for that of any other."[7]

On another occasion he wrote:

> It is well known, that I have been opposed to a convention to nominate a President, because; it is unwarranted by the Constitution, and is intended to supercede its provisions, in reference to his election, as far as the party is concerned. To that extent the nomination is in effect the election. Because; it destroys the compromises of the Constitution between the larger & smaller members of the Union, as it relates to his election, by securing to the former their preponderance, in the electoral college, & depriving the latter of theirs in the eventual election by the House. Because; as constituted, the Convention is an unequal & unfair representation of the party. . . . The effect of that is, to give several States, in which the democratick party has no weight . . . as much weight as others, which give a unanimous vote in both houses, and an undivided

[6] To Henry W. Conner, July 9, 1848, herein.
[7] To Anna Maria Calhoun Clemson, February 20, 1848, herein.

electoral vote . . . . the effect of the nomination is, to give a minority of the party, & the least sound portion of the Union, in a party view, the control of the election.[8]

Calhoun was not alone in his feeling for the decline of public virtue. Nor were his fears limited to the South. A New York clergyman wrote him:

Since you and I have come upon the stage of active life; there is a very perceptible diminution, in that, high-minded strait-forward, moral and political integrity, which characterized the earlier period of this Republic. We are fast becoming a nation of political gamblers, and Stock jobbers; and among a certain Lot of men, Politics, is about as much a matter of trade, as any thing that can be named in the market. The thought is humiliating to the last degree, to every good man—And unless it can be arrested in some way, short, I fear, will be the career of our Liberty, between the Cradle & the grave.[9]

An Ohio physician concurred:

Although the principles of our republic are, like christianity, good in themselves, like it also, all that is good, is neutralised in the administration. Associations of all kinds embrace a majority who are far below mediocrity both in a moral and intellectual point of view. And of consequence when we attach ourselves to them we are compelled to descend below that graduation, to be on the same level, or be unpopular should we hold ourselves above it. . . .[10]

The Wilmot Proviso

Calhoun's largest concern, which would be the main theme of the rest of his career, was the struggle over slavery in the Territories, specifically the determination of the Northern majority to deny the South any share in them and any hope of new States. Matters came to the fore in this session with what was called the "Oregon bill," a measure to provide a Territorial government for the region. The Wilmot Proviso, barring slavery in all the Territories, was brought forward and affixed to the bill by the House of Representatives, precipitating debate and maneuver that prolonged the session and led to extraordinary evening and night sessions.

[8] To Henry W. Conner, April 4, 1848, herein.

[9] From John D. Gardiner, January 10, 1848, herein.

[10] From James Wishart, June 24, 1848, herein. Wishart had recently moved from Ohio to St. Louis.

The matter was complex. It was an election year, and prospective Presidential candidates tended to take refuge in the complexities. Did the Missouri Compromise line apply? Did or did not the restriction on Oregon set a precedent for California and New Mexico, waiting in the wings? Upon what could the Senate and House agree? What were the powers of Territorial governments and of the Congress before Statehood in regard to domestic institutions such as slavery? If the acts of the Territorial governments were accepted, should these be approved by Congress or merely tacitly left in place? In the last days of the session, the Senate finally submitted to an obdurate House majority and agreed to the Oregon bill with the Proviso. Polk reluctantly signed it, against Calhoun's recommendation.

Calhoun's stand in this controversy has arrested the attention of historians, for it would frame the national debate up to secession: the Territories were the common property of the States and the citizens of no State could be excluded with their property by Congress, the common agent of the States, nor by Territorial governments, which were mere temporary devices that did not embody the sovereignty of the people.

Privately, Calhoun was willing to accept the Missouri Compromise line, as he had been when it was originally proposed, as a reasonable compromise and settlement, which would allow the South further growth and, most importantly, force the North to go on record as conceding to the South its honor and its rights within the Union. Publicly, his position was adamant on the right of slaveholders to settle the Territories without a ban on their property, but it was understood that the Compromise would be accepted as a fallback position.

So President Polk gathered from conversation.[11] So reported a Philadelphia newspaper:

> Mr. Calhoun, in his speech of yesterday [that is, June 27], himself admitted that if the South were permitted to carry their slaves to any part of the new territories of California and Oregon, the natural consequence would be that a practical line would be established not far from 36° 30', which would mark the extreme Northern boundary of slavery. I take it for granted that this was no casual nor incidental remark of the great Southern statesman, and that Mr. Calhoun . . . meant, by that means, to hold out, or at least to let the North perceive, the line which, on average, he and his friends

[11]Allan Nevins, ed., *Polk: The Diary of a President, 1845–1849* (New York: Capricorn Books, 1968), pp. 331–332 (entry for February 14, 1848).

are willing to accept as a compromise. He said that the question does not admit of further delay, and that whatever is to be done, whatever the North is willing to do in the premises, to satisfy the South, had to be done now; and that to wait would be giving to passion a fearful momentum, and would lead at once to the establishment of geographical parties.

There can be no doubt, in the minds of reasonable men, that Mr. Calhoun is right in the estimate of the importance of this subject, and the inevitable consequences to which it may lead. . . . The matter is not less important because it is of little practical utility, and *requires per se* no legislation. It is the theoretical part of it which is agitating the country, and most difficult to settle. It must not be forgotten that the thirteen original colonies of North America went to war with England for an abstraction, for the theory of freedom, and not to shake off an actual oppression . . . . "No taxation without representation" was an abstract doctrine. . . .[12]

In the end, a slim but bipartisan Northern majority denied the South even an inutile token of compromise. Calhoun had sought not so much the "expansion of slavery" as a semblance of the fellowship that ought to characterize the relations of the Union. This repudiated, he warned, in a speech of August 10 a few days before the session closed, a speech perhaps more weighty and dramatic than any he had delivered since the days of Nullification, that a crisis had been reached in the balance of the Union and the South must look to itself.

Critics at the time and historians have speculated upon Calhoun's stand, nearly always putting it in the light of the bitterness of thwarted ambition or obsession with slavery. It is not really necessary to resort to such polemical explanations. Calhoun's range of vision was long. He had never believed in short-term solutions for long-term issues. With his power of intuition and forecasting of trends, he sensed a new aggressiveness in the North that threatened the brotherly comity that had until now underpinned the Union. The South was to receive no more benefits from the Union in the new political scramble, only burdens and insults.

The temper of the free-soil agitation and the submission of both parties in the North to it signalled the power of the forces to be confronted. The militance, not to say conspiracy paranoia, against the South was well illustrated by verses promulgated at this time by the "gentle Quaker poet," John Greenleaf Whittier, entitled "To a Southern Statesman," obviously referring to Calhoun:

[12] Philadelphia, Pa., *Public Ledger*, June 30, 1848, p. 1.

Sore-baffled statesman! when thy eager hand,
With game afoot, unslipped the hungry pack,
To hunt down Freedom in her chosen land,
Hadst thou no fear, that, erelong, doubling back,
These dogs of thine might snuff on Slavery's track?
Where's now the boast, which even thy guarded tongue,
Cold, calm and proud, in the teeth o' the Senate flung,
O'er fulfilment of thy baleful plan,
Like Satan's triumph at the fall of man?
How stood'st thou then, thy feet on Freedom planting,
And pointing to the lurid heaven afar,
Whence all could see, through the south windows slanting,
Crimson as blood, the beams of that Lone Star!
The Fates are just; they give us but our own;
Nemesis ripens what our hands have sown.

.   .   .   .

So, Carolinian, it may prove with thee,

.   .   .   .

. . . It may be,
That the roused spirits of Democracy
May leave to freer States the same wide door
Through which thy slave-cursed Texas entered in,
From out of the blood and fire, the wrong and sin,
.   .   .   .[13]

Wrote Ellwood Fisher, one of Calhoun's Ohio friends: "The South may rest assured of the fact that hostility to their institutions is becoming more and more inveterate—and is extending."[14]

As Calhoun's correspondence and the Congressional votes would seem to indicate, Calhoun had at this time the South with him as never before. No longer was he a lonely prophet, out in front with a small group of disciples, but rather the leader of a growing throng.

A non-political neighbor from Pendleton represented this swelling tide when he wrote: "We are gratified with the prospect of peace with Mexico, but feel a little restrained in giving it indulgence by the prospect it brings with it, of a war with the Abolitionists."[15]

Was Calhoun, as has so often been charged, engaging in agitation for agitation's sake? In debate with John P. Hale of New Hampshire, the most overt antislavery man in the Senate, he said that he had hoped to be relieved "from the necessity of ever again speaking upon this subject," but:

[13] *National Era*, vol. II, no. 56 (January 27, 1848), p. 15.
[14] From Ellwood Fisher, May 19, 1848, herein.
[15] From Ozey R. Broyles, March 3, 1848, herein.

When this subject was first agitated, I said to my friends, there is but one question that can destroy this Union and our institutions, and that is this very slave question . . . . that if the thing were permitted to go on, and the Constitution to be trampled on; that if it were allowed to proceed to a certain point, it would be beyond the power of any man, or any combination of men, to prevent the result. We are approaching that crisis . . . .[16]

Calhoun knew that the North was not monolithic on the question, except in terms of expedient party machinations. He hoped to solidify the South in self-defense but also to rally thoughtful, conservative men of the North. Historians have consistently underestimated their presence. Not a few nor insignificant Northerners agreed with Calhoun's position. Paulding wrote: "All things considered, I think the Wilmot Proviso is the most impudent political movement of my time."[17]

Another New Yorker, the pioneer anthropologist Lewis Henry Morgan, wrote:

. . . the Mass of the people have no disposition to encroach upon the Constitutional rights of the Southern States. But I think it must be regarded as certain, that if a conviction seizes the public mind, that Congress has power to make the territories of the Republic free without impinging the rights of any portion of the Country, this conviction will be persisted in to the last extremity. If the South gets the better of the argument, and it certainly will, if in the right, then the people of the North will be satisfied to see slavery spread. But if it should be otherwise and the South should be unwilling to yield—we shall find our Republic in the greatest peril.[18]

Here is another New Yorker, Fitzwilliam Byrdsall, quondam leader of the Locofocos:

If the South cannot maintain its equal rights to the territory of the United States—here then we have the beginning of the end. There is no constitutional right of the Southern people clearer than their right to go with their property of any kind into the territories of the Union. . . . If the Southern people cannot maintain their equal rights as to their settling in new territory, what other rights under the Constitution can they maintain? If defeated on the Wilmot proviso principle, will the crusade began against them stop at that point? They are self deluded who imagine an affirmative. . . . The Statements of those Whigs and democrats who are

[16] Remarks on the Disturbances in the District of Columbia, April 20, 1848, herein.

[17] From James K. Paulding, January 24, 1848, herein.

[18] From Lewis Henry Morgan, June 30, 1848, herein.

now uniting with the Abolitionists, that they mean not to interfere with the Slavery existing in the Slave States are all hollow.[19]

Sylvester Graham, noted dietary reformer, reported to Calhoun a speech he had made at a political meeting in Massachusetts in which he:

> presented exactly the same views on the subject that you have in the Speech [of June 27] before me. I showed, by precisely the same course of reasoning, that Congress has no constitutional, no legitimate right nor power to abolish slavery in the several States, nor in the District of Columbia . . . nor to abolish nor prohibit Slavery in the territories . . . .[20]

A citizen of New Hampshire wrote to Calhoun:

> The controversy that now agitates the country in regard to new Territory is one of vital interest to the south. I do not hesitate to say that your friends in this quarter are equally strong with you on this point. They agree fully with you that there is nothing in the Constitution to prevent, in fact it gives to all the right of living and enjoying their property at the north or south as they please, or taking it from a State into a territory and there enjoy it as they please. Doctrines contrary to these are anti-democratic. Every lover of free principles and every lover of his country cannot consistantly take any other position.[21]

Since the Civil War, American society has tended to define itself in terms of grand, rootless abstractions, a different thing from the Constitutional principles and fair play insisted upon by Calhoun. Thus, the first post-war biography of Calhoun, that of Hermann von Holst, portrayed Calhoun's career as the defense of an abstract, reified "Slavery," and therefore a pursuit for evil and against progress. But Calhoun was not defending an abstraction. He was defending a Constitutional legacy and a living society and way of life, a society which asked nothing from a hostile majority except non-aggression. He had in 1838 described the South as "an aggregate, in fact, of communities, not of individuals," and had asked: "When did the South ever place her hand on the North?"[22]

[19] From Fitzwilliam Byrdsall, July 31, 1848, herein.

[20] From Sylvester Graham, July 21, 1848, herein.

[21] From George Dennett, June 24, 1848, herein.

[22] *The Papers of John C. Calhoun*, 14:84, 95 (January 10 and 11, 1838). An exemplary description of one of the communities that Calhoun was defending has recently appeared: James E. Kibler, *Our Fathers' Fields: A Southern Story* (Columbia: University of South Carolina Press, 1998).

The Science of Government

In the spring of 1848 revolution broke out in France and spread across Europe. Calhoun was called upon to give his opinion upon this phenomenon, and he did so in his role as guardian of republican institutions. In a speech of March 30, in a letter of May 28 in reply to a request from the Prussian minister, and in private correspondence, Calhoun gave his views. His hopes were all in favor of the establishment of the New World's principles of free government in the Old World, but he was not optimistic.

To a son at college, he wrote that he was anxiously awaiting further news which would allow him "means of forming some opinion, as to what is to follow." He added: "I have no confidence that France will be able to establish a Republick. That is a task of far greater difficulty, than is generally supposed."[23]

To his daughter in Europe he wrote:

There is no prospect of a successful termination of the efforts of France to establish a free popular Government; nor was there any from the beginning. She has no elements out of which such a government could be formed; & if she had, still she must fail from her total misconception of the principles, on which such a government, to succeed, must be constructed. Indeed, her standard of liberty is false throughout. Her standard of liberty is ideal; and belongs to that kind of liberty, which man has been supposed to possess, in what has been falsely called a state of nature—a state supposed to have preceded the social & political, & in which, of course, if it ever existed, he must have live[d] a part, as an isolated individual, without society, or government.[24]

Reflections on these matters turned Calhoun's thoughts to his own legacy that was to become *A Disquisition on Government.* He wrote his trusted brother-in-law, James Edward Colhoun:

What I propose to publish on the subject of Government is not yet prepared for the press. I had hoped to have had it prepared last fall, but was so interrupted, as to fall short of my calculation. . . . I do not think any thing will be lost by the delay. I do not think the publick mind is yet fully prepared for the work, nor will be, until there has been such failure and embarrassment in the French experiment . . . as will bring into distrust & doubt, Dorrism, so as to prepare the publick mind to have its errors and consequences

[23] To James Edward Calhoun, Jr., March 23, 1848, herein.
[24] To Anna Maria Calhoun Clemson, June 23, 1848, herein.

pointed out, and to reflect seriously on the question; What are the elements, which are indispensable to constitute a constitutional popular Government?[25]

He went on to describe his plan of work and promised to submit his writing for Colhoun's perusal by the following fall. Whether or not Calhoun had read the comment of the French observer Alexis de Tocqueville that "a new science of politics is indispensible for a new world" cannot be known, but that was the mission he had undertaken.

Personally, Calhoun does not seem much to have been bothered in 1848 by the health problems that were soon to overcome him. He continued his customary activities. Amelia Gayle, daughter of an Alabama Representative who lodged in the same Washington house, left an interesting recollection of Calhoun at this time. (She was later to marry Josiah Gorgas, the able Chief of Ordnance of the Confederate Army, and be the mother of William Crawford Gorgas, Surgeon General of the U.S. notable for his contributions to public health.)

She reported on March 29 that "Mr. Calhoun tapped at my door this morning for me to take a long walk with him before breakfast. Fortunately I was awake and soon dressed for I enjoy of all things a walk with him." As was his custom with ladies and young men, Calhoun discussed current events, especially the French revolution, with the same seriousness he would with mature and important men. Then the ambulatory conversation turned to housekeeping. Calhoun, reported Miss Gayle, "gratified me by saying that of all things in the world he disliked an over-particular house-wife, nothing to him was half so annoying."[26]

It was about this time that Calhoun confided to his daughter the philosophy that had guided his life and public career in a statement that has often been quoted: "I hold, the duties of life, to be greater than life itself, and that in performing them manfully, even ag[ai]nst hope, our labour is not lost, but will be productive of good in after times."[27]

[25] To James Edward Colhoun, April 15, 1848, herein.

[26] Amelia Gayle to [Sarah Gorgas Crawford], March 29, 1848. ALU in University of Alabama, Amelia Gayle Gorgas Scrapbook.

[27] To Anna Maria Calhoun Clemson, March 7, 1848, herein.

THE PAPERS

of

JOHN C. CALHOUN

Ⅲ

Volume XXV

DECEMBER 6, 1847–
JANUARY 31, 1848

◊

The first session of the 30th Congress convened on December 6. The next day Senator Andrew P. Butler presented Calhoun's credentials for a new six-year term to expire in March 1853, and he was sworn in by Vice-President George M. Dallas. "Mr. Calhoun," wrote one reporter, "looks the very picture of health, and appears to be in fine spirits." (Philadelphia, Pa., Public Ledger, *December 15, 1847.) At his own request, Calhoun received no committee assignment.*

An American army had been occupying Mexico City for three months but there appeared to be no prospect of early negotiations for peace. Calhoun was deeply concerned about the Polk administration's intention to raise more troops and extend the war so as "to conquer peace." On December 15 he introduced resolutions against further prosecution of the war. Though the resolutions were eventually tabled without a vote, they allowed him to make a much-praised speech on January 4 in which he outlined the desirability and feasibility of a defensive policy rather than a further expansion of the war, warning that the latter would be a violation of American principles and potentially disastrous.

On January 8, a Whig Representative from Illinois, Abraham Lincoln, serving his one term in the House of Representatives, made a speech affirming the right of any people to withdraw from existing governments and establish new ones. It is probable that he found an opportunity during the session to be introduced to Calhoun, whose proposals to cede the federal public lands to the States he had praised.

Calhoun's speech had been attacked in force by supporters of the administration, but the public reaction seemed favorable, including that of the Army. On the same day that Lincoln made his speech, which was the anniversary of the battle of New Orleans, the Virginia volunteers stationed at Buena Vista held a celebration. Calhoun was toasted in the highest terms as the "polar star" of the South and the "brightest star in the galaxy of American statesmen." (Petersburg, Va., Republican, *February 14, 1848.)*

On January 22, Calhoun found time to write some advice to his

3

son James at South Carolina College: *"Knowledge is like architecture. You must lay the foundation deep & strong in order to sustain a noble superstructure. When that is done, the mind may go on increasing its vigour & store of knowledge, long after the physical faculties have commenced their decay."*

⫘

From H[ENRY] W. CONNER

Charleston, Dec[embe]r 8 1847

My Dear Sir, I rec[eive]d last night the letter of which the enclosed is a copy—& I hasten to communicate it to you. The Mr. [Samuel J.] Peters refer[r]ed to you know I think. He is a whig of the worst sort being averse to any movement adverse to the Wilmot proviso. As he said nothing to my correspondent touching Gen[era]l [Zachary] Taylor[']s views on that subject I infer if any thing was said at all it was not favourable to his (Mr. Peter[']s) views.

I called up at the Hotel the morning after you left—& then only learned you were gone.

I have encouraged our friends here to keep quiet for the present as to Gen[era]l Taylor & all other Candidates for the Presidency & have written to Col. [Arthur P.] Hayne at Columbia who would see Col. [Franklin H.] Elmore advising them of the information I have (which I think is about the earliest) & recommending them to keep our friends quiet for the present. The feeling however in favour of Gen[era]l Taylor I perceive is *very, very* strong ["feeling beginning to show itself" *canceled*] in his favour even here & it will I think increase rapidly. The sooner his position can be made definite with regard to us is therefore the better.

When you write us it were perhaps better you should write 1st with a view to informing our friends here generally as to the state of things & the policy ["to be" *interlined*] adopted to them & next to give some of us your views & wishes more fully in private. Your own better judgment will however best determine. Very Truly Y[ou]rs, H.W. Conner.

[Enclosure]

—— to Henry W. Conner, "Copy"

New Orleans, 2d Dec[embe]r 1847

My Dear Sir: You are no doubt aware that General [Zachary] Taylor is here, or rather at the Barracks, six miles below the City.

I have just seen Mr. Peters, who, in company with several gentlemen, committee of arrangements ["&c" *canceled*] for his reception &c, met him at the Balize and accompanied him to his present quarters. To Mr. Peters, he expressed himself openly and frankly, *stating unequivocally that he is a candidate for the Presidency, and this position he intends to maintain,* no matter how many Richmonds there be in the field or whatever may be their present political position or standing, and *that under no circumstances will he withdraw.*

If popular feeling be any test of success, Gen[era]l Taylor is certain to be the next President—nothing, I apprehend, short of Omnipotent power can prevent this result.

Whatever may be the feeling towards other prominent men, it amounts to nothing, compared with the universal sentiment in favor of the General.

What I now state in regard to the General's determination, is so direct that you may rely upon its accuracy, and those who scrutinize the effect of change may discover the probable influence such an event may have on the future action of the Government and on the prosperity of the Country. Yours truly [unsigned.]

ALS with En in ScCleA; variant PC with En in Jameson, ed., *Correspondence,* pp. 1147–1148. NOTE: Henry Workman Conner (died 1861) was a native of N.C. who became a banker and railroad president in Charleston. He was a member of the secession convention. His son James Conner became Brig. Gen. in the Confederate Army and held various public offices in S.C.

From THO[MA]S W[ILLIA]M WARD

Austin [Tex.,] Dec[embe]r 8th 1847
Dear Sir, Permit me to introduce to you my friend Dr. [S.W.] Baker of Maine who has resided in Texas with us the past summer and who in the morning leaves for his home in Main[e]. He is a gentleman of much merit and individual worth. During his sojourn here he was engaged per contract in his profession for the frontier troops and as he is not familiar with the business of the departments in the City of Washington he may require your counsel and aid in the adjustment of his claims as he is from the ill health of his family obliged to reach home with as little delay as possible. Such courtesies as you may extend to the Dr. shall be reciprocated by Your Very Ob[edien]t Serv[an]t, Thos. Wm. Ward.

ALS in ScCleA. NOTE: The above letter was enclosed with that of S.W. Baker to Calhoun, dated 1/10/1848.

From JAMES GADSDEN

Charleston S.C., Dec[embe]r 9 1847

I greatly regret I did not meet you on your way to Washington. You stated you would be in the city on [November] 25 and I postponed my visit to the 29th. My presence was necessary in Columbia on that day.

I was exceedingly anxious of a long & friendly conversation—and on many matters which escape you on the sheet. The Political movements are pregnant with events. The election of [Robert C.] Winthrop [as Speaker of the House of Representatives] would argue more harmony in the W[h]igs than was generally supposed. Their union will stimulate union among that wing of Democracy with which Carolina does not fraternize. The No Convention Ante Wilmot Proviso candidate is the man for the South. To you your immediate friends look with a fidelity which has never been shaken; and in candor I was sanguine that your course on the Mexican war, the Oregon Boundary &c &c had placed you in the very position which I have always desired to see you—The Independent Ante Convention Candidate. But [Zachary] Taylor will occupy the same ground, and his great military popularity (I don[']t speak merely of its availability) will be a serious impediment I fear to any movement for you on same grounds, with success. Many of Taylor[']s most ardent admirers & who are bound to him by other ties than military fame or political statesmanship, are likewise your friends. They feel a divided influence & these with others, and the People in many cases will create a deversion probably fatal to both. What are your views? What can be done to promote Union[?] I am individually so opposed to the Spoil party, who have more than once deceived us, that I can take no part with any other but an Ante Convention Candidate. My preferences have always & continue for you, above all in the Country but if your high claims are to be again postponed, let us know early the intentions, that concert of action may be certain to secure the triumph of one who will not court our influence to deceive & who will stand by the guarantees of the cons[t]itution as the Political Bible of the States. I write in *confidence*, expecting a response in the same feeling. I have individually been drawn into, or reconciled to political movements in the past that my judgement did not approve at the time. I went however with others with whom I have always associated politically—but they like myself perhaps now see how we have been deceived. I desire an early Answer. See [Isaac E.] Holmes [Representative from S.C.]. Our views correspond. Yours truly, James Gadsden.

ALS in ScCleA; PC in Jameson, ed., *Correspondence*, pp. 1148–1149. NOTE: Found among Calhoun's papers in ScCleA is an undated, unsigned wrapper with an unidentifiable or missing En, but which may date from about this time. The unknown correspondent writes: "For the Hon[ora]ble John C. Calhoun[,] Care of Col. [James] Gadsden[,] President So. Carolina R.R. co. To be opened by the latter in case of Mr. Calhoun's absence from Charleston—and the writer would ask the further favor from Col. G. of laying it before such other gentlemen of influence in his vicinity—afterwards forwarding to Mr. Calhoun."

Calhoun and 53 other members of Congress to "the Right Reverend Bishop [John Joseph] Hughes," 12/9. They invite Hughes [Roman Catholic Bishop of New York] to preach to a joint session of Congress on "Sunday morning next," 12/12. LS in CSmH, Huntington Manuscripts.

From MARIA D[ALLAS] CAMPBELL, "Private"

Philadelphia, Dec[embe]r 10th [1847]

My ever dear friend, Seeing you announced as already at your post of duty, [I] take the earliest moment of your arrival, & before you become so *immersed* in the *business* of your life, (when you *neglect*, if you do not *forget* your friends) to thank you kindly for your prompt reply to my perhaps importunate request, that my son [St. George T. Campbell] should be honored by a letter, or letters, of introduction from you—it so happened that he could not avail himself of them. Mr. [Richard] Cobden was on the Continent, when St. George was in England, & [Hiram] Powers was in Italy, where however anxious my son was to have been, his time & health did not permit him to seek that sunny clime. Mr. [Thomas G.] Clemson was in Paris, when he passed through Brussels, but St. George had the pleasure of spending an hour with your daughter [Anna Maria Calhoun Clemson], whom he found looking well in health, & much pleased with her residence abroad. I wish I could add that my son's health has been improved by his trans Atlantic trip, but I grieve to say since his return, his attacks have recurred, & he is now, by the express command of his

7

physicians required to relinquish the practice of his profession, having I fear broken down his constitution by too intense a pursuit of it. It is a sad trial for him and the ambitious hopes of distinction, which were so nearly realized[,] are not crushed without great pain, & which a mother's heart can too acutely sympathize with. I need not tell you how anxious I am to hear from *yourself* what are your views and intentions, on the great questions agitating the public mind. Enlarged and liberal as I have believed your ideas are on all subjects, where your country's welfare was concerned, I shall never believe you actuated by any other than truly patriotic motives, the *little influences* of mere politicians, I have ever known you to despise, therefore do not suppose that *woman as I am*, with understanding enough to appreciate your superiority, I am to be influenced solely by personal partialities. Therefore write to me, as you have ever heard me speak to you, with fearless frankness—and believe me you cannot have better friends *personally* & *politically* than [my husband] Mr. [Alexander] C[ampbell,] my son, & myself. My anxieties for my son and his family, will keep me from Washington this winter where I had hoped to have passed many weeks. I wish I could induce you to pay us a visit here, it seems to me, it would be a natural wish to see our growing & improving city, when a few hours would bring you, where you have more friends than you perhaps imagine. Should all be right in my own immediate circle I may come on to Washington in the Spring, if you will summon me. I have many things to talk over with you, which I do not like to write, and in fact, you give me very little encouragement to hope you care, or feel interested in our opinions or hopes.

Tell me where you are located for the Session, whether your family have accompanied you, how you are in health & spirits and how far you mean to *draw the line*, not between yourself and the Mexicans, but between the *Whigs* & yourself—for my sake do not *unite* yourself with that *no* principle party. Mr. C[ampbell] & my son unite with me in the kindest remembrances to you. Ever & truly your old friend, Maria D. Campbell.

ALS in ScCleA.

To T[homas] G. Clemson, [Brussels]

Washington, 10th Dec[embe]r 1847
My dear Sir, I wrote you just before I left home for this place; and now write principally to give you an account of my visit to your place [in Edgefield District, S.C.].

I took it in my way to Aiken; & stayed one day there. There has been a good deal of sickness among the negroes; but not more than in all the country around. There has been, however[,] no death, & the negroes, with one or two exception, had recovered & looked well, and appeared conten[t]ed. The crop of corn about equals last year's, but the cotton will not much exceed a half crop, owing to the cold spring & long continued wet spell in the summer. It appears to have been pretty well cultivated, & is quite equal to Mr. [John] Mobley's, or any other, I understand, in the neighbourhood. The crop will yield about 16,000 ["pounds" *interlined*] of clean cotton. I rode over the place. It is in tolerable order. I saw the horses, mules & hogs, but not the cattle, or sheep. The horses & mules & hogs were in good order; but the hogs were small. The overseer expected to put up & slaughter about 20; but, I do not think, they would much, if any, exceed 100 pounds on an average.

I have employed another overseer, R[e]uben H. Reynolds, to set in on the 1st Jan[uar]y next. He came well recommended from those, who had formerly employed him, & also from Mr. [James] Vaughn, Col. [Francis W.] Picken[s]'s overseer. The Col. was not at home. He has had much experience, as an overseer over large gangs of negroes; and hope he will do well. He will plant 150 acres of cotton, of which 55 will be the new ground over the river, & the fresh lands adjoining, which ought to yield well. Should the season not be unfavourable, like the three last, I think you may calculate on a good crop. I agreed to give him $235, and to find bread, meat & milk for himself & family; a wife & three children. I could [not] get him for less & Mr. Mobley thinks it moderate for an experienced overseer. He first insisted on $300.

I have not been here long enough to form an opinion, what course parties will take during the session. The whigs have have [*sic*] a small, but apparently decided majority in the House, & the democrats a large, but not a very reliable majority in the Senate. The session will be an eventful one. It will be difficult for either of the old parties to hold together. I anticipate much confusion & distraction. I send a copy of the [annual] Message [from President James K. Polk to Congress]. It is very long, very undignified & full

9

of false assumptions. You will see that things have progressed to a point, where it is difficult to advance or retreat; but I will write you more fully on political subjects hereafter.

My love to Anna [Maria Calhoun Clemson] & the children [John Calhoun Clemson and Floride Elizabeth Clemson]; and say to her I will write her next. Your affectionate father, J.C. Calhoun.

ALS in ScCleA; PEx in Jameson, ed., *Correspondence*, pp. 740–741.

From J[OHN] B. JONES

Philad[elphi]a, Dec[embe]r 10th 1847

Dear Sir, I was much gratified to receive y[ou]r favour of the 15th Nov., and to be assured that my humble efforts had merited your approbation.

About a week ago I issued the 5th No. of the Compact, which is now in the hands of the agents in the different cities. Mr. [W.] Adams, Pa. Avenue, Washington, has them, as I see by an advertisement in the [Washington Daily National] Intelligencer.

The leading article in the 5th No., I cannot venture to suppose would be approved by you. It was written without consultation with any one; but I deemed something of the kind advisable, to indicate to those gentlemen who think they may always offer insult and indignity to the South with impunity, that there ["is" *canceled*] not only [is] a remedy for violated Constitutions, but a means of applying it. I wished to show them that *ultimate operations* might be calmly meditated, and *final results* dispassionately contemplated by those who are resolved never to submit to any abridgement of their rights, ["perpetrated by means of" *interlined and* "by" *canceled*] a violation of the Constitution.

Hereafter I shall endeavour to avoid novel suggestions, and rather follow the lead of others, better qualified by their experience and location to indicate the proper course to be pursued.

My proposition for those ["in the North" *interlined*] who see the wrong meditated against the South, and have the boldness to declare their disapprobation of it—to organize, has brought upon me a column of assault in the N.Y. Evening Post (7th inst.), which is repeated in the [New York] Tribune—one Whig, the other Democratic—but both abolition papers. This is a good indication. I shall not now be surprised, if I ultimately succeed in getting a hearing in the North.

But I do hope that some of those who feel as deep an interest as I can do in the prevalence of right views, will be equally as fo[r]ward in manifesting it. If some of the Southern members of Congress would use a little exertion, the paper could be firmly established. I have, it is true, some little fortune, just sufficient to yield me a moderate income—but still I have a family to support, and would prefer to avoid unnecessary sacrifices. I will make them if *necessary*. But I do not think the time for that yet arrived. Each No. of the paper has cost me some $40—the sales just about defraying the advertising bills &c. Now, if I could have the printing of some twenty speeches, addresses &c during the winter, on the same terms that it is done ["for" *interlined*] in Washington, I could go on without losing more than $20 per number—and this I would be willing to do, for the sake of maintaining the *right*. I approve the series of resolutions introduced by you last winter, and intend to advocate the doctrines embraced in them to the utmost of my ability. And if the North should ultimately triumph—and cause a dissolution of the Union— I shall sell my estate here, and go with those who are in the *right*.

Should you, or any of y[ou]r political friends travel this far north, I should feel happy to entertain you or them at my house—No. 8 Franklin Row[,] 9th St. between Walnut & Locust. There are some men of high standing and wealth in this city, who see the right, and declare in favor of the South, in their private conversations—but they are reluctant to organize. I trust that those who entertain such sentiments, however, will yet be stimulated to action. Truly & Sincerely yours, J.B. Jones.

P.S. I do not wish to tax y[ou]r time by replying to this letter.

ALS in ScCleA. NOTE: An AEU by Calhoun reads "The Compact."

From Jos[eph] J. Singleton

Dahlonega [Ga.,] 10th Dec. 1847
My Dear Sir, I promised you in my last, that I would see Mr. R.B. Lewis on his return, and inquire of him in reference to the toll due you from Mr. E[dward J.] C. Milner. I have done so, and it appears from what Mr. L[ewis] informed me, that Mr. [William G.] Lawrence was to have paid the said toll, which he has failed to do, after repeated calls by Mr. Lewis for it. Now the question is, what is to be done with insolvent Gold Diggers for a noncompliance of contract.

11

I design this as a general question, to be answered at your leisure, if atall. Mr. Milner has left the Country, and Mr. Lawrence is one of those very independent kind of Gentlemen not atall uncommon in Gold Regions. You have been deceived by such men here, and I fear I have been as your agent, with all my vigilence and importunities. At the expiration of the Lease on your Cain Creek interest, I shall not renew it to the same individual. The truth is, the existing lease has been long since forfeited, on the part of the Lessee, and had you been the entire owner of the property, the terms of said lease should have been complied with, or abandoned.

The operators on your Obarr Mine are still few, only 2 or 3, and doing small business at that, tho' they say they will be able to make a Deposite of 2 or 3 hundred Dwts. by Christmas. I wish they may of course.

I discover by the papers that Gen[era]l Duff Greene is about to publish a paper at Washington to be called the Times the principles of which I am exceedingly well pleased. Should he start such a paper, I will thank you to have my name enrolled amongst his subscribers, and I will enclose him the price of it, on the reception of the first number.

I would be much pleased with a short specimen of your views, as regards the anticipated action of Congress upon the two principal topics of present national interest. To wit the Mexican War, and the slave question as involved under the provisions of the Wilmot proviso. There are various conjectures in this part of the Country with regard to the probable course which Congress will take in those important matters. So far as I can learn a decided majority are in favor of the course pursued by yourself during the last session (and especially so, since Mr. [Henry] Clay[']s recent Speech & Resolutions) and appear to express an anxious hope that you will adopt the same course, and stren[u]ously insist upon it at the present Session of Congress.

Mr. Clay has certainly lost ground with his own party since his late Lexington speech; they say it is too much of a milk & water concern to promote even the interest of the whole Country much more its Southern portion. His views are evidently intended for popular favor; will he obtain it to the extent of his desires is the question. "He cannot please God & Mammon" at the same time. If he can get Gen[era]l [Zachary] Taylor coupled in with him, he will try it no doubt, and they will be hard to beat; nothing short of a united action of the South, with some other help could promise itself ["with" *canceled*] a hope of success. Could this be attained, and that by one of our own would be exceedingly gratifying to your very humble servant. I have the honor Sir of being yours very truly &c, Jos. J. Singleton.

ALS in ScU-SC, John C. Calhoun Papers. NOTE: On 11/13/1847, Henry Clay, who at this time held no public office, made a widely reported speech at Lexington, Ky. He blamed the Mexican War on the Polk administration, hoped that Mexico would not be dismembered, suggested that the U.S. accept San Francisco Bay as settlement and compensation for all claims against Mexico, and opposed the acquisition of territory for the purpose of extending slavery.

From JAMES G. BENNETT

Herald Office, New York [City], Dec. 11, 1847
Dear Sir, Mr. [John] Nugent who will hand you this, goes to Washington as confidential correspondent of the *Herald.* By affording him any information in your power on matters of public interest, you will much oblige very truly yours, James G. Bennett.

ALS in ScCleA.

To A[NDREW] P[ICKENS] CALHOUN, [Marengo County, Ala.]

Washington, 11th Dec[embe]r 1847
My dear Andrew, I was not much disappointed to learn by your last, that the late fall would not add as much to our cotton crop as I once expected. The effects of the severe frost ["had" *canceled*] were the same with us in Carolina as ["it was" *canceled*] with you, and I presume all over the cotton region. I am of the impression now, that the crop will fall short of 2,200,000 bales & will not greatly exceed 2,000,000 & that we ought not to sell at the present prices. I think, the late accounts from England not unfavourable. The indication is, that the storm has passed. I wish you to keep me advised, as to what will be the probable amount of the crop of cotton in the Gulf States, so that I may be enabled to form a definitive opinion as early as practicable when we ought to sell. We must not dispond. Good times will yet come. The consumption is going on, & the deficient crops of late will one day tell.

I was surprised and mortified to learn, that Patrick [Calhoun] had drawn on our factors in the way he had. He ought to have ["had" *interlined*] the manliness to inform me of his wants. I saw that he was not in sperits, and I fear that the $600 may not relieve him from his difficulties. I am uneasy about him. I have heard nothing from him since he left Charleston. I hope the draft was taken up. But you must write him, that he must not again draw without my consent. Write him kindly, but firmly, & state the reasons, why you cannot hereafter honor his drafts, except through me. Carefully avoid anything like censure, and all unkind expressions. He is at a critical point; and it will require great judgement & discretion to give him a right direction. He has fine qualities, but is too easily seduced by unworthy companions. I agree with you, he ought to go to Mexico. It may brake his present associations, and habits. As he has drawn for an amount greater than what you were to remit me, I must endeavour to get along without that, or at any rate, ["you may" *interlined*] postpone the remittance until the crop is sold; and it is ascertained whether it can be spared. I hope you wrote to our factors to accept the draft, but with a caution, not accept any hereafter unless authorised by you.

Let me know in your next, whether the cotton seed & & & has been sent by the factors to Mr. [James Edward] Boisseau to be forwarded to Mr. [Thomas G.] Clemson, & if not have it done immediately.

You of course have seen the Message [of President James K. Polk] & the course it indicates to be pursued towards Mexico. The impression here is, that it is intended ["to" *interlined*] conquer & subject the whole country. That at least will be the result if the course should be pursued; and if it should be, the end will be to hold it as a conquered Province or incorporate it in the Union. Either will overthrow our system of Government. It may, indeed, have a different termination, which few yet dream of; and that is, to be held by the Army & volunteers as an independent country. Keep this to yourself. I have never whispered it before to anyone; but it is not an improbable result. The country is in a most critical condition. It will be hard to save it.

My love to Margaret [Green Calhoun], & the children. Your affectionate father, J.C. Calhoun.

[P.S.] I wrote you from Charleston. I hope you got my letter.

ALS in NcD, John C. Calhoun Papers; PEx in Jameson, ed., *Correspondence*, p. 741.

REMARKS ON THE DISTRIBUTION OF
BOOKS TO SENATORS

[In the Senate, December 14, 1847]
[In the previous session, some 10,000 copies of various volumes of public and semi-public documents had been purchased and distributed to Senators. Under consideration was a resolution to present new members of the Senate with the same books that had previously been distributed.]

Mr. Calhoun. I have been a good many years in this body, and believe I have voted steadily against all these propositions to distribute these books, and yet I have felt a good deal of embarrassment upon the subject. When the books have been offered to me, I have hesitated whether I should take them, but knowing they must go to somebody, I concluded in my own mind I ought to take them. I have always believed, that among the smaller abuses of the Government expenditures this is the greatest; and I am willing to give up to any new member that may desire them, that portion of the books which have fallen to my share. I have never derived five dollars advantage from them since the first day they encumbered the shelves of my library. I was not a little surprised when I received a letter from one of the messengers of this body, informing me that there were two boxes of books for me, for I knew not a word about the resolution which passed at the last session. The books were, by my direction, sent to my rooms in this city. I found them packed in two large boxes, which I have not opened, and which I do not believe I shall open during this session. I appeal to the new members of this body whether this thing ought to go on forever; and if not, when can there be a more favorable time for putting a stop to it. It is a very great abuse. These books have accumulated from year to year, and if the system be allowed to go on for ten years longer, as it has done for the last ten, a whole library will be voted to each new Senator. I shall vote for the reconsideration [*which subsequently passed*].

From *Congressional Globe*, 30th Cong., 1st Sess., p. 23. Also printed in Houston, ed., *Proceedings and Debates*, pp. 21–22; the New York, N.Y., *Morning Courier and New-York Enquirer*, December 16, 1847 (Supplement), p. 1. Variants in the Washington, D.C., *Daily Union*, December 14, 1847, p. 3; the New York, N.Y., *Herald*, December 16, 1847, p. 4.

From JAMES DAVIS, "Confidential"

Enon Grove[,] Heard County Georgia
December 15, [18]47

Dear Sir, Permit me an humble individual to claim ["your attention" *interlined*] to the affairs of state. Never since I have been a man, has the clouds thickened and lowered, so dark and portentious, as at present. In fact I am unable by any keen of human foresight to unravel or look into the future. In retrospecting the past, I now see clearly that the staunch Old republican Independant party, has lost much ground by *Compromises* and *availables.* This is illustrated In the defeat of Mr. [Martin] Vanburen before the nominating convention and takeing up of Mr. [James K.] Polk as an available. For had Mr. Vanburen run the Independant party would now be in the majority—but as it is we have now to take a groound start, without the Texas question to aid us forward. I am perplexed and bewildered at the course of the Administration in conducting the Mexican war, yet I am a war man and proud of the achievements of our arms. I am shocked at the speech and resolutions of Mr. [Henry] Clay, yet there is in Mr. Clay's exposition much to admire and commend. The Wilmot Proviso stands out threatening the dismmemberment of our Union and with it the last hope of human liberty—until Prince Imanuel shal[l] reign King of nations as he is now King in Zion and from the reading of scripture the day is to be dark im[m]ediat[e]ly antirior to the dawn of that bright morn which will rise and continue in its resp[l]endant glory three hundred and sixty five thousand of years and six thousand hours during which time the earth ["will be" *interlined*] regenereted and redeemed from the misrule of Kings and Tyrants, and the ambition of aspiring demagouges: denominated in scripture, *"a thousand years"* which in Prophetic language stands a day for a year, and is called in parabolical language "the new heavens and the new earth." Yet even in this dark day I hear the voice of his servant to trust in the name of the Lord at evening time it may be light; In looking to the future the only ray of light which fligts acoross my mind is your resolutions submit[t]ed in the U.S. Senate February 19, 1847. It is my earnest prayer that you may be blest with a clear head as I trust you have already a patriotic heart ["in Discusing them" *interlined*] in all their h[e]ight, lenght and bre[ad]th; which discus[s]ion promulgated as I trust It will be into every nook, hole and corner of this Union as I trust It will ["be may" *canceled*] go far to enlighten the Pub[l]ic mind, and raise the great platform; upon which the patriotic of all parties may rally to the rescue of *Constitutional* liberty. And it is to be hoped that the patriotic of all parties will behold the justice of General [Zachary] Taylor's Views in conducting the Mexican war, and to my mind there is ["but" *interlined*] little difference in your views and his—the principal is the same and which differs widely from the views both of the *opposition* and the *administration*.

I see it stated in some paper, that Gen. [Duff] Green, is about [to] establish at Washington City and [*sic*] Indepen[den]t press[;] this is [c]ertainly wise. But is he the man, for so responsable a position; to my mind, it is problamatical. However, this I leave to the judgement of abler & Wiser heads. My Location for next year will be Cedar Town, Paulding County where I would like to Receive any communication from you, or any public Documents. I am Stationed there next year, as Domestic Miss[ionary] for the Southern Baptist Convention. I shall leave my Temporal interest in this County—where I have been, living for the last 13 years and which place I may return after the expiration the term of my Mission. On all these State affairs I would like to hear from you fully, My mind being turned to you as the the [*sic*] great instrument for the Salvation of the South & of the whole country. I am in high consideration your Sincere Friend, James Davis.

ALS in ScCleA. NOTE: An AEU by Calhoun reads "Re[veren]d Mr. Davis. Send doc[umen]t."

Petition of Maria Caldwell Robertson, presented by Calhoun to the Senate on 12/15. This document, dated 2/20/1847 at New York [City], asks payment for $587.31 in loans made by James Caldwell during the American Revolution, the certificates for which have been lost or destroyed. (The petition was referred to the Committee on Revolutionary Claims, which reported adversely.) DS in DNA, RG 46 (U.S. Senate), 30A-H18.

RESOLUTIONS ON THE MEXICAN WAR

In Senate of the U.S.
Dec[embe]r 15 1847

Read & ordered to be printed

Mr. Calhoun submitted for consideration the following Resolution[s:]

Resolved; that to conquer Mexico and to hold ["her" *canceled and "it" interlined*] either as a Province, or to incorporate ["her" *canceled and "it" interlined*] in our Union would be inconsistent with the avowed object for which the war has been prosecuted; a departure from the settled policy of the Government; in conflict with its character and genius, and in the end subversive of our free & popular Institutions.

Resolved; that no line of policy in the further prosecution of the War should be adopted, which may lead to consequences, so disasterous.

ADU in DNA, RG 46 (U.S. Senate), 30A-B6; PC in Senate Document No. 8, 30th Cong., 1st Sess.; PC in *Congressional Globe*, 30th Cong., 1st Sess., p. 26 and p. 53; PC in Houston, ed., *Proceedings and Debates*, p. 24; PC in the Washington, D.C., *Daily Union*, December 15, 1847, p. 3; PC in the Washington, D.C., *Daily National Intelligencer*, December 16, 1847, p. 2.

To H[ENRY] W. CONNER, [Charleston]

Washington, 16th Dec[embe]r 1847

My dear Sir, When I parted with you & other friends in Charleston, I hoped to be able, in a short time, to inform you, what would be the probable direction, which events would take in reference to the great questions, which now agitate the country; but I regret to say, that I have, as yet, been able to form no definite opinion. I have, however, seen enough to satisfy me, that we have much to fear & little to hope, in reference either to the abolition, or Mexican question. I fear that even the South will be fatally divided in reference to the former. You have of course seen the resolutions [of 12/14] of Mr. Dickerson [*sic*; Daniel S. Dickinson, Senator from N.Y.]. They, I doubt not, originate with the administration, and are intended to cover both questions, but more especially the abolition, and to form a ["rallying" *canceled*] point around, which the whole democratick party may rally. Much circumlocution is used, in order to disguise their real meaning, but their real object is to affirm, that the territorial Legislatures may exclude the introduction of slaves, while they deny that Congress can. The plain intent, taking the two resolutions together, is, to errect whatever part of Mexico we may acquire, or choose to take[,] into territories & let the people of the territories, Mexicans and all, decide whether slavery shall be excluded or not. Now, when we reflect, that the Mexicans are all abolitionists, it is easy to see, that the scheme will, as effectually exclude slavery, as would the Wilmot proviso itself. Indeed, I would rather concede to Congress the right of deciding whether slavery should or should not exist in ["the" *canceled and* "a" *interlined*] territory, than to leave it to the Mexicans to decide. In the one case we would at least have some control; but in the other none; and yet there are Southern men, who I fear will be either too blind to see the truth, or too much devoted to party & President making to act on it.

["Should" *canceled and* "Such" *interlined*] a state of things clearly show[s], that a press such as we propose is indispensable here; but at the same time, I regret to say, that I, as yet, see no prospect of any cooperation from any other Southern State, in the way of funds, or even sympathy with such a press. It would be, if established now, a Carolinian press exclusi[ve]ly, which, I fear, would very greatly diminish its usefulness. Thus thinking, my impression is, that it would not be advisable to establish it yet. It may be that the farther developements of the session will bring the South more together, when it may be established with advantage. I will keep my attention directed towards it.

As to the Mexican war, the great danger is, that it will terminate in leaving no choice, but to hold it as a conquered Province, or incorporate it in the Union. I have moved ["the resolutio(?)" *canceled*] on the subject to bring the ["fact before" *canceled and* "danger to the notice of" *interlined*] the people & the govern[men]t, with all the ["dangers" *canceled and* "calamities" *interlined*] to which it will expose us, so that they may deliberately decide with their eyes open, ["whether they" *canceled*] whether they will presist [*sic*] in a course of policy, which must lead to such results, or not. In making the movement, I have changed no opinion, or views which I have heretofore entertained or expressed. The future is as uncertain and menacing, as it was the day the war was declared. What will be the end no one can tell, but let what will come I shall do my duty.

As to the remain[in]g question, the Presidential election, the indications are strongly in favour of General [Zachary] Taylor. The Whigs, I do not think will run [Henry] Clay. Indeed, the Southern Whigs cannot; and they will, I think, rally to a man around ["him" *canceled and* "Taylor" *interlined*]. I can get nothing authentick as to his opinion; but the impression is strong, that he will be with us on the questions of the Convention, slavery & the Tariff of '46.

Show this to [Franklin H.] Elmore, [Ker] Boyce & other friends. I cannot write to all, and I hope that a letter to one will be regarded as to all.

I shall take up my resolutions after the holy days. I hope our papers will come out ag[ai]nst Dickerson's resolutions; & that some able pen will expose them in the Mercury. Should they be adopted our situation will be more critical than ["they" *canceled and* "it" *interlined*] ever has been. The resolutions passed unanimously by the Senate of Georgia are well drawn up & the ["two first" *canceled and* "second" *interlined*] directly negatives his, as far as territories are concerned. Yours truly, J.C. Calhoun.

ALS in ScC; photostat of ALS in DLC, Henry Workman Conner Papers.

From WADDY THOMPSON, [JR., former U.S. Minister to Mexico]

Greenville [S.C.,] Dec. 18, 1847

My Dear Sir, I see that the madness which rules the hour is increasing and seems literally to grow by what it feeds on. I have already spread upon the record my protest from the very commencement of this ill advised Mexican war. I have no wish or purpose to publish another line on the subject. But if the suggestions which I now make have any weight they will be more useful in your hands than any other. Will the governments of Europe[,] France & England especially[,] consent to our subjugating Mexico? I have very many reasons for saying they will not—some of these reasons not in the possession of every one. Can we prosecute the war if those countries interpose[?] Our supplies & reinforcements must be sent by sea. Their combined navies in the Gulph of Mexico without a single soldier on land would at once put an end to the war. Shall we run the risk of such intervention and all the consequences of the conflict which will ensue—or the equally painful alternative of being forced to abandon the war. There will *certainly* be such an intervention unless we assume the debt of Mexico. If we take the foreign we must take the domestic debt also. That debt is not less than 100 millions. Is the country worth this sum to us besides the annual cost of keeping in subjection an insubordinate & habitually rebellious people—a people indolent[,] vicious and producing nothing for foreign commerce but the precious metals—and this their single product costing more than its value. The same labor in manufactures or agriculture is much more profitable than the average labor in mining operations in Mexico. To say nothing of the difficulty of keeping in subjection as a province eight millions of people. Does history furnish any instance of such a result[?] I know of none. To receive them into the union is impossible—such a measure would ipso facto dissolve the union. To which segment would Mexico belong—and would that fraction have power to retain it[?] Before this war a majority of the people of the northern departments would have been in favor of a union with us. I do not believe that one per cent of our people would have consented to such a union. How much more onerous and less desirable would such a union be when forced upon Mexico[?] All the incompatibilities of language[,] race[,] religion[,] education and institutions will occur to every one. Is the country desirable per se—even if we could get it free from the incumbrance of its hetero-geneous—vicious & hostile population[?] I do not think that it is. I am quite sure that there is no portion of our own vacant territory which is not more desirable to such a population as ours.

We have the authority of [Baron Alexander von] Humboldt that in the latitude of Mexico sugar and cotton will not grow above the elevation of 2000 feet. On the whole Gulph coast the mountains come down almost to the sea shore. I believe that from Matamoros to [*partial word canceled*] Alvarado the average distance from the sea at which that elevation is attained is not more than fifty miles. On the route from Vera Cruz to the city of Mexico—it is not twenty miles. This narrow belt is generally ["the" *canceled*] sterile and precipitous mountains and the worst climate on this contine[n]t[,] the very home of yellow fever. Would any sensible farmer abandon the advantages of the valley of the Mississippi or of Texas for such a country[?] Beyond this narrow belt the land is generally poor and entirely destitute of timber—generally more sterile than any equal portion of the United States with which I am acquainted. But if it were otherwise[,] if well timbered and as rich as the Nile[,] there is the conclusive & insuperable objection that there is not & never can be the means of transportation. Suppose a farmer having corn & wheat (and the grains are all that can be cultivated) one hundred and fifty miles from the sea coast[;] will the price for which he can sell them pay for the transportation[?] The average distance will be more than twice that. If he raises stock what can he do with it[?] If he kills it he cannot cure it even on the table lands. The coldest weather even there is very much like our warm April weather—and meat cannot be well cured. But if it could can it be transported by land two or three hundred miles and compete with the supplies from our inexhaustible West—which are sent by water from the very doors of the farmers[?] If they drive it to the seaboard and kill it putrefaction will begin before it is cut up & salted. These are no new opinions advanced now for the sake of argument. I have always believed that Mexico never could become a great farming country for the simple reason that it has not and never can have the means of transportation to market. The climate is delicious and the country just suited to a lazey people like the Mexicans—whose highest idea of happiness is the "dolce farniente.["] What earthly good can come of diffusing our people over such an extent & sending them to a country where their labor will be so much less profitable[?] But to us of the South it is positive madness. If it was proposed to annex Canada & the Brittish possessions all would see what an overwhelming addition would be made to the power of the free States. It is not more certain that those States would be non slave holding than that these Mexican States will.

It is nakedly a proposition to add fifteen or twenty non slave holding States to our union—woe to the Southern man who lends his aid to doing that.

This Mexican country is the natural outlet to some extent for our negro population. If any thing can prevent this it will be the erection of dykes to arrest it by planting non slave holding American States on our Mexican border.

I do not design this as even a summary of the argument upon this vitally important question. All the leading views I know have occurred to you. It may be that some of these have not and I cannot give you a higher evidence of my conviction of the deep importance of the issues involved nor of my respect for your course upon the subject than by suggesting them to you. Respe[ct]f[u]lly & truly Yours, Waddy Thompson.

ALS in ScCleA; PC in Jameson, ed., *Correspondence*, pp. 1149–1152.

From J[OHN] A. CAMPBELL

Mobile, December 20, 1847

Dear Sir, You have heard before this of Mr. [Dixon H.] Lewis' election [as Senator from Ala.] & Col. [William R.] King[']s defeat. As Col. King was bound up with the Northern democrats of a very doubtful order, & as he was the candidate of the Hunkers here this was a work very well done. Mr. Lewis I fear has made pledges which will greatly embarrass him & estrange his friends in this section. He pledged himself I learn to abide a national convention for the selection of a candidate[,] *preferring* a Northern man. He pledged himself to sustain Mr. [James K.] Polk further than his message calls for support.

In this he will not be upheld. You know what a rough piece of work we have had to perform in this State.

The overthrow of [Martin] Van Buren & his dynasty ["and" *canceled*] has not been completed without an effort. With me (and I can say the same as to the most of our friends) the spoils principle was the great & cardinal principle in their party government to which our hostility was directed. That principle had its entire force communicated to it by the use they made of the caucus system. I thought I observed a decided change among some of our friends ["after" *canceled and* "upon" *interlined*] my return in reference to that system.

They supposed that the party organisation had passed into our hands in consequence of the movements in New York. It is not so. Even here in Alabama we cannot defeat them. I tell you and Mr. Lewis too that if Silas Wright had lived we could not have prevented his nomination except by the use of Mr. [James] Buchanan[']s name.

It was a profound conviction of our inability to meet those men successfully with any democrat I could name that induced me (of course there were other reasons) to favour the [Zachary] Taylor movements. They (Hunkers) at once spoke of [Levi] Woodbury to hush our mouths on the subject of Taylor. The plain reason of this is, that the mountain democracy command the State and our politicians defer to their wishes. The whole of the talent of the democratic party in this State is with us but, the county leaders are not— and our leaders are unwilling to ["lead" *canceled and* "combat" *interlined*]. They succumb continually to those mountaineers.

The whole strength of the Hunkers of this State will be given to Buchanan. He is the administration candidate in the South. He expects the South to aid him against a Wilmot proviso Northern man. How can we get rid of him[?] There is but one mode. It is for some public man to take bold decided ground against him. I will not vote for him myself. I will vote for no man whose foreign policy has been so shamefully defective in sound judgement & whose personal character is so equivocal. I refer now to his transactions between Gen[era]l [Andrew] Jackson & Mr. [Henry] Clay in 1825 & his assertion that Mr. Polk was a better friend of a protective Tariff than Mr. Clay.

What can we do? [Lewis] Cass has taken so much pains to estrange us that it would be a pity if we disappointed him.

[Vice-President George M.] Dallas loses caste from his connections with Polk. He seems to want position & character.

Mr. Woodbury has reached quite as high a place as nature ever intended he should fill. He has been true to us. He can be depended on as a party man. I am willing to vote for him, as a party candidate. Looking above the party can we hope any good from his nomination[?] It would create a schism in every Northern State in the democratic party. He has no hold on the popular favor. He has no public services to gild his pretensions. He was a prominent member of the Senate and supported the party creed & that is all we can say. He would be nominated as the Southern candidate at the North. Has he any popularity in the South? His connection as Vice President with a ticket having your name as President upon it induces some to think kindly of him. His fidelity on the Texas & Tariff ["endears" *canceled*] struggles endears him to others.

Has he any popularity with the voters? Could one in ten thousand repeat a single word that he has ever spoken[?] Is he identified with anything save the Pet bank system & [Samuel] Swartwout[']s failure[?] If you encourage Mr. Woodbury's pretensions you may take my word, that you will ["en" *canceled*] only receive in return defeat. I do not think at the North he can unite the Barnburning democrats to him in any of the States & in the South he has no popularity. The contest in his absence is then between Dallas & Buchanan supposing Cass & Van Buren out of the way. In that contest Buchanan has the advantage all over the country. The signs point to him directly as the ["future" *interlined*] nominee of the party.

It comes then at last to this[,] what can we do? The perils of a party contest seem to me so imminent—the introduction at [the coming convention at] Baltimore of the disgraceful scenes that were witnessed at Syracuse appears so probable that for one I am disposed to part with a party organisation.

At present there is but one principle on which it is sought.

That principle is deadly to the Constitution & Union. It is to give full support to Mr. Polk and his administration. To carry out the infamous design of destroying the nationality of Mexico.

We cannot support Mr. Clay nor [John] McLean—nor [John J.]

Crittenden—nor [Thomas] Corwin—we cannot be transmuted into whigs.

We must find a man who will not accept a party nomination.

General Taylor is that man.

In reference to the territory question. It appears to me that the Southern people will be found in a weak position if they insist on the acquisition of territory.

In reference to that subject it appears to me that the just grounds upon which to place ourselves is that we desire none & ask for none for the purpose of strengthening our institutions but we will not suffer those institutions to be weakened by the action of Congress. If territory is acquired we insist on our share but we have no wish to make the acquisition. I was pleased with Mr. Clay[']s resolution of disavowal. It was of the same nature as your own opposition to the war. I have continually disavowed for the South & have indignantly resented the imputation of a purpose on the part of our people to spread slavery or any other institution by means of this war. The impression has been industriously made upon the Northern people that this was the end for which the war was proclaimed. Your opposition to the war has been the most ready answer to such aspersions. We require vindication. We require a moderate & even ["a" *interlined*] self denying course of conduct in all matters connected with the settlement of the terms of the peace. Let us have peace[;] we shall not quarrel about the terms. In having a peace ["with Mexico" *interlined*] we must not transfer the war so that it shall reach our homes. I say we should leave the Northern people to settle the peace as they like & to arrange the question, of territory (within proper bounds) but always with the *proviso* that no inequality should result. We should be the *Proviso* men[;] on that ground we should make our stand.

I have written to New Orleans for the information you desire in regard to Gen[era]l Taylor. Very Respectfully Y[ou]rs, J.A. Campbell.

[P.S.] Write to me at Montgomery so that it may reach me before the 8th Prox.

ALS in ScCleA; variant PC in Jameson, ed., *Correspondence*, pp. 1152–1155.

Documents relating to the petition of Hugh Wallace Wormeley, presented by Calhoun to the Senate on 12/20. Calhoun submitted additional documents in support of a claim for a pension previously referred to the Committee on Pensions. Abs in *Senate Journal*, 30th Cong., 1st Sess., p. 59; Abs in *Congressional Globe*, 30th Cong., 1st Sess., p. 50.

From WILSON LUMPKIN,
[former Senator from Ga.]

Athens [Ga.,] Dec. 20th 1847

My dear Sir, I am in receipt of your letter of the 12th Inst. Upon the subjects of our Internal, & External affairs—I find every one in suspense, from the President [James K. Polk] down to the humblest Citizen; we have to wait for the developments of time, to write the history of the future. We have no divinely inspired prophets in whom we can confide.

I have no doubt, the *President makers*, of *both parties*, are disposed at present, to avoid any action in Congress, on the slave question. But as a private Citizen of the South, I am wearied with annoyance, & menace on this subject. The Wilmot Proviso, is but one item in our Bill of Complaints. I am tired of skirmishing on this subject. Let us have no more *bush* fighting. I want an issue, that will embrace the whole subject.

I want nothing but a literal & faithful adhereance to the compromises of the Constitution on the slave question, & nothing less can be satisfactory to the people of the slave-holding States. Violations of our rights, & assaults upon our peace & quiet—whether they come from Congress, or State Legislation, are equally provoking, & tend to allienate our affections & produce those sectional prejudices, which endanger the perpetuity of our system.

It is often, much less difficult to get into trouble, than to get out of it.

Solomon said, "a Wise man foreseeith the evil & avoideth it." As a public man, I have often been accused by my friends, of extending my prudence, to the point of timidity. But I still think, it is much better to do but little than to do great mischief. It is the present state of ["the" *canceled*] our Mexican relations, that gives rise to the foregoing reflections. I don[']t know how we can best get out of the war. Mr. [Henry] Clay[']s plan won[']t do. His Lexington speech may be considered his political Epitaph. But a very small portion of the people will sustain Mr. Clay[']s views. It will require the united wisdom of every patriot at Washington, to make the best of the Mexican War.

I am uncompromising in my aversion, to the idea of annexing the whole of Mexico to our Union—Either by a speedy or more gradual process. It is best for Mexico to retain her national character. I am equally averse to the idea of our governing it, for a long course of years, as a conquered province.

All things considered, as they exist at present—I can see nothing better, than to seize & retain a proper Territorial indemnity. Notwithstanding the extended argument of the President in his message, against the course which I suggest—I think he magnifies the difficulties of changeing the Mexican War, into a *defensive* war. Unpleasant as a border war may be, allmost every State of this Union, have proved their capacity & ability, to maintain such wars successfully—& at a limited expense, compared with that of an invadeing war. However, I don[']t assume to know, what is the best policy to be pursued. Your individual position, is an extremely delicate one. You stand aloof from the corruptions & intrigues of both the great political parties of the Country. The selfish of both parties look upon you with an Evil Eye. Strictly speaking, you are attached to no party whatever. Yet you have a strong hold on the confidence of honest intelligent men every where. Connect your name, with the idea of official power & station, and the party leaders of all parties are at once united, in leveling their heaviest metal against you. And yet I do not entertain a single doubt, if your name could be brought directly before the people, for the first office of the Country—in opposition to any one man, in the U.S. of either, any, or no party—you would be overwhelmingly the choice of the American people. And yet strange to see, the combination & machinery of party is such, that your influence is limited, to comparatively a small circle. Your position, ["is" *interlined*] rather limited to ["the" *interlined*] work of preventing evil to the country, than that of devising & carrying out great measures of utility to the country.

You have however much to console you, on reviewing the past. The efficiency & glory of our triumphant army in Mexico, is by no means disconnected with your labors, while at the head of the War Department.

Our present Treasury system, with all its multiplyed advantages to the Country—points to you as one of its founders. The present admirable state of our Currency & commercial Exchanges, must be connected with your name. Your *Free Trade* views, long entertained & nobly advocated, will pervade the Civilized world, & its

27

inestimable benefits be felt, by every consumer of food & raiment. I might enlarge, but enough for the present. At your leisure, please keep [me] apprized of such under currents, as cannot be seen upon the surface. Truly Yours, Wilson Lumpkin.

ALS in ScCleA; variant PC in Boucher and Brooks, eds., *Correspondence*, pp. 412–413.

REMARKS ON HIS RESOLUTIONS ON THE CONQUEST OF MEXICO

[In the Senate, December 20, 1847]

Mr. Calhoun. I hope that the resolutions which I offered the other day [12/15] may now be taken up, in order to fix a day for their consideration.

The resolutions were then taken up and read, as follows:

> *Resolved*, That to conquer Mexico and to hold it, either as a province or to incorporate it into the Union, would be inconsistent with the avowed object for which the war has been prosecuted; a departure from the settled policy of the Government; in conflict with its character and genius; and in the end subversive of our free and popular institutions.
> *Resolved*, That no line of policy in the further prosecution of the war should be adopted which may lead to consequences so disastrous.

Mr. Calhoun. I shall be regulated in fixing the day by the wishes of the Senate. I have no particular desire in regard to a very early consideration of the resolutions. All I wish is, that there should be no unnecessary delay. If it be agreeable to the Senate, I propose that they be taken up on the first Tuesday in January next—two weeks from to-morrow [1/4/1848].

[*William Allen of Ohio declared that Calhoun's resolutions were "ambiguous" and that he wished them to be clarified.*]

Mr. Calhoun. I will answer the Senator from Ohio with a great deal of pleasure. It is not my intention to involve any question in reference to territorial indemnity, or any other subject apart from that which is presented in the resolution itself. I believe the pressing question at this moment is, whether we shall conquer Mexico, and hold her as a subjected province, or incorporate her into our Union. That, of course, would involve the nationality of Mexico; and it was to that point that my resolution referred. I think, sir, it is a question which ought to be first decided, because, Mr. President, if I am any judge at all of the operation of existing causes, the certain tendency of all that we are now doing is to the annihilation of the nationality of Mexico; and that we shall thus find ourselves, unless the greatest caution is exercised, at the end of another campaign, or at some future time, with eight or nine millions of Mexicans, without a government, on our hands, not knowing what to do with them, and forced to one or other of the alternatives which I have presented. This is a question which I consider as exceeding in importance all others at this time. After that is decided, we may then consider what course, in accordance with that decision, it may be wise to pursue. I, for one, wish to guide my own course, and I offered the resolution for the double purpose of bringing it before this body and before the country, and putting myself in reference to this Mexican question where I wish to stand.

[*Daniel S. Dickinson of New York remarked that his own resolutions, previously introduced, should have precedence on the Senate calendar.*]

Mr. Calhoun. I perceive that one of the morning papers supposes that my resolutions were introduced with reference to those offered by the Senator from New York. Not at all. My resolutions were written several days before his were introduced. The Senator may fix any day he pleases for the consideration of his resolutions, either before or after the day fixed upon for the consideration of mine.

[*Allen suggested that there would be many resolutions concerning the war during this session and that therefore the best course would be to refer all to a committee of the Senate. (He was chairman of the Committee on Foreign Relations.)*]

Mr. Calhoun. I do trust that the course suggested by the Senator shall not be pursued. What is the object of the reference? Reference is made to committees for the purpose of considering and perfecting details; but here there are no details to settle. In fact, it is a simple proposition. The Senate have only to determine whether it is intended or desired that the whole of Mexico shall be conquered—her nationality destroyed—and that we shall be placed in a position in which we shall be compelled either to hold her as a subjected province, or incorporate her into our Union. We have carried this business of reference far beyond the parliamentary rules, and have encroached, in my opinion, in no small degree on the rights of individual Senators here. As to the number of resolutions that may be offered, I have no reason to believe that there will be many. Only two have been introduced, and they upon entirely different subjects.

One I understand refers to the slave question—mainly, at least—and the other to a question entirely aside from that. Sir, I do not believe that there will be a long discussion. Unless I am very greatly deceived, there will be no great division—at least there is not at present a great division in the country on this point, and I trust there will not be in this body. The end against which I wish to guard, is one which heretofore has not been contemplated. I do not know that such an end is now contemplated. I trust that it is not intended. But we may find ourselves in a position not intended, and from which we cannot extricate ourselves. My object in introducing the resolutions, is to guard against such a result. I trust they will have that effect, and that the Senator will not agree to refer them to the Committee on Foreign Relations.

[*Allen spoke at length.*]

Mr. Calhoun. I rise principally to correct an error into which the Senator from Ohio has fallen, doubtless from having misunderstood my remarks. I by no means said that I considered the annihilation of the nationality of Mexico and the acquisition of a portion of her territory as identical; on the contrary, I said expressly that I did not understand the resolution as involving the question of territory at all. I agree with him that we may take a part—very large parts of Mexico without touching her nationality. My object is very different; and to satisfy the Senator I will tell him that I have changed not a single opinion, which I have ever expressed, in relation to this Mexican war. I hope that this will satisfy him.

Now, sir, if I understand the drift of the Senator's remarks, and of his motion, it is this—that he wishes these resolutions of mine to go to the Committee on Foreign Relations in order that they may make a report upon them before I myself have an opportunity of being heard upon them. I ask, is that fair? I introduced a general subject here, and the Senator proposes to take it out of my hands before I am heard—sending it to the Committee on Foreign Relations, where it is to be discussed and reported on in advance of my own explanation of it. Is there any precedent to be found in this or any other parliamentary body for a procedure of that kind? As he believes, there is no instance of such resolutions being introduced and not referred to a committee before discussion. I do not know an instance in which any such reference has been made. I myself at the last session introduced important resolutions on the subject of slavery. They were discussed here and everywhere.

Mr. Allen, (in his seat.) There is no committee of the Senate on slavery.

Mr. Calhoun. You have a Committee on Territories, and that involved a territorial question. You may raise a special committee. There is no difference in that view between a special and regular committee. The whole drift of his motion—on which I shall say no more—is to take my own resolutions out of my own hand, so that the committee may make the first speech on them, to which I will be called upon to reply, instead of explaining my own resolutions. I submit whether that be fair.

[*Allen spoke again, withdrawing his motion. Calhoun's resolutions were ordered to be considered on 1/4/1848. Then Daniel S. Dickinson moved that his resolutions be taken up on the day before Calhoun's were to be considered. These resolutions stated that the true policy of the U.S. was to annex such "contiguous territory" as could be justly acquired and would strengthen the government's "political and commercial relations upon this continent." Further, that in new territories to be organized, "all questions concerning the domestic policy therein" should be decided by the legislatures of such territories. Dickinson's motion provoked further discussion.*]

Mr. Calhoun hoped that the Senator would fix an earlier day for the consideration of these resolutions than that fixed for those which he (Mr. C[alhoun]) had offered.

Mr. Dickinson was desirous only of an opportunity of explaining his resolutions before the entrance of any other subject, which, by giving rise to discussion, might prevent him from doing so.

Mr. Calhoun suggested that the Senator could have the opportunity which he sought on the morning of the day after that fixed for the consideration of his (Mr. C[alhoun]'s) resolutions.

Mr. Dickinson. I am not so sure of that; and I prefer that my resolutions retain the priority, to which they are entitled in the order in which they were offered. I may not trespass long on the attention of the Senate in addressing it on the resolutions, but what little I have to say I desire to offer before discussion arises on other subjects.

Mr. Calhoun. I must make a remark here. The Senate has already fixed a day for the consideration of my resolutions; and the Senator now proposes the day immediately preceding for the consideration of his—thus anticipating mine. That his resolutions shall pass without discussion is impossible. There will be, as I take it, great diversity of opinion on the subject, at least as the resolutions now stand. They may lead to a long discussion. Now I do not think that it would be treating my resolutions fairly, if, after having fixed a day for their consideration, the day immediately preceding should be set apart for the consideration of others which must give rise to discussion, in consequence of which mine may be cut off. If the Senator wishes to be heard, he can be heard on any intermediate day, or on the morning immediately after the day set apart for the consideration of my resolutions.

[*Dickinson defended his position. Lewis Cass of Michigan argued that the two sets of resolutions ought to be considered together, but that, at this stage of the war, it would be unwise to make any declaration of intentions, which might aid the enemy or prove foolish in the eyes of the world.*]

Mr. Calhoun. I should be very glad indeed to think with the honorable gentleman from Michigan, that there is no person in the country who thinks of the extinction of the nationality of Mexico. Why, you can hardly read a newspaper without finding it filled with speculation upon this subject. The proceedings that took place in Ohio, at a dinner given to one of the volunteer officers of the army returned from Mexico, show conclusively that the impression entertained by the persons present, was, that our troops would never leave Mexico until they had conquered the whole country. This was the sentiment advanced by the officer, and it was applauded by the assembly, and endorsed by the official paper of that State.

But this is not the point. The question is not now whether such a thing is contemplated. I attribute no such motive to any one. I look at the progress of events. I look at what is proposed and the end of it—those consequences which I propose to avert by this resolution. Sir, let any man look at the progress of this war—let him consider how we got into it, not expecting to get into it at all, for certainly the Executive officers expressed, in the strongest manner, their conviction that there was not the slightest hazard of war at the time when our troops marched to the Rio Grande. What next? After the war was commenced we were told that the Government was to conquer a peace; and what have we been told since? That we must carry on the war vigorously. Where is this to end? The whole progress towards the accomplishment of this avowed object of the President, to conquer a peace, has been marked by an earnest desire eagerly to prosecute the war; to go on and go on, until we find ourselves where no man expected. Sir, instead of being an abstraction, these resolutions are eminently practical; they are intended to present to the people of this country a *finale*, probably not now anticipated, but which will come if proper precautions be not taken. It is while the public mind is yet sound, and while the Senate, as I believe, is prepared almost unanimously to vote against such an end of the war, that I wish this expression of opinion to be made. Sir, we begin now to find the misfortune of entering into a war without a declaration of war—without a declaration setting forth to the people the causes of the war, and one upon which they may hold the Government responsible. We have got into a war by a recognition of war, and not a declaration, and hence the necessity for this resolution, to negative a result which we do not contemplate. No, sir, it is as practical as any measure that can be brought forward; for, until the question which arises upon these resolutions is decided, we shall be at a loss to know what amount of supplies, how many men, and how much money to grant. If it be declared, that it is not intended to conquer Mexico so as to destroy her nationality, this will throw a great deal of light upon our vote; but if it be contemplated to do this, then more men and more money will be required; and hence the decision upon these resolutions is the preliminary step to be taken. Sir, it was a good old practice in the early stages of this Government, when the President of these United States sent an address to Congress, that an answer to that address was prepared in a Committee of the Whole, and the whole affairs of the nation were discussed before any measures were adopted. That is the course pursued in the British Parliament, and in the French Chamber of Deputies. That practice has been dropped, and the various subjects now come before us piecemeal, and are referred to committees, and we have no opportunity of knowing what the state of the Union is, until we are called upon to vote upon the various propositions so submitted. Now, I hope that a discussion will be had, if discussion be necessary, and that a vote will be taken, though, if what I hear from the Senator from Michigan be correct, that no man contemplates the entire conquest of all Mexico, then we need not have a long discussion; and it will be very satisfactory to myself, at least, and I believe it will be highly satisfactory to the people generally, to have it declared that such a thing is not contemplated.

[*After further extended discussion on the floor and private conversation between Calhoun and Dickinson, Dickinson withdrew his motion.*]

From *Congressional Globe*, 30th Cong., 1st Sess., pp. 53–55. Also printed in the Washington, D.C., *Daily National Intelligencer*, December 22, 1847, p. 1; the Washington, D.C., *Daily Union*, December 22, 1847, p. 2; the New York, N.Y., *Morning Courier and New-York Enquirer*, December 22, 1847, p. 2; the Richmond, Va., *Whig and Public Advertiser*, December 24, 1847, p. 2; the Charleston, S.C., *Courier*, December 29, 1847, p. 2; the Charleston, S.C., *Mercury*, December 29, 1847, p. 2; Houston, ed., *Proceedings and Debates*, pp. 30–32. Partly printed in *Niles' National Register*, vol. LXIII, no. 17 (December 25, 1847), p. 272; the Nashville, Tenn., *Whig*, December 30, 1847, p. 2; Wilson, ed.,

The Essential Calhoun, p. 160. Variants in the Washington, D.C., *Daily Union*, December 20, 1847, p. 3; the Washington, D.C., *Daily National Intelligencer*, December 21, 1847, p. 2; the Alexandria, Va., *Gazette and Virginia Advertiser*, December 21, 1847, p. 3; the New York, N.Y., *Herald*, December 21, 1847, p. 4, and December 22, 1847, pp. 3–4; the Petersburg, Va., *Republican*, December 23, 1847, p. 2; the Charleston, S.C., *Courier*, December 28, 1847, p. 2; the Columbia, S.C., *South-Carolinian*, December 31, 1847, p. 2; the Memphis, Tenn., *Daily Appeal*, January 5, 1848, p. 2.

To F[RANKLIN] H. ELMORE, Charleston

Washington, 22d De[cembe]r 1847

My dear Sir, I have not neglected your request to ascertain, as far as I could here what would be the probable amount of the cotton crop, & to let you know the result.

I have made frequent enquiries, but can get nothing satisfactory. From a variety of causes, it is more difficult this year to form an estimate, than it has been for several past years. The general impression is, that it will be about 2,200,000. Such also is mine; but it is but an impression. I shall act on it, but have not sufficient confidence in it, to advise any friend to act on it. Should it not exceed that amount, I am of the impression the price will rise in the spring.

I wrote to Mr. [Henry W.] Conner not long since in reference to the state of things here, and requested him to show the letter to you & other friends.

Since then there has been nothing calculated to change the opinion I then expressed. If any thing the occurrences since have but served to impress me more deeply, as to the critical state of both the Mexican & slave questions, and the impossibility of finding any reliable candidate at the North, and the hazard of looking on our part to that quarter for a candidate. It is impossible for the South to unite with the North on any of their prominent men ["for" *canceled and* "as" *interlined*] a candi[d]ate without making dangerous concessions on the slave question, of which Dickerson's [Senator Daniel S. Dickinson's] resolutions furnish conclusive proof. As dangerous as ["are" *canceled and* "is" *interlined*] the concession which they make, I find many Southern men disposed to make it. I fear they will be adopted. If they should, I shall regard it as a surrender on our part of the whole ground. Yours truly, J.C. Calhoun.

ALS in DLC, Franklin Harper Elmore Papers.

34

Remarks on the reception of an anti-slavery petition, 12/22. John P. Hale of N.H. presented a petition from the Anti-Slavery Friends of Ind. requesting abolition of slavery in D.C. In accordance with usual Senate practice, a question was called on a motion to table the motion to receive the petition. "Mr. Calhoun hoped the usual course would be pursued. We had never been troubled with but one petition of this sort in this body." The Senate by a vote of 33 to 9 laid on the table the motion to receive the petition. From the New York, N.Y., *Herald*, December 24, 1847, p. 2. Variant in the Washington, D.C., *Daily Union*, December 23, 1847, p. 2; *Congressional Globe*, 30th Cong., 1st. Sess., p. 63; Houston, ed., *Proceedings and Debates*, p. 37.

From FRANKLIN SMITH

Barnum's Hotel Baltimore
Dec[embe]r 22d 1847

Sir: I believe you to be the only great man that has been in Washington for the last two years and the only statesman worthy of the name between this point & the Isthmus of Panama and though personally a stranger to you yet you have no friend in the United States this day whose heart throbs with a truer devotion to you or with a higher admiration for your character than mine does. I have watched you nearly & weighed your purposes well & it is clear to my mind that you have stated the truth that for the last eight or ten years you have held parties in contempt & looked solely to the good of your country. You have looked over the mole hill of the presidency and fixed your eye on the far off mountain of principle. The Presidency could confer on you no honor. The Caesars are forgotten but Cato lives in imperishable renown. A party is springing up in our country enamoured with the spoils of war & eager for plunder. A party is forming that expects to live by war individually & to fill the national exchequer by the same means, a proconsular party ["that" *canceled*] destined if not checked to run the same career as they did in old Rome cheat the Senate & beggar the provinces plunder both sides those who give them power & those over whom they rule. All your predictions of the war have so far proved true. It is now admitted that the general who ["first" *interlined*] conquered Mexico *must be President.* Henry Clay is no body, Martin Van Buren is no body, John C. Calhoun is no body. There are no eyes to see, nor

35

hearts to beat for any body else but General Zachary Taylor. You warned the small potatoe men at the head of the Government what would be the result but they like cowardly enchanters having raised the devil are afraid to look him in the face. You saved your country's Constitution when you came to the aid of a hated rival in 1837 on the subtreasury bill. You saved the South from Bondage when you struck for free trade years before. You ["ha"[?] *canceled*] saved your country when you got us out of the Oregon difficulty. Had your voice been listened to in the Spring of '46 you would have saved us from this war. Had your counsels been [*partial word canceled*] followed in Febr[uar]y '47 this war would have been long since honourably closed, all our rights protected, our republican institutions & glorious Constitution freed from the cor[r]oding canker of a public debt, and the hearths of thousands & tens of thousands of the victors & the vanquished would have remained unshrouded in mourning. You are the true warden on the watch tower—your eye is ever open—& when you see the foe approach in the distance you ring the alarum bell in time to bring the tenants of the castle to their posts. To show the utter degradation of the press—how completely it is sold to party—though both sides denounced your speech at Charleston (except the Union [newspaper] at Washington) so far as I know neither side dared to publish it. Yet it has entirely dissipated the dark cloud that lowered upon us. *The Polititians of the North expecting* ["government" *canceled and* "national" *interlined*] *offices* have been compelled to take a stand against the Wilmot Proviso. Had you waited until they had become committed it would have been too late. You are now right in your course in reference to the resolutions recently offered ["by" *canceled*] by you. Let great men or little men sneer & say what they please—there is a disposition not loud but deep fast growing ["among"(?) *canceled*] up in the country in which hundreds of thousands participate to seize all Mexico[,] confiscate the church property & seize ["& work" *interlined*] the mines ["fa"(?) *canceled*]. I look on the President's Message as contemplating the extinction of Mexican nationality. No man but a fool (& it would be a species of treason to say the President [James K. Polk] is one) can believe for a moment that if the Congress of the United States once organize a governmental occupancy (even through the military) ["of" *canceled and then interlined;* "that" *interlined and canceled*] Mexico that it will be ever given up. It is not in the nature of power to release its grasp. And in the career of plunder & conquest there will constantly arise leaders more unscrupulous than their predecessors. Unless this war is stopped our epitaph is written. It is recorded in the history of Rome & France. Propagandists of liberty at the point of the bayonet, & levying contributions to carry on the kindly work while in the mean time we are sowing the dragon's teeth of corruption & robbery to spring up in armed men & to destroy us. "What does it profit a man if he gain the whole world & lose his own soul or what shall a man give in exchange for his soul"? What ["it" *canceled*] will it profit us to gain the whole world & lose the soul of our institutions? Mr. Clay is in his dotage or he must think the people fools. How he can reconcile his speech at New Orleans with his late speech in ["La." *canceled*] Ky. is a question which all men ask. It can [*ms. torn*] done [*ms. torn*] thought the war popular when at o[*ms. torn*] tide changing when he spoke [*ms. torn*] & every body sees the dif[f]erence between your course & his. You stood up for principle alone; he decides after the event, you before. Sir I wish to vote for you for President. I was a most ardent supporter & friend of the President until I saw the course adopted to wards you on the [Thomas] Ri[t]chie affair & in reference to that great measure of humanity sense & national salvation your defensive line. For sustaining you, for upholding to the best of my humble abilities & with all the zeal natural to me your course & character I have been read ["of" *canceled*] out of the Democratic party in Missi[ssippi] where I reside. Malim cum Scaligero errare quam cum maevis recte sapere. I have learned to look to you for wisdom. I hope you will allow your name to go before the people for President. I want to vote for you. You owe it to your country to allow your friends to use your name. I don[']t wish to vote for a mere general—& I don[']t want to vote for small men who shape their course not *from principle* but from party. If you will allow your name to be used for the Presidency there is one in Missi[ssippi] who will see that your name & character shall not go undefended who will bear aloft your banner whether in bright days or dark days whether for victory or defeat & will use every exertion to call the people to the support of a great statesman in preference to a general or some small abortion of conventional corruption. I live at Canton Missi[ssippi]. Very respectfully your ob[edien]t s[ervan]t, Franklin Smith.

ALS in ScCleA. NOTE: An AEU by Calhoun reads "Franklin Smith."

From E[stwick] Evans

Philadelphia, Dec[embe]r 24, 1847

Sir: I have the honour, at this late period, to acknowledge your letter, in answer to mine, of the 21 March of the present year.

I am still waiting for an advantageous opening for the publication on State Rights, which is a subject of deep import—the embers of this fire being spread beneath the service of the whole country. The great immediate question, however, is whether new States are entitled to establish slave institutions. This is a splendid question—(although I candidly confess that I *like* not the subject,) because it involves *deep principles*, & *nice discrimination*, & close reasoning, which I think is a great feast to the mind. I *like* not slavery; but be pleased to mark that I do not *know* that it is *Relatively* wrong, (not *abstractedly*, which is not, by any means, always the question;) & very far am I from knowing that it is not eminently useful. I mean not to the master, which I will not take into the question, but to the slave him-self—& to the race.

I used to reside in Wash[ington]. I might be induced to reside there again, if I should find an advantageous situation in the Senate or House—particularly the former. The Whigs of that body would be friendly, & probably some not whigs. I am against the war. The [James K.] Polk dynasty (if I may so speak) if they cared at all one way or the other, would not be friendly. Had I an offer, I might accept it; & then employ leisure time in advancing what is *constitutionally*—& *politically* right in relation to the great question which interests you & your friends. Few, Sir, very—very few are *capable* of grasping the subject. It must be constitutional—a gubernatorial sort of mind; & a mind of comprehension—of reach—of depth, & of close, discriminative acumen. The man must have the Genius—the key from above, to unlock the chambers of this great *moral* subject. What do the generality of politicians—even among the shrewd & ambitious & laborious, ["know" *interlined*] of the depths of political being in free States—combined, too, with the complexities of a central system?

Be pleased [", Sir," *interlined*] to excuse this long & hasty letter, & to accept the very high consideration of Your Humble Ser[van]t, E. Evans.

ALS in ScCleA. NOTE: Evans (1787–1866) was a native of N.H. He was the author of *Essay on State Rights* (Washington: William Greer, Printer, 1844). A copy of this work in PHi contains Evans's record of purchasers, including eight copies to Calhoun and to Levi Woodbury, and four to Abel P. Upshur, among others.

From AND[RE]W TURNBULL

Esperanza near Princeton
Washington County, Miss. [*ca*. December 25, 1847]

My Dear Sir, When in New York [City] in the fall of 1846, I expressed to Mr. [James] Bogle, artist, my great desire to have your Portrait taken; and requested him, should he go to Washington the ensuing winter which he proposed doing, to give me timely information, that I might write to you, soliciting the favour of your sitting for me; & in case of my letter not reaching in time to solicit the favor for me himself. Business calling me unexpectedly to the west, Mr. Bogle[']s letter did not come to hand until my return to [South] Carolina, in succeeding summer when I deemed the time past: on visiting New York again, last fall however I was most agreeably surprised to find an almost finished portrait of one so highly valued & so justly beloved by every Carolinian as yourself. I cannot My dear Sir, express to you, the grateful sense, I have, of the obligation conferred upon me, and I sincerely thank you for your condescension and kindness in granting me so much of your invaluable time. Since leaving Charleston the Portrait has been finished, & sent on, & Mrs. [Gracia Rubine] Turnbull, yielding to the wishes of many friends, had it placed at [John] Russell[']s [bookstore in Charleston] in order that your fellow citizens, might have an opportunity of seeing it, & I am happy to learn that it has given great satisfaction. In the hope that this may find you, in the enjoyment of health, and that, you may be long spared to your Friends, to So. Carolina, and your Country is My Dear Sir the sincerest wish of Y[ou]r Assured friend & Most Ob[edien]t Servant, Andw. Turnbull.

ALS in ScCleA. NOTE: The above undated letter has been assigned the date of its postmark, "Columbia, S.C., 25 Dec.," though it was obviously composed earlier. The Charleston, S.C., *Courier*, October 21, 1847, p. 2, reported as follows: "We had the pleasure of seeing yesterday at Mr. Russell's Book store on King Street, an admirable portrait of our distinguished fellow-citizen, Mr. Calhoun, just completed by Mr. Bogle. It arrived a few days since from New York, purchased from Mr. Bogle by our fellow townsman Andrew Turnbull, Esq. It is regarded by members of the family of Mr. Calhoun, who have seen it, as the best likeness ever taken of him. It is certainly, according to our judgment, unexceptionable, both in feature and execution. The artist, Mr. Bogle, is a native of Georgetown, in our State; and it may be remembered, associated with his brother, exercised his art in this city some years since very successfully. He has however, to judge from the specimen before us, greatly improved in many respects, and now ranks considerably higher among portrait painters than he did then. He has established himself permanently in New York, and from the encouragement afforded him bids fair in a short time to realize an ample reward for his talents. He has taken several portraits of distinguished men at the North, which have been much admired for their fidelity and as specimens of fine art. A friend who has visited Mr. Bogle's studio in New York, where he saw the portrait of Mr. Calhoun to which we are now inviting attention, reports to us it was much admired there and confirms the favorable judgment we have passed upon it. It will remain a few days longer at Mr. Russell's on King Street." Andrew Turnbull was one of the few Southerners with whom Ralph Waldo Emerson was acquainted, they having been classmates at Harvard.

To A[NNA] M[ARIA CALHOUN] CLEMSON, [Brussels]

Washington, 26th Dec[embe]r 1847
My dear daughter, I was quite disappointed in not receiving a letter from either you, or Mr. [Thomas G.] Clemson by the last steamer. I, however, got the box & the books transmitted by you & Mr. Clemson. Say to him, I am very much obliged ["to him" *interlined*] for the latter. The Vist patren [*sic*] you sent me is very beautiful, & I have already put it in the hands of a taylor to be made for me. The other articles, intended for your mother [Floride Colhoun Calhoun] and [Martha] Cornelia [Calhoun], are very han[d]some; & no doubt will be very acceptable to them. I will send the box containing them by the first opportunity.

I had a letter from William [Lowndes Calhoun] about a week since. They were all well. He, your Mother, Cornelia, & Mrs. [Margaret Hunter] Rion are the only white persons at Fort Hill, except the overseer [—— Fredericks] & his family. William's health is quite restored. He has grown much, & has apparently a good constitution. I am gratified to add, that he has resumed his studies, with vigour & appearantly with a determination to persevere. He had recommenced his Latin, & was making, when I left home, excellent progress. I have much hope of his doing well. It is also gratif[yin]g to add, that James [Edward Calhoun] & John [C. Calhoun, Jr.,] have become studious. Both have improved much, especially the former, and promise to do well. I am sure it will delight you to have such favourable intelligence in reference to them.

I wrote Mr. Clemson a short time after my arrival here, and gave him as full account as I could of his [plantation] business. I hope he has received my letter.

The ground is covered with snow & winter has set in, in good earnest. I have had, as usual on my arrival here, an [*sic*] cold; but it has been lighter, than what it has been for several years. I am taking more than ["my" *canceled*] usual care of my health, & hope to be less afflicted with colds, than I was the last Winter. My friends think I look unusually well.

Congress, as yet, has done but little, & will not do much more, until after the 1st Jan[uar]y. On the fourth of that month my resolutions, in reference to the Mexican war, will come up, when the discussion on that exciting and important subject will begin. The prospect is, that I shall be able to carry them. If I should, it will do much to arrest the war. If they should be defeated, we may look for the entire conquest & subjugation of Mexico. What a fearful result it will be for our country & institutions! Already the interest in favour of its entire conquest & subjugation is exceedingly strong; & will, if not arrested by the vote of the Senate, become overwhelming so. Our people have undergone a great change. Their inclination is for conquest & empire, regardless of their institutions & liberty; or rather, they think they hold their liberty by a devine tenure, which no imprudence, or folly on their part, can defeat. When my resolutions where [*sic*] first introduced they were regarded by many as of little importance & uncalled for; but at present they are veiwed [*sic*] in a very different light. For my part, I consider them, as among the most important I ever introduced, regarded in their practical bearing on the course of events hereafter. I only hope, I shall be able to do them full justice in what I may say. If I should, I feel much confidence, I shall be able to arrest the presant headlong enthusiasm for war, which is rapidly impelling the country to its distruction.

Give my love to Mr. Clemson, & the children [John Calhoun Clemson and Floride Elizabeth Clemson]. Kiss them, also, for their Grandfather & tell them how much I wish to see them. Your affectionate father, J.C. Calhoun.

ALS in ScCleA; PEx in Jameson, ed., *Correspondence*, pp. 741–742.

41

From J[AMES] D. B. DeBow

New Orleans, Dec[embe]r 26, 1847

My dear Sir, I was honored by the receipt of your esteemed favor of the 12th Dec[embe]r and fort[h]with forwarded the Number of [my] Review containing Dr. [Josiah C.] Nott[']s paper on the health of negroes north & South—which it appears you had not previously received. I have nothing further before me on this subject now, though I endeavored last summer to obtain information at the north. The fact is they are unwilling in that quarter to divulge more than can be helped and almost neglect entirely this branch of Statistics.

I noted your enquiries about Gen[era]l [Zachary] Taylor. His most intimate and particular friend in Louisiana[,] Col. Maunsel White, a democrat, also a very dear friend of mine, knows more perhaps of Gen[era]l Taylor than any one else. They have been companions from Youth upward. I was at Col. White's on Gen[era]l Taylor[']s arrival in the State previously to his visiting the City. The Col. has been in close correspondence with Taylor. In answer to a note which I directed him the other day Col. White made this response[,] "Gen[era]l Taylor is an honest man and a true patriot and said when asked of what party he was that 'in the battles he fought for his Country a whig fought bravely on one side of him while a democrat fought as bravely on the other—he knew no party but country.' I know that his politics are those of Mr. [Thomas] Jefferson for he told me so. He is a Southern man and will of course be opposed to the Wilmot Proviso. [*Interpolation*: "Was not Mr. Jefferson opposed to the principles even of the Missouri Compromise?"] He is in favor of peace provided it can be had without any dishonor or danger to the Country—as to Tariffs & Banks I don[']t believe he has ever given them much thought; in short he is no politician and has often said so, and as to Caucusses I don[']t believe he would have anything to do with them. I don[']t know of a man in this Parish (a democratic one) of both parties that won[']t vote for him."

You will see that this still leaves his Tariff views in the dark. I know however that it is Col. White[']s opinion that Taylor would not willingly have the Tariff of [18]46 touched. In fact [I] can hardly believe that that issue is to be sprung upon the Country again for a very long time to come.

The whigs here have taken mortal offence about Mr. [Henry] Clay[']s course on the Proviso, *all his old friends*. The movement in receiving Taylor began with them, but extended to all parties. The Democrats of the State are strongly administration which abates the strength of their Taylorism. However, I think the Gen[era]l clearly has carried the State. The same may be affirmed positively of Alabama. All Mississippi is enthusiastic in his support.

South Carolina is you know where. Did it please God and could political honesty combined with intellectual greatness ever again be rewarded with that high chair—she would see her own proud son occupy it. If this must not be so, on the issue of the South & North she will stand to Taylor. I know of no man in Louisiana however who does not regard it a compliment to the Presidency to couple *your* name with it.

Gen[era]l Taylor[']s position in view of the Presidency is to a great extent dependent upon the slavery agitation. What effects the previous settlement of that question may have the future will show. The strength of feeling in opposition to the Proviso here though not as great as in South Carolina is marked. The contemplated Southern paper at Washington has elicited many considerable subscriptions from planters etc.

Our election for the U.S. Senator in place of [Henry] Johnson comes on in a few weeks. A whig or Taylor democrat (i.e. this is a distinct branch of the democratic party proper here) will be elected. If a whig perhaps J[udah] P. Benjamin an eminent jurist, formerly of South Carolina, if a Taylor democrat probable [*sic*] Judge [Robert Carter] Nicholas of Rapides [Parish], formerly in the Senate for a short time. The Democrats speak of [John] Slidell most prominently.

I am afraid that the present low prices of sugar will be interpreted unfavorably to the Tariff by those of the planters who had previous doubts—this is natural with men who have not studied the subject in all its bearings.

I think the Legislature [of La.] will pass very strong resolutions on the ground you have taken on the Wilmot proviso—if not previously determined. With great respect Y[ou]r ob[edien]t s[er]v[an]t, J.D.B. DeBow.

ALS in ScCleA; variant PC in Boucher and Brooks, eds., *Correspondence*, pp. 413–415.

To [Francis] Markoe, Department of State, 12/27. "I will thank you to place the enclosed [letter of 12/26 to Anna Maria Calhoun Clemson] in the foreign bag of the Dept." ALS in DLC, Galloway-Maxcy-Markoe Papers.

From O[zey] R. Broyles

[Pendleton, S.C.,] 28th Dec[embe]r 1847
Dear Sir, As guardian of the orphan children of a deceased friend [Chester Kingsley], the responsibility of investing the sum of thirty thousand dollars or more devolves upon me in a very short time. I have no experience in matters of this sort and intended to have consulted you on the subject before you left for Washington, but missed the opportunity by unavoidable absence from home.

In a letter to Col[o]n[el Benjamin F.] Perry in which I solicited his views of the subject, I expressed doubts as to the United States government stock on the ground that I had but little confidence in the permanency of our Institutions, and a better confidence in our State stocks since as a Carolinian, I was disposed to sink or swim with my native State. In his reply he insists upon the United States stock as being decidedly the proper investment, and that a dissolution of the government would not be followed by a failure to pay the debts of the government.

This was to me a new idea ["for me" *canceled*], as falling from the pen of a statesman in this Era of repudiation.

But apart from any errors or prejudices of my own I will thank you kindly to advise me as to the best investment as combining the greatest security and the best profits.

The children are young[:] the eldest twelve[,] the youngest two years of age[,] *three in number.*

We have no local news of interest except the sudden death of Mr. [John L.] North which will have reached you. Very truly yours, O.R. Broyles.

ALS in ScU-SC, John C. Calhoun Papers. NOTE: Ozey Robert Broyles (1798–1875) was a Pendleton planter and physician who wrote and lectured on scientific agriculture.

From H[enry] W. Conner

Charleston, Dec[embe]r 28, 1847
My Dear Sir, I rec[eive]d your fav[our] of the 16th & have shewn it to a few of our confidential friends here. Col. [Franklin H.] Elmore is absent & Mr. [Ker] Boyce quite sick.

44

We notice what you say of the paper & will await your directions in the matter.

Judge Beverl[e]y Tucker wrote to Gen[era]l [James H.] Hammond approving of the project & recommending in the highest terms a young friend of his own[,] a Mr. Holmes[,] now engaged in some of the departments about Washington. Judge Tucker is a prominent man I believe in Virginia & no doubt well known to you.

The Mercury has been silent[,] too much so latterly—owing to the abscence of its first Editor [John E. Carew?] but we will have the fire opened anew.

I regret to learn that the South is not united. Difficulties are made to be overcome & it only remains for those that both see & feel the necessity of meeting the danger to stand up firmer & closer together. To my mind the enemy should now be met & fought upon the field they have selected.

You will have seen Gen[era]l [John A.] Quitman I suppose. We talked together some on Mexican affairs & upon questions of Southern politicks. He possesses a great deal of information & I beg[ge]d him to see & converse with you. I think from what I saw of him he is right himself on all Southern questions & appeared to be a very sensible & judicious man.

I asked him about Gen[era]l [Zachary] Taylor[']s sentiments. He knew nothing himself[,] not having seen him for months, but cannot doubt but that he is right on the slavery question & thinks he is equally sound on the subjects of a convention & Free trade. My impression is Gen[era]l Quitman would like a free & confidential conference with you.

We hope to bring [Daniel S.] Dickinson[']s resolutions properly before the people in the Mercury in a day or two. In the mean time continue to advise us as may be necessary. Very Truly y[ou]rs &C, H.W. Conner.

ALS in ScCleA.

From J[AMES] GADSDEN

Charleston So. C., 28 Dec[embe]r 1847
My Dear Sir, I am in receipt of your note enclosing an article on manufacturing on the Ohio &c—which will claim early attention.

I write on a more important subject—The one on which all the sober minded portion of our Union, who value the honor & perpetuation of our institutions should rally; before the People are bewildered in mists of Glory: or misled on the false pretense of national honor. God knows we have had Glory in Abundance: in our wonderful triumphs in Mexico overwhelmed with it. It is for you & others who have at heart the real welfare of our Republican States, and the wise principles which originated them, to see that they are not overwhelmed in a hallow[?] of Glory. The conquest of Mexico, would be a conquest of us. Don [Luis] Onis asserted it 20 years ago, & really we are advancing with rapid strides to that period when the 13 States will be lost—The anniversary of the 4 July forgotten & these States hereafter only known under the more alluring & powerful name of the United Mexican States. I must confess untill this morning I have been in a state of much alarm—witnessing what I have seen in this State, and heard, I did not suppose it possible even in your own Carolina to arrest the military spirit of Conquest. We all—all from the Governor [David Johnson] down have been bewildered in the spirit of military Glory & conquest. That [John M.] Niles [Senator from Conn.] however, a thorough partisan as he is, should have come to the support of your views, and declared the *Truth* which he did that every military man was for conquest, is somewhat cheerling [*sic*], that the Senate will yet arrest the mad designs of those in power. They may disclaim but their recommendations are enough for me. They lead to inevitable unavoidable war.

I can say with Niles that I have not yet seen the officer that is not for conquest. Like the Roman all our American Generals are for War & American Provinces. Each probably claim a state as their share of the spoils. Gen[era]l [James] Shields did not disguise his views. Indeed he was so bold at a dinner party & addressing himself direct to me that we were involved in a very unpleasant argument for the time. [John A.] Quitman, with whom I had no conversation of this subject, but who I found exceedingly well balanced in his opinions on other subjects, it is said would regret the conquest. Thinks it would be fatal &c &c but at the same time he was for holding our positions & admitted that the vigorous prosecution of the war as recommended would end in *Conquest*. You must therefore rally all the powers of your mind & influence to force the declaration adverse & if possible to take up (don[']t say retire) that word choakes some of the over sensitive) a line which will amply indemnify this country for the expenses of the war. You may rest assured that this is the strong point of the administration, and so resolved on it that I have been suspicious that [Nicholas P.] Trist[']s moderation in assuming the Rio Grande and upper California, was under the impression it would not be succeeded & that the Pres[iden]t would gain strength for his assumed moderation. We must take *Territory therefore* to reconcile the indemnity part who are very strong. In taking Territory & *defining a Line* let this be done after most thorough examination by a competent commission aided by military science; so that the line assumed be one which for years & ever (untill contiguity absorbs differences of opinions & institutions) shall be the best for a *permanent Border* between The Two Great Republics of the Saxon & Castilian Races. My predilection has been for the mountain Range—The Entire valley of the Rio Grande ought to be under the same Government. If we take some strong position on the Gulf, say San Marino, & the River from thence to the mountains & then along the Sierra Madre to the Latitude by which we strike west, which should be to take in the head of the California Bay. But these are matters of examination & consultation. In the mean while establish the Fact of Line & arrest[?] the military spirit or fire[?] a Conquest we cannot avoild[?]. Yours Tru[ly], J. Gadsden.

ALS in ScCleA.

From F[RANCIS] LIEBER

Columbia S.C., 29[t]h December 1847

Dear Sir, The class of [South Carolina College of] which your son [James Edward Calhoun] is a member has requested me to resume a certain kind of lectures which I call Newspaper Lectures, and in which it is my endeavour to explain all the leading events and transactions as they occur around us, and to teach the students how to read the papers of the day with profit so as to extract and properly to deposit in the mind all that is important in this fleeting and perishable species of literature, reminding them continually of the two facts that what happens to-day is history to-morrow and that no history is more difficult to be got at than that of the 25 or 30 years immediately preceding us.

I requested your son to beg you to send us in documents or papers whatever you do not want. I will turn ["it" *interlined*] to the best account according to my poor abilities. I know, you will approve of my plan, and I beg to repeat here the same request which your son may already have communicated to you.

47

I can only give you the best accounts of your son. He is a gentleman and a student.

Will you permit me to beg of you the kindness to send the enclosed to the address?

Why do so few Southern papers mention your resolutions? At least so it seems to me.

In England I make little doubt but that in a conjuncture as the present one in the Congress is, an administration must resign. Our Constitutional fabric does not admit—or, at least not require it. I am with sentiments of high respect Your very obed[ien]t, F. Lieber.

P.S. I suppose I hardly need add that in my Newspaper Lectures I am constantly mindful that I am paid by the *State*, and have no right to use my chair for propagandism of specific and personal views, although I am aware that a professor is no abstract being—no empty bottle, and that what he considers sacred truth he may not only, but ["his" *changed to* "is"] bound to teach; so, for instance, Free Trade with me. It is for the trustees to see that they appoint the right man as to vital points. I stand in this respect upon the same footing, I think, with [James H. Thornwell] our professor of Christian evidence. He must not use his chair to preach sectarian views, but he cannot float in the clouds of indifferentism above protestantism and Catholicism. F.L.

ALS in ScCleA; PC in Jameson, ed., *Correspondence*, pp. 1155–1156.

Remarks on a supplemental military appropriations bill, 12/29. The bill asked funds to cover a shortfall of four million dollars. Calhoun queried for what period had the shortage been accumulated, and later argued, with other Senators, to postpone the bill for further study. From *Congressional Globe*, 30th Cong., 1st Sess., p. 75. Also printed in Houston, ed., *Proceedings and Debates*, p. 45. Variant in the Charleston, S.C., *Mercury*, January 4, 1848, p. 2.

Remarks on the Bill to Raise an Additional Military Force

[In the Senate, December 30, 1847]
[Lewis Cass of Michigan, Chairman of the Committee on Military Affairs, moved immediate consideration of a bill to add ten regiments to the regular Army.]

Mr. Calhoun. I hope the honorable Senator does not intend to press the bill to a decision at this time. The Senate is extremely thin, and it is a question of so much importance, as everything must be which is connected with the war, that I submit to the Senator, inasmuch as what supplies we shall grant must depend on what we shall determine in the next few days is to be done, that it would be proper to allow the consideration of this bill to be postponed. If the Senator is determined to press the question upon us at this early period, and before any one has had time to fix his own mind in regard to the subject, I shall be constrained to oppose the Senator's motion.

[*Cass urged action on the bill, which was similar to one of the previous session. He did not believe the bill had any relation to Calhoun's resolutions on the war. Cass said that the President (James K. Polk) had stated that he did not intend "to prosecute this war, with the view of extinguishing the nationality of Mexico." The ten regiments were needed to secure an honorable peace.*]

Mr. Calhoun. As the Senator has avowed his intention to proceed with this bill, and to press the question upon us now, I shall be compelled to oppose it.

Mr. Cass. For the personal accommodation of the Senator, I will consent that the bill shall lie over until Monday [1/3/1848]. Beyond that day I cannot consent that it shall be postponed.

Mr. Calhoun. My ideas, sir, extend far beyond that. I am very happy to hear the Senator say that the President is entirely opposed to the conquest of Mexico and the extinguishment of her nationality; and I am very happy, also, to hear that the chairman of the Committee on Military Affairs repeats the same thing. That being admitted as among the greatest calamities that could happen, the important question comes up—how shall we escape it? Sir, we often get into situations which we never intended to get into. We got into this war although we never intended to get into it; for I will venture to say, that in this body, if the question had been propounded to them of war or no war, independent of the exigency of the occasion, there would not have been one-fourth of the Senate in favor of it. Now, my object is to guard, not against consequences that are contemplated, but against consequences that may follow from the measures proposed, which consequences are not contemplated. That is the object. Now, whether this additional force shall be granted, will depend on the fact whether the mode recommended by the Executive to carry on this war will not, in its practical consequences, end in the extinction of the nationality of Mexico. Now, I submit to the Senator himself, whether there is nothing due to those who differ from him

49

in opinion in regard to this point? He may think that the policy recommended by the Administration will not end in the extinguishment of the nationality of Mexico; but I differ with him in that opinion; and until I am satisfied that he is correct, I am not prepared to vote in favor of the measure that is now proposed. Sir, though the honorable Senator himself is very properly opposed to the extinguishment of the nationality of Mexico, we know that there are many of a totally different opinion; and we know that there are many who believe that such will be the result, whether intended or not, of the measures proposed by the Administration. And I am one of those who entertain this belief. Now, I do think we ought to postpone action on this bill for some little time, until we shall have determined the course which it will be proper for us to pursue; and, with this view of the question, I shall vote against the motion of the honorable Senator.

[*Cass read a passage from an official message of the President to Congress, disavowing any intent for the permanent conquest of Mexico. He urged that the military bill be considered without a general discussion "of the origin and progress of the war."*]

Mr. Calhoun. A word only in reply. I am aware of the views of the President in regard to the war. I have examined with great care the policy which is recommended in the message, and, in my opinion, the result of that policy, if carried out, will tend to the precisely opposite course to that professed to be contemplated therein. If such should be the danger, we must guard against it in some way; but if this danger does not exist, then there will be no necessity for any steps on our part to guard against it. But with my present information, I am not prepared to give an intelligent vote upon the subject.

[*John M. Clayton of Delaware also urged postponement of the bill, until Senators had had time to read reports from the Secretary of War. John M. Berrien of Georgia argued that the Senate should discuss Calhoun's and Daniel S. Dickinson's resolutions before considering the military bill. Cass replied and was supported by William Allen of Ohio.*]

Mr. Calhoun. It appears now, sir, that the object in calling up this bill at present is not to pass the bill, but to get a parliamentary advantage—to compel the Senate to discuss this bill before an opportunity is afforded for discussing the resolutions which I have offered. It is a mere parliamentary move. The Senator shakes his head. Well, sir, if we follow the advice of the Senator from Ohio, we shall consume just as much time in discussing this bill as if we were first to discuss the resolutions. The Senator from Ohio talks of the necessity of proceeding to act upon this bill now, and tells us in the next breath that we are to have the whole discussion upon the subject of the war upon this bill.

Mr. Allen. The honorable Senator misrepresents what I said. What I said was, that we ought to take up this bill and go on with its consideration at on[c]e.

Mr. Calhoun. Exactly. We are to go on with the discussion upon this bill instantly, we are told, both by the Senator from Ohio and the Senator from Michigan, and not let the discussion upon the resolutions have precedence. The Senator from Ohio says that it is a parliamentary advantage to have the discussion upon this bill previous to discussing the resolutions. Well, I acknowledge that it is so. I acknowledge that we should be tied up, in a great measure, in the discussion upon the bill, and prevented from going so freely into all these questions regarding the war as we would in discussing the resolutions. It will then be, strictly speaking, out of order. Besides this, we will not have (what is most important) in the discussion of the bill an expression of the sense of this body upon the great point as to whether Mexico is to be conquered and held as a subject province, or incorporated into the Union, or not. Sir, I know there are many, as staunch friends of the Executive as the Senator from Ohio, who believe that the policy recommended by the President, and now about to be carried out by this bill, will end in her subjugation and the extinguishment of her nationality. Now, sir, it is due to the country that this question should be distinctly presented, that the people of the country may see what is to be the probable result of the war, and determine whether they will meet it or not; for that is to be the end of the whole of the contest, unless the most decisive measures are taken on the part of the Senate to prevent it.

Sir, I cannot be mistaken. I wish to go into the subject. I deem it to be due to my constituents, to the American people, that this, the greatest of all questions, the extinguishment of the nationality of Mexico, should be distinctly voted upon by this body.

The Senator from Ohio is unwilling that I should have a vote upon this question, I presume. Sir, it is my object to have a vote upon my resolutions, and to have the response of the country upon the question embraced in them; for the debate will bring forth the response of the country. Now, according to my apprehension, there is no greater calamity that can befall this country than the subjugation of Mexico and the extinguishment of her nationality, and the transfer of all her territory to us. Sir, from the beginning I had great forebodings about this war, and my forebodings, among others, related to this very thing—the absorption of Mexico. And I reiterate, sir, that if it takes place, we are very near to the end of our political career. Sir, the Senator from Ohio made an announcement of doomsday, in the event of any delay in the action of the Senate upon this bill, although necessary information is to be extracted by that delay. The Senator need not suppose that discussion will be avoided by giving precedence to the consideration of this bill. He never can escape from a full and thorough investigation of the designs of the Executive in the prosecution of this war. My object is not opposition to the Administration. Whenever I intend to assail the Administration, I will do so directly, and to their face. My object is to have the sense of the Senate and the country upon a point which I deem of the first magnitude to the safety of the country and its institutions; and I do trust, sir, that the Senate will not deprive me of the opportunity of having a clear vote upon this point, after full discussion.

[*There was further extended discussion, until the vote was taken on Cass's motion. The Senate divided 19 to 19 on the motion, and Vice-President George M. Dallas made his casting vote in the affirmative.*]

From *Congressional Globe*, 30th Cong., 1st Sess., pp. 78–80. Also printed in the Washington, D.C., *Daily Union*, January 1, 1848, p. 2; the Washington, D.C., *Daily National Intelligencer*, January 3, 1848, p. 3; the New York, N.Y., *Morning Courier and New-York Enquirer*, January 3, 1848, p. 2; the Richmond, Va., *Whig and Public Advertiser*, January 4, 1848, p. 2; Houston, ed., *Proceedings and Debates*, pp. 49–51. Variants in the Alexandria, Va., *Gazette and Virginia Advertiser*, December 31, 1847, p. 3, and January 3, 1848, pp. 2–3; the New York, N.Y., *Herald*, January 1, 1848, p. 4.

To Mrs. —— Rowand, [*ca.* 1847?]. "With his best wishes for the long life & happiness of Mrs. Rowand. J.C. Calhoun." AES in a copy of *The Floral Year* (Boston: Benjamin B. Mussey, 1847) owned by Norman W. Pratt; copy of AES in ScU-SC, John C. Calhoun Papers.

To ——, [*ca.* 1847?]. "Mr. [John T.] Towers is the printer of the speech you refer to, and I suppose you can get from him as many copies as you want." (This undated document has been assigned an approximate conjectural date.) ALS in ScU-SC, John C. Calhoun Papers.

To "Doctor [James A.] Houston, Reporter, Senate," [*ca.* 1848?]. "I will be glad to have the notes of my speeches of yesterday that I may correct them, this afternoon." LS in ScU-SC, John C. Calhoun Papers.

J[ames] E[dward] Calhoun, Columbia, to [Edwin W. Seibels], President, Clariosophic Society, [South Carolina College], 1/1. "Permit me to present through you to the Society in my Father[']s name, a vol. of the Constitution of the United States printed under the order of the Senate." Copy in ScU, University Archives, Clariosophic Society Papers, Minutes, Letterbook and Constitution, 1842–1849, p. 324.

FURTHER REMARKS ON HIS RESOLUTIONS

[In the Senate, January 3, 1848]
[*Under consideration was the bill to add ten regiments to the regular Army.*]

Mr. Calhoun. Believing that I probably might not have the opportunity to speak to-morrow, I had a conversation with the Senator from Michigan [Lewis Cass], and expressed to him my desire of addressing the Senate. If I have that opportunity, it is all I ask.

[*John J. Crittenden of Kentucky moved to postpone consideration of the bill until after Calhoun had spoken tomorrow. Cass objected.*]

Mr. Calhoun. I certainly am desirous of knowing in advance whether I can have an opportunity of speaking to-morrow or not. I introduced my resolution before the Senator's bill was reported, and fixed a day for its consideration. Now, if I am to be prevented from addressing the Senate, by reason of a measure subsequently introduced, which has obtained a parliamentary advantage, all that I can say is, it will be the first occurrence of this kind that I have ever known. All I ask is the opportunity of being heard. I do not choose to speak upon this bill, and my reason for it is, that it does not give me the scope which I desire. I wish to have it understood whether I am to have to-morrow or not.

[*There followed a long and complicated discussion among Cass and nine other Senators about the next day's calendar and the priority of the military bill or Calhoun's resolutions.*]

Mr. Calhoun. I rise to say that I am perfectly satisfied with the course [of postponement] which is suggested by the Senator from Arkansas [Ambrose H. Sevier] and the Senator from North Carolina [George E. Badger]—either will be satisfactory to me.

[*After further discussion, Sevier's motion to postpone consideration of the military bill until the afternoon of 1/5 was agreed to.*]

From Houston, ed., *Proceedings and Debates*, pp. 57–58, 61. Also printed in
the Washington, D.C., *Daily Union*, January 4, 1848, p. 2; *Congressional Globe*,
30th Cong., 1st Sess., pp. 89, 92. Variants in the New York, N.Y., *Herald*, January 5, 1848, p. 4; the Alexandria, Va., *Gazette and Virginia Advertiser*, January 5,
1848, p. 2.

From D[AVID] O. HAWTHORN

Due West Corner[,] Abb[eville] Dist[rict] S.C.
January the 4th 1848
Sir, I Wrote to you Some time Last Spring [5/9/1847] in regard to
an account I held on your Son [William Lowndes Calhoun] that attended college at D[ue] W[est] Corner in W[h]ich I Received
answer from you certifying that as soon as your Son Returned from
the West & he would See the account that you would Settle the Same.
You also Wrote to Mr. [E. or J.W.] Agnew acknowliging all the the
[*sic*] accounts that he Sent & My account was embraced in the List of
accounts he Sent. You Said you would Settle them all before you
would Start to the city of Washington. But it appears from Some
Reason that you have not complyed with the promise. The[re]fore
I wish you would Send the Money to Due W[est] Corner By Some
Means of [*sic*] other Before Long Because I Stand in need of the
Same.

The account was made With D[avid] W. Hawthorn. Respectfully your Friend, D.O. Hawthorn.

ALS in ScU-SC, John C. Calhoun Papers. NOTE: Calhoun's AEU reads, "Money
to be sent by 1st April."

SPEECH ON THE WAR WITH MEXICO
(First Report)

[In the Senate, January 4, 1848]
On motion by Mr. [Ambrose H.] Sevier, the Senate proceeded to the
consideration of the special order of the day, being the following
resolutions submitted by Mr. Calhoun, on the 15th December:

Resolved, That to conquer Mexico and to hold it, either as a province or to incorporate it into the Union, would be inconsistent with the avowed object for which the war has been prosecuted; a departure from the settled policy of the Government; in conflict with its character and genius; and in the end subversive of our free and popular institutions.

Resolved, That no line of policy in the further prosecution of the war should be adopted which may lead to consequences so disastrous.

Mr. Calhoun said: In offering, Senators, these resolutions for your consideration, I have been governed by the reasons which induced me to oppose the war, and by the same considerations I have been ever since guided. In alluding to my opposition to the war, I do not intend to notice the reasons which governed me on that occasion, further than is necessary to explain my motives upon the present. I opposed the war then, not only because I considered it unnecessary, and that it might have been easily avoided; not only because I thought the President [James K. Polk] had no authority to order a portion of the territory in dispute and in possession of the Mexicans, to be occupied by our troops; not only because I believed the allegations upon which it was sanctioned by Congress, were unfounded in truth; but from high considerations of reason and policy, because I believed it would lead to great and serious evils to the country, and greatly endanger its free institutions.

But after the war was declared, and had received the sanction of the Government, I acquiesced in what I could not prevent, and which it was impossible for me to arrest; and I then felt it to be my duty to limit my course so as to give that direction to the conduct of the war as would, as far as possible, prevent the evil and danger with which, in my opinion, it threatened the country and its institutions. For this purpose, at the last session, I suggested to the Senate a defensive line, and for that purpose I now offer these resolutions. This, and this only, is the motive which governs me. I am moved by no personal nor party considerations. My object is neither to sustain the Executive, nor to strengthen the Opposition, but simply to discharge an important duty to the country. But I shall express my opinion upon all points with boldness and independence, such as become a Senator who has nothing to ask, either from the Government or from the people, and whose only aim is to diminish, to the smallest possible amount, the evils incident to this war. But when I come to notice those points in which I differ from the President, I shall do it with all the decorum which is due to the Chief Magistrate of the Union.

When I suggested a defensive line, at the last session, this country had in its possession, through the means of its arms, ample territory, and stood in a condition to force indemnity. Before then, the successes of our arms had gained all the contiguous portions of Mexico, and our army has ever since held all that it is desirable to hold—that portion whose population is sparse, and on that account the more desirable to be held. For I hold it in reference to this war a fundamental principle, that when we receive territorial indemnity, it shall be unoccupied territory.

In offering a defensive line, I did it because I believed that, in the first place, it was the only certain mode of terminating the war successfully; I did it, also, because I believed that it would be a vast saving of the sacrifice of human life; but, above all, I did so because I saw that any other line of policy would expose us to tremendous evil, which these resolutions were intended to guard against. The President took a different view. He recommended a vigorous prosecution of the war—not for conquest: that was disavowed—but for the purpose of conquering peace; that is, to compel Mexico to sign a treaty making a sufficient cession of territory to indemnify this Government both for the claims of its citizens and for the expenses of the war. Sir, I opposed this policy. I opposed it, among other reasons, because I believed that if the war should be ever so successful, there was great hazard to us, at least, that the object intended to be effected by it would not be accomplished. Congress thought differently. Ample provisions, in men and money, were granted for carrying on the war. The campaign has terminated. It has been as successful as the Executive of the country could possibly have calculated. Victory after victory has followed in succession, without a single reverse. Santa Anna was repelled and defeated, with all his forces. Vera Cruz was carried, and the Castle with it. Jalapa, Perote, and Puebla fell; and, after two great triumphs of our army, the gates of Mexico opened to us. Well, sir, what has been accomplished? What has been done? Has the avowed object of the war been attained? Have we conquered peace? Have we obtained a treaty? Have we obtained any indemnity? No, sir: not a single object contemplated has been effected; and, what is worse, our difficulties are greater now than they were then, and the objects, forsooth, more difficult to reach than they were before the campaign commenced.

Now Senators have asked what has caused this complete discomfiture of the views of the Executive for which men and money were granted? It is not to be charged to our troops; they have done all that skill and gallantry was capable of effecting. It must be charged somewhere, and where is it to be charged, but upon the fact that the plan of the campaign was erroneous; that the object pursued was a mistake? We aimed at indemnity in a wrong way. If we had aimed directly to it, we had the means to accomplish it directly; they were in our hands. But, sir, we aimed at indemnity through a treaty. We could not reach it by a treaty with Mexico, and Mexico, by refusing to treat simply, could defeat the whole object which we had in view. We put out of our own power, and in her hands to say, when the war should terminate.

We have for all our vast expenditure of money, for all the loss of blood and men, we have nothing but the military glory which the campaign has furnished.

We cannot, I presume, estimate the expenses of the campaign at less than forty millions of dollars. I cannot compute the sum with any degree of precision, but I believe I may say about that sum, and between the sword and disease, many thousands of lives, probably five, six, or seven thousand have been sacrificed; and all this for nothing at all.

But it is said that the occupancy of a defensive line would have been as expensive as the campaign itself. The President has assigned many reasons for that opinion, and the Secretary of War [William L. Marcy] has done the same. I have examined these reasons with care. This is not the proper occasion to discuss them; but I must say, with all possible deference, they are to my mind utterly fallacious. I will put the question in a general point of view, and satisfy the minds of Senators that such is the case.

The line proposed by myself, extending from the Pacific Ocean to the Paso del Norte, would have been covered by the Gulf of California, and wilderness peopled by hostile tribes of Indians; and for its defence, nothing would have been needed beyond a few vessels of war stationed in the Gulf, and a single regiment. From the Paso del Norte to its mouth, we can readily estimate the amount of force necessary for its defence. It was a frontier between Texas and Mexico when Texas had not more than 150,000 of a population; without any standing army whatever, and very few troops. Yet for seven years Texas maintained that frontier line; and that, too, when Mexico was far more consolidated than she is now, when her revolutions were not so frequent, her resources in money were much greater, and Texas her only opponent. Can any man believe that Mexico, exhausted as she now is, prostrated as she has been, defeated—can any man believe that it will cost as much to defend that frontier as the last campaign has cost? No, sir. I will hazard nothing in asserting that the very interest of the money spent in the last campaign would have secured that line for an indefinite period, and that the men who have lost their lives would have been more than sufficient to defend it.

So much for the past; we now come to the commencement of another campaign; and the question is, What shall be done? The same measures are proposed. It is still "a vigorous prosecution of the war." The measures are identically the same. It is not for conquest—that is now as emphatically disowned as it was in the first instance. The object is not to blot Mexico out of the list of nations, for the President is emphatic in the expression of his desire to maintain the nationality of Mexico. He desires to see her an independent and flourishing community, and assigns strong and cogent reasons for all that. Well, sir, the question is now, What ought to be done? We are now coming to the practical question. Shall we aim at carrying on another vigorous campaign under present circumstances?

Mr. President, I have examined this question with care, and I repeat, that I cannot support the recommendations of the President. There are many and powerful reasons, stronger than those which existed at the commencement of the last campaign, to justify my opposition now. The cost in money will be vastly greater. There is a bill for ten additional regiments now before the Senate, and another bill providing for twenty regiments of volunteers has been reported, making in all, not less, I suppose, than twenty-five thousand troops; raising the number of troops in the service—as, I presume, the chairman of the Committee on Military Affairs [Lewis Cass] can inform you—to not much less than seventy thousand in the whole. Well, sir, the expense will be much more than that of the last campaign. It will cost not much short of sixty millions of dollars.

Now, sir, what is the condition of the money market at present? Last year it was most flourishing. An unfortunate famine in Europe created a great demand for our agricultural products. The balance of trade was in our favor. If money poured out at one end of the sub-treasury, it poured in at the other. But how stands the case now? We stand now with a drain both ways. The exchanges are in our favor, and therefore, instead of gold and silver, drafts founded on exports will be remitted. The exchanges in Mexico must be met either by remittances in gold and silver, or by drafts drawn in favor of British merchants, or other capitalists there, which must be cashed here and also transmitted abroad. Now, sir, what will be the operation of this state of things? How long can this continue? What is the present price of treasury notes and of stocks in the market? Are they above par? No, sir. I see them quoted below par. I understand the treasury notes are sensibly below par, and stocks still lower. Now, what is to be the result? So long as treasury notes are below par—so long as they are the cheaper medium—the end of it will be, that treasury notes will go into the treasury, and specie come out of it. There is very great danger that at last your treasury will be drained to the bottom.

Now, sir, in this state of things, what can possibly follow? A great commercial crisis—a great financial crisis—even, possibly, a suspension of the banks. I do not pretend to deal in the language of panic; but there is danger of all this, of which there was not the slightest apprehension at the commencement of last session. At present, there is great danger. The great difficulty in prosecuting your campaign will be to obtain money. Men you may raise, but money it will be difficult to get. I lately conversed with a gentleman who ought to know these things better than myself, and he supposed that forty millions of dollars would be required, either in the shape of treasury notes or stocks, to carry on the campaign. I asked at what price money could be had; and the reply was, that it would be at the rate of ninety for one hundred; which would be rather more than seven per cent., I believe.

But, sir, these are not the only objections, formidable as they are. The farther you proceed, the difficulties will increase. I do not see the slightest chance that can tend to the realization of what it is avowed the prosecution of the war is intended to accomplish. The object is to obtain a treaty. We no longer hear of conquering a peace, but of obtaining an honorable treaty; the meaning of which is, neither more nor less than that we are to obtain a treaty from Mexico, giving us a cession of land equal to the whole indemnity already stated in the former part of my remarks. Well, sir, as it strikes me, whether the war is successful or unsuccessful, it must certainly end in the defeat of the object, for the attainment of which it is avowedly prosecuted. If the war be unsuccessful, I need not argue the point. If we should be baffled in our arms—as I trust we will not be, and I think is not very likely to be the case—but if circumstances should prove unfortunate for us, and we should not be able to accomplish, in a military point of view, what is characterized as a vigorous prosecution of the war, then certainly there will be no treaty. I take higher ground. I insist upon it that the more successfully this war is prosecuted the more certain will be the defeat of the object designed to be accomplished, whilst the objects disavowed will be accomplished.

How is a successful war to be carried on? What is the object of it? What is it intended to effect? I can see but one thing to be effected. It is to suppress all resistance in Mexico, to overpower and disperse her army, to overthrow her civil Government, and to leave her without any further power of resistance. Well, Mr. President, if that be done, what is the result? How are you to get an honorable peace? It takes but one party to make war—two parties to make peace. If all authority in Mexico be overthrown, if there be no legitimate power with whom to negotiate, how are you to accomplish those objects which it is proclaimed this vigorous prosecution of the war is intended to effect? Sir, you are defeated by your success. That will be the clear and inevitable result. But what do you accomplish? The very object which you disavow. For if the war should be so prosecuted, where will be the nationality of Mexico? Where her separate existence? Where this free Republic with whom you desire to treat? Gone! We have blotted her out of the list of nations. She has become a mere mass of individuals without any political existence, and the sovereignty of the country, at least for the time being, is transferred to us. Now, Mr. President, this is not only a conclusion from reasoning upon this subject, but it is one to which, if I understand the President aright, he comes, with a single exception, and that a mere contingency not likely to take place. The President has very much the same conception of the object of a vigorous war as I have presented. He says that the great difficulty of getting peace results from this, that the people of Mexico are divided under factious chieftains, and that the chieftain in power dares not give peace because his rival would then be able to turn him out; and that the only way to remedy this evil and obtain a treaty, is to put down the whole of them. Well, what is to be done then? Is the thing to stop there? No. We are then to build up again, and establish, under our power and protection, a republican form of government from the citizens who are well disposed, which he says are numerous, and are prevented from obtaining it, only by fear of those military chiefs. And it is with this government, sir, which is to grow up under the encouragement and protection of our army—to be established by their authority—that it is proposed to treat, in order to obtain peace. I must confess I am a little at a loss to see how a free and independent republic can grow up under the protection and authority of its conqueror. I do not see how such a government can be established under his authority. I can readily understand how an aristocracy—how a kingly government—a despotism, might be established by a conqueror. But how a free and independent republic can grow up under such circumstances, is to me incomprehensible. I had always supposed that republican government was the spontaneous work of the people—that it came from the people—from the hearts of the people—that it was supported by the hearts of the people, and that it required no support—no protection from any quarter whatever. But, sir, it seems that these are antiquated notions—obsolete ideas— and that we may now manufacture republics to order, by authority of a conquering government.

But suppose, sir, all these difficulties surmounted: How can you make a free government in Mexico? Where are your materials? It is to be, I presume, a confederated government like our own. Where is the intelligence in Mexico adequate to the construction of such a government? That is what she has been aiming at for twenty-odd years; but so utterly incompetent are her people for the work, that it has been a complete failure from beginning to end. The great body of the intelligence and wealth of Mexico is concentrated in the priesthood, who are altogether disinclined to that form of government. Then the owners of the haciendas—the large planters of the country—who comprise almost all the remaining mass of intelligence, are without opportunities of concert, and destitute of the means of forming such a government. Sir, such a government would be impossible; and if put up, would tumble down the very next day after our protection was withdrawn.

It appears to me to be a far more plausible plan, if it is determined to have peace, to sustain the Government that now exists in Mexico, or rather, to refrain from putting it down. Let it grow up and mature itself. I have conversed with several of the officers of the army— men of intelligence—on this subject, and all agree in the opinion that the mere shadow of a government which now remains at Queretaro, will have no authority whatever; and that if we were to make a peace in any degree conformatory to our view of what a peace ought to be, the very moment we withdraw, it would all be overthrown; and what then? The very country assigned to us by the peace for an indemnity, we must either hold defensively and be brought back ultimately to the defensive line, which would be the end of the whole of it; or, return and renew this war till it terminates in the conquest of the country.

I protest utterly against this Government undertaking to build up any government in Mexico with the pledge of protection. The party placed in power must be inevitably overthrown, and we will be under the solemn obligation to return and reinstate them in power; and that would occur again and again, till the country would fall into our hands precisely as Hindostan fell into the hands of the English. This very conquest of Hindostan, which we have been censuring for years and years, ever since I recollect, was the result of mistaken policy, leading on from step to step, each one deeper and deeper—scarcely any design of conquest being entertained; but ultimately conquest became unavoidable, and it was necessary not only to hold the country, but to conquer the adjacent territory.

Well, sir, if this contingency follows—if the Executive fails in establishing another government there under our encouragement and protection, and if the Government itself shall refuse to make a treaty with us on such terms as we will accept in regard to indemnity, then the President himself agrees that he must take the very course which I have said would be the inevitable consequence of a vigorous prosecution of the war. The President says in substance, after having attempted to build up such a government—after having employed the best efforts to secure peace upon the most liberal terms, if all fail—I now give his own words—if all fail, we must hold on to the occupation of the country; we must take the measure of indemnity into our own hands, and enforce such terms as the honor of the country demands. Now, sir, what is this? Is it not an acknowledgment, that if this factitious government, which is aimed at, cannot be built up, we must make a conquest of the whole country and occupy it?—can words be stronger?—"Occupy the country." Take the full measure of indemnity—no defensive line—no treaty; and enforce terms—terms on whom? on the government? No—no—no. It is to enforce the terms on the people individually; that is to say, to establish a government over them in the form of provinces.

Well, the President is right. If, in the vigorous prosecution of the war, as the President proposes, the contingency should fail—and the chances of its failure are many—there will be no retreating. Every argument against calling back the army, as they designate it—against taking a defensive line—which is now advanced, will have double force after you have spent sixty millions of dollars, and have acquired possession of the whole of Mexico. The interests in favor of keeping us there will be much more influential then than now. The army itself will be larger. Those who live by the war—a large and powerful body: the numerous contractors, the sutlers, the merchants, the speculators in the lands and mines of Mexico, and all engaged every way, directly or indirectly, in the progress of the war, and absorbing the whole expenditures—will be all adverse to retiring, and will swell the cry in favor of continuing and extending conquest. The President talks, sir, of taking indemnity into our hands then; but why not take indemnity now? We are much nearer indemnity now than we will be at the end of the next campaign, when we shall have sixty millions added to the expenditure of the last forty. What will you then have to indemnify you? Nothing but a Mexican population, on whom you are to impose taxation in all forms and shapes, and amongst which you will have to maintain an army of at least forty thousand men—according to the Senator from Mississippi, (Mr. [Jefferson] Davis,) not a very large number, for he says that the seventy-three thousand men now there are in danger. That, then, is no indemnity at all. You will never get enough in that way to meet your expenditures. It will all have to come out of the pockets of the people of the United States; and, after all the talk of indemnity—of pushing on this war vigorously to success—at the end of the next campaign, instead of indemnity, you will have a heavy pecuniary burden imposed upon the present and succeeding generation.

Well, Mr. President, we have now come to the solemn question proposed by these resolutions. I have shown where this line of policy will, in all probability, lead you—I may say, will inevitably lead you, unless some unexpected contingency should prevent. It will lead to the blotting out of the nationality of Mexico, and the throwing of eight or nine millions of people without a government, on your hands. It will compel you, in all probability, to assume the government, for I think there will be very little prospect of your retiring. You must either hold the country as a province, or incorporate it into your Union. Shall we do either? That's the question. Far from us be such an act, and for the reasons contained in the resolutions.

The first of these reasons is this: it would be inconsistent with the avowed object for which the war has been prosecuted. That needs no argument, after what has been said. Since the commencement of the war till this moment, every man has disavowed the intention of conquest—of extinguishing the existence of Mexico as a people. It has been constantly proclaimed that the only object was indemnity. And yet, sir, as events are moving on, what we disavow may be accomplished, and what we have avowed may be defeated. Sir, this result will be a dark and lasting imputation on either the sincerity or the intelligence of this country: on its sincerity, because so opposite to your own avowals; on your intelligence, for the want of a clear foresight in so plain a case as not to discern the consequences.

Sir, we have heard how much glory our country has acquired in this war. I acknowledge it to the full amount, Mr. President, so far as military glory is concerned. The army has done nobly, chivalrously; they have conferred honor on the country, for which I sincerely thank them.

Mr. President, I believe all our thanks will be confined to our army. So far as I know, in the civilized world there is no approbation of the conduct of the civil portion of our power. On the contrary, everywhere the declaration is made that we are an ambitious, unjust, hard people, more given to war than any people of modern times. Whether this be true or not, it is not for me to inquire. I am speaking now merely of the reputation which we bear abroad—everywhere, I believe; for as much as we have gained in military reputation abroad, I regret to perceive, we have lost in our political and civil reputation. Now, sir, much as I regard military glory; much as I rejoice to behold our people in possession of the indomitable energy and courage which surmount all difficulties, and which class them amongst the first military people of the age, I would be very sorry indeed that our Government should lose any reputation for wisdom, moderation, discretion, justice, and those other high qualities which have distinguished us in the early stages of our history.

The next reason which my resolutions assign, is, that it is without example or precedent, either to hold Mexico as a province, or to incorporate her into our Union. No example of such a line of policy can be found. We have conquered many of the neighboring tribes of Indians, but we never thought of holding them in subjection—never of incorporating them into our Union. They have either been left as an independent people amongst us, or been driven into the forests.

I know further, sir, that we have never dreamt of incorporating into our Union any but the Caucasian race—the free white race. To incorporate Mexico, would be the very first instance of the kind of incorporating an Indian race; for more than half of the Mexicans are Indians, and the other is composed chiefly of mixed tribes. I protest against such a union as that! Ours, sir, is the Government of a white race. The greatest misfortunes of Spanish America are to be traced to the fatal error of placing these colored races on an equality with the white race. That error destroyed the social arrangement which formed the basis of society. The Portuguese [in Brazil] and ourselves have escaped—the Portuguese at least to some extent—and we are the only people on this continent which have made revolutions without being followed by anarchy. And yet it is professed and talked about to erect these Mexicans into a Territorial Government, and place them on an equality with the people of the United States. I protest utterly against such a project.

Sir, it is a remarkable fact, that in the whole history of man, as far as my knowledge extends, there is no instance whatever of any civilized colored races being found equal to the establishment of free popular government, although by far the largest portion of the human family is composed of these races. And even in the savage state we scarcely find them any where with such government, except it be our noble savages—for noble I will call them. They, for the most part, had free institutions, but they are easily sustained amongst a savage people. Are we to overlook this fact? Are we to associate with ourselves as equals, companions, and fellow-citizens, the Indians and mixed race of Mexico? Sir, I should consider such a thing as fatal to our institutions.

The next two reasons which I assigned, were, that it would be in conflict with the genius and character of our institutions, and subversive of our free government. I take these two together, as they are so intimately connected; and now of the first—to hold Mexico in subjection.

Mr. President, there are some propositions too clear for argument; and before such a body as the Senate, I should consider it a loss of time to undertake to prove that to hold Mexico as a subjected province would be hostile, and in conflict with our free popular institutions, and in the end subversive of them. Sir, he who knows the American Constitution well—he who has duly studied its character—he who has looked at history, and knows what has been the effect of conquests of free states invariably, will require no proof at my hands to show that it would be entirely hostile to the institutions of the country to hold Mexico as a province. There is not an example on record of any free state even having attempted the conquest of any territory approaching the extent of Mexico without disastrous consequences. The nation[s] conquered have in time conquered the conquerors by destroying their liberty. That will be our case, sir. The conquest of Mexico would add so vast an amount to the patronage of this Government, that it would absorb the whole power of the States in the Union. This Union would become imperial, and the States mere subordinate corporations. But the evil will not end there. The process will go on. The same process by which the power would be transferred from the States to the Union, will transfer the whole of this department of the Government (I speak of the Legislature) to the Executive. All the added power and added patronage which conquest will create, will pass to the Executive. In the end, you put in the hands of the Executive the power of conquering you. You give to it, sir, such splendor, such ample means, that, with the principle of proscription which unfortunately prevails in our country, the struggle will be greater at every Presidential election than our institutions can possibly endure. The end of it will be, that that branch of the Government will become all-powerful, and the result is inevitable—anarchy and despotism. It is as certain as that I am this day addressing the Senate.

Sir, let it not be said that Great Britain furnishes an example to the contrary—that she holds provinces of vast extent of population without materially impairing the liberty of the citizens, or exposing her to anarchy, confusion, or corruption. It is so. But what is the explanation? Of all Governments that ever existed, affording any protection whatever to liberty, the English Government far transcends them all in that respect. She can bear more patronage in proportion to her population and wealth, than any Government of that form that ever existed; nay, to go farther, than can despotism in its most absolute form. I will not go into the philosophy of this. That would take me farther from the track than I desire. But I will say in a very few words, it results from the fact that her Executive and the House of Peers, the conservative branch of her Government, are both hereditary. The Roman Government may have exceeded, and did exceed the British Government in its power for conquest; but no people ever did exist, and probably never will exist, with such a capacity for conquest as that people. But the capacity of Rome to hold subjected provinces, was as nothing compared to that of Great Britain, and hence, as soon as the Roman power passed from Italy beyond the Adriatic on one side, and the Alps on the other, and the Mediterranean, their liberty fell prostrate—the Roman people became a rabble—corruption penetrated everywhere, and violence and anarchy ruled the day. Now, we see England with dependant provinces of vastly greater territorial extent, and probably not less in population—I have not examined—we see her going on without impairing personal liberty or exposing the Government to violence or anarchy. Yet the English have not wholly escaped. Although they have retained their liberty, and have not fallen into anarchy and despotism, yet we behold the population of England crushed to the earth by the superincumbent weight of debt. Reflecting on that Government, I have often thought that there was only one way in which it could come to an end—that the weight of the superstructure would crush the foundation—that the wealth accumulated in part by these very conquests by the higher classes, would crush the laboring masses below. But has she obtained indemnity from all her subjected provinces? On the contrary, instead of drawing the means of supporting herself from them, has she not been compelled to resort to the labor of her own population to hold them in subjection? And has she not thrown a burden upon them, which, with all their industry and skill—with all their vast accumulation of capital and power of machinery, they are incapable of bearing without being reduced to poverty? Take even her earliest and nearest conquest—the neighboring island of Ireland—is it not to this day a source of heavy expense, and a burden to her, instead of a source of revenue?

But while the English Government has such vast power of holding subjected provinces in subjection without impairing her liberty, without the evils incident to it, our Government, of all free Governments that ever existed, has the least capacity to bear patronage proportionate to its wealth and power. In this respect, the genius of the two Governments is precisely the opposite, however much alike in their exterior forms, and their laws and customs. The cause of this difference I cannot undertake to explain on the present occasion, but must content myself by saying that it results from its Federal character, and the nature of its conservative principles. Shall we, then, with these certain and inevitable consequences in a Government better calculated to resist them than any other, adopt such a ruinous policy, and reject the lessons of experience? So much, then, Mr. President, for holding Mexico as a province.

I come now to the proposition of incorporating her into our Union. Well, as far as law is concerned, that is easy. You can establish a Territorial Government for every state in Mexico, and there are some twenty of them. You can appoint governors, judges, and magistrates. You can give the people a subordinate government, allowing them to legislate for themselves, whilst you defray the cost. So far as law goes, the thing is done. There is no analogy between this and our Territorial Governments. Our Territories are only an offset of our own people, or foreigners from the same regions from which we came. They are small in number. They are incapable of forming a government. It would be inconvenient for them to sustain a government, if it were formed; and they are very much obliged to the United States for undertaking the trouble, knowing that, on the attainment of their majority—when they come to manhood—at twenty-one—they will be introduced to an equality with all the other members of the Union. It is entirely different with Mexico. You have no need of armies to keep your Territories in subjection. But when you incorporate Mexico, you must have powerful armies to keep them in subjection. You may call it annexation, but it is a forced annexation, which is a contradiction in terms, according to my conception. You will be involved, in one word, in all the evils which I attribute to holding Mexico as a province. In fact, it will be but a Provincial Government, under the name of a Territorial Government. How long will that last? How long will it be before Mexico will be capable of incorporation into our Union? Why, if we judge from the examples before us, it will be a very long time. Ireland has been held in subjection by England for seven or eight hundred years, and yet still remains hostile, although her people are of kindred race with the conquerors. A few French Canadians on this continent yet maintain the attitude of a hostile people; and never will the time come, in my opinion, Mr. President, that these Mexicans will be heartily reconciled to your authority. They have Castilian blood in their veins—the old Gothic, quite equal to the Anglo-Saxon in many respects—in some respects superior. Of all nations of the earth they are the most pertinacious—have the highest sense of nationality—hold out longest, and often even with the least prospect of effecting their object. On this subject also I have conversed with officers of the army, and they all entertain the same opinion, that these people are now hostile, and will continue so.

But, Mr. President, suppose all these difficulties removed; suppose these people attached to our Union, and desirous of incorporating with us, ought we to bring them in? Are they fit to be connected with us? Are they fit for self-government and for governing you? Are you, any of you, willing that your States should be governed by these twenty-odd Mexican states, with a population of about only one million of your blood, and two or three millions of mixed blood, better informed [*sic*], all the rest pure Indians, [or] a mixed blood equally ignorant and unfit for liberty, impure races, not as good as the Cherokees or Choctaws?

We make a great mistake, sir, when we suppose that all people are capable of self-government. We are anxious to force free government on all; and I see that it has been urged in a very respectable quarter, that it is the mission of this country to spread civil and religious liberty over all the world, and especially over this continent. It is a great mistake. None but people advanced to a very high state of moral and intellectual improvement are capable, in a civilized state, of maintaining free government; and amongst those who are so purified, very few, indeed, have had the good fortune of forming a constitution capable of endurance. It is a remarkable fact in the history of man, that scarcely ever have free popular institutions been formed by wisdom alone that have endured.

It has been the work of fortunate circumstances, or a combination of circumstances—a succession of fortunate incidents of some kind— which give to any people a free government. It is a very difficult task to make a constitution to last, though it may be supposed by some that they can be made to order, and furnished at the shortest notice. Sir, this admirable Constitution of our own was the result of a fortunate combination of circumstances. It was superior to the wisdom of the men who made it. It was the force of circumstances which induced them to adopt most of its wise provisions. Well, sir, of the few nations who have the good fortune to adopt self-government, few have had the good fortune long to preserve that government; for it is harder to preserve than to form it. Few people, after years of prosperity, remember the tenure by which their liberty is held; and I fear, Senators, that is our own condition. I fear that we shall continue to involve ourselves until our own system becomes a ruin. Sir, there is no solicitude now for liberty. Who talks of liberty when any great question comes up? Here is a question of the first magnitude as to the conduct of this war; do you hear anybody talk about its effect upon our liberties and our free institutions? No, sir. That was not the case formerly. In the early stages of our Government, the great anxiety was how to preserve liberty; the great anxiety now is for the attainment of mere military glory. In the one, we are forgetting the other. The maxim of former times was, that power is always stealing from the many to the few; the price of liberty was perpetual vigilance. They were constantly looking out and watching for danger. Then, when any great question came up, the first inquiry was, how it could affect our free institutions— how it could affect our liberty. Not so now. Is it because there has been any decay of the spirit of liberty among the people? Not at all. I believe the love of liberty was never more ardent, but they have forgotten the tenure of liberty by which alone it is preserved.

We think we may now indulge in everything with impunity, as if we held our charter of liberty by "right divine"—from Heaven itself. Under these impressions, we plunge into war, we contract heavy debts, we increase the patronage of the Executive, and we even talk of a crusade to force our institutions, our liberty, upon all people. There is no species of extravagance which our people imagine will endanger their liberty in any degree. But it is a great and fatal mistake. The day of retribution will come. It will come as certainly as I am now addressing the Senate; and when it does come, awful will be the reckoning—heavy the responsibility some-where!

Mr. President, with these impressions I cannot approve of the policy recommended by the Executive, nor can I, with my present views, support it. The question is now, what shall be done? It is a great and difficult question, and it is daily becoming more and more difficult. What is to be done? Sir, that question ought not to be for me to answer—I, who have used every effort in my power to prevent this war, and after its commencement have done everything in my power to diminish the evil to the smallest possible amount. But I will not shrink from any responsibility, whether it properly belongs to me or not. After saying that I cannot support the course recom-mended by the Executive, I will proceed to state that which I would propose as the best to be pursued. Well, then, I will say that there is not the smallest chance of our disentangling ourselves from this Mexican concern, which threatens us so much—there has not been, in my opinion, the smallest chance, from the commencement of the war until this time—but by taking a defensive line; doing that now which the President recommends should be done finally after the conquest, and taking indemnity into our own hands. To do this depends on our own volition, and not on the fleeting consent of Mexico. Sir, if time had been allowed to the Senate when the mes-sage of the President recommending war was before them; if time had been allowed to the Senate, I would have announced the course of policy which I thought right; but time was not permitted. My opinion was, that we should have simply voted [Zachary] Taylor the means of defending himself. That ought to have been done. There then should have been a solemn report from the proper com-mittee, going into all the circumstances, showing that the Republic of Mexico had not yet recognized these hostilities, recommending a provisional army to be directed to a proper point, giving time to the Mexican Congress and Mexican people to have considered whether they would avow or disavow the attacks upon us; and if no satisfaction were obtained, not to make war in this set form, but seize upon the portions of the country contiguous and most convenient to us, and then have assumed the defensive line. These are my views; but, unfortunately, we were all acting here under an urgency, with-out time to reflect. We were pushed on, and told, If you do not act to-day, nothing can be done.

Well, now, sir, as to where the defensive line should be at the present time, I do not presume to offer an opinion. I suggested a line at the last session. I am not prepared to say what would be the proper one at the present time; but I do say that we must vacate the central parts of Mexico. We must fall back, if you choose to use that word, or take a line that shall cover ample territory for indemnity.

For my part, I am not for charging Mexico with the whole expense of the war; but I would take ample territory, and hold it subject to negotiation. Now, sir, I know it will be said that this will be as expensive as the war. I think I have said enough to show that that cannot be; that it will fall far short of it; but I will not repeat the argument. But admitting it should: admitting that, by no means concludes the argument; for the sacrifice of men would be infinitely less, and, what is more important, you will thereby be able to disentangle yourselves. That is the only way by which it can be done. You are tied at present, as it were, to a corpse. My object is to get rid of it as soon as possible.

I look not to Mexico; I look to our own country and her institutions. I look to the liberty of this country, and nothing else. Mr. President, if we but preserve our liberty by a proper course of moderation, acting justly towards our neighbor, and wisely in regard to ourselves—if we remain quiet, resting in idle and masterly inactivity, and let our destinies work out their own results, we shall do more for liberty, not only for ourselves, but for the example of mankind, than can be done by a thousand victories.

Sir, I find I am becoming old; I almost feel that I live among strangers. If I have expressed anything that is uncongenial to the feelings of this body, put it down as proceeding from the old associations of thirty or thirty-five years ago, which are still clinging around me. Sir, this is not the first time that I have taken my stand against war. When [in 1836] General [Andrew] Jackson recommended letters of marque and reprisal against France, I arose alone in the Senate and remonstrated against such injustice. And in point of fact, the treaty which was subsequently concluded with France, was ratified with the express understanding, which was known to our Government when the treaty was formed, that it would require a vote of the Chambers, on the part of France, to sustain it, as it would require a vote to sustain it on the part of this country; and that they were no further responsible than to use their best efforts to obtain that vote. And yet, though it was acknowledged that the Executive of France had done all in his power to obtain the vote, we were nearly pushed into a war. Nothing but the interposition of Great Britain prevented it. As for myself, standing on this side of the Chamber, I raised my voice singly against it.

Mr. President, in my opinion, all parties are interested in giving

this matter the only direction that can be given to it with any prospect of a favorable result. Let me say to the friends of the Administration, if you go on, and some accident does not meet you—if you
go on in the prosecution of this war from year to year—you will find
that it will overthrow you. Do you not see that, as far as the internal
affairs of the Government are concerned, you are reversing the
policy of which you have heretofore professed to be the advocates?
What party has been opposed to the re-creation of a great national
debt? The Democratic or Republican party. Well, sir, this war is
involving you in a greater debt than the opposite party could have
done, perhaps, in any circumstances short of war. This very campaign, which you look upon so lightly, will be almost as great a charge
upon the country as the debt of the Revolution. What party has
always been against the extension of the patronage of the Executive?
Well, sir, you are doing more towards the extension of that patronage,
and, above all, towards the continuance of that extension, than has
ever been done under our Government. Well, sir, what party profess-
es to be most in favor of a metallic currency? And do you not see
that, as your treasury notes and stocks accumulate, you are in danger
of being plunged again in the paper system to the utmost extent?
What party has always been in favor of free trade? Do you not see
that, by accumulating charges and burdens upon the people by the
debts which have now been contracted, you never will, during your
time, have an opportunity of making any considerable reduction in
the tariff?

Sir, I know what is at the bottom of the course of policy which is
recommended to be pursued. It is that pride of opinion to which we
are all subject. No doubt it was thought that that course of policy
would lead to the consequences which were contended for; but it
has not. But, sir, the alternative is pressing. You will have but the
choice between that and worse, in my opinion. It is magnanimous
and honorable to retract, when a course of policy which has been
pursued turns out to be wrong. It would do great credit to the party
in power to act now precisely as they would have acted if they had
had all the lights of experience at the commencement of this war
which they now have. It would be doing a high act of patriotism to
sacrifice their feelings of individual pride to the good of the country.

Now let me say, that in asserting that a defensive line was the
only alternative to the plan recommended by the President, I have
put out of the question the course which most of you advocate—
taking no indemnity of territory; because I believe that the voice of
the country has decided irrevocably against it; and that to keep it

as the alternative would but render more certain the adoption of the policy recommended by the Executive, and, in consequence, the conquest of the whole country. Let me say further, to my [Whig] friends on the other side of the Chamber—for I regard them as such—(it is our good fortune to differ in politics here, without permitting our personal feelings to be affected)—that they have contributed by their course to give the public opinion that strong and fixed determination not to terminate the war without some suitable indemnity. I do not allude to your voting on the bill recognizing the existence of war between the Republic of Mexico and the United States. No one knows better than myself, that you voted for the bill with the view of furnishing immediate relief to General Taylor and his army—and not in reference to the war; that you even protested and remonstrated against that interpretation being put upon your vote. But after the bill passed, and the war was authorized, most of you have continued to vote appropriations to prosecute the war with the object expressed of acquiring territory as an indemnity. Now, I must say, I cannot see how the two can be reconciled—how your vote to acquire territory can be justified, and at the same time your opposition to the acquisition of territory as means of indemnity, when it is acknowledged on all sides, that that is the only means by which it can be acquired. The people will find it hard to believe that it was necessary to vote so much money for the purpose of getting territory for indemnity, which you intend to throw away when you get it. But, whatever may be the causes which have led to this state of public opinion, it has, beyond all doubt, decided against any conclusion of this war that does not involve territorial indemnity to some extent. Hence, I repeat, the alternative whether this war shall go on and consummate itself, is between taking a defensive line and adopting the course pointed out by the Executive, and that the decision must be made now; for if it be passed over until another session, the end will be, I doubt not, the subjugation of the whole country, thereby involving us in all the difficulties and dangers which must result from it.

Now, I have delivered my opinion with that candor and frankness which, I hope, become my position on this floor. I shall now propose nothing; but if I find that I can be supported in these my views, I will undertake to raise a committee to deliberate, after consulting with those officers who are now fortunately in this city, upon the best defensive line that can be taken. If it should be fortunately adopted, we may not get peace immediately. The war may continue for some years, but we will accomplish that all-important consideration, the extrication of ourselves and the country from this entanglement with Mexico.

Mr. Sevier moved to lay the resolutions upon the table.

Upon this motion the yeas and nays were demanded.

Mr. Calhoun said he hoped the motion would be allowed to prevail. It was perfectly right, in the present circumstances, that the motion should prevail. He would take it as a personal favor that no opposition should be offered to it.

Mr. Sevier observed that it was, of course, to be expected that this speech would be replied to; but he was desirous that this debate should be suspended for a time, in order to proceed with the consideration of the army bill.

The motion to lay [Calhoun's resolutions] on the table was then agreed to.

From *Congressional Globe,* 30th Cong., 1st Sess., pp. 96–100. Also printed in Houston, ed., *Proceedings and Debates,* pp. 62–67. This version was the earliest report of the speech, which is printed above. Compare the following, slightly later version, corrected by Calhoun, with occasionally different and more concise and polished language, but no difference in substance, which is printed below. Other printings of these two related versions: the Washington, D.C., *Daily Union,* January 6, 1848, pp. 1–2; the New York, N.Y., *Morning Courier and New-York Enquirer,* January 6, 1848, p. 2; the Alexandria, Va., *Gazette and Virginia Advertiser,* January 7, 1848, p. 2; the Washington, D.C., *Daily National Intelligencer,* January 8, 1848, p. 2; the Charleston, S.C., *Mercury,* January 10, 1848, p. 2; the Charleston, S.C., *Southern Patriot,* January 10, 1848, pp. 2–3; the Richmond, Va., *Enquirer,* January 11, 1848, p. 1; the Richmond, Va., *Whig and Public Advertiser,* January 11, 1848, p. 1; the Charleston, S.C., *Courier,* January 12, 1848, p. 2; the Louisville, Ky., *Morning Courier,* January 13, 1848, p. 2; *Niles' National Register,* vol. LXXIII, no. 20 (January 15, 1848), pp. 316–319; the Nashville, Tenn., *Whig,* January 18, 1848, p. 2, and January 20, 1848, p. 2; the Camden, S.C., *Journal,* January 19, 1848, pp. 1–2; the Tuscaloosa, Ala., *Independent Monitor,* January 20, 1848, pp. 2–3; the Pendleton, S.C., *Messenger,* January 21, 1848, pp. 1, 4, and January 28, 1848, p. 1; the Greenville, S.C., *Mountaineer,* January 21, 1848, pp. 1, 4; the Tallahassee, Fla., *Floridian,* January 22, 1848, pp. 1–2; the Huntsville, Ala., *Democrat,* January 26, 1848, pp. 1–2; the Athens, Ga., *Southern Banner,* January 27, 1848, pp. 1–2; Wilson, ed., *The Essential Calhoun,* pp. 114–115 (part). Substantially variant reports: the New York, N.Y., *Herald,* January 5, 1848, pp. 2–3; the Baltimore, Md., *Sun,* January 5, 1848, p. 4; the Charleston, S.C., *Courier,* January 8, 1848, p. 2, and January 10, 1848, p. 2; the Louisville, Ky., *Morning Courier,* January 8, 1848, p. 3, and January 11, 1848, p. 2; the Petersburg, Va., *Republican,* January 10, 1848, p. 2; the Charleston, S.C., *Southern Baptist,* January 12, 1848, p. 3; the Nashville, Tenn., *Whig,* January 13, 1848, p. 2. NOTE: Negative commentaries on Calhoun's speech appeared in the Washington, D.C., *Daily Union,* January 31, 1848, p. 3, and in *The American Review,* vol. 1, no. 3 (March, 1848), pp. 217–230.

SPEECH ON THE WAR WITH MEXICO
(Revised Version)

[In the Senate, January 4, 1848]

Resolved, That to conquer Mexico and to hold it, either as a province or to incorporate it in the Union, would be inconsistent with the avowed object for which the war has been prosecuted; a departure from the settled policy of the Government; in conflict with its character and genius; and in the end, subversive of our free and popular institutions.

Resolved, That no line of policy in the further prosecution of the war should be adopted which may lead to consequences so disastrous.

Mr. Calhoun said: in offering, Senators, these resolutions for your consideration, I am governed by the reasons which induced me to oppose the war; and by which I have been governed since it was sanctioned by Congress. In alluding to my opposition to the war, I do not intend to touch on the reasons which governed me on that occasion, further than is necessary to explain my motives upon the present.

I then opposed the war, not only because it might have been easily avoided; not only because the President [James K. Polk] had no authority to order a part of the disputed territory in possession of the Mexicans to be occupied by our troops; not only because I believed the allegations upon which Congress sanctioned the war untrue, but from high considerations of policy; because I believed it would lead to many and serious evils to the country, and greatly endanger its free institutions. But, after the war was declared, by authority of the Government, I acquiesced in what I could not prevent, and which it was impossible for me to arrest; and I then felt it to be my duty to limit my efforts to giving such direction to the war as would, as far as possible, prevent the evils and danger with which it threatened the country and its institutions. For this purpose, at the last session, I suggested to the Senate the policy of adopting a defensive line, and for the same purpose I now offer these resolutions. This, and this only, is the motive which governs me on this occasion. I am moved by no personal or party considerations. My object is neither to sustain the Executive nor to strengthen the opposition, but simply to discharge an important duty to the country. In doing so, I shall express my opinion on all points with the freedom and boldness which becomes an independent Senator, who has nothing to ask from the Government or from the People. But when I come to notice those points on which I differ from the President, I shall do it with all the decorum, which is due to the Chief Magistrate of the Union.

I suggested a defensive line because, in the first place, I believed that the only certain mode of terminating the war successfully was to take indemnity in our own hands by occupying defensively, with our military force, a portion of the Mexican territory, which we might deem ample for indemnity; and, in the next, because I believed it would prevent a great sacrifice of life and property; but, above all, because I believed that it was the only way we could avoid the great danger to our institutions against which these resolutions are intended to guard. The President took a different view. He recommended a vigorous prosecution of the war—not for conquest—that was emphatically disavowed—but for the purpose of conquering peace—that is, to compel Mexico to sign a treaty ceding sufficient territory to indemnify the claims of our citizens and of the country for the expenses of the war. I could not approve of this policy. I opposed it, among other reasons, because I believed there was no certainty that the object intended to be effected would be accomplished, let the war be ever so successful. Congress thought differently, and granted ample provisions, in men and money, for carrying out the policy recommended by the President. It has now been fully tested under the most favorable circumstances. It has been as successful as the most sanguine hope of the Executive could have anticipated. Victory after victory followed in rapid succession, without a single reverse. Santa Anna repelled and defeated with all his forces at Buena Vista—Vera Cruz, with its castle, captured—the heights of Cerra Gorda [*sic*] triumphantly carried—Jalappa, Perote, and Peubla [*sic*] occupied—and after many triumphant victories under the walls of Mexico, its gates opened to us, and put us in possession of the Capital. But what has all these splendid achiev[e]-ments accomplished? Has the avowed object of the war been attained? Have we conquered peace? Have we compelled Mexico to sign a treaty? Have we obtained indemnity? No. Not a single object contemplated by the campaign has been effected; and what is worse, our difficulties are greater now than they were at the commencement, and the objects sought more difficult to be accomplished. To what is this complete failure to be attributed? Not to our army. It has done all that skill and gallantry could accomplish. It is to be attributed to the policy pursued. The Executive aimed at indemnity in a wrong way. Instead of taking it into our own hands, when we had territory in our possession, ample to cover the claims of our citizens and the expenses of the war, he sought it indirectly through a treaty with Mexico. He thus put it out of our own power, and under the control of Mexico, to say whether we should have indemnity or not, and thereby enabled her to defeat the whole object of the campaign by simply refusing to treat with us. Owing to this mistaken policy, after a most successful and brilliant campaign, involving an expenditure not less, probably, than forty millions of dollars, and the sacrifice, by the sword and by disease, of many valuable lives, probably not less than six or seven thousand, nothing is left but the glory which our army has acquired.

But as an apology for all this, it is insisted that the maintenance of a defensive line would have involved as great a sacrifice as the campaign itself. The President and the Secretary of War [William L. Marcy] have assigned many reasons for entertaining this opinion. I have examined them with care. This is not the proper occasion to discuss them, but I must say, with all due deference, they are, to my mind, utterly fallacious; and to satisfy your minds that such is the case, I will place the subject in a single point of view.

The line proposed by me, to which I suppose their reasons were intended to be applied, would be covered in its whole extent, from the Pacific ocean to the Passo del Norte, on the Rio Grande, by the Gulf of California and the wilderness peopled by hostile tribes of Indians, through which no Mexican force could penetrate. For its entire occupancy and defence, nothing would be required but a few small vessels of war stationed in the Gulf, and a single regiment to keep down any resistance from the few inhabitants within. From the Passo del Norte to the mouth of the river, a distance of a few hundred miles, a single fact will show what little force will be necessary to its defence. It was a frontier between Texas and Mexico, when the former had but an inconsiderable population—not more than an hundred and fifty thousand at the utmost, at any time—with no standing army, and but very few irregular troops; yet for several years she maintained this line without any, except slight occasional, intrusion from Mexico, and that too when Mexico was far more consolidated in her power, and when revolutions were not so frequent, and her money resources were far greater than at present. If, then, Texas alone, under such circumstances, could defend that frontier for so long a period, can any man believe that now, when she is backed by the whole of the United States, now that Mexico is exhausted, defeated, and prostrated—I repeat, can any man believe that it would involve as great a sacrifice to us of men and money, to defend that frontier, as did the last campaign? No. I hazard nothing in asserting, that, to defend it for an indefinite period, would have required a less sum than the interest on the money spent in the campaign, and fewer men than were sacrificed in carrying it on.

So much for the past. We now come to the commencement of another campaign, and the question recurs, what shall be done? The President, in his message, recommends the same line of policy— a vigorous prosecution of the war—not for conquest, that is again emphatically disavowed; not to blot Mexico out of the list of nations; no, he desires to see her an independent and flourishing community, and assigns strong reasons for it; but to obtain an honorable peace. We hear no more of conquering peace, but I presume that he means by an honorable peace the same thing; that is, to compel Mexico to agree to a treaty, ceding a sufficient part of her territory, as an indemnity for the expenses of the war, and for the claims of our citizens.

I have examined, with care, the grounds on which the President renews his recommendation, and am again compelled to dissent. There are many and powerful reasons, more so, even, than those that existed at the commencement of the last campaign, to justify my dissent. The sacrifice in money will be vastly greater. There is a bill for ten additional regiments now before the Senate, and another for twenty regiments of volunteers has been reported, authorizing in all the raising of an additional force of something upwards of thirty thousand. This, in addition to that already authorized by law, will be sufficient to keep an effective army in Mexico, of not much, if any, less than seventy thousand men, and will raise the expenses of the campaign to probably not less than sixty millions of dollars.

To meet so large an expenditure, would involve, in the present and prospective condition of the money market, it is to be apprehended, not a little embarrassment. Last year money was abundant, and easily obtained. An unfortunate famine in Europe created a great demand for our agricultural products. That turned the balance of trade greatly in our favor, and specie poured into the country with a strong and steady current. No inconsiderable portion of it passed into the Treasury, through the duties, which kept it full, in spite of the large sums remitted to meet the expenses of the war. The case is different now. Instead of having a tide flowing in, equal to the drain flowing out, the drain is now both ways. The exchanges now are against us, instead of being in our favor, and instead of specie flowing into the country from abroad, it is flowing out. In the mean time the price of stocks and Treasury notes, instead of being at or above par, have both fallen below, to a small extent. The effects of the depreciation of Treasury notes will cause them to pass into the Treasury in payment of the customs and other dues to the Government, as the cheaper currency, instead of gold and silver; while the expenses of the war, whether paid for by the transmission of gold and silver direct to Mexico, or by drafts drawn in favor of British merchants or other capitalists there, will cause whatever specie may be in the vaults of the Treasury to flow from it, either for remittance direct, on account of the ordinary transactions of the country, or to pay the drafts which may be drawn upon it, and which, when paid, in the present state of exchanges, will be remitted abroad. But this process of paying in Treasury notes, instead of gold and silver, and gold and silver flowing out in both directions, cannot continue long without exhausting its specie, and leaving nothing to meet the public expenditure, including those of the war, but Treasury notes. Can they, under such circumstances, preserve even their present value? Is there not great danger that they will fall lower and lower, and finally involve the finances of the Government and the circulation of the country in the greatest embarrassment and difficulty?

Is there not great danger, with this prospect before us, and with the necessity of raising by loans near forty millions, of a commercial and financial crisis—even possibly a suspension by the banks. I wish not to create panic; but there is danger, which makes a great difference in a financial and monied point of view, between the state of things now and at the commencement of the last session. Looking to the future, it is to be apprehended that not a little difficulty will have to be encountered in raising money to meet the expenses of the next campaign, if conducted on the large scale which is proposed. Men you may raise, but money will be found difficult to obtain. It is even to be apprehended that loans will have to be negotiated on very disadvantageous terms for the public. In the present state of things, if they grow no worse, there can be no resort to Treasury notes. They cannot be materially increased, without a ruinous depreciation, and a resort must be had, exclusively, or almost entirely so, to borrowing. But at the present prices of stocks, to borrow so large a sum as will be necessary, can only be done at a greatly increased rate of interest on the nominal amount of stock. In a recent conversation with a gentleman, well informed on this subject, he said, that in his opinion, if forty millions are required, a loan could not be had for more than ninety for one hundred, which would be about at the rate of seven per cent.

These are formidable objections, but they are not the only ones that are more so than they were at the commencement of the last campaign. I hold that the avowed object for the vigorous prosecution of the war is less certain of being realized *now*, than it was then; and if it should fail to be realized, it will leave our affairs in a far worse condition than they are at present. That object, as has been stated, is to obtain an honorable treaty; one which, to use the language of the President, will give indemnity for the past and security for the future—that is, a treaty which will give us a cession of territory, not only equal to our present demand for indemnity, but equal to the additional demand—equal to the entire expenses to be incurred in conducting the campaign; and a guarantee from the Government of Mexico for its faithful execution. Now, Senators, I hold that whether the war is successful or unsuccessful, there is not only no certainty that this object will be accomplished, but almost a certainty that it will not be. If the war be unsuccessful; if our arms should be baffled, as I trust and believe they will not be; but if, from any unfortunate accident, such should be the case, it is clear that we shall not be able to negotiate a treaty that will accomplish the object intended. On the contrary, if the war should be successful, it is almost equally certain that, in that case, the avowed object for prosecuting the war vigorously, will not be accomplished. I might take higher ground, and maintain that the more successfully the war is prosecuted, the more certainly the object avowed to be accomplished will be defeated, while the objects disavowed would as certainly be accomplished.

What is the object of a vigorous prosecution of the war? How can it be successful? I can see but one way of making it so, and that is by suppressing all resistance on the part of Mexico, overpowering and dispersing her army, and utterly overthrowing her Government. But if that should be done; if a vigorous prosecution of the war should lead to that result, how are we to obtain an honorable peace? With whom shall we treat for indemnity for the past and security for the future? War may be made by one party, but it requires two to make peace. If all authority is overthrown in Mexico, where will be the power to enter into negotiation and make peace? Our very success would defeat the possibility of making peace. In that case the war would not end in peace, but in conquest; not in negotiation, but in subjugation; and defeat, I repeat, the very object you aim to accomplish, and accomplish that which you disavow to be your intention, by destroying the separate existence of Mexico, overthrowing her nationality, and blotting out her name from the list of nations, instead of leaving her a free Republic, which the President has so earnestly expressed his desire to do.

If I understand his Message correctly, I have his own authority for the conclusion to which I come. He takes very much the same view that I do, as to how a war ought to be prosecuted vigorously, and what would be its results, with the difference as to the latter, resting on a single contingency, and that a remote one. He says that the great difficulty of obtaining peace results from this, that the people of Mexico are divided under factious chieftains, and that the chief in power dare not make peace, because for doing so he would be displaced by a rival. He also says, that the only way to remedy this evil and to obtain a treaty, is to put down the whole of them, including the one in power, as well as the others. Well, what then? Are we to stop there? No. Our Generals are, it seems, authorized to encourage and to protect the well disposed inhabitants in establishing a republican Government. He says they are numerous, and are prevented from expressing their opinions and making an attempt to form such a Government, only by fear of those military chieftains. He proposes, when they have thus formed a Government, under the encouragement and protection of our army, to obtain peace by a treaty with the Government thus formed, which shall give us ample indemnity for the past and security for the future. I must say I am at a loss to see how a free and independent Republic can be established in Mexico under the protection and authority of its conquerors. I can readily understand how an aristocracy or a despotic Government might be, but how a free republican Government can be so established, under such circumstances, is to me incomprehensible. I had always supposed that such a Government must be the spontaneous wish of the people; that it must emanate from the hearts of the people, and be supported by their devotion to it, without support from abroad. But it seems that these are antiquated notions—obsolete ideas—and that free popular Governments may be made under the authority and protection of a conqueror.

But suppose these difficulties surmounted, how can we make a free Government in Mexico? Where are the materials? It is to be, I presume, a confederated Government like their former. Where is the intelligence in Mexico for the construction and preservation of such a Government? It is what she has been aiming at for more than twenty years, but so utterly incompetent are her people for the task, that it has been a complete failure from first to last. The great body of the intelligence and wealth of Mexico is concentrated in the priesthood, who are naturally disinclined to that form of Government; the residue, for the most part, are the owners of the haciendas, the larger planters of the country, but they are without concert and destitute of the means of forming such a Government. But if it were possible to establish such a Government, it could not stand without the protection of our army. It would fall as soon as it is withdrawn.

If it be determined to have a treaty, it would be a far preferable course, as it appears to me, to abstain from attacking or destroying the Government now existing in Mexico, and to treat with it, if indeed it be capable of forming a treaty which it could maintain and execute. Upon that point I do not profess to have any information beyond that derived from conversations with those who have been in Mexico; but from all that I can hear, it may be doubted, whether we have not already pushed, what is called a vigorous prosecution of the war so far, as not to leave sufficient power and influence in the Government to enter into a treaty which would be respected, when our forces are withdrawn. Such I know to be the opinion of intelligent officers. They concur in thinking that the existing Government at Queretaro, if it should enter into a treaty in conformity with the views expressed by the Executive, would be overthrown, and that we should be compelled to defend that portion of Mexico which we require for indemnity, defensively, or be compelled to return and renew the prosecution of the war. If such is its weakness, it may be apprehended that even now, without pushing the vigorous prosecution of the war further, we are greatly exposed to the danger which these resolutions are intended to guard against, and that it requires great discretion and prompt action on our part to avoid it.

But before leaving this part of the subject, I must enter my solemn protest, as one of the Representatives of a State of this Union, against pledging protection to any Government established in Mexico under our countenance or encouragement. It would inevitably be overthrown as soon as our forces are withdrawn, and we would be compelled, in fulfilment of plighted faith, implied or expressed, to return and reinstate such Government in power, to be again overturned and again reinstated, until we should be compelled to take the Government into our own hands, just as the English have been compelled again and again to do in Hindostan, under similar circumstances, until it has led to its entire conquest. Let us avoid following the example which we have been condemning, as far back as my recollection extends.

The President himself entertains doubt, whether the plan of forming a Government in the manner which I have been considering, and treating with it for indemnity, may not fail. In that case, he agrees that the very course to which I have said the vigorous prosecution of the war will inevitably lead, must be taken. He says, after having attempted to establish such a Government—after having employed the best efforts to secure peace—if all fail, "we must hold on to the occupation of the country. We must take the full measure of indemnity into our own hands, and enforce such terms as the honor of the country demand." These are his words. Now, what is this? Is it not an acknowledgement, that if he fails in establishing a Government with which he can treat, in Mexico—after putting down all resistance under the existing Government, we must make a conquest of the whole country, and hold it subject to our control? Can words be stronger? "Occupy the whole country"—"take the full measure of indemnity"—no defensive line—no treaty, and "enforce terms." Terms on whom? On the Government? No, no, no. To enforce terms on the people individually. That is to say, to establish a Government over them in the form of a province.

The President is right. If the vigorous prosecution of the war should be successful, and the contingency on which he expects to make a treaty fails, there will be no retreat. Every argument against calling back the army and taking a defensive line will have double force, after having spent sixty millions of dollars, and acquired the possession of the whole of Mexico, and the interests in favor of keeping possession would be much more powerful then than now. The army itself will be larger—those who live by the war, the numerous contractors, the merchants, the sutlers, the speculators in land and mines, and all who are profiting directly or indirectly by its prosecution, will be adverse to retiring, and will swell the cry of holding on to our conquests. They constitute an immense body of vast influence, who are growing rich by what is impoverishing the rest of the country.

It is at this stage that the President speaks of taking the indemnity into our own hands. But why delay it until the whole country is subdued? Why not take it now? A part of Mexico would be a better indemnity now, than the whole of Mexico would be at the end of the next campaign, when sixty millions of dollars will be added to the present expenditures. We would indeed acquire a control over a much larger portion of her population, but we would never be able to extort from them, by all the forms of taxation to which you can resort, a sum sufficient to pay the force necessary to hold them in subjection. That force must be a large one, not less certainly than forty thousand men, according to the opinion of the Senator from Mississippi, (Mr. [Jefferson] Davis,) who must be regarded as a competent judge upon this point. He stated in debate the other day, that the army now there, exceeding that number, are in danger; and urged, on that account, the immediate passage of the bill to raise ten regiments. On this subject, it is as well to speak out plainly at once. We shall never obtain indemnity for the expenditures of the war. They must come out of the pockets of the people of the United States; and the longer the war is continued, and the more numerous our army, the greater will be the debt, and the heavier the burden imposed upon the country.

If these views be correct, the end of the policy recommended by the President, whether contemplated or not, will be to force the Government to adopt one or the other alternatives alluded to in these resolutions. With this impression, I cannot support the policy he recommends, for the reasons assigned in the first resolution. The first of these is, that it would be inconsistent with the avowed object for which the war has been prosecuted. That it would be so, is apparent from what has already been said. Since the commencement of the war until this time, the President has continually disavowed the intention of conquering Mexico, and subjecting her to our control. He has constantly proclaimed that the only object was indemnity, and that the war is prosecuted to obtain it by treaty. And yet, if the results should be as I have stated, the end will be, that what was disavowed will be accomplished, and what has been avowed to be its object, will be defeated. Such a result would be a deep and lasting impeachment of the sincerity or the intelligence of the Government—of its sincerity, because directly opposed to what it has continually and emphatically disavowed; or of its intelligence, for not perceiving what ought to have been so readily anticipated.

We have heard much of the reputation which our country has acquired by this war. I acknowledge it to the full amount, as far as the military is concerned. The army has done its duty nobly, and conferred high honors on the country, for which I sincerely thank them; but I apprehend that the reputation acquired does not go beyond this, and that in other respects we have lost instead of acquiring reputation by the war. It would seem certain, from all publications from abroad, that the Government itself has not gained reputation in the eyes of the world, for justice, moderation, or wisdom. Whether this be deserved or not, it is not for me to inquire at present. I am now speaking merely of reputation; and in that view it appears that we have lost abroad, as much in civil and political reputation as we have acquired for our skill and valor in arms. But much as I regard military glory—as much as I rejoice to witness the display of that indomitable energy and courage which surmounts all difficulties—I would be sorry indeed that our Government should lose any portion of that high character, for justice, moderation, and discretion, which distinguished it in the early stages of our history.

The next reason assigned is, that either holding Mexico as a province, or incorporating her into the Union, would be unprecedented by any example in our history. We have conquered many of the neighboring tribes of Indians, but we have never thought of holding them in subjection, or of incorporating them into our Union. They have been left as an independent people in the midst of us, or been driven back into the forests. Nor have we ever incorporated into the Union any but the Caucasian race. To incorporate Mexico, would be the first departure of the kind; for more than half of its population are pure Indians, and by far the larger portion of the residue mixed blood. I protest against the incorporation of such a people. Ours is the Government of the white man. The great misfortune of what was formerly Spanish America, is to be traced to the fatal error of placing the colored race on an equality with the white. That error destroyed the social arrangement which formed the basis of their society. This error we have wholly escaped; the Brazilians, formerly a province of Portugal, have escaped also, to a considerable extent, and they and we are the only people of this continent who have made revolutions without anarchy. And yet, with this example before them, and our uniform practice, there are those among us who talk about erecting these Mexicans into territorial Governments, and placing them on an equality with the people of these States. I utterly protest against the project.

It is a remarkable fact, in this connection, that in the whole history of man, as far as my information extends, there is no instance whatever, of any civilized colored race, of any shade, being found equal to the establishment and maintenance of free Government, although by far the largest proportion of the human family is composed of them; and even in the savage state, we rarely find them any where with such Governments, except it be our noble savages; for noble I will call them, for their many high qualities. They, for the most part, had free institutions, but such institutions are much more easily sustained among a savage than a civilized people. Are we to overlook this great fact? Are we to associate with ourselves, as equals, companions, and fellow-citizens, the Indians and mixed races of Mexico? I would consider such association as degrading to ourselves, and fatal to our institutions.

The next remaining reasons assigned, that it would be in conflict with the genius and character of our Government, and, in the end, subversive of our free institutions, are intimately connected, and I shall consider them together.

That it would be contrary to the genius and character of our Government, and subversive of our free popular institutions, to hold Mexico as a subject province, is a proposition too clear for argument before a body so enlightened as the Senate. You know the American Constitution too well, you have looked into history, and are too well acquainted with the fatal effects which large provincial possessions have ever had on the institutions of free States, to need any proof to satisfy you how hostile it would be to the institutions of this country, to hold Mexico as a subject province. There is not an example on record of any free State holding a province of the same extent and population, without disastrous consequences. The nations conquered and held as a province, have, in time, retaliated by destroying the liberty of their conquerors, through the corrupting effect of extended patronage and irresponsible power. Such certainly would be our case. The conquest of Mexico would add so vastly to the patronage of this Government, that it would absorb the whole powers of the States; the Union would become an imperial power, and the States reduced to mere subordinate corporations. But the evil would not end there; the process would go on, and the power transferred from the States to the Union, would be transferred from the Legislative department to the Executive. All the immense patronage which holding it as a province would create, the maintenance of a large army, to hold it in subjection, and the appointment of a multitude of civil officers necessary to govern it, would be vested in him. The great influence which it would give the President, would be the means of controlling the Legislative department, and subjecting it to his dictation, especially when combined with the principle of proscription which has now become the established practice of the Government. The struggle to obtain the Presidential chair would become proportionably great—so great as to destroy the freedom of elections. The end would be anarchy or despotism, as certain as I am now addressing the Senate.

Let it not be said that Great Britain is an example to the contrary; that she holds provinces of vast extent and population, without materially impairing the liberty of the subject, or exposing the Government to violence, anarchy, confusion, or corruption. It is so. But it must be attributed to the peculiar character of her Government. Of all Governments that ever existed, of a free character, the British far transcends them all in one particular, and that is, its capacity to bear patronage without the evils usually incident to it. She can bear more, in proportion to population and wealth, than any Government of that character that ever existed. I might even go further, and assert than despotism itself in its most absolute form. I will not undertake to explain why it is so. It will take me further from the course which I have prescribed for myself, than I desire; but I will say, in a few words, that it results from the fact that her Executive and the House of Lords, (the conservative branches of her Government,) are both hereditary, while the other House of Parliament has a popular character. The Roman Government exceeded the British in its capacity for conquest. No Government ever did exist, and none probably ever will, which, in that particular, equalled it; but its capacity to hold conquered provinces in subjection, was as nothing compared to that of Great Britain; and hence, when the Roman power passed beyond the limits of Italy, crossed the Adriatic, the Mediterranean, and the Alps, liberty fell prostrate; the Roman people became a rabble; corruption penetrated every department of the Government; violence and anarchy ruled the day, and military despotism closed the scene. Now, on the contrary, we see England, with subject-provinces of vastly greater territorial extent, and probably of not inferior population, (I have not compared them;) we see her, I repeat, going on without the personal liberty of the subject being materially impaired, or the Government subject to violence or anarchy! Yet England has not wholly escaped the curse which must ever befall a free Government which holds extensive provinces in subjection; for, although she has not lost her liberty, or fallen into anarchy, yet we behold the population of England crushed to the earth by the superincumbent weight of debt and taxation, which may one day terminate in revolution. The wealth derived from her conquests and provincial possessions may have contributed to swell the overgrown fortunes of the upper classes, but has done nothing to alleviate the pressure on the laboring masses below. On the contrary, the expense incident to their conquest, and of governing and holding them in subjection, have been drawn mainly from their labor, and have increased instead of decreasing the weight of the pressure. It has placed a burden upon them which, with all their skill and industry, with all the vast accumulation of capital and power of machinery with which they are aided, they are scarce capable of bearing, without being reduced to the lowest depths of poverty. Take, for example, Ireland, her earliest and nearest conquest, and is it not to this day a cause of heavy expense, and a burden, instead of a source of revenue.

On the contrary, our Government, in this particular, is the very reverse of the British. Of all free Governments, it has the least capacity, in proportion to the wealth and population of the country, to bear patronage. The genius of the two, in this particular, is precisely opposite, however much alike in exterior forms and other particulars. The cause of this difference, I will not undertake to explain on the present occasion. It results from its federal character and elective Chief Magistrate; and so far from the example of Great Britain constituting a safe precedent for us to follow, the little she has gained from her numerous conquests and vast provincial possessions, and the heavy burdens which it has imposed upon her people to meet the consequent expenses, ought to be to us a warning never to be forgotten; especially when we reflect that from the nature of our Government, that we would be so liable to the other and greater evils from which she, from the nature of her Government, is, in a great measure, exempted. Such and so weighty are the objections to conquering Mexico, and holding it as a subject-province.

Nor are the reasons less weighty against incorporating her into the Union. As far as law is concerned, that is easily done. All that is necessary is to establish a Territorial Government for the several States in Mexico, of which there are upwards of twenty, to appoint governors, judges, and magistrates, and to give to the population a subordinate right of making laws, we defraying the cost of the Government. So far as legislation goes, the work will be done; but there would be a great difference between these Territorial Governments, and those which we have heretofore established within our own limits. These are only the offsets of our own people, or foreigners from the same countries from which our ancestors came. The first settlers in the Territories are too few in number to form and support a Government of their own, and are under obligation to the Government of the United States, for forming one for them, and defraying the expense of maintaining it; knowing as they do that when they have sufficient population, they will be permitted to form a constitution for themselves, and be admitted as a member of the Union. During the period of their Territorial Government, no force is necessary to keep them in a state of subjection. The case will be entirely different with these Mexican Territories; when you form them, you must have powerful armies to hold them in subjection, with all the expenses incident to supporting them. You may call them Territories, but they would, in reality, be but provinces under another name, and would involve the country in all the difficulties and dangers which I have already shown would result from holding the country in that condition. How long this state of things would last, before they would be fitted to be incorporated into the Union as States, we may form some idea, from similar instances with which we are familiar. Ireland has been held in subjection by England for many centuries, and yet remains hostile, although her people are of a kindred race with the conquerors. The French colony in Canada still entertain hostile feelings towards their conquerors, although living in the midst of them for nearly one hundred years. If we may judge from these examples, it would not be unsafe to conclude that the Mexicans never will be heartily reconciled to our authority. The better class have Castilian blood in their veins, and are of the old Gothic stock—quite equal to the Anglo-Saxons in many respects, and in some superior. Of all the people upon earth, they are the most pertinacious; they hold out longer, and often when there would seem to be no prospect of ever making effectual resistance. It is admitted, I believe, on all hands, that they are now universally hostile to us, and the probability is, will continue so.

But suppose this difficulty removed. Suppose their hostility should cease, and they should become desirous of being incorporated in our Union. Ought we to admit them? Are the Mexicans fit to be politically associated with us? Are they fit not only to govern themselves, but for governing us also? Are any of you, Senators, willing that your State should constitute a member of a Union, of which twenty odd Mexican States, more than one-third of the whole, would be a part, the far greater part of the inhabitants of which are pure Indians, not equal in intelligence and elevation of character to the Cherokees, Choctaws, or any of our Southern Indian tribes?

We make a great mistake in supposing all people are capable of self government. Acting under that impression, many are anxious to force free Governments on all the people of this continent, and over the world, if they had the power. It has been lately urged in a very respectable quarter, that it is the mission of this country to spread civil and religious liberty over all the globe, and especially over this continent—even by force, if necessary. It is a sad delusion. None but a people advanced to a high state of moral and intellectual excellence are capable in a civilized condition, of forming and maintaining free Governments; and among those who are so far advanced, very few indeed have had the good fortune to form constitutions capable of endurance. It is a remarkable fact in the political history of man, that there is scarcely an instance of a free constitutional Government, which has been the work exclusively of foresight and wisdom. They have all been the result of a fortunate combination of circumstances. It is a very difficult task to make a Constitution worthy of being called so. This admirable federal Constitution of ours, is the result of such a combination. It is superior to the wisdom of any or all of the men by whose agency it was made. The force of circumstances, and not foresight or wisdom, induced them to adopt many of its wisest provisions.

But of the few nations who have been so fortunate as to adopt a wise Constitution, still fewer have had the wisdom long to preserve them. It is harder to preserve than to obtain liberty. After years of prosperity, the tenure by which it is held, is but too often forgotten; and I fear, Senators, that such is the case with us. There is no solicitude now about liberty. It was not so in the early days of the Republic. Then it was the first object of our solicitude. The maxim then was, that "power is always stealing from the many to the few;" "the price of liberty is perpetual vigilance." Then no question of any magnitude came up, in which the first inquiry was not "is it constitutional"—"is it consistent with our free, popular institutions"—"how is it to affect our liberty." It is not so now. Questions of the greatest magnitude are now discussed without reference or allusion to these vital considerations. I have been often struck with the fact, that in the discussions of the great questions in which we are now engaged, relating to the origin and the conduct of this war, their effect on the free institutions and the liberty of the people have scarcely been alluded to, although their bearing in that respect is so direct and disastrous. They would, in former days, have been the great and leading topics of discussion; and would, above all others, have had the most powerful effect in arousing the attention of the country. But now, other topics occupy the attention of Congress and of the country—military glory, extension of the empire, and the aggrandizement of the country. To what is this great change to be attributed? Is it because there has been a decay of the spirit of liberty among the people? I think not. I believe that it was never more ardent. The true cause is, that we have ceased to remember the tenure by which liberty alone can be preserved. We have had so many years of prosperity—passed through so many difficulties and dangers without the loss of liberty—that we begin to think that we hold it by right divine from heaven itself. Under this impression, without thinking or reflecting, we plunge into war, contract heavy debts, increase vastly the patronage of the Executive, and indulge in every species of extravagance, without thinking that we expose our liberty to hazard. It is a great and fatal mistake. The day of retribution will come; and when it does, awful will be the reckoning, and heavy the responsibility somewhere.

I have now shown, Senators, that the conquest of Mexico, and holding it as a subject-province, or incorporating it into our Union, is liable to the many and irresistible objections assigned in the first resolution. I have also shown that the policy recommended by the President, if carried out, would terminate, in all probability, in its conquest, and holding it either in one or the other mode stated; and that such is the opinion of the President himself, unless in the mean time, peace can be obtained. Believing, then, that this line of policy might lead to consequences so disastrous, it ought not, in my opinion, in the language of the second resolution, to be adopted. Thus thinking, I cannot give it my support. The question is then presented— What should be done? It is a great and difficult question, and daily becoming more so. I, who have used every effort in my power to prevent this war, might excuse myself from answering it, and leave it to those who have incurred greater responsibility in relation to it. But I will not shrink from any responsibility where the safety of the country or its institutions are at stake.

The first consideration in determining what line of policy, in the present state of things, ought to be adopted, is to decide what line will most effectually guard against the dangers which I have shown would result from the conquest of Mexico, and the disastrous consequences which would follow it.

After the most mature reflection which I have been able to give to the subject, I am of opinion now, and have been from the first, that the only one by which it can be certainly guarded against, is to take the question of indemnity in our own hands—to occupy defensively, and hold subject to negotiation, a portion of the territory of Mexico, which we may deem ample to cover all proper claims upon her, and which will be best suited to us to acquire, and least disadvantageous to her to lose. Such was my impression when the message of the President of the United States recommended to Congress the recognition of the existence of a war with Mexico. My view, at that time, as to the proper course to be pursued, was to vote the supplies, to rescue Gen. [Zachary] Taylor and his army from the dangers which surrounded them, and take time to determine whether we should recognise the war or not. Had it been adopted, I would have insisted on raising a provisional army, to be collected at some proper point, and to be trained and disciplined: but to postpone the declaration of war until the Congress of Mexico, in which, according to her Constitution, the war-making power resided, should be allowed time to disavow the intention of making war on us, and to adjust all differences between the two countries. But if she refused, even then I would have advised to seize, by way of reprisal, the portion of her territory which we might select, and hold it defensively, as I have just stated, instead of declaring war formally against her; and that mainly for the purpose of avoiding the very dangers against which these resolutions are intended to guard. But such was the urgency which was supposed then to exist, that no time was allowed to present or press these views upon the Senate. Such a course, besides the saving of an immense sacrifice of men and money, and avoiding the many other evils to which the course adopted has already subjected the country, would have effectually prevented our being entangled in the affairs of Mexico, from which we find it now so difficult to extricate ourselves. This consideration alone gives it decisive advantages over the course adopted, and makes it vastly superior, even if it should involve the same sacrifice of men and money to maintain a defensive line, as would, to use the usual phrase, the vigorous prosecution of the war. Mexico is to us as a dead body, and this is the only way that we can cut the cord which binds us to the corpse.

In recommending this line of policy, I look not to the interests of Mexico, but to those of our own country, and to the preservation of its free popular institutions. With me, the liberty of the country is all in all. If that be preserved, every thing will be preserved; but if lost, all will be lost. To preserve it, it is indispensable to adopt a course of moderation and justice towards all other countries; to avoid war whenever it can be avoided; to let those great causes which are now at work, and which, by the mere operation of time, will raise our country to an elevation and influence which no country has ever heretofore attained. By pursuing such a course, we may succeed in combining greatness and liberty—the highest possible greatness with the largest measure of liberty—and do more to extend liberty by our example over this continent and the world generally, than would be done by a thousand victories. It may be, in expressing these sentiments, that I find no response in the breasts of those around me. If so, it must be attributed to the fact that I am growing old, and that my principles and feelings belong to a period of thirty or thirty-five years anterior to the present date. It is not, however, the first time I have ventured in their maintenance to stand alone on this floor. When General [Andrew] Jackson, some years since, during the latter part of his Administration, recommended to Congress to issue letters of marque and reprisal against France, I stood alone in my place here, and raised my voice against it, on the ground that there was no just cause of war with her; that in entering into the treaty to indemnify our citizens for old claims against her, the King of France [Louis Philippe] and his Ministers declared to our Minister, that it required a vote of the Chambers to make the appropriation to carry it into effect; and that they were no further responsible than to use their best efforts to induce them to do so. This was all communicated to our Executive, and the treaty accepted and ratified, with this condition attached. And yet the President, although he admitted that the King and his Ministers had fully redeemed their pledge to use their best efforts to obtain the necessary appropriation, recommended the adoption of the measure to which I have alluded, and which would have been tantamount to war. Fortunately the Government of Great Britain, by her interposition, prevented it. This example, I fear, has contributed much to give the strong tendency, which we have since witnessed, to resort to menace and force in the settlement of our differences with other powers.

According to my opinion, all parties are interested in adopting a line of policy which will with certainty disentangle us from the affairs of Mexico, and avoid the great sacrifices of men and money, and the many other evils to which the war exposes us. Let me say to my friends, who support the Administration in their policy, that if you persist, and if peace by some good fortune should not be obtained, the war will go on from year to year, and you will be utterly overthrown as a party. Do you not see that its effects, in reference to our internal affairs, is to drive you into a course of policy directly contrary to that which you have professed to support, and in favor of that which you have charged your opponents with supporting. You have ever professed to oppose, as a party, a national debt, and charged your opponents with being its advocates. But what, I ask, are the effects of the war in this respect? Is it not to create an immense national debt, greater than that which the party which you are opposed could possibly have created by any other policy, had they been in power. This campaign, on which you look so lightly, will add to it a sum more than half as great as the entire debt of the revolution. You have been opposed to the extension of the patronage of the Executive, at least in profession. But this war is doing more to enlarge his patronage than any other policy which your opponents could have adopted. You profess to be in favor of a metallic currency. Do you not see that, with the increase of stocks and Treasury notes, you are in danger of being plunged again into the lowest depths of the paper system? You, as a party, have advocated the doctrine of free trade. Do you not see that, by the vast increase of the expenditures of the country, and the heavy interest which you will have to pay on the public debt, you are creating a necessity of increasing the duties on imports to the highest point that revenue will admit, and thus depriving the country of all the practical benefits of free trade, and preventing the Government from making any material reduction, until the whole debt is paid, which cannot be expected during this generation? What could your opponents have done more, or even as much, to destroy a system of policy which you claim to distinguish you from them, and to establish that which you allege to be the reason why they should be excluded from power? Has not, and will not, this war policy, if persisted in, effectually and finally obliterate the line of policy which you have insisted as distinguishing you from them? Why, then, to save yourselves from such a result, do you hesitate to adopt the course of policy I have suggested, as the only certain means of preventing these and other evils, and the danger to which our institutions are exposed? The pride of opinion may resist. I know the difficulty, and respect it, with which we yield measures that we have advocated, even when time has shown them to be wrong. But, true magnanimity and the highest honor command that we should abandon them, when they threaten to be injurious instead of beneficial to the country. It would do great credit to the party in power to adopt the policy now, in reference to the war, of taking indemnity into our own hands, by assuming a defensive position, which, it can hardly be doubted they would have done when the war was recognised, if they had foreseen the difficulties and dangers to which it has led. It would be a noble sacrifice of individual pride to patriotism.

In asserting that the only alternative is between the policy recommended by the President and the adoption of a defensive position, I have put out of the question the policy of taking no territory. I have done so, because I believe the voice of the country has decided irrevocably against it, and that to press it as the alternative, would render almost certain the final adoption of the policy recommended by the President, notwithstanding the disasters which it threatens. Let me say to my friends on the other side of the chamber, (for as such I regard them, for political differences here do not affect our personal relations,) that they have contributed by their course to fix the determination not to terminate the war without some suitable indemnity in territory. I do not refer to your vote recognising the existence of war between the Republic of Mexico and the United

States. I well know that you voted with a view to furnish immediate support to General Taylor and his army, then surrounded by imminent danger, and not with the intention of recognising the war, and that you remonstrated and protested against that interpretation being put upon your votes. But since it passed, and the war was recognised, most of you have continued to vote for appropriations to prosecute the war, when the object of prosecuting it was avowed to be to acquire territory as an indemnity. Now, I cannot see how the two can be reconciled—how you can refuse to take indemnity in territory, when you have voted means for the express purpose of obtaining such indemnity. The people are not able to understand why you should vote money so profusely to get indemnity, and refuse to take it, when obtained; and hence public opinion has been brought so decidedly to the conclusion not to terminate the war without territorial indemnity. But if such indemnity is to be had without involving the hazard of conquering the country, with all the dangers to which it would expose us, we must decide whether we shall adopt a defensive position or not, now—this very session. It will, in all possibility, be too late at the next.

I have now, Senators, delivered my sentiments with freedom and candor, upon all the questions connected with these resolutions. I propose nothing now. But if I find that I will be supported, I will move to raise a Committee to deliberate upon the subject of the defensive line.

The opportunity is favorable, while there are so many officers from Mexico now in the city, whose opinion would be of great value in determining on the one to be adopted. If the course of policy which I have suggested should be adopted, we may not get peace immediately. The war may still continue for some time; but be that as it will, it will accomplish the all-important object—will extricate the country from its entanglement with Mexico.

From *Speech of Mr. Calhoun, of South Carolina, on His Resolutions in Reference to the War with Mexico. Delivered in the Senate of the United States, January 4, 1848* (Washington: printed by John T. Towers, 1848), a 16-pp. pamphlet (a copy of which addressed and franked by Calhoun to D.W. Lewis, Sparta, Ga., is found in GU). Also printed in *Congressional Globe,* 30th Cong., 1st Sess., Appendix, pp. 49–53; Crallé, ed., *Works,* 4:396–424.

Further Remarks on the Bill to Raise an Additional Military Force

[In the Senate, January 5, 1848]
[Under consideration, in Committee of the Whole, was the bill to raise ten additional regiments for the regular Army, which was defended by Lewis Cass and Jefferson Davis.]

Mr. Calhoun said that there were two or three points of difficulty still unexplained in answering the objection to the bill. If he understood aright the Senator from Kentucky [John J. Crittenden], during a period of the last fifteen months not more than about eleven thousand recruits had been enlisted.

[Cass and Crittenden debated whether eleven thousand or twenty thousand men had been recruited in the period.]

Mr. Calhoun continued: He would, then, assume the number stated by the chairman of the Military Committee [Cass]. If only twenty thousand men were raised during the last year, it was very evident that in the present state of the market—for the recruiting had taken up a great deal of the loose portions of society disposed to enlist—it would be very difficult indeed to raise, during the present year, the men necessary to fill these ten additional regiments. Well, they had been told that this additional force was required immediately, when, in all probability, with the strongest recruiting force, it could not be obtained in less than six or eight months after the passage of the bill, allowing the greatest success. Yet they had been emphatically told that this force was so immediately necessary, that not a day could be allowed here for debate. He did not doubt that regulars were the best description of force. He wished to know if the eight thousand included the entire deficit.

Mr. Cass replied, that the general deficiency amounted to eight thousand men.

Mr. Calhoun. That, added to the ten regiments, would make eighteen thousand or twenty thousand to be raised. Then the defect must be in the recruiting service. Eight thousand was very near the number which it was proposed to raise by this bill; and yet a deficit to that extent existed in the present force. The remedy seemed to be in the creation of a sufficient number of recruiting officers—not of generals nor colonels—not of officers of the higher grades, but of officers suited for that service.

This business of war was a serious one. War created the means of its own continuance. It called into being mighty influences which were interested in carrying it on; and few nations ever terminated

96

war, so long as they possessed the means of carrying it on. A single regiment could not be raised without the creation of new interests in favor of the war. If these views were correct, the cheaper plan would be to strengthen the recruiting service, rather than create additional regiments, officers and all. The volunteers, if their services were needed, could be called out at once. The spirit of gallantry which characterized the people, was not yet exhausted, notwithstanding the disasters of the war, as far as deaths were concerned, and all the regiments had been thinned to an extraordinary extent. He presumed that the mortality had been not less than twenty per cent. Yet recruits, he had no doubt, could be still had plentifully. If, then, the chairman of the Committee on Military Affairs wanted an immediate augmentation of the military force, he should ask for volunteers.

He (Mr. C[alhoun]) was glad to perceive that the Senator from Mississippi (Mr. Davis) was not averse to a defensive line at the proper time. In his (Mr. C[alhoun]'s) opinion, the present was the proper time. In view of that policy he would prefer regulars to volunteers. He objected, though, to regulars, because that force gave greatly increased patronage, and greatly added influence to the support of the war. He knew not how other gentlemen felt; but as for himself, he was convinced that the patronage of this Government had gone beyond all bounds, and already exercised a most dangerous control over the deliberations of Congress. He felt the awkwardness of his position. He was utterly averse to pursuing this war for any view yet presented, even taking the strong view presented by the Senator from Mississippi. He put it to that gentleman, Was there any certainty of peace? and if not, where would the country stand? That was the question. It would be in a position worse than ever. Every step they took only plunged them deeper and deeper into difficulty. If his memory served him, the Secretary of the War Department [William L. Marcy] stated seventy thousand men as adequate to conquer and hold in subjection all Mexico. Was that not the view of the Secretary? He could not at the moment lay his hand on the report of the War Department; but if he had not correctly stated the views of the Secretary, any Senator could set the matter right. The Secretary then disavowed the plan of entire subjugation. The Executive [James K. Polk] disavowed it; and yet a force, according to the Senator from Kentucky [Crittenden], of ninety or one hundred thousand men, was demanded. He could not believe that it was the intention of the Executive, because it had been again and again disavowed. But when he saw such a force asked for in the report of the Secretary; when he saw, in the President's message, the declaration which he had quoted yesterday, to the effect that he himself believed, that unless in a certain contingency they must take possession of the country, and take the measure of the indemnity into our own hands, he could not but think there was a strong impression on all sides that the end would be to conquer and hold Mexico.

If they could have the question first submitted to the deliberative consideration of that body, and it were decided what was to be the proper course of conducting this war; if it were known whether they were to go on, or take a defensive line, they would then act understandingly. But voting and voting, without knowing what was to be ultimately done, threw him, and he believed every member of the Senate, into a state of great difficulty to determine how to vote.

From *Congressional Globe*, 30th Cong., 1st Sess., p. 115. Also printed in the Washington, D.C., *Daily National Intelligencer*, January 7, 1848, p. 2; the Washington, D.C., *Daily Union*, January 7, 1848, p. 2; the New York, N.Y., *Morning Courier and New-York Enquirer*, January 10, 1848, p. 2; Houston, ed., *Proceedings and Debates*, p. 74.

From GEORGE H. THATCHER

Ballston Centre [N.Y.,] Jan. 5th 1848

Hon. & dear Sir, I regret exceedingly that I had not time when in Washington a few days since to converse with you at length on the subject which most interests us as patriots & friends of the Republic— I mean the subject of the present war as it relates to slavery. Perhaps you will recollect my saying to you just as you were leaving the Capitol for your lodgings a few days ago that in my judgement you Southern gentlemen do not appreciate the *real* state of things at the North in regard to slavery, & the war. I intimated to you that I intended writing you on the subject. Hence this communication. What I am about to say is of course in confidence. I am a Clergyman (Presbyterian) & do not, for prudential reasons, wish my name made public—tho' if the *matter* of this letter would in any way serve you you are at liberty to use it as you choose. Much of my information I gather from Abolition sources, & from men who are well acquainted with that class of our Northern people who style themselves opponents of slavery. From what I can gather I think I am safe in asserting that the project of an extensive acquisition of Mexican

Territory is fast gaining ground among anti-slavery men at the North. Familiar as I am with political & religious factions at the North I was not a little surprised to see how rapidly this idea is making a favorable lodgement in the public mind—or rather in the minds of this class of men. I refer now not simply to nominal Abolitionists but to that large portion of anti-slavery men at the North who do not belong to Abolition organizations technically so called. It is this class of men & to the South the most formidable class who are fast becoming converts to the idea of *extensive annexation.* In their view the *more extensive the better.* Whether slavery be extended over this territory or not they think its annexation will ultimately overthrow the institution. Mind you, however, they connect this effect with *extensive annexation.* They are coming to adopt this ground—"Territory without slavery *if they can,* but *with it rather than not have the territory."* On the supposition that large territory be acquired & slavery extended over it they reason thus: "In proportion as you extend slavery over a greater area in that proportion, you weaken it." In a conversation with one of these men who has the reputation of great shrewdness as a man of *policy* I took occasion to reprove him for inconsistency in some of his views. In reply he used as nearly as I can remember the following language—"Why Sir," said he, "we understand this matter perfectly. The South are committing political suicide with this annexation project. They are over-reaching themselves. Do you not know, Sir, that just in proportion as you extend slavery over a greater area in that proportion you weaken it? Suppose they extend it over half or two thirds of Mexico? The slaves they remove there they must take from the old slave States. You cannot deny that in those States after a large portion are removed fewer slaveholders & friends of the institution are left to bear up against the onsets of their enemies. More. White labourers will immediately take the places vacated by the removed slaves. You know how this class of men will act. They will at once throw their influence—their sympathies & their acts & votes in favour of emancipation. Immigration & the laws of population will soon give such a preponderance to the whites that will ere long overwhelm slavery. More still. As the effect will be to make the slave population exceedingly sparse (i.e. in a short time—) we can set up our anti-slavery presses right among them without fear of molestation. We cannot do it now because they are *too many.* But thin them out, & the non-slaveholding whites will defend us. When we can do this more than half the battle will be won. This is one of the most important points we are striving to gain. Let us attain this & we may defy them. Now what is true of the old States will be true of the States newly created out of this territory. The same cause will operate—the same effects will follow sooner or later.["]

["]The fact is the South have not *slaves enough* to take permanent possession of this territory—& yet hold their own in the old States. They might get along very well if they were to stop with Texas. But by extensive expansion they divide their forces & distract their energies. When Napoleon fought the Allied Powers he adopted the policy of attacking detachments of the enemy & thus cut them up *in detail.* Whereas had they ["the" *interlined*] enemy kept concentrated & combined, his force would have been insufficient to overcome them. So in this case will we do with slavery. We will attack it in detail if the slave-holders expand the institution." But, said I, would not the creation of new States out of this territory give the South, the preponderance in Congress? "Temporarily it might. Not permanently. For while they gain slave States at the South they would lose them at the North. Virginia, Maryland, Dellaware, Tennessee, Kentucky, & North Carolina would soon become free. What then would the South gain? If they cut off a foot from one end of the stick & add it to the other will they increase its length?" These are among the views he advanced on the supposition that large territory be annexed & slavery extended over it. Anticipating these effects he seemed willing to wink at its extension over this territory rather *than not have the territory.* But on the supposition that he could get the Territory & keep it *free* he thought they could also bring about the downfall of slavery sooner than in the other case. ["]Out of this territory there would be many free States created. These would unite with the Northern free States in opposition to slavery. That would prevent the South from dividing the Union. Slavery would be between two fires. Besides, the facilities for the escape of slaves would be greatly multiplied. Thus the South would be like a barrel tapped at both ends &c &c." Whether this reasoning be sound you are better able to judge than I am. But to an anti-slavery Northerner it is very plausible. It is fast reconciling this class of men to the idea of extensive annexation. From what I can learn I think the signs of the times hereabouts indicate that the Abolitionists & their coadjutors will go for extensive annexation at all hazards. If they can enforce the Proviso they will. But if not they will favour *secretly* if not *openly* what they regard as the *next best*—i.e. a great extension of territory & a *corresponding* expansion of slavery. This will, perhaps, explain the reason why the National Era—the anti-slavery ["paper" *interlined*] at Washington goes for the acquisition of territory & yet strenuously urges the Proviso. It betrays their *secret* intentions. But, Sir, my reasons for writing you relate not to the merits or demerits of these questions but to the preservation of the Union. I love the Republic. To you Sir, I convey no information when I say that in view of this state of things & the movements of political parties the times are pregnant with mighty events—events which are to affect matterially the interests of the Republic. Deem it not flattery either when I say that to *you* all eyes are turned—especially of the sober, intelligent, & reflecting portion of this great people with the most earnest solicitude. Your position as foreshadowed in your resolutions I fully believe will meet their unqualified approbation. Let that policy be adopted & the Union is safe. Let these antagonist schemes be carried out & Heaven only knows the disasters that may follow. For your encouragement, if indeed any thing can add to *that* courage which derives its virtue from conscious rectitude & love of country, let me say, you have with you the hearty good wishes of those of our citizens whose approbation is of the most value. Persevere, then, my Dear Sir, & may success under the blessing of God crown your praise-worthy efforts. Save the Union. If you succeed in confining our territory to nearly its present limits you will place our national compact on a firmer basis than ever.

If at any time I could afford you information as to anti-slavery developments of the North I will cheerfully do so. My opinion is if you Southern men would keep an agent here at the North to ascertain what new movements are started from time to time—one who would devote his time to it & give you accurate intelligence you would be the better prepared to meet future political emergencies. Abolitionists have their disguised agents among you, & you would do well to counteract them with their own weapons. Were it not too expensive I would come & see you personally & talk with you more fully on what I have said in the fore-part of my letter. Please do me the favour to acknowledge this & oblige one who entertains for ["you" *interlined*] the profoundest respect. George H. Thatcher.

P.S. Various causes operate to predispose different factions to entertain favorably the idea of an extensive acquisition of territory. Anti-slavery men for the reasons before stated. The more ardent friends of the [James K. Polk] Administration favour it because it affords them a ready apology for a vigorous prosecution of the war with a view to conquest. Speculators favour it because it affords increased facilities for speculation & that in a variety of ways. Kindred to these are the great cap[i]talists who think it will stimulate enterprize & thereby create a permanent demand for money—irre-

101

spective ["of" *interlined*] that which must arise from Government loans. Then the manufacturing classes & high tariff men think the effect will be to increase the National debt to a degree that will of necessity require a high rate of duties in order to carry on the Government. Besides these, are the military who see in this scheme employment & openings for military renown. Others favour the scheme for still other reasons. The more I think of it the more am I convinced that you have hit the nail on the head. Let it be driven & clinched *now*. Six months hence may be too late. Surely no benefits can adequately compensate for the political convulsions & the manifold disasters that will inevitably ensue in case the policy antagonist to yours be carried out. My dear Sir, let not the golden opportunity pass. Fix the policy of the Government by your resolutions & all will be safe. G.H.T.

ALS in ScCleA; variant PC in Boucher and Brooks, eds., *Correspondence*, pp. 415–419.

From H[ENRY] W. CONNER

Charleston, Jan[uar]y 7, 1848
My Dear Sir, You have seen the Editorials of the [Charleston] Mercury some days since upon [Daniel S.] Dickinson[']s resolutions & more recently upon [Lewis] Cass's letter, & I hope they were not far from the mark. We are much in the dark out here however as to passing events & from the position the Mercury ought to occupy upon the great questions of the day it is essential that they should have *the best & earliest* intimation of what is in project & the course that is proper for the occasion. You are too much occupied & it is not necessary you should appear in a matter of the kind but I have thought that Mr. [Armistead] Burt [Representative from S.C.] might under your direction keep us posted up both as regards the present & the future. If more agreeable he might communicate with some of us—myself if preferred—*in confidence* & we would see that the views proper for the objects should be carried out promptly & with as much Judgment & propriety as possible. Last summer a few gentlemen of character & ability were associated together to write for the Mercury & are ready now to continue their services but we want the *programme*. The feeling here now is to let drive at Cass

& his coalition, but we are not sufficiently in possession of the whole case except what appeared in the Mercury two day's since.

Our people begin to feel wearied with suspense & are becoming impatient to act. The feeling is with Gen[era]l [Zachary] Taylor & if a proper vent is not soon given the feeling will seek its own vent. Very Truly y[ou]rs &c, H.W. Conner.

P.S. J. Hannan, the agent of the Rothchilds [*sic*] at New Orleans begged me a few days since to put him in communication with you, that he might confer with you upon the standards for gold & silver coins & I took the liberty of giving him a letter to you.

ALS in ScCleA.

From W[ILLIAM] F. DeSaussure

Columbia, Jan[uar]y 7, 1848
My dear Sir, It may be that in the course of the debate upon the Mexican War some one may object that the South Carolina Senators have taken a course opposed to that of their State and cite certain resolutions & a report passed by our Senate at the late session, and which I find have been published. I desire to say that the Senate report and resolutions were not adopted by the House, but laid on the table. As Chairman of the Com[mit]tee on Federal Relations I made a report, which with the resolutions appended were adopted by the House, but were not passed by the Senate. I send by this mail the [Columbia] Palmetto [State] Banner of 14 Dec. 1847 which contains both Reports.

The contest with Mexico is exciting our liveliest apprehensions. The curtain is lifting, and the future becoming daily more alarming. What is to be done with this unhappy country which can neither make war, nor peace.

I believe the prudent portion of our people desire no Mexican Territory, beyond what may be necessary to pay for past spoliations and the expenses of the war; but a large proportion will not be satisfied short of this, no matter what may be the consequence.

The letter of Gen[era]l [Lewis] Cass plainly indicates that the Wilmot proviso is an abortion. The Administration party seem to be sensible that the South will withhold the supplies unless this insolent claim is abandoned. But I do not see what pledges we can take;

especially against people who deal in bad faith with the Constitution, habitually, as well upon this as upon other matters. The treaty making power and the veto are sheet anchors, and that the last may continue to be available, it is manifest that we must look well to the Presidential election.

Alas for the South—who would have thought twenty years ago that we should have to fall back so soon upon this last line of defence. I am my dear Sir with most sincere respect & regard Yours &c, W.F. DeSaussure.

ALS in ScCleA; PC in Boucher and Brooks, eds., *Correspondence*, p. 420.

To H[ENRY] W. CONNER, [Charleston]

Washington, 8th Jan[uar]y 1848

My dear Sir, I send herewith my speech on my resolutions, corrected by myself. The Report of it was in several respects erroneous & imperfect. I would be glad to have it published from the corrected copies by our papers.

The speech will give you my views fully on the war, & the consequences, if it is to go on, and makes up the issue fully, between conquest & subjugation & a defensive line. My object in offering the resolutions was to present that issue directly to the country, so that it might be deliberately decided by the people, which they will take. I shall call ["up" *canceled*] my resolutions up, as soon as the Army bill will permit, & force them to a vote, if I can.

The issue is one of the greatest ever presented to the country, and, I do hope, our State will be found on the side of liberty and our free institutions; & that Charleston will take the lead in giving the impulse in the right direction to the State & the South. I trust ["our" *canceled and* "its" *interlined*] press will be united on the occasion. If such should be the case, the present dangerous sperit of ag[g]randizement may be quelled, & the Country & its institutions saved.

I am now satisfied, that all the North is opposed to our having any part of Mexico. The movements of our State & my resolutions have killed the [Wilmot] Proviso; but it is resolved to effect, what it aimed at directly, by a more circuitious [*sic*] route. The present scheme is, to give the Mexicans, who we have conquered, the [*partial word canceled*] power to ["do so" *canceled and* "exclude us" *interlined*] by forming them into territories. It would be a sad result of our valor

& sacrafice to be deprived of their fruits by the very people we have conquered, and to lose, at the same time, our equality as members of the Union; and yet such, I apprehend, will be the end. I hope to have some early opportunity to present my views on the present state of the abolition question, in reference to this ["point" *canceled*] aspect of the subject. Truly, J.C. Calhoun.

ALS in ScC; photostat of ALS in DLC, Henry Workman Conner Papers.

From A[NDREW] J. DONELSON, [U.S. Minister to Prussia], *"Private"*

Berlin, Jan[uar]y 8, 1848

D[ea]r Sir, Young Mr. [Edward Wyatt] Geddings & his companion [—— Ball] have arrived safely at this place; and I have secured to them admission to one of the best Gymnasiums where they will be under the direction of Professor [Carl Eduard] Bonnell, and will, I trust, realise the hopes of their parents. I have a son at the same school with whom they will be associated, which will make it more easy for me to assist them with such advice as may be useful.

The President[']s [James K. Polk's] annual message as published in the *British Times* reached Berlin yesterday. It will be severely criticised by the European press as exhibiting the spirit of defiance rather than of conciliation. We cannot expect monarchs to relish the intimation that our example is a proof that their agency in Government ought to be dispensed with. But such criticism cannot hurt us much. The main thing is to be sure that we do nothing wrong or that will lessen the confidence inspired by the past that the agencies which have thus far made our Union the instrument of the general prosperity will be preserved. Whilst such is our conduct the force of our example will increase and the liberal party on this Continent may gradually introduce and strengthen the Representative principle. In this point of view it is all important that our war with Mexico should cease, and it is fortunate that the brilliant atchievements of our arms will enable our Government to exhibit a forbearance and magnanimity in the negotiation for peace which under other circumstances would not have been tolerated by the people.

You are aware that I was one of those who regretted the movement of Gen[era]l [Zachary] Taylor to the Rio Grande, in as much as the question of limits was one of negotiation unless Congress gave

105

it a different character. Foreseeing that Mexico could give us no indemnity but land and dreading the application of the annexation principle to the Territory west of the Rio Grande, I would have preferred almost any expedient to an aggressive measure.

In my argument with Gen[era]l [Samuel] Houston [when U.S. Minister to the Texas Republic] I treated the annexation of Texas as the only step that could check the spirit of aggression and wild adventure on that frontier. His idea was that without money or arms he could dismember Mexico—that he could defeat our negotiation with England—that under European auspices he could form a new empire embracing Oregon, which would be a counterpoise to the United States. He was not mistaken. This he could have done; but it was his merit to abandon the ambitious temptation, and I thought I had done something beneficial in commending his self denial. In other words my belief was that in annexing Texas, a compromise was secured by which the nationality of Mexico was confirmed, and a war with England on account of Oregon avoided.

But it may be that no conduct on the part of the United States would have prevented war with Mexico and that for this reason the movement by Gen[era]l Taylor was considered immaterial in determining the judgement of Congress. At all events after the declaration that the war existed the public will seems to have overlooked all previous irregularity and made it imperative on the President to chastise Mexico in the most exemplary manner with the means voted by Congress.

Yet the original difficulty remained. What could we do with a nation that seemed to have lost all character, and to have no other policy but that of opposition to the United States? Must our chastisement of her necessarily throw upon us the dangerous responsibility of taking care of her hereafter?

I state these questions, not to answer them for remote as I am from the scene of action, it would be presumptuous in me to intrude a suggestion upon your time. I have referred to them as connected with the Message, and to express my hope that Congress will give them a satisfactory solution.

In European affairs the Swiss are now the agitating people. The question of intervention[,] always dangerous, is complicated by many surrounding difficulties. England and France have different views: and this King [of Prussia, Frederick William IV] as Prince of Neufchatel has been prematurely committed. But I do not think there will be war unless Louis Philippe should die before there is a cordial understanding between his & the English Government. A great guarantee for peace is also found in the personal character of the King of Prussia whose power has been much increased by the reform which he has admitted in his Government.

I find our relations with the Zoll Verein not capable of much improvement, unless we can concede something for the reductions proposed to be made on our staple articles. We could now gain much more than the Treaty of 1844 stipulated for, but to do so it would be necessary to change our Tariff in some particulars.

If Mr. [Isaac E.] Holmes [Representative from S.C.] is with you be kind enough to give him my respects, and believe me very truly Y[our] ob[edien]t ser[van]t, A.J. Donelson.

ALS in ScCleA; PEx in Boucher and Brooks, eds., *Correspondence*, pp. 420–422. NOTE: An EU on the address sheet of this letter indicates that it was received in the Department of State on 2/18.

From JAMES GADSDEN

Charleston S.C., Jan[ua]r[y] 8, 1848

My Dear Sir, I am unable to comprehend the necessity of more Troops in Mexico, or of acting with precipitation on the Bill introduced by [Lewis] Cass. There is now in Mexico a well organized army of some 30 to 40 Thousand men, and General [James] Shields openly avowed, not merely to me Individually, but to many others, that he could conquer, & *hold the whole of Mexico with 5000 men.* Would it not be as well therefore to examine both [Gen. John A.] Quitman & Shields as to the force necessary to prosecute the views of the Administration[?] Why have more men than is necessary, and involve the Government ["the" *canceled*] not only in additional expense, but all the hazards of *conquest* ["and" *canceled and* "without" *interlined*] design. Of what avail is it, if an evil is to come, whether we bring it upon ourselves unintentionally or not. If the Executive [James K. Polk], if Secretary [*sic*] Cass are sincere in their declarations, and I have no right to doubt either, why not pause & reflect, survey all the ground we have to act on before by precipitation we accomplish what leaves us no remedy for or avoidance of what they say, they do not desire, but would rather deprecate. No Proposition in Mathematics is so clear to my mind as the entire Conquest of Mexico *if we continue to prosecute the War* ["as we have" *interlined*] *to conquer Peace.* The latter we may not obtain, but by conquering Country[?] & denationalizing Mexico. By the by[e], from information derived from many sources, our Army cannot be supported by subsidizing the Country, and they can only be maintained ["and" *interlined*] at great expense by *purchasing from the People.* This matter should be looked into. Why not require of the Secretary of War [William L. Marcy] a Report, as to the management of expenditures for supplies, drafts &c.[?] I am well informed that double & treble prices are paid for every article of consumption. That the prices are the temptation to the People to seek the markets to attempt to forage & take from them would prove a failure & irritate the population. To subsidize the Cities & make them pay cannot last long. It would soon depopulate them. The payment of the high prices for every article of consumption will make the war popular in Mexico. The People at large will not care how long the Army of occupation remains among them. Indeed the danger is that their profits & prosperity may reconcile them to our Government & thus both Army & People favor conquest. Each state will form a Province for a General.

Have you reflected on what may be the effects of the Foreign Commercial Houses remitting by Government Bills through us to Europe[?] If Exchange is high, all of the subtreasury deposits must find their way by shipments of specie to England. It is true we avoid remitting the metals to pay Army expenses in Mexico, but the Mexican productions of the mines thus remain at Home, and the U. States bled [*sic*] at every pour[?]. At least this seems to me to be the operation.

I perceive 18 to 19 millions reported as one Quarter[']s expenditure. This only includes moneys actually drawn from Treasury, & not what is due, continually increasing.

If this Government escapes with 25 millions per Quarter during the continuance of the Mexican war, I shall be much deceived. The Revenue, including the Mexican subsidy will not probably exceed 50 millions for the year, leaving 50 millions deficient. Yours resp[ectfully,] James Gadsden.

ALS in ScCleA.

To W[ILSON] LUMPKIN, [former Senator from Ga., Athens]

Washington, 8th Jan[uar]y 1848

My dear Sir, I cannot give you more fully my opinion of the present state of the Mexican war; what will be its termination, if not stopt, & its consequences; and what is the only practical mode, by which it can be done, than by enclosing you a corrected copy of my speech on my resolutions.

I intend to push them to a vote, as soon as we shall get clear of the Army bill.

The Speech presents the issue directly & & [*sic*] fully between conquest & subjugation on one side, & liberty & our free institutions on the other. My object is, to present it directly for the consideration of the people, ["before they should be" *canceled and* "to prevent them from being" *interlined*] forestalled before they reflected on consequences. Be assured, there are already a considerable party ["already" *canceled*] in favour of conquest & subjugation; notwithstanding the disavowal of Gen[era]l [Lewis] Cass and other leaders; and that they will become formidable, unless the sound portion of the country shall be roused & present a stern resistance.

The Wilmot Proviso is killed. My resolutions & the movements at the South have destroyed it; but be assured, the North is united in the determination, that we shall not have an inch of Mexico. The object ["is" *canceled*] at present is to do that indirectly through territorial Govern[men]ts in Mexico, which it aimed to do directly; as if it was of any importance to us, whether we should be excluded by Congress, or the subordinate territorial Governments they may establish in in [*sic*] Mexico, consisting of the very population, we have conquered. I hope to have an opportunity before long to present my views of the deception intended to be imposed on the South, in this new turn, which the proviso has taken.

Excuse a short letter. I am much pressed for time. Your old friend, J.C. Calhoun.

ALS in NcD, John C. Calhoun Papers.

From "MERCATOR"

New York [City,] Jan. 8th 1848

Sir, At the risk of being considered intrusive I take the liberty to enclose the accompanying communication, sent to the [Washington, D.C., Daily] Nat[ional] Intelligencer in Feb. last, as being coincident ["to" *canceled and* "with" *interlined*] the state of the public finances, represented in your just and admirable remarks upon our present position with Mexico, an outline only of which I have as yet seen. The awful condition of England has caused the drain of coin from this country to be greater and more *sudden* than even *I* had anticipated. It is a convulsive action on her part—the final result of which is to be seen—and may it not be well worthy of question, whether she is not now in the premonitory struggles of Revolution, mainly the result, of this very system of Conquest and Empire—her giant colonies like vampires feeding upon her life's blood—her home population ground to dust to pay for Navies, and Armies and *Wars* to protect and retain them?

This drain has now continued for some ninety days, and still continues, altho' in somewhat a diminished ratio—every merchant in England realizing all that is due to him from abroad as far as practicable in specie. Unprepared for this unnatural state of things, a requisition for specie to pay indebtedness, when this country was really creditor, (caused by the paralysis of England's credit) the Banks of the Northern and Eastern section of the United States, were at first taken at disadvantage, but immediately upon becoming aware that the current of specie was really setting from this country they commenced, and have continued a contraction which has been, and still is, stern and steady. I presume, at least, as a whole, that *twenty* per cent of the volume of the currency has been drawn in within the period alluded to—happily, thus far, without serious individual disaster; but I fear the same strain continued for a few weeks longer may tell a different tale.

The coin, as you may suppose, dragged away on both sides, by foreign demand on the one, and the Sub-Treasury on the other, has been and is, exceedingly reduced. By the Sub-Treasury, aside from the shipments to Mexico, it has been spread all over the country, particularly through the valley of the Mississippi, (where the extinguishment of a great number of Banks has caused *its requisition as a currency*,) so broken up in volume ["as" *canceled and* "that" *interlined*] for all the purposes of immediate demand, it might as well

110

be meandering in its original veins in the mines. Its return by this contraction appears to be comparatively slow—mainly to be accounted for, from the general prosperity of the Agriculturists.

The ability of the Banks to sustain this *foreign* drain turns simply upon the question of time. I believe that the present judicious system of contraction, will enable them to meet that demand until the tide turns, (*not so* had Europe been a *heavy creditor* country) but, of this I am sure, that if the government attempts to realize within sixty days any material requirement for the war in specie according to the Sub-Treasury provisions *that a suspension of specie payments is inevitable.* It remains to be seen whether the drafts already negotiated in Mexico are to be realized in bullion to be remitted abroad, if so, I am not sanguine as to *their* being met save at very great inconvenience.

Apparently, all that the Government can now do to meet their calls without producing disaster, is to authorize the issue and re-issue of Treasury notes to government creditors drawing interest at the rate of six or seven per cent.

Should they issue three or four millions of the denomination of *fifty* dollars at *"one mill"* interest, as heretofore under Mr. [John C.] Spencer [Secretary of the Treasury during the John Tyler Administration], they would sweep up that amount of claims at par, and the saving of interest perhaps meet the sacrafice which may be judicious for the obtainment of specie in peculiar exigencies. This issue of government paper will afford a medium approachable to specie— that is, of definite value, to fill the chasm, until the laws of trade restore the ["mass of" *interlined*] specie through its natural channels to the great sea-ports, its proper reservoirs.

Writing anonymously, I will not apologise for this hasty letter, in the hope that some hint may be afforded which may be of use in the conflict in which you are engaged in the great question of putting an end to this wicked and ungenerous war.

It may not be improper for me farther to say, that professionally connected with the currency, these remarks are made advisedly, [*several words canceled.*]

Should you, Sir, require any information of a statistical character relative to the currency, perhaps it may be in my power to furnish it, (I need not say, devoid of expense) from a correct and trustworthy source.

By addressing a line to Mercator, 73 Remsen Street, Brooklyn[,] New York, with such questions formally propounded, I will submit

111

them to the party to whom I allude, who will answer them, if in his power, in his own name. I am Sir, with high respect for your unbending integrity and patriotism, Your obedient Servant, Mercator.

ALS in ScCleA. NOTE: "Mercator" in Latin means "a wholesale merchant." It is not certain whether there was a separate "accompanying communication" enclosed with this letter or if the letter itself is the "communication" referred to in the first sentence. If there was a separate En, it has not been found.

From W[ILLIA]M EMMONS

Southboro [Mass.], Jan. 9th 1848
Honored Sir, I feel at a loss for words when I reflect on the present state of my country and contemplate the supineness of so many of our public men, connected with the fatal lethargy prevailing among the people, in connection with the doubtful policy of the present Administration.

While thus desponding however, I feel to rejoice that you now stand on a proud eminence as you have ever done on all vital questions touching the dearest interest of the great whole, as a faithful sentinal on the watch-Tower of American Liberty, ready to sound the alarm to your fellow Citizens, when any danger to our free gover[n]ment seemed to threaten a connecting link in the chain of our glorious bond of Union.

Turning to the fatal policy persuing in relation to our affairs with Mexico, (if persisted in) cannot fail to fasten a cancer on the very vitals of our Republic; which will prey upon it, until, it effects a seperation of the States, erecting an "Imperial" gover[n]ment, and that gover[n]ment but the echo of the milatary who, as in ages past were in fact the Gover[n]ment. Already what do we whitness but one of its Milatary leaders in the field claiming the Presidency from a nomination of our Army on the 4th of July last then, as now, in Mexico.

During my absence from the capitol in my traveling, often has it done me good to hear New England men [(]those of understanding,) remark that John C. Calhoun was the most honiest man in the Senate "for he never hides his opinions." Recently however Sir, even among a class known as Anti Slavery men they exclaim you to be "the noblest Roman of them all." The views embodied in your Resolutions has endeared your name and made it become as household words in this section of the country. I have a favor to ask, Viz. that you will be pleased to forward me a copy of any speech you may deliver this Session, or public Documents as they come to hand at your rooms.

Looking to your great experience and such as may co-operate with you in this peculiar crisis, to save my country's dearest int[e]rest from the its [*sic*] present impending fate I have the honor to be Very Respectfully Your Ob[edien]t S[er]v[an]t, Wm. Emmons.

ALS in ScCleA. NOTE: An AEU by Calhoun reads, "Mr. Emmons." Emmons was a well-known writer and publisher in behalf of the Democratic party in Mass.

From S. W. BAKER

Saccarappa [Maine,] Jan[ua]ry 10th 1848
Dear Sir, Inclosed is a letter of introduction to yourself [dated 12/8/-1847], given me by Hon. Tho[ma]s W. Ward[,] Commissioner of Gen[e]r[a]l Land Office [in] Texas. I had promised myself the honor & pleasure of delivering this letter in person, and permit me Sir to assure you that by doing so, while I should [have] enjoyed a high degree of the latter, I could not have been entirely insensible to the former. Circumstances to which the inclosed letter alludes imperiously demanded my hasty return to Maine. Should however a future time present an opportunity, when I might avail myself of the privilege extended by my Friend, I would Sir most respectfully ask permission to do so. I am Sir with Sentiments of high Consideration Your Ob[e]d[ien]t Serv[an]t, S.W. Baker.

ALS in ScCleA.

From JOHN D. GARDINER

Sag Harbor [N.Y.,] Jan[uar]y 10th 1848
My Dear Friend, I have just finished reading your very able speech in the Senate, on the Mexican question on the continuance of the War; or the withdrawment of our army and taking a defensive line—And I need not say that I read ["it with" *interlined*] great interest and pleasure.

Could the government be induced to adopt this Policy, it would, in my view, not only be honorable and magnanimous, but be a

113

great saving of blood and treasure. But so intoxicated have the people become, with the spirit of Military glory, and the desire of conquest, that I much fear, that argument and reasoning, however strong, will prove unavailing. If we are to judge from the past, as well as the present course of the government, in relation to Mexico, there seems to be but little hope, that any thing will satisfy them, but the entire prostration of that Country; establishing therein a Military government; and ultimately annexing it to this Union in some form or other. The longer the war is continued, the more I am convinced, that this will be the final result; than which nothing could be more disasterous to the country, or ["more" *interlined*] injurious to her high reputation abroad, and to her free institutions at home.

The sooner, therefore, the war can be arrested, and a treaty of some sort, be formed between the two contending nations the better. To effect this, so important and desirable object, much depends upon the action of the Senate of the United States. In this body, and throughout the whole Country your influence, with all parties is great, and extensively felt. In these days of Fanaticism and wild extravagance, we need somewhere a great conservative power, as a kind ["of" *interlined*] balance wheel, to regulate and control their precipitate movements. And if this power, ["is power" *canceled*] is not found and exercised in that grave and dignified body, where is the Country to look for it?

War, in almost every point of view, is one of the greatest evils that can befall a Nation. In ninety instances out of an hundred, this tremendous evil, with all its calamities, has been brought upon Countries, by the ambition, pride, folly or selfishness of the few, and not of the many—And these few, too often the most reckless and unprincipled. It is no difficult task to find pretexts to rouse the worst passions, and set men or nations to war with one another. It is easy to raise the storm, but much more difficult to controul it. Contention is like the letting out of water. A Child can make a breach in the dam, through which the torrent soon becomes irresistible; until its power is exhausted in the work of desolation. Nothing can justify war on the part of this Republic, but the defence of our Liberty and independence. We have no right to war for power, wealth ["power" *canceled*] or conquests—The Policy, peace, and prosperity of this Union, is to avoid alliance, with all nations and to war with none.

We have however gotten in ["to" *interlined*] a quarrel with ["our" *interlined*] neighbor. It is almost universally deplored; nothing that can be gained, will compensate for the loss already sustained—And the longer the contest is continued, the deeper we shall plunge into

114

difficulties, and the harder will it become to extricate ourselves from them. The further we go, the harder will it be to retrace our steps. We have fought many bloody battles, and gained many victories. Our army have done nobly—They have done all that bravery and blood could do, and still a "conquered peace," seems to retire further from their graspt every step they take in their march. How this avowed object of pursuit is ever to be obtained is yet unknown. Would it not be wise to pause in our career, until we discover some tendency in the means to accomplish the end? To rush on, without such discovery, is to proceed blindfold. Notwithstanding all that has been done, there remains still much land to be conquered. And if this be conquered, the Cananites will yet continue in the Land, and be nothing but a source of perpetual trouble and vexation, sores in our eyes and thornes in our sides—we neither want them nor the¹ Country. That the Mexicans have done ["us" *interlined*] much wrong is readily admitted; but how we are to obtain redress and satisfaction for the injuries sustained, does not so readily appear.

The great body of the people desire peace, an honorable peace and ["the sooner" *canceled*] the sooner this can be effected the better—And those who contribute most to bring it about, will give the greatest evidence of patriotism, and regard to the best interest of their Country.

The old Democracy of this State has become, of late, much divided. The Leaders, are fiercely contending with each other, so that the former strength of the party is much weakened; and I see no prospect of their soon becoming again united. The Whig Party is now in the poss[ess]ion of full power—And all parties are beginning to plan and scheme and organise in reference to the approaching Presidential election. Caucuses, Conventions, and Cliques are now holding meetings in different parts of the State for that purpose. Those behind the Curtain will soon begin to pull the wires; and then he who is the most expert, in this nefarious business, is deemed, the best fellow. To every enlightened and honest Patriot, such political manoevering is detestible, and ought to be denounced by all the friends of a free gover[n]ment. It opens the door to all sorts of corruption. Since you and I have come upon the stage of active life; there is a very perceptible diminution, in that, high-minded straitforward, moral and political integrity, which characterized the earlier period of this Republic. We are fast becoming a nation of political gamblers, and Stock jobbers; and among a certain Lot of men, Politics, is about as much a matter of trade, as any thing that can be named in the market. The thought is humiliating to the last degree, to every good man—And unless it can be arrested in some way, short, I fear, will be the career of our Liberty, between the Cradle & the grave.

There was one remark in the close of your speech on Mexico, which struck ["me" *interlined*] with peculiar force; and I can ["not" *interlined*] forbear to Notice it. Addressing the Chair, you say, "Sir, I find I am becoming old, and almost feel that I live among strangers." To the truth of this remark I can truly respond from experience. I feel that I too am becoming old, and live almost among strangers in my own Neighborhood—And is ["it" *interlined*] possible that we have become old men, so soon, and stand in the front Ranks of the grey-headed. It is even so. Another generation has risen up around us, with most of whom we are unacquainted. We stand comparatively alone like solitary oaks upon the mountain, amid the dust of the once surrounding Forest. From the things of time I can hope for no higher enjoyments than ["those" *interlined*] which I have possessed—to find higher and purer, I must look to another state of being, to a brighter and more enduring scene. On this I must fix my hopes, and draw my chief comforts during the residue of my continuance here. My health is good, and my wife & children are around me, and every thing I could desire. Please to write me when ["you" *interlined*] have a leisure moment, for old friends are like old wine the better for age. With great respect & esteem I remain your friend & [Yale College] Classmate, John D. Gardiner.

ALS in ScCleA.

John A. Monroe and Walter Preston, New York City, [to the public], 1/10. They announce the opening of a law office and promise to attend promptly to any business referred to them from S.C. They give as references the "Hon. John C. Calhoun" and four other prominent South Carolinians. PC in the Charleston, S.C., *Mercury,* January 19, 1848, p. 3, and subsequent issues.

Petition of the pilots of Charleston harbor, presented by Calhoun to the Senate on 1/10. In this undated document, eighteen signers ask for the repeal of a law of 1837 which took from state legislatures the regulation of pilotage. They state that "we the Pilots of Charleston are willing and desirous that our own State Authorities should have the management and control of this matter." (The petition was referred to the Committee on Commerce and ordered to be printed.) DS in DNA, RG 46 (U.S. Senate), 30A-H3.2; PC in Senate Document No. 25, 30th Cong., 1st Sess.

From W[ILLIAM] F. VAN AMRINGE

Montgomery Orange Co. New York, Jan[uar]y 10, 1848
Dear Sir, Relying on your known love of literature & science, I have taken the liberty of sending to you a prospectus of a work I have written on the Natural History of Man, in the hope that you will favor me with your name to the subscription list, which now contains over 200 names of the highest literary & scientific character.

That you may more fully understand the scope of the work, I make the following extract from the conclusion of the Introductory chapter—

"We expect to prove by the following pages—That the ["whole subject" *canceled and* "scientific investigation" *interlined*] of the Natural History of Man, as it regards one or several species, is not forbidden by Scripture, but is as much open for discussion & investigation as the Natural History of any animal.

That the zoological classification of man by his animal properties, excluding his psychical attributes is unphilosophical[.]

That there are, at least, four distinct species of Man in the world, which is proved by their physical & psychical powers.

That although there were several centres of distribution, or creation, of animals & vegetables, every known fact proves an original single centre of distribution, or creation, of Man, in the neighborhood of the Euphrates.

That the progressive development & improvement of the human species, in morals & intellect, are laws of human nature, the equivalent of the series of creations anterior to man.

That the differences in the races of men cannot be accounted for by climate, mode of living, or any natural causes now in operation, or which have been in operation within the period of history.

That they cannot be accounted for by accidental, or congenital varieties springing up in the human family.

That there is no analogy between man & animals which can assist us to classify man, or to understand his history.

That the principles of Zoology, if applied to man in the same manner they are applied to animals, establish specific differences among men.

That the Anatomical & Physiological differences of the races of men constitute specific differences[.]

That the Psychical Attributes of the different races of men, in every point of view in which they can be considered, establish specific differences.

117

That the history & condition of women in the different races establish specific differences.

And lastly—That the natural law of sexual love, by which the races have been kept distinct from time immemorial, establish a distinction of species."

Although specific differences appear, on the face of the above statement, to be objects of primary importance, they are, in fact, subordinate to the general psychical, sexual, anatomical, & physiological history of man, from the earliest to the latest period. You will immediately perceive, from the above, as well as the prospectus, that my method of treating the subject is original, & owes nothing to the European artificial systems.

I am aware that the doctrine of specific differences among men is unpopular; but truth is regardless of prejudice or prepossession.

If you [shou]ld think proper to subscribe please send me your name at your earliest [con]venience. The Book will be delivered to you, at Washington, free of expe[nce.] Very resp[ectfull]y Y[ou]r Mo[st] Ob[edien]t S[er]v[an]t, W.F. Van Amringe.

ALS in ScCleA. NOTE: The book referred to was Van Amringe's *An Investigation of the Theories of the Natural History of Man, by Lawrence, Pritchard, and others, founded upon Animal Analogies: and an Outline of a New Natural History of Man, founded upon History, Anatomy, Physiology, and Human Analogies* . . . (New-York: Baker & Scribner, 1848). W.F. Van Amringe (1791–1873) was the author of several other scientific works and the father of a later president of Columbia University, John H. Van Amringe.

REMARKS ON THE TEXAS ANNEXATION TREATY

[In the Senate, January 13, 1848]
[*Under consideration was the bill to add ten regiments to the regular Army. James A. Pearce of Maryland, a Whig, was speaking at length about the war and its causes.*]

Mr. Calhoun. Will the Senator yield the floor that I may make a short explanation in reference to that treaty? It is a treaty which I negotiated [as Secretary of State] in reference to the admission of Texas, and which was rejected by the Senate.

In making that treaty, and entering into it, I by no means assumed that the Rio del Norte was the western boundary of Texas. On the contrary, I assumed that the boundary was an unsettled one between Mexico and Texas. No provisions were made in reference to it, because Texas, by the provisions of that treaty, was to come into the Union as a Territory; and as such, the right of the Government of the United States to settle the boundary was unquestionable: there was an express provision to that effect. It was different in reference to the resolutions under which Texas was actually admitted into the Union. They proposed to admit her as a State, not as a Territory; and, coming in that character, it would have been necessary to have had the consent of Texas to establish a boundary between her and Mexico. Those resolutions, to avoid the difficulties which might result, very properly contained a provision which provided that the matter in dispute should be settled by the Government of the United States.

I am far from thinking that the treaty which I negotiated established the Del Norte as the boundary. Immediately after the negotiation, I despatched [on 4/19/1844] a messenger to our chargé in Mexico [Benjamin E. Green], and, among other things, intimated to him that the Government of the United States was prepared to settle the boundary on the most liberal terms. What boundary was contemplated at the time, it is unnecessary to state, and would be improper, perhaps, on the present occasion.

From *Congressional Globe*, 30th Cong., 1st Sess., p. 174. Also printed in the Washington, D.C., *Daily National Intelligencer*, January 18, 1848, p. 2; *Niles' National Register*, vol. LXXIII, no. 22 (January 29, 1848), p. 349; Houston, ed., *Proceedings and Debates*, p. 111; *Congressional Globe*, 30th Cong., 1st Sess., Appendix, p. 98.

From JOHN R. CHAMBLISS

Hicksford, Greensville c[oun]ty Va.
Jan[uar]y 14/1848
Dear Sir, Permit me to thank you for the speech lately delivered by you in the Senate of the U.S. on the Mexican War. I[t] comes freighted with wisdom; full of sound practical good sense, and deserves the warm admiration of your fellow citizens. The relation we all sustain to our country, imposes upon us all peculiar obligations to Labour for its best interest and welfare and the period once was, when this statement would have been universally rece[ive]d as a truism—and you still acknowledge ["the" *canceled*] its truth & force.

I have some[time]s differed with you; often concurred in opinion with you; and at *all times*, held your virtue, patriotism and *honesty* in exalted Regard—and your Recent effort to arrest the corrupting tendency of the times, confirms me in the estimate I had formed of your character.

It is my fortune to be an humble individual, and my opinions, can not add "one whit to your Stature." Yet it must afford the public man, some satisfaction to know that his course has Rec[eive]d the commendation of the public—or any portion of the public, however little the individual who expresses it, may be known to public fame.

If your views are not right & just, then let them be exposed, and their fal[l]acy pointed out. Let the country know what is to be the end of this War. How can it be terminated, otherwise than you propose, without blotting out the nationality of the Mexican nation, without the conquest and subjugation of the whole country?

I am a stranger to you, but hope you will forgive me for this expression of my thanks. I am very Respectfully Your ob[edien]t Ser[van]t, John R. Chambliss.

ALS in ScCleA. NOTE: Chambliss was a planter at Hicksford, which was later renamed Emporia. His son of the same name was a Confederate Brigadier General killed in action in 1864.

To Tho[mas] G. Clemson

[Washington, January *ca.* 15, 1848]
.... but it is difficult to say, who or what party will be successful at the approaching election. The appearance is in favour of Gen[era]l [Zachary] Taylor, run[n]ing ag[ai]nst conventions, as the peoples candidate.

I shall make another effort to get an answer from [J.B.] Crockett & [D.C.] Briggs. Their conduct has been extr[a]ordinary, and speaks badly for the morality or attention of the Western attorney's. Mr. [John J.?] Crittenden [Senator from Ky.] can give me no information in relation to them.

I accidently tore off the cover of one [of] the letters enclosed, supposing it to be addressed to me. It will explain why the address is in my handwriting. Your affectionate father, J.C. Calhoun.

ALS (fragment) in ScCleA. NOTE: In his letter of 1/17/1848 to Anna Maria Calhoun Clemson, Calhoun refers to this letter. In his letter of 2/4/1848 to

Thomas G. Clemson, Calhoun explained that the first page of this letter was found under his Senate desk several days after the remainder had been mailed through the State Department. Since it contained nothing of importance, he decided not to forward it.

To HENRY GOURDIN, [Charleston]

Washington, Jan[uar]y [*ca.* 15] 1848
My dear Sir, Our papers are pursuing a very judicious course in reference to Dickerson[']s [*sic*; Daniel S. Dickinson's] resolutions, [Lewis] Cass' letter, & [Robert J.] Walker's toast. They, as well as [James] Buchanan's letter & [Vice-President George M.] Dallas' speeches, are intended to delude the South. They all oppose the [Wilmot] Proviso, but not the end at which it aims; to exclude the South from whatever Territory may be acquired from Mexico. Among them, Dallas' is the least objectionable, & Dickerson's resolutions & Walker's toast the most so. The ["author of the" *interlined*] latter is not at all Southern in his feelings. [David L.] Yulee's amendment to Dickerson's resolutions and [Arthur P.] Bagby's resolutions are both correct, as far as they go, and ought to be favourably noticed, as taking the right ground. The whole will ["whole will" *canceled*] be fully discussed. I shall take a full share in the discussions. The subject will be brought up, as soon as the questions connected with the war are disposed of in the Senate. I thought it was advisable for me to hold back, & let others show their hand. The whole will rece[i]eve a thorough examination. If the South is to be deluded, it shall not be my fault. There has been one continued, effort thus far, to delude it, and I am sorry to say with the approbation & concurrence of no small portion of the Southern delegation, democrats & whigs.

As to the presidential question, every thing is still in a state of uncertainty. The indication, however, is, that the majority of both parties are disposed to go into Convention. Mr. [Henry] Clay has been using all his efforts & influence to induce the whig party to take that course, with no small success. Great efforts will be made to force Gen[era]l [Zachary] Taylor in, but I hope without success. Should he yield, we could not, consistently with our principles, or propriety, support him. I hope our State will wait farther developements before it takes its stand. We ought not to move until we can see our way clearly. Otherwise we might be thrown into a position, which would greatly embarrass ["us" *interlined*] & force us to back out, with great loss of credit & influence. The next two months will shed much light on the subject, which may enable us to take & maintain the stand, which our character & principles demand.

There are many rumours of peace; but, I fear, no solid foundation to hope for so desirable an event. It may be even doubted, whether there is any power left in Mexico competent to make good any stipulations, into which it may enter. If such should be the case; any treaty, which may be made, may leave us in a worse condition than ever.

You are of course at liberty to show this to any of our friends you ["may you" *canceled*] may desire. Yours truly, J.C. Calhoun.

ALS in ScC; photostat of ALS in DLC, Henry Workman Conner Papers. NOTE: Henry Gourdin (1804–1879) was a prominent Charleston merchant, formerly a Nullifier member of the S.C. General Assembly, and a director of the Bank of Charleston. During the 1850's he was president of the Blue Ridge Railroad (serving without pay) and of the Charleston Chamber of Commerce. Gourdin was one of the men most active, after Calhoun's death, in raising funds for his widow and in concealing Calhoun's remains from federal vandalism in 1865. Dickinson had introduced in the Senate on 12/14/1847 resolutions that would leave slavery up to territorial legislatures. On 12/24/1847, Cass, a front-runner for the Democratic Presidential nomination, had written to Alfred O.P. Nicholson of Tenn. Cass opposed the Wilmot Proviso, suggesting that it could only apply to territories and that slavery was not likely to be established in any of the Mexican cession. In a public letter of 8/25/1847 Buchanan, another Democratic Presidential contender, appealed to the compromises of the Constitution and the spirit of the Missouri Compromise, but added that slavery was not likely to exist in the new territory. Therefore it was best not to agitate a question which would divide the party and cause sectional discord. In several speeches Dallas had said he dissented from the Proviso and that compromise was needed. Robert J. Walker, James K. Polk's Secretary of the Treasury, was a native of Pa. and a former Senator from Miss. In a toast on 1/12/1848, Walker declared that no State, North or South, could force its local institutions on the people of the territories. Such would be a violation of the "fundamental principle of self-government." (Washington, D.C., *Daily Union*, January 15, 1848, p. 1.) In a speech at Pittsburg on 9/18/1847, Vice-President George M. Dallas made a somewhat evasive speech on the Wilmot Proviso, stating at one point that he would keep an open mind until all the arguments were heard at the next session of Congress but also stating that the matter would best be settled by leaving it to the people of the territories. (Washington, D.C., *Daily Union*, September 24, 1847, p. 2.)

To A[NNA] M[ARIA] CALHOUN [CLEMSON, Brussels]

Washington, 17th Jan[uar]y 1848

My dear Anna, I have received safely the box containing the presents to your mother, [Floride Colhoun Calhoun, Martha] Cornelia [Calhoun] & myself. They are all very han[d]some. I have had mine made into a vest. It is thought to be very han[d]some; & will send the box by George McDuffie Calhoun, who expects to go south shortly, to your mother. I have no doubt she & Cornelia will be much pleased with their presents.

I enclose letters for [you] from both of them. They will give you all the home news, as my letter to Mr. [Thomas G.] Clemson will give you the political here.

I have only to add, that my health is as good as usual, though troubled as usual here, with a cold. It is very common at present in the city. Indeed most of my acquaintances think I look unusually well.

There are many strangers in the city, but I understand (for I do not go out) that the winter thus far has been unusually dull.

I hope you all have escaped the Influenza, which has been so prevalent in Europe, if we may judge by the papers, and are in good health.

Kiss the children [John Calhoun Clemson and Floride Elizabeth Clemson] for their Grandfather. Your affectionate father, J.C. Calhoun.

ALS in ScCleA. NOTE: George McDuffie Calhoun was the youngest of eleven children of J.C. Calhoun's brother William and his wife Catherine de Graffenreid Calhoun.

From H[ENRY] W. CONNER

Charleston, Jan[uar]y 17, 1848

My Dear Sir, Yours of the ——— [8th] Inst. is rec[eive]d. The Mercury published at an early day your speech as then reported. The Courier & other papers have since published what they called a revised copy. The Mercury will republish the copy as corrected by yourself. The Courier may also.

You will perceive an Editorial in the Mercury of today. It is intended to cover the ground presented in your letter to me which I rec[eive]d on the 15th.

The Courier in a late Editorial approved your views. They have published since a well written article it is said (I have not read it) on the Mexican war signed Lowndes by W[addy] Thompson [Jr.]. The other papers here are with you. The Senior [editor] of the Courier [Aaron S. Willington] is a whig & will go with that party & tho with you now will go against you & with the whigs whenever necessary. The Junior [editor, William S. King,] is a democrat & goes for the Conquest of Mexico, but his voice is not heard through the paper.

The Mercury *is true & sound* & you can rely upon it most implicitly. This I will answer for.

You will notice their Editorial of this morning. It is intended to carry out the views expressed to me in your letter rec[eive]d on Saturday (15th). The Editors have been prompt & decided in responding to your sentiments in every instance & in every particular as far as they were known. Mr. [John E.] Carew the Editor is gone to Columbia this morning. He will see Col. [Franklin H.] Elmore who has been there for a month past & endeavour with him to get the Columbia & up country papers to respond to your views. Mr. [Henry] Gourdin has written Col. Elmore fully on the subject.

I wrote you a week since pointing out the necessity as I conceived of our being kept better advised of the progress of events & the line of policy to be pursued in reference to the same. Very Truly y[ou]rs &c, H.W. Conner.

ALS in ScCleA.

From R[ichard] K. Cralle

Lynchburg [Va.,] Jan[uar]y 17th 1848

My dear Sir: Your favour reached me some ten days since, and your Speech as reported in the Newspapers a day or two ago. I have read carefully, as have every body else, and confess it opens a chapter I had not before contemplated. Your friends, as far as I am acquainted with them in this section seemed to think that, however wise was your proposition at the last Session, events had since intervened which rendered it at least very doubtful in policy, if not, in fact, irreconcilable with the rights and honor of the Country. I confess to a strong impression that it would not now suit the emergency—but

I an[d] others judged from a very partial view of the subject. We contemplated only one of its bearings; and that, indeed, not the most important. We fell into a like error in regard to Dickerson's [*sic*; Senator from N.Y., Daniel S. Dickinson's] Resolutions, which were warmly applauded when they first made their appearance. These things only show how important it is to exercise perpetual scrutiny and vigilance.

The general impression here is that your last is the ablest Speech you have ever delivered. It certainly traverses a wider field—and deals deeper in the philo[so]phy of man and government than any I have yet seen—and must exercise a powerful influence on the public mind. The administration men are completely staggered by it, while many of the leading Whigs are loud in their applause. The truth is, the Party here is completely broken up; and hundreds who, a few years ago, were ready on all occasions to denounce, are now the foremost to applaud. There is but one sentiment expressed by those who think at all, and that is, that if your views are not adopted the Country will be in danger of disgrace, if not something worse. Ought you not immediately to follow up this blow by a full exposé of the dangers of Dickerson's "*wooden horse*"? The subjects are connected, and it seems to me that the time is propitious for the free and full discussion of the whole subject. What would be the result of a motion to substitute the Resolutions by those you introduced some years ago [on 12/27/1837] in the Senate? I see that Mr. Dickerson has called up his resolution; and I suppose, of course, it will not be allowed to pass out of notice without the proper stamp on its brow.

But to return to the War question. Much interest is felt and many inquiries made as to the precise line of defence you propose. I know it was designated with some care in your Speech during the last session; and I suppose, from what you say you adhere to that line. But as the question of indemnity is intimately connected with the territory proposed to be occupied, will that which would have sufficed twelmonths ago be sufficient at the present time? In other words, many inquire whether you propose to secure indemnity for the whole expenses of the war, notwithstanding what you have said lately in the Senate, which appears to them inconcluclusive [*sic*]. Every thing you say on this as on other subjects is subjected, as you see, to the most rigid scrutiny. I think we ought to have indemnity for the past; but if the Administration go on to expand it is obvious that to secure this for the future, we must occupy the whole territory of Mexico—and the effect of this, strange as it may appear, never seems to have been realized by the public, nay scarcely to have been considered at all, until your late speech. Judge [Daniel A.?] Wilson told me a day or two ago that even he had never, for a moment viewed it in the light in which you have presented it. This is true almost universally; but how far your exposition of consequences will go to check the mad career of ["the" *interlined*] military mania of the day is to be seen. I doubt its efficacy as well as that of every other antidote. We are, in my humble opinion, rushing on to the end of our history. The curtain, as you have well observed, has already fallen on the first Chapter—and what remains to be written will, I fear, be only the echo of the past. The Executive is already nearly omnipotent; and this war will complete the measure of his power.

From the tone and tendency of your letter, I infer that Gen. [Zachary] Taylor will be the Candidate of the Southern States—as the only alternative left us. It is a dangerous experiment, and in my opinion, settles for all time to come, the military tendencies of the Republic. But considering the circumstances in which the Country is placed—the vile and ignoble herd which has so long fattened on the plunder of the Government, and the consequent inmorality and corruption which have been introduced into its administration, I am persuaded your friends will justify your course and follow your lead. For one, I shall, should you think it wise to sustain Taylor, do so likewise, but *despairingly*. There is however one condition—he must by all means keep clear of the infernal machinery of faction which has already wrought such disastrous effects on the body politic. If he is to wait for the *imprimatur* of a National Convention, he will only perpetuate a system whose evils must greatly overbalance every benefit his election can confer. Permit [me] to ask have your friends in Congress surrendered all purpose of placing your name before the Country? If they have it will only be in keeping with their past conduct. Their timidity—or in other and plainer words—their want of that high devotion to principle, moral and political, has seriously injured themselves and the Country. It has not injured you; for your fame stands not in need of their support—nor the support of any other set of men. You are its own and sole author and supporter. On that score I care not for their time serving and obsequiousness. *I know* that your name must go down to posterity clothed with honor and veneration, when theirs and their four years' idols' will have utterly perished. But it is only [on] public account I lament their want of nerve. If the Republic be lost, they will not be without a negative responsibility, and this result, I fear, is inevitable. The great change which you have so forcibly and feelingly depicted in your late Speech, can only be the effect of deep, and, I fear, incurable causes. All history is a fable if they who have forgotten the *tenure of liberty* shall long remain free.

I shall be much obliged to you for a Copy (in Pamphlet) of your late Speech, as well as that which I hope and expect you will deliver on Mr. Dickerson's Resolution; as I am collecting all that you have made during the last twenty years, which I wish to have bound in a single volume.

If Mrs. [Floride Colhoun] Calhoun and your family be with [you], be pleased to present my warmest regards with those of all my house hold. With highest respect and veneration I remain, dear Sir, ever truly yours, R.K. Crallé.

ALS in ScCleA.

From ELLWOOD FISHER

Indianapolis, 1 mo[nth] 17, 1848

Dear Friend, I learned with much regret from thy last letter the probable intention of the Southern whigs to support [Zachary] Taylor, and with still more regret that there was a disposition on the part of the southern democrats also to support him. I do not see clearly that any important advantages would result from his success. The slavery question would be evaded instead of settled: it would be postponed to arise at a future day under circumstances probably less favourable to the rights involved. It is not now at all clear even that Taylor remains in favour of a defensive line much less opposed to the War. The course of his friends in Congress indicate[s] the contrary. And if the Whigs of the north should give way to him, he will probably consent to go into a Convention, and thus that abuse will remain untouched.

On the other hand the incapacity of Taylor, and his Whig principles, his exclusively military pretensions, his hostility to thyself, his pledge well known here to appoint a Whig Cabinet, present altogether an array of objections to him which could hardly be made worse. Of his opposition to thee personally I became aware on going up the river the other day from Louisville to Cincinnati. [Former] Senator [William S.] Archer [of Va.] was on board—no friend of thine is he either—and sat at the dinner table with an officer recently from Mexico, both near enough for me to hear their conversation.

This officer said General Taylor had an unfavourable opinion of ["th" *canceled*] Mr. Calhoun and entertained a much higher regard for Mr. [Thomas H.] Benton—and had so stated to him.

Thee will have observed that the Dem[ocratic] Conventions of Ohio and Indiana waive the Wilmot proviso. That of Ohio declared for [Lewis] Cass. As for the Convention here it is more doubtful although W[illiam] J. Brown [2nd] Asst. P.M. General wrote a letter here advising no expression of preference to be made but that Cass delegates to the National Convention should be selected. If we should be compelled to choose between Cass and Taylor it would be emphatically a choice of [*partial word canceled*] evils: a choice between the negation of moral principle and the negation of intellectual ability. Surely we cannot acquiesce in that. Surely there is no necessity for it. There are ample materials throughout the country for another and a victorious party. And for one I will not submit to the miserable alternative of voting either for Cass or Taylor.

I have just had the pleasure of reading thy speech on thy resolutions. It is worthy of the occasion and the author. And but for party feeling it would command the approbation of three fourths of the people. It is condemned in very feeble terms by the vigorous prosecution War Democrats; it is approved by the Whigs generally who however are becoming more reserved on the War question as the prospect of nominating Taylor becomes stronger.

I got here after the Conventions of the two parties had ["been" *canceled*] adjourned—but before the members generally had left. The Whigs were generally friends of [Henry] Clay but generally yielded to the expediency of making no nomination before the National Caucus, and are preparing to go for Taylor. But to show the curious condition of sentiment now existing—I had a conversation the other night with two of the electors among the most distinguished of their party one on each side, E[dward W.] McGaughey and J[oseph] A. Wright both ex-members of Congress [from Ind.]—both said they would be ready at once to vote for thee if thy election could be made probable.

I do not think that Taylor or Cass can unite their respective parties. And the more I see of public sentiment, the more am I satisfied of the predominance of opposition to the War. The only thing is to detach the friends of peace from both parties, and unite them. If General Taylor[']s friends [John J.] Crittenden [Senator from Ky.] and [Henry] Johnson [Senator from La.] represent the position of his party on the War question, I am certain that the Whigs of the West and North will not support him. On the other hand if General

Taylor[']s position were satisfactory to the friends of peace, there are many of the latter among the Democrats favourable to free trade who could scarcely be prevailed on to support him. Under the influence of these views I have written an article for the New York Journal of Commerce and intend to present similar ones in ["one" *canceled*] some of the Western papers, ["so as" *possibly canceled*] that no reasonable effort ["however humble" *interlined*] shall be left untried to avert the evils which threaten us.

If General Taylor should become committed in favour of a prosecution of the War—should be nominated, and the Democratic candidate should be brought forward on the other side in favour of the same policy in that respect, the impending commercial embarrassment of the country if it were to burst forth in the spring would confound the friends of both. It would of necessity arrest the War. If the friends of peace were then ready, they might elect a President of their own. I confess I look to the threatening aspect of monetary affairs with hope. I believe we shall have an explosion. The Banks of New York State have but six or seven millions ["for" *changed to* "of"] specie for ["sixt" *canceled*] sixty odd of immediate liabilities. They are therefore at the mercy of circumstances[;] the rumour of an hour may suspend ["them" *interlined*]. Much as I should regret such a catastrophe of itself, I should hail it as a blessing, as a kind interposition of Providence, to terminate the War, after the reason and principle of the country had failed.

On the whole the changes ["continually" *canceled*] occurring in party movements are so frequent and important, and are so much complicated by events as to impress me with a determination to stand by all our principles until the very last moment. If then something must be sacrificed in order that something must be saved, then and then only would I be willing to acquiesce in the necessity.

I intend to be in Washington by the beginning of Spring—the condition of my family not admitting of an earlier trip.

I have heard nothing recently about the paper proposed last session. We shall be ready and willing to give it our full share of support at an early day. With great regard thy friend, Ellwood Fisher.

ALS in ScCleA; variant PC in Boucher and Brooks, eds., *Correspondence*, pp. 422–424.

From J[AMES] GADSDEN

Charleston S.C., Jan[ua]r[y] 17, 1848

My Dear Sir, I am in rec[eip]t of yours of 8 containing copy of your speech which I had previously read, as corrected in the Intelligencer. You have the political policy & argument in your favor, but what are we to hope from those in Congress, who *have not either the moral courage or firmness* to act up to their judgements, but constantly immagine a Popular Tornado out of Doors, under the full blasts of military Glory to overwhelm them, if they don[']t administer to their aspirations[?] When men of yesterday, are by accident suddenly elevated & to positions even above their own aspirations, when the young & ambitious witness the honors showered on heads whom good luck alone saved from decapitation, when all these immagined halloos of Glory are spiced with the fears of little politicians affraid of loosing their places, more than ["their" *canceled*] reputation, which they never expect to achieve, when an administration with all its patronage consults with & is influenced only by that Class, what I ask are we to hope[?] Even those who certainly do not come within the category ["of" *canceled*] seemed alarmed at the mere imputation of not furnishing men & means in time of war—and will not combine to resist, what every obligation to country, & not party [*sic.*]

[Lewis] Cass in his Speech, disproves every position he wished to established [*sic*].

He clearly shews by his own arguments that Conquest of Mexico, and not Peace, is the object of the Administration. The latter is but the pretext to quiet the People at home & to blind foreign powers. Can any one doubt that an avowal of Conquest on our Part would & ought to arrouse Great Britain & France on their part[?] Would those Governments not be recreant to their own People to see us absorb the Country on which alone is their reliance for a heavy debt, unless we recognise the debt[?] But she was not to consent & to concentrate a combined Fleet of French & Spanish & English in the Gulf just as our last reinforcements were on the way. What then[?] It is true that too much confidence makes us regardless of the powers of others & our success in Mexico, against a cowardly copper race, may mislead us. But I am not one of that number, & I must confess I have witnessed the Great preparations in England under the pretext of Sea Coast defence, with some distrust. If England takes part, she will be forced into it & she won[']t engage hastily or without preparation. Her blow will be at our financial ability as well as physical power. She will abide her time & wait untill the first are deranged, and recruiting slumbers under the unfavourable influence of an exhausted treasury. I don[']t believe there is much of the stamina of the Revolutionary spirit remaining, unless in [South] Carolina; our Western & Northern People have been too long speculative—Too long estimating their prowess by the indemnities in land &c to be acquired, to embark in a war of privations, hard fighting, disease & every evil to which war is incident, with the prospect of nothing but Glory. It is the enlargement of our domains, the prosperous condition of our Country & the Poor miserable half starved savages we whip so eas[il]y that is the strong stimuli to those, who now embark & who will be first to fail[?] on such a War, as we may be forced into.

Cass' documents prove that the President [James K. Polk] needs no more authority than what he has to enlarge his army to the extent desired. He may under existing Laws raise 50,000 men & if [needed] some 7 or 10,000 more may be necessary as a reserve. [Andrew P.] Butler [Senator from S.C.] has taken the true view[:] increase the Rank & file, & give a supernumerary Recruiting officer. Push recruiting, & hold the Recruits in readiness properly organized to move at a moment[']s warning. A camp of instruction at some healthy spot is the true policy. This will restrict the patronage of the Govt. to R[e]g[imen]t[s,] will involve 30 Field & some 800 Company officers, all of whom may be saved under the present organization somewhat modified. The army in Mexico is large enough, unless Conquest is resolved on. An increase of force will prevent the *Conquest of Peace* & may force the Conquest of Country and city.

The War is becoming one of Speculation. High officers are for Glory & Power, a province when no more victories are to be achieved. The subalterns stimulated in a greater & less degree by same motives. Retainers & sutlers all looking to the spoils & the Mexicans, who are to profit most under the policy pursued, will want the largest numbers to tax & feed. What if we do & with success attemp[t] to derive revenue from immense[?] Cities & direct taxation. It returns a gain to the People from whom extorted & in a four fold rate. For the most sanguine have not estimated the subsidy from these sources at more than 9 millions. Say 10—But the War will cost 70,000,000—of which at least 50 millions will be expended in Mexico. So for 10 extorted from the country 50 will be returned. Can no one figure out this Problem in Washington[?] Can Mr. [Robert J.] Walker [Secretary of the Treasury] be blind to results[?] It is clear to me that the war as pursued in Mexico & you can pursue no other must become popular with the People & we shall enrich & probably reconcile them to our Government—or we shall by enriching & by example, when our Soldiers become careless & confident, enabled [*sic*] them to achieve as did the Castilians of old another Moorish expulsion.

You have indicated the true policy, & I would add our Govern[or']s [David Johnson's] recommendation. Take a line, such as will give ample indemnity; select it well with the wisdom & eye of the State[s]man & Engineer, & then blockade all her Ports, cut her off from all trade untill they by treaty recognise that line. In haste Y[our]s, J. Gadsden.

ALS in ScCleA.

From H[ENRY] GOURDIN

Charleston, Jan[uar]y 17th 1848

My Dear Sir, Mr. [Henry W.] Conner has put into my hands your letter [of 1/8?] to him for perusal, and I now enclose to you two articles that have appeared in the Charleston Courier under the signature of Lowndes, written by Mr. or rather Gen[era]l [Waddy] Thompson [Jr.], of Greenville. I send them to you because they relate to the subject matter of your letter, and altho' you may have seen them, you may not have known the author.

They have more importance as coming from Gen[era]l Thompson, for I take it, that from the resolutions lately offered in the Senate by Mr. [Andrew P.] Butler, that you do not exactly agree as to the best mode of arresting the Mexican War, and Thompson's connexion with the Butler family renders ["his" *changed to* "an"] opinion from him, ["agreeing with you" *interlined*] of more consequence at this time, when it is desirable to have but one opinion in the State on the subject. The papers in Charleston have all come out in support of your views, and I doubt not that those in the interior will do so also.

The only doubt in the minds of some seems to be whether it would be politic or prudent to abandon the Country between Vera Cruz and the City of Mexico that has been won by so much hard fighting and loss of life. Many fear that such a course would give great strength & spirit to the Mexicans, and render more difficult the holding of any line that might be fixed upon.

I am obliged to you for the copy of your speech. It is without flattery a production which cannot fail to be felt every where, and the Country owes to you another debt of gratitude for it. I am My Dear

Sir Very resp[ectfull]y & truly Your Ob[edien]t S[er]v[an]t, H. Gourdin.

ALS in ScCleA. NOTE: Thompson was married to Andrew P. Butler's sister.

From ASHER W. GRAHAM

Bowling green Ky., Jan[uar]y 17, 1848
D[ea]r Sir, Although, ["from" *canceled*] the elevated position which you so deservedly occupy in the councils of our nation may render you comparatively indifferent to the approbation or censure of any obscure citizen, yet as I have just now enjoyed the high satisfaction of perusing your speech in the senate on the subject of the Mexican war, permit me to say, as I feel, that the thanks and gratitude of the whole people, are due to you for the noble effort you have made to save our country from disgrace, and it may be, from ruin ["and" *canceled*].

Permit me also, as one unknown to you, and who never expects to have the pleasure of your personal acquaintance, to say, that as one of the people, one who prefers his country and her glorious institutions to any and all parties, I tender you my thanks, and pray that He in whose hands are the destinies of the nations of the world may bless you, and give success to your effort to save our common country from misrule, degradation, disunion, and anarchy. Trusting to your kindness to excuse this hasty effusion of a stranger, I am very respectfully Y[ou]r ob[edient] Ser[van]t, Asher W. Graham.

ALS in ScCleA.

Remarks on the bill to raise an additional military force, 1/17. In a long speech, Andrew P. Butler of S.C. mentioned that supporters of the administration had previously declared that New Mexico and California would be the minimum demand made on Mexico for peace. Calhoun interjected: "Upper California." Butler replied, "All of California, Upper and Lower." From *Congressional Globe,* 30th Cong., 1st Sess., p. 186. Also printed in Houston, ed., *Proceedings and Debates,* p. 120.

From LOUIS MCLANE

Baltimore, Jan. 18, 1848

My dear Sir, I make you my thanks for the printed copy of your Speech, which I have read with the deep interest I always feel in your public acts. If I cannot in all respects concur in your views, I do not the less appreciate your motives, or the ability with which you have maintained the policy you would adopt.

I must confess to you that, in my opinion, after the annexation of *Texas*—which I advocated at that hazard—a war with Mexico could not well have been avoided; and, even if that had been *possible*, I do not think the *President* [James K. Polk] should be held responsible for the occurrence of a war which it was next to impossible to avoid. I am of opinion too that after it was commenced, the war should have been prosecuted with the utmost vigour and energy, until, by the subdugation of the Mexican power, peace could have been dictated upon just and liberal terms; and I cannot help thinking that the remissness of the administration in this respect, constitutes its real weakness. I cannot doubt that Mexico has been much encouraged by the opposition in this country, and that if the war had been promptly & vigorously pushed, less mischief would have arisen from that source. I am not capable of adding to the embarrassments of the Administration, in the present crisis; but it has always appeared to me that, from the capture of Monterey, there has been a greater desire to give eclat to the civil diplomacy of the administration than to realize the legitimate results of military operations. Indeed, I am persuaded that the actual achievements of our army have transcended any reasonable expectation that could have been entertained.

The policy of the "*Whigs*" is evidently, by discrediting the war, to break down the Democratic party, and reduce our acquisition of territory within the smallest possible compass; and although my notions as to new territory are by no means immoderate, I should be sorry to see such a scheme succeed; and I could not be brought to accept less than would afford just indemnity, and a reasonable security against the future, in all its bearings. The present war appears to me to have hastened a crisis in Mexico, full of the gravest interest to us; and I have a strong conviction that whatever we leave of that Country will immediately become an object of European interference. If that is to be depracated by our Statesmen, the mode of preventing it ought to enter largely into their notions of *future security*, and not be without weight in deciding upon the best [*one word canceled and* "means" *interlined*] of prosecuting the war.

I tender you my cordial wishes for your health and prosperity; and am Dear Sir, Most respectfully, Your friend & obedient Servant, Louis McLane.

ALS in ScCleA; PC in Boucher and Brooks, eds., *Correspondence*, pp. 424–425.

From H[ENRY] GOURDIN

Charleston, Jan[uar]y 19, 1848

My Dear Sir, I wrote to you yesterday [*sic*; on 1/17], and alluded to resolutions offered in the Senate [on 1/13] by Mr. [Andrew P.] Butler. It seems that we had not a correct representation of them—this day[']s mail gives them to us as they were offered, and they appear to me to be right & proper, viz. to increase the Army by filling up the rank and file of regiments already in existence. This mode of increasing the Army would be in keeping with the long established & well understood principles of the Miltary Organization of the Army [", as" *canceled*].

In your letter [of 1/8?] to Mr. [Henry W.] Conner you seem to be under the impression that Mr. [Daniel S.] Dickinson[']s resolutions have not been noticed in the Mercury. They were very ably reviewed some days since, and I will endeavour to obtain the paper and send it to you. There was a very good Article in it this morning also on the Wilmot Proviso & Gen[era]l [Lewis] Cass' opinions, to which I would call your attention. The two articles referred to were indicated by your two letters; If you desire that the papers in this State should continue to agitate these questions you should I think intimate, as far as you can, what they should do, or in other words, on what platform they should stand. Thus far, all that has been said and done, has been merely to object to the various schemes put forward by [David] Wilmot[,] Dickinson[,] Cass &c. No scheme has been offered, or recommended by us, and unless something be defined, our papers may run on beyond the point desired, and you may find them some day running counter to your own views & opinions, in anticipation. We presume that your opinions are embodied in Mr. [David L.] Yulee's resolutions viz. that neither Congress, or the Legislatures in the Territories, have any Constitutional right to abolish or prevent Slavery in them.

I give the Substance, not the words. It would be an excellent thing, and very desirable, that some course should be determined on that the whole South ["will" *canceled and* "would" *interlined*] unite upon, and then, through particular parties having influence with the press throughout the Country, get them to come out [and] advocate the plan adopted. I think that it might be done by yourself and the representatives of the Southern States in Washington.

We are well pleased here with the Resolutions of the Legislature of Maryland. I am Dear Sir, Very truly & resp[ectfull]y Your Ob[edien]t S[er]v[an]t, H. Gourdin.

ALS in ScCleA; variant PC in Jameson, ed., *Correspondence*, pp. 1159–1160.

Remarks on the appointment of committees, 1/19. When a number of vacancies needed to be filled on Senate committees, the presiding officer [Vice-President George M. Dallas] expressed embarrassment as to "whether the chairmen were to be designated by him, or merely appointed to complete the number." This led to a discussion among several Senators during which Calhoun said: "I think the practice has been different. I know there have been cases where the chairmen have been appointed by the Presiding Officer; but I think the principle is, that the Chair appoints the committee men, and it belongs to the committee, where it is not otherwise provided for, to say who shall be chairman." From *Congressional Globe*, 30th Cong., 1st Sess., p. 209. Also printed in the Washington, D.C., *Daily Union*, January 20, 1848, p. 2; Houston, ed., *Proceedings and Debates*, p. 133. Variant in the New York, N.Y., *Morning Courier and New-York Enquirer*, January 21, 1848, p. 2.

From F[ITZ]W[ILLIAM] BYRDSALL, "Confidential"

New York [City,] Jan[uar]y 20th 1848

Dear Sir, I have received your speech of the 4th instant in pamphlet form. It was my intention to have written to you for it, as the report of it in the New York Herald which I read, was not full, but your anticipation of my request is only the more gratifying to me, and the more especially so, as you could not have sent me a better intellectual present.

I will not attempt to convey to you my impressions of the most remarkable speech ever uttered in the Senate, a speech calculated ["to excite" *interlined*] the most serious and even melancholy reflections as regards our future. I hold that our Republican system is the greatest good ever achieved by the human race, a system fitted to keep pace with every step, even to the highest of human progress. Indeed our Institutions are not only "wiser" but they are better than ourselves. With all our advancement beyond other nations in this respect, we have in our country a very large portion of our people not sufficiently intelligent and capable for the proper exercise of their political privileges. The addition of the less intelligent and less capable millions of Mexicans to this large portion of our own unreflecting people, may well be apprehended as fraught with danger to our confederated system. It is a portentous fact, that such is the Negrophilism of the North & East, that it can easily embrace the mongrell races of Mexico. Pass the Wilmot proviso, or satisfy its fanaticism that its object can be accomplished without the action of Congress, and the North & East will go at once for the whole of Mexico. The crisis has come which is to determine our future. No evil can befall us, our posterity or all humanity so disastrous as the overthrow of our Institutions.

The next presidential contest will present the great issue. Already the minor politicians of both parties affraid of not seeming sufficiently patriotic before the people, are out or coming out for the prosecution of the war, and the annexation of Mexico, regardless of any inward convictions they may hold to the contrary. The popularity of Gen[era]l [Zachary] Taylor is reviving over the land and is becoming so troublesome to the friends of Mr. [Henry] Clay that they are sorely perplexed. The most of those in the Whig party who have come out for Gen[era]l Taylor here, greatly prefer Mr. Clay as their first choice, but their fears of defeat since he came out against the war, induce them to abandon their favorite. Under these circumstances the Old leaders are devising a plan of pursuing a sure game of all chances in their favor, in this way namely—to induce the Whig National Convention to make no nomination for the Presidency, but to recommend the Whigs of each State to run one electoral ticket, each voter to endorse the name of Clay or Taylor on the back of his ticket, according to his preference. Now, as there is no law requiring the Inspectors of election to make returns of such endorsements on the ballots, it is easy to foresee to whose elevation such an arrangement would enure. The foregoing plan is privately concocted but not yet brought out. If it can be pursued it will—I give it to you for your own use.

A letter was published some time ago addressed by M[artin] Van

Buren to the Editor of a Wilk[e]sbarre Penn. newspaper, in which V.B. expressed himself in effect that those who were instrumental in elevating the present administration ought to sustain it in its measures. I recur to this point because of a co-incidence which took place in our Rep[ublican] Gen[era]l Committee for the year 1848. Immediately after the election of the annual chairman & on the same evening, a Resolution in favor of the war, sustaining the administration, was adopted and a sub-committee thereupon appointed to call a public meeting.

A majority of the General Committee are Van Burenites. M. Van Buren has been in our city for some short time past and is still here. I have some grounds for believing that he is working for a ["nomination" *altered to* "re-nomination"] of the present Executive in 1848. Gen[era]l [Lewis] Cass is no favorite with the Barnburners. If V. Buren can bring them to the support of Mr. Polk there will be no opposition on the part of those called Conservatives the friends of Gov[erno]r [William L.] Marcy. In fact Mr. Polk would unite the party in this State far better than Cass and if the union of the party would carry the State under the management of V.B. the latter would stand high with the administration thereafter.

When the public meeting takes place we shall have more light as to the under workings. Probably John Van Buren will figure in a speech. John McKeon says he will make one. I should not be surprised if he will present the nomination of Gen[era]l Cass to the meeting. Should he do so—it will test matters yet in embryo. With Veneration & esteem I am Dear Sir Yours &c &c &c, F.W. Byrdsall.

ALS in ScCleA.

AMENDMENT Offered to [John M.] Berrien's Resolution

[In the Senate, January 20, 1848]

Mr. Berrien submitted the following resolution:

Resolved, That the President of the United States be requested to furnish to the Senate copies of the letters, reports, or other communications which are referred to in the letter of General Zachary Taylor, dated at New Orleans, July 20, 1845, and addressed to the Secretary of War [William L. Marcy], and which are referred to as containing the views of General Taylor, previously communicated, in regard to the line proper to be occupied at that time by the troops of the United States.

Mr. Calhoun suggested as a modification—

"And any similar communication from any officers of the army on the same subject, unless he be of opinion that a communication of the same be inconsistent with the public interests."

PC in *Congressional Globe*, 30th Cong., 1st Sess., p. 214; PC in *Niles' National Register*, vol. LXXIII, no. 22 (January 29, 1848), p. 342; variant PC in the New York, N.Y., *Morning Courier and New-York Enquirer*, January 22, 1848, p. 2. NOTE: Berrien accepted Calhoun's amendment. By standing rule, the resolution was to lie over for later consideration.

REMARKS ON THE CAPTURE OF VERA CRUZ

[In the Senate, January 20, 1848]
[In a speech on the bill to raise an additional ten regiments, Henry S. Foote of Miss. attributed to Calhoun the statement at the beginning of the war that Vera Cruz was impregnable.]

Mr. Calhoun—That's a mistake, sir.

[Foote continued.]

Mr. Calhoun—As the Senator has said so much, I desire to say one word upon this point. This is a point upon which I had a conference with the Chief Magistrate [James K. Polk] himself.

Mr. [John M.] Clayton—A little louder.

Mr. Calhoun—Upon this subject I had a conversation with the Chief Magistrate himself. In that conference, the President did me the honor to ask my opinions on the plan to be pursued in the war; and upon the contemplated attack on Vera Cruz. I had two objections to it. The first was, that the movement would prevent us from taking up a defensive line. The second was, that if we captured Vera Cruz, we should be compelled to go on to Mexico [City]. The one movement would of necessity involve us in the other. Third, that if the war could be closed with the occupation of Mexico [City], it would not be so bad a policy, but that I had no hope of that. My opinion was, that the castle could not be taken in a direct attack; but that the city of Vera Cruz could be taken and that the castle would fall with it.

From the New York, N.Y., *Herald*, January 22, 1848, p. 4. Variant in Houston, ed., *Proceedings and Debates*, p. 145. Other variants in the New York, N.Y.,

Morning *Courier and New-York Enquirer,* January 21, 1848, p. 2, and January 22, 1848 (Supplement), p. 1.

From F[RANCIS] LIEBER

[South Carolina College]
Columbia S.C., 21st January 1848

My dear Sir, Last night I received your note, after having had the copy of your speech on the Resolutions some time before. I wrote an article on the speech in the Columbia Telegraph, in the form of an editorial; but I found it the next day changed into the form of a communication. I did myself the honour of sending you a copy.

There is but one thing your plan does not cover, and which nevertheless I look upon as one of the noblest ["truest" *interlined*] things we could do as the pioneers of mankind and the missionaries of civilization, and, therefore, ought to do. I mean the Ship Canal from the ["Pacif" *canceled*] Atlantic to the Pacific. We ought at least to bring about this work as one of the fruits of so rash a war.

Have you seen Mr. [Richard] Cobden's speech to the electors of Stockton (I think)? It is extolled in my English papers as an Essay of Free Trade, complete and cogent; but they donot [*sic*] give it.

I am much obliged for the promise of documents &c for our N[ews]paper lecture. Pray Sir, has the Message with all the Reports &c ["never" *canceled and* "not" *interlined*] yet been printed?

The remains of Cols. [Pierce M.] Butler and [Lt. Col. James P.] Dickinson [of the Palmetto Regiment, killed in the Mexican War] were interred with great pomp, but I cannot help saying that, to my individual feeling, too much time had been allowed to elapse between their arrival and interment, so that every day of delay took away something from the original spontaneous and natural manifestation of feeling and added to ["the" *interlined*] character of exhibition. But such things depend upon individual feeling and taste. I am most respectfully my dear Sir Your most obed[ien]t, F. Lieber.

ALS in ScCleA.

J[ohn] C. Calhoun and Others to President [JAMES K. POLK]

[Washington, *ca.* January 21, 1848]
We recommend to the President of the United States, the appointment to West Point, as Cadet, Mr. Benj[amin] Huger [Jr.], son of Capt. B[enjamin] Huger, now serving with the Army in Mexico, and great grandson of Gen[era]l Thomas Pinckney, a soldier of the Revolution & war of 1812. (Signed), J.C. Calhoun, I[saac] E. Holmes, A[lexander] D. Sims, A[rmistead] Burt, Ja[me]s A. Black [Representatives from S.C.], A[ndrew] P. Butler [Senator from S.C.], Tho[ma]s S. Jessup [*sic*; Jesup, Quartermaster General], R[oger] Jones [Adjutant General], Geo[rge] Gibson, C[ommissary] G[eneral] S[ubsistence], G[eorge] Talcott [Chief of Ordnance], N[athan] Towson [Paymaster General], A[rthur] P. Hayne, G[eorge] M. Dallas [Vice-President], Lewis Cass [Senator from Mich.], Ja[me]s M. Wayne [Associate Justice of the U.S. Supreme Court], Rob[er]t C. Winthrop [Representative from Mass.].

Copy (in Benjamin Huger, Jr.'s, handwriting) in DNA, RG 94 (Adjutant General's Office), Application Papers of Cadets, 1805–1866, 1848, 143 (M-688:171, frames 429–430). NOTE: "Capt." Benjamin Huger was later a Major General in the Confederate States Army; his son Benjamin Huger, Jr., attended Princeton and worked on the U.S. coastal survey for nine years before serving as a Capt. in the Confederate Bureau of Ordnance. A Clerk's EU indicates that this undated communication was received on 1/21.

To JA[ME]S ED[WARD] CALHOUN, Jun[ior], [Columbia, S.C.]

Washington, 22d Jan: 1848
My dear James, I received your letter of the 2d Jan[uar]y when I was in the midest pressing official engagements, which prevented me from giving it my immediate attention. In the meane time the portion, which stated that you would want an im[m]ediate remittance of $60 unaccountably slip[p]ed from my memory, until I took it up to answer ["it" *interlined*] this morning. I am much mortified that such should be the case; but hope you have not experienced any serious inconvenience. I wish you to explain the cause of the delay to whomsoever the money may be due.

I am glad to hear ["of" *canceled*] such good account of you, and to perceive by your letter, that you take so much interest in your studies. Those which will claim your attention this and the next year, are of the most interesting character; and, if you should be as studious, as I have no doubt you will, you will find yourself making more rapid progress than ever you have in the same time, in accumulating knowledge, and the increased vigour of your reasoning faculties. This & the next year are pre[e]minently your seed time. What you acquire now will be as durable as life, &, if well and accurately acquired, will prove to be the means of greatly enlarging the sphere of your knowledge hereafter. Knowledge is like architecture. You must lay the foundation deep & strong in order to sustain a noble superstructure. When that is done, the mind may go on increasing its vigour & store of knowledge, long after the physical faculties have commenced their decay.

I am much gratified to perceive, that not only yourself, but John [C. Calhoun, Jr.], & William [Lowndes Calhoun] have evinced, within the last year, so greatly increased a desire for improvement. William seems to have undergone an entire change. He is devoted to his studies & makes great progress. His aversion to Latin & Greeke seems to have disappeared entirely. I hope you will write to him occasionally in a manner to encourage him.

I sent you & James Rion copies of my speech on the Mexican war. I hope you both received them. The speech has been exceedingly well received, as far as I have heard, all over the Union; and the opin[ion] is, that it has made a deep impression on the publick mind. There is clearly a strong reaction against what is called the vigorous prosecution of the war. I am waiting to see whether I would be supported in the movement I indicated towards taking a defensive line. I entertain but little doubt if a peace should not be patched up, that in a few months, both Congress & the country will be with me. As soon as the debate on the ten regiment bill is closed I shall call up my resolutions & have a vote on them, to be followed up, if favourable, at the proper time, with raising a Committee to consider what line should be adopted.

I will have the [New York] Herald ordered on for you; & herewith enclose a check on the rail road bank for $60. Write me as soon as it is received, so that I may know you have got it. I will shortly remit the amount necessary to meet your debts of the last year.

Give my respects to James Rion. I am glad to hear that he stands so well in College. Your affectionate father, J.C. Calhoun.

[Marginal P.S.] I had letters by the last steamer from your sister [Anna Maria] & Mr. [Thomas G.] Clemson. ["I hope" *canceled.*]

They were all well. She expresses great pleasure to hear you & your brothers are doing so well. I hope you will not fail to write to her. It would make her happy to get a letter from you.

ALS in ScU-SC, John C. Calhoun Papers.

From Jos[eph] J. Singleton

Dahlonega [Ga.,] 22d Jan[uar]y 1848
My Dear Sir, I am very much obliged to you for your Speech in support of your recent & important Resolutions. As the saying is, it "takes here like hot cakes." "Truth is mighty and will prevail," ever throughout this "land and nation" I hope. What more could be said, or done, than you have strove to do for the benefit of the whole Country, certainly no one can suggest, and but for the puny time serving Politicians of the present day, we never would have gotten into our unnecessary difficulties with Mexico. Now to get out of them certainly requires the best Wisdom of the Wisest, and I would ["ask" *interlined*] the whole Country for a better plan than you suggested twelve months ago, although I believe the question would be asked in vain. "Never be wary in well doing[.]" A retrospective action must be the result, as well on our Mexican dif[f]iculties, as on our Orrigon, altho you think the former produced the lat[t]er, and no doubt of the fact, yet as an humble cipher in this great Republic, I must repeat "hang on," and depend upon the Renowned Institutions of our Fathers. You are one in the purest History (Recollection) and so am I. Nothing so pure. Excuse me if you please; if I am in error[,] attribute it not to my Heart.

I accompany this letter with two of my last papers for your amusement, the Editorials of which I have marked, just for you to see how little Dogs will bark when something scares them. They are [Howell] *Cobb* papers, with but little corn left on the *cob*, altho' the Editor is a former member of Congress, with some degree of tact, in a strong head wind; nevertheless you will perceive he is disposed to hang onto the cob, corn or no corn. Be pleased to recollect that I am writing to a farmer as well as &C. &C.

To turn to private business. [John] Pasco[e], on your Obarr lot has realized his expectations with regard to the Am[oun]t he expected to deposite before Christmas. The Deposite has been made, of which I have in my hands subject to your order $49.$^{58}/_{100}$, and,

143

some prospect of renewed energies for the present year. I cannot say any thing satisfactory to you at this time, in regard to your other Lessee [Robert H.] (Moore). I never have been more disappointed in any man; I am fearful it is owing to his having entire controll over two thirds of the property in which you are only one third interested. After every effort in my power, thus far, neighborly and friendly I cannot get him to a settlement; am apprehensive that there is some wrong intentions affloat some where; and I am also fearful that I shall have to resort to some legal steps before it is ended, unless you will instruct me otherways. I would be truly glad of some instruction by you, be it whatever it may, as I am nearly at the end of my row.

The Superintendent of our Br[anch] Mint [James F. Cooper] is about to resign his office, if he has not already done so, for a State appointment on our State Rail Road. So look out for his successor. I have 1728 respectable Petitioner[s] before the President for a restoration. I fear it will avail me nothing on account of the p[r]esence of the Great *cob* above alluded to. A reconciliation is all that is necessary, but how it is to be brought about is the question. Help me if you can consistent with your own dignity. Yours very sincerely, Jos. J. Singleton.

ALS in ScU-SC, John C. Calhoun Papers.

To ——, 1/22. "D[ea]r Sir, Unless tomorrow should prove to be a *very* bad day, I will do myself the pleasure of taking a family dinner with you. Truly, J.C. Calhoun." Transcript in DLC, Carnegie Institution of Washington Transcript Collection.

From J[AMES] GADSDEN

Charleston So. C., Jan[ua]r[y] 23, [18]48

My Dear Sir, The enclosed [*not found*] express so strongly the views I have previously conveyed to you, that I have cut them out, least they should have escaped your notice in the columns of the Mercury. The great object at this time is to arrest the mad designs of Conquest, involving the still more dreaded but unavoidable policy, if the first succeeds[,] of the annexation of the whole of Mexico, in States to this Union. I cannot reflect on the measure without the most fearful apprehensions for the character & security of this Government or confederation. The Question of indemnity however, and the certainty that it can only be met on the part of Mexico in the surrender of Territory is no longer debatable with our People. The cry of the administration on that subject has been echoed and the whole pack of hungry land hounds have opened on the scent. If the W[h]igs therefore don[']t give up their repugnance to any extention of Territory, you will be left in an awful minority, in your wise position to stop short of conquering anything but *Territorial indemnity*. If the W[h]igs & sober minded Patriots of the Democratic party coales[c]e on this subject, you may carry your restrictive measures, and thus the Country [be] rescued from a catastrophe into which Presidential making & a blind ambition of conquest is hurrying Poke [*sic*; James K. Polk] and his advisers. I am the more persuaded likewise that whatever we do should be permanent; our Landmarks of future boundaries should be so fixed by *strong natural features* as to put a limit to future extensions. A River will not answer. The whole of a Valley must be settled by the same People, & the valley of the Rio Grande is so susceptible of a large population, that it will constitute a barrier population, which with the difficulties of the Sierra Madre will always make us safe on that frontier. The Sierra Madre was intended by nature to seperate the People of Texas & New Mexico, from what is old Mexico & the more the map is examined, and the more information received from those who have traversed & crossed the range, the more are we confirmed that it is the great natural barrier which should be placed between the Anglo Saxon & the Spanish Race, untill, what will probably be the fruits of "Masterly inactivity[,]" the latter are absorbed in, if not destroyed by the former. The details as where to begin on the Gulf & where to rise[?] the mountain, and where to terminate on the Pacific must all be the matter of examination with the skilful eye of the soldier, & judgement of the Statesman, for what may escape the eye of the soldier looking only to defence may suggest itself to the State[s]man who looks to country, production, and their natural connections with political communities. I think however the writer of the Article, goes too low in the Gulf. He has evidently set his affections upon Tampico & possibly San Luis Patosis [*sic*] mines, which will bring us into too close connection with portions of Mexico which will be settled & capable of cultivation. It would be better for us that the Mexicans work their own mines, and purchase with their gold & silver the works of our ingenuity & labor. The vicinage which the Sierra Madre boundary will give, the markets of Sallao[,] Monterey & Soto Marina [*sic*] will divert most of the Mexican trade in that quarter & prove the great Pacificator on a line, which Mr. Polk & Marcey [*sic*; Secretary of War

William L. Marcy,] think we cannot defend. It is impossible to comprehend their boldness on other positions & their apprehensions on this. They can conquer & hold all Mexico, & they cannot conquer & hold a part. But to return, Soto Marina, or mouth of the Santandre River in latitude 24', should be our position on the Gulf & the sea coast gate between that & the mountain[,] & the gap is reported to be very narrow[,] should be fortified with small Ports, or Ma[r]tello Towers. A Fort at Soto Marina, and works at the different passes with mounted men in part composing the Garrison & the whole Line could be maintained ultimately with 3 or 4000 men. At first it might be prudent to commence with 10,000 not merely to overawe the Guerrillas or disaffected Mexicans, but to encourage by protection American emigration. Once decree that up to that line is indissolubly united to us & every Town in the rear will be filled with American Traders, and new farms opened by American enterprise, as they are now opening in every part of the West. When sober judgement, free from party ties is permitted to dwell on the President[']s & Secretary's labored documents to prove the difficulty of defending a line it will appear ridiculous & must recoil on them either as evidences of *insincerity* or of great want of confidence in our Army & *institutions*. On the latter I most rely & 12 months after the Line is drawn & Posts established we shall see an American Population in their rear making that frontier as strong as that towards Canada. Yours, J. Gadsden.

ALS in ScCleA; PEx in Boucher and Brooks, eds., *Correspondence*, pp. 425–426.

From D[avid] J. McCord

Langsyne, near Fort Motte [S.C.], Jan[uar]y 23d 1848
Dear Sir, I received a few days since your speech on the Mexican War, in pamphlet form, for which I must thank you. I had already read it with great pleasure in the Newspapers. I am extremely pleased with its style and substance. Its simplicity, purity and dignity is admirable. [William C.] Preston says it is antique, and an imitation of Demosthenes. He could not have paid it a higher compliment. In assuming an independent course, it is not likely that either party, into which our country is divided, will be pleased, but it does seem to me impossible for any honest patriotic man to agree on all occasions with any party, where people submit themselves so

blindly to party leaders. Our great men must do what is right and look to posterity alone for their justification; for in these days the interest of the country is lost sight of in the greater interest felt for party and sections. It does seem to me, that whether men think you right or wrong, your self devotion and independence ["pla" *canceled*] must give you a position of high patriotism quite above any thing of the day. With most of our leading men, patriotism seems defunct. The prospect a head is alarming and mortifying. The Constitution! We have none. It is the will of the majority.

I most fully concur with you as to the practicability of taking and keeping a line, at a much less expense of life and money, than must be expended on a War of General Conquest of Mexico, and in the great danger of such a conquest. When in Texas just before their annexation, I noticed that their whole line of the Rio Grande had no other defence than Capt. [John C.] Hays['s] company of Spies, containing 40 men; and Texas just preceeding the act of annexation, ["found" *canceled and* "thought" *interlined*] it only necessary to add another company of 40 men under Capt. [Samuel H.] Walker, who were stationed at Corpus Christi. Here were upwards of 300 miles frontier guarded from invasion and depredation by 80 men against the whole Mexican nation, and the Camanches besides! No attempt for years was made upon the peace of Texas, notwithstanding all the threats of Mexico. In guarding the line across from the Rio Grande to ["the" *interlined*] Californian Gulph, the Indians tribes would be more to be feared than the Mexicans. Indeed by a few regiments the Mexicans would feel themselves protected from the savages.

As to Slavery. By the Mexican law of Master and Servant, which I have before me—(their laws relating to peones) the labouring classes are placed in a condition inferior to our slaves. If they work for any one, as they must do, for the lands are owned by few great proprietors, they must enter into articles or apprenticeship, and receive their supplies of food, clothing and otherwise from their masters the owner of the hacienda or rancho, who for that purpose always keep a store of such things as are necessary or tempting to the peon. As long as he remains indebted to his master or the contract lasts, he cannot quit his master ["at his will" *canceled*]. He may be punished, imprisoned and "shackled" by the master, and if he attempts to run away the Alcalde is expressly directed to apprehend him and punish him by imprisonment and *shackles*. Such is the language of the law. He cannot discharge the slave, for he is a slave, *even if he is punished to excess by the master.* If in sickness the master furnishes him with sustenance and medicine, it is to be charged to the servant, and he

147

remains to all purposes the slave of the master as long as he owes him one cent. The contract cannot be rescinded but by consent of both sides. Such was the law of Coahuila & Texas ["Judge Hemphill, the chief justice of Texas, informed me" *canceled*] under the Mexican rule before the Texan Revolution. How rediculous then to raise an outcry against *establishing* and *extending* slavery there.

Judge [John] Hemphill the chief Justice of Texas, a very intelligent gentleman to whom I am indebted for much information and various documents on this subject, informed me that after two years residence at San Antonio, and much intercourse with the Mexicans, he came to the conclusion that the state of *Peonage* in Mexico, as it existed in Texas among the Mexicans before the Texian Revolution, was more profitable to the master, and more oppressive to labourers on haciendas and agricultural ranchos than slavery in its worst ["state" *canceled*] condition in the U.S. Indeed he said that some of the old Mexicans complained to him of the injury done to them by this alteration of the law of servitude, and wished it enforced against their peons. And while in Texas I was surprised to find that the prisoners, (*not white,*) taken at San Jacinto had not left Texas, (and all with whom I spoke declared their unwillingness to return & to be forced into the army against their will) and were to be found on plantations in every part of Texas I visited, willing enough for their clothes and victuals and for permission to marry one of the negro field wenches, (being actually scorned by the house servant maids) to remain on the plan[tation] in the same condition as any other slave ["of the" *canceled*]. They were generally employed about the stables ["and" *canceled*] and horses and as stock minders. This I saw with my own eyes. Some ["few" *interlined*] of the better class of them get employment as servants in Hotels & steamboats. But in all cases associating with the slaves. Can we admit such *people* into our Union? They are not *"people"* embraced within the meaning of our Constitution. They are not *"free white."* They can form no territory—and never can we consent they should constitute an equal component part of our great & free people. Can they participate in making laws for this Union? Let every man under the Palmetto Banner die first.

But I beg your pardon for thus obtruding so much on your time and patience ["which can be" *interlined*] so much better bestowed.

Should you be kind enough to send me any thing hereafter, pray direct to *Fort Motte* my post office, and not "St. Mat[t]hews" which last is 9 miles off & where I never send. Very Respectfully Yours, D.J. McCord.

[P.S.] Having been very little at home since I was[?] called off to Alabama, I have not written yet what I designed writing for the papers, on the subject we are talking of.

ALS in ScCleA; PEx's in Boucher and Brooks, eds., *Correspondence*, pp. 426–427 and 283–284. NOTE: McCord (1797–1855) was Thomas Cooper's successor as editor of the laws of South Carolina and was the husband of the noted writer Louisa Cheves McCord, daughter of Langdon Cheves. The second large extract printed in Boucher and Brooks, pp. 283–284, was appended erroneously to a letter of 2/19/1845 from J[ames] S. Mayfield.

From J[AMES] K. PAULDING

Hyde Park[,] Du[t]chess County [N.Y.,] January 24th 1848
Dear Sir, It was with great pleasure, I received the day before yesterday, a little Packet bearing your Frank, and containing a copy of your Speech on the Mexican War. In my opinion, it is a wise and masterly exposition of a subject presenting many difficulties on all sides; and though I may not precisely coincide with you in every view, yet I frankly confess, I should be not a little puzzled to say wherein we differ. We have got into one of those unlucky positions from which it is impossible to move without committing a blunder.

You however are I think beyond all question right in the course you have taken on this question. As the steady inflexible guardian of the rights of fourteen States you could not do otherwise, than oppose the acquisition of Territory from which their citizens were to be virtually excluded, after having expended their blood and treasure in its conquest. All things considered, I think the Wilmot Proviso is the most impudent political movement of my time. I know nothing of Mr. [David] Wilmot [Representative from Pa.], but presume he is a catspaw in the hands of others, who wish to ride into power on the back of the Fiery Dragon of Slavery. I think they will fail as heretofore; and they *must* fail, if the States equally involved in one great interest paramount to all others, are true to themselves. There is no such bond of Union in the other States, and some of them will certainly refuse to rally under the Black Flag, unless I am greatly mistaken.

Much will depend on New York, and New York is not to be depended upon. What she is now, is no indication [*with the "c" interlined*] of what she will be six months hence, except as ["*it" interlined*] affords grounds for concluding that she will present a complete contrasting at that time. Our Governor [John Young] puzzles me not a little, and at this moment I am at a loss to decide whether he is most knave or fool. I think however he will turn out, an equal compound of both. Our Legislature is a compound of ignorance, and fanaticism; and it is only necessary to watch its daily proceedings to be convinced that ["they" *changed to* "the" *and* "had" *canceled,* "majority has" *interlined*] not the slightest perception of the limits of Legislative authority, or the true functions of Government.

But I am not yet discouraged. I have made up my mind as to the ultimate destinies of The United States, and am somewhat of a Fatalist in this respect. It seems clear to me that, this country is most emphatically under the direction of Providence. I mean to say, that its fortunes will be shaped by certain great universal causes, inflexible in their operation, and which constitute the instruments of omnipotence in governing the world. It seems to me that no human power, can arrest or control them, and that so long as our people preserve their present habits, characters, and physical superiority, they will run their race, not in spite of Fate, but in fulfilment of what is decreed. I do not rejoice in this prospect, because I know from all history and experience, that nations never become great but by the sacrifice of their happiness. It is impossible to be both at once. As you intimate in your speech, we shall become [*one or two words canceled*] the most illustrious nation of the world, and exhibit another example of the uniform fate of all that have gone before, as well as all that shall come after. This will happen, whether we are governed by sages, fools, or madmen; and for that reason I look on the struggle of the present moment with less solicitude than I used to do, when I remember I fell out with you for differing with me in opinion.

I have become wiser now as all men do—or at least think they do, when they grow old. But wise as I am, I have never yet been able to decide, whether on the score of happiness—which after all is the only rational pursuit of rational beings—it is best to exhaust ourselves in opposing the current, or lay on our oars, and float quietly along with the ["Currents" *canceled*] stream. I am now quietly and permanently settled down, in a pleasant spot in a pleasant country, where thus far, I have found content and repose. I am not indifferent to Public affairs, ["and" *canceled and* "but" *interlined*] if I ever meddle with them again it will be only with my Pen.

I have written you a long letter, having plenty of leisure during the winter, and from long habit finding pleasure in writing. You have plenty of business on hand, and I presume take greater pleasure in speaking, than writing, from long habit, too. I therefore don['']t expect you to answer this; and assure you your silence will not the least diminish that early esteem and sincere admiration with which you inspired me long, long ago. I am Dear Sir Yours very truly, J.K. Paulding.

ALS in ScCleA; variant PC in Aderman, ed., *The Letters of James Kirke Paulding*, pp. 468–470; PEx in Boucher and Brooks, eds., *Correspondence*, pp. 427–428.

From J[OHN] E[WING] BONNEAU

Charleston, So. Ca., Jan[uar]y 25th 1848
My dear Sir, I received on 15th Inst. 26 Bales of your Cotton the quality of which I am sorry to find is very inferior to your crop of 1846. The Cotton is badly prepared and the packages in bad order. The most the Cotton would command now would be about 7¼ cts. I shall not offer them for sale until I am instructed by you to do so, as requested in your letter of 13th ult. With respect yours truly, J.E. Bonneau.

ALS in ScU-SC, John C. Calhoun Papers.

To [John] Nugent, [Washington], 1/28. "I wish you to have the weekly [New York] Herald sent to my son Ja[me]s Ed[ward] Calhoun Jun[io]r, Columbia, S. Carolina." [John Nugent was the Washington correspondent of the *Herald*]. ALS in ScU-SC, John C. Calhoun Papers.

From U. S. WILSON

Greenville, Floyd Co[unty], Ind., 28 Jan. 1848
Sir, I have no confidence in this government, & I have much reason, individually, to say this. The legitimate object of all government is *to protect good men from rascals*, & that government, whatsoever the form may be, which fails to accomplish this grand object, so far from being desirable, may truly be said to be a grievous burthen, if not a judgment & a curse, upon the people. The government which does not fulfil its lawful purpose, *only works oppression*. I admit there are comparative degrees in the unlawful work, while it may be justly

said, by way of comparison, also, that the worst of such governments
is the Devil's Head Quarters. The most humble & the poorest person
in the community has a right to be protected; if he is not, his government is in fault which oppresses him or allows him to be oppressed, & the time of retribution will surely come. I would rather
live under an absolute monarchy, with security as to the rights &
privileges of a citizen but especially those of a Christian, than in a
republic where ["each" *interlined*] man makes his own laws, using his
own right arm to enforce them; where almost every man is an infidel,
under the dominion of his lusts & passions, licentious, & in practice
a tyrant; where Christians, honest men, & the weak, are left at the
mercy of the wicked & vile, victims, without protection, without a
shield, the objects of insult, mockery, reproach, & detraction; where
liberty is but a name, *nominis umbra*; where Christianity itself is almost universally a *mere profession*, a shadow, existing chiefly in the
imagination. If I must live under tyranny, I prefer *one* tyrant to a
thousand. Yes, I would rather live under the government of *one
virtuous man, a Christian prince*, than under the tyranny & oppression of *ten, twenty, or a hundred, thousand or million of devils in the
shape of men.* Men who are governed by their lusts & passions, &
who are *not*, therefore, *capable of governing themselves*, are *not fit
to govern others.* In the conduct of the people of the Jews, the Roman
Soldiers, & the rabble, towards our Divine Saviour, generally, ["generally" *canceled*] but particularly at the time immediately before, at,
& immediately after, his crucifixion, before Pilate & afterwards, as
related by St. Matthew & the other Evangelists, there is the strongest
& most conclusive argument, with Christians & good men, *against the
fantasies, deceits, & wickedness, of all popular governments!* ! ! What
a mournful & gloomy picture presents itself, when we take a view
of the *levelling system* which is put in practice by the people of this
republic, whose will does not acknowledge the obligation even of a
Divine law, who reject all superiority whatsoever, & whose boundless
self-conceit exalts them above God, while it makes gods of themselves! ! ! As Cain envied & murdered his brother, the impious & profligate infidels & reprobates of this country, stimulated by pride, self-
conceit, envy, & other unbridled passions, & availing themselves of the
facilities afforded by the actual licentiousness of the democratic system of government, are carefully endeavouring, with indefatigable
zeal & by all means in their power, to establish an *equality* among
men: this is done by destroying all moral & religious distinction; by
throwing down any rampart which good men by law may build up for
the protection of faith, piety, virtue, ["&" *interlined*] chastity, against

infidelity, impiety, wickedness, & lust; &, especially, by scoffing & mocking, & by elevating themselves, by the help of female infidelity & female influence, to the rank & level of good men & Christians! The theory, so fashionable in modern times, that *all men are by nature equal*, is only true in part. All men have a natural right to live when they come into the world, &, when they grow up, to make their living by some honest means proper & suitable for the purpose. Those who deny me the means of making my living honestly by my own industry, or take the bread I have made from my mouth, might be accessary to my death. All men, then, have an *equal* right to select & establish some kind of government & laws for the protection & security of life, property, & honest pursuits. Again, all men have, that is, every man has, a natural right to believe in God, & to worship & serve Him accordingly. Here is *equality*. But, can it be said that the monster, the deformed person, the blind, the deaf, the dumb, who are so by nature, are on an *equality* with those who, from their birth, grow up to be beautiful & well proportioned, samples of symmetry, who can see & hear & speak? Is the natural idiot on an *equality* with him who is endowed with a good understanding? Not so; nor is the unlearned man on an *equality* with the learned; nor is he who travels the road which brings him to the gallows, on an *equality* with him who lives a Saint & dies a martyr; nor is the Irish Apostate, nor the Prussian Heretic, who cries, *Donnez moi du pain*, but does not ask for the *Bread of Life*, on an *equality* with the humble & devout believer who is hungry for this heavenly bread.

In this war with Mexico, in which some that are called Catholics unite with Protestants in afflicting & distressing others that are likewise called Catholics, how are Christians to be benefitted? Who are the enemies of the Holy Church of God but those who fight against her? Such are all Apostates, (who do not even help the church by prayers) Heretics, & Infidels. This war will continue, perhaps, until a strong *European Alliance* will be formed against this country; the result of this would doubtless be *the downfall of this government*. Terrible will be the *crash*, when that *licentiousness* which is called liberty, & that *popular tyranny, injustice, & oppression*, which are cloaked under the *democratic system*, will have an end. God protects his people & punishes their enemies: those who do not believe this, will believe it when it is too late. See Josephus' Antiquities of the Jews, book the 4th, chapter the 6th, & part of the 7th; which is testimony in aid of the Sacred History in Numbers, chapters 25 & 31; ["as introductory" *interlined*] to which, chapters 22, 23, 24 of the same book, may be read with advantage ["as introductory" *canceled*].

The particular history to which I refer you, begins with *Balaam*, & ends with the *war with the Midianites*. The history of Josephus is more in detail than the Sacred History in regard to some things, & less so in regard to others. By a careful perusal of this history, which is most remarkable, you will discover what *lust* is & what it does. You will see how men can be seduced from their religion & their God; yea, & be made to worship the false gods of women. That *beastly lust*, which results from infidelity & also occasions it, & which is so universally prevalent in this country, among all classes, that men seem to imagine they come into the world, like the hog or the horse, merely to eat, drink, & sleep, & propagate the species, will take a most active part, doubtless, in overthrowing that *democracy* by which it is even fostered & promoted. Between *lust* & such a revolution, while the congruity may be denied, the connexion, also, may not, at first sight, be visible; yet, the effect may be traced to the cause, with as much accuracy & certainty, perhaps, as the war with the Midianites & their total defeat, may be traced to their proper cause. *Lust* is a great & a grievous sin; it is the cause of many other great & grievous sins, to say nothing of innumerable smaller offenses; &, consequently, it must constantly produce many & great evils & sad calamities! When men's minds are so much occupied by *lust*, that they can hardly conceive a thought, utter a speech, or perform an action, without its defiling & corrupting influence, would it be wonderful if they should be utterly denied the previlege & opportunity, as they have not the capacity & qualifications, to govern themselves?

The government, although not old, is in the decline of life: it has evident marks of decay, if it is not already rotten: *ergo*, it must fall. There is no virtue in the government, because there is no virtue in the people. Among the absurdities & enormities of that *democracy* which bears rule in this country, that system of infidelity which would place rogues & rascals, free-booters & cut-throats, upon a *level* with good men & Christians, of which I have spoken, is not the least nor the least detestable! To think of it shocks the senses, astounds the powers of reason, &, were it possible, would strike terror & dismay into the hearts of Christians! ! Yet, all this is for the sake of that *liberty* which presumes to do what it pleases, right or wrong, good or bad, lawful or unlawful, murder, robbery, slander, every thing else. This is not liberty but licentiousness, wickedness, depravity, crime. There is, in fact, no liberty where there is no restraint. That is not liberty ["but *licentiousness*, wickedness" *canceled*] which Christianity & reason both condemn. Therefore, while rational liberty, Christian liberty, may be good for men, licentiousness, wickedness, impiety, depravity, crime, are fit only for devils. Is not the political press in the U. States, instead of being the palladium of liberty, *the devil's slop-tub* for beasts?

If Texas once belonged to the U. States, & had not been ceded away by treaty, there could have been no necessity for the *annexation* of it, nor for a war of conquest to secure it. Should it not be ascertained by whose agency this was done, if by any person's in particular? Should not a regular inquiry be instituted for that purpose, & all the facts be made known to the public? Respectfully, Your humb[le] Serv[an]t, U.S. Wilson.

ALS in ScCleA.

From SARAH MYTTON MAURY

Liverpool, Jan[ua]ry 29th, 1848

My dear Mr. Calhoun, The accompanying pamphlet was put into my hands a few days ago; with a remark that the conversation detailed in page 32 had been held with you.

This pamphlet is read by some Abolitionists in this country, and as I think it very desirable that your sentiments should not be misunderstood, I have enclosed it for your examination. The pamphlet altogether is a very insignificant production, and were it not that "Massachusetts Junior" claims connection with your name, I should have thought it quite beneath your notice.

I have snapped a small blood vessel in my right eye, which makes it an imprudence to write; therefore I will only add that I anxiously watch your political success, and am ever, my dear Mr. Calhoun, your faithful and affectionate friend, Sarah Mytton Maury.

ALS in ScCleA. NOTE: The pamphlet by "Massachusetts Junior" was entitled *A Plea for the South* (Boston: S.P. Seaman, 1847), apparently an abolitionist treatise. It contained a reported conversation with "a southern gentleman" on racial prejudice in the North. The "gentleman," whose description excludes the possibility that he was Calhoun, said that Northern States had deprived Negroes of rights out of racial prejudice while they granted the same rights "to the lower orders of Irish and Dutch, their inferiors both in intellect and morality. . . ."

From Jos[eph] W. Lesesne

Mobile, January 30th 1848

My dear Sir, I am very much obliged to you for the volume you were kind enough to send me; but still more so for the copy of your masterly and *best* speech. I have never felt more completely satisfied by any argument out of ["the" *canceled*] pure mathematics, than I have been by this of yours and I do most earnestly pray that your veiws may be adopted. I can not see how those of the [James K. Polk] Administration can stand up against the herculean assaults that they are now undergoing. If it were not for the party which the war has built up by executive patronage there would be little difficulty in carrying through your veiws. But this is one of the horrid consequences of war—that it always breeds a mercenary host who clamor for its continuance.

I should have written you long since in relation to the establishment of the Paper; but soon after I received your last letter I accepted the office of Chancellor from the Governor [Reuben Chapman], and have since been elected by the Legislature; and the duties of the office called me almost immediately from home and have scarcely given me a moment of entire leisure, until now. I, however, became well satisfied that little could be done to promote the enterprise in Alabama. Some of our friends who ought to have been most active in its favor, and were so at first, ["dropp" *canceled*] abandoned it altogether in the end. You can probably conjecture the cause—if you have seen the answers of [Dixon H.] Lewis to certain questions propounded to him ["on" *interlined*] the night before his election [as Senator], by half a dozen Hunker democrats. [John A.] Campbell tells me that he has explained to you the circumstances of that election—and I can only add that I look upon the conduct of Lewis as the most disgraceful piece of political perfidy, truckling and time serving that has ever fallen under my observation—such as sinks him utterly below the confidence of Gentlemen. I took great interest in his election before I reached Montgomery; but I do not for a moment hesitate to say, that on the morning when the election took place, if I had had a vote to give it would have been cast for [William R.] King; who with all his emptiness and weakness behaved at least like a gentleman and told the truth. You have doubtless remarked also the recent proceedings of a Democratic meeting ["at Montgomery" *interlined*] composed principally of members of the Legislature, at which [William L.] Yancey acted a very conspicuous part. This is part of the *res gentae* of the Senatorial election; and our friends at

Montgomery in whom I had the greatest confidence have no doubt been persuaded or constrained to this unmanly and insincere course in order to give weight and respectability to the course persued with the Hunker party by Lewis. He has thus stabbed us in the most vital part. *Yancey's* course did not disappoint me—I was prepared for it. But I confess I am greatly surprised and deeply mortified at the Course of the *Elmores* [that is, John A. and William A. Elmore], and some few other old, and, as I thought, tried friends at Montgomery. Our Legislature, however, so sadly lacks both talent and character that it is not surprising that a few selfish intriguers have been able to turn the current to suit themselves.

I strongly suspect that another element has ["largely" *interlined*] entered into these proceedings of ["the" *canceled and* "Mr. Lewis and his" *interlined*] friends ["of Lewis" *canceled*]—and that he is looking for a nomination for the vice presidency on a Northern or northwestern ticket. If such be the case I sincerely hope, as I beleive, that he will be do[o]med to disappointment. When the South begins thus to bid for Northern votes ["it is high time" *canceled*] our safety is at an end.

Possibly I may speak to[o] strongly of Lewis' conduct—possibly I may do him injustice. I hope it may turn out so. But I fear he is utterly lost to us and what still more concerns him—to himself.

I beleive the happiest event that could happen to the country would be the overthrow of both the political parties that now distract it. The leaders of both of them are utterly selfish. But how to effect this object is the great problem. I confess I can not silence my conscientious scruples against attempting it by the nomination of Gen[era]l [Zachary] Taylor, and I can not doubt that the evils resulting from his election like those that sprang from Gen[era]l [Andrew] Jackson's elevation to the Presidency would be greater than any ["security" *canceled*] equivalent benefits ["we should realize" *interlined*] in the shape of security to the South. Taylor if elected will inevitably fall into the hands of the whigs and his want of experience in public affairs, ["&" *interlined*] of information ["and" *canceled*] would I fear as in the case of Gen[era]l Jackson lead him into great errors.

I heartily concur with you in your veiws with regard [to] the mischi[e]vous effects of the Caucus system. But I fear that it has become too firmly fixed in affections and the philosophy of parties in this country ever to be overthrown until some great and signal national calamity results from it. I shall never give my consent express or implied to the action of a Caucus in advance, but I can

157

readily see that a conscientious man fully sharing my feelings on this subject might be greatly embarrassed by committing himself in advance to Taylor and afterwards finding, in the nominee of the Baltimore convention, a Republican, in every way, unexceptionable. I should myself feel very painfully the awkwardness of such a position—if for example Mr. [Levi] Woodbury should be nominated— an event I admit not likely to happen—but since the nomination of Mr. [James K.] Polk who can predict what may be the result of the action of ["such" *canceled*] a Baltimore Convention? ["The labour(?) of" *canceled*.] I acknowledge freely that my mind has been sorely troubled and perplexed on this subject. I can not vote for a Whig nominee—and on the other hand I would escape the decrees of that monstrous tribunal that has already overshadowed the Constitution, ["and is fast approaching the institutions of the States" *canceled*] and in effect repealed one of its most salutary provisions. If I can under any circumstances support Taylor it must be as the candidate of the people and without the intervention of Caucuses and conventions. But I shall patiently wait events; and I am very glad that I am in a [judicial] position that not only enables me, but makes it in some measure a duty to do so, and to abstain from any public participation in ["the conven(?)" *canceled*] the movements of parties. You may however, be assured, that I shall always be found in the right place; and that you and our tried friends who still remain proof against the corruptions of the day may always look to me for any cooperation or aid in any thing consistent with the new sphere of duty in which I am acting. Neither the allurements of office nor the possession of its honors shall ever induce me to sell myself to the advocacy of men or measures that I can not approve, or induce me to hold my peace when it is proper that I should speak out my honest sentiments. And I am glad, that poor as our Legislature was in spirit, I was elected against strong opposition without the necessity of concealing a single sentiment in relation either to men or measures. But on the contrary with a distinct and oft-repeated avowal of my opinions whenever the course of conversation afforded an opportunity. Falsehood and hypocrisy are the instruments of cowards, who succeed with them only ["by" *canceled and* "to" *interlined*; "incurring" *changed to* "incur"] the contempt of those who have been deceived or betrayed.

This long and ill looking letter needs an ample apology. Pray do not consider it important enough to waste any time in deciphering its obscurities. We would be pleased to know whether the enterprise of the paper has been altogether abandoned. Very truly Your friend &c, Jos. W. Lesesne.

ALS in ScCleA.

From W[ILLIA]M H. CHASE

[Pensacola, *ca.* Jan. 1848?]
My dear Sir, In adopting your line policy I think I understand that you would embrace also all the important points on the Sea coast of Mexico. The possession of the Castle of S[a]n Juan D'Ulloa and its dependent islands and anchorages is of great importance to the United States.

Previously to the landing of General [Winfield] Scott's army at Vera Cruz, I suggested that, in any negotiation with Mexico resulting after the reduction of S[a]n d'Ulloa, the retention of the Castle and its dependenceis should be insisted upon as a guaranty for the faithful performance of future treaty stipulations.

I trust now that no Treaty will be made that does not secure to us the permanent possession of the Castle and its dependent islands; and that, we shall lose no time in increasing[?] the strength of the castle, and constructing strong works at Sacrificios to command that anchorage.

The castle should be provided with 12 inch Columbiad and the batteries of the main work made bomb proof. Its magazines & store Rooms should be enlarged, so that, three years provisions of men ["and" *interlined*] ammunition could be lodged therein. Whilst at Sacrificios a depot for three years supply of coal should be established.

In connection with this possession the military man will readily perceive how important it *is that no more time be lost in completing the fortifications at Tortugas & Key West*.

A wise policy led Congress some years since to make ample appropriations for the commencement and vigorous prosecution of the Fortifications in the Florida States [*sic*]; and the same policy will, I hope, insure the possession of the Castle of Vera Cruz and its dependencies, and their increase of defence by all the means of art.

The fortified possession of Tortugas, Key West, and S[a]n D'Ulloa leaves no fortified harbor uncontrolled by the U. States within the Gulf of Mexico, save the Havanas. The Gulf then becomes an

159

American Sea, and its control gives power to the U. States to settle *the Cuban question* whenever circumstances may render it necessary.

I think it would be well that the military Committees should enquire into the expediency of the measu[r]es above suggested.

Although the permanent possession of S[a]n Juan D'Ulloa might not ["be" *interlined*] deemed advisable if it were obstructive of peace, the imp[*ms. torn*] of the early completion of the defences in the Florida Straits would not be denied. I urged, three years ago in a report to the War Department, that the works should be commenced & completed *in 3 years.* Three years have elapsed and you will find but little progress made. Congress has constantly given ["what" *canceled*] (nay much more,) what has been asked by the Engineer Department. That Department is not aware of the importance of the rapid prosecution of those Fortifications, and look forward to some quarter of a century to their completion. This should be looked to, and as I am without power save that of suggestion, I can only act in the premises by suggesting [that] $1,000,000 be applied this year to Tortugas & Key West, [and] a declaratory clause be inserted in the Fortification bill to the effect, *that these fortifications should be prosecuted with all possible vigour.* I remain most Respectful[l]y & faithful[l]y Your O[be]d[ien]t S[ervan]t, Wm. H. Chase.

ALS in ScCleA. NOTE: William Henry Chase (1798–1870) was a native of Maine, a grandnephew of John Hancock, and a West Point graduate in 1815. He was for some years the senior Army engineer officer on the Gulf Coast, responsible for building defenses in the area. He resigned from the Army in 1856, having become a prominent citizen of Pensacola. He served as a major general of Fla. state troops in the early days of the Confederacy.

FEBRUARY 1–MARCH 31, 1848

◫

The war was, after all, coming to an end without the escalation that Calhoun had feared. Polk received an unauthorized treaty that had been made by Nicholas P. Trist, and, after some hesitation, he submitted it to the Senate on February 23. On March 10 it was ratified 38 to 14, most of the negatives being cast by Democratic hyperexpansionists. An attempt to attach the Wilmot Proviso to the treaty was rejected 38–15. On the same day that Polk sent the treaty to the Senate, John Quincy Adams collapsed and died in the House of Representatives, a sign perhaps that an era was nearing close. He was fifteen years Calhoun's senior.

A friend from home, Dr. Ozey R. Broyles, reflected a lot of Southern opinion when he wrote on March 3: "We are gratified with the prospect of peace with Mexico, but feel a little restrained in giving it indulgence for the prospect it brings with it, of a war with the Abolitionists."

The administration's expansionist proclivities were still not entirely at an end, and it was necessary for Calhoun to make speeches on March 16 and 17 against a proposal to increase the Army by ten more regiments. These speeches were also a profound examination of Constitutional questions about the powers of the President and of the U.S. in warmaking and in the occupation of foreign territory.

Meanwhile, large events were at work in the world, another portent of changing times. In February there was revolution in France. Louis Philippe fled and a republic was set up. Upheaval soon spread across the Continent. Calhoun spoke on March 30 against resolutions congratulating the French on their revolution. Congratulations should await something much more difficult and doubtful than a revolution—the successful establishment of a durable free and popular government.

◫

"Progress of the American Union," 2/ ——— . This article in the February number of *De Bow's Commercial Review*, written by William Darby, a noted American geographer, described the growth of the Mississippi basin. According to Darby, the population of the trans-Appalachian region had grown "*seven-fold*" in the years 1810 to 1830. The editor prefaced Darby's article by saying that it had been elicited "by a communication to him directed, from the Hon. John C. Calhoun." PC in *De Bow's Commercial Review*, vol. V, no. 2 (February, 1848), pp. 191–196.

From J[AMES] WINSLOW

N. York [City,] 1 Feb[ruar]y 1848

Sir, The undersigned though a native of New England and a decendant directly of the first governor of Plymouth colony [Edward Winslow?] is not however either a protectionist or anti slavery advocate. On the contrary from a personal view of the laboring classes of Europe and the free negroes of the British West indies he is convinced that as a whole, no class of people of this description exist, so happy and comfortable as the slaves of our southern country. Not only is the writer impressed with this opinion—but he has adopted the yet bolder one, that the attempted suppression of the slave trade, as now carried on by several civilized nations, is erroneous and productive of far more injury than benefit to the Africans themselves. Some letters of mine in the New York "Albion" of the last year may have met your view. In those I boldly and in advance of the age advocated the regulation rather than the suppression of the slave trade and proposed that it be legalized under such regulations as now prevail in respect of emigrant ships, whereby a trade that it is impossible to suppress might be so regulated as to afford relief and comfort to the superfluous population of Africa and tend to destroy the custom of sacrificing prisoners in war so long prevalent before the slave trade arose.

It would appear that the British Colonial Secretary in view ostensibly of the decadence of the West India islands, but probably aware of the impossibility of suppressing the slave trade—or perhaps both, gave permission for the exportation of free laborers from such parts of the coast of Africa as lay within the British possessions to the W. India colonies, as passengers & laborers. I do not see that the same privilege can be denied to other nations and who having no possessions on the coast, must naturally select their laborers at large along the shore. As respects Spain, France &c such laborers are likely to be converted into slaves as soon as landed in Brazil, Cuba &c and it may be, that under this facility of providing black labor, new conquests and settlements may be effected by European Powers in the Southerly neighborhood of the U. States. And now, I arrive at my intended suggestion, whether a system of African emigration as proposed by Great Britain might not be useful to our Southern States? If we are to occupy yet more territory in Southern latitudes the earliest desiderata are capital and labor. To retain the markets of Europe for Cotton[,] Rice and Tobacco—to enter them with Sugar & Indigo the lowest cost of production is an essential point. This object is not to be obtained by spreading the slave population of our Southern States over a large space of newly acquired territory—although the value of the slave himself may be increased.

Hence, how far would the prosperity and extension of the United States in general and the weight of the Southern States in particular be promoted, by the introduction of free black laborers, who should be bound for a certain period, to pay the cost of their transit?

I approach a subject capable of so many considerations not in its advocacy, but as one for older and wiser heads to bestow serious reflection upon. No objection that I can see will arise from other nations—these must be founded upon domestic considerations more of which will occur to you as one of our most experienced and upright Statesmen and well versed in Southern interests, than can possibly present themselves to Y[ou]r ob[edient] S[er]v[an]t, J. Winslow.

ALS in ScCleA; PC in Boucher and Brooks, eds., *Correspondence*, pp. 428–429. NOTE: Winslow (1815–1874) was a N.Y. banker. His greatest claim to fame was during the Abraham Lincoln administration when he was active in raising war loans and establishing the national banking system.

From J[OHN] S. BARBOUR

Gadsby's Hotel [Alexandria, Va.,] Feb[ruar]y 4th 1848
My Dear Sir, Many of your friends in Virginia are embarrassed by the rumors which are carrying to the public mind a belief that you are hostile to the present administration. With you those friends gave their aid to the election of the present Chief Magistrate of the Confederacy [James K. Polk].

The principles that brought him into power, and which he

brought with him into power were believed by us all to be the true principles of the Constitution. And in several instances we have seen him steadily and we believe honestly & firmly maintaining them in the face of perplexing difficulties. Under these circumstances a lapse from his support by one so prominent as yourself, has come upon your friends with a surprise that afflicts them with pain.

Upon the war question the stronger impulses of patriotism are naturally with the Country. And these impulses are the more active & vigorous ["because" *canceled*] because its energetic prosecution is looked to as the surest means for its speedy termination—an object within the wish of every lover of humanity. It is quite apparent that faction is lending its influence, to defeat these measures, for purposes on its part, that cannot consort with any of the duties of patriotism.

Measures seem to be retarded, that an influence may be worked out, for the ensuing election of President; the aim & end of which *must be* the overthrow of the party & the principles, which we have always cherished, & in support of which, (to your own fame & the public weal,) you have devoted those abilities that distinguish you.

That perfect wisdom should mark the measures of any human agency, is not to be ["expected" *with several letters canceled and the* "cted" *interlined*] and the most zealous friend of the Executive will not assert a claim to infallibility. It is to the general scope that we must direct a fair & candid scrutiny; & if this be true & comprehensive for right results: forbearance to passing error in minor matters, is the right of the servant; & the duty of the public. No man can draw to himself the titles of an exclusive patriotism, however pure his virtues, nor can he set up *his judgment*, as the standard of infallibility, however exalted his talents. Men *will think*, & it is the misfortune attendant on human imbecility, that suspicion invariably pursues the course of every public man, that is considered to be desultory, and inconsistent. The displeasure this awakens falls not alone on the statesman, (who however guiltless of it,) is drawn within the vortex of distrust. His friends share his fate. The instinct of consistency, is as powerful as any other sentiment, that is imbedded in our nature, and with the multitude it is stronger than in enlightened minds. I have learned from your own authority "that much is to be deferred to party," and that the inclinations of the mind & the persuasions of the sensibilities, should *yield often*, to the impulses of party—unless those impulses [*several words canceled and* "are condemned by the" *interlined*] settled convictions of the judgment. It is to this that I appeal; and if your deliberations are in doubt, as I learned from you; may not the wishes of your friends, be the dust on the balance, & let it preponderate for them. These wishes thus expressed to you have not been the subject or result of *any conversation with any one here.* I have held communication with no one but our friend Gen[era]l [Henry S.?] Foote [Senator from Miss.]. They result entirely from what I learn from home—*from your friends,* tried & true, through many a year of trial, who are unofficed, & unambitious of office, who have nothing to hope & less to fear from any administration. Seductions sometimes lead ["the" *canceled*] astray the highest ambition, from its sternest duties. No such temptations are before those of whom I write, whose great wish is *for the Country* & its best interests, and among these interests, the power and the renown of our trusted leaders, is not the least and to preserve that power & celebrity in our statesmen is among the first of my wishes. It will add to the pain of addressing, you, if one syllable of this letter, give you pain. With anxious & cordial wishes for your welfare, joined to the highest respect & Regard I am y[ou]rs Sincerely, J.S. Barbour.

ALS in ScCleA.

To T[homas] G. Clemson, [Brussels]

Washington, 4th Feb: 1848
My dear Sir, The Steamer just arrived brought your's of the 30th Dec[embe]r, with the others ["from" *canceled*] accompanying it. I received by the Steamer immediately preceeding, your two letters of the 14th of the same month, a day after I had forward[ed] mine to go by her on her return, with letters from home for Anna [Maria Calhoun Clemson], & one or two for yourself, which I had received under cover to be forwarded to you. I also sent you a couple of copies of my speech on my resolutions. I conclude you would be very much surprise[d] & disappointed, on opening mine, to find it was only the latter part of my letter. A few days after it was sent, I was surprised to find in the morning the first sheet of my letter on my Desk in the Senate Chamber. On enquiring, I found that it had been picked up by one of the pages under the desk, where it must have fallen, while I ["was" *interlined*] in the act of putting up the package, without being observed. I immediately dispatched a note to the State Dept. to ascertain, whether the bag containing its dispatches & letters, among which were mine, still remained in the Department, in order, if ["it did" *canceled and* "so" *interlined*] to restore the sheet to its

165

place; but found it had left, & that it was too late to reach the steamer before its departure.

I would now enclose it, but as it contained nothing of importance, I do not deem it worth while.

My speech has had a very wide circulation & the impression is, that it has made a deeper impression than any I ever delivered. It brought to the surface the strong feeling, which had been working below in favour of the conquest & holding as a Province, or annexing all Mexico; and which I can hardly doubt, if not intended, was looked to by the administration, as not an undesirable result. It has done more. It has turned the tide and brought the [Washington, D.C., Daily] Union to a disavowal; but, I fear, that things have gone so far, that it will be found difficult to avoid a result so disasterous, as it would prove, should it occur. It seems, at least, pretty certain, if I had not promptly made the movement, & taken the stand I did, such would have been the result of the war. Strange as it may seem, neither side, had the least conception, that there was any danger of it, when I introduced my resolutions. Both were disposed to regard them, as a mere abstraction, and an unnecessary precaution, but now all take a different view.

The effect has been, to give a new direction to the debate on the supplies of both men & money; and one, on the part of the opposition, far more effecint. It is [*one word canceled and* "making" *interlined*] on their side far ["more" *canceled*] deeper ["impression" *interlined*] on the country, so much so, that nothing short of a treaty, or adopting the plan I suggested, can save the administration, if even that now can. The indication at present is, a disposition on their part to adopt the policy of a defensive line. If nothing else, the financial difficulties will compel them to treat, or fall back.

The Presidential question is of course a leading topick. [Henry] Clay's friends have made great efforts to bring him forward, but, it is said, in quarters which ought to know, without success. My impression still remains, that [Zachary] Taylor will be the Whig, or rather the popular candidate, ag[ai]nst what may be called the Administration Candidate. Who that will be is doubtful. At present the prospect of [Lewis] Cass [Senator from Mich.] would seem to be the most promising.

Your letter by the last Steamer brought your statement of your account. I do not deem it necessary to examine it with care, or to make any remarks now, as I have not ["my" *interlined*] papers to refer to, and as you will return next summer, when the whole, I cannot doubt, may be readily adjusted, & placed on a satisfactory footing.

I enclose a letter to Anna [Maria Calhoun Clemson] from her mother [Floride Colhoun Calhoun].

My health is as good as usual; and I am very happy to learn that you, & she & the children [John Calhoun Clemson and Floride Elizabeth Clemson] are in the enjoyment of such good health, & that ["they" *interlined*] grow & improve so fast.

Give my love to Anna & them, and tell them how happy their Grandfather will be to see them next summer. Your affectionate father, J.C. Calhoun.

ALS in ScCleA; PEx in Jameson, ed., *Correspondence*, pp. 742–743.

From H[ENRY] GOURDIN

Charleston, Feb[ruar]y 4, 1848

My Dear Sir, I have to own rec[eip]t of your favor, but cannot refer to its date as Mr. [Henry W.] Conner has it for perusal. Mr. [Arthur P.] Bagby's resolutions [of 1/25], and Mr. [David L.] Yulee[']s amendments, will be noticed in the Mercury in a day or two.

A report has reached Charleston that Gen[era]l [John A.] Quitman, & Mr. [George M.] Dallas will be the Democratic candidates for President & Vice President. From all I can learn, Gen[era]l Quitman would be ["a" *interlined*] more desirable candidate for us than any one who has yet been named. He was a Nullifier with us in 1832, and this is the best guarantee for his Southern feelings, and his States rights opinions. Mr. Dallas is also the best man we can find in the North after Mr. [Levi] Woodbury. The combination is a good one, and the party who has named them strongly urges their immediate nomination in our State. I do not concur in this move however, and have discouraged it as far as I am concerned. The combination is a good one; but can they be elected? My impression is that the nomination, especially should it be first made in South Carolina, w[oul]d be regarded as a Southern one, and that would be quite sufficient to unite a large portion of every party in the North against it, while in the South, so great is the progress which Gen[era]l [Zachary] Taylor has made in Louisiana, Alabama, & Georgia, that unless he comes out with some declarations which the Southern States cannot stomach, he will carry the South against any party or ticket that can be named. At the same time he ["will" *canceled and* "would" *interlined*] have a much larger vote in the West than Gen[era]l

167

Quitman. However favorable therefore to the nomination suggested, we may be compelled ourselves to support Gen[era]l Taylor to over- throw those of our opponents, who, on the Slave question, are entirely opposed to us, & it would not be wise to place ourselves in a hostile position to him. Besides So. Ca. cannot make the President, and we have consequently nothing to lose by delay, and it would therefore be madness to commit ourselves to any nomination or party. Let others nominate; we will select & decide afterwards, as they may declare themselves.

The nomination to which I have referred comes from Washington. Pray have you heard any thing about it? I have only heard ["it" *interlined*] from one quarter and thus far regard it more as a feeler than any thing else. I am very resp[ectfull]y & truly Your Ob[edien]t S[er]v[an]t, H. Gourdin.

[P.S.] There is little chance of any portion of our people or the press, committing themselves by any hasty nomination. I write the above, but with no apprehension of its being done, however anxious some may be to bring it about. Mr. Yulee [Senator from Fla.] opposes, I understand, the confirmation of the Contract made with ["us by" *canceled*] our Havana Company by the Post Master General. Can you not put him right in the matter[?] The Bill as passed required us to go into St. Augustine, which is impossible, because there is not water on the bar by three to six feet, and if the Post Master had insisted on an impossibility, the enterprize must have been abandoned. Our Florida friend & Mr. T. B[utler] King of the House of Representatives [from Ga.] are most unreasonable, and I do hope that their selfishness in this matter may ["not" *interlined*] be permitted to be exercised to our injury, & the injury of our Port.

ALS in ScCleA; PC in Jameson, ed., *Correspondence*, pp. 1160–1161.

From W[illia]m W. Lea

Nashville, Feb[ruar]y 4th 1848

D[ea]r Sir, Knowing the deep interest you feel in the carrying out the m[a]gnificent scheme of connecting the Atlantic with the Mississippi River, through Tennessee, suggested by you some years since, I take the liberty of sending you the enclosed documents, addressed to the Legislature of Tennessee now in session. This body will adjourn on Monday next after a long session, in which but little has been done. Some few acts passed will, however, redeem it from the charge of having spent a great deal of time and money without any beneficial result to the State. A Bill has passed both houses, lending the credit of the State, by way of endorsement on the bonds of the Companies, for $500,000 to the Nashville and Chat[t]anooga and $350,000 to the Hiwassee, alias Georgia and East Tennessee, Rail Road. This will doubtless enable those works now to progress vigorously, and I have no doubt the former will be extended to the Tennessee River, if they take the route recommended by Engineer Thompson [*sic*; J. Edgar Thomson], in three or four years, and probably to Chat[t]anooga in five years. In the mean time we have obtained a charter for the "Tennessee Central Rail Road", and are going to work under it, with zeal and energy, for the connection of the Mississippi River with this great work. Our charter contains the most favorable provisions that have ever been granted, in the United States, to any enterprise of the kind, and we ["have" *interlined*] every assurance of Legislative aid, two years hence. This being but an extension of the noble works of South Carolina and Georgia to their ultimate destination, we shall also expect aid and cooperation in that quarter. I need suggest nothing to your comprehensive mind in relation to the incalculable benefits that must result to those States as well as to Tennessee, from the completion of this great enterprise.

I received some months since your favour in answer to mine enclosing a copy of the memorial addressed to our Legislature, in behalf of the Central Rail Road, and shall be pleased to hear from you again. Please to address me at Trenton, Tennessee, as heretofore. I hope to have the pleasure of seeing you, in Washington, in the month of May. With the highest respect, I remain, Dear Sir, your ob[edien]t servant, Wm. W. Lea.

[P.S.] You will perceive some typographical errors in the printed documents, the correction of which will readily suggest itself.

ALS with Ens in ScCleA. NOTE: Enclosed are two printed memorials signed "West Tennessee" and addressed to the Tenn. General Assembly. One is entitled "The Central Rail-Road"; it discusses "supplemental facts and statistic calculations" concerning the proposed railroad to link Tenn. with Atlantic ports. The other is entitled simply "To the Members of the Legislature" and discusses the advantages to be gained by linking Southern Atlantic ports to the Miss. River through the Central Railroad.

From W[ILLIAM] T. THOMPSON

Baltimore, Feb. 4, 1848

Dear Sir, When I was in Washington, some two weeks ago, I desired to have some conversation on the subject of the paper which I am now publishing in this city. Believing that you, as a southern man, feel some interest in the success of the only neutral journal devoted to southern interests, I have determined to appeal to you for aid in my present emergency. The course of the Continent, is, I presume, not unknown to you. The stand which it has taken in opposition to the abolition movements of the day, has rendered it obnoxious to a large portion of the northern press and people, who desire to stifle all opposition to the aggressive movements of the north, and has arrayed against it the private and open opposition of the enemies of the south. I have thus far stemmed the current without any direct aid from southern friends, ["but" *canceled*] and though I have succeeded in obtaining a very respectable circulation at the South, I have become involved by my efforts to sustain my position. Rather than submit to the humiliation of a failure, in which, under existing circumstances I feel that the south would necessarily participate, I have determined to seek pecuniary aid.

The Western Continent has now been in existence about two years, and the present income from its subscription list is just about equivalent to its expenses, so that with its present steady increase from subscriptions, I might soon have a living business. But the debt which I have incurred in bringing the paper to its present position is oppressing me, destroying my credit, and must crush my enterprize unless speedy aid is afforded me. I have thought of many plans by which my southern friends might assist me, but the following seems to me the most favorable, viz.—

I propose to borrow, say $4000, at 6 or 7 per cent interest, ["The principal" *interlined*] to be paid say in five years from date of the loan. I propose to secure this ["amount" *interlined*] by a mortgage of the Continent establishment, copyright &c to the lender, or by a good endorser. This arrangement would at once place me upon vantage ground, and secure the permanent prosperity and usefulness of the Continent.

Now Mr. Calhoun, I address you to request that you will give me your influence to ["enable me to" *interlined*] obtain this accommodation, either from some individual or association of gentlemen of your acquaintance. I hope you will not consider my request importunate or presumptuous. Were my individual interests alone involved, I would never think of making such an application. I feel that I have no personal claim upon you or the gentlemen with whom I conversed, in Charleston, in reference to the matter, last fall. But I appeal to you as one whose well known devotion to the rights and interests of the South, enables you to appreciate my motives, and will prompt you to aid my efforts in her behalf, should you deem them worthy.

Unfortunately I know no one in Washington except Senator [James D.] Westcott [of Fla.], to whom to refer you. [Alexander H.] Stephens and [Robert] Toombs [Representatives from Ga.] are my acquaintances, but they are both of them unfriendly to the Continent. Judge [Augustus B.] Longstreet of Georgia is my warm personal friend. Many of your friends in Carolina are well acquainted with the course I have pursued in the Continent, and I am gratified to know that they unanimously (so far as I can learn) approve its tone and character.

I hope, sir, you will excuse the liberty I have taken and that you will attribute my course to the proper motive. I cannot quietly contemplate the taunts and jeers ["of our enemies," *interlined*] which would follow the discontinuance of the Continent; and ["I" *interlined*] feel that with a little pecuniary aid at this time, I could do efficient service to the cause of the South. Will you do me the favor to let me hear from you in reference to this matter at your earliest convenience? I shall wait with anxiety your answer to my request. Very Respectfully Your very ob[edien]t serv[an]t, W.T. Thompson.

ALS in ScCleA. NOTE: An AEU by Calhoun reads "Editor of the Western Con[tinen]t[,] 8th Feb. An[swere]d that I could do nothing." William Tappan Thompson (1812–1882) was a native of Ohio, had been an assistant to Westcott in the Fla. territorial government, and had been associated with Longstreet's newspaper in Augusta, Ga. He apparently continued to publish the Baltimore *Western Continent* until 1850, when he returned to Georgia. By 1848 Thompson had already published three volumes of the "Major Jones" stories which were his greatest claim to fame.

ANNOUNCEMENT by Calhoun and Others

[Washington, February 5, 1848]
Lectures on the Connexion between Religion and Learning. The Rev. Dr. [James M.] Mathews, late Chancellor of the University of New York, at the request of several distinguished gentlemen of that

city, has been engaged for some time past in preparing various courses of Lectures on the harmony between Science and the Christian Religion, with the object of vindicating and illustrating the truth of Christianity. He has delivered several of them, not only in New York, but in other cities, and with great satisfaction to the numerous and intelligent audiences who have attended them.

The obvious importance of such lectures, maturely prepared, has induced many to express a wish for their delivery in this city; and the undersigned have much pleasure in stating that Dr. Mathews has kindly agreed, so far as it may be in his power, to comply with the request made to him on the subject. The nature and object of the lectures render the Lord's day the most fitting season for their delivery; and the first lecture will be delivered in the Hall of the House of Representatives on Sunday morning next, at the usual hour, accompanied by the usual devotional exercises. [Signed:] John Q[uincy] Adams, H[enry] Clay, Thomas H. Benton, R[obert] J. Walker, Lewis Cass, J[ohn] Macpherson Berrien, J[ohn] J. Crittenden, J.C. Calhoun, R[obert] B[arnwell] Rhett, P[atrick] W. Tompkins, George P. Marsh, Fred[erick] A. Tallmadge, W[illiam] B. Maclay, James M. Wayne, Samuel Nelson, John McLean, Levi Woodbury, Daniel Webster, D[aniel] S. Dickinson, Willie P. Mangum, Rob[er]t C. Winthrop, Thomas Corwin, W[illiam] L. Dayton, E[lisha] Embree, James Dickson, D[avid] Wilmot.

PC in the Washington, D.C., *Daily National Intelligencer*, February 5, 1848, p. 3. NOTE: The *Daily National Intelligencer*, February 7, 1848, p. 1, reported that Mathews's lecture was presented "yesterday morning" and that "amongst the densely crowded audience were noticed President [James K.] Polk and his lady, several members of the Cabinet, Senators, and Members of Congress."

From E D W [A R] D M. G L E N N

Rio de La Vaca[,] near Texana, Texas [Feb. 5, 1848]
Respected Sir: I have just been reading & re-reading your Speech, (or extracts from it) delivered in the Senate of the U.S. on the 4th January 1848—the views, sentiments & arguments of which have made so deep an impression on my mind, that, I must beg your pardon, for requesting you to enclose, if at all convenient, to my address, at Texana, your full speech on that occasion, & the one or more speeches to which you refer as containing your views and arguments upon, & against the Mexican War. I know, as you say, you have nothing to

"gain" even should you be elected President. At least, it could not add anything[?], to your merits, or your patriotism, but allow me to say it is an event which many of our *truly good* citizens devoutly pray for—and for one, I believe it will occur, because the pure, and disinterested ought, & must, in the natural course of things, receive their reward. It is true, you say in your speech, that good constitutions, or forms of Govt. depended upon, or were the result of accident, or some peculiar conjunction of circumstances, rather than on the previous decisions of of [*sic*] the human mind. The idea to me is new but true & striking—in a word—even the garbled extracts I have seen in papers, have so interested me in your though[t]s on that singular question that I have *dared* to request you, to forward it to me. I was born & bred on the Bank of Enoree, Laurens District, and your name & publick services are associated with my earliest recollections. And, Sir, when I read your declaration, in your place, that you were an "old man" that your views were, perhaps, antiquated—that you stood among strangers—and above all, when you announced the solemn warning to the Senate, & the country, that the day of retribution would come for the er[r]ors & mistakes of the Govt. if it should persist in its unhallowed conquests—I confess that my heart sunk within me, & I felt for the first time ["the" *canceled*] apprehension for our institutions.

I beg you to excuse me for thus writing to you, for I am no public man, or politician, but an humble cultivator of the soil—and worshiper of senatorial independence. Very truly & respectfully, Edwd. M. Glenn.

ALS in ScCleA. NOTE: This letter is undated, but the content places it in 1848 and the postmark is 2/5.

From JOHN HENRY, [former Representative from Ill.]

Jacksonville Illi[nois,] Feb[r]uary 5th 1848
Dear Sir, I have just read your late Speech on the Resolution in relation to the prosecution of the Mexican war. I am well aware that you are much troubled with communications, from dif[f]erent parts of the union. Your manly course in this matter in what I conceive to be purely for the best interest of this Republick, is the appology I make for troubling you with a few lines. That you may know some-

thing of the writer, I will merely state that I was elected from this District, to fill the vacancy occasioned by the Resignation of Col. [Edward D.] Baker. My time was short, only haveing about four weeks to serve. I promised myself to call and see you while there and cultivate a personal acquaintance with you, but you seemed allways to be so much engaged, and me a stranger that I neglected to do so. I have ever since regret[t]ed it very much indeed. I went to Washington like thousands of others in the United States, with wrong views and some predjudice as to your real position as a Statesman. Nothing affords me more pleasure than to change my views of a man, when I am ["covinced" *changed to* "convinced"] that he is governed by honest Statesman like views.

I had the pleasure of standing in the Senate Chamber last Feb-[r]uary, and hearing your Speech on the present war. I distributed 300 Copies of them in this District, which were well received, and made you many friends. I ["had" *canceled*] heard of the miserable attack that [Hopkins L.] Turney of Tennessee, made on ["you" *inter-lined*]. Your defence on that occasion divested me of all predjudice that I had entertained towards you as a Statesman.

Your defence on that occasion satisfied me that you had been actuated by higher motives than mear party opinions. Your late Speech has confirmed me in that belief. I hope you will place me on the list amongst your friends. If you have a few Copies to spare (I mean your late Speech) send them to me for distribution. I hope you will not think I desire to flatter you. I think I know the Statesman to whom I am writing. If your time would permit nothing would afford me more pleasure than to receive a few lines from you at any time. I remain your sincere friend, John Henry.

ALS in ScCleA.

From J[OHN] S. BARBOUR

Gadsby's [Tavern, Alexandria, Va.]
Sunday morning [February 6, 1848]

My Dear Sir, I did not receive your note until after dark of the last evening, and of course too late to fulfil the request it made for a call on you between one & four o'clock. The tone of the note makes me uneasy. You will not think that I have any purpose in view, but that which my letter [of 2/4] indicates by its terms. And least of all will you suppose that I have any wish to draw from you any expression of opinion, that is to be used for any other object than the perusal of my two sons now in Richmond [John S. Barbour, Jr., and James Barbour], one in the Legislature & the other a Delegate to the Democratic convention about to meet in that City. I know they wish to uphold you against all & any misrepresentation. They must also maintain their own consistency as friends of this administration. Many of their political opinions they have derived from you, and they find the task both difficult & painful to defend you & preserve themselves. But I was not without the hope, that if your own judgement deliberated in doubt on the measures now before the Senate for the support of the war & the objects we all have in view, (a speedy peace), that the wishes of your friends might have some influence, however light.

You will probably recollect your letter to me immediately preceding your determination to return to the Senate, some what in these words[,] that in your return to the Senate, you wished it known that your "object was not the presidency, but to perform your duties to the Country. To support the administration whenever you could do it consistently with your principles. To avoid war if war could be avoided, consistently with the rights & Honor of the Country—if war ["not" *canceled and* "could" *interlined*] not be avoided, then to use your exertions in calling forth all the energies of the Country for ["its support" *interlined*], and if you *should differ* with the administration, to do so in moderation & in kindness."

On that letter one of my Children wrote a communication for the [Richmond] Enquirer & the Fred[ericksbur]g Recorder a copy of which was sent you setting forth these views—and on these grounds my sons have both vindicated & defended you. It is due to our ancient friendship to speak frankly to you, if I speak at all and to add that your friends, do not see the consistency of any course of opposition to the war measures now under deliberation with the views expressed by you in the letter of Oct[obe]r 1845.

It was to this point that I wished to call your attention, besides expressing my anxious wish that the doubts you freely expressed to me, whether you would or would not support the war measures, might be resolved in their favour.

I hope that this hasty & explanatory note may displace any cause for misconstruction which you may have discerned in my letter.

In great haste & with Sincere Regard y[ou]r friend, J.S. Barbour.

N.B. My ["pen" *canceled and then interlined*] is so bad I can with difficulty use it.

ALS in ScCleA. NOTE: Barbour addressed this to Calhoun at "Mrs. Reads." This letter, undated except for "Sunday morning," has been supplied a date from its apparent relationship to Barbour's letter of 2/4 above.

To [FRANCIS] LIEBER, [Columbia, S.C.]

Washington, 6th Feb. 1848

My dear Sir, I have not seen Mr. [Richard] Cobden's speech to which you refer in your note of the 21st Jan[uar]y. Should I receive a copy, or find it in any papers, I will enclose it to you.

I restricted my speech of which you speak so kindly to the great object of cutting loose from Mexico & her concerns. That to my mind, is so great an[d] urgent, that all other considerations are as nothing. I am happy to say, that I think, the prospect of doing so, is not so gloomy as it was. I see symptoms, which induces me to believe, that the people are begin[n]ing to recover from the intoxicating dose of glory, & to come to their senses.

As to the canal or ship Chan[n]el between the Atlantick & the Pacifick, I am not sanguine as to its early execution, nor am I inclined to think, that its advantages will be so great as is generally believed; and certainly, not so much so, as to impede our extrication from Mexico & its affairs.

I send by the Mail that takes this the annual Treasury report. Yours truly, J.C. Calhoun.

ALS in CSmH, Francis Lieber Papers.

From Jo[SEPH] PICKENS

Eutaw Alabama, 6th January [*sic*; Feb.] 1848

Dear Sir, By the last mail, I was much gratafied to receive your speech [of 1/4] in pamphlet form, which you had the kindness to forward me, and for this mark of kindness I thank you, and shall be very thankfull to receive any thing from you at any time. Your Speech I had read in the Intel[l]igencer which paper I take, and I am pleased to say to you that every sentiment and views in that speech meats my entire approbation and that of every Whig friend that I have conversed with without one solitary exception. Some of the Old Hunkers hear don[']t like it so very well thinks you rather indapendant.

I have from the first thought that the war might have been avoided if propper prudence had been use[d; "by" *interlined*] Mr. [James K.] Polk. I think he lacks the *bump* of of [*sic*] Caution if nothing ["elss"(?) *canceled*] else.

I have no hesitation in believing that the President violated the Constitution knowingly and willfully in rushing us into this uncalled for and unnatural war with Mexico, and if his acts are allowed to go unrebuked the Constitution is a perfect dead letter.

In thus believing I could not vote him either men or money to carry on the war, only so much money to march the armey out of Mexican territory to Corpus Christie if you please—and then treat for boundary. We may then have a permanent peace and not untill then, can we expect any thing permanent.

It has always been a sourse of much grattification for me to agree with you, as I do now on this Mexican War and its management, as also your entire course on the Oregon question, and I hope ever to see so going for Country in preference to the dictation of a party. We are all in good health. Very Respectfully, truly your friend, Jo. Pickens.

ALS in ScCleA; variant PC in Boucher and Brooks, eds., *Correspondence*, p. 419. NOTE: This letter was postmarked in Eutaw, Ala., on 2/8. Joseph Pickens (1791–1853) was the last child of Gen. Andrew Pickens and Rebecca Calhoun Pickens and thus a distant cousin of Calhoun.

W[ILLIA]M EVELEIGH to Calhoun and Others

[Statesburgh, S.C., Feb. 7, 1848]

To the twelve Tribes scattered abroad, greeting

D[ea]r Brethren, Being myself a Jew I feel great concern on your account when I consider the great danger to which we are exposed by the temptations of the enemy, who is now making his last & greatest effort. He is enticing us by all the allurements of pride, of power, & of wealth to seduce us from the standard of our King; offering us the honours & glory of this world. Let me, then, exhort you to be upon the watch. To remember, that, if we leave the laws of our God, there is no such thing as a standard of right & wrong, of honour & glory among men. That which is considered by one people to be right &

honourable, is regarded by another as the reverse, & yet the enemy entices them all by the p[h]antasm of honour & glory. How clearly is this fact manifested in the scene exhibitted in Jalapa on the twenty fourth day of Nov[embe]r last, when the bodies of the two Mexican officers, who had been shot by order of [Winfield Scott] the American General, for the infamous crime of violating their parole, were buried with all the honours, both civil & military, which the people of Jalapa could confer on them. Here the very act which we consider to be most infamous, the Mexicans regard to be a "deed of noble daring." "Lord, who shall abide in thy tabernacle? Who shall dwell in thy holy hill? He that walketh uprightly, & worketh righteousness, & speaketh the truth in his heart. He that back biteth not with his tongue, nor dost evil to his neighbour, nor taketh up a reproach against his neighbour. In whose eyes a vile person is contemned, but he honoureth them that fear the Lord. He that sweareth to his own hurt, & changeth not. He that putteth not out his money to usury, nor taketh a reward against the innocent. He that doeth these things shall never be moved." But the people of Mexico honoured the bodies of those officers. Poor fellows! They were insensible. They could neither see nor hear the honours & praises confer[r]ed upon them. Perhaps, if General [Robert] Patterson had lent the people of Jalapa a few pieces of cannon, their war might have roused them from the dead, as Cortes roused the people of Mexico to a sense of duty at Cholula. Then they would have seen that the only "deed of noble daring", which was performed among them, was done by the woman who was killed when giving drink to her wounded enemies. She fell in the act but she fell to rise to immortal honour, while those who fell in the violation of the laws of rectitude, will rise to shame & everlasting contempt. [*Marginal interpolations:* "15 Ps."; "12 ch. Dan."]

How clearly are the truth & judgment of our God manifested in the history of America! "Thou shalt have no other Gods before me; Thou shalt not make to thee any graven image, or the likeness of any thing ["that is" *interlined*] in heaven above, or that is in the earth beneath, or that is in the water under the earth. Thou shalt not bow down thy self to them, nor serve them; for I the Lord thy God am a jealous God, visiting the inquity of the fathers upon the children, unto the third & fourth generation of them that hate me, & showing mercy unto thousands of them that love me, & keep my commandments." Count the number of human victims sacrificed in the idolatrous Temples in the capital & other cities of Mexico. The thousands of people butchered by Cortes & the Spaniards. They slew them & why? What wrong had they done either to Cortes or the

Spaniards? None. But there were gold & pearls full in their view; & military fame. But it was the fame of the Eagle destroying a nest of mice to come at the serpent. "O Lord, deliver our soul from the wicked, which is thy sword; from men which are thy hand, O Lord, from men of the world which have their portion in this life."

Cortes & the Spaniards took possession of Mexico: & they & their posterity, in their several generations, have enjoyed the fruits of their labour for three score years & ten up to the present time. Their Cathedrals glitter with gold & golden images. See now the cities which they had taken from the natives, falling into the possession of the American army with the loss of thousands of their people. The blood of Montezuma, & of Gautemozin, & their people cries aloud against them. "The way of the just is uprightness; thou, most upright, dost weigh the path of the just. Yea, in the way of thy judgments, O Lord, have we waited for thee. The desire of our soul is to thy name, & to the remembrance of thee." For "thy judgments are true, & righteous altogether." [*Marginal interpolation:* "19 Ps., 26 ch. Isa."]

But what have the Mexicans done to us that we should invade their territory? The President of the United States [James K. Polk] tells us of the many wrongs which the government of Mexico, & the people have done to the people of the United States. But he tells us that these wrongs had been settled to the mutual satisfaction of both parties. The Mexican Minister complains of acts of injustice done them by the citizens of the United States in aiding the Texans with men, arms & ammunition. The American Minister at Mexico, & the Secretary of State admit the facts; but justify them upon the ground that Texas is an independent government; & say, that the Mexican Minister cannot but understand that the United States do not regard Texas as still being an integral part of the Mexican Republic. But the American ["Minister" *canceled and* "Secretary" *interlined*] cannot but understand that the Mexican government do not regard Texas as being an independent state. Yea, he cannot but understand that the government of the United States did not regard her as being absolutely such—& that the government of the United States regarded her as being in a state of warfare with Mexico. This is evident from the words of President Polk, of the Secretary, & of the Minister at Mexico. The President says, in his Message 1846, that when the Texians had made early application to be received into the union, the government refused to receive them "untill it should be manifest to the whole world that the reconquest of Texas by Mexico was impossible." This is a plain & fair admission, that notwithstand the government of the United States had acknowledged the independence of Texas for commercial purposes, yet they did not consider her, ["yet they did not consider" *canceled*] as being absolutely independent of ["Texas" *changed to* "Mexico"]. If the government of the United States regarded Texas as absolutely independent, why did they refuse to admit her into the union upon the principle assigned by the President? If she was absolutely independent, both parties had the right to act as they pleased in the matter; & the reasons which induced the government to receive her into the union in 1844 existed in 1837. But the government refused then to receive her untill "it should be manifest to the whole world that the reconquest of Texas by Mexico was impossible." The government of the United States, therefore did ["not" *interlined*] regard Texas as being absolutely independent, & consequently they must have considered her as an integral part of the Mexican Republic, in rebellion against the government. That they considered her to be in a state of warfare with Mexico in the years 1841 & 1842 is plain from the words of Mr. [Waddy] Thompson & Mr. [Daniel] Webster. Mr. Thompson says, "within the last six months two armed schooners, built in the United States, & known to be intended expressly for the Texian war, were permitted to leave our ports." Mr. Webster says, "on a recent occasion, complaint was made by the representatives of Texas, that an armament was fitted out in the United States for the service of Mexico against Texas. Two vessels of war it was alledged, built or purchased in the United States, for the use of the government of Mexico, & well understood as intended to be employed against Texas, were equipped & ready to sail from the waters of New York. The case was carefully inquired into, official examination was made, & legal counsel invoked. It appear[e]d to be a case of great doubt: but Mexico was allowed the benefit of that doubt, & the vessels left the United States with the whole or a part of their cargo actually on board." Now it is evident from what is said above that the authorities of the United States did consider Texas & Mexico to be in a state of warfare in the years 1841 & 1842: & that the declaration of Mexico of her design to assert her claim to Texas by military force was no idle threat. The representatives of Texas had lodged their complaint. The complaint was legally inquired into; & the case found to be doubtful, & the Mexicans allow[e]d the benefit of the doubt. Mr. Webster does not tell us what gave rise to that doubt; & being unacquainted with the cause, I can only judge from general principles. Now if Texas & Mexico stood precisely in the same relation to the United States, both being independent Powers at war with each other, then, it is evident that the equipment of those vessels, & their departure from New York by the permission of the United States' authorities was a violation of the law of nations, our relation to both parties being equally friendly. I know of no circumstance of the case as stated either by Mr. Thompson or Mr. Webster, which could create a doubt as to the unlawfulness of the case as it regards Texas. But if the government of the United States regarded Texas as still being a part of the Mexican ["government" *canceled*] Republic in rebellion against her government, not having sufficiently established ["their" *canceled and* "her" *interlined*] independence, then, the doubt as to the validity of her claim is easily seen. In this respect she had no separate existence from Mexico, & therefore, the vessels fitted out, & sent to the service of Mexico was no just cause of complaint—neither the vessels, the men, the military stores, nor any part of their cargo of whatever description, could have been considered as contraband, because they were not to be employed by Mexico against any power with whom the United States were at peace. Surely it is not an unlawful commerce for one nation to trade with another in articles of war, when the nations so trading are at peace with all other nations. Hence it is, I presume, that Mexico was allowed the benefit of the doubt. But it clearly proves that the government of the United States did not regard Texas as absolutely independent of Mexico—altho' they had for commercial purposes, acknowledged her independence. For if they had so considered her, the permission of those vessels to depart from the United States would have been an act of injustice towards her. But Mr. Webster says, the government will not act unjustly towards her neighbours. The government, therefore, regarded Texas as a part of the Mexican Republic, in rebellion against her government.

"Public Meetings"—Any assemblage of the people with the avowed purpose of violating the laws of the country, & consequently of the laws of nations, which are a part of those laws, is an insurrection, & the authorities of the country are bound to suppress it.

"If a regular military expedition is fitted out, then, it is not only our right, but our high duty to prevent it." Whether the rendezvous be at Charleston, Washington, New Orleans, or any city or place in Texas, it is the duty of the authorities of the country to arrest any person or persons, whether "one, ten, a hundred, or a thousand, the principle is the same," who shall be found on their way to such rendezvous. "Contraband goods." The penalty of confiscation was not intended to justify the neutral nation in authorizing such trade upon submitting to the penalty, but to aid her in enforcing the laws of neutrality upon her citizens or subjects. "Vattel says, "Recourse is had to the expedient of confiscating all contraband goods that we can seize on, in order that the fear of loss may operate as a check on the avidity of a gain, & *deter* the merchants of neutral countries from supplying the enemy with such commodities."

Now, my brethren, I have said, that I know not the cause of the doubt alluded to by Mr. Webster, in the case of the two vessels which left New York for the service of Mexico. But I do know, that, the eye of our God, who ruleth over the destiny of nations as well as of individuals, is upon the truth. He sees through all fallacies & knows whether we act contrary or not to the conviction of our understanding & conscience. We shall all be judged by him, who has said, "Wo unto them that seek deep to hide their counsel from the Lord, & their works are in the dark, & they say, who seeth us, & who knoweth us." [*Marginal interpolation*: "1 ch. Rev., 29th ch. Isa."]

While speaking of the gold & silver mines, & the pearl fisheries of California, & the great value which the possession of the territory would be to the United States, Mr. Thompson says "That our language & laws are destined to pervade this continent, I regard as more certain, than any other event which is in the future. Our race has never yet put its foot upon a soil, which it has not only not kept, but has advanced." I may not understand what Mr. Thompson means by the phrase "our race"; But that we who are Jews will get possession of the country, & that at no very distant period, is absolutely certain, for it is ours by the gift of our God. "I will establish my Covenant between me & thee, & thy seed after thee, in their generations, for an everlasting Covenant: To be a God unto thee, & to thy seed after thee; & I will give unto thee, & to thy seed after thee, the Land wherein thou art a stranger, all the land of Canaan, for an everlasting possession, & I will be their God." "I will declare the decree; The Lord hath said unto me; thou art my Son, this day have I begotten thee: Ask of me, & I shall give thee the heathen for thine inheritance, & the uttermost parts of the earth for thy possession." "Those that wait on the Lord, they shall inherit the earth. The meek shall inherit the earth. Such as are blessed of him shall inherit the earth. The righteous shall inherit the land & dwell therein forever. Wait on the Lord, & keep his way, & he shall exalt thee to inherit the land, When the wicked are cut off, thou shalt see it." [*Marginal interpolations*: "Recollections of Mexico"; "2 Ps."; "17 ch. Gen."; "37th Ps., 30 ch. Deu., 31 ch. Jere., 36 ch. Eze."]

Now, my brethren, the land is ours by Divine right. The people of other nations have usurpt it, & in their generations, have had possession of it for three score years & ten; & other nations may yet, for a little while have the same. But the everlasting possession is secured to us by the guarantee of him, who has all power in heaven & in earth. Let us then wage continual war, not with carnal weapons, but with the weapons of our King, untill we shall have reconquered the possession of it, no more to be disturbed by the power of God & Magog. [*Marginal interpolation*: "50, 51, 52, 53 chs. Isa., 36, 37, 38, 39 chs. Eze., 6 ch. Eph. 10 to 18 vs. inclusive."]

That you may all arrive safely at your eternal inheritance is the prayer of a Son of your Father Abraham, Wm. Eveleigh.

P.S. Since writing the above I have read Mr. Calhoon's [*sic*] speech [of 1/4] in the Senate of the United States relative to the Mexican war. I do love Mr. Calhoon, but I hate the Syrian who dwells in the natural heart of every man.

Mr. Calhoon says, "The great misfortune of what was formerly Spanish America may be traced to the fatal error of placing the coloured race on an equality with the white." Now this assertion is indeed a fatal error. The putting of the coloured race on a national equality with the white is not the source of the misfortunes of Spanish America but just the contrary conduct is the true source of their calamities. Mr. Calhoon says, "none but a people advanced to a high state of moral & intellectual excellence are capable, in a civilized condition, of forming & maintain[in]g free governments." But how could the people of Mexico advance in moral & intellectual exceulence [*sic*] when their Priests, by both civil & eccleasiastical [*sic*] authority, forbade them to use the grand means which God himself has given for the improvement of their morals & intellect: & compelled them to violate the first & great command, "Thou shalt have no other Gods before me" & thus training them to the way of impiety, immorality & servility. This is the cause of their misfortunes. "At what instant I shall speak concerning a nation & concerning a Kingdom, to pluck up & to pull down & to destroy it, If that nation against which I have pronounced turn from their evil, I will repent of the evil that I thought to do unto them—& at what instant I shall speak concerning a nation & concerning a Kingdom to build & to plant it, If it do evil in my sight, that it obey not my voice, then I will repent of the good wherewith I said I would benefit them." Disobedience to the voice of God therefore, is the root of all their calamities, & not their incorporating the different races in the same national association. Where this association does not exist, the mass of the people excluded must remain in ignorance & vice, as is plain in the experience of our own government. To put the different races on a national equality does not necessarily involve individual connexion. Mankind naturally divide into parties according to their different education, customs habits &c. & there is no greater distinction in these matters in Monarchical governments than what exists among us. The only difference is, that in Monarchical governments these distinctions are sanctioned by law; in our country by custom. [*Marginal interpolation*: "18 ch. Jere."]

Mr. Calhoon tells us of the great evils to which the Mexican war is likely to expose us. Truly it will expose us to tremendous evils; for God will reward us according as our works shall be. He has already given, in part, to Spanish America & to Mexico as their works have been, & he will give to us as our works shall be—According to the motive which has led us into this war. If our motive is just, we may expect his blessing. If otherwise, his wrath is impending over us, & will in the end consume us, unless we avert it by timely repentance. Let us then consider. No person can doubt that the annexation of Texas was the occasion of the war, & consequently God will, according to his positive declaration, judge us by the motive which induced us to receive Texas into the union. The wrong thereby done to Mexico, I have already shown from the words of the President, of the Secretary of State, & of the Minister to Mexico. Therefore I shall now speak of the motive which induced us to receive Texas into the union. Whatever may be the motive of other States, it is apparent from the open declaration of many private citizens, the resolutions proposed for adoption in our State Legislatures, & in Congress by our representatives, that the motive of the Southern States is, the hope of strengthening our influence in Congress by an additional number of slaveholding States to be formed in the territories to be obtained from Mexico, so that we may be enabled to defend our system of slavery from attack. Now in this consists the great evil to which the war, occasioned by the annexation of Texas, exposes us. We can only maintain our system of slavery by abusing the two great gifts of God to man. His scriptures & the institution of marriage, & keeping our slaves under moral & intellectual depression. This is evident beyond dispute. The legislatures cannot give them the use of the scriptures, or which is the same thing, the privilege of learning to read, & the privileges appertaining to marriage & hold them in bondage. This is evident to every person who coolly reflects upon the subject. Give them the use of the scriptures, & the privileges appertaining to marriage & they are free. & are we so hardened as to presume that God will suffer us to continue to abuse his gifts with impunity, when he has so peremptorily declared that he will reward us according as our works shall be. That, at what instant he shall speak concerning concerning [*sic*] a nation & concerning a Kingdom to build & to plant it, if it do evil in his sight, & that it obey not his voice," but refuse to repent, "He will repent of the good wherewith He said He would benefit them." We cannot maintain our system of slavery without disobeying the voice of God. We cannot do it without going counter to the spirit of our political constitutions. Slavery is the reverse of freedom. But our political constitutions are founded on the principle that all men are free by divine right. Slavery, therefore, cannot be consistently sustained under a free & republican government. It can only be sustained by the subversion of such a government, by "an her[ed]itary executive & Senate"; & under such, only by the loss of piety & virtue. Are you, my brethren, willing to see that order of things established among us, under which you will be compelled to pull of[f] your hats to the aristocrats whom you may meet in the streets & high ways, as your slaves now pull of[f] their hats & ["put" *canceled*; "hold" *interlined and canceled*] hold them in their hand, untill you have past. Oh! let them be free, that you may be free.

Again Mr. Calhoon says, "It is a remarkable fact, in this connexion, that in the whole history of man, as far as my *information extends*, there is no instance whatever of any civilized coloured race of any shade, being found equal to the establishment of free governments—& he would regard it a degradation to be politically associated with them." From whom did Mr. Calhoon obtain his information? From men of like prejudices & passions with ourselves, who could only look to the past & see some truths through a thick mist, while others were hid from their view—& when they looked to the future they were totally in the dark. But Jesus Christ sees all things from the beginning to the end. Hear him, through Moses & the Prophets, narrating the history of man from the days of Adam to the end of time. Hear him telling us that Joseph, the greatest man of his time in Egypt, thought it no degradation to marry the daughter [of] Potipherah, Priest of On, by whom he had two sons, from whom sprang two of the tribes of Israel. Hear him telling us that Moses, his great legislator, thought it no degradation to marry an Ethiopian woman. It seems however, that Miriam was a white woman, & therefore took great offence at Moses' marriage. See our Lord himself association those of the coloured races who were willing so to be associated in the political Kingdom of Israel, for he gave but one law for him that was born in the land & for the stranger—& hear him telling the Ephesians, through St. Paul, that he has not repealed that law, that

185

they were no longer strangers & foreigners, but fellow citizens with the Saints & of the household of God." Oh! my brethren, let us dip seven times in Jordan that we may prove that we are indeed of the Caucasian race. This is no time to appeal to parties. If we are truly desirous of the salvation of our country & of our own, we must tell the people the truth in plain language. God has declared that sin will destroy all political constitutions. His wrath is upon us. But blessed be God we may prolong our national tranquility & prosperity, & secure our individual salvation, by repentance towards God & faith in our Lord Jesus Christ. The Kingdom of ["Syria" *changed to* "Assyria"] was doomed to certain distruction, but the people were brought to repent by the preaching of Jonah, & God granted them a respite. Verily we are inexcusable. The way is plain. "The wayfaring men though fools shall not err therein." "Write the vision & make it plain upon table[t]s, that he may run that readeth it." God says He will visit the sins of the fathers upon the children unto the third & fourth generation of them that hate him; & show mercy unto thousands of them that love him & keep his commandments." We are the eleven sons of Jacob selling their brother to the Ishma[e]lites, & this sin visited upon themselves & their posterity to the third & fourth generation. When they cried unto the Lord, he sent them Moses, who delivered them from their bondage. When they again rebelled against the Lord & made a King over them, he suffered their enemies frequently to oppress them: & finally ten of the tribes were carried into bondage by the Assyrian, & afterwards the two remaining tribes by the King of Chaldea—& though the two tribes were partially liberated by Cyrus, yet they were never perfectly free from the yoke of the Persian, Macedonian & Roman Empires; & when they had completed the measure of their iniquity by rejecting their King, God dispersed them all over the face of the earth, where they have ever been under oppression. Besides all this, God has given us seven examples of the execution of his wrath; six of them we see clearly accomplished in the distruction of the heathen Kingdoms which have gone before us. See the distruction of the Kingdom of Egypt, of Assyria, of Chaldea, see their ribs in the mouth of the Persian, see him swallowed up by the Macedonian & he in his turn by the Roman—& where is the Roman? Gone with his fellows, & why all this distruction? Because of the oppression ["of the oppression" *canceled*] of the people of Israel, & shall we expect to escape, when God has told us that his wrath is upon all the present Kingdoms of the world? Oh! my brethren, our government is winding up the machinery to the final catastrophe. Nationally we can only hope for a respite. Let us then follow the example of Nineveh. We may free ourselves from the evils of slavery, & take our slaves into political association without following the example of Joseph & Moses. I refer you to them to convince you that the crime of individual connexion, arises, not from the nature of things, or from any natural superiority of one race to another, but from our own prejudices & passions. It is undoubtedly a great crime for a white man to marry a coloured woman, for he would subject his children to all the evils of slavery, if his wife should be a slave or if she should be free, to all the evils arising from the prejudices of mankind. In this the crime consists & not in any natural superiority of one race to another, & consequently the pride of mankind is the root of the crime. Pride naturally leads them to divide into classes: & among us such distinctions are formed by custom. In monarchical countries, these distinctions ["these distinctions" *canceled*] which are ["heritary" *changed to* "hereditary"] by established law, are the source of oppression & poverty to the lower classes, as Mr. Calhoon has shown. But under the genuine spirit of our government this evil is in a great measure avoided, for every citizen being equally free, talent & virtue have free scope, in all classes for developement & exercise. W.E. [*Marginal interpolations*: "8th ch. Isa."; "25 ch. 8 v. Isa., 2 ch. 2 v. Hab."; "7 ch. Dan."; "17 ch. Rev."]

ALS in ScCleA. NOTE: This letter was addressed to the President of the U.S., the President of the Senate, the Speaker of the House of Representatives, the Secretary of State, Calhoun, and [Waddy] Thompson, [former] U.S. Minister to Mexico. Though undated it was postmarked in Statesburgh, S.C., on Feb. 7 and bears Calhoun's AEU reading "Mr. Eveleigh."

From G[EORGE] F. LINDSAY

Mobile, 9 Feb[ruar]y/48

Hon. Sir, I herewith send you today[']s "Mobile Tribune" that you may peruse "No. 5" of "Geo. Mason," written by our distinguished ["Townsman" *canceled and* "townsman" *interlined*] J[ohn] A. Campbell.

If I am not mistaken "Mason" has taken the right ground—but still I confess, in my ignorance & youth, that this whole subject is filled with clouds & darkness. If I understand you aright, you maintain that the Sovereignty of any Territory we may acquire belongs to *all* the States, *individually*—& that what the laws of any one recognize as property must be held as such if taken to that Territory.

And yet is not "Geo. Mason" right—that, as Slavery does not exist *now* in Mexico, there must be "an Enabling Act" of some competent authority passed before we can hold Slaves there? ["And yet" *canceled and* "But" *interlined*], if so, has the *Treaty-making power* that authority—& if it had, would or could it be exercised at present?

All these questions, respected Senator fill my mind with doubt & difficulty & almost make me curse the hour when the recklessness of the President [James K. Polk] brought about such fearful difficulties. *My* only remedy is in "no territory," but that you say is impossible in the present state of the public mind. I hope you are mistaken—but if not—to you, Mr. Calhoun, do the youth of our Country look with prayerful solicitude & anxiety for guidance in our dark hour. I have ventured thus to intrude merely to call your attention to the articles of "Geo. Mason" as perhaps deserving some notice, and as suggesting some things for reflection. We have no other medium through which to speak our sentiments in this region but this small neutral paper. The Register, with the other papers of that ilk, sails quietly down "Duck River," & hopes for "*pap*" to feed its ravenous maw. But, thank God, the leaven of your views is spreading, & every day I find a wholesome state of public sentiment. Will you allow me to make, most humbly a single suggestion. If, when you again speak on the war question, you would *yourself* send some 20 or 30 of your speeches to *prominent administration* men here, it would do a vast deal of good. [Former] Gov[erno]r [John] Gayle [Representative from Ala.] I know would take great pleasure in directing them for you to such as I allude to.

May God in Heaven bless & long preserve you among us as our "*Pillar of fire*" is the ardent prayer of Hon. Sir Your most humble Servant, G.F. Lindsay.

ALS in ScCleA.

From W[ILLIAM] T. THOMPSON

Baltimore, Feb. 9, 1848

Dear Sir, Your letter has been received and my last hope of being able to sustain the [Baltimore, Md., Western] Continent has been dissipated. I shall publish the number for this week, and if possible one more, when I will be compelled to give it up. You allude to the money which has been raised in Carolina for the establishment of a press in Washington City. As the movement for the establishment of this press, by diverting the attention of influential men of the south from the Continent has materially affected my interests, am I asking too much to request you to use your influence to induce the projectors of the new press to purchase of me at a fair price my subscription list &c &c. The present circulation of the Continent is about 3000, and would serve as a very good basis for the new press. I wish as far as I can to indemnify those friends who have assisted me while I have been relying on promises of aid from southern gentlemen. My paper is worth to day to any one who can carry it on at least four thousand dollars. If I am compelled to stop it—to let it die—the type and fixtures are the only things valuable about it. But for the agitation of the Southern Press at Washington, my paper would now be able to sustain itself. As that scheme has been fatal to my enterprize have I not a right to expect those interested in the new paper to spare me all the loss they can?

I beg your pardon for troubling you on this subject, but I know that your word will have great influence with those southern gentlemen who have the controll of this matter, and believe that your sense of justice will prompt you to protect my interest, under the circumstances.

I have been most sadly deceived and disappointed, and had I known what I do now, when I came home from the South last fall assured by promises of assistance, I should have saved myself and friends from damage and mortification for which I now see no remedy.

If you can give me any encouragement to hope for the arrangement I have suggested, please do me the honor to write me immediately, that I may know how to act. Very respectfully Your very ob[edien]t serv[an]t, W.T. Thompson.

ALS in ScCleA.

From JOSEPH GRISHAM

West Union
Pickens District S.C.
10th February 1848

Dear Sir, My Eldest son John O. Grisham has settled in Pontotoc[,] Miss. He writes me that it is expected the office of Receiver in the

Land Office at that place will become vacant soon and he would be glad to have it. You are acquainted with the family, his Mother[']s only brother Samuel L. Watt who went to Pontotoc before the Indians left, and my son has been there two years, he is a business man[,] a good Surveyor of sober industrious habits, [and] if you feel interest enough to procure the appointment it will be considered as another favor to those heretofore confer[r]ed on your friend & Humble Servant, Joseph Grisham.

P.S. I hope & pray that this Session of Congress may be harmonious, that our difficulties at home and abroad may be amicably & speedily settled. I thank [you] for the Speech and Documents sent me. J. Grisham.

ALS in ScCleA.

From JAMES W. TAYLOR

Orangeburgh [S.C.,] February 10th 1848

Respected Sir, I am your fellow citizen, one of your constituents and long an admirer of your publick, as well as private character.

I admire your political wisdom and foresight, and particularly the high moral courage you exhibit, in your fearless and noble support of truth and sound principles. For none of your acts do I esteem you more, than for the stand you have taken on the Mexican question; your course must endear you to all who love their Country, truth and justice.

I believe that you could long since have been President of the U.S. had you stooped to the management usually resorted to by politicians; but I rejoice to know that you have "long ago aspired to something higher than the presidency"—to a fearless and consciencious discharge of duty.

For this you have the love and admiration of every honest heart. Permit me my Dear Sir to hope that you seek an honour still higher than this, the honour which comes from God only: that of being an humble follower of the meek and lowly Saviour. Deem me not presumptuous in thus addressing you, for you have not a fellow-citizen that loves and venerates you more than the writer.

I speak thus to shew you that there are hearts (and many I believe) while rejoicing in your well earned fame, that has won for you the respect and admiration of the civilized world, yet love you too well to have you fail of winning "eternal life." I doubt not that from many a Christian heart, the prayer often ascends to heaven, that you may not rest satisfied with the praise of man, and the honour that you receive and justly merit; but that you may be led to seek that "honour which comes from God only."

I thank the Lord for having blessed the Country, and particularly our *beloved* State, in raising you up for good, to the present, and future generations.

I write not this for any publick exhibition, the contents are known only to myself, and an allseeing eye.

I desire it only as a "still small voice", that may reach you amidst your incessant engagements, and through the agency of God[']s Blessed Spirit lead your mind to such reflections as shall induce you, (if you have not already done so) to cast all your honours at the foot of the *Cross*, that when done with earthly renown, you may receive an "Eternal Crown" "that fadeth not away." This has *long* been, and I trust will *ever* be the prayer of Dear Sir ["of" *canceled*] Very Respectfully Your friend and fellow-Citizen, James W. Taylor, M.D.

ALS in ScCleA.

To Jos[eph] W. Lesesne, [Mobile]

Washington, 11th Feb. 1848

My dear Sir, The defection of the State rights party in and about Montgomery, with [Senator Dixon H.] Lewis at their head, has been the cause of much greif to me. I had hoped, after it became the Seat of Government, that the combined efforts of our friends at two points so influential as Mobile & Montgomery would ultimately place our principles & policy in the ascendancy in the State. I fear now there is no hope of effecting so desirable a result.

Lewis appears a shamed of his course, as he ought to be; but I do not see how he can ever disentangle himself from his new association, or how he can ever recover the confidence of those he has forsaken.

I am happy to inform you, that my views seem to have made a deep impression on the Country, and that there is reason ab(page torn) to believe, if no treaty is (page torn) the policy of a defensive line which I recommend, will be adopted. I feel confident it will, if the Whigs will cooperate, which they seem disposed to do. The

191

debate going on in the Senate has been thus far very able on the side of the opposition; & cannot fail to make a deep impression. What I propose to do is, to make no movement towards adopting a line until the administration shall have a fair opportunity to make a treaty with [José Joaquin de] Her[r]era [President of Mexico,] which I hope they will be able to do; but if they should not make one, then to adopt the course of raising a Committee, as I suggested in my speech. I do not think that Congress ought to terminate the session until something decisive is done to bring the war to a close. Our friends here and [in] our State will take (page torn) the Presidential election, until (page torn) (b)e able to see our way clearly when our course will be to throw our weight, where it can best aid in establishing our principles and carrying out our policy. Our present impression is, if Gen[era]l [Zachary] Taylor will refuse to ac[c]ept a nomination, & rely on the people for his election, that we can best do that by supporting him, but not otherwise.

I congratulate you on your elevation to your highly respectable office [of Chancellor]. It is hon[or]able to you, coming as it did without sacrafice of principle, amidst such degeneracy & subserviency, as marks the present time. Yours truly & sincerely, J.C. Calhoun.

Transcript in NcU, Southern Historical Collection, Joseph W. Lesesne Papers.

From ANNE JANE COLQUHOUN

Address Prospect Terrace Leek Staffordshire
England, February 14th 1848

My dear Sir, You may think it strange why I should write to you, but having few relations myself, and unfortunat[e]ly being a widow with four Children, I am anxious to find out my dear Husband[']s relations for their welfare, and having frequently heard their Grand Father and Grand mother speake of relations that were in America and. moreover saying, that they used to export Flour to Liverpool in great quantities, and that they resided in Charleston South Carolina United States North America I take the liberty of addressing you upon the subject. My husband[']s Father[']s name was John Colquhoun (for that is the way we spell our name, but your Americans cut matters short as well as names and are go head Boys) and he had a brother Angus, and another one but I forget his name, for at that time I was just married, and did not pay particular attention to their conversation. My husband[']s Father died in a few months after our marr[i]age, in the month of July 1831 and he had not heard from his American relations for more than twelve months before he died. My husband[']s father was a Scotch man from the neighbourhood of Dumbartonshire in Scotland & he enlisted for a Soldier in the 48 Regiment, and he listed against his Father's will, for he was the Eldest Son but if I recol[l]ect right, his Father, and Family went to America shortly after, their eldest son enlisted for a Soldier. My husband[']s Father had a brother in Glasgow, James, steward to Lord Douglas, but he has been dead a many years, and what has become of his two daughters I know not. I am this particular, for you may have only heard of the same from your Father. Your Grandfather must have been dead a many years, for my husband[']s Father was 80 years old when he died. I have been introduced to Henry Russell the Singer, who has seen you, & he describes you, as a man about 50 or 52 years of age, & that convinces me more than what I have thought, that you are the cousin of my dear lamented husband, whose name was Daniel Colquhoun & he has been dead two years aged 45 years. My Family consists of Two Boys and two Girls, the eldest a Girl Rosa, aged 14 years, the second a boy John, aged 12 years, the third a boy Angus, aged 10 years, the youngest a Girl Emily, aged 8 years. Now if you think it would be advantageous to us to come out to America, & that you would be disposed to do something for our welfare, *for which we shall feel most gratefull,* & I have no doubt if you are convinced we are your relatives, you will show us the light of your Countenance, & render us every assistance in your power. Do not think I am wanting bread, no but I want protection, & as I have no husband it is natural I should seek out for his nearest relative, for the sake of my dear Children who I think would have a better chance of getting on in America than here. If you do not feel favourable disposed towards, or have a large family of your own, at least write to me, or I shall think this has never reached you. Hoping that yourself, and Family are in perfectly good health & prospects, & as you will have no boundary but the Pac[i]fic, let your bond & word be peace, not forgetting justice in all things. Let me hear from you. Believe me True & faithfully Yours, Anne Jane Colquhoun.

ALS in ScCleA. NOTE: This letter was addressed to Calhoun, "Charleston[,] South Carolina[,] North America."

To E L [L] W O O D F I S H E R, [Cincinnati?]

Washington, 14th Feb. 1848
My dear Sir, The position you assumed for yourself, in reference to the pending presidential election, accords entirely with that, which I have prescribed to myself, and which I hope South Carolina will adopt. If she should not, it will not be because, I have not endeavoured to place her in that position. As things now stand, it would be impossible for me, consistently with the views that govern me, to take any active part in the election. Indeed, I have ceased almost to hope for any beneficial change in the administration of the government through the presidential election. I do not see how any man who has the ability and the disposition to correct abuses & reform the Govern[men]t can in the present state of parties be elected. The governing, I might with truth say, the exclusive object of both parties in electing the President, is to obtain the spoils. They are both equally ready to sacrafice every other consideration to it.

There is at present great confusion in the ranks of both. The larger portion of the Northern Whigs are appearantly resolved to support Mr. [Henry] Clay, while the almost entire portion of the party ["south" *interlined*] appear equally resolved to support Gen[era]l [Zachary] Taylor. It seems, as yet doubtful, which will prevail. Nor are the Democrats less distracted. [Lewis] Cass, [James] Buchanan, [George M.] Dallas, [Levi] Woodbury & [James K.] Polk all have their supporters. The two latter would at present seem to be the strongest. Woodbury would run best in the South, and some think he has the best chance, ["and" *canceled*] I think ["he" *interlined*] would take the electoral vote in that quarter, unless Gen[era]l Taylor should run, as an independent candidate in opposition to the dictation of a caucus. In that event, I would think the chance is in his favour, as far as the Southern section is concerned. I give the impression made on my mind from what I hear. I am passive. It is due to Gen[era]l Taylor to say, that the impression here is, that his feelings towards me, personally, is different from what you infer it to be, from the conversation you heard. But be that as it may, it will have but little weight in reference to my course. I personally desire nothing from any of the aspirants.

I am happy to inform you, that the prospect of car[ry]ing out the line of policy, in reference to the war, which I advocate daily brightens. My present object is to wait, before I make a movement, in order to afford an opportunity ["to the administration" *interlined*] to treat with Gen[era]l [José Joaquin de] Her[r]era, if they are disposed to do so. But if they do not make a treaty with him within a reasonable period, I shall, if I can see a reasonable prospect of success, make an effort to carry out the policy, which I proposed. I am deeply impressed with the necessity of brin[g]ing the war to a close, or if that cannot be done, to bring it under control of Congress, before its adjournment. Unless one or the other is done, I fear it will prove impossible to prevent the conquest & subjugation of the Country.

As I hope to see you ere long here I shall postpone what else I have to say until then. Yours truly, J.C. Calhoun.

ALS in ScU-SC, John C. Calhoun Papers.

From FRANCIS LIEBER

Columbia S.C., 14th February 1848

My dear Sir, I acknowledge the receipt of your obliging lines, as well as of the copy of the Letter of Mr. [Robert J.] Walker.

To us at a distance—at least to myself—it appears like a calamity that there seems to be no concentrating, invigorating and shaping mind—in short no leading and commanding intellect in the H[ouse] of R[epresentatives], ["in" *canceled and* "at" *interlined*] this momentous period. The H[ouse] seems to have come to no consciousness ["yet" *interlined*] of what it wills, ["and" *canceled*] perhaps, because, as House, it does not will anything. I call myself one of the most patient newspaper readers; I am willing to wade through long distances of loose ground of longsome debate, in order to keep up with the times; but this year the H[ouse] baffles the most Germanic perseverance. I have given up reading the debates, and if I have done so, I know, there are few that have not. On the other hand we find no definite, energetic, clear action in the H[ouse]. What then is ["to be" *interlined*] the result of all this loss of time, energy and absence of statesmanship?

The *degree* is different, but in character I think the H[ouse] somewhat resembles the French Assembly after the death of Mirabeau and before the Jacobins again acted. I mean in the self-complacent talk on generalities and protestations of patriotism. And the accusation of the distant and victorious general furnishes another little item of similitude. Most truly Yours, Francis Lieber.

ALS in ScCleA.

Remarks on interference with the franking privilege, 2/18. Under consideration was a resolution aimed at preventing the Post Office from making the franks of members of Congress invalid on mail that was addressed in a handwriting different from the frank. "Mr. Calhoun. I really doubt the propriety of adopting this resolution. There is no authority, as I understand, by which the Postmaster General is authorized to put such a construction as he may think proper upon a law of Congress. The resolution ought to be in the form of an assertion of our rights." [George E.] Badger agreed with Calhoun and suggested the propriety of making it a punishable offence in U.S. courts for any government officials to interpret or amend U.S. laws "to suit their own views." "Mr. Calhoun. I submit to the honorable Senator whether or not the right exists on the part of any officer of the Government to put his own interpretation upon a law of Congress. I am not aware that it is so. I would suggest as the proper course to be purs[u]ed, to call upon the Postmaster General to state upon what principle it is that he gives the construction to the law which he has given; and after we have received a reply from him, then let a resolution be passed indicative of the sense of this body in regard to it." From *Congressional Globe*, 30th Cong., 1st Sess., p. 380. Also printed in the Washington, D.C., *Daily Union*, February 26, 1848, p. 1; Houston, ed., *Proceedings and Debates*, p. 316.

To A[nna] M[aria Calhoun] Clemson, [Brussels]

Washington, 20th Feb: 1848

My dear daughter, The Hibernia has arrived, brin[g]ing a letter from Mr. [Thomas G.] Clemson to me, with one enclosed for his overseer [Reuben H. Reynolds], & one from you to [Martha] Cornelia [Calhoun] undercover to me. I have forward[ed] them both to their respective post offices.

I am happy to hear, that you are all in such good health, & that the children [John Calhoun Clemson and Floride Elizabeth Clemson] are growing & improving so finely.

I had letters from home a few days since. All were well. Your mother [Floride Colhoun Calhoun] in particular is in fine health, and is busey about the yard, the garden & the buildings. Her Constitution is excellent; and all she needs to preserve her health & sperits is continued emp[l]oyment. My own health is about usual. I am never entirely free from a cough, and am subject to colds; but, notwithstanding, enjoy reasonably good health.

I continue to receive favourable intelligence in reference to the boys. They all seem at last sensible of the necessity of improving themselves. William [Lowndes Calhoun] is making very good progress in his studies, & will be prepared to enter college next fall. He is studious & seems to have acquired the sperit of perseverance, which I feared he would lack. James [Edward Calhoun] stands well in College & is studious. John [C. Calhoun, Jr.,] appears much devoted to his medical studies. The winter course in Charleston is drawing to a close; & I expect him here next week on his way to Philadelphia, where he will take a summer course. He had a severe attack of the Measeles, & is slowly recovering from its effects.

Patrick [Calhoun] has not been here this winter. I hear he looks well, & is much in fashionable society. He does not often write.

All were well in Alabama, when I last heard from Andrew [Pickens Calhoun].

Our winter has been remarkably mild & pleasant, but I suppose we shall pay for it before March is over. There have been but little gaiety & few parties as I understand, in consequence of so many families having lost friends & relatives in Mexico.

As to politicks things are very much as they were, when I last wrote Mr. Clemson. We have constant rumours of peace, but I can see no certain prospect of getting ["one" *canceled and* "it" *interlined*]. The policy I recommended in my speech is gaining friends; and I am of the impression, if peace is not made in a reasonable time, there will be a majority for it in both Houses & the Union.

The Presidential election is the constant topick of agitation & conversation; but is involved in perfect uncertainty. The Whigs are divided between [Henry] Clay & [Zachary] Taylor; the latter I think will prove the stronger. The democrats are still more divided, as to the individual to be selected. But these are not the only devisions. There are others in reference to measures, which prevade both, & the two combined leave every thing uncertain.

I keep aloof, standing independently on my own ground, seeking nothing either from the Govern[men]t or the people. I would not change my position for that of any other.

I enclose a letter for Mr. Clemson received some days since. Give my love to him, & kiss the dear children for their Grandfather. I look forward to next fall with pleasure, when I hope to see you all. I would not be surprised, if we should be in session when you arrived. I do not think we ought to adjourn until something definitively is done in reference to Mexico. Your affectionate father, J.C. Calhoun.

[P.S.] Since finishing I received your mother[']s letter to you, herewith enclosed.

ALS in ScCleA; PEx in Jameson, ed., *Correspondence*, pp. 743–744.

From JOSEPH HALL

Boston, Feb[ruar]y 22d 1848

Dear Sir, With this, you will please receive by the hands of our mutual friend Hon. John D. McCrate, a cane manufactured from the original wood of the Constitution—as you will notice by the memorandum herewith annexed.

The cane is perfectly plain, without ornament, purely democratic, and valuable only as being framed from the Constitution—that noble ship which has been so instrumental towards establishing respect for the flag of our beloved country, and compelling foreign nations to yield due rights to the sailors & merchants of the United States.

That this cane may prove a support and staff to you until a good old age, and that God may preserve, prosper, and make you and those connected with you happy, is the earnest wish and desire of your friend and Obedient Servant, Joseph Hall.

P.S. I have a favour to request of you if perfectly convenient. I am in want of a President[']s message with accompanying documents. It is very valuable as a book of reference. I have been promised one by a friend in Washington, but it has not arrived. I therefore name my wish to you. Should it be convenient to forward me one, please direct the same to Joseph Hall[,] Navy Agent[,] Boston Mass., as there are several of the same name in this city.

[Enclosure]

The wood of which this cane is composed is selected from the Lower Scarf of the middle peice of the stem, it being the original timber of United States Frigate Constitution.

Presented by Samuel Pook, Naval Constructor to Joseph Hall.

ALS with En in ScCleA.

To A[NDREW] P. CALHOUN,
[Marengo County, Ala.]

Senate Chamber, 23d Feb: 1848

My dear Andrew, The treaty with Mexico, has just been laid before the Senate, & read. It will be warmly opposed, but I think will be approved by the body. It will be a fortunate deliverance, if it should be. A sudden impulse, in that case, would be given to commerce, accompanied by a rise of price of our great staple so soon as it is known in England.

The slave question will now come up, & be the subject of deep agitation. The South will be in the crisis of its fate. If it yeilds now, all will be lost.

I enclose a speech of Mr. [David L.] Yulee [Senator from Fla.] on his amendment to Mr. Dickerson resolutions [*sic*; that is, those offered by Daniel S. Dickinson, Senator from N.Y.] They express substantially my views. Indeed, (in confidence), he is one of the members of our mess & has conversed with me freely on the principles, which control the questions involved; but the execution is all his own.

Love to all. Your affectionate father, J.C. Calhoun.

ALS in NcD, John C. Calhoun Papers; PC in Jameson, ed., *Correspondence*, p. 744.

From B[ENJAMIN] F. PERRY

Greenville S.C., Feb: 23rd 1848

My dear Sir, I had the honor of receiving from you, some weeks since, a copy of your speech on the Mexican War, for which you will please accept my sincere acknowledgements.

I need not say to you, that I read, with profound interest, your views, as to the future policy of the United States, in regard to Mexico. They have had a most salutary influence upon the State, and I hope, the whole country in allaying that aggressive war feeling, which has pervaded it, for the last eighteen months.

Your views as to the annexation, or subjugation of the whole of Mexico, by the destruction of her nationality, should meet the cordial approbation of every just & patriotic bosom. They are founded in wisdom as well as in justice & patriotism.

In regard to the termination of the war, it seems to me, that there should not, now, be two opinions. We have acquired all the glory & honor which can be achieved in this war; and we are in possession of an ample "indemnity for the past & security for the future." There is little probability of a permanent treaty with such a Government [as that in Mexico]. The expenses of the war & the sacrifices of human life, in carrying it on, are enormous.

I hope you will pardon me, in the seeming presumption, in saying that I had hoped you would submit to Congress & the President, a distinct proposition or plan for closing the war. Such a plan might not be *entirely* acceptable to either of the great parties, & yet command a majority of both Houses of Congress. Should it be adopted the President would, of course, feel himself bound to act in conformity to it.

The suggestion of Judge [Andrew P.] Butler [Senator from S.C.], to send an Embassy, & make an effort, once more, to accomplish a peace, before taking a defensive line, is a good one. The Mexican Government should be warned, that if no peace can be made with them, their fortresses & castles & the walls of their towns will be destroyed, their public property, cannon & ammunition carried off, and their country occupied as far as the *Sier[r]a Madre.* I would take the mountains as a line of defense instead of the Rio Grande, because they can be more easily defended.

This destruction of fortified places & public property may seem Vandal like, but it is in accordance with the Law of Nations, & should be resorted to, where all offers of peace have been rejected. It may be adopted for the purpose of weakening & disabling an enemy, so as to prevent her aggressions hereafter.

Should a defensive line be adopted, it will be a matter of very little consequence, whether the Mexican Government makes peace or not. In a few years the country occupied by our armies will be *settled by our citizens,* & they will be able to defend the line themselves. The Mexicans will have to retire before them, as the Indians have done.

I hope you will excuse the liberty I have taken in addressing you. I could not resist expressing my approbation, however humble it may be, of the policy designated in your speech. At first I did not suppose the idea of destroying the nationality of Mexico by annexing her to the U. States or holding her as a conquered Province, could be seriously entertained by any portion of the Democratic Party. But I am now satisfied, from the expressions of General [Lewis] Cass &

Mr. [George M.] Dallas that I was mistaken[.] With great respect I am &C, B.F. Perry.

ALS in ScCleA; PC in Boucher and Brooks, eds., *Correspondence*, pp. 429–430.

Remarks on the proposed repeal of the 40th rule of the Senate, 2/23. William Allen of Ohio proposed repeal of the rule which required the Senate to conduct "Executive business" with closed doors (a move clearly aimed to embarrass opponents of the administration's war measures). "Mr. Calhoun thought there was an intimate connection between the ten-regiment bill and the subject which had been alluded to, which pertained to Executive business. He hoped the honorable chairman of the Military Committee [Lewis Cass] would not, therefore, persist in his determination to press the passage of the bill. As to the resolution of the Senator from Ohio, he was utterly opposed to it, even if so modified as to embrace only the present subject for Executive consideration. It would be opening the door to a dangerous precedent, and would throw down the barrier which the Constitution had wisely placed round the consideration of questions involving peace or war." From *Congressional Globe*, 30th Cong., 1st Sess., p. 384. Also printed in the Washington, D.C., *Daily National Intelligencer*, February 24, 1848, p. 2; the New York, N.Y., *Morning Courier and New-York Enquirer*, February 25, 1848, p. 2; Houston, ed., *Proceedings and Debates*, p. 321. Variant in the Washington, D.C., *Daily Union*, February 23, 1848, p. 3; the Baltimore, Md., *Sun*, February 24, 1848, p. 4.

From ELLWOOD FISHER

Cincinnati, 2 mo[nth] 26, 1848

Dear friend, I received and read thy last letter with great pleasure. I am satisfied that besides the intrinsic objections to General [Zachary] Taylor[']s election, but little if any collateral benefit would result from it. I saw a fortnight since a copy of an extract of a letter from him to [Henry] Clay, binding the General, if Clay is nominated, to support him. And day before yesterday I saw a letter from Clay himself direct from Washington in which he reserves the decision as to being a candidate until some time next month. He evidently intends to see the complexion of the delegates to the Whig Nat[ional]

Convention before he determines. The Kentucky convention has nominated Taylor delegates all but two. This the Clay men say they found it expedient to permit in order to commit the Taylor men to the Convention, relying on enough Clay delegates from other States to outvote them.

I send herewith a copy of the Cin[cinnati Morning] Signal containing the only public statement of Taylor[']s views ["on the Wilmot Proviso" *interlined*] by himself that has appeared. The Editor of the Signal is a Wilmot Proviso [Martin] Van Buren man of New York. He tells me that he recently wrote to the General at the instance of John Van Buren to say that if he would adhere to the plain interpretation of his letter in the accompanying paper on the Wilmot proviso he should have the support of the New York Barnburners. General Taylor replied that his views on that subject being already publicly known he had nothing further to say. In addition to this we have it here on good authority that Maj[o]r [William W.S.] Bliss is now assuring leading men at the North that the General is opposed to the extension of slavery. It is evident to me therefore that if General Taylor is not friendly to the Wilmot Proviso, he is not frank. And although the South may rely on his being a slaveholder and cotton planter yet it must not be forgotten, that a military chieftain [Andrew Jackson] formerly in the same situation was for a judicious tariff &c &c. We know here also as I presume it is equally well known at Washington that although in his Signal letter he sanctions the suggestion of forming a cabinet from both parties, yet that he has written to [John J.] Crittenden that his Cabinet should be exclusively and purely Whig, although some subordinate offices should be given to the other party. Such is the candor of a soldier candidate—such the liberality of his no partyism—such is the security of the South.

I suppose that before this will arrive the Treaty will have been acted on by the Senate, and approved: although if it contains a clause admitting the Mexicans in the acquired territory to citizenship I don't see how that can be sanctioned. In any event however we shall now have issues more distinctly made than we could otherwise have expected. And I know of none of the questions now pending which had not better now be decided than hereafter. I see no signs of moral or political progress to warrant a sounder judgment from delay.

There is reason to believe that a junction will be formed between the Abolitionists and National reformers; so as to make a combined assault on the entire institution of property. The Democratic party in this State has already made concessions to both. The Whigs have always sympathized with the Abolitionists. I see that the National Reformers have already begun to analyze the relations of property pretty thoroughly in New York. In Rens[s]ellaer county they find that two thirds of the voters have no land, and about seven eighths less than one hundred and sixty acres.

Since the foregoing was written we have received the letter of General Taylor to Peter Sken Smith disavowing still more emphatically than ever all Partyism. This alarms the Whigs and may secure Clay the Convention, although I yesterday saw a letter from Andrew Stewart [Representative from Pa.] stating that there were some seventy odd Taylor men in Congress.

I perceive that the old opponents of the Oregon treaty ["in the Senate" *interlined*] are opposed to the Mexican. I believe that they will have even less sympathy on this occasion than that. For the general opinion is favourable to Peace whatever it may cost if there be no sacrifice of honor—which is scarcely possible. A peace will jostle both parties out of position. The Whigs had gained here materially by opposition to the War, and nevertheless the Democrats had almost concluded to make it their exclusive test. The Whigs cannot revive their old notions with success, nor can the Democrats with much face claim now to be ["much" *canceled*] devoted to free trade after smothering it under high War taxes. The War has excited such general alarm and hostility as to render the election of a military chieftain in a great degree obnoxious: and I cannot but regard the nomination of Taylor, even on the score of immediate expediency as a critical experiment. It may prove a total failure.

It seems to me that events have once more turned in our favour. And I intend to insist among our friends on seizing the golden moment, and acting with decision.

Our friend W[illia]m M. Corry will accompany me to Washington whither we expect to start in three weeks perhaps sooner. With greatest regard thy friend, Ellwood Fisher.

ALS in ScCleA. NOTE: Peter Sken Smith was a Philadelphia editor and nativist leader.

From JOS[EPH] J. SINGLETON

Dahlonega [Ga.,] 27th Feb. 1848
My Dear Sir, Yours of the 11th Inst. was duly rec[eive]d. Your request in regard to paying over whatever toll there may be in my

hands to Mr. [Francis W.?] Pickens or [William] Sloan, or whomso-
ever they may authorize to receive the same, to be handed to Mr.
[John S.] Lorton of Pendleton for you, will be strictly attended to.

Since my last letter to you, I have received from the Obar lot
$37.$^{85}/_{100}$ which added to $49.$^{58}/_{100}$ makes in my hands subject to
the above disposition $87.$^{43}/_{100}$. With all my importunity I am not
able to give you any satisfactory result of your Lease on the cane
Creek lots. The Lessees or Lessee have acted in very bad fait[h].
The fact is, I consider myself trifled with, which I do not intend to
acquiesce in. I have determined to have first, a legal survey made
arround the said lots, as I may be the better enabled not only to define
the lines in a Court of Justice if necessary, but that I may detect any
swindling which may be attempted upon the said lots.

In the mean time I shall obtain the best counsel, not only for the
past, but for the future management of your said interest, on account
of the joint & undivided ["onership" *canceled*] ownership of the said
Cane Creek lots.

I hope you do not think that I wish, any sacrafice of the independent course which you are pursuing in reference to your duty. I so
much admire such a course, that I would not have you to abandon it
for any office whatever as I look to such a course alone as the only
safeguard of our liberties. By a recurrence to my letter you will
discover it ["is" *interlined*] not desire[d]. May you yet succeed in
your views, especially so far as regards your Resolutions introduced
at the commencement of the present session is my most ardent desire.

I am very much obliged to you for the two Documents sent me
(To wit) the map of Florida & Dr. D[avid] D. Owen[']s Report on
the mineral lands of the U.S. I would be very glad to have a map of
Mexico, such an one as described by Mr. [Thomas J.] Rusk's Resolution, which I think passed the Senate.

At all times glad to hear from you, and allways ready to obey
your commands, While I have the hon[or] of being your humble
serv[an]t, Jos. J. Singleton.

ALS in ScU-SC, John C. Calhoun Papers. Note: Calhoun's AEU reads: "Dr.
Singleton[,] Has $87.43 toll gold in his hands for me."

WILLIAM GARRETT to Calhoun and Others

Washington City, Feb[ruar]y 28th 1848
Gentlemen, Unexpectedly finding myself out of office, as a South
Carolinian, and, for many years previous to 1844, a resident citizen
of Alabama, I take the liberty of addressing you, jointly, in regard
to my situation, and respectfully soliciting your kind offices, with
the Administration, in my behalf. The situation, I lately held, was
that of Clerk in the General Land Office, at a compensation of $1200
per annum; and I believe I was the only South Carolinian who held
an appointment in any of the Executive Departments, in this City.
The following note from the Commissioner of the Gen[era]l Land
Office, to me, will, I trust, bear sufficient testimony to my qualifications, whilst, at the same time, it will inform you of the *manner* of
my going out of Office, and the present distressed situation of my
family.

"General Land Office
February 25, 1848
At the request of Mr. William Garrett, formerly of South Carolina,
and late a Clerk in this Office, I take pleasure in stating, that he is an
experienced Clerk, writes a good hand, and expeditiously, and has
few superiors as a Patent writer (in which service he has been chiefly
employed) in this office. Withal, he has an amiable wife and a
family of small children dependent upon him for a support; and he
has no means of living except by daily employment within my knowledge. I would be gratified, therefore, to learn that he had received
some suitable situation, which would enable him to provide for
himself and wants of a helpless family. Richard M. Young, Commissioner."

"P.S. Mr. Garrett was not removed, by me, from his situation
of temporary Clerk in this office; but was discontinued with some
twenty or thirty others, for the want of means to afford them further
employment. R.M.Y."

Any aid you may feel at liberty to give me, Gentlemen, in, again,
obtaining employment, under the Government, will be kindly and
gratefully remembered. I am very Resp[ectfull]y Your ob[edien]t
S[er]v[an]t, William Garrett.

ALS in ScU-SC, John C. Calhoun Papers. NOTE: This letter is addressed "To
the South Carolina and Alabama Delegations in Congress." Appended to it are
signed endorsements from S.C. and Ala. Senators and House members. Armi-
stead Burt wrote: "I concur in desiring that Mr. Garrett be provided for and that

his family in South Carolina is of the highest respectability." Calhoun added: "I concur cheerfully in the above [statement by Burt]. J.C. Calhoun."

From W[ILLIAM] F. VAN AMRINGE

Montgomery[,] Orange Co[unty,] New York
Feb[ruar]y 28, 184[8]

Dear Sir, It is both an advantage & a disadvantage to be so much distinguished as to be made the depository of notions which are often of no value beyond the pleasure bestowed on him who conceived them. The advantage lies in often receiving valuable hints, which may produce a train of thought leading to results often different from, but of greater value than, those detailed. The disadvantage is that your time is taxed to read a long epistle on a subject which your correspondent thinks of importance, but which is of no value, & should be consigned to the fire. I know not to which of these you will place this letter; I venture it because your late speech on Mexican affairs gives me an assurance that the subject I have to propose is deeply interesting to you, although the views I entertain of it may be crude, or impracticable. I al[so] select you, because, of all of our distinguished statesmen, you have been the most independent in your course—less influenced by party considerations—&, therefore, more likely to adopt any measure permanently beneficial to the [*word missing.*]

From the earliest history of our government it has been apprehended that Executive patronage would become a mean[s] of corruption, & endanger the institutions of our Country. It was an objection to the Constitution in the Convention which framed & adopted it; & was a prominent reason given to their cons[t]ituents by most of the patrio[tic] members of that body who refused to sign that instrument. Mr. [James] Madison, in his celebrated Virginia Report & Resolutions of '98, made the increasing patronage of the Executive a chief topic of his animadversions. In the political campaign of Gen[era]l [Andrew] Jackson the fear of it operated powerfully against Mr. [John Quincy] Adams. In short in every important political contest it is used as a tocsin of alarm, which is an evidence of the sensitiveness of the people in regard to it; but although it has constantly been sounded, & the people have frequently responded to it, no exertions have been made to remove the evil. Parties have, apparently, been satisfied by using it as an instrument [of] power, without any other object; as if the evil required to be retained for future use by the vanquish[ed] & for spoils by the victorious party. It is not necessary to inquire whether the leaders of parties acted with good & patriotic motives, or otherwise, by directing the minds of people to this subject; for it is sufficient [to] know that, from the very commencement of our government to this hour, it has been a subject of fear [to] the people—an instrument of corruption by the government—(unintentional, & the natural consequence of the rapid growth of the country it may be,)—and the great bond of union of corrupt party leaders, who seize upon ["any" *interlined*] individual for the Presidency furnished by accidental circumstances, who will be likely to an[swer] their purposes. From this cause, alone, the Presidency has become a stake, played for between military chieft[ains] & political partisans, the one seeking the honor, & the other the profits of the game, while the high minded & ho[*ms. torn*] statesmen of the country are disgusted spectators of the scene. Nay, from this cause the Presidency has fallen so low that some of our most eminent statesmen prefer to seek their fame by their own exertions, in more humble situations, without being obliged to submit to party trickery, party machinery, & party corruptions.

The time has at length arrived when this subject can be no longer neglected by patriotic public men, without a culpable disregard of the future permanence & prosperity of our institutions. I do not mean to say that danger from this cause is now actually knocking at our doors; for this would indicate that the time had actually passed for deliberation on a peaceful remedy. A peaceful, a constitutional remedy can only be applied before corruption has destroyed the principles of the people, after which a republican government is not worth saving—if it could be saved.

A new; & an alarming element has recently sprung up among us, which is becoming a predominant feature of public [*two or three words missing*] has not become a predominant feature of the policy of the Administration. Conquest, military glory, & the consolidation of the whole of North America (insular & continental) into one great empire, constitute this new element, which has many partisans whose sagacity might be supposed to be above such seductions. I fear that even your warning voice will not arrest this desire, this passion for extension. Our fathers were alarmed at the corruptions brought among us by European immigrations, although they were protected by naturalization laws, & the fact that immigrants were scattered among the native population, acquiring our habits, and becoming familiar with our institutions; but we are willing to admit nations of millions without [the] probation required by the naturalization laws, & consequently, without the possibility of acquiring our habits, or being familiar with our institutions. If, therefore, Executive patronage [was] a just object of fear when we were only 13 States— a strip along the Atlantic—with less than 4,000,000 of a homogeneous people—what should it be when we extend from the Rio Grande to the [Great] Lakes, & from the Atlantic to the Pacific, with a heterogeneous population nearly six fold greater than it was, to say nothing of the desire to possess Mexico, Cuba, Canada &ca.!

Executive patronage is productive of all the mischief we deplore, & will, if not prevented, consummate all we fear. It is the only instrument of corruption incorporated in our system of government, which can be advantageously separated from the Executive Office [wit]hout impairing the important functions for which it was established. The foreign relations [and a]n independent treasury were the two great principles of a national government which the [old?] Confederation did not secure, & which induced the adoption of the Federal Constitution. [T]he foreign relations are necessary incidents of the Executive; consequently diplomatic appointments should be made by him. The superintendance of the relations of the States, one with another, is also a necessary incident of his Office, which is chiefly discharged through the instrumentality of the Supreme Court, which has also jurisdiction of foreign matters; consequently the appointment of the Officers of this Court should belong to him. The Navy brings us in contact with all the world, &, in discharge of its duties, is more generally connected with foreign than domestic relations. Besides the Navy can never be a subject of fear; Consequently the Navy Department might safely abide with the President. These embrace all the functions necessarily incident ["to the incident" *canceled*] to the President, & should be the extent of his patronage. The Departments of War, of the Treasury, & of the Post Office are, according to the genius of our institutions, essentially domestic, the appointments to which are not required to be possessed by the President, either for the efficiency of the several Departments, or the honor, dignity or efficiency of the Executive. No good reason can be given why the President should be commander in Chief of our Army unless we contemplate aggressive wars. It was adopted in our Constitution from the British type without considering the difference between a monarchy & a [Rep]ublic.

You will, therefore, perceive that the remedy I propose is to amend the Constitution so that the Secretaries of the Treasury, of War, & the Post Master General, shall be elected by the people, at the same time they elect the President & V. President; and give to the head of each Department the appointments appropriate to each, subject to the ratification of the Senate. The separation of these Officers, & the appointments under them from the Executive, would deprive him of dangerous power and, at the same time, increase his dignity by lifting him above the tricks & strifes of politicians of principles in proportion to their interests. An important object is also obtained by elevating these offices from subordinates to Coordinates, which would make them objects to gratify the ambition of military chieftains, & other aspirants, whose claims to the Presidency' are founded on a single quality, which might ["not" *canceled*] be suitable for a Department, but not ["be" *interlined*] at all suitable for the higher qualifications necessary for a President. These Coordinates would also be important checks, each on the other, which would, probably, preserve the purity of our institutions from corruption by the government, which is all a statesman can guard against by a prospective permanent measure. When the mass of the people, in the progress of time, shall become so corrupt as to infect the government, the most patriotic statesman can only hope to make them fall into the arms of despotism in the most easy & comfortable manner. But corruptions do not generally originate with the people, & from thence infect the government: On the contrary they commence with the government, from whence they rapidly spread among the people, & liberty is frequently strangled before she is much diseased. The statesman, therefore, who protects the people from the government, by checks against Corruption, confers a lasting benefit on posterity, which can only be fully appreciated at particular periods of a nation's history. At such epochs the people, protected by these bulwarks of liberty, make his name their war cry, &, by the enthusiasm it inspires, overcome every danger, & reestablish their original principles, & return to their primitive habits, or at least secure as much liberty as they deserve to possess, which is all their virtues can appreciate.

I am aware that the practicability of the measure I propose will much depend on the details constituting the amendments, & the mode by which they should be made to harmonize with other parts of the Constitution. For example—The President, from the nature of his Office, & the duties he is required to perform, should always possess, or have it in his power to possess, a ["knowledge of" *interlined*] matters in contemplation, or transacted by other Coordinate Departments. For this purpose these Departments should ["be" *interlined*] required to report to him at certain periods, or when required by the President. Also, although the President should not have the power of directing a thing to be done by a Coordinate Department, it might be proper to invest him with power to suspend action in a particular matter until the action of Congress on the subject. It might also be advisable to constitute a Cabinet Council of all the heads of Departments, by an Article of the Constitution, the details of which would require consideration. But all the details will be readily suggested by your experience & sound judgment, if you should approve of the project.

Permit me to recapitulate the advantages I suppose would be derived from the proposed amendments.

1st. The patronage of the government would be divided between four Coordinate branches, in their appointments independent of each other, but all subject to the [vote] of the Senate. Patronage would thus be disarmed of dangerous power, while the advantage of having appointments m[ad]e by a single responsible officer would be reta[ined].

2nd. By elevating these Offices to the dignity of Coordinates (instead of being mere head clerks, as was asserted by a President who assumed the responsibility) military chieftains, & others, could find appropriate objects of ambition, & we should be more likely to have distinguished statesmen for Presidents, because the peculiar talents of each would be appropriated to a proper Department.

3rd. Efficient checks would be embodied in our Constitution sufficient to guard against improper ambition, & to insure the faithful administration of the laws, until the people had become so corrupt as to require a stronger government.

4th. The President would retain the power to appoint to the Navy Department, the State, & all the high & dignified offices, to obtain which tricks, frauds, bargains &ca. are seldom necessary; and would be relieved from those which are a burden, & a constant source of vexation to any high minded patriotic man. These minor offices would also be more carefully filled, & more faithfully executed, because the appointments would be made by the Department on which the responsibility rests.

5th. Our national elections would be less bitter & not so corrupt; because patronage, (being divided) would divide the attention of interested politicians to several objects, instead of having them all concentrated on one object.

6th. Wars would be more cautiously encountered, because the War making—or rather the diplomatic department, which is nearly equivalent to it—and the War conducting departments would be distinct, each responsible for his own acts. But when entered upon they would be more efficiently conducted, because each department, feeling a direct responsibility to the President, to Congress, & to the People, would do his utmost, without improper interference or embarrassment, to discharge his duties.

The great object, however, is to divide patronage—to take from the President this powerful instrument of corruption, & to lodge it where it will be as much as possible deprived of poisonous properties. If left with the President it will certainly accomplish our destruction, & probably at no very distant day. It cannot be lodged with Congress, nor with either House, without corrupting legislation by converting the halls into political shops. I know not where it could be as safely lodged as in the Departments to which the respective duties properly belong. Nor would it answer the object to bestow the appointments appropriate to each department to the head of it, leaving his appointment with the President; for this would relieve the President of the responsibility, while he would hold the solid power of the department. The examples of Mess: [Samuel D.] Ingham & [William J.] Duane, who were dismissed for not being obsequious, prove the insecurity of such a measure.

A prudent man regards not only the importance of a measure, but the means of carrying it into effect, which, in this matter, is its probable popularity. I am so sanguine as to believe, that, if brought before the nation in a proper & imposing manner, by a man already high in the confidence & affections of the people, it would control the next presidential election, notwithstanding the glare of military glory which is now attracting the gaze of [the] people. But as you are much better qualified to judge of the merit, & probable success [*words missing*] project than I am, I leave this part [of] the subject without further remark.

Three objections may be made to the proposed constitutional amendments. 1st. They would destroy the unity, & therefore the efficiency of the Administration. But, [if] the amendments should be judiciously drawn, all the powers necessary to be lodged with the President may be as perfectly possessed by him as they are now. Experience proves that we have more to fear from the strength than the weakness of the Executive power. 2ndly. By making the Sword, the Purse, & the Post Office coordinates with, & but a step below the President, the wheels of government may be obstructed by cabals & jealousies. Instances might occur, but only in cases when the policy of prompt action should be doubtful, & when each officer would feel confidence in appealing to Congress & the people for the soundness & purity of his conduct. 3rdly. The proposed amendments may be supposed to be too democratic—giving the people too much power. Who will prescribe limits to the power of the people? Where is the limit under our present institutions? The popular will controls every thing by methods unknown to the Constitution—by inferences from elections, by which momentous constitutional constructions have been claimed to have been decided by the people who never thought of them at the polls. Would it be more dangerous to give to the people, in the Constitution, a power which any Executive may infer they have exercised unconstitutionally by inference, by a sanction of a construction as he understands it? I have no fear of the people, but I have of the Executive; & therefore I am for giving to them all the power not absolutely necessary to be lodged with the Executive. A republican government will be efficient when it acts in harmony with public opinion, & weak when opposed to it, [what]ever may be the Constitution; but it is important to take from the administration the power of manufacturing public opinion.

I mention these things in this very general way because I know it to be unnecessary to argue these topics with you, because you will see, at a glance, all that could be said in regard to them, more fully than I could represent them. But I believe you will agree with me that some measure should be devised to remedy the great & growing evil of patronage. Whether that which I have proposed will answer the purpose, without introducing other evils equally to be feared, I leave to your better judgment. My object is accomplished by laying the subject before you, being well assured that what is proper will be attempted by you, without the fear of losing, or the hope of gaining popularity by the course you may adopt.

I offer no apology for sending you this long letter, because I am only using the right in you which belongs to my share. There are few members of Congress with whom I would take such a liberty, because there are very few who aim at being more than the partisan representative of a district, and still fewer whose talents & patriotism make them the common property of the nation.

You will readily discover, from my letter, that I am no politician; but I am, with very high respect, Your Mo[st] Ob[edien]t S[er]-v[an]t, W.F. Van Amringe.

ALS in ScCleA. NOTE: In the above transcription many words and parts of words have been conjectured within brackets for parts of the manuscript that are unreadable due to deteriorated margins.

From JOHN A. CAMPBELL

Mobile, 1 March 1848

Dear Sir, I have received your letter of the 23rd Inst. together with a speech of Mr. [David L.] Yulee of the Senate. I have read the letter carefully. I think Mr. Yulee establishes that the inhabitants of a territory have no right to determine for themselves their municipal laws or domestic institutions but are dependent upon congress ["or the States" *interlined*] for them.

I think congress has the power ["has the right" *canceled*] to organise the inhabitants of a territory of the U.S. into a body politic, and to determine in what manner they shall be governed. As incident to this power I think that congress may decide what shall be held and enjoyed as property in that territory, and that persons should not be held as property. I think farther that when a territory is acquired by conquest or by treaty and the ["municipal" *interlined*] laws ["of the" *canceled*] in force in the territory are not changed by the treaty of cession or by an act of congress that they remain in force. That they do not remain in force as "temporary" acts or among a portion of the inhabitants but they remain in force as laws to which all the people in the territory ceded & all that may emmigrate to it owe obedience. I think further that slavery is purely a municipal institution and falls under this principle. With these opinions I hold Mr. [James K.] Polk[']s war, as likely to produce the most disastrous consequences to the Southern States.

I have, as far as in my power I could do, ["have" *canceled*] opposed the lust for territorial acquisitions he has encouraged. I have viewed with mortification & disgust the abasement of our politicians at the feet of his administration and I wrote the resolutions offered by Mr. [William L.] Yancey ["& offered" *canceled*] to the Montgomery convention requiring the rejection of territory unless the treaty or an act of congress provided guarantees against Mexican & abolition legislation & laws.

My reasons for my opinions are that slavery is an institution dependent upon the laws of the State that has adopted it. That the slave master cannot carry ["those" *canceled*] his slave property to a State in which the relation is not sanctioned. That we must produce a law or custom which sanctions slavery operative in the territory where the slave is or the relation will be at an end. That the Constitution of the United States does not sanction the tittle of a master in his slaves except in certain specified cases. It provides for the recapture of a fugitive—for the suppression of insurrections by federal authority—it allows an enumeration of them for the purposes of representation & taxes—it no where provides that the rights of the slave owner shall be protected in all the territories of the U.S. or that the master shall be free to carry them as slaves to those territories. If there is any such ["provision in" *canceled and* "right under" *interlined*] the Constitution it is derived from some clause, it is no where expressed. Mr. Yulee does not derive it from any clause in the Constitution but that it is a right *reserved*—a right enjoyed before the formation of the Constitution & not conveyed away. I do not think his argument well founded. His argument is 1. That the people of the several States are sovereigns of the territories. 2. That congress is an agent or trustee & bound to hold the property for the common use of the people of the several States. 3d. That each individual of each of the States may carry any article that the laws of the State in which he lives calls property to the territory and that he can hold[,] use & enjoy it as property there—without hindrance from congress or any government it may form.

The premises do not at all uphold the conclusion.

When you admit that congress may form a *government* you concede the right to it to define what shall be property and how it may be enjoyed[,] transferred or inherited. It may decide that persons shall or shall not be property. There is nothing about slave property that I know of, that takes it from the sway of legislative authority. It is true our State constitutions have in many cases limited the powers of the legislature ["over them" *interlined*] but in the absence of such limitations *slaves* fall under the influence of the legislature in the same manner as any other property. I have always understood that the laws of the place where the property is must determine the tenure by which it is to be holden and that no other laws were ever regarded except as a matter of comity & in the absence of a prohibitory law. I have especially understood that the relations of master & slave depended particularly upon the municipal laws of the place where the slaves were.

I think Mr. Yulee has applied to slaves principles that he would shrink from applying to any other species of property or to any other relation of persons.

Suppose the Society of Newyork was arranged on the principle of the superiority of females and that the existence of the ["male" *canceled and* "husband" *interlined*] by those Laws was merged in that of the wife.

Would that be the condition of things between those persons in a territory ["of the U.S." *interlined*] in which the common law was adopted after their immigration to that territory[?]

Suppose children & wives were vendible by the husband ["and Father" *interlined*] in New Hampshire, would that right be carried with an emigrant to Wisconsin or Oregon[?]

The strength of our position is that slavery is the central point about which Southern Society is formed. It was so understood at the formation of the Constitution. It has been dealt with by the country since in the same spirit. This territory is the fruit of common expenditure & toil. We must insist that for the future the same spirit shall be maintained. We must not submit to disparagement on account of this institution. We must have an organisation of the territory that admits us as equals.

Now altho these are facts I see no provision in the Constitution which provides against an opposite temper. Nor can I gather a *legal* right from what rests simply as a moral obligation upon congress. If congress does the people of the Southern States wrong their appeal must be to a higher authority—and in the last resort—we may overthrow the congress.

Allow me to call your attention to the weight of authority & precedent against the position of Mr. Yulee—The repeated sanctions to the ordinance of 1787 ["by congress" *interlined*]—the implied sanction in the compacts of Georgia & North Carolina ceding territories & stipulating for the extension of the ordinance except in one particular—["In" *canceled*] The Missouri compromise—The admission of Texas ["with a restriction" *interlined*]. The Supreme courts of Kentucky[,] Virginia—Mississippi[,] Louisiana & Missouri have all decided upon the validity of the clause in the ordinance that ["repeals" *canceled*] restricts slavery. They ["have" *interlined*] maintained the right of the children of slaves born after the ordinance to freedom & that freedom was obtained in virtue of that ordinance.

See what a contradiction is given in the acts of every territorial government restricting the introduction of property from other States in some form or other and continually changing the tenures on which it is held & regulating the mode of its enjoyment.

As to that other proposition that the laws remain in force not for limited terms & transient purposes but as laws of a permanent & abiding character the history of Louisiana furnishes strong proof. One case is that of Indians held as slaves by the French prior to 1762. The Spanish regulations forbade the servitude of slaves. The french law was never directly repealed nor were the Spanish regulations of

Charles 5th specifically introduced. The Indians claimed their freedom on the ground that the laws of ["the conqueror" *canceled and* "Spain" *interlined*] by the treaty were extended to Louisiana. The court declares the principle in these words "it is an incontrovertible principle of the laws of nations that in cases of the cession of *any part of the dominions* of one sovereign power to another, the *inhabitants of the part ceded retain their ancient municipal reg[ulations?] until they are abrogated by some act* of their new sovereign" 5 Martins Rep. 284.

The Spanish laws remained in force in La. until repealed in 1828 & furnished the rules of action upon all subjects when alterations had not been made. The fact is implied in the law, for organising the ["Louisiana" *interlined*] territory & in which the freedom of religion is expressly guarded.

My object in writing the articles you refer to signed "George Mason" was to warn our people not to rest upon *opinions* however well founded but to insist on *guarantees* in advance of a cession of territory that we should suffer no harm. I write you my opinion as a lawyer that you would not be safe in going to California or New Mexico without a change of laws with your slaves. That in all probability in a suit for freedom commenced by your slaves ["against you" *interlined*] you would be lost. That those arguments that courts most value are opposed to you—and at last the thing settles down to a controversy between the slave & his master in a court of justice.

I have written to you more at length than I desired. I have written frankly & openly to you. I see we are on the eve of collisions & conflicts worse than those with Mexico. I see we at the South will come out of these conflicts with the loss of everything—I fear honor—as well as influence[,] stability[,] strength. I have felt to you and for you, since your conduct on the declaration of war more ["strongly" *canceled*], warmly than I ever expected to feel in regard to a public man. I know you will have no such support as you ought to have.

The public opinion around you is all corrupted and is adverse and we at the South have hardly an opinion at all. Our editors are engaged in recruiting for the Presidential struggle and insult every man, if such creatures can give insults, who is not willing to be as prostrate as themselves. Our public men are all fettered to party and do not give sound and independant judgements to the people.

I have thought over this subject for a long time and I can only say that were I a member of congress I would let the war continue forever before I would take 697000 of territory which must be free territory—and that I would not let the war continue an hour with the hope of getting any territory that belongs to Mexico. I firmly believe that the ["propositions" *canceled*] position and policy of [John P.] *Hale* is far more favorable to the Southern States than that of the President or any of his counsellors. With great respect Your friend, John A. Campbell.

ALS in ScCleA; variant PC in Boucher and Brooks, eds., *Correspondence*, pp. 430–434. NOTE: The speech of Senator Yulee of Fla. can be found in *Congressional Globe*, 30th Cong., 1st Sess., pp. 302–306. John P. Hale of N.H. was the most dedicated freesoiler in the Senate and had opposed any acquisition of territory.

From PATRICK O'SULLIVAN

Sumterville S. Ca., March 1, 1848
My Dear Sir, As one of your greatest admirers and humble constituents, I take the liberty of addressing you in relation to my unfortunate and much persecuted country (Ireland). The famine which has been raging there for the last two years & better has awakened all my Sympathies in relation to her *wretched and deplorable* condition, that I have been endeavouring as in my feeble efforts lay in my power to awaken not only the Sympathies of all Irishmen and their descendants, but that of all good philanthropists in her favour, and amongst the many plans that I have thought of for her *effectual* relief I am confident there can be none better devised than to get the poorer classes of people away from there and in order to do so to *advantage* it would be *most essentially necessary* that they should have some particular spot dessignated where they could go to at once after their arrival in this country which they could call their own instead of being running to & fro, as they now are like *sheep without a shepherd*, on the idea of which I have drafted a petition to send to your Congress, the object of which you will see stated therein, but before sending it in due form one of my respectable friends has suggested to me the propriety of subjecting it to your consideration and attentive perusal whether you think it feasible that your honorable body would take ["it" *interlined*] into due consideration and whether there is any thing contained in the petition that would make it objectionable and if so, that you would have the extreme kindness to draft one that would meet your views and forward it to me in Sumterville, as I have the assurance of the most respectable Citizens of the State to give the measure their full support. Besides the objects mentioned

in the petition the advantages of its success would be innumerable to the *poor people* that it is intended for, it would prevent unprincipled speculators from taking advantage of them in time to come, and have them in the same position that they are in now by those heartless land lords of Ireland. All that Congress has to do is to dessignate the place where the Irish Societies can send them to, at once which they can't take the liberty of doing now, although there is liberty for all to squat on the public lands. The citizens of this district are going to hold a meeting next Monday at our Court-House at which the most distinguished men of the district will preside. I am also getting the wealthiest & most respectable planters of the District to prof[f]er lands, implements & food for one year to as many as will make their way into the district. Your expression last year when there was a petition sent to Congress to grant half a million of dollars to the distressed Irish, that "you had no Constitutional scruples on that subject," has already endeared you to every Irish heart that wishes well to his country, and should you with your characteristic benignity, use your influence to grant them this favour, it would endear you to them a thousand times more, and if it could ["add" *interlined*] any thing to your present enviable position, they would place you on their Scrole of fame. I have the honor to be my dear Sir, with the most profound respect your most ob[edien]t and humble Servant, Patrick O'Sullivan.

[Enclosure]

To the Honorable the Senate and House of Representatives of the United States of America—

The petition of the undersigned citizens of South Carolina, most humbly sheweth—

That as the object of all governments from the foundation of the world to the present time has been the amelioration of the condition of such portions of the human family as would place themselves under their protection[,] laws and jursidiction—and the object of our far and wide spread Republic is that of "the greatest good to the greatest number" affording a safe asylum to the oppressed of all nations who choose to take refuge under the wings of the Eagle, the emblem of our nationality, the banner of liberty, and conform to our laws and institutions and determine to maintain them.

That your petitioners see with sincere & heartfelt sorrow the famine which is now raging in Ireland which like an incorrigible disease to the human [*one word altered to* "frame"] hangs to them so closely and is sweeping them off the stages of life daily and by thousands without any likelihood of its mitigation or cessation causing such of them as can afford it to fly from the impending calamity & emigrate to our shore as their last haven of safety of affording them relief in this world causing the hearts of thousands who are naturally endowed with true feelings of sympathy to bleed for their misery and squalid wretchedness without possessing any effectual means of affording them immediate relief when they reach our shores.

That your petitioners actuated from a pure love of sympathy for their helpless and forlorn condition would suggest both on the principles of humanity and sound policy of making a grant to them of such a portion of territory as in the wisdom of your honorable body as you [*one word altered to* "may"] think proper together with your judicious designation of its location on the condition of their paying the government price for it at such times as your honorable body may think proper to stipulate with them for the payment of the grant.

That your petitioners know from actual facts and the idea may very forcibly strike the attention of some members of the house that in case your Honorable body would grant their petition it would be a pleasing announcement to the inhabitants of the Atlantic cities of this country who are so much annoyed by the presence of those poor emigrants not so much from the trouble they take (for that is given freely) but the concern they feel for their situation, and for that reason alone would cause the measure to be hailed by ["every" *canceled*] every good citizen, philanthropist and Sincere Christian with not only approbation but applause in every State in the Union. It would relieve the friends of Ireland in the Atlantic Towns and Cities from a great part of their responsibilities and labors and enable them the more effectually and a thousand times greater cheerfulness to put all the means in their power into operation of sending them to their destination, where the poor exile might sit down with contentment and exclaim with ecstasies of rapture and delight (so characteristic of the Irish people and a heart filled with gratitude to their humane benefactors) this shall be my future home.

And your petitioners as in duty bound, will ever pray—.

ALS with En in ScCleA.

To [Edmund Burke, Commissioner of the Patent Office], 3/2. "Mr. Calhoun's respects to the Com[missione]r of Patents & will thank him to enable him to answer the enclosed [*not found*] by furnishing him with papers referred to. Return the letter." ALU in DLC, Edmund Burke Papers, 2:472.

From O[zey] R. Broyles

[Pendleton, S.C.,] 3d March 1848
My dear Sir, Your views in reference to the relative value and security of the United States and State stocks are precisely those I anticipated. Since the reception of your letter however both have in a good degree ceased to be objects of interest or inquiry, from an entire willingness on my part to accede to the proposition you think you will probably make to take the whole amount.

I regard a Mortgage on real and personal property that is untrammelled as the very best security that could be offered, and particularly satisfactory if on an estate within the limits of the State. That I have not answered you on the subject sooner, has resulted from a wish to acquire correct information not only as to the amount of the estate [of Chester Kingsley], but also as to when it can be obtained and made available. W[illia]m Magee[,] the former ordinary[,] by an act of favouritism much censured by many, gave the Administratorship to a couple of his brothers in no way related to the family of Kingsley. Their object of course was to make of it a very profitable speculation, and although their securities are considered responsible the opinion is entertained by many that there will be some dif[f]icu[l]ties to encounter before the money will be obtained. I have addressed them a letter requesting them to meet me at Anderson sale day in March, prepared to pay over all that they may have collected. And I shall there avail my self of the occasion to demand the balance at as early a period as it can be collected. The Commissioner in Equity informed me that the estate was worth between thirty and thirty-five thousand dollars. The personal property and bonds if in this he is correct must amount to almost twenty-five thousand I should suppose as I have been informed that the land sold for about eight thousand. The above large amount will be coming through the hands of the Administrators, and was all due either in October or November last. The lands were sold by the Commissioner on a credit of one, two, three, and four years, in equal instalments, and only one-fourth of that amount can be had now, and another fourth will be due the ensuing fall. I am quite correct in all the above statements, and only uncertain as to the full amount of the whole.

In addition to the above I had promised to loan to two individuals a year ago[,] to one the sum of five thousand dollars, and to another three thousand if they could give satisfactory security which I understand they are likely to do. Except the above I do not stand committed to any one, and the remainder will be subject to your order. So that after paying out the above eight thousand and making a reasonable allowance for expences, it would seem that you might calculate on the sum at least of twenty thousand dollars. As I shall visit Anderson on Monday next expressly for the purpose of obtaining all necessary information on the subject I will in a few days give you the result of my investigations, so that you may be prepared to adopt a final conclusion on the subject, and communi[c]ate your determination as soon as convenient.

We have no local news of interest. After a few months of unusually fine and dry weather, we have had heavy and repeated rains for the last few weeks, and the prospect of a forward spring. We are gratified with the prospect of peace with Mexico, but feel a little restrained in giving it indulgence by the prospect it brings with it, of a war with the Abolitionists. Very truly yours, O.R. Broyles.

ALS in ScU-SC, John C. Calhoun Papers.

From A[NDREW] J. DONELSON

Berlin, March 3d 1848
D[ea]r Sir, I take the liberty of enclosing you a note addressed to me by Lord Westmoreland to whom I had given a copy of your speech on the Mexican war, in order that you may see the favorable impression it has made.

The revolution in France has taken all the world by surprise; so much so that no one yet pronounces on the result. It is to be hoped that France will make no aggressive movement. If she does not she will not be disturbed by her neighbors. If her leaders are able to improve upon the charter of 1830, it is encouraging to find that the great powers have also learned that the principles of the Holy alliance have become inapplicable. Except in the case of an ambitious state seeking to destroy the ballance of power by conquest, intervention is no longer thought of; and a league of monarchs, as contradistinguished from the people, with the view of guaranteeing and maintaining their personal pretentions, is admitted every where to be an absurdity. This is the fruit of our example as a free Government, which is destined to do still more if it can be preserved in its original purity. Hence as you justly remark in your speech the necessity of our continuing to cultivate peace. When we can say to the old world that our system is administered with a less tax than that of any other, and that it secures life and property, we do more for freedom than we could if we had all the soldiers of Europe under our orders. This is not an American vanity, but is admitted ["even" *interlined*] by many Princes, as I have had occasion to know in repeated instances. One of them declared to me at a party recently attended by the King [Frederick William IV] and many of the Royal family, that he was reading with great interest the correspondence of [George] Washington as published by [Jared] Sparks, and saw nothing to object to in the opinions of that Father of our country.

I am so far off and receive the news so much in arrear of the times, that I know scarc[e]ly any thing of the great question which agitate[s] at Washington. I do not however flatter myself the less that some lucky turn will give us peace with Mexico and that you can go back to the more noble business of retrenching expenses and developing the resources of our country.

Do you notice the debates in the British Parliament on the slavery question? The facts prove that our mode of treating this subject is the only practicable one, whether we look at the interests of the Negroe or the white man. England's mistake in this respect is reacting powerfully and concurs with other causes to bring upon her a change of commercial policy which will be as important in its results as the establishm[en]t of a Republic in France. Mr. [Richard] Cobden[']s party must in the end go into the Ministry and it will be their work to retrench expenditures and set the great example of promoting peace by disowning[?] the parades of useless armies and warlike fleets. This movement will be hastened if the National convention about to be called in France have the wisdom to persevere ["and succeed" *interlined*] in the attempt at Republicanism, and should found it on a declaration against standing armies except when employed to repel invasion.

Great events now turn on the experiment at Paris. If it takes the direction of peace and moderation, do not be surprised to see it followed by all Europe, permitting new Territorial ["divisions" *canceled and* "associations" *interlined*], and admitting the representative principle so as to combine under one Governm[en]t all homogeneous interests. If on the other hand it breaks up in anarchy and seeks refuge in a monarchy, we may consider the cause of European reform as consigned again to the doctrines of 1815.

Your young friends Messrs. [Edward W.] Geddings & Ball are well. I am v[er]y truly y[ou]r Ser[van]t, A.J. Donelson.

[Enclosure]
[Lord] Westmoreland to [Andrew J.] Donelson
Berlin, Thursday [*ca.* March 2, 1848]
My D[ear] Mr. Donelson, With my best thanks I return you the admirable Speech of Mr. Calhoun. Y[ou]rs most sin[cere]ly, Westmoreland.

ALS with En in ScCleA.

From ALBERT GALLATIN

New York [City,] March 3d 1848
My dear Sir, The issue, on the subject of peace with Mexico, seems to be altogether changed by the contingent Projet negotiated by Mr. [Nicholas P.] Trist and submitted by the President [James K. Polk] to the Senate. The annexation of Texas was both expedient and natural, indeed ultimately unavoidable; and, whether annexed or not, it must necessarily be a slave holding State, so long as slavery existed in the United States. I differed in opinion with you, as to the time and manner of effecting the object, under the strong apprehension that these would produce a war with Mexico. But now I am confident that we ["agree, as to" *changed to* "agree on"] the importance of making the projet, the foundation of a speedy termination of the war, and of a solid and permanent peace.

One of the great obstacles is the question of slavery; and it is highly desirable, that this should not impede the progress of the negotiations for peace, and that, if practicable without committing either party, the discussion ["shou"(?) *altered to* "of"] that subject should be postponed for the present and left open for subsequent consideration. I will also acknowledge that I have the most rooted aversion to the annexation of New Mexico to our Union.

In the next place, without regard to right, and only in reference to a solid and permanent peace, I lay under the most intimate conviction, that the desert between the Nu[e]ces and the Rio Norte should be made the boundary between Texas and Mexico; and that if the lower part of the Rio Norte is adhered to, it will necessarily produce collisions and the renewal of a war of conquest.

I have ventured to commit to paper my view[s] on both points, and submit them to your consideration. My suggestions on the first subject may appear fanciful and appear impracticable: and I hope that some better mode, having the same object in view, may be devised. On the subject of the Rio Norte boundary, I have no hesitation and feel that it is of paramount importance.

But I pray that, on this occasion, [I] may be altogether kept out of view. I send it confidentially only to the six ["or seven" *interlined*] Senators with whom I am acquainted. (Exaltados [those who are exaggerated and violent in political ideas] excepted).

Pleased to accept the reiterated assurance of my most distinguished consideration and of my most sincere personal regard. Respectfully your obed[ien]t & faithful Servant, Albert Gallatin.

[Enclosure]

The projet of a Treaty, communicated by the President to the Senate, comes in a questionable shape, prepared, on the part of the United States, by one whose powers had been revoked; on that of Mexico under duress, and by persons whose authority is doubtful and perhaps transient. Yet a speedy termination of this lamentable war is so desirable, and so generally wanted by the great body of the nation, that no effort should be omitted, to make this overture the foundation of a just, honourable, real and lasting peace. Every month of the war, during its continuance, is a sacrifice of hundreds of valuable lives, and costs the nation about four millions of dollars.

The line designated by the Projet, as the northern boundary of Mexico is generally and with only one important exception, founded on rational principles, so far at least as relates to Mexico itself.

The independence of California is a fact accomplished, which not the joint efforts of the United States and of Mexico could recall. The Majority of its white inhabitants already consists of European emigrants not of Spanish descent, and of citizens of the United States; and it must necessarily, in a short time, be almost exclusively occupied by emigrants from this last quarter. The same observation applies, with still greater force, to the districts situated north of the proposed boundary, which are not yet inhabited by either the Mexicans, or the Americans. Neither those provinces, nor even New Mexico are of any real utility to the Mexican Republic. They are either deserts, or distant outposts and colonies, which add nothing to her strength, and which she may yield without impairing her Nationality. But the Mexican inhabitants of both California and New Mexico have rights which ought to be respected: and they should not be considered as Cattle, that may be transferred without their consent.

It may also be, that the people of the United States are not prepared, for the absolute and unconditional annexation of those provinces, which is contemplated by the Projet. They may object to the admission, as a State, and to the introduction into the National Councils, of the representatives of sixty or seventy thousand Mexicans, and cultivating Indians, who are the sole inhabitants of New Mexico. It is also well known, that differences of opinion, entitled to the most serious consideration, do exist—and that there are several difficult and important questions to be settled, respecting the conditions on which new territory should be acquired by, and annexed to, the United States.

The paramount importance of the termination of the war, is such, that it is most highly desirable, that some mode might be devised of postponing for the present, a decision, or even a discussion of those intricate and delicate questions; provided it can be done, without in any way committing either of the parties concerned. Sensible of its intrinsic difficulties and my own incompetence. I hardly dare emit an opinion on that subject. The following suggestions are submitted with unfeigned diffidence, and principally for the purpose of illustrating the object I have in view.

Instead of an absolute and direct cession to the U. States of the whole territory north of the intended boundary; let the Mexican Republic, recognize by the Treaty, the unconditional independence of the states of Texas, New Mexico, and California, with limits defined by the Treaty; and cede to the United States, only the residue of the territory north of the boundary, not included within the limits of those three states. This residue will consist ["of" *canceled*] almost exclusively of the Country drained by the great Colorado of the west, and its tributaries, which contains about 250,000 square miles, and still remains unoccupied by any inhabitants of European descent.

The annexation of Texas is an accomplished fact, and cannot in any way be affected by any treaty. The recognition of its independence, would be a mere matter of form, and the same thing as its cession to the United States, contemplated by every plan of treaty which has been proposed.

According to the arrangement suggested, there would be no conquest: and the objections in that respect would be altogether removed. But every body knows that the great ["obstacles" *changed to* "obstacle"] to any acquisition of territory, however legitimate, is to be found in the conflicting views respecting slavery. And without discussing the question itself, the effect in that respect of the arrangement must be fairly stated.

The States of California, and New Mexico, being declared unconditionally independent; will, each of them respectively admit, or forbid Slavery, as they may think proper. Whichever way they decide, the question of annexation, and ["of" *interlined*] its terms will remain open: and those which relate to Slavery may be then discussed, as free of any previous commitment as at this time. The discussion may therefore be ["discussed, as free of any previous commitment," *canceled*] postponed for the present, without inconvenience or disadvantage to either of ["the Parties" *interlined*].

The people of the two States respectively, on the one part, and the United States on the other, will be at full liberty, to remain independent Sovereignties, or to be but one nation, as may suit their mutual convenience. This is conform with natural justice: and provided the provisions of the Constitution of the United States be adhered to, these will afford a sufficient guarantee, on the subject of slavery and on any other, that the ultimate decision will be proper; and that a bare majority will not dictate terms to the other party. For no territory can be acquired otherwise, than by a fair treaty approved by two thirds of the Senate: and no new state can be erected, or admitted in the Union, in any other manner ["be" *imperfectly erased*] than by Congress, and therefore, with the co-operation and approbation of the House of Representatives.

But the treaty must be real and solid. Negotiated, on the part of Mexico, under duress, without the assent of the Congress of Queretaro, and, as it seems by men not vested with sufficient legitimate powers, it must afford a well founded expectation, that it shall be ratified freely by a Government truly representing the Mexican Nation. And its terms must also be such, as shall afford security for its permanence and solidity. They must, for that purpose, provide as far as practicable, against collisions, and against any other ["collisions" *canceled*] incidents which might produce, or afford pretences for a renewal of hostilities.

In this respect ["that" *altered to* "there"] is but one part of the proposed northern boundary of the Republic of Mexico, which is truly objectionable, and of any real and immediate importance, but its importance is such as to require the most serious consideration. It is obvious, that I allude to the condition which makes the Rio del Norte; from its mouth to the southern boundary of New Mexico, the boundary between the two countries. Setting altogether aside the question of right, and considering only the expediency of the measure. I have no hesitation in saying that, probably the ratification ["of" *canceled*] by Mexico of the proposed treaty, and most certainly the solidity and permanence of peace depend on the rejection of that line.

No one can deny, as an abstract proposition, that no more natural and eligible boundary can be devised, than the desert of 120 miles in breadth which separates the River Nu[e]ces from the Rio del Norte. None could be contrived more calculated to produce collisions, than a narrow river, fordable in many places, and to which there is a common right of navigation. Nothing can be more provoking, a greater nuisance to the weaker party, than a commanding and threatening position, from which its towns on the opposite side may be bombarded. It cannot be denied, that this boundary leaves Mexico, without a defensive frontier, exposed at all times to be invaded, and its interior provinces to be occupied by a powerful neighbour. Nothing finally can be more dangerous than to place, under such circumstances in immediate contact, the Texans and the Mexicans, with such feelings as have been generated by their relative position and long warfare. Alluding only to one of the many sources of collisions. I said on another occasion[,] "Where there was nothing but a fordable river to cross, slaves would perpetually escape from Texas; and where would be the remedy? Are the United States prepared to impose on Mexico, where slavery is unknown the obligation to surrender fugitive slaves?["]

It is idle to suppose, that the occupation of the left bank of the ["river" *canceled*] Rio Norte is wanted by the U. States, either as a defensive position, or as a security for the future good behaviour of the Mexicans. No candid man can believe, specially of [*sic*] the desert be made the boundary, that the Mexicans, after the severe lesson they have received, ever will begin an aggressive war. With such an immense superiority in every respect, and particularly with the indisputable command of the sea, the United States want no special defensive boundary in that quarter.

The desert itself would be a sufficient barrier against invasion. No other reason can be alleged for insisting on the Rio Norte Boundary, than a compliance with the claim advanced by Texas.

Not only will the abandonment of this pretension secure the permanence of peace: but no measure can better ensure the free ratification of the treaty by the Government of Mexico and the unreluctant and general acquiescence of that Nation. The high degree of importance, which Mexico justly attached to the continued possession of the left bank of the Rio Norte, has been manifested on every ["respect" *canceled*] occasion, and never more forcibly than in the negotiation with Mr. Trist, when he was an authorized agent. Kind and even grateful feelings will be restored, when the Mexicans find, that the United States leave them compact and secure, and that their true strength and their nationality remain ["unimpaired" *interlined*].

With respect to Texas, she will not deny, that her claim was disputed, and that by the act of annexation, the right to decide on the boundary was reserved by the United States. Moreover this detached belt of land, separated from the compact body of the State by the wide desert, and owned as far as it is fit for cultivation, by Mexicans, is of no intrinscis [*sic*] value, and adds nothing to the real strength of the State. It is only an outpost and, unless Texas entertains ulterior views, it is with her little more than a question of pride.

This has been fully gratified by her invincibility in the field; and she might afford to be even generous. Texas should also remember that, however ["entertains" *canceled*] convenient the annexation may have been to the United States, it will have cost them, besides thousands of invaluable lives, one hundred millions of dollars of destroyed capital, and will impose on them a debt of nearly the same amount. Yet if it would remove opposition from that quarter; it would be expedient to deduct three millions from the sum, which may be thought due to Mexico as a compensation for her cessions, and to pay that sum to Texas.

But if [the] state should notwithstanding every effort to obtain its assent, persist in opposing the cession of her claim it may reasonably be suspected, that there are some ["claim, it may reasonably be suspected, that there" *canceled*] other ulterior ["views" *canceled*] projets in view, that this obstinate retention of the left bank of the Rio Norte is only an entering wedge; through which, the Exaltados of the United States expect, that collisions will necessarily take place and may be encouraged, that a new war with Mexico will thus be provoked, or forced upon her, and that the plans of conquest dismemberment, subjugation, or annexation, may be carried into effect.

Additional Note. Though of much less immediate importance, but still for the same reasons, the river Gila, is an improper boundary. Here something more is wanted than is provided for by the Projet. For the sake of peace, the whole of the Country drained by the Colorado and its tributaries should belong to the U. States. The ridge which separates the waters from the South that empty into the River Gila, from the sources of the Rivers that fall into the Gulf of California, is the natural and proper boundary. An exception may be necessary in order to afford to Mexico a land communication with lower California. But the right of the free navigation of the Rio Colorado, from that point to its mouth should be expressly reserved; and, in order to secure it, the island of Algodones (in the Rio Colorado) should be included in the cession to the United States—See Coalter, Coalter 5th Vol. [of the Transactions of the] Royal Geog[raphical] Soc[iet]y London.

ALS with En in ScCleA; variant draft with En in NHi, Gallatin Papers; PC in Jameson, ed., *Correspondence*, pp. 1161–1162. NOTE: An autograph note affixed to the draft by Gallatin indicates that copies of this were also sent to [Thomas H.] Benton, [Daniel] Sturgeon, [John A.] Dix, [John M.] Berrien, and [John] Davis. The ALS and the variant draft with its En are published in the microfilm edition of the Albert Gallatin Papers, roll 44, frames 619 and 623–626.

To GEORGE W. BARTON, Philadelphia

Washington, 6th March 1848
My dear Sir, I take the liberty of introducing you to my son, J.C. Calhoun Jun[io]r who will deliver you this.

He visits Philadelphia with the intention of taking the summer course of medical lectures, which will commence I understand, about the 15th of this month. I will be obliged to you to introduce him to the Professors and to aid him in obtaining suitable quarters. With great respect Yours truly, J.C. Calhoun.

ALS in ScU-SC, John C. Calhoun Papers. NOTE: Barton was the brother-in-law of Calhoun's son-in-law Thomas G. Clemson.

To A[NNA] M[ARIA CALHOUN] CLEMSON, [Brussels]

Washington, 7th March 1848
My dear Daughter, The letters from home enclosed with this, & mine to Mr. [Thomas G.] Clemson will give you all the Pendleton & political news, so that you must regard this but as brief answer to yours by the Britannia.

I am happy to hear, that you all, except yourself, escaped the Influenza, & that you have recovered from its effects.

You must not suppose, that in contending ag[ai]nst corruption & interest, that I am impelled by the hope of success. Had that been the case, I would long since have retired from the conflict. Far higher motives impel me; a sense of duty; to do our best for our country, & leave the rest to Providence. I hold, the duties of life, to be greater than life itself, and that in performing them manfully, even ag[ai]nst hope, our labour is not lost, but will be productive of good in after times. Indeed, I regard this life very much as a struggle ag[ai]nst evil, & that to him, who acts on proper principle, the *reward is in the struggle, more than in victory itself*, although that greatly enhances it. So strong is my faith in this belief, my dear Daughter, that no appreciation of my efforts, either by the present, or after times, is necessary to sustain me in struggling to do my duty in resisting wrong, especially where our country is concerned, although I put a high value on renown. You will thus see, that in struggling ag[ai]nst the downward tendency of our country, it is not because, I do not take a just view of human nature, as you suppose, but because, I am actuated by higher motives, than what you attribute to me. But enough of this.

I am not surprised, that the powers of Europe so much dread changes. They are right; because what are called reform, will lead to anarchy, revolution & finally to a worse state of things, than now exists, ["in" *canceled and* "through" *interlined*] the most erroneous opinions now entertained ["by the popular party" *canceled*] both in Europe & this country by the movement, or popular party, as ["to" *interlined*] in what liberty consists, & by what means, it can be obtained & secured. Their opinion of liberty is, neither more nor less, than Dorrism.

I had a letter from Patrick [Calhoun] yesterday. He is well & looks I am told remarkably so. He expects to be here in a few days. He rarely writes to any one. I think, he has a mind, at last, to leave the Army, & get married, if he can find a girl to his fancy. I do hope he may. I am anxious to see him married & settled down. John [C. Calhoun, Jr.] has been with us a week & left yesterday for Philadelphia to take the summer course of medical lectures. He looks well, although not entirely recovered from a severe & dangerous attack of the measeles. I continue to receive good account of James [Edward Calhoun] & William [Lowndes Calhoun].

I am gratified to have so good account of your children [John Calhoun Clemson and Floride Elizabeth Clemson], & believe them to be all you say of them. I shall be very happy to see them & you & Mr. Clemson, as I hope to do next summer at Fort Hill. It will be a joyous & happy occasion.

Kiss the children for their Grandfather & tell them how much I want to see them. Your devoted father, J.C. Calhoun.

ALS in ScCleA; PEx in Jameson, ed., *Correspondence*, pp. 744–745.

To T[homas] G. Clemson

Washington, 7th March 1848
My dear Sir, The last Steamer brought a letter from Anna [Maria Calhoun Clemson] to me, the only one received by it. I am happy to learn by it, that she had entirely recovered from the attack of the Influenza, & that you & the children [John Calhoun Clemson and Floride Elizabeth Clemson] had escaped and were in such excellent health.

Since I wrote you last, the only occurrence, in the political world on this side, of marked importance, is the treaty with Mexico. It is now under deliberation in the Senate, and has been for the last nine days. No decisive vote has yet been taken; but I do not doubt, ["but" *canceled*] that the Senate will give its advise & consent to its ratification. The final vote will probably be taken tomorrow, or next day at fartherest. Its fate will, however, be still uncertain. Some important amendments have been made, to which the Mexican Governm[en]t may object, although I do not think it probable. The greatest danger is, that the Governm[en]t may not hold together until the treaty is exchanged. Nothing but the countenance of our Governm[en]t, & the support of capitalists interested in preserving it, can continue it in existence. It is, indeed, but the shadow of a Govern[m]ent.

As to the terms of the treaty, they are not such as to confer any éclat on the war, or the administration. I cannot of course speak of them in detail, but may say, that the end of all ["of" *canceled*] our expenditure of blood & money is, to pay the full value in money for the country ceded to us, and which might have been had without a war, or ["at" *canceled and* "for" *interlined*] the 10th part of its cost by taking a defensive line from the first, as I advised. The desire for peace, & not the approbation of its terms, induces the Senate to yield its consent.

The presidential election is in as great uncertainty as ever. The whigs are violently devided between [Henry] Clay & [Zachary] Taylor; and the democrats know not who to rally on. It is, indeed, a mere struggle for the spoils, and the selection of both parties will in the end be governed sol[el]y by the availability of the candidate, and not his qualifications.

I enclose two letters for Anna, which will give all the home news.

The winter has been delightful, & highly favourable for agricultural operations.

My health is good. Your affectionate father, J.C. Calhoun.

ALS in ScCleA; PC in Jameson, ed., *Correspondence*, pp. 745–746.

To A[lbert] Gallatin, [New York City]

Washington, 13th March 1848

My dear Sir, I read with much interest your letter [of 3/3] & the accompanying paper on the subject of the Mexican treaty. I concur in most of your views; but so great was the division of opinion in the Senate on the question of boundary & the other points, on which you touched, that on no one proposition in reference to them could a bare majority be had, much less that of two thirds. No alternative was left, but to pass the treaty, or to continue the war; and as between ["them" *interlined*] I could not hesitate.

The course of events have been unfortunate both to us & Mexico. It commenced with the rejection by the Senate of the treaty I negotiated for the annexation of Texas. Had it not been, I feel confident, that the true boundary between the United States & Mexico, and all questions of difference between them, would have ["been" *interlined*] settled & permanent peace established between them. I had at the time, full & free conversation with [Juan N. Almonte] the Mexican Minister, and explained to him all my views on the subject of boundary and the other points of difference. I proposed to draw the line through the desert to the East of the del Norte, so as to seperate the waters flowing into it and those flowing into the streams east of it, until it struck the mountain, which seperated the waters of the Red river and Arkansas from those flowing into it, and thence along the mountain to the 42 degree, and thence along it to some suitable point, from which it should be drawn, so to strike the Pacifick Ocean Some where between the Bay of St Francisco and Monterey. I also proposed to make adequate compensation for the cession of Territory, out of which the sum due to our citizens should be deducted; & also to pay the Texian portion of the debt of Mexico, at the time of her declaration of Independence. I had reason to believe, that the propositions were favourably received, & that a treaty on them, as a basis, might have been made. These expectations were all blasted by the rejection of the Texian treaty for the time. But I am under strong conviction, that had I been permitted to finish the Oregon negotiation, and consummate the arrangements growing out of the annexation of Texas, I could have ultimately ["have"(?) *interlined and imperfectly erased*] made a treaty with Mexico on the same basis. When I left the ["State" *interlined*] Department ["of State" *interlined and imperfectly erased*; "State" *canceled*], my intention was first to close the Oregon dispute on the 49th parallel, before any movement was made to adjust our difference with Mexico, which would give us the advantage of the British inf[l]uence with her Governm[en]t, in the adjustment of our difference with her. With that advantage, and the hopeless prospect of resisting us single handed, I had no fear, on such reasonable terms, of succeeding in making a treaty, and preserving peace between the two countries. Such still is my opinion.

I am happy to hear, through mutual acquaintances, that time has treated you so kindly, as to leave you in full possession of your faculties & much of your physical powers. That they may be long spared, to one who has so long & so well served his country is my sincere prayer. With great respect yours truly, J.C. Calhoun.

ALS in NHi, Gallatin Papers (published microfilm, Gallatin Papers, roll 44, frames 642–643).

Petition of Robert Monroe Harrison, presented by Calhoun to the Senate on 3/14. Calhoun moved that this petition "on the files of the Senate," be referred to the Committee on Foreign Relations. In a document dated 12/12/1846, Harrison, U.S. Consul at Kingston, Jamaica, asked Congress for indemnity against loss by the failure of a U.S. citizen (for whom he had acted as security) to appear in court in a suit in Jamaica. (The petition was referred, and a bill for Harrison's relief subsequently reported out.) DS in DNA, RG 46 (U.S. Senate), 30A–H6.1.

Remarks on the bill for an additional military force, 3/15. "Mr. Calhoun said, if no other gentleman desired to speak to-day, he would prefer the postponement of the bill till to-morrow, as he wished to show why he should not give the bill his support." Later in the day's proceedings, Calhoun said: "I had intended in any event to vote against this bill. Recent occurrences have rather increased than lessened the force of this resolution. If there is no objection I would prefer that the Senate adjourn [which it did]." From the New York, N.Y., *Herald*, March 17, 1848, p. 4. Variant in the Washington, D.C., *Daily Union*, March 19, 1848, pp. 1–2; *Congressional Globe*, 30th Cong., 1st Sess., pp. 467–469; Houston, ed., *Proceedings and Debates*, pp. 343–349. Other variants in the New York, N.Y., *Morning Courier and New-York Enquirer*, March 16, 1848, p. 2; the Philadelphia, Pa., *Public Ledger*, March 16, 1848, p. 3; the Petersburg, Va., *Republican*,

March 17, 1848, p. 2; the Charleston, S.C., *Mercury*, March 20, 1848, p. 2.

To F[RANCIS] W. PICKENS, [Edgefield, S.C.]

Senate Chamber, 16th March 1848

My dear Sir, I received by the last mail from Mr. [Thomas G.] Clemson's overseer, Mr. [Reuben H.] Reynolds, a letter, by which he informed me, that he would require additional horse force & supply of meat for the use of the plantation, without stating how much of either would be needed.

As it is impossible for me, with the imperfect information I possess, to act in the case, I must ask you, as a favour both to Mr. Clemson & myself, to act for me.

In order you may have all necessary information, I have enclosed this to Mr. Reynolds, with the request that he should deliver it to you himself.

I regret to give you this trouble, but the necessity of the case must be my apology. You will, of course, draw on Mr. [John Ewing] Bonneau for whatever sum will be necessary.

We have no news but such as the papers will give you. Yours truly, J.C. Calhoun.

ALS in ViLxW, Francis W. Pickens Papers. NOTE: Appended to this ALS is the following AES by Pickens: "This written after Mr. Calhoun had wounded my feelings at his own house the Fall before, & did it deliberately as he said to Judge [Andrew P.] Butler because his sons requested it of him, but he did not wish it. My Cousin Mrs. [Floride Colhoun] Calhoun I met with my family at Glen Springs, & she was very affectionate & visited & pressed us to visit them at Fort Hill. She went with us to Greenville and we went to Table Rock for a few days & promised her to go & see her. My wife [Marion Antoinette Dearing] was a stranger & never saw them before. We did go & Mr. C[alhoun] refused to meet us or to come into the house until late dinner & then acted out-rag[e]ously for a gent. in his own house, after his wife had pressed us, & after he had before written me expressly dated 27th Dec[embe]r[?] 1846 saying 'that it ["afforded" *canceled*] is a source of great gratification to me, that our relations should, after being for a time, apparently interrupted, stand where they have so long stood,' & besides this writing several very friendly letters, which threw me completely off my guard—And then after that to attempt to write me as if nothing had occurred!!" The address sheet of this letter is endorsed: "From Hon. J.C. Calhoun[,] March 1848[,] strange letter."

First Speech on the Bill for an Additional Military Force

[In the Senate, March 16, 1848]
The Senate having resumed the consideration of the bill making provision for an addition to the regular military force—

Mr. Calhoun addressed the Senate as follows:

After a very careful examination, I have not been able to find a single argument, which, in my opinion, would justify the passage of this bill, at this time, and under existing circumstances. I cannot but feel that those who have come to a different conclusion have overlooked the actual condition of the Mexican Government, and of the people of Mexico, in supposing that this bill was necessary either to intimidate or to coerce that Government into a ratification of the treaty recently acted upon here. If that Government were strong and vigorous, if the people of Mexico were united in resistance to us, and capable of sustaining a war in the event that the treaty shall not be ratified, there might be strong reasons for passing this bill. But such is not the case. On the contrary, the very opposite is. The Government itself is little more than a shadow; without an army and without revenue; the people in a state of distraction, with a large and powerful party in opposition to the Government and for a continuance of the war—not in hostility to us, but in hostility to their own Government, which they desire should be overthrown. The Government itself exists by our forbearance, and under our countenance; they have been induced to treat with us from the dread of their annihilation, and we to treat with them from the same consideration. For, strange as it may appear, the very motive that induced Mexico to treat with us, induced us to treat with her. She dreaded her annihilation, and so did we. It is difficult to say which would be subjected to the greatest evil in consequence of her annihilation. The danger is, not that the Mexican Government, in the event of the rejection of the treaty, would be able to resist, but it is, that it may perish before she can ratify it. But, if I am mistaken in all this, one thing is clear: without these ten additional regiments, we have the means of intimidating or coercing that Government to any extent we please. A single brigade can annihilate it. But even if we should choose to avoid this, we hold another power in our hands, that is ample to induce her to ratify the treaty, provided there be any hesitation on her part. We would, in that case, have but to tell her that we will adopt the boundary agreed upon in the treaty, and thus save ourselves the vast sum of twenty millions of dollars, which rumor states we are to give for the ceded territory. To obtain this sum was her inducement to agree to the treaty, and the fear of losing it would be sufficient to induce her to ratify it, provided the Mexican Government can maintain itself until it has acted upon the treaty, including the amendments made by this body.

In this view of the subject, I regard the passage of this bill, if it be intended either for the purpose of intimidation or coercion, to be entirely useless—an unmeaning bravado. But it is worse than useless; it is mischievous, and will prove to be mischievous both here and there. Mischievous here, for if this body, conversant with all the secret proceedings in reference to the treaty, and supposed by the country to be fully informed of everything in relation to the subject, should pass the bill now before us, it will be received by the public as an apprehension on our part that there is great danger that the treaty will not be ratified, and the effect upon our commerce, and upon the money interest of the country, will be highly injurious. It will be mischevious there, for the real danger that the Mexican Government has to fear, is this: there is a large party in Mexico called Puros, which is unwilling to see a peace concluded between the Mexican Government and this country; unwilling—not because they are our friends or enemies, but simply for the reason that they wish to see that Government annihilated, and the power placed in their hands. Now if the impression produced there by the passage of this bill should be, that there is danger that the treaty will not be ratified, it will arouse and animate that party to double exertion, in order to fulfil their object.

But I consider it not only useless, not only mischevious in the light which I have indicated, but it will be a costly bravado. I take it for granted that the honorable chairman of the Committee on Military Affairs [Lewis Cass] does not intend simply that this bill shall pass this body—that would be unworthy of his character. He then expects that it will also pass the other branch of Congress, and become a law, and that the force will be raised and be employed, if the treaty should fail, in carrying on the war with Mexico. Well, if the bill passes—and I must consider it in that light—in that case, what will be the result? There will be no difficulty in getting officers and men. Officers will greedily seek the honors and the emoluments attached to command, and the men will readily enlist, for they will have no apprehension of going to Mexico or fighting future battles. The enlistment will turn out to be a profitable speculation. Each recruit will receive, on enlistment, a bounty in land of 160 acres, and in money of twelve dollars. He will also receive the issue of clothing usual on such occasions, equal, at the present time, to about twenty-one dollars; estimating the bounty in land at on[e] dollar and twenty-five cents an acre, that item alone would make $2,000,000. Add the other two items and the whole would not be less than two millions three or four hundred thousand dollars. Add to this the pay and emoluments of the officers, the pay to the soldiers, the expense for their subsistence, and the expense of their recruiting, and it will be found that the passage of this bill will subject the Government to the sum of three millions of dollars, even if the treaty should be ratified and not a man ever go to Mexico—no small sum for an unmeaning bravado. But the mischief will not end here; the appointment of five hundred officers and this great expenditure would confer vast patronage on the President, and that, too, on the eve of a Presidential election, when it is always brought into the highest degree of activity. I will not attempt to show that it would be a great evil to increase the patronage of the Executive. It is already enormously great, as every man of every party must acknowledge, if he would candidly express his sentiments. Now I submit to my friends on this side of the chamber [the Democrats], who would be responsible for the passage of this bill, are you prepared to add this great additional sum to the already heavy debt incurred in the prosecution of this war, and this great increase of patronage to that which the war has already added, for an idle bravado, unbecoming a great and magnanimous Government, as I have already clearly shown.

But I not only object to the passage of this bill at this time, and under existing circumstances, but I take higher ground; I am opposed to the bill at all times and under all circumstances. I would have voted against it if the treaty had not been made, for reasons conclusive to my mind, as I shall next proceed to state.

We all know the history of the origin of this bill. It was reported early this session, and originated in the message of the President recommending a vigorous prosecution of the war. Its leading and main object was to carry that recommendation into effect, as has often been stated on this floor by the chairman of the Military Committee, and others, who have advocated its passage. Indeed, it has been repeatedly acknowledged that it would not be necessary but for that purpose. If, then, we should pass this bill, according to my conception, it would be, in fact, to give a pledge to the Executive, and to the country, that if the treaty should fail, we will resort to the vigorous prosecution of the war, in conformity to the President's recommendation at the opening of the session. I, for one, am unwilling to give such a pledge—unwilling, because I think it ought not to be given, if it could be redeemed; and unwilling, because, if given, I am of the impression it never could be redeemed.

I have assigned fully, on a former occasion, the reasons why I am opposed to what is called a vigorous prosecution of the war. I will not repeat them here, further than to state that I am opposed to it: first, because it will annihilate the Mexican Government, and leave no authority in that distracted country with whom we could treat; and next, because the effect of that would be to subject the whole country, and throw on us one of two alternatives, either to create a Government by our own authority, with which to treat, (to which no true republican would ever assent,) or to hold it as a conquered country, to be governed as a subject province, or be incorporated into this Union. Now, as I am utterly opposed to either of these results, I cannot give this pledge.

Nor can I give it, because I have not the least expectation that, if given, it will ever be redeemed. The sentiment of the whole country is remarkably changed, since the commencement of this session, in reference to the war. There was, at that time, a large party scattered over every portion of the country in favor of conquering the whole of Mexico. To prove that such was the case, it is only necessary to refer to the proceedings of numerous large public meetings, to declarations repeatedly made in the public journals, and to the opinions expressed by officers of the army and individuals of standing and influence, to say nothing of declarations made here and in the other house of Congress. But this sentiment is now changed. And why is it changed? Because the people were not aware, at that time, that what was called a vigorous prosecution of the war would, under existing circumstances, inevitably lead to the consequences I have stated, whether intended or not. But as soon as they saw that such would be the consequences, they drew back, and put the seal of their reprobation upon them, not only for the present, but I trust forever. Such being the case, it is an idle dream to suppose that, in the event of the failure of a treaty, this war would ever be renewed to be carried on vigorously, with a certain knowledge of the results to which it will lead. It is, indeed, highly honorable to the good sense and patriotism of our people, that seeing that the result of the policy recommended would be to conquer Mexico, to be held as a subject province, or incorporated in this Union, they have raised a nearly unanimous voice of reprobation against it, in despite of the temptation held out to their pride, ambition, and cupidity, by the advocates of a vigorous prosecution of the war.

But, it may be asked, what shall be done if the treaty be not ratified by Mexico? Should such be the case, no alternative would remain but to adopt the line of boundary established by the treaty, to take possession of the country covered by it, and defend it against Mexico, if she should ever attempt to disturb our possession, which is hardly probable. She is too weak, distracted, and exhausted, even if she should be so inclined. Nor would we be subject to any additional cost, compared to what we would be subject in holding the country in our possession under the treaty; for it would take fully as large an army, and as great expense to protect Mexico, under the stipulations of the treaty, against the Indians, falling on our side of the line, as it would take to protect ourselves against the Mexicans, by assuming the line without the treaty; while we would save the large sum of twenty millions of dollars, in the latter case, to be paid to Mexico in the former. Indeed, the whole affair is in our own hands, whether the treaty fails or not, if we do but exercise a little common sense, and avoid, what I detest above all things, a system of menace and bravado into which we have lately fallen in the management of our negotiations. I had hoped that this system had been abandoned forever after the bad success which has attended it. It was resorted to in the Oregon negotiation, and would have terminated in involving us in a war with England, but for the firmness and wisdom of this body. It was resorted to in our negotiations with Mexico. The order to Gen. [Zachary] Taylor to march to the Rio Grande constituted a part of it. I cannot believe that the President [James K. Polk], in giving the order, contemplated, or even believed, it would lead to a conflict between the armies of the two countries, because, if he did, it would have been an impeachable offence. It was intended but as a menace, to bring Mexico to terms, but, unfortunately, under circumstances which prevented the interposition of the Senate to prevent conflict, as in the case of Oregon, and this unhappy war, which we now so much desire to terminate, was the consequence.

But the vigorous prosecution of the war was not the only avowed object for introducing this bill; it was, indeed, the primary and principal one; but there was another, secondary, it is true, though not much less important. It was intended, in part, to carry into execution a system of imposts and taxes, imposed by the President, by his own authority, upon Mexico. The army, including the very force to be raised by this bill, was intended to be used for collecting these duties and imposts; and for that purpose, as it was avowed, and officially announced, was to be spread all over Mexico.

Now, I hold we cannot pass this bill without sanctioning the act of the President in imposing this system of impost[s] and taxes. This

I never can do, because I am under a deep conviction that the President has no right whatever to impose them, and that in so doing he acted without the authority of constitution or law, and established a precedent, which, if it be not reversed, will be fatally dangerous to the liberty and institutions of the country. Thus thinking, I would not be true to my trust if I did not raise my voice against it. I would, indeed, have been glad not to have been forced, at this time, to do so. My friends around me know that I was anxious that this bill should not be pressed to its passage now. Not that I desired to shun the responsibility of expressing my opinion, because I preferred postponing it until after the treaty was ratified, when there would be no pretence for raising the cry of giving "aid and comfort" to the enemy. But as it has been resolved to force the bill through, and as this is the first measure proposed since the adoption of the system, a vote on which would sanction it, I feel myself compelled by the highest obligation of duty to state my reasons for opposing it. If, under circumstances, it involves any responsibility, it ought to fall, not on me, but upon those who, without any necessity, as I have shown, have forced me to express my opinions.

But, to return to the discussion. I ask, where can the President find authority for laying duties and taxes on the commerce and people of Mexico? If it exists at all, it must be found in the Constitution or the laws; can it be found in the former? If so, point it out. Can it be found in the laws? If so, point it out. It will not be pretended that either confer[s], expressly, any such authority upon him; but it may be said, that it is embraced in his implied powers; that is, the powers necessary and proper to carry into execution those expressly invested in him. If so, point out the powers expressly vested in him by the Constitution, to which this is necessary and proper, to carry into execution. But, let me say to the advocates of this bill, if you could succeed in doing this, which you cannot, it will not remove the difficulty; for, by showing that it is an implied power, you but impose upon yourselves the necessity of pointing out some act of Congress authorizing its exercise. The framers of our Constitution had the sagacity of vesting in Congress all implied powers; that is, powers necessary and proper to carry into effect all the delegated powers wherever vested. I refer to what is usually called its residuary clause, which provides that "Congress shall have power to pass all laws necessary and proper to carry into execution the foregoing powers, (that is powers vested in Congress,) or powers vested in any of the departments or officers of the Government." It matters not then, in what department or branch of the Government a power may be vested, whether in the legislative, the executive, or judiciary, or in this or that officer of the government, it belongs to Congress, and exclusively to Congress, under this express provision, to pass all laws necessary and proper for carrying it into execution.

The effect of this important and sagacious provision is to vest Congress with all the discretionary power; and of course, making it necessary for the other departments to show an express provision of the Constitution or some act of Congress to authorise the exercise of any power whatever. It is thus that this Government is made a Government of Constitution and law, and not of discretion. And of course the advocates of the bill, even if they could show it to be an implied power, must still show an act of Congress authorising its exercise.

But it may be said that the President is commander-in-chief of the army of the United States, including the portion in Mexico, and that it is essential to his power, in that character, to impose a system of taxation in case of a foreign war in the enemies['] country. If, indeed, it be essential to his power, as is supposed, it results that it cannot be separated from it without destroying the power itself, and it must of course belong to him, as commander-in-chief, wherever he exercises its powers, and, of course, as well in the United States as in Mexico, or any other conquered country. But it is manifest that it cannot be essential to his power in that character within the limits of the United States, because the constitution expressly invests the power of taxation, not in the President, but in Congress. To this it may be replied, that there is a distinction between exercising the power in the United States and exercising it in Mexico, or any other place beyond the bounds of the United States, where our army may be operating. To those who make this reply, I put the question, why so? What makes the distinction? What possible reason can be assigned why the power may be exercised in one and not in the other? Who can answer these questions?

But if it be a fact that the President can exercise in Mexico a power expressly delegated to Congress, and which he cannot exercise in the United States, I would ask what are the limits to his power in Mexico? Has he the power also of appropriating the money collected by the taxes without sanction of Congress, when the Constitution expressly provides that no money shall be appropriated without authority of law? Has he the power to apply the money to whatever purpose he may think proper, and among others, to raise a military force in Mexico, without the sanction of Congress, when the Constitution expressly vests the power of raising and maintaining armies in Congress? If he can exercise these important powers expressly given to another department, what is there to prevent him from exercising all the powers of the Constitution, or any other that he may think proper? If so, he stands in a two-fold character in the two countries—the constitutional President of the United States, and the absolute and despotic ruler of Mexico. To what will this lead? What may he not do? He may lay taxes at his pleasure, either as to kind or amount—he may establish rules and regulations for their collection. He may dispose of them as he sees fit, without passing their proceeds into the Treasury. He may of course raise armies, and pay them out of the proceeds of the taxes. May, do I say—he has already done all this, upon his own exclusive authority, without deigning to consult Congress. How much further may he not go? May he not wage war on his own authority against the adjacent country of Guatamala and the South American States, to the extreme limits of the continent? May he not equip a fleet and attack the islands of the South sea, or conquer Japan, or the adjacent parts of the continent? May he not, finally, turn his army against his own country, and make it the instrument of her subjugation? All this he may do, if it once be conceded that he has the power of doing what this bill is in part intended to enable him to do, without the possibility of Congress preventing.

But, it may be asked, do I deny him all power, and if not what are the limits of his power in Mexico? No: I admit that he has power and important powers—nor am I at a loss to assign its limits. The Constitution assigns to him the power of commanding in chief the army, wherever stationed—a power which gives him the command in chief, and no more, that is, the supreme control in conducting and directing the army in its military operations. Such is the true interpretation of the word. They confer neither more nor less power. Instead of conferring an absolute power, as is supposed, they confer relatively a very restricted one, of which the Constitution and legislation of the country furnish many evidences. The very act which recognizes this war with Mexico, furnishes a striking illustration. Upon its face it shows that the act of recognising or declaring war did not necessarily carry with it the authority even of employing either the army or navy for its prosecution—for the power of employing both is expressly vested in him by the act. If we look back to other acts declaring war, we shall find that they, in like manner, confer the same power. If we turn from these to the laws for suppressing insurrection, or repelling invasion, we shall find their framers deemed it necessary to authorise the President to employ the militia and the army for the purpose. If we turn to the Constitution, we shall there find decisive evidence of its being regarded by its framers as a power within narrow limits. For if there be any power which one would suppose might be inferred to belong to the commander-in-chief, it would be that of establishing rules and regulations for the government of the army and navy, and yet this very power is given by an express provision to Congress. Is it not strange that with all this evidence and much more that might be added, going to show how restricted the power of the President as commander-in-chief is, there should be any one, and especially any professing popular principles, who would give the unlimited and despotic power claimed for the President in Mexico?

But, it may be asked, has the conqueror no power to impose taxes on a conquered country? Yes, he certainly has. When an army invades a country and subdues it, in whole or in part, the conqueror has unquestionably the right; but under our system of Government, the question occurs, who is the conqueror? I answer, the people of the United States. It is they who have conquered Mexico—not the Government—not the President—not the Generals—not the Army! These are but the instruments by which they effected the conquest; and it is the people of the United States, in the character of our conqueror, that have the exclusive right to impose taxes. But who represents the United States—who is the organ through which they must act for the purpose? I answer this Government—the Federal Government of these States—consisting of the executive, legislative, and judicial departments—each in its proper sphere. The question then is, within what sphere does the President properly and exclusively represent the United States in a conquered country? The answer is, to no other but as the commander-in-chief of the army and navy. In almost all other respects Congress is the sole representative, and to them especially belongs, by express delegation, the power of laying and collecting taxes, without restriction or distinction, as far as the authority of the United States extends. Now, it is an established principle of international law, that wherever a country is subdued, even in part, its sovereignty is for the time suspended, and that of the conquering, substituted in its place. Of course, in our case, with the sovereignty of the people of the United States the authority of their Government, through its respective departments, attaches to it, in like manner as if it were a part of the United States, each acting in its appropriate sphere. The opposite doctrine, which would make the President the sole and exclusive representative of the sovereignty of the United States in such cases, is entirely destitute of authority, and would lead to all the monstrous consequences which have been traced. All this is so clear, that it is not a little surprising that it should have been overlooked in the prosecution of this war, or that there should have been any division or diversity of sentiment in reference to it; and as the taxes, which are the subject of these remarks, were imposed by the President in the interval between this and the preceding session, and as this is the first opportunity I have had to express my opinion in reference to the subject, as I have already stated, I avail myself of the occasion to put in my most solemn protest against the power. If it should become a precedent in future wars, it would lead to consequences of the most fatal character. It would elevate the power of the President above that of the other departments and the Constitution itself, and end, almost necessarily, in establishing despotic authority in that branch of the Government. The danger is imminent. We are a warlike people, rapidly increasing in numbers, population, and wealth—well fed and well clothed, and having abundance of leisure—like all such people, we seek excitement; and there is no excitement more seductive to the young and ardent portion of our population than war. It is difficult to prevent such a people from rushing into war on any pretence; and if they should frequently recur, and this precedent be not reversed, nothing can prevent the Executive power from overshadowing the Constitution and liberties of the country. We now have an opportunity to reverse it, if we think proper, by giving a strong and decided vote against a bill, the passage of which, as has been shown, is perfectly useless, and even worse than useless.

It is proper to remark, in conclusion, that I am aware that there are some doubtful questions as to the extent of the power of the President, in his character of commander-in-chief. Among these may be ranked that of levying contributions, in the strict sense of the term, and establishing temporary governments. I will not now enter in the investigation whether they belong to him or not, but my impression is, that in the portion of the enemy's country in which the authority of the United States is established for the time, he has not the right, without the sanction of law, to levy contributions, or to establish temporary governments. In coming to this conclusion, I readily concede to the President, as commander-in-chief, many and great powers, but they are such as arise out of exigencies immediately connected with the operations of the army, and its success or safety—among them I include the power of seizing supplies of every description, and to remove every obstacle necessary to be removed for security or victory. For that purpose, town[s] and cities may be battered down and destroyed; but when he undertakes to exercise power, on his own authority, over subdued territories, unconnected with the operations of the army, he exercises, in my opinion, a power not belonging to him. Congress may, by law, indeed, authorise him to levy contributions, or to establish temporary governments in such territory; but it is one thing to exercise it on his own authority, and another to exercise it under the authority of law. The one places him under the control of law, while the other places him above its control.

I have now expressed my opinion. In all I have said I have put myself, I trust, above party feelings or personal consideration. I am actuated by the single motive, a desire to prevent an unconstitutional and dangerous act from becoming a precedent, which there is great cause to fear it would, if not noticed or exposed.

From *Speeches of Mr. Calhoun, of South Carolina, on the Ten Regiment Bill; and in Reply to Mr. Davis, of Mississippi, and Mr. Cass. Delivered in the Senate of the United States, March 16 and 17, 1848* (Washington: printed by John T. Towers, 1848), pp. 3–10. Also printed in Crallé, ed., *Works*, 4:425–439. A slightly variant report in *Congressional Globe*, 30th Cong., 1st Sess., pp. 477–479; Houston, ed., *Proceedings and Debates*, pp. 351–353; the Washington, D.C., *Daily National Intelligencer*, March 18, 1848, p. 2; the Alexandria, Va., *Gazette and Virginia Advertiser*, March 20, 1848, p. 2; the Richmond, Va., *Whig and Public Advertiser*, March 24, 1848, p. 2; the Charleston, S.C., *Mercury*, March 28, 1848, p. 2; the Columbia, S.C., *South-Carolinian*, March 28, 1848, p. 2; the Georgetown, S.C., *Winyah Observer*, March 29, 1848, p. 2; the Nashville, Tenn., *Whig*, March 30, 1848, p. 2. Variant reports in the Washington, D.C., *Daily Union*, March 16, 1848, p. 2; the New York, N.Y., *Morning Courier and New-York Enquirer*, March 16, 1848 (Supplement), p. 1; the Alexandria, Va., *Gazette and Virginia Advertiser*, March 17, 1848, p. 2; the Louisville, Ky., *Morning Courier*, March 17, 1848, p. 3; the New York, N.Y., *Herald*, March 17, 1848, p. 2; the Philadelphia, Pa., *Public Ledger*, March 17, 1848, p. 3; the Baltimore, Md., *Sun*, March 17, 1848, p. 4; the Charleston, S.C., *Courier*, March 20, 1848, p. 2; the Charleston, S.C., *Mercury*, March 20, 1848, p. 2; the Richmond, Va., *Enquirer*, March 21, 1848, p. 1.

SECOND SPEECH ON THE BILL FOR AN ADDITIONAL MILITARY FORCE

In Senate, March 17, 1848

The same subject being again under consideration, Mr. Calhoun addressed the Senate as follows:

I rise to make a very few remarks. When I addressed the Senate yesterday, in reply to the question, What shall we do if the treaty is not ratified, I answered—take possession of the country which is ceded to us by that instrument, occupy it, and defend it. The worthy

245

Senator from Michigan (Mr. [Lewis] Cass) says, he is at a loss to understand what I mean by that. Well, there is not much difference between us. I am at a loss to understand why he cannot understand it. It appears to me to be one of the plainest propositions in the world. He has hunted up a thousand imaginary difficulties that never did exist, and never can exist, in order to make good his case. Does he wish to know how my plan can be carried out? I point to the case of Texas. The whole of the eastern frontier, according to the line ceded to us by the treaty, was the boundary which Texas claimed as against Mexico. Now, does not every man know, that for seven long years, Texas held possession of that frontier to the Nueces, without a single invasion on the part of Mexico, and that at a time when Texas had not more than three or four companies of regulars altogether? Now, sir, if Texas could hold that line then, is there any difficulty with Texas in doing it now, as far as the Rio Grande, when she has doubled her population, and is backed by the whole of the United States? And yet the worthy Senator from Michigan cannot understand it! It is impossible that he can understand it! Again, as to California, he is, if possible, more at a loss with regard to that. His first great difficulty is as to our occupying the Gulf of California. If the Senator will remember, the line that I proposed passed through the whole extent of the Gulf of California, and if he will look at the map he will find it is a very broad expanse of water. He will find that it covers a very large portion of California—all the settled and inhabited portion of California. If he will look at the statistics of Mexico, he will find that she has not a single armed vessel. Now, what I asserted was, that a few armed vessels—one or two steamers among them—occupying that expanse of water, would be sufficient to secure us against all attacks of Mexico on that portion of the line; and yet the Senator could not understand it! It is, as I understand, with him, a sort of metaphysical idea! Now, as to the residue of that line. The whole length of it is about four or five hundred miles from the head of the Gulf to the Paso del Norte. That is all that remains to be defended. Well, the whole of the country covered by that line is inhabited by Indian tribes, so powerful that there is no fear of Mexico invading it. They invade Mexico! They are too powerful for her; and it will not require a single soldier to be stationed on its whole extent to protect us against Mexico. There may be some protection necessary against the Indians. Indeed, California is so remote from Mexico, and the difficulty of approach so great, that the mere handful of people in California have been enabled, in fact, to have almost an independent government there. I venture to say that not a single regiment will be needed there—that the Americans now there, together with the natives who are well affected towards us, and desirous of seeing our authority established, will be quite adequate to defend it against Mexico forever, with the aid of a few vessels in the Gulf of California.

Now, I venture to present, what no doubt will appear to the Senator, a very bold proposition: the cost would be vastly less to fall back and occupy the country without the treaty, than to occupy it under the treaty. I beg the especial attention of the Senator. Under the treaty—I may speak of what every one knows perfectly well—a large mass of Indians is thrown on our side of the line, and, from the necessity of the case, we shall be compelled to defend Mexico against these Indians; or, if we should not, and Mexico should have force enough, she will have the right to pass over and attack these Indians within our line, to which we could not submit. For that purpose, then, we will be obliged to establish a line of military posts along the whole length of the Gila, from the Paso del Norte to the head of the Gulf of California. But it would require a larger and more expensive force to occupy this long line of posts, so as to defend Mexico against the Indians, than would be necessary to occupy and defend the country against the Mexicans themselves. The reason is obvious. The Gulf of California, as I have stated, will cover, with a few vessels, the whole of the settled part of California; and the intervening Indian tribes between the head of the Gulf of California and the Paso del Norte would effectually cover us from the possibility of an attack on that part of the line from the Mexicans. Nor would it be necessary to have any considerable force to protect us against the Indians, as their hostility to Mexico, and their love of plunder would direct their warfare exclusively against Mexico. Thus the long line, of which the Senator spoke, of fifteen hundred miles, could, to its whole extent, from the Pacific Ocean, to the Paso del Norte, be defended by a small force, and at an inconsiderable expenditure, if held without the treaty. The only remaining part is that from the Paso to the Gulf of Mexico, along the Rio del Norte; and we know from the experience of Texas how little that will probably cost. Now, if we add to this difference, in the cost of defending the country without the treaty, and of defending under the treaty, the large sum of fifteen or twenty millions of dollars, which will be saved if Mexico refuses to ratify the treaty, there can be no doubt but we will be great gainers, in a pecuniary point of view, if she should refuse to ratify.

But I understand the drift of the Senator's remarks in this particular. He and I entertained directly opposite opinions as to what should be done, in case the treaty should not be ratified. He is, in that event, for a vigorous prosecution of the war, and hence his vigorous attack upon the policy of which, in that case, I am in favor, and exaggerated statement of the expense and difficulty of maintaining it. Indeed, there has been a standing conflict between the two lines of policy, almost from the commencement of the war, and hence the repeated assaults of a similar character, which have been repeatedly made on that which I have maintained, and with the same view, by those who support the policy maintained by the Senator. But I have no fear—none in the world—that we shall ever return to a "vigorous prosecution of the war." That day is gone. You cannot vitalize the policy. It is buried. The country would consider it the greatest misfortune that could befall us, if we were to reopen and renew the Mexican war. The tide of public opinion is running with irresistible force against it. I have no apprehension of it. But I do desire that in the meantime the public mind shall not be occupied with an idea which will prevent it from falling readily into its natural position, if this treaty should be ratified. If the treaty should not be ratified, it is plain that we must keep possession of the country, and defend it.

Every Senator can speak of his course and his votes in the secret session. I voted for the treaty, and I supported it. But did I do that because I regarded it as preferable to the course which I indicated at the commencement of this and last session? No, sir, not at all. I did it for two reasons: In the first place, I was anxious to terminate this war on any reasonable ground, and was determined to avail myself of the earliest opportunity of terminating it; for I hold it to be pregnant of evil of the most dangerous character, if it continues. In the next place, it is the natural way of terminating hostilities between nations; and many of my friends whom I see around me will testify that I have declared, for the last three or four weeks, that I was in favor of allowing the Administration reasonable time to make a treaty. But at the same time I was not ignorant of the many advantages of a defensive line. And again, I take this opportunity to say, that, so far as my voice is concerned, I wish it now to be established, as I hope it will be, by the ratification of the treaty. I hope we never shall take, by an aggressive war, one foot of territory by conquest. We pay by the treaty the full value—more than the full value—a hundred times more than the full value, as far as Mexico is concerned; for it is worse than useless to her, and the full value as far as we are concerned, and I rejoice it is so. I wish to square accounts liberally and justly with Mexico, and we have done so, and hence my desire that Mexico shall ratify this treaty, and receive this money.

These are my views. As to the other remarks which the Senator was pleased to make, with regard to my speech of yesterday, I pass them by without comment, except as they relate to the right of the President to establish a system of taxes in Mexico. I listened to the Senator, as I always do, with attention, and I must say, if I could have entertained a doubt as to the truth of the position which I assumed yesterday, all doubt would be dispelled. We know that the gentleman is deeply versed in the principles of law, of great intelligence, capable of investigating questions of this character. I expected when he rose, that he would meet the points which were presented; that he would attempt to show their fallacy, and exhibit the true principles which ought to govern us in this case, if mine were false. I was disappointed. As far as I understood the Senator—and if I be in error, I hope he will correct me—he assumes one broad position, which, in my judgment, I say it with great deference, is without a particle of truth to sustain it. He assumes that the President [James K. Polk], in consequence of the declaration of war, has an unlimited power in Mexico. Am I right?

Mr. Cass. Unlimited, except by the restrictions imposed by the law of nations.

Mr. Calhoun. Well, then, the law of nations does not prohibit an order of nobility. Can he create nobles in Mexico? Give me the answer.

Mr. Cass. Is that one of the incidents of the war-making power?

Mr. Calhoun. I repeat it. Can he establish an order of nobility?

Mr. Cass. I would not give much for the patents of nobility.

Mr. Calhoun. Can he establish an order of nobles?

Mr. Cass. Without going into any detail, I may state, that the commander-in-chief and his generals may do any act, in the prosecution of the war in Mexico, which is not prohibited by the law of nations. All I can do is to lay down general principles. It cannot be expected that I should go into details of all that may or may not be done.

Mr. Calhoun. I did not intend this as an irrelevant or impertinent question, and I must regard the Senator's refusal to deny, as an admission, on his part, that the President has the power. Indeed it followed necessarily from the principle laid down by him. It would indeed be an important power in the hands of the President to bring, and subject, a conquered country under his arbitrary rule. The Senator acknowledges that the power is a very dangerous one. It is indeed a dangerous power, if it be as unlimited as he contends for. Can he create a field-marshal in Mexico? The Senator will not doubt that if the President could raise an army there, he can create a field-marshal. I hold it to be the most monstrous proposition ever uttered within the Senate, that conquering a country like Mexico, the President can constitute himself a despotic ruler, without the slightest limitation on his power. If all this be true, war is indeed dangerous! If that be the fact, we ought never to engage in a war of conquest. If that be the fact, there are double reasons for the ratification of the treaty, and fleeing the country.

There is a tendency in all parties, when they have been for a long time in possession of power, to augment it. It has been the fortune of the popular party in this country to hold possession of the Government for a great length of time, and it is no more than human nature that the effect of that long continued tenure should be the creation of the fondness of power, that, necessarily, diminishing [*sic*] the love of liberty. This love of power leads men to strike at those provisions of the Constitution which restrict power. I believe that the popular party in this country [the Democrats] have resisted this tendency for a great length of time to a considerable extent; but it is impossible for any man who reads the early history of that party not to be impressed with the conviction that it has departed from the principles which then characterized it. The declaration of the Chairman of the Committee on Military Affairs this evening, proves a great departure beyond all controversy. I did not believe that there was a man in this country—certainly not that there was one in the Senate—who would declare that the President of the United States, as commander-in-chief of the army in Mexico, has no restrictions on his power but those imposed by the law of nations.

Mr. Cass. After the Senator has concluded I may say what I did declare.

Mr. Calhoun. I will gladly hear the Senator now.

Mr. Cass. When the honorable Senator from South Carolina has finished—

Mr. Calhoun. Then I shall finish now.

Mr. Cass. What I maintain is, that the commander-in-chief and the generals under him have a right to do any act of war justified by the law of nations, and it belongs to every officer of the army, from a general down to a corporal. I went at large into the question, in the remarks which I had the honor to make to-day. The course taken in Mexico has been fully justified by the practice of war in all ages.

Whether the contribution be in cash or kind, the principle is the same. One word as to the line which the honorable Senator has laid down. I have presented the objections to it which, to my judgment, are decisive, and I need not repeat them. No public opinion in the world could permit such a thing as the establishment of a line behind which an operating army must retire. If you are at war with an enemy, you cannot stop upon a given line. But Texas pursued the enemy; and whenever you follow the enemy beyond the line, the project is abandoned.

Mr. Calhoun. But the Senator puts the question, How can I justify the army in performing any act not authorized expressly by law? I take the ground, that the army may do under the President, as commander-in-chief, any thing that properly belongs to him in that character. Now, the extent is not defined; it is governed by the exigencies of war. I believe I use the very terms employed in the elementary works upon this subject. But these acts must relate to war, and not to legislate for a conquered country. Now, if you mean that an army in operation can seize provisions of every description, means of transportation, and so on, I never denied it; but if you mean to say, that after the country is conquered, the commander-in-chief may levy either taxes or contributions, I deny the doctrine altogether.

Mr. [Jefferson] Davis, of Mississippi. The President has clearly the right to move the army of the United States into any portion of its territory.

Mr. Calhoun (in his seat). Certainly not into disputed territory.

Mr. Davis. The Senator says that the President has not the right to move the army into any disputed territory. When we annexed Texas, we left this boundary question open for negotiation. The Administration sought assiduously to settle the question by negotiation. What, then, is the argument of the Senator? When the opposite party refuse to settle the question by negotiation, are we to be estopped? Are we to allow the enemy to wrest from us the dominion which we claim as ours of right? If so, what is this but a broad invitation to every land to dispute the boundary with us? But I would ask the honorable Senator, how comes it, that even before the annexation of Texas, the navy of the United States was ordered to the Gulf of Mexico for the protection of Texas?

Mr. Calhoun. The answer is obvious. The Gulf of Mexico is the common property of all nations. It is not disputed. But though we had a right to lay off Vera Cruz, we had not the right to enter the harbor of Vera Cruz.

Mr. Davis. Was it not the gentleman's own order [while Secre-

251

tary of State] to make a naval demonstration against Vera Cruz?

Mr. Calhoun. I have no knowledge of such an order. Will the Senator permit me to notice another point? He indicated that the President had a right to march the army into any disputed territory. Am I right?

Mr. Davis. I do not consider it disputed territory.

Mr. Calhoun. The Senator says he does not consider it disputed territory, in what he differs from the resolutions annexing Texas, for they expressly admit the country to the east of the Del Norte, to a certain extent at least, to be disputed territory, by providing that the boundary between Texas and Mexico, shall be settled by the Government of the United States. Now, as Texas never claimed any country beyond the Del Norte, it results necessarily, that the point to be settled was, whether the boundary of Texas extended to that river or not, admitting, of course, that country lying east to some extent, was disputed territory. Now, I ask, how is a question of disputed territory to be settled? There can be but two modes. By negotiation or war. As far as it relates to the former, the President, with the Senate, represent exclusively the United States; but when negotiation fails to settle a disputed boundary, nothing is more clear, that if it becomes necessary to resort to war to establish the boundary, in that case, the power passes out of the hands of the President into that of Congress, which, under the Constitution, exclusively possesses the war-making power, and that it belongs, in that case, exclusively to Congress, to determine where the boundary is, and, if it thinks proper, to authorize the President to establish it by force. The great mistake of the Senator, and those who think with him, is to look exclusively to the question between Mexico and the United States, and to overlook entirely the question, between the departments of our own Government. As between the United States and Mexico, there can be no doubt, that when negotiation failed, the United States had the right to establish by force the boundary for themselves. But the question is, through what department. Through the President, or through Congress? The very statement of this question is sufficient to decide it to all who have the least knowledge of our Constitution. The error of the Senator consists in supposing, that when the President failed to negotiate with Mexico in reference to the boundary, his failure gave him the right to determine on his own authority, without consulting Congress, which was the boundary, and to occupy by force the disputed territory, when in fact the failure of the negotiation exhausted his power, and left him no means of acting but by submitting the question to Congress for its decision. It is really wonderful to those who have been in this body for any considerable length of time, that there should be any question on these points.

It may be proper to add, that the power of the President and Senate is so rigidly restricted to negotiating and making treaties, that although they may make, they have no authority to set aside a treaty when it is violated by the opposite party. That power belongs not even to the Judiciary, but to Congress—of which there is a remarkable instance in reference to the treaty made between France and the United States, during the war of the Revolution. That treaty was so outrageously violated by France during her revolutionary struggle, that it became necessary, on our part, to disavow any further obligation under it; and that was made by a joint resolution of Congress, declaring it to be null and void. This precedent has never been questioned. It shows that the power was restricted within the limits I have assigned.

Assuming these views to be correct, I put the question to the Senator, how could the President, on his own authority, order General [Zachary] Taylor to occupy a territory which the resolutions of Congress and the act of Texas acceding to them, admitted to be disputed territory between her and Mexico, and that, too, without consulting or even advising Congress of the order, although Congress was at that time in session? I hold that the President had no more right to order the army to march into the disputed territory, than he had to order it to march into Mexico. I might appeal to the whole history of our country, in reference to this point, for the truth of this position. There are many cases that bear upon it. Among others, I might cite those which occurred under the Administration of General [George] Washington. It is known to all the least conversant with our history, that Great Britain, after the treaty of peace, held on not only to Detroit, which was near the frontier, and then in the woods, but to Fort Stanwix, now Rome, in the very heart of the State of New York, from 1783 to 1794, without any attempt on the part of General Washington to disturb her possession. He never dreamt of attacking either without authority of Congress; and if he had, there was no one at that day that would not have considered it as a flagrant violation of the Constitution. To this I may add, we had a question of disputed boundary in Maine, arising out of the same treaty, which remained open under all Administrations down to a very late period, that of Mr. [John] Tyler's Administration; yet there was not any attempt whatever on the part of the many Presidents, in the long intervening period, to assert by force, the right of the United States to the disputed territory. I never heard the principle laid down anterior to this war with Mexico, that the President, on his own authority, had the right to march the army into a disputed territory.

From *Speeches of Mr. Calhoun, of South Carolina, on the Ten Regiment Bill; and in Reply to Mr. Davis, of Mississippi, and Mr. Cass. Delivered in the Senate of the United States, March 16 and 17, 1848* (Washington: printed by John T. Towers, 1848), pp. 11–16. Also printed in *Congressional Globe*, 30th Cong., 1st Sess., pp. 496–497; Houston, ed., *Proceedings and Debates*, pp. 368–370; the Washington, D.C., *Daily Union*, March 30, 1848, p. 1; Crallé, ed., *Works*, 4:439–450. Variants in the New York, N.Y., *Herald*, March 20, 1848, pp. 3–4; the Charleston, S.C., *Courier*, March 21, 1848, p. 2; the New York, N.Y., *Morning Courier and New-York Enquirer*, March 21, 1848, p. 1. NOTE: Debate continued until the question was called, when the bill was passed 38 to 19. However, the bill was not passed by the House of Representatives.

Further remarks on the bill to raise an additional military force, 3/17. When Calhoun had finished his speech on this date, James D. Westcott, Jr., of Fla. remarked: "I beg to remind the Senator that Mr. [Thomas] Jefferson and Mr. [James] Madison seized upon the country west of the Mississippi." Calhoun was reported as replying: "Oh! that was a trifling case. You could cover the whole country with a blanket!" Davis remarked that he could not see how Calhoun could justify the orders sending the Navy to the Gulf [in 1844] before annexation, but deny that the President could occupy the disputed territory after annexation was completed. Calhoun replied: "They were issued when Congress was in session. If any attack had been necessary, application would have been made to Congress for authority." Later in the debate, Calhoun reiterated that the President "has no right to order it [the Army] into disputed territory." From *Congressional Globe*, 30th Cong., 1st Sess., pp. 497–498. Also printed in Houston, ed., *Proceedings and Debates*, p. 370; the Washington, D.C., *Daily Union*, March 30, 1848, p. 1.

From R[ICHARD] K. CRALLÉ

Lynchburg [Va.,] March 19th 1848

My dear Sir, Private engagements, combined with ["the" *interlined*] absence of any matter of interest have hitherto prevented me from acknowledging the receipt of your last letter, and thanking you for a copy of the Constitution which accompanied, as also for copies of your Speeches on the Ten Regiment Bill.

The recent political movements in the State you have already seen in the Papers, and can appreciate far better than I. As yet they have not been followed up by either Party; nor will any general or vigorous action be had until after the two Conventions shall have settled on their respective candidates. In the meantime, however, *"the noise of hammers, closing rivets up, give drea[d]ful note of preparation."* The next will be one of the most excited elections which ever occurred in the State. The Parties are more nearly balanced; and the zeal of the minority will be greatly stimulated by the fair prospect they now have of success. On the other hand the Party so long dominant in the State will move heaven and earth to maintain its ascendancy. The contest must, of course, be regarded as doubtful; and much will depend on the action of the Philadelphia Convention. If [Henry] Clay be the nominee I think the State will be lost to the Party; while if [Zachary] Taylor receive the nomination (the Baltimore Convention uniting either on [James] Buchanan, [Lewis] Cass or any other of the old Party hacks,) I think *it certain* that the Democratic Party will lose the State. Indeed there is, in my opinion no other individual but yourself, who can carry the State for the Party; and I presume they would as soon unite on Taylor as on you. [Levi] Woodbury would make some favourable division, but his influence, chiefly amongst your friends, would not be sufficient to change the result. I regard the State, *under present appearances*, notwithstanding the acquisition of [Henry A.] Wise, [John M.] Patton, [Richard K.] Meade and others, as certain for the opposition, if either you or Taylor should receive the nomination. The present position of these gentlemen, strongly contrasted as it is with that they so recently occupied, will rather tend to detract from than add to the strength of the Party.

By the bye, in regard to Wise, I cannot but remember your predictions about the time you left the [State] Department. Things have turned out precisely as you then anticipated. I suppose he has been deluged with flattering letters; and has, perhaps, some private interests, connected with his late mission [to Brazil] to subserve. Be this as it may, his course has excited strong remarks, and I doubt not will tend to his entire political destruction. He will never be trusted by those whom he now serves; while his sudden conversion [to the Democratic Party] will be regarded by his former associates as dictated by every other consideration than that of the public good. Patton, [James] Garland [former Representative from Va.] & Meade will share in the suspicions which attach to him, and participate in his fate.

Intelligence has lately reached us here, direct from Washington, that the contest between the friends of Clay and Taylor, daily more and more embittered, will probably result in a permanent breach, and that some third person will have to be taken up in order to unite the opposition. I should be glad to know whether there be any probability of such a result.

You see that the Resolutions of the Democratic Convention in Richmond have deliberately endorsed the movement of Mr. [Daniel S.] Dickinson [Senator from N.Y.]. This makes it very important that the Resolution introduced into the Senate should be fully discussed; for I am persuaded that many honest men have been misled by its tone and verbiage. Now that the Treaty is off your hands, it seems to me a favourable time to give the whole subject a thorough scrutiny. If the principle embodied in the resolution lead to the *practical results* which you apprehend, it is obvious that we are giving up every thing for a *sett of well-strung words*. I intend, if I can find leisure, to prepare some comments on these Resolutions at an early day, and to have them published in the newspapers here. In the meantime I should like much to see your views expressed fully in a speech on the Resolution itself. Many thinking men of both Parties look to you with firmer confidence than any one else, and especially on this great question [slavery in the newly-acquired territory]. This is the only tribute their Party fealty allows them to pay, but it is the highest. It is lately rumoured here that you will not improbably remain neutral on the Presidential Contest, should it be between Buchanan or Cass and Clay. But that if Woodbury be the Candidate you will co-operate with the Party. This is a matter where your own judgment is the safest counsellor—and, of course, I shall presume to offer no advice. He is the only man amongst the whole sett that I could trust at all, and even he I should trust *tremblingly*. The object of such a nomination would, doubtless be to secure your influence; but not to advance it. I see that the war of the Administration Presses has suddenly ceased—the usual symptom of an *approaching election*. I could almost wish, from a keen perception of the injustice of the past—I could almost wish, even at the sacrifice of the public interest that you would have nothing to do, one way or the other in their vile scramble for plunder, for the whole contest is for nothing else. Your fame is too high—your name, character and conduct stand too prominently out of and above them to participate in any mode[,] manner or degree in such an inglorious strife. It suits such men as Buchanan, Cass, Clay &C, but not you. And should the public interests constrain you to take an active part I shall regret the necessity, yet not without the proud confidence that you will not suffer, except in feeling, in the conflict; for your friends can say with just pride that you alone, of all our distinguished public men have escaped suspicion in the very worst of times. It was high fame, indeed, that, amongst all nations the Lacedomonian matrons alone could walk naked in the public streets without the slightest imputation on their chastity.

I am very anxious to know what is the true political position of our old friend [Dixon H.] Lewis. Since I last heard from him, I have read his letters written on the eve of his election, which has surprised me no little. Has he clothed himself in full administration armour? I fear he will tread too exactly in the footsteps of Wise. By the bye, did you preserve the letter written to you by the latter, soon after [James K.] Polk's election? It is a strange document, and I hope you have laid it away amongst your papers. I thought I had preserved it for you, but do not find it amongst mine. I well recollect its chief contents. That with another written by Col. [Francis W.] Pickens from the Nashville Convention, written before the election ought to be preserved as memorials for history.

I am gratified to learn that you voted for the Treaty, though I presume, from what I see in the public Prints, it amounts, *in results,* to no more than you anticipated viz.—that we have had to *establish* the Governments that negotiate, and must sustain the Treaty and those who make it. Still this is better than a longer continuance of the war, with more fearful results in prospect. The universal sentiment here is favourable to a Treaty on almost any terms.

I have taxed your time and patience too far on public matters to say anything of domestic concerns. We are, however, preparing to spend the summer, at least, if not the next winter, in the mountains; for I am anxious to test, in person, the advantages of grazing, which, I cannot but think, are greater than those either of cotton or sugar planting. Good grass fed bullocks are now selling here at $50 per head—and I am sure I can raise them at an average cost of $18 or less.

With the affectionate regard of my whole household I offer the assurances of [*one word changed to* "both"] regard and respect, R.K. Crallé.

ALS in ScCleA.

From KER BOYCE

Charleston, March 20th 1848

My dear Sir, Your favor of the 12 Instant is duly received, and I notice your remarks as to the debt of Andrew P[ickens] Calhoun Esq[.] This debt I have Made My Calculations on from the promise of Last year and Made my Ar[r]angements Accordingly. I Need Not say how Long this debt has been made and If you Can borrow the Mon[e]y any other place I would be Much oblidged by having the debt. Still I would rather put My self to great inco[n]v[en]ience than sell his property. But if you Cannot Borrow the Mon[e]y, I will try and allow it to stand over Untill Next Winter. But under No Circumstance, will I Allow it to stand over unless the In[tere]st is payed up to this time to My [Mobile] agent Mess[rs.] Crawford & Gowdey; be pleased to let Me Know if you Suc[c]eed, in borrowing the Mon[e]y as soon as posiable so as I may Make such Ar[r]angements as will, Meet the amount in another way. Your most sinsare friend, Ker Boyce.

ALS in ScU-SC, John C. Calhoun Papers.

From GEO[RGE] H. CHRISMAN

Harrisonburg, Va., March 20: [18]48

Sir, I have read your speech on the Ten Regiment bill, and as a Citizen of Virginia who feels some solicitude for the preservation of our Institutions, I thank you most sincerely for it. I look upon it as a Master-piece of real eloquence, concise, able and demonstrative. It is a stream of light, illuminating the darkness around. If this & your speech upon your resolutions, shall have the effect to open the eyes of the people of the U.S. to the dangers of this Mexican War, and the precedents which have been set in making, & prosecuting it; and if for the end, they shall have the effect of saving us from the great evil of the annexation of Mexico, to which it has seemed to me we have been blindly rushing, you will have added greatly, greatly indeed to the many claims which you have upon the gratitude of your Country.

Patriotism I consider a very rare, and a very exalted Virtue. It is as [sic] ascribed to many, who are wholly strangers to so exalted a sentiment. But when a man raises himself above party & personal interests, and steps out of the narrow circle of his selfish feelings, and takes his stand upon the platform of his Country's good, regardless of himself, as I conceive you have done, upon the Oregon & Mexican questions, then he may have some claim to patriotism. Regarding you as one of the three great intellectual men of the Country, and considering you the first, in that far reaching sagacity, which foresees coming events, I look upon you, as placed, upon the Watch Tower, to warn your Countrymen of coming dangers. Standing on a position more honorable than the presidency itself, were it not, to save the Country from such bitter[?] evils as we have lately experienced from the rule of Weak & vicious men, you ought scarcely to be willing to descend to the Presidency. And I am sorry that Mr. [Henry] Clay does not see, that the presidency is not necessary to his fame, and that he cannot conquer his passion for it.

I hope Sir, you will give me credit for more sense, than a desire to flatter you. Humble & unknown myself, I would be weak indeed to suppose I could ["succeed" *canceled*], accomplish it, if I had any motive for doing so. He Sir, who deserves well of his Country, is entitled to the cheering approbation of his fellow-Citizens of all classes, who have intelligence & virtue to appreciate his efforts. This is my motive for thus addressing you. I was very glad to hear you say that a great change had taken place in public Sentiment, in relation to the annexation of Mexico, for I have been afraid, that if any thing should defeat the peace, it would become a growing Sentiment of the Country. I have been afraid that the democratic Party, would stake themselves upon it in the Presidential election, and that the uncontrolable influence of party feeling would make it popular.

That you may long continue to watch & guard the true interests of the Country is the sincere prayer of your Obed[ien]t S[er]v[an]t, Geo. H. Chrisman.

ALS in ScCleA. NOTE: An AEU by Calhoun reads "Mr. Chrisman. Send Speech."

REMARKS ON THE MISSION TO THE
PAPAL STATES

[In the Senate, March 21, 1848]
[*Under consideration was an omnibus appropriation bill to supply "deficiencies" in previous appropriations. George E. Badger of N.C. moved to strike out the appropriation for a diplomatic mission to the Papal States.*]

Mr. Calhoun. I have had some hesitation in determining upon

the vote which I intend to give on this question, and I rise to state the reasons which induce me to vote against the proposition to strike out. In the first place, I may refer to those considerations which have, with me, little or no weight. I do not favor this mission because the Pope [Pius IX] is a reformer, though I do not at all doubt that he is a very wise and liberal reformer. I am inclined to think that he has gone as far as he ought to go, considering the nature of his power and the people whom he governs; and I do not think the less of him on that account; but, on the contrary, I am the more favorably impressed by his wisdom in proceeding cautiously. There is very little confidence to be reposed in any reform that originates in force and violence. But, sir, I do not think the fact that the Pope is a reformer, furnishes a sufficient reason for the establishment of a diplomatic mission to the Papal States. I am in favor of non-interference in the highest sense. I wish him well. I desire his success. Although, as I believe, the Pope will not be able to proceed far, yet he will succeed to some extent in ameliorating the condition of his people. Again: it is to be considered that recent occurrences in Europe may put an end to the present movement of the Pope. A counter movement may be made. He is in favor of proceeding slowly; but there is a people north of his dominion, who are of a very different temperament, and who spring at a bound to the object at which they aim. How far the Pope may be intimidated or influenced by these occurrences, time will show.

As to another consideration which has been presented in this debate, according to my conception, the Federal Government has nothing whatever to do with religion. The States may act upon that subject, but certainly there is no power here to do so; and we have no right to be influenced at all by considerations of that nature. And here let me say, in reference to a remark made by the Senator from Michigan [Lewis Cass], that I do hope that rule which he says prevails in Europe with regard to the precedence of the Pope's legate, will not be permitted to operate here. Our established rule is, that the minister bearing the oldest commission in each grade, takes precedence. I feel assured, that to give precedence here to the Pope's legate, upon spiritual grounds, which is the case in Europe, would produce a very undesirable and dangerous excitement. If the Pope should entertain any design of sending a legate to this Government, I trust that the precaution of informing him with regard to the difficulty on this point will be observed.

Nor do I vote for this mission upon commercial grounds. Our

commerce with Rome is inconsiderable, and is not likely to improve. It is not sufficiently important to require the presence of a chargé, and has been heretofore very well attended to by our consul. The fact, alluded to by an honorable Senator, that Rome was a point of confluence for great numbers travelling for amusement and instruction, ought not to influence our action.

It may, then, be asked, why I am induced to favor this mission? My reason is to be found in the present political condition of affairs. The Italian States, not under the authority of Austria, and perhaps, I may add, some of those under the control of that Power, are in a state of revolution, which, in Italy, may very likely run to some excess. We know that the Pope is the central moving power of this reform. We know that the Pope has the power of controlling these movements. Now, reform in Italy may run into a certain degree of violence and disorder and it may be very important that we should be able through the Pope to guard our commerce, and protect our citizens engaged in commerce from injury. I believe that Rome is the most favorable point at which you could place a minister, if events in Italy should take a certain direction. The reason is a temporary one, and I should therefore put this mission on a temporary basis. It is possible, that besides affording protection to it, in the event of certain occurrences, through the influence of the Pope, a liberal turn might be given to our commerce in Italy. Though that under his immediate direction is not important, yet the commerce of the whole of Italy is very important, and may be made still more so. A large portion of Italy is admirably cultivated—better perhaps than any other portion of Europe, and is inhabited by a thriving and vigorous population. For these reasons I am induced to cast my vote against striking out the provision of the bill.

[*Lewis Cass reiterated the importance of the Pope's precedence in Europe and added: "I really do not see how the Government can be called on to settle such a question."*]

Mr. Calhoun. It has settled it.

Mr. Cass. Well, I cannot imagine how such a question could arise, except as a matter of etiquette in going to the dinner table.

Mr. Calhoun. The Senator certainly must know that as between the diplomatic corps this is a point insisted upon, and that it has been passed upon here. Within my recollection a case has occurred in which swords were drawn between the French and English ministers [Alphonse Pageot and Richard Pakenham] in the ante-chamber of the Presidential mansion; and during the short period in which I was in the department of State, the point was presented, requiring grave deliberation, so much so, that in that case I thought proper to consult Mr. [John Quincy] Adams, who had had more experience in such matters.

Mr. Cass. That case does not apply to the point of my remarks.

Mr. Calhoun. It was then established that any minister should take rank according to the date of his commission. Though as between ourselves there may be no question of this kind, yet there can be no doubt that if the Pope's legate, if sent here, should take precedence of all the other members of the diplomatic corps in the face of this established principle, I take it for granted that his claim would not be respected; and the Pope should be apprized of it.

[*Cass asserted that if the Pope's minister were here, every member of the diplomatic corps would allow him to pass first to the table. The vote was then taken and the effort to strike out the appropriation was defeated by 7 to 36.*]

From *Congressional Globe*, 30th Cong., 1st Sess., Appendix, p. 410. Also printed in Houston, ed., *Proceedings and Debates*, p. 395. Variants in the New York, N.Y., *Herald*, March 23, 1848, pp. 3–4; the Alexandria, Va., *Gazette and Virginia Advertiser*, April 29, 1848, p. 2.

To T[homas] G. Clemson, [Brussels]

Washington, 22d March 1848

My dear Sir, The Cambria brought me your's of the 24th Feb: with a letter from Anna [Maria Calhoun Clemson] to her mother [Floride Colhoun Calhoun].

I explained in a former letter, how it happened, that a sheet of the letter to which you allude, was omitted to be enclosed.

It would be difficult in the present state of the money market to raise the money we owe you. Although there is a fair prospect of peace with Mexico, very considerable loans will have to be raised by Governm[en]t to meet the heavy balance ag[ai]nst the treasury, resulting from the war, which will create an active demand for money, until the whole is taken up, and make it difficult to negotiate individual loans.

I am glad to learn, that you are all well, & that the children [John Calhoun Clemson and Floride Elizabeth Clemson] are doing so well.

I enclose a letter, which came under cover to me, a few days since, and also one from your overseer [Reuben H. Reynolds] to me. It indicates a good disposition on his part to do his duty, & I hope he may succeed in making you a good crop. I answered him, & enclosed a letter for Col. [Francis W.] Pickens, which I directed him to deliver in person, in which, I asked as a favour, that he would act for you in purchasing, whatever additional Horse force, and supply of meat the place might require for the year. You will see, in your overseer's letter, that he declined on his application to act in the case, assigning for reason, that I had not even informed ["him" *interlined*] when I met him at Aiken, that I had employed him. Such is the fact; but I did not, because the former overseer, Mr. [John?] Mobl[e]y, wrote me, that he had made application to him, when he was out of meat last fall or summer, to order a supply, & that he had refused on the ground that he had nothing to do with the place. I hope there was some mistake on the part of Mr. Mobl[e]y, as to his reply; as it would seem from Mr. Reynolds' letter, he only declined because I had not mentioned to him, that I had employed him; and I accordingly took the course I did. Indeed, it was impossible for me, with the information before me, to determine what additional force, or supply was needed.

The Cambria brought us the intelligence of the Revolution in Paris, the overthrow of the late dynasty & the establishment of a Republick. Your letter, tho' dated as late as the 24th Feb., makes no allusion to it; from which I infer the intercourse by the rail road had been inter[r]upted. It is, indeed, a great event—I would say a terrifick one for Europe. No one can say where it will stop. France is not prepared to become a Republick. I hope the Governm[en]ts of Europe will look on without interference, and let the process take its natural course. It seems to me, looking on from this distance, that interference would but increase the flame and spread it more widely. But it is too early yet to speculate. We wait impatiently for the next arrival.

As to ourselves, I feel pretty confident, we shall have peace with Mexico, or if we fail in that, we shall take a defensive position, which would in effect terminate the war. That closed, we shall have no exciting question, but that connected with the Wilmot proviso, & the Presidential election. The fate of both is still in a state of great uncertainty. It is impossible to say, with any certainty even now, who will be the candidate of either party.

All were well when I last heard from home. My health is as good as usual, & I have been less subject to colds than what I was last winter & the one before.

Love to Anna & the Children. Your affectionate father, J.C. Calhoun.

ALS in ScCleA; PEx in Jameson, ed., *Correspondence*, pp. 746–747.

From W[ILLIAM] F. VAN AMRINGE

Montgomery[,] Orange Co[unty] N.Y., March 22 1848
Dear Sir, I have the honor to acknowledge the receipt of your favor of 13th inst., in reply to mine [of 2/28] in relation to Executive patronage. I was aware of the difficulty of carrying any measure to abridge power, both because the possessors were desirous of keeping, & the expectants of acquiring it. But being satisfied that the subject will receive from you all the consideration it deserves, I will not trouble you with any further speculations in relation to it. I had an idea of draughting the proposed amendments, & of incorporating them with the existing Constitution, to exhibit distinctly their nature; for arguments *about* an important measure are seldom as useful as when the thing itself is placed before the eye. This might be useful if I were communicating with a gentleman whose perspicacity was questionable, but can be of no service in the present instance.

My work on the Natural History of Man has probably been rec[eive]d by you. It is with regret I perceive, by a hasty examination of the copy I have received, that there are a number of typographical errors in it, some of which are important to the sense, although most of them will be apparent to the reader as errors of the press. By reason of my residence in the interior, & of my long confinement by indisposition, it was impossible for me to correct the proofs; consequently, I contracted with the printer to attend to this matter, who assured me of the great accuracy of his proof reader, who had only to follow a plainly written copy. I hope, therefore, to be exonerated from carelessness in the matter. At foot I furnish a list of those I found by a hasty reading, except errors of punctuation, which I have not thought it necessary to notice.

The view I have taken of this important subject being entirely new, & opposed to the universally received European theory, it will afford me much pleasure to have your opinion of my work, if you can find time, & have the inclination, when you shall have read it. With great respect I am Your Mo[st] Ob[edien]t S[er]v[an]t, W.F. Van Amringe.

264

ALS in ScCleA. NOTE: In a postscript marked "Errata" Van Amringe listed twenty-five substantive typographical errors in his book, *An Investigation of the Theories of the Natural History of Man.* . . . (New York: Baker & Scribner, 1848). This letter was addressed to "Hon[ora]ble John C. Calhoun LLD."

To JA[ME]S ED[WARD] CALHOUN, Jun[io]r, [Columbia, S.C.]

Senate Chamber, 23d March 1848

My dear James, Your letters afford me much pleasure, as they evince on your part a due appreciation of the advantages, which a Collegiate ["education" *interlined*] affords, and a disposition to make the most of them. They afford additional pleasure, as they state, incidentally, facts, which indicate that you have the esteem & confidence of your class mates. That they should appoint you their monthly Orator, & and [*sic*] the Chairman of the Committee, on the occasion, to which you refer, I regard in that light. I am happy, also, to add, that I am gratified to perceive, that you take such just views of the duties belonging to the former, & ["have" *interlined*] performed so well, those belonging to the latter. Your class & & [*sic*] Committee took the right course, and acted well throughout. It is a good rule always to make sure that you are right before you take your stand, and to listen clamly [*sic*] to those, who oppose, before you act. By doing so in this case, you saved yourselves & the Institution from much difficulty.

You request me to write you fully my views in reference to the treaty. I have expressed them in debate, on the 10 regiment bill, as far as I was at liberty to do, before the injunction of secrecy is removed. It is true, that much is disclosed surreptitiously, but that would not justify a Senator in his place to use, or refer to what they disclose in debate. My remarks will be printed in Pamphlet form & will be ready for delivery to day, or tomorrow. If they should be received to day, in time, I will send you a copy with this; but if not, one tomorrow. My remarks were well received, & made a deep impression. I hope they will be printed in the Columbia papers. They treat of subjects of deep import.

We have not sufficient intelligence to pronounce with certainty on the great events, which have occurred in France. The next steamer, which will be in, probably, in three or four days, will shed much light on them, and afford means of forming some opinion, as to what is to follow. I wait for it with great anxiety. In the meantime,

I have no confidence that France will be able to ["form" *canceled and* "establish" *interlined*] a Republick. That is a task of far greater difficulty, than is generally supposed.

I am glad to see you take so lively an interest in the politicks of the Country; but you must not, at present, permit them to divert your mind from your studies. I would not advise you to take the Congressional Globe or Appendix at this time. They contain a vast deal of trash, & are not necessary to keep you up with the general train of events.

I had letters from your sister [Anna Maria Calhoun Clemson] & Mr. [Thomas G.] Clemson by the last steamer. They & the children were well. I do hope you will not fail to write her the first leisure. She often mentions you kindly, but complains that you do not write to her.

I enclose, agreeably to your request a check for $83; $68 for your board & $15 for the other items. I hope it will ["be" *interlined*] sufficient to carry ["you" *interlined*] through to the close of the ["next" *interlined*] term, which will close the session. Your affectionate father, J.C. Calhoun.

[P.S.] Acknowledge the receipt of the check so that I may know that it has been received.

ALS in NcD, John C. Calhoun Papers.

From JOSEPH HENRY, [Director of the Smithsonian Institution]

Washington, March 25th [18]48

My Dear Sir, I beg leave to introduce to your attention my young friend Charles Lanman[,] author of "A Summer in the Wilderness" and several other works which gave him the reputation of a man of letters before he was scarcely a man in years. He is about starting on a tour to the South for the purpose of making pen and pencil sketches in your State and you will oblige me if you can furnish him with a letter of introduction to some literary Gentleman in your neighbourhood. I remain very respectfully and truly yours &., Joseph Henry.

ALS in ScCleA.

From J[OHN] T. TREZEVANT

Memphis, March 25 [18]48

D[ea]r Sir, A friend has sent me your speech on the Mexican war. Permit me to request that you will send me one which I see it stated you have made on the right of our Government to levy contributions &C in Mexico. I trust I may not be deemed a trespasser upon your delicacy[?] when I express my admiration of your general positions on the great questions of government; and to the exposition of them as given in your sundry speeches I have generally looked, for the soundest views of our national policy. Having ever been a Republican (I do not mean a *rabid* Democrat) I can but approve of most of the leading measures of our present administration; and the successful operation of them I consider as the best commentary upon their merits or demerits. Upon one question, however, the south here & the west, are much divided—the division not being governed indeed, by party lines. It is the power of the gen[era]l Government over internal improvement. The *necessity* for ["the" *interlined*] care of our government over our interests on the great waters in the West, tells us that the power *should* be lodged there to protect us; but the question is how will such a system of jurisdiction end, and what effect will it have upon the *moral force* of candidates for popular favour? Will it not engender such a mania as is gradually spreading among the abolitionists? Will not each candidate be compelled to go farther, in his promises to carry out the wishes of his constituents, than his predecessor? and will not this eventually result in the exaction of pledges from all, that they will get Congress to improve all their little creeks, rivers, lakes &C? This is the great, latent evil of abolitionism. Ambition must be fed; and the candidate who will do most & go farthest to abolish slavery in the District of C[olumbia] & then, in the States, will become the choice of partisans whose ruling passion he promises so liberally to gratify. I say, will not this be the *end* of the beginning, as to the power of internal improvements. A middle course is desired, and it seems to me that when *rivers* are the *boundary of States*, the power might be safely exercised, upon the ground that the *entire* jurisdiction of the waters is in neither State or no one State.

Let me say to you, that, by the intelligent & the reflecting of both parties out here, your course is anxiously watched; and regarding you, as they do, as attached to neither party in all things, they are the more prepared to respect & defer to a judgment ripened by experience, and influenced by no political bias. Your position before the people is now higher than it has been for years, because it is deemed an independent one—not sought or taken, as the popular breeze might indicate. Thus, a proper direction of the public mind (and let me say that it seldom *leads*, but is almost always *led*) on a question in which every man in the growing west is deeply interested—a direction that might give the power of improvement a limit, but at the same time, a *liberal view*, would place you, in the estimation of a people that must soon control all great elections, in a position which would gratify the most noble aspirations of ambition.

I am a stranger to you sir, though I might claim perhaps the honor of having been with you, some little, while you were here several years since; but I am acquainted with your political views sufficiently to admire them, & to wish light from you, on any subject of so great moment as that of internal improvement. With respect Yours, J.T. Trezevant.

ALS in ScCleA.

To J[OHN] Y. MASON, Sec[retar]y of the Navy

Washington, 26th March 1848

Dear Sir, I am not acquainted with [R.E. King] the applicant, who is recommended by the enclosed [*not found*] for a birth [*sic*] in the Navy, but know the writer to be very respectable. I wish his letter to be placed on file with the other recommendations in favour of the applicant, & would be obliged to you to inform me, whether there are any vacancy, in the quota allotted to the State, & what I may say to the writer of the enclosed as to the prospect of success. With great respect I am & &, J.C. Calhoun.

ALS in DLC, Gideon Welles Papers, 35:25454–25455.

From R[ICHARD] E. MERRILL

North Conway, N. Hampshire, 27th March 1848

Dear Sir, I take the liberty of addressing you, for the purpose of requesting you to favour me with one or more copies of ["both" *interlined*] your speeches delivered in the Senate this present session upon the Mexican war &c & the Ten Regiment Bill. I am always desirous of reading all your speeches, but am sorry to say that, I cannot obtain *all* for Northern prejudice, & partizan political feeling condemns many of them & for that reason do not publish them, because they imagine that "no good thing can come out of Nazareth," or no one, but themselves can claim to be a Democrat *par excellence* but those who cringe at the footstool of power, forgetting who it was in the South that was the pioneer in the divorce of government & banks & free trade, the greatest of reforms. I am one who can appreciate talent & emminent public services by whoever performed, & should ever be glad to be noticed by receiving any favour from one whom I so highly honour as a Statesman. I say this as no unmeaning flattery, but the real sentiments of one northern man, whose aspirations are for the good of the whole Country. I think that different views in relation to the policy of an administration, may be held without conflicting with the great principles of Republicanism, progress & reform.

Would to God France, generous, & patriotic as she is[,] could settle down upon the great & im[m]utable principles of Liberty & order, & the enjoyment of those principles which alone renders nations ["happy" *altered to* "prosperous"] & happy. Are they not capable of self government? Place them in the enjoyment of the unalienable rights of man, & would they not be an orderly, contented & prosperous people?

"In fifty years," said [Napoleon] Bonaparte at St. Helena, "Europe will be Cossack or Republican"—it may [be] the struggle has begun in France already. But I have troubled you too long. I beg to be remembered by you hereafter & believe me to be Your ob[edien]t Serv[an]t, R.E. Merrill.

[P.S.] Nothing would afford me greater pleasure than a few lines from your pen, relative to matters so simply reffered to in this letter. I ask it for my own private use & a memento from one so justly distinguished. Yours &c, R.E.M.

[P.P.S.] Public Sentiment appears to be setting in strongly for Judge [Levi] Woodbury in preference to Gen[era]l [Lewis] Cass here in N.H. & Mass.

ALS in ScCleA.

From CHARLES LANMAN

Washington, March 28th 1848

My dear Sir, I am very sorry that I shall not be enabled to present the enclosed letter of introduction [from Joseph Henry to you, dated

3/25], in person. It was written several days ago, but was unfortunately mislaid, and it is important that I should leave the city this afternoon. I am about to travel throughout the length and breadth of the Alleghany mountains, and while at the south intend to visit the section of country where you reside. It was with this idea in my mind, that I asked Professor Henry for the enclosed note. On my way to the south, I shall stop for a week or so in *Eastville*[,] *Northampton Co*[*unty*], *Virginia,* and if you will do me the kindness prayed for, I should be happy to hear from you at that place.

By way of letting you know a little more about me, I may mention, as among the friends of my father, such gentlemen, as Senator [Alpheus] Felch [of Mich.], Senator [Lewis] Cass [of Mich.], Senator [Roger S.] Baldwin [of Conn.,] and Ex-Senator [William] Woodbridge [of Mich.]. The Hon. James Lanman [of Conn.] who was in the United States Senate in 1824 was my Grand Father. Among my friends I number Hon. Henry Clay—but I am no politician. With great respect your unknown friend & servant, Charles Lanman.

ALS with En in ScClea. Note: Charles Lanman (1819–1895) was to acquire considerable note as writer, painter, and explorer.

From Lt. M[ATTHEW] F. MAURY, U.S. N[avy]

National Observatory
Washington, March 29th, 1848

Dear Sir, I have the pleasure of sending you as you requested I would do, a chart shewing the relative distances to Monterey & the Columbia river from some of the principal points on the Atlantic coast. I have added such other information as in my judgement is calculated to throw light on the interesting subject as to the best route across the country for reaching by Rail Road the Pacific coast of the U. States.

I am clearly of the opinion that a Rail Road through the heart of the country to the most convenient point of our Pacific coast, is greatly more in accordance with the true interests of the U. States, than any route by canal, or Rail Road, that can be constructed across that narrow neck of land between North & South America.

A chief value of a Rail Road, or canal, consists in its collateral advantages, so to speak; by which I mean, the advantages which the country & the people in the vicinity of the improvement [*one word erased*] derive from it; such as the increased value of land & property of various kinds.

The increased value which such property has derived from the Rail Roads & canals in the U. States, exceeds I suppose, the original cost of the works themselves. This therefore may be considered a permanent value attached to property of our fellow citizens which no reverse of fortune, no enactment of laws, nothing, but a destruction of the works themselves, can ever destroy.

A canal between the two Continents would not pass through U. States Territory & consequently the Citizens of the U. States would derive no such collateral advantages from it, nor her statesmen the prerogative of taxing such increased value for the revenues of the country: but they would derive them abundantly from a Rail Road running through the heart of the Union & connecting its Atlantic with its Pacific ports.

In this fact is included one of the many reasons which induce me to favor a Rail Road across the country in preference to a canal out of the country, for connecting the two oceans.

The question therefore is, where shall the Rail Road begin on the Atlantic, & where shall it end on the Pacific?

Unfortunately the present state of topographical information as to the several routes that have been prop[os]ed for reaching the Pacific by Rail Road, is not sufficient to afford a satisfactory reply to this question. I propose to consider it therefore only in a *geographical* & commercial point of view, leaving the final decision of the question for hydrographers & engineers after they shall have made the necessary examinations & surveys.

If we continue to increase our tonnage for the next two or three years at the ratio of increase for the last two or three, the tonnage of the U. States will then exceed that of Great Britain & the commercial supremacy of the seas will be ours, so far at least as the business of fetching & carrying is concerned.

If you will examine the accompanying chart [*not found*] you will observe that I have drawn *geographically*, the dividing line of commerce between England & the Atlantic ports of the U. States. Any point ["in" *altered to* "on"] this line is equi-distant from us & from England, consequently England is nearer to all places, including the ports of Europe, the Mediterranean, & of Africa north of the Equator, which are to the East of that dividing line, & *geographically* speaking, therefore ["she" *interlined*] can meet us on that side of it at advantage. Whereas all ports on this side of it, including her American

Colonies, the West Indies & the states of Central & South America as far as the Equator, are *geographically* more favorably situated for commerce with the U. States than with England.

Now it so happens that this dividing line crosses the Equator at what may be considered the great thoroughfare of vessels trading to the south of it, whether they be English or American, or whether they be bound around Cape Horn, or the Cape of Good Hope. The winds are such as to make this the common & best place of crossing for all such vessels.

Consequently, *geographically* speaking, the ports of Brazil, of the Pacific ocean, China & the East Indies are as convenient to the Atlantic States of the Union as they are to England, & the merchandise of the two countries may be said to meet there precisely on equal terms.

Hitherto the great channels of trade have led to Europe, yet notwithstanding that the position of England is much more central than that of the U. States with regard to Europe, (the vessels of the former making in a week voyages which it takes ours months to accomplish,) we have under these disadvantages never ceased to gain on our competitor & are now about to pass her with our ships in the commercial race.

The coasts of Oregon & California are just beginning to feel the energy of American enterprise & are fast filling up with our citizens. Where they go, there commerce will come. The peopling of those coasts will greatly enlarge the commercial limits of the U. States, extending them from lines into a greatly elongated ellipse with its conjugate centres, the one on the Pacific, the other on the Atlantic.

Having determined what port on the Pacific offers the most advantages for the commercial focus there, it will then be easy to project the major axis of this new commercial curve; for the line across the country which joins these two centres will shew geographically the best route for a Rail Road between the two oceans.

The shortest distance between two places that are not on the Equator, or in the same Longitude, is the arc of the Great Circle included between them, & this arc appears on the chart as a curve. I have drawn such curves on the chart & called them Great Circle routes, because they shew the route by which a traveller may go from place to place by travelling the smallest number of miles possible, supposing he could follow a line through the air.

You will observe that the Great Circle which shews the shortest navigable route between Chili[,] all the ports of Peru, Ecuador, Central America & Mexico passes so near Monterey that if a steamer, bound from Chili to Shanghae in China, were to pursue the shortest route which it is possible to go, she would make Cape St. Lucas in Lower California, & might touch at Monterey by going less than 100 miles out of her way.

But if the point of departure were Panama, then it would be 1000 miles nearer to take the Great Circle route via Monterey, than to follow the straight compass course by way of the Sandwich Islands.

Monterey, therefore, may be regarded as the great half-way-house on the commercial road between Pacific America & the Indies; and this route ["as" *interlined*] the commercial circle of the Pacific Ocean.

It will be observed that Astoria in Oregon occupies by no means, such a central position with regard to the commerce of the world.

The line commencing on the Pacific coast mid way between Monterey & the mouth of the Columbia river & drawn to Philadelphia, I have called the dividing line of travel between Monterey & the mouth of the Columbia. It is so drawn through the country that any given point on it is equi-distant from those two places; so that a traveller who starts from any point to the South of this line, is nearer to Monterey, but if he starts from a point to the North of it, he is nearer to the mouth of the Columbia.

Table of distances

From the English Channel to Boston
(shortest navigable distance for steamers) 2670
Boston, via Albany & the Lakes to Chicago 1000
Chicago by an air line to Columbia river 1650
[*total*] 5320

From English Channel, via Phila[delphia]
& Baltimore, to Monterey 5100

From English Channel to Charleston[,] S.C. (by water) 3360
From Charleston to Memphis (Rail Road) 510
From Memphis to Monterey (air line) 1500
[*total*] 5370

It thus appears that Monterey is quite as central to the European travel as is the mouth of the Columbia River, & with this advantage, that the Lakes are frozen up half the year, when the Columbia route is impassable; whereas, if the traveller from Europe comes as far South as Philadelphia, Monterey then is the most convenient port.

In truth, Chicago is quite as near to Monterey as to the mouth of the Columbia.

While Monterey is, therefore, altogether as convenient a halting place as the Columbia river for travellers from Europe to China, it has decidedly the advantage with regard to the travel from three fourths of the States of the Union, from Brazil, the West Indies & even from the Pacific ports of South America.

Were a Rail Road constructed from Memphis to Monterey, passengers from Chili, Peru &c. on arriving at Panama, would save two or three days by crossing over to Chagris, taking a steamer thence to New Orleans & up the river to the Memphis and Monterey Rail Road; & so, across the country.

For this region therefore, that is, for all the travel South of us, the route to China via Charleston or New Orleans to Memphis & thence to Monterey, would be some thousand or two miles nearer, than up to Chicago, & thence to the Columbia river; nearer from most of the States of the confederacy, & as near for the rest.

The harbours of San Francisco and Monterey are good, easy of ingress and egress. The mouth of the Columbia is difficult both of ingress and egress. In 1846, Lieutenant [Neil M.] Howison, one of the most accomplished seamen in the Navy, was wrecked in attempting to get to sea from that river. He chartered another vessel for himself and crew to get to Monterey, 600 miles, and though in sight of the open sea, and drawing but eight feet of water, he was detained there *sixty three* days, waiting for an oppertunity [*sic*] to cross the bar. He was wrecked where the [U.S.] Exploring expedition [of 1838–1842] found water enough to float a [warship carrying] 74 [guns].*

* Note: "The Cadboro anchored in Baker(')s Bay (Mouth of Columbia river) Nov. 17th. (1846) where we remained, pent up by adverse winds & a turbulent sea on the bar, until the 18th of January. Her master, an old seaman, had been navigating this coast & river for the last 18 years, & his vessel drew but eight feet water; yet in this long interval of sixty two days he could find no oppertunity of getting to sea safely. This is in itself a commentary upon the dangerous character of the navigation of the mouth of the Columbia." Report of Lt. Neil M. Howison(,) U.S.N. H(ouse of) R(epresentatives) 30(th) Congress 1st Session, Mis. No. 29.

"I lay at anchor in Baker(')s Bay, some three hundred yards inside the cape, from November 17th 1846 until Jan(uar)y 18th 1847; & although we were unfortunately destitute of barometer & thermometers, we had a good oppertunity of observing during these two winter months the wind & weather. The heavens were almost always overcast; the wind would spring up moderately at E. haul within four hours to S.E., increasing in force & attended with rain. It would continue at this point some 20 hours, & shift suddenly in a hail storm to S.W., whence, hauling westwardly & blowing heavy, accompanied with hail & sleet, it would give us a continuance of bad weather for three or four days, & force the enormous Pacific swell to break upon shore with terrific violence, tossing its spray over the tops of the rocks more than 200 feet high. A day of moderate weather, with the wind at N.E. might succeed this; but before the sea on the bar would have sufficiently gone down to render it passable, a renewal of the South Easter would begin & go on around the compass as before."

Vessels in distress off the mouth of the Columbia river have been baffled in their attempts to enter; & finally, after sundry trials, have found themselves compelled to run down to the ports of California, where they are sure of getting an anchorage.

The Rail Road to the Pacific, should terminate at that port which presents the most advantages for our future dock yard & great naval station on the Pacific. That port is not the Columbia river, for the reasons just stated. Moreover, the mouth of that river will be overlooked by the English from the excellent ports of Quadra and the straits of Fuca. While our crippled vessels should be standing off & on, waiting to get in, they would fall an easy prey to inferior British cruisers, which, in safety, could watch their movements from the straits of Fuca.*

 * Note: A very snug harbor has within a few years been sounded out & taken possession of by the Hudson's Bay Company on the southeastern part of Vancouver's island. They have named it Victoria, & it *is destined to become the most important British seaport contiguous to our territory.* Eighteen feet water can be carried into its inmost recesses, which is a fine large basin. There is besides pretty good anchorage for frigates outside this basin. The company are making this their principal shipping port, depositing, by means of small craft during the summer, all their furs & other articles for the English market at this place, which is safe for their large ships to enter during the winter season (.) *They no longer permit them to come into the Columbia between November & March.* Lt. Howison's report.

Monterey & San Francisco are beyond the reach of any such surveillance; moreover they are in a better climate, & mid way our line of Pacific coast. They are in a commanding position. During the Naval operations in the Pacific, against Mexico, our men of war beat out of the harbor of San Francisco in a gale of wind: so easy is it of ingress & egress.

 The harbors of California are convenient for, & are even now frequented by, our whalemen. Columbia river is not.

There is a fleet in the Pacific of 300 vessels, engaged in this business, manned by six or eight thousand of the best seamen of America. In money & in kind, they expend annually among the islands & ports of the Pacific not less than one million of dollars. The facilities which a rail road to California would afford in ennabling [sic] them to overhaul, refit & communicate with friends & owners in New England, would attract this whale fleet there. And this vast sum of money would be expended in our own country & among our own citizens, instead of being disbursed, broad cast, as it now is, over that wide ocean. As long as there are breakers & a bar at the mouth of the Columbia, there can be no attraction there for our whale ships.

The coast of California is a favorite place of resort for the whale. They come there to herd ["& feed their young" *erased*].

The chart has two circles of a radius of 3000 miles each: one drawn from the mouth of the Columbia as a centre, the other from Monterey. The latter from its facilities of ingress & egress, is in a geographical position to command the trade with all places within these circles, except perhaps the ports of British & Russian America.

The chart also exhibits the geographical dividing lines of travel & of commerce. The red line through the island of Japan, shews the dividing line of travel from London by the overland route to India; & from London through the U. States, by rail road from Charleston, via Memphis, to Monterey. The nearest route to London from all places to the east of this line, is through the U. States; but from all places to the west of it, the nearest route is through the Red sea & across the Isthmus of Suez. These lines, as before stated, are all drawn without regard to time. They are mere geographical lines intended to represent distance in *nautical miles*. Were the rail road across the country completed, & the lines drawn with regard to time, they might probably be extended a thousand miles or two, further to the westward; for much of the distance to be overcome by the overland route [across the Isthmus of Suez] is by water, & there is much less rail road travelling by that route than there would be by a rail road across the U. States.

A passenger can accomplish as many miles in two days by rail road as he can in a week by water.

The other red line shews the dividing line of travel between the overland route to London, & the Atlantic & Pacific rail road to this part of the country.

The blue, & most westerly line shews the dividing line of commerce between England, on the one hand, & our Pacific ports on the other, supposing the English ships to pass, as they have to do, the Cape of Good Hope.

This line exhibits interesting facts, consequences and significations. Among them, it shows that the United States are now in a position which will soon enable them, geographically, to command the trade of the entire East—And that, commercially speaking, our country is in the centre of the world, and occupies a position for trade & traffic which no nation that ever existed, has held.

Hitherto in all parts of the world, except Europe and the West Indies, the ships of the two great competitors on the Ocean, have met on barely equal terms. An American and a British ship met in India, China, New Holland, the Islands of the Pacific, or the ports of South America: one was owned in London or Liverpool, the other in some one of our Atlantic ports. To reach home they both had to pursue the same route, and sail the same number of knots.

But now, that Oregon and California are *Americanized,* all of these ports are nearer, and the chief among them, as Bombay, Calcutta, Singapore, the ports of China, Japan, New Holland, Australasia, Polynesia, and the Islands of the East, many thousand miles nearer, to the U. States than they are to England.

Table of Distances by Sea

		To England	To Monterey
From	Persian Gulf	11,300 miles	10,400 miles
"	Bombay	11,500 "	9,800 "
"	Calcutta	12,200 "	9,300 "
"	Singapore	12,300 "	7,400 "
"	Canton	13,700 "	6,100 "
"	Shanghae	14,400 "	5,400 "
"	Jeddo	15,200 "	4,500 "
"	New Guinea	14,000 "	6,000 "
"	N.W. Point of New Holland	11,800 "	7,800 "
"	N.E. do do do	13,500 "	6,900 "
"	New Zealand	13,500 "	5,600 "

From Memphis—a central point in the immense valley of the west, and one on the great natural and national highway from the Gulf to the Lakes—the distance via Panama and the Sandwich Islands (the usual route) to China, is 11,700 miles: but by the proposed rail road to Monterey, and the Great Circle thence to China, the distance is but 6,900 miles.

A rail road across the country, in this direction, would therefore, it may be observed, place us before the commercial marts of *six hundred millions* of people, and enable us, *geographically*, to command them. Open the needful channels, unbridle commerce, leave it to the guidance of free trade, and who shall tell the commercial destiny of this country!

Rightly and wisely profiting by the advantages which are now opening to us, how long will it be before our sturdy rival will cease to be regarded as such, and when we shall have no competitor for maritime supremacy among nations?

From Monterey to Shanghae is 5400 miles. Midway between the two, and right on the wayside, are the Fox or Eleoutian Islands, with good harbors, where a depot of coal may be made for a line of steamers: for the establishment of which, I understand, Mr. [Thomas B.] King [of Ga.], the Chairman of the Committee of Naval Affairs in the House of Representatives, is preparing a bill.

Coal has been found on the surface at San Diego, and San Francisco, and Vancouver's or Quadra Island. Formosa and the Islands of Japan abound with the most excellent qualities of this mineral. Supposing the vessels to be put upon this line to perform not better than the "Great Western," and that the rail road from Charleston, on the Atlantic, be extended to Monterey, on the Pacific, you might, then, drink tea made in Charleston within the same month in which the leaf was gathered in China.

The passage from Shanghae, allowing a day for coaling at the Fox Islands, can be made in 26 days to Monterey, and thence to Charleston by rail road, at the English rate of 40 miles an hour, in less than three days.

Hydrographical surveys & topographical reconnoissances [*sic*] may show San Diego or San Francisco to be the best terminus for the great rail way. I have spoken of Monterey merely from its *geographical* position.

San Francisco is a better harbor, and has in its rear a more fertile country. But whichever of the three be adopted, the selection will not alter the point I have been endeavoring to establish.

A rail road from Charleston to Tennessee is already completed. Memphis is above the yellow fever region of the Mississippi valley. It is on the great river and in a central position. A road thence would cross the head waters of Red, the Arkansas and the Colorado [rivers]. It would facilitate the overland trade with Mexico, and perhaps be the principal channel of foreign commerce for her people.

Large amounts of bullion are annually shipped from Western Mexico, in British ships of war, for England. Owing to the route and the uncertainties as to the time when a vessel of war may come for it, it may be assumed that this bullion does not reach England for eight or ten months after it is taken from the mines: during all of which time, it is, of course, idle. Moreover, it pays a freight of 2 per cent to the British Officer and Greenwich Hospital, for conveying it in one of Her Majesty's vessels.

Now all this bullion would come as fast as it is taken from the mines, over this road, and would perhaps be coined in our own mints, instead of those of Europe.

This route as compared with one to the Columbia river, is more convenient for a large portion of the citizens of Pennsylvania, all of Delaware, Maryland, Ohio, Indiana, Illinois, Missouri, and all the States to the south of them: and, considering the present routes of travel, quite as convenient to the people of New England, as is the proposed route to the Columbia. Besides, this last will be obstructed by snows and ice, in winter: the other never. Therefore, California offers the most convenient terminus for the commerce & business of all the States, and the most desirable one for the purposes of the General Government.

There is a line of steamers already in operation from Valparaiso, Lima, Guyaquil, and the intermediate ports to Panama. Under Mr. King's bill of the last Congress, contracts have been made for another line to connect with this, and to run to the mouth of the Columbia, touching at Monterey or San Francisco.

From Panama to China, via Monterey is 8,600 miles, and from Panama by water to Monterey is 3,200 miles.

Thus it will be observed that Steam Communication has already been provided for more that [*sic*; than] one third of the distance from Panama to China; a rail road to Monterey, and a line of Steamers thence to China, would place our citizens only half the distance that they now are, and, without such rail road, must continue to be, from Japan and the Celestial Empire.

The most equitable location of a great national rail way to be constructed for the convenience of all the States from the banks of the Mississippi to the shores of the Pacific, would be along the line which divides the U.S. Territory west of the Mississippi into two equal parts. The main trunk would then be in the most favorable position for receiving lateral branches from all the States hereafter to be formed out of that Territory. But the ports on the Pacific and the character of the country do not admit of such a location.

I have endeavored, as you suggested, to find the geographical centre of the present States of the Confederacy.

By one method, Memphis is as near that centre as may be; by the other it falls in Kentucky.

A Geodetic line, drawn diagonally across the States, from the N.E. corner of Maine, to the S.W. corner of Texas, intersects another from the N.W. corner of Iowa to Cape Sable in Florida, within a few miles of Memphis, and Memphis is just about half way between the mouth of the Mississippi and the head of the Lakes at Chicago.

But if we divide the States by two lines, one drawn from North to South, the other from East to West, these two lines will cross each other in Kentucky, nearly midway between Nashville & Louisville.

Now if we take a position about midway between these two points of intersection, we shall have very nearly what may be called the Geographical centre, not of the Territories, but of the States of the Union. I have marked the point (A) on the chart. It is on the Cumberland, not far from its mouth.

The centre of population is near the same parallel but much farther to the eastward. But it is a shifting centre, and is on its way westward. The territorial centre is the point which is most convenient to all the States, and if from this centre we project the arc of a Great Circle to San Francisco we shall have geographically the fairest and most suitable route that the harbors on the Pacific will admit of being drawn. Continue it to the Atlantic & it will come out exactly mid way [on] that coast line.

What the most *practicable* route may be for a rail road from the valley of the Mississippi to the shores of the Pacific I have not the knowledge to designate. The best route, and the precise location of the road, must be left to the decision of the Topographer, the Engineer, and the Hydrographer.

There is however another light in which this road is to be considered. In the choice of routes, an eye should be had to the military character of the road, for, in such a work, the common defense, as well as the convenience of commerce, has to be considered.

Vancouver's Island abounds in excellent harbors. Coal of superior quality has been found there. The *"Cormorant"* has carried specimens of it to England which she obtained at 4 shillings the ton. The English Steamers in the Pacific use it, and pronounce it to be of the most excellent quality. It crops out in large seams on the banks of a river, and mounds of it are already found on the surface. It is so accessible that the Indians mine it, and deliver it on board at a mere nominal price. That Island is in a position to command Pugets' Sound, the straits of Fuca & the mouth of the Columbia. It overlooks those places more effectually than Cuba does the mouth of the Mississippi, and it belongs to England.

In view of these facts, surely no man with a military eye in his head, would think of leading this great inland channel, through which we aim to control the commerce of the East, so as to bring it out either at Columbia River, or Pugets' Sound, where its terminus would be right under the muzzles of British cannon. Were the terminus of the rail road established at either of these points, it would be in the power of our commercial rival to shut it up at will.

The mouth of that river can never become a naval station of importance. It is too near a better one, and one that is to become the principal naval station—aye, the Portsmouth of England, in the Pacific.

Its approaches are exposed and dangerous, its egress difficult, and its navigation, whether going or coming, always perilous, being often impracticable for weeks and months together during the winter season.

Were these difficulties out of the way, its position is not central enough to make it our great naval station in that sea: Our Pacific coast is 1000 miles long, and the Columbia River is 800 miles from the southern terminus of this coast line.

San Francisco, with every facility for safety, ingress & egress, that the navigator can desire, is midway between our Southern boundary and the straits of Fuca, and is in a position to command so much of that coast line; and Monterey is not a day's sail from it.

Suppose the Island of Cuba were in the hands of Great Britain, it would be quite as reasonable for us to plant a great naval station at Pensacola, for the protection of New York, as it would be to expect in war that a fleet in the Columbia river could escape the surveillance of British cruisers from Vancouver's Island, and reach the coast of California unmolested.

Owing to its dangerous navigation, the close proximity, and the commanding position of Vancouver's Island, both Astoria, and whatever ports we may have on Pugets' Sound, are rendered incapable of commanding so much, even, as their three marine leagues at sea. Respectfully &c, M.F. Maury, Lt. U.S.N.

LS in ScCleA; PC in *Hunt's Merchants' Magazine*, vol. XVIII, no. 6 (June, 1848), pp. 592–601; variant PC in *De Bow's Commercial Review*, vol. VI, no. 2 (August, 1848), pp. 205–214. Note: The chart described by Maury was not found with the LS and was not reproduced in *De Bow's Commercial Review*.

From J[OHN] Y. MASON,
[Secretary of the Navy]

Navy Department, March 30th 1848

Sir, I have the honor to acknowledge the receipt of yours of the 26th inst. and have caused the application in behalf of young [R.E.] King, therein enclosed, to be placed on file.

By the act of March 3d 1845 South Carolina is entitled to thirteen Midshipmen—it now has that number in the service. A vacancy recently occurred to which a son of Dr. [William] Butler [former Representative from S.C.] was appointed. It is quite uncertain when another appointment can be made from that State; when it can be done young King's application will be respectfully considered with those of other applicants from that State.

A large proportion of the officers now in the service from South Carolina were appointed from Charleston and its immediate vicinity and the selection of lads from other parts of the State is [s]trongly urged whenever an opportunity offers to make such appointments. Without deciding now, on the application[s] from the State, I may say, that, I have always thought that such claims have much force in view of the law requiring appointments to be made in the proportion of representatives in Congress. I am respec[tfull]y yours, J.Y. Mason.

FC in DNA, RG 45 (Naval Records), Miscellaneous Letters Sent by the Secretary of the Navy, 1798–1886, 39:444–445 (M-209:14). NOTE: James L. Butler, appointed Midshipman, was the nephew of former Governor of S.C. Pierce M. Butler and Senator from S.C. Andrew P. Butler; and nephew on his mother's side of the naval heroes Oliver Hazard Perry and Matthew Calbraith Perry.

SPEECH ON THE REVOLUTION IN FRANCE

[In the Senate, March 30, 1848]

[*William Allen of Ohio had introduced resolutions by which Congress, on "behalf of the American people," tendered congratulations "to the people of France upon their success in their recent efforts to consolidate liberty, by embodying its principles in a republican form of government." Roger S. Baldwin of Conn. moved to refer the resolutions to the Committee on Foreign Relations.*]

Mr. Calhoun. I do not perceive the slightest necessity for referring this resolution to the committee, and on that point I entirely concur with the views of the mover of it. The resolution is simple; it requires no examination of details, and the Senate is just as competent to form an opinion of its merits as any committee can possibly be.

I do not intend to enter at present into the great question presented in the resolution. To act upon it now, would, in my judgment, be premature. The people of France have done much. They have made a mighty revolution. They have overthrown an old and powerful monarchy, and decreed the establishment of a republic. All this they have accomplished in a very short period, and without any extraordinary bloodshed or confusion. It is indeed calculated to excite our wonder, and, so far as the aim of the French people extends, our lively sympathy. But the time has not yet arrived for congratulation. Much remains to be done. The real work to be performed is yet before them. They have decreed a republic, but it remains for them to establish a republic. If the French people shall succeed in that—if they shall prove themselves to be as wise in constructing a proper constitution, as they have proved themselves to be skillful in demolishing the old form of government—if they shall really form a constitution which shall on one hand guard against violence and anarchy, and on the other against oppression of the people, they will have achieved, indeed, a great work. They will then be entitled to the congratulations, not only of this country, but of the whole civilized world. But if they fail, what then? What then? Can there be a more important inquiry? If France fail, under what form of government will she find herself? I suppose it will be out of the question to go back to a constitutional monarchy. The Bourbon family in all its branches, is, I take it, now odious to the French people. They will hardly think of reinstating the old imperial dynasty of Napoleon. An aristocracy they cannot think of; and what then must be the result, if they fail to establish a republic? If it come to contests within, or wars without—if it shall be necessary to resort to force, to repress internal discord, or overcome foreign assailants—quite a possible case—France may find herself in the embrace of a military despotism. Such a result would furnish no ground for congratulation either on our part, or that of the civilized world.

This is, indeed, a mighty movement. It is pregnant with mighty consequences. Whether the result shall prove to be a blessing or a curse to France and the world, depends upon what is coming, rather than upon what has been already done. A revolution in itself is not a blessing. The revolution accomplished by the French people is indeed a wonderful event—the most striking, in my opinion, in history; but it may lead to events which will make it a mighty evil. It is therefore premature to offer our congratulations merely upon a revolution. We must look to the consequences and the end. We must await the termination of the movement. I wish well to France—sincerely do I wish her well! There is no man that breathes who has a deeper or more profound love of constitutional government than I have—not one. But I have never known a period when there was so great a necessity for wise, deliberate, cautious procedure. Great events are before us. There lives not the man who can say what another year may bring forth.

I offer no opinion as to the success or failure of the French people in this effort. I see tremendous difficulties in the way of success—difficulties resulting from the social condition of France, and the composition of her people. I see, on the other hand, a good deal of encouragement. The success of the French people will, in my opinion, depend, at least in a very high degree, upon the fact whether she can prevent war—that again depending upon two circumstances: one, whether she may have the self-control to abstain from improper interference with surrounding countries; the other, whether they may have the moderation and good sense to abstain from assailing France. Thus far the leading Power of Europe has certainly discovered great good sense and foresight. Great Britain has done as she ought to have done; and I trust that every other Power in Europe will stand and look on; giving France a fair opportunity to consummate the great work in which she has engaged. It is due to France, to the civilized world, and to themselves, that European Powers should observe strict non-interference. If she succeed, it will be an admonition to all Europe, that the time has arrived when they must agree to yield to liberty in a constitutional and stable form. Thrones will fade away, and freedom and republican institutions become the order of the day. If, on the contrary, standing aloof and avoiding all contest, France shall fail in this great undertaking, after a fair trial, without the interference of other Powers, it will do more to put down liberty under a republican form of government, than any other event which could occur.

Now, I think that it is due all round, that there shall be a fair trial. The first step to that, in my opinion, consists in quiet looking on, and as little interference as possible. To France, the people every where will extend their sympathy; but I do contend that the governments themselves ought to be prudent and abstemious in the expression of their sentiments. If we, as a Government, extend our congratulations in this formal and solemn manner, others may take the opposite and denunciatory course, and between the two, that result will be produced which must inevitably overthrow the revolution—an appeal to arms. That is one reason why this Government, looking to the interests of France alone, and with the kindest feeling, ought to be cautious and abstemious in making a move. My opinion, then, is, that the wisest course will be to lay this resolution on the table, expressly on the ground that it is premature. The circumstances by which we ought to be regulated in expressing or withholding our congratulations, have not yet presented themselves. When these circumstances do occur, the time for taking up the subject will have arrived. We know that a national convention, called by the provisional government, is to assemble about the middle of next month.

Mr. [Thomas H.] Benton, (in his seat.) It will meet on the 20th of next month.

Mr. Calhoun. Let us await that important event. Let us await the action of the convention. That will be wise and prudent. Let us not act with precipitation. I move, then, to lay the resolution on the table.

[*Calhoun's resolution to table was defeated by 14 to 29. Later in the debate, Henry S. Foote of Miss. remarked that Calhoun "desired a postponement of the resolution till the public sentiment had been matured."*]

Mr. Calhoun. Not at all. I said that I desired a postponement of the resolution till we had an opportunity of judging whether the movement in France was a subject of congratulation or not.

From *Congressional Globe*, 30th Cong., 1st Sess., pp. 568–570. Also printed in the New York, N.Y., *Herald*, April 1, 1848, p. 3; the Washington, D.C., *Daily National Intelligencer*, April 3, 1848, p. 2; the Alexandria, Va., *Gazette and Virginia Advertiser*, April 4, 1848, p. 2; the Columbia, S.C., *South-Carolinian*, April 11, 1848, p. 1; the Charleston, S.C., *Mercury*, April 13, 1848, p. 2; the Greenville, S.C., *Mountaineer*, April 21, 1848, p. 1; Houston, ed., *Proceedings and Debates*, pp. 429, 431; Crallé, ed., *Works*, 4:450–454. Variants in the Alexandria, Va., *Gazette and Virginia Advertiser*, March 31, 1848, p. 3; the Washington, D.C., *Daily National Intelligencer*, March 31, 1848, p. 4; the New York N.Y., *Herald*, March 31, 1848, p. 2; the New York, N.Y., *Morning Courier and New-York Enquirer*, March 31, 1848, p. 2; the Philadelphia, Pa., *Public Ledger*, March 31, 1848, p. 3; the Baltimore, Md., *Sun*, March 31, 1848, p. 4; the Charleston, S.C., *Mercury*, April 3, 1848, p. 2; the Richmond, Va., *Enquirer*, April 4, 1848, p. 4; the Philadelphia, Pa., *Pennsylvania Freeman*, April 6, 1848, p. 3.

From Ch[arles] Aug[ustus] Davis

Newyork [City,] 31 March 1848

My D[ea]r Sir, I was much gratified with y[ou]r views regarding the french question. I have letters from sources ["in Europe by last Steamer" *interlined*] I w[oul]d rely on more than I w[oul]d on political sources, for when a man is writing on matters involving $ & cents and markets in which his own pocket is interested, is apt to understand himself—and not apt to allow his fancy or his wishes to blind him. Now from those sources I predict that the present *provisional Gov't. even* will not last till 20 Ap[ril]. If it does it will be by "a combination of miracles"—and as for France settling down into a republican form of Govt. *such as we w[oul]d approve* (for a *name* is not always the *thing*) I have not the least hope or expectation. I think it can be demonstrated—it is in my mind quite clear—people sh[oul]d remember that no Gov't. in Europe can be created that has not the confidence of capitalists. What capitalist w[oul]d trust France as a republic? They scarcely incline to trust us. Gold will float away from the continent & go to England. She will of course become stronger as the continent becomes weaker—the continental Govt's (if republics) will find it not only impossible to borrow money to carry on Gov't. but can't pay debts—*repudiating* will soon be no fable. Every act of this nature will of course weaken the weak & strengthen the strong.

England will be too cunning to interfere for such w[oul]d only quiet factions. These factions will destroy one another if left alone. I predict that this revolution on the continent will result in giving England renew'd assendency there—which she was fast losing.

As regards our Country this trouble in Europe will for a time be most disastrous to the cotton portion and I fear it will go very low—besides this, the South will lose largely by bad debts—or *bad bills* of Ex[change] taken for late Ship[men]ts—for I fear every continental agency will go by the board.

Now my notion is that it becomes us to wait—before throwing up our caps for any party in Europe. "It is a rascally world (there) at best (politically & morally) and the fewer we praise in it the better." We are superior to the best among them and what claims has any portion of Europe upon us? A very brief period since an *American* in Europe was a *shun'd* person—(vide the European press (passim)—now to be sure we are rightly appreciated by our own merits. I sh[oul]d not be at all surprized to hear a blow up in france between the *Troops of the line* and the other Troops, for the National guards will have been sadly changed by reason of an infusion of "all sort of people" and their "esprit de Corps" somewhat diluted ["and a large portion join the Line Troops" *interlined*]. The provisional Gov't. has unfortunately been constrain'd to promise too much to the masses— more than can be complied with. It is not as easy a matter in Europe to create a republic out of a monarchy as the reverse. There is not *the right kind of stuff* to readily create & sustain a republic like ours, or one that w[oul]d strike our fancy & meet our approval. And the world will see in the current contest the striking difference between a European republican & an American republic—& we shall not be losers by the contrast.

The Senate w[oul]d do well to let those Resolutions lie on the table till 4th July next. Esteemfully & regardfully Y[ou]r friend, Ch: Aug. Davis.

ALS in ScCleA.

Remarks on the bill for the relief of Patrick Walker, 3/31. Several Senators wished to reconsider the passage of the bill, so "that a general system should be established for all cases of disability by wounds received in the service, in preference to legislating on individual cases." Calhoun joined these Senators: "I voted for this bill, but on reflection I have been induced to change my opinion. I understand that the subject has engaged the attention of the Military Committee, and that they are preparing a bill which will cover this and similar cases; and under this view, in order to test the principle whether we shall defer this matter a little, and give that Committee an opportunity to act upon the subject, I move that, for the present, this bill lie upon the table." (Calhoun's motion was ruled out of order, as a motion to reconsider was pending.) From Houston, ed., *Proceedings and Debates*, p. 433.

APRIL 1–MAY 31, 1848

〖〗

Calhoun's warnings about the dangers of warmaking, even for the victorious, seemed to be confirmed by a letter to him penned on April 6 at Mexico City. The writer was John G. Tod, who Calhoun knew well as a high level despatch bearer during his time in the State Department. Tod described at length demoralization and criminality among the American occupying troops.

Calhoun's correspondence and Senate duties were heavy at this time. One of the major themes of the correspondence, both letters written and letters received, was the ongoing revolutions in Europe. Calhoun and his correspondents approved the end of monarchies, but were only cautiously optimistic about the possibilities of new regimes that reflected American-style freedom and self-government.

This was a Presidential election year and the politicians who favored men over measures had been busy since the beginning of the year. A large factor in the political equation, as everyone understood, was the immense popularity of General Zachary Taylor, who was admired for his military victories, his plain and honest character, and also probably for his lack of known political opinions. He could doubtless have had the nomination of either party. Many Southerners took comfort in the fact that he was also a Louisiana planter. Calhoun, for his part, urged non-participation in the spoilsmen-controlled nominating process of the Democrats. Whatever nominee was selected and whatever pledges were made to the South, the spoilsmen would be sure to betray Southern interests.

The party convention met in Baltimore in May and nominated Lewis Cass of Michigan, a known proponent of "squatter sovereignty," that is, the right of territorial governments to exclude slavery prior to Statehood. Calhoun had known Cass well for thirty years and had no great opinion of his ability or character.

Calhoun's largest concern at this time was the continued threat of war and the accompanying aggrandizement of Presidential power and danger of imperializing republican institutions. A war between whites and Indians raged in Yucatan, which was or was not a part of Mexico. James K. Polk asked Congress to authorize occupation of the province to prevent any European power from taking advantage of this situation and "to rescue the white race from extermination." From April 29, when he first heard of this proposal, Calhoun fought against it with all his powers. The battle culminated in one of his timeless speeches on May 15, containing much matter still relevant to the relationship between foreign interventionism and republican government. The Charleston Courier *(May 23, 1848, p. 2) commented, correctly: "The Yucatan measure is considered dropped. Mr. Calhoun's speech against it made a deep impression."*

Internal improvements was another continuing concern, in its various forms. A number of South Carolina papers reported in May that Calhoun, as a stockholder in the South Carolina Railroad, had approved a change of terminus from Aiken to Greenville.

Another concern, a pervasive one, was the rising intensity of anti-slavery. A bill had been under consideration throughout the session for organizing a territorial government for Oregon, and this carried with it, since the appearance of the Wilmot Proviso, certain conflict over the power of Congress and territorial governments over slave property in the common territory. There was an incident in Washington itself in April when an attempt (unsuccessful) was made to carry off eighty-some slaves belonging to citizens of the federal District. Antiabolition riots ensued. On April 20 Calhoun had an extended debate on these matters with John P. Hale of New Hampshire, who had already accepted the Presidential nomination of the Liberty Party. (The party, though, merged with the Free Soil Party, which met in June and nominated Martin Van Buren.)

Many and substantial Northerners agreed with Calhoun on all of his positions, including those on slavery. James K. Paulding was a member of the old Dutch aristocracy of New York, of Revolutionary family, a literary man, and had been Van Buren's Secretary of the Navy. On April 5 he wrote to Calhoun in praise of his anti-war speech of March 16: "After reading your speech, I fell into a speculation on the grandeur of the position you now occupy. You are decidedly in a minority in the Senate, and yet your opinions have more influence over the People of the United States than probably those of all the majority combined."

Ⅲ

To T[homas] G. Clemson, [Brussels]

Washington, 1st April 1848

My dear Sir, I am very happy to learn by your's and Anna's [Anna Maria Calhoun Clemson's] letters by the Caledonia, that you were all well, & that Belgium was so quiet, & disposed to pursue, what appears to me at this distance, so wise a course; to maintain her institutions & nationality & to prepare to defend them. I hope there will be the same good sense on the part of other European powers. Thus far the revolution in France exhibits to the inexperienced eye a fair prospect; but I see much to excite in me deep distrust as to the result. Indeed, I have on [sic] no hope, that she will ever be able to establish any government deserving to be called a republick. She has on this side of the Atlantick much sympathy but little confidence among the thinking. The subject ["of tendering our congratulations" *interlined*] was brought up in the Senate yesterday, on resolutions offered by Mr. [William] Allen. A short running debate took place in which I took part. I send the sheet containing it, which will give the views presented by myself & others. There is a decided majority in the Senate ag[ai]nst hasty action, or expression of opinion. The Senate will wait the action of the National Convention.

I enclose also my remarks on the 10 Regiment Bill. They are badly reported & printed, but will give a correct conception of the grounds on which I placed my objections to the bill.

I also enclose a letter from her Mother [Floride Colhoun Calhoun] to Anna, & two letters received under cover for you.

Since I wrote you by the last Steamer we have had no political occurrence worthy of note. The prospect of a peace with Mexico still continues good, & the uncertainty, in reference to the Presidential election is still as great as ever.

My love to Anna & the children [John Calhoun Clemson and Floride Elizabeth Clemson]. Your affectionate father, J.C. Calhoun.

ALS in ScCleA; PC in Jameson, ed., *Correspondence*, pp. 747–748.

To Charles Lanman, [Eastville, Northampton County, Va.]

Washington, 1st April 1848

Dear Sir, I enclose you letters to Mr. [Joel R.] Poinsett & Mr. [Waddy] Thompson [Jr.], who reside in GreenVille, a short distance from the base of the Mountains, and on your route to my immediate vicinity, near the village of Pendleton.

I hope to be home before you reach that portion of the great chain, and will expect you to make my residence a resting place in your tour. There is no part of the chain, which I have ever seen, more wild and picturesk than that in my vicinity. With great respect I am & &, J.C. Calhoun.

ALS in ScU-SC, John C. Calhoun Papers.

To W[ADDY] THOMPSON [JR., Greenville, S.C.]

Washington, 1st April 1848

My dear Sir, I take pleasure in introducing you to Mr. Charles Lanman, who will deliver you this.

He is the author of "A Summer in the Wilderness" & several other works, which has given him reputation, as an author.

He intends travelling during the coming season, through the length & breadth of the Alleganey Mountains; and will probably visit Greenville in his tour. While there, I feel assured you will take pleasure in making his stay agreeable to him. Yours truly, J.C. Calhoun.

ALS in ScU-SC, John C. Calhoun Papers.

To H[ENRY] W. CONNER, [Charleston]

Washington, 4th April 1848

My dear Sir, Understanding from your letter to Mr. [Armistead] Burt [Representative from S.C.], that it was desired to know my opinion, whether it would be advisable for the State to be represented in the Baltimore convention, I thought it most respectful to have a meeting of our delegation, to ascertain their views before I undertook to express my opinion.

After full consideration, they were of the opinion, the State ought not to be, unanimously & decidedly, with the exception of Mr. [Alexander D.] Sims [Representative from S.C.], who felt disposed to differ, but declared he would take no part. It was, however, decided, that it would be unadvisable to make an Address to our Constituents, as it might look like dictation. Each was left to write & express his opinion.

It is well known, that I have been opposed to a convention to nominate a President, because; it is unwarranted by the Constitution, and is intended to supercede its provisions, in reference to his election, as far as the party is concerned. To that extent the nomination is in effect the election. Because; it destroys the compromises of the Constitution between the larger & smaller members of the Union, as it relates to his election, by securing to the former their preponderance, in the electoral college, & depriving the latter of theirs in the eventual election by the House. Because; as constituted, the Convention is an unequal & unfair representation of the party. Instead of giving to each State a representation in the Convention, in proportion to its relative party strength, it gives each the relative weight it has in the electoral college, without the least regard to its party strength. The effect of that is, to give several States, in which the democratick party has no weight, which have not a vote in either House of Congress, and which can command not a single electoral vote, as much weight as others, which give a unanimous vote in both houses, and an undivided electoral vote the other way. Now, as the non slave holding States are much more populous, than the slave holding, while they are far less democratical, it is appearant, that the effect of the nomination is, to give a minority of the party, & the least sound portion of the Union, in a party view, the control of the election. The effects of that, again, is to sacrafice the interest of the slave holding States, & to expose them, ultimately, to great danger, if not certain distruction.

The first effect, is to give a minority of the party ["in the non slave holding States" *interlined*] a control over the Executive Department of the government. Let, who will be elected, if he desires a reelection, or ["the election of" *interlined*] a favourite to succeed him, as he always will, one or the other, he must, to accomplish his object, court the minority in those States, as they have the control over the nomination. To do that, he must bestow his patronage freely on it, and accommodate his measures to their interest, to the neglect & sacrafice of the interest of the majority of the party in the other States. But still worse; he becomes for the time the leader of the party, and, in order to sustain him against the assaults of the opposition, the delegates from the States, whose interest are thus sacraficed, are forced by party ties to defend him in the ["very" *canceled and then interlined*] measures, by which they are [sacrificed]. Under this influence, a minority of the party, in the non slave holding States, are absorbing & assimilating a majority in the slave holding to their views, on the most vital of all questions to ["them" *canceled and* "us" *interlined*]; I allude to that, which relates to slavery. It is owing to this cause, that ["they" *canceled and* "we" *interlined*] have not long since united, & put down abolition in the other States, as ["they" *canceled and* "we" *interlined*] might easily do, if united. So long as it is permitted to operate, there is no redemption for the slave holding States. Their certain distruction, if it is permitted to continue, will be the end. The process has already commenced and made great progress, of which no stronger evidence can be furnished than that they should consent to go into the Convention proposed to be held in May next in Baltimore.

Heretofore they would have met with indignation ["a proposal" *interlined*] to meet in Convention avowed & knowen [*sic*] abolitionists. A single individual of that discription would have been sufficient to ["would have" *canceled*] deter every delegate from the slave holding States from taking a seat in the Convention. But time, with the influence of the cause stated, has already effected so great a change, that all those States, with the exception of ours, have already, as is believed, ["have" *canceled*] appointed delegates to that Convention, although it is well known, that it will consist of numerous individuals, as hostile, to our domestick institutions, as [Joshua R.] Giddings [Representative from Ohio], or any other abolitionists. Indeed, there will be very few delegates from the non slave holding States, who will not on this all important question be decidedly opposed to us. Many of them, it is true will disavow the Wilmot proviso; but they will support other measures having the same object and not less fatal in their consequences to us. To show how little reliance we can place on the delegates from those States on this, to us vital question, it is sufficient to state, that the Legislature of N. York has just passed an act to make it penal in any of its citizens to aid, even the federal officers, in delivering up fugitive slaves to their masters. It was, with the exception of two votes, passed unanimously; whigs, Barnburners & Hunkers all voting for it. Similar acts have been passed by Michigan and other States, at the last session of their legislature ["this session" *canceled*] by the joint consent of all parties. And yet, such is the progress, which has already been made to assimilate our feelings with that of the non slave holding States, on even this question, that the entire slave holding States, with, as stated, the exception of ours, have agreed to go into convention to be thus composed, to nominate by their joint action & votes a candidate for the Presidency. What is this, but, in effect, to merge the

293

abolition question, as far as the Presidency is concerned? And what is that, but a decleration, in effect, that abolition of slavery with us, is a less evil—less to be dreaded than ["any one of the questions" *canceled and* "the defeat of the party in the presidential struggle" *interlined*] which now divides the two parties?

But it is said, that the delegates from the slave holding States go in with a fixed determination not to agree to the nomination of any one, who is not decidedly with us on the subject of abolition. Whether they can be brought to take firmly such a stand, remains to be seen. It is to be feared, they will not; that the desire to avoid defeat in the election, and to preserve the ascendancy of the party will make them yield to the majority of delegates from the non slave holding States. But, be that as it may, it will not avert the danger, which must result from agreeing to cooperate & fraternize with known abolitionists. When it comes to be fully established, that the abolition question is not to enter into the Presidential issue, & that Southern planters may fraternize with abolitionists, in nominating & making Presidents, there will be little difficulty to take the next step; to reconcile them to the election of an abolitionists [*sic*]. The first step, in all such cases, is the most difficult. The powerful cause, which has reconciled them to unite in Convention, with abolitionists to make a president, is sufficient, if permitted to continue to operate, to reconcile them to the election of an abolitionists [*sic*].

Thus thinking, I trust, our State will never agree to take so debasing & fatal a step. It may be, if she should resist the bad example, that other States will follow her example hereafter, and that this, otherwise fatal step, may be prevented from becoming a president [*sic*].

I might add many other & weight[y] reasons, against going in at this time; & among others the disorganization of the party and the danger of being committed to the support of a candidate, in whom we ought not, & cannot confide. And, also, that we would have a far greater control by standing aloof, ready to throw our weight, where it can be done with the most effect, to promote our principles & policy, than we possibly could by going into the Convention; but I do not think it can be necessary, after the weighty objections, which have been stated. Indeed, it would seem strange, that the State, after having refused to connect herself with Conventions for so long a period, should go into one now, when the objections are so much strong[er] than they ever were before.

I must ask the favour of you, to consider this addressed to all our friends, who take an interest in the subject, as well as to yourself.

I hope, if you & they concur in the views, that our papers will take such grounds, as will be calculated to discourage any movement in favour of a Convention, if, indeed, there should seem to be any danger of any of the kind. Yours truly, J.C. Calhoun.

ALS in ScC; photostat of ALS in DLC, Henry Workman Conner Papers.

From F[RANCIS] W. PICKENS

Edgewood [Edgefield District, S.C.,] 4 April 1848
Dear Sir, I recieved ["your kind letter" *interlined and* "yours" *canceled*] yesterday & immediately purchased a mule & a mare for Mr. [Thomas G.] Clemson's place.

I will do any thing that a gentleman ought to do for Anna [Maria Calhoun Clemson] & Mr. Clemson, & would have done so all along, but for the very *extraordinary treatment* I ["recieved" *canceled*] met with at your own house last Fall, which I have too much selfrespect [*sic*] to forget. Your ob[e]d[ien]t Serv[an]t, F.W. Pickens.

ALS (retained copy) in NcD, Francis Wilkinson Pickens Papers.

To RICHARD RUSH, [U.S. Minister to France, Paris]

Washington, 4th April 1848
My dear Sir, I understand, that Robert Greenhow E[squi]r[e] of the State Department, is an applicant for the place of Secretary of Legation in the mission, of which you are the head, & which has been vacated by the appointment of Mr. [J.L.] Martin to the place of Charge to Rome. I, also, understand, that he is recommended to you by the Secretary of State, Mr. [James] Buchanan.

It affords me much pleasure to add my recommendation to his. I know Mr. Greenhow well, and can with confidence recommend him to you as well qualified in every respect to fill the place for which he applies. Permit me to add, that I take much interest in his success and would be much gratified, if his application should meet your approbation. With great respect yours truly, J.C. Calhoun.

ALS in NjP, Rush Family Papers (published microfilm of The Letters and Papers of Richard Rush, reel 21, item 11432).

From J[AMES] K. PAULDING

Hyde Park[,] Duchess C[ount]y [N.Y.]
April 5th 1848

My dear Sir, Though you could not furnish me the correspondence of Mr. [Henry A.] Wise [former U.S. Minister to Brazil], you have sent me something much better, and I congratulate myself on the delay of the Public Printer. After reading your speech [of 3/16], I fell into a speculation on the grandeur of the position you now occupy. You are decidedly in a minority in the Senate, and yet your opinions have more influence over the People of the United States than probably those of all the majority combined. Your speech on the Mexican War, by pointing out clearly & specifically the certain consequences of the acquisition of that country was, I am convinced, one ["of" *interlined*] the principal causes of that great change which has taken place in the feelings of the People on that subject. It arrested the career of Conquest, and though the Resolutions were lost in the Senate they were triumphantly carried in the nation, which has shown itself to possess more good sense than its Representatives. Your argument on the Ten Regiment Bill, will have the effect of strengthening their just views on the subject, and you will receive ample compensation for failing in the Senate, from the approval of a People who have understanding to perceive what is right and I firmly believe virtue enough to follow its dictates.

I see with pleasure you are adopting the sound[?] course in regard to the new French Revolution which I fear, now that we have no [George] Washington at the Helm, may eventually involve the United States in the vortex of European politics, and what in my view is equally dangerous, lead us astray from the sober path of American Democracy, into the barren field of European Radicalism.

The extreme Radical Democrat of Europe is a very different Person from the sober Democrat of the United States. The theory of one is altogether destructive, that of the other essentially conservative. The former wishes to pull down, the latter to build up, or at least preserve. The great grievances of Europe are a surplus population, a heavy load of Debt leading to burdensome Taxation, and an unequal division of Property, which while it enables a few to revel in luxury, entails on the masses a load of hopeless poverty, approaching almost to absolute destitution. Hence, in my opinion, all effectual relief in that quarter must be based on a new division of Property, either brought about by the slow and salutary operation of wholesome regulations gradually depriving the few of the monopoly, and giving the many an opportunity for honest acquisition untrammelled by artificial restraints, or by a violent revolution.

No mere change from a monarchy to a Republic; no civil institutions, can at once relieve the necessities of the masses of Europe. They want Bread, and cannot wait the slow process of the Harvest. While the grass grows the steed starves; and I greatly fear that when the sovereign power passes into the hands of People without property, and they find as undoubtedly they will do, that the mere possession of civil ["liberty" *canceled and* "rights" *interlined*], does not immediately and at once relieve their necessities, they will become disgusted with Liberty & seek in licentious anarchy, a remedy for what freedom has failed to cure. For anarchy there is no cure but Despotism, and I cannot but apprehend, that the struggle now commencing in Europe, will eventually reduce that quarter of the globe, to something like the state of Asia. It is not easy to resuscitate old Nations or old men; and all former experience seems to have demonstrated, that the course of Nations is equally uniform and inevitable. They must go the rounds from Barbarism to civilization; from civilization to Luxury and effeminacy, and so to barbarism again. There is no cross-cut—they must make the circle. Europe has had her day. She has worn the sceptre her due time; the Old World is Passé, and the New One must have its turn, before that of the other comes round again.

I fear the example about to be presented by Europe will be eventually pernicious to the United States, which are always imitating where they should set the example, and following where they ought to lead. All our efforts are directed to the preservation of Liberty, those of the Democracy of Europe to a removal of the evils of despotism. Our cue is prevention; theirs is cure. Hence, I think I am justified in the conclusion, that we of the United States, can derive no benefit from the political example, or political precepts of Europe, in its present or future state, except as they may operate as warnings. The Old World is beyond the reach of ordinary remedies, and the regimen necessary to her renovation would if adopted in the New, eventually bring it precisely to that state, from which the former is striving to relieve itself. A revolution in Europe might possibly end in freedom; in the United States it would infallibly produce a Despotism. When Europeans talk of Liberty, equality, and self-government, it is without any definite idea, which can only be thoroughly acquired by living under the system, and becoming practically accustomed to its enjoyments. The obstacles to the acquisition of Freedom in the Old World, will require a force to overcome them which when once they give way will carry the People far, very far, beyond the sober limits of Democracy in the United ["States" *interlined*]. We see it already peeping forth in France, where among the first acts of the Provisional Government, are the robbery of the West India Planter and an interference in the relations of the Labourer and Employer— both savouring of the worst Species of Despotism. Frankly, I should be very sorry to see Republics throughout Europe, for I verily believe they will bring Liberty into disgrace like those of South America, and in the end worry the People back into despotism as the only refuge from anarchy and Licentiousness. Those who think the people of the present age better or worse than those of the past, will I fear find themselves mistaken. We may know more than our ancestors. But knowledge is not wisdom[;] much less is it virtue; and the latter is a much more important ingredient in the composition of a free People than the former. There can be no rational [*or* "national"] Liberty except among a people well grounded in the principles of reason and justice, which are the only substitutes for brute force.

I wish my letter were worth as much as your speech, and then I might hope you would receive it as an equivalent. But as I don[']t tax you with an answer, you will only have the trouble of reading it or not just as you please. I am Dear Sir with great respect & regard yours very truly, J.K. Paulding.

ALS in ScCleA; variant PC in Aderman, ed., *The Letters of James Kirke Paulding*, pp. 474–477.

From J[OHN] E[WING] BONNEAU

Charleston, So. Ca., 6 April 1848

My Dear Sir, I have delayed for a few days to reply to your letter of 23rd ult. in relation to the Sale of your Cotton, with a view of seeing what effect the late news from Europe would have on our market. It has produced a decline of one & one half cents on all descriptions. There were sold yesterday about 2600 Bales, which brought from $5\frac{1}{4}$ to 7 cents as to quality; the latter being the best[?] since[?] paid for the best brands in the market. I received on 29th[?] Feb[ruar]y last the remainder of your Pendleton Crop, say 24 Bales which with the 26 Bales received on 15th Jan[uar]y last makes 50 Bales now on hand. The quality of the Cotton is very inferior & would not command today over $5\frac{1}{2}$ cents. The Cotton has been badly prepared for market. I shall reserve a sample of each Bale in order that you may see yourself the quality of the Cotton as you pass through on your return home.

I see no prospect of things being better. With great respect yours truly, J.E. Bonneau.

ALS in ScU-SC, John C. Calhoun Papers. NOTE: An AEU by Calhoun indicates that on 5/4 he authorized Bonneau "to sell my cotton to the best advantage he could."

To H[ENRY] W. CONNER, [Charleston]

Washington, 6th April 1848
My dear Sir, After I mailed my letter [of 4/4] to you yesterday, Mr. [Armistead] Burt [Representative from S.C.] put in my hands yours to him of the 3d Inst.

I regret to learn, that there ["should be" *canceled and* "is" *interlined*] so strong a disposition to send de[le]gates to the Baltimore convention. I have stated the objections to it in my letter to you. They seem to me to be overwhelming strong; and I hope such will be your impression and other friends. If we go in, we shall take the yolk [*sic*] of party, & will become as insignificant as N. Jersey or any other State, that has no will of its own.

It is too late to write to Mr. [Robert F.W.] Allston, as you suggested; and I would be at a loss to whom it would be proper to write in the different parts of the State, to counteract the tendency to go in, as I do not know who is, or is not committed to the move. Besides, it would be a heavy burthen to give to each my opinion at large, with my objections to going into the convention. I intended to state them in my place in the Senate, had an opportunity offered, but none has.

My letter to you was intend[ed] as a private letter to you and such of our Charleston friends as might desire to know my opinion; but, if you & they should think it necessary to use it more largely, by sending copies to influential persons in different parts of the State, or to use it in any other way, I leave it entirely to your's & their discretion to do so. My opinion, with my reasons for entertain[in]g it, could be, probably, more promptly & generally made known ["that" *interlined*] than any other way. But you must judge for yourselves, without being influenced by any suggestion of mine. Truly, J.C. Calhoun.

ALS in ScC; photostat of ALS in DLC, Henry Workman Conner Papers.

From Ch[arles] Aug[ustus] Davis

Newyork [City], 6 Ap[ril] 1848

My D[ea]r Sir, There is not a man among us—not even a frenchman whose opinion is worth a straw—who can yet say whether the late revolution in Paris is to be a one act Farce—or a 5 act Tragedy. One thing seems pretty clear (and this the more confounds) that *a monarchy* without a strong hereditary aristocracy is a pretty dangerous *experiment*—it is like a dictatorial Commodore going to sea in a 74 gun ship—with no officers except such as may wear a mere ribbon— but hold no other *rights*—or *pay* above any man before the mast. This may work safely where every man is as good as the Commander and takes so much pride (individually & nationally) as to be willing to do the rough work & let him & the ribbon'd folks enjoy the ease & best cuts—but assuming the fact to be as it is in france—a King there without the appendages of *estated nobility* about him—holds by a very attenuated string. And it seems to me it matters not by what name he is call'd—"King"—"Emperor"—"President"—"Chef de People"—"President" [*sic*] or what—the moment he attempts *to rule*— he begins to feel the want of something besides the badge of office. And the question to my mind seems to turn upon this—they must try a republic and prove and show its inadequacy—& then ten to one they will drift into a stronger form than they have had for many years, for their own safety. In the mean time the *"war of opinion"* may be a very bloody one. So my own opinion is that france *just now* is as unfit for a *republic* (such as we understand it) as she is just now for a *strong monarchy* as they understand it.

They seem to have kick'd the staves of the barrel into a heap and broken the hoops—and neither a cooper or a carpenter has the means at hand to reform the barrel or construct a square box out of the ruins, & they have no other materials to use, & there they are dancing and carousing about it.

As yet it appears as complete a break up or break down as was ever presented to the world—and I never knew *intel[l]igence* here so completely in a puzzle in even *surmising* results. France contains much of intel[l]igence & polish'd skill—but no Country perhaps contains a larger portion of opposite qualities and when these attempt a mixture no one can tell what kind of a pudding may come out of the pot.

The first great practical difficulty will be in obtaining means—a *Provisional* Govt. may find a lack of *provision.* A row may follow— and then another *run*—and no one can say where the *necessities* of the people may carry them. Who can say they may not resort to *confisca-* *tion* & *sequestration* or in other land *grabbing*—at even our Property—, or property of our Citizens within reach—and plead as an excuse "the dire necessities of the State." If such sh[oul]d occur we may see cause to regret any hasty *approval* of what has been done in *Paris.*

For one I feel that we are not call'd on to take by the hand any people who chuse to cry "Vive la Republique"—until they have proved themselves worthy of our countenance.

Our standard of republicanism reaches beyond the mere "huzza." It is based on Virtue—self denial—self restraint—respect for Laws— and years of Probation. I for one am not ready to believe that such a republic as our own is to be made out of *any kind of material.* Hence I am somewhat *aristocratic* on this point.

I was struck by the fact that at the late meeting in the Park here I saw very few of our own or foreign citizens of that Cast which w[oul]d gather on an occasion where no doubt or fear or misgiving of result existed—a very different collection gathered there. A few days now will tell us more & enable us to look a little deeper into the dust that has been so suddenly kick'd up abroad. Very truly Y[ou]r friend, Ch: Aug. Davis.

ALS in ScCleA.

From JOHN G. TOD

City of Mexico, April 6th 1848

Mr. Calhoun, I have been mortified to find that the letters that I sent by the British Courier of the 13th of Feb: had not reached New Orleans by the 9th of March!

I sent you a half sheet by that conveyance, believing that it would go forward with despatch, & that the news with us, about the Peace prospect, would interest you.

The Treaty has arrived, and great difference of opinion prevails as to its probable fate. Those having the responsibility of affairs think we will have Peace in sixty days, or less time. The truth is, that thus far all the efforts of the Executive Government to get the Congress together have failed; but the prospect is in favor of its assembling in all of this month. Many good Mexicans, however, do not desire Peace, they want the Country to be occupied by our Troops, this policy gives them and [*sic*] assurance of security for life and property, and affords them a prospect of diminishing the power & influence of the Church, which doubtless, is a greater Curse upon the People, than every thing else put together. The Roman Religion here is not what it is with us in the U. States. If it is was [*sic*] not for some of its forms & ceremonies, and its professions, it might as well be call[ed] by any other name.

The public mind at present here appears absorbed entirely, by one of those horrid murders that shock a community & disgraces humanity.

Some twelve individuals attempted the other night, to rob, in the most thronged part of the City, an extensive mercantile house, by going from the top of the adjoining building, and letting themselves down by a rope-ladder. The Chief Clerk, a gentleman of great worth, was killed: the robbers did not succeed in getting any money, as the firing of Pistols attracted different persons, and they fled; not however, in time for all of them to escape, as one, or two, were apprehended, sin[c]e then five or six more have been caught.

Amongst those already in custody are two Officers, the 1s[t] & 2nd Lieutenants of Captain [Charles] Naylor[']s Company of Penn: Volunteers. The Adj[utant] of the 2nd Regiment of Penn: Vols: is also implicated, and they are after him at present. This horrible and lamentable affair, has done more to degrade the American Character in this Country, and will wherever known, than any thing that has occurred since the Declaration of our Independence. If the Texas Rangers had been in this ["city" *interlined*] and these scoundrels had not been apprehended, I am sure they ["former" *canceled*] would have been suspected—for they have been made the 'scape goats for all acts of barbarity, as the Mexicans were ready to believe that they would do every thing, no matter how horrible.

If you were in this City for one day, to see and observe the dreadful state of morals amongst our Troops, you would ["not" *interlined*] be surprised at the outrages committed here daily against society & humanity.

I have always, on proper occasions, denounced the course pursued here by our authorities, in legalizing Gambling houses, and places of resort called "Ball Rooms," which are mere receptacles for a profligacy & corruption unknown, since the downfall of Venice! Not one decent Mexican Lady would dare even to think of going to a Ball here—And no American Gentleman, according to the acceptation of that word at home. Yet the rooms are crowded with our officers night after night.

As for the Gambling houses, there is a constant crowd, Sabbath as well as week days, around the Tables—Colonels, Majors, Captains, & Lieutenants, Grey headed men & beardless youths, married & single: hundred[s] of whom keep women, and openly appear in public with them. These things, with drinking, brings down the standard of our morals to a degree, below the conception of Americans at home. Our Generals and superior officers looking for political preferment at a future day, do not possess the firmness and moral courage sufficient to discountenance, and rebuke the vicious habits, that are degrading the Character of our Flag: and that is destined in time to roll back a tide of vice & corruption upon our Country, that will be felt by many, when the glory of this war has departed.

Bands of desperate men—Gamblers and vicious Soldiers—prowl about, robbing and murdering—extending their outrages to the neighboring Haciendas—all resulting from vices that have been winked ["at" *interlined*] and tolerated by those to whom are entrusted the honor of our Flag. Many young men, who were the pride of the'r friends, and the hope of their Parents, will return home to bring down their grey hairs with sorrow to the grave. Like causes produce like results, and nine-tenths of the inmates of our Penitentiaries, and Criminals, whose outrages shock humanity, terminated their Career in the path that is crowded here to excess by our officers. I say nothing about the common soldier. My desire "to see the world and study mankind" never yet has induced me to visit the "dark places of the Earth," or the purlieus and sinks of villainy, as shadowed forth in this City. Vice does not degrade the Mexican ["(in his own mind)" *interlined*], it is a part of his religion; but with our people, it is different. It makes us abandoned to all the restraints of Society, and many who are now here, that were an honor to our country, would doubtless, if they were Sailors turn Pirates, when this war is over; but as it is, they will return home to add to the number of those who are a curse to any community.

I do not wish you, Mr. Calhoun, to think that I set myself up as a regulator of ["other" *interlined*] men's morals, or possess the spirit of the Pharisee—but the outrages here at times, would make any man reflect, who is not drawn within the vortex of dissipation. What is to be the result of it, God only knows. This is a melancholy subject to write ["upon," *interlined*] let alone to *send* to a Patriot, and a lover of his country. Yet it is well that the truth should be known at times, however disagreeable. Foreign wars if conducted with results that seem likely to accrue from this, would so degrade an Army that they would be ready for any thing, that would give them ["an lift" *canceled*] "a lift" without the efforts of honest industry.

I have just had a conversation with an agreeable, intelligent Mexican, who is lately from Queretaro. He is an advocate for Peace, but fears it will be a long while before it can be brought about. The President [Manuel de la Peña y Peña] is doing all in his power to get the Members of Congress together, even sending them money to travel upon, as the want of it was their apology for not appearing in their seats. They have written back, that it was not received! A party there, are for bringing back Santa Anna & make him *Dictator*, but it is thought they will not do so, until Peace is ratified. Y[ou]r ob[edient] Serv[an]t, Jno. G. Tod.

ALS in ScCleA; PC (misdated 4/5) in Jameson, ed., *Correspondence*, pp. 1163–1166. Note: John Grant Tod (1808–1877) was a native of Ky. and had been a ranking officer of the Texas Republic Navy. He was well-known to Calhoun as a carrier of despatches between Washington and Texas when Calhoun was Secretary of State.

Remarks on the Supreme Court Bill

[In the Senate, April 7, 1848]
[*Under consideration was a bill from the Committee on the Judiciary which would relieve the Justices of the Supreme Court from their customary duties as Circuit Court judges.*]

Mr. Calhoun. I rise simply to state, in a very few words, the reasons that will govern me, in giving my vote on this occasion. It must be admitted on all sides, that this is intended to be only a temporary measure, and that the present system ought to be continued. I believe this is the general impression; such is mine, very strongly. The bill is presented on the ground, that the cases upon the docket have so accumulated, that it requires an extraordinary law—to relieve the judges from their circuit duties for one year—in order to clear them off. Well, what possible assurance have we, that at the end of the year the same reason will not exist for enacting such a law for the next year? It appears to me that we are inverting the order of things. The first object should be to adopt some measure that would prevent the accumulation of cases in future, and then some measure for disposing of those which now exist. But proceeding as we are, it appears to me, it will be tantamount—without intending it to be so—to a permanent change in the circuit system. Now, I believe there are very few Senators prepared for this; I believe the judges themselves are not. We have ample time during the remaining part of the session—it will probably last three months, yet I should be very glad to think it would terminate in three—surely this will furnish ample opportunity to the Judiciary Committee, or if that committee be overloaded with business, to a select committee to take the subject into consideration, and propose some measure that will prove an effectual remedy for the evil that is complained of.

[*William L. Dayton of N.J. said that there was a bill such as Calhoun suggested now before the House of Representatives, but that the accumulation of cases still had to be dealt with.*]

Mr. Calhoun. I was not aware that there was a bill before the House relating to this subject; but that being the case, it is a reason why this bill should lie upon the table until that bill passes. Let us apply first the general remedy, and then adopt any additional measure that may be necessary. Being strongly desirous that the system should not be changed, and fearing that this bill if adopted will change it, I feel myself compelled to vote against it.

[*A vote was then taken on the engrossment of the bill, which failed 17 to 19.*]

From *Congressional Globe*, 30th Cong., 1st Sess., p. 598. Also printed in Houston, ed., *Proceedings and Debates*, p. 464; Benton, ed., *Abridgment of Debates*, 16:173. Variant in the New York, N.Y., *Herald*, April 9, 1848, p. 4.

From E. and J.W. Agnew, Due West, [S.C.], 4/8. They have received Calhoun's letter containing a check for $271.18, which they acknowledge to be payment in full for the following creditors: D[avid] W. Hawthorn, $18.73; William Norton, $41.37; R.C. Sharp, $15.29; Thomas Robertson [*sic*; Robinson?], $3.25; and E. and J.W. Agnew, $192.52. Calhoun's AEU indicates that the debts were incurred by his son William [Lowndes Calhoun] while at Erskine College. DS in ScU-SC, John C. Calhoun Papers.

From O[zey] R. Broyles

[Pendleton, S.C.,] 8th April 1848

Dear Sir, I have delayed the communication I promised for the purpose of obtaining full information in reference to the Estate [of Chester Kingsley], its available amount et cetera. I have ascertained that of the Notes due Mr. Kingsley previous to his death some four or five thousand dollars of them are considered not good, and that consequently not more than twenty-six thousand dollars will in all probability be realized. Of this amount as I before stated eight thousand dollars were preengaged, which will leave eighteen thousand dollars, which is all I could venture to promise with a near approach to certainty. From the above the ordinary expenses will have to be deducted[,] with some small debts, but both of them I presume can be met by the interest that will accrue on the whole amount of the estate before it will be collected.

The personal property amounted to a little more than thirteen thousand dollars, all of which was due last fall. The lands sold for a little the rise of seven thousand[,] payable in equal annual instalments for four years, the first for one-fourth was due last fall, the next, or one-half will be due the ensuing fall. From all the facts then it appears that in October next the full amount of the personal estate, one-half of the land, and six thousand dollars in Notes in hand previous to the decease and long since due, in all twenty-two thousand five hundred dollars will be due, and notwithstanding the great dif[f]iculty in collecting money at present by reason of the low price of Cotton, the Administrators are of the opinion that they can collect the above during the present year.

I was not a little astonished to find so large an amount of the bonds not available in the hands too of one so cautious, and so generally successful as Mr. Kingsley was. But I understand they came into his hands at the winding up of an old mercantile concern.

I have fears now that the sum will be so inconsiderable that you may not wish to avail yourself of it. You have made no intimation to me as to when you would like to make the investment. If the ensuing fall or winter, I presume there can be little or no doubt but that I can have subject to your order fourteen or fifteen thousand dollars and the remaining instalments on the land as fast as they become due; in all I can promise you about eighteen thousand dollars.

If this sum will be an object with you it would give me great pleasure to collect it as soon as possible and pay it over, there to remain if it suited your wishes until the orphans become of age.

You will do me the favour to write me on the subject as soon as you can determine the course you wish to persue. If you conclude to make the investment, and could say when you would wish me to make the advance I could arrange it with the Administrators in such way as to insure a prompt complyance on the part of debtors and yet have the funds profitably at interest up to the time. Very Truly Yours, O.R. Broyles.

ALS in ScU-SC, John C. Calhoun Papers. NOTE: In an AEU Calhoun indicated that he wrote a letter to Broyles on 4/25 [*not found*] and "acceded to his offer to loan whatever surplus might be in his hands."

From F[ITZ] W[ILLIAM] BYRDSALL, "Private"

New York [City,] April 9th 1848

Dear Sir, On Tuesday next an important Election will take place in this County, important because the Democratic Candidate for Mayor [William F. Havemeyer] is a Wilmot proviso man and a Delegate to the Baltimore Convention from the State Convention recently held at Utica. Two years ago he refused the *unanimous* nomination of the County Convention and now he accepts with a bare majority of *one*, and that obtained after three long meetings of the Convention and nearly forty ballotings.

The nomination was procured with a view that his success ["in the Election" *interlined*] should furnish a plea for his admission into the Baltimore Convention instead of the Delegate chosen by the District; and this plea founded on the popular Vote in his favor for Mayor, would be available to his Colleagues for their admission. But this is not all, the fact of his election as Mayor would furnish strong proof that this County is like a large portion of the Democracy of the State, in favor of Wilmot provisoism. And furthermore as the Van Burenites avow that a defeat in the next presidential contest, is necessary in order to cause a reorganization of the Democratic party and an expulsion of what they term the "Conservatives," "Old Hunkers" &c. which generally means in this State at this time, the opponents of the Proviso, we can easily arrive at the ultimate they contemplate, that is to reorganize the Democracy on the Wilmot proviso platform, to which the Democracy of the New England States have always had a strong tendency, (for generally, wherever the New Englanders, either in old States or new States are settled, there Abolitionism in some form or other takes root,) and thus create *a Democratic party of the North* with John Van Buren as the Autocratic Leader.

But many of us feel that we are under no party obligation to vote for a Candidate when such Vote would place us on the same platform with Henry Clay, Horace Greel[e]y, the last Whig State convention at Syracuse, and John Van Buren[']s Conventions at Herkimer and Utica, as regards the Republican party of the Confederacy. It is not

307

our duty to the Constitution of our Country, or to ourselves, to cast such Vote. If he be elected, I shall be greatly mistaken in my calculations as to the signs around me. There must be insincerity to a great extent amongst the people—there must be a buying up of Votes—there must be fraudulent Voting to a great amount, if he shall be elected. We have about Eighty Polls or places of Election in this County, and being without a Registry Law, there are facilities for frequent voting by the same individuals.

As regards this State in the next presidential Election I see no probability of carrying it for the Democratic Candidate—even if the Van Burenites should go in union with the Old hunkers for him, unless the Candidate were General [Zachary] Taylor. If the Democratic Convention at Baltimore would nominate him, it would accomplish several great ends at once. First it would defeat and disorganize the Whig party. Second it would frustrate and disband John Van Buren and his faction—Third it would strengthen the Constitution of the U.S. and Fourth the election of a Southern man would facilitate the settlement of the constitutional point between the States and the General Government, as to political power of the latter over our Territories, whether its power is not confined "to dispose of and make all needful rules and regulations, respecting ["respecting" *canceled*] the territory or other property belonging to the United States." Far better would it have been that this point had been settled years ago, than to have agreed upon the Missouri Compromise.

I am weary of the continual onslaught upon ["upon" *canceled*] the Southern States, coming up in some form or other every few years.

The News from Europe indicates the progress of Revolutionary principles, but there is no Republic yet—that has yet to be formed. The French have begun well, but the greatest difficulties have yet to be surmounted i.e. the creation of a Republic. If it shall be created much will be due to the mind and tact of one great man [Alphonse de] La Martine. His manifestoes to other nations and to the French people are beautifully expressed and breathe a fine spirit. He is a God sent man. I am Dear Sir with the highest Respect, F.W. Byrdsall.

ALS in ScCleA.

308

From WILSON LUMPKIN

Athens [Ga.,] April 10th 1848
My dear Sir, I read & keep myself informed, upon most subjects connected with the great Events of the times, at home & abroad, & hold but little correspondence with any one at present. I think my own thoughts & form my own Opinions, from the facts presented in connection with every subject.

I was pleased to find from your late speech, on the "ten regiment Bill," that you entertain the opinion, that whether the Treaty with Mexico, shall be ratifyed or not—that public opinion has been so modifyed, as to put a final stop to the spirit of conquest—which will tend to hasten the day for peace & quiet, once more within our borders. I most fully concur with all your feelings & opinions, in a strong desire for peace. The curse of war, is not fully comprehended, by the great mass of our people. Our whole fabrick of govt., is based on principles of peace, & good will to all men & nations.

I am astonished, that the present & prospective financial condition of the country, growing out of this Mexican War, should receive so little consideration, by the popular party, now in power. They are evidently in danger of overturning, all their long professed cherished opinions, in favor of an economical govt., low Taxes, no national debt, small army—Limited Executive patronage & &C. &C. Indeed parties seem to me at present, to be little more, than mere combinations of office seekers, banded together for purposes little better, than rob[b]ing the people, through the instrumentality of the government. All the present party combinations seem to me, to have lost sight of the real opinions & principles of the good old Republican party. Mr. [James K.] Polk has professed well, & acted well, upon many subjects connected with our internal affairs—but I cannot see how his views upon these subjects, (which I highly approve) can be long maintained, in connection with the policy pursued in regard to our Foreign relations. The Elements of society in our Country at this time, is in a state of Chaos. And time alone can develope the future.

I could feel easy & quiet, for my short day, to stand still & look for the salvation of God—If my Country had permanent peace, & we could have an honest Constitutional administration of the govt. There is however, one annoyance which must last to ["the" *canceled*] my end of Earth, Viz. The debts & inevitable consequencies arising out of this Mexican War. The appal[l]ing list of unset[t]led balances, pensions &C &C &C must come.

309

Have you any idea, what will be the result of the labors of the political managers of both parties—upon the subject of the next Presidency?

The machinery of party, is too well organized & too powerful, to be successfully resisted, by the patriotic, honest portion of the Country. Hence we are necessarily driven, to make a choice of evils. And hence we adhere, to the party which profess our principles, while it fails to maintain its faith, by its works.

I have scarcely the shadow of a hope, that our govt., will ever again, be brought back to a constitutional administration. The Constitution has been so long, & so often trod[d]en under foot, & that by all parties—That it will never be a legible instrument, to the young men & boys, who are now in our Colleges and schools. The politicians of the present day, have no regard for the Constitution. The only consideration is, will the people sustain us, in this, or that measure? And thus, they put all their machinery into opperation, to bring the people to the support of their measures. Our government is rapidly tending, to the single principle—That the majority shall govern, *in all cases*, regardless of our written Constitution. May we be preserved from this awful Despotism, before we come under the absolute controul of the mighty West.

The wise men of the East & the North, ought at once, to unite with the South, and strike for the Constitution. Put down promptly & at once, fanaticism upon the subject of Slavery.

For be assured, if the good ["old" *interlined*] 13—The States bordering on the Atlantic, are not brought to sustain the Constitution, our government is destined to revolution. If our Constitution was strictly adhered to—considered sacred—venerated by all men, in & out of office—Then our Empire might be safely extended, as fast, as we could find material for Republican govt. But disregard the Constitution, & adopt the principle, that the majority, shall govern in all cases, Extend your Empire—Annex to your Union, people & States unqualifyed for wise self government—and ere long, it will be recorded, The U.S. of America "*WAS.*" Truly Y[ou]rs, Wilson Lumpkin.

ALS in ScCleA.

From F[ITZ]W[ILLIAM] BYRDSALL

New York [City,] April 13th 1848

My Dear Sir, New York City and County Election is over and if the vote in favor of [William F.] Havemeyer, a disciple of the Evening Post School is any test, then is this a Wilmot Proviso City by Nine hundred & twenty majority. By my Calculation he lost above one thousand Democratic votes and gained over two thousand Whig, Native and abolition votes. [William V.] Brady the Whig Candidate being a [Zachary] Taylor man, one of those very troublesome to the Clay Whigs of these days, of course the latter traded him off by voting for Havemeyer and obtaining democratic or rather Wilmot proviso votes for Whig Aldermen. [*Marginal interpolation:* "(Moses G.) Leonard's majority over (Jefferson) Berrian Whig is 4,264."] Indeed the extraordinary exertions made use of to elect Havemeyer presented a new feature in New York politicks, namely the Zeal of the Wilmot proviso fanatics induced a temporary absence of all consideration of the spoils. But the rejoicings of the Whigs on this point, has waked up the Zealots from their temporary hallucination and they are weeping and wailing and charging in their Chagrin, their loss of the prey to the Conservatives. Now they are sorry that the proviso was ever agitated. Many of them declare that it is a humbug, because they find that a proviso mayor is a shadow of a Victory, for the sake of which, they have lost the Common Council and all the Offices.

The indefatigable exertions, sacrifices of time and money on the part of these men to induce Havemeyer to stand as Candidate, and to carry him successfully through the contest were worthy of a better cause. But there is a coming event which made this course very essential to John Van Buren & company, that is, the annual address of the Democratic members of the Legislature to the people. This address was probably prepared in this city by or under the supervision of John [Van Buren]. It was certainly in this city a few days ago in manuscript in the hands, not of the head of the Custom House or of the Treasury here, I mean neither Laurence [*sic*; Cornelius Van Wyck Lawrence] nor [William C.] Bouck, but of those next to them in official rank. This address takes Wilmot proviso ground and therefore the election of a Wilmot proviso mayor is necessary to sustain the proclamation and hence the efforts to elect him. Had he been defeated some difference might have been necessary in that Docuement. The News of the Election of mayor reached Albany by Telegraph on Wednesday morning and the Caucuss adopted the address late in the afternoon.

311

Mr. [Henry] Clay in his Lexington Resolutions and speech has gone over to some extent to the Wilmot proviso men and Abolitionists. He and [William H.] Seward of this State will be the Candidates of the Whig party for the Presidency and and [*sic*] Vice presidency. Such a ticket would gain so many votes from the fanatics of provisoism in ["the" *interlined*] Democratic party, from the Abolitionists and from the adopted Citizens with whom Seward is popular, that I know of no man in the Union that could have any chance of carrying this State against them except General [Zachary] Taylor. But if the Democratic Convention at Baltimore does not nominate him, I hope some of the Southern States will run him and throw the election into the House [of Representatives] and there I would like ["it" *interlined*] to remain never to be completed, so that the Vice president elected by the Senate shall become the president of these United States.

I never in my life felt that the election of President was of so much importance to the integrity of this Union as now. I do not see as bright a future for these United States as I saw in 1844. I had thought that our system of Government was calculated for any and every stage of human progress even to the highest degree of civilization and enlightenment, but the balances which have been conservative will have to give way to the majority which is apt to be a despotism regardless of Constitutions. These things I fear, but I hope they are mere phantoms of my own mind. Yet I sometimes contemplate the past history of the race[,] a history of demons in the human form of Conquerors and Kings, Revolutions, Republics[,] crimes and sufferings; the masses or rather the best portions of the people oppressed and ill used by every form of Government and I ask myself is our Country to rise to decline and ["fall" *interlined*] like the other great nations which have gone before, and if so how little will be gained for humanity. Some years ago when I contemplated that our system of Government had its exemplar in the heavens in our sun, and planets revolving around ["him" *interlined*] I thought the one would last as long as the other.

Excuse my digression and allow me to subscribe myself Yours very truly, F.W. Byrdsall.

ALS in ScCleA.

To T[HOMAS] G. CLEMSON, [Brussels]

Washington, 13th April 1848

My dear Sir, I was disappointed in not receiving any letter by the Hibernia from Brussels.

Since I wrote you by the preceeding steamer, nothing material has occurred on this side of the Atlantick. The prospect of peace with Mexico has not changed, & the presidential question ["is" *canceled*] continues as doubtful as it was.

Our attention now is turned from ourselves to your side of the Ocean. We are all gazing with intense interest on the mighty scenes, which are exhibiting there, and wondering where they will terminate. Germany seems to be in a fair way to be in a fair way to be [*sic*] completely revolutionised, and I hope permanently improved. I have much more hope for her, than France. Her old institutions, as I suppose we may call them now, furnish an excellent foundation, on which to errect, if not a federal Republick like ours, a federal constitutional Government, united at least in a Zollverein league, & something more intimately united politically, than at present. If the states of Germany should not attempt too much, the events, which have occurred may do much to strengthen them & better their condition. With these impressions, I shall look with anxiety to the proceedings of the Diet, which was to meet on the 2d of April.

I am glad to see Belgium acting so wisely. Thus far the course ["of" *interlined*] events there indicate much moderation & wisdom, as they appear to me, looking on at this distance.

I fear the prospect for France is not so good. I look more to the reaction from Germany to save her, than any other cause. If the latter should take a firm stand to preserve its nationality[,] to adopt wise constitutional reforms, & to form a more intimate commercial & political union, it could not but have a powerful & salutary reaction on France, and might lead to some stable constitutional form of government with her. Otherwise, I see little hope of such a result.

You must regard all this, as little more than the expression of hopes.

I received by the last mail the enclosed from your overseer, which although addressed to me on the outside, is addressed to you within.

I hope you all continue well. My health still continues good, although subject to colds, & never entirely free from a cough.

I hope, notwithstanding the state of things in Europe, you will be able with your family to make us a visit in the summer or fall.

My love to Anna [Maria Calhoun Clemson] & the children. All

were well, when I last heard from home, a few days since. Your affectionate father, J.C. Calhoun.

ALS in ScCleA; variant PC in Jameson, ed., *Correspondence*, pp. 748–749.

From H[ENRY] W. CONNER

Charleston, April 13, 1848

My Dear Sir, I have rec[eive]d your letters, of the 4th & 6th & have lost no time in giving currency to your views upon going into the convention. The Mercury will in editorial give the substance of your remarks in a day or two but beyond this & the circulation of your views through private channels we have thought it not advisable to go at present. In truth we *are afraid* to excite discussion or even attention to the subject knowing as we do the strong & decided ["repugnance" *interlined*] the people have to a passive or neutral line of policy. It is not the going into the convention that they are anxious for. On the contrary most people see numerous & strong objections to such a course but all concur I think in the propriety ["of" *canceled*] & necessity of definite & combined action of some sort amongst the Southern States & in which So. Ca. will play her part & it is with a view to this result that the going to the convention finds so many advocates.

On the receipt of your letter a conference ["of a few" *interlined*] of your principal friends was held here to talk the matter over & see what was best to be done to keep ourselves in position & at the same time prevent a d[i]vision amongst ourselves & they all admitted your arguments to be unanswerable as to ["the" *canceled*] a convention both in principle & in practice but they were equally unanimous that we ought *to do something* in common with the other slave holding States who participate in our views & principles. This is the whole secret of the desire to move upon the Baltimore convention—not because it is a convention but that the other Southern States are going there. Some of them with the declared intentions of resisting every nomination & every move adverse to the rights of the South & particularly because it is thought some combined action of the South may then be adopted whose influence will be felt there & that may also be brought effectively into play hereafter.

A plan was suggested by Col. [Isaac W.] Hayne that was thought might obviate some of the difficulties & I was requested to submit it for your consideration & I now enclose it & will be glad to hear from you in reply as early as convenient. The paper was sketched off hastily by Col. Hayne with no other intention than of submitting it as a memorandum of the views he himself & others with whom he assosciated entertained. It will be sufficient however for the purpose of expressing its own views to you. All present concur in these views & they consisted of Mr. [George A.] Trenholm, [Charles M.] Furman, Hayne, [Andrew G.] Magrath, [Henry] Gourdin, [John E.] Carew & Hart [*sic*; John Heart]. Col. [Franklin H.] Elmore is not here but from the conversation I held with him some days since I am sure he concurs in most part at least if not in the whole.

If deemed best I think we may evade for the present any movement at all touching a convention in any way as the public mind is sufficiently occupied with subjects nearer home to them. Even this however depends upon accident. If a move is attempted by any person or persons of influence it can[']t be stop[pe]d but admitting that any decided move is evaded now ["&" *canceled*] it is sure to come at another time unless some definite mode of action is given to the people. *They will not stand idle & aloof.* Very Truly y[ou]rs, H.W. Conner.

[Enclosure by Isaac W. Hayne]

Arguments ag[ain]st Convention *upon principle* unanswerable, but the ill effects of *isolation* great and manifold.

Besides this, *impossible to be preserved.* Association with Whiggery too dangerous to be thought of. Has *destroyed* the old Nullification party every where *out of South Carolina,* and in time *would destroy it here.* Not one Nullifier in Fifty, out of So. Ca., who has not utterly *abandoned* his States Rights creed.

Something must be done to prevent the possibility of such a result here. A *passive* course will bring about, to some extent, such a result. There will be a split & rupture in So. Ca. and in a short time a regular Whig party and most probably the other division ["will" *interlined*] side *submissively* with the Democracy.

For So. Ca. to go regularly into Convention, as a *constituent part*—even on the Alabama restriction—would be *inconsistent* and an *abandonment* of Mr. Calhoun and *our Delegation* in Congress.

I would suggest that the Mercury take ground against So. Carolina's going into Convention, and urge the Arguments at large, and with re-iteration, but *affirm* our *adherence* to the principles of Democracy. *Denounce Whiggery,* and *eschew all association with Whigs,* as Whigs. Show that *as a party* they are *worse* on the slavery question, than even the Democratic party proper. Claim that there are *some* Democrats going into Convention whose principles are

315

sound, and who have resolved that these *principles* shall be *paramount* to *party.* With *these we have sympathy.* Express a hope that *possibly* these may *leaven the mass*—and ["if" *interlined*] they cannot, our conviction, that they will *secede. These men* deserve our *confidence* and *aid,* and we should have in Baltimore *representatives of some* sort to express to *these men* our views.

If they can *succeed* in securing the nomination of a *good man and true,* we pledge our *support,* tho' taking no part in the nomination. If they *fail* we are *there* to co-operate in some *new* organization for the protection of Southern rights.

The only ["practicable" *altered to* "practical"] difficulty the selection of—or rather the *mode of selecting* proper representatives. If meetings are called there is danger of *discord.* I would suggest that our Delegation at Washington or a Delegation *from our Delegation* attend at Baltimore, on request of the Mercury, and other *presses,* and that *informally* some of our discreet citizens at home be requested to drop in on the occasion.

That the active men at home of every district be *conferred with, at once* by the *representatives* of the Districts respectively, giving the views of Mr. Calhoun and the delegation, and furnishing a *programme* of the *action* proposed. The *Press* particularly to be *kept advised.* I.W.H.

ALS with En in ScCleA; variant PC in Jameson, ed., *Correspondence,* pp. 1166–1167.

From Ch[arles] Aug[ustus] Davis

Newyork [City,] 13 Ap[ril] 1848

My D[ea]r Sir, I notice that a bill has pass'd House of Rep[resentatives] unanimously—(Mr. [Joseph] Grinnell[']s [Representative from Mass.] bill) regarding the ventilation and better regulation of Imigrant passenger Ships—and which bill is now perhaps awaiting action in the Senate.

I understand that certain interests ["(more alien than native)" *interlined*] are at work here to delay the passage of that Bill, or if it passes, to urge that the 4 Section be struck out. This section imposes on the vessel to have certain food on board. I hope sincerely in common with every humane man that this bill will neither be delay'd nor alter'd.

Every day[']s delay but adds to the accumulating misery. Thousands & Thousands of poor & ignorant families are now daily taking their passage for U.S.—totally unconscious of the misery & suffering that is to await them on the voyage on board some of these vessels which are totally unfit to carry human beings to sea. It is said in extenuation that many of these miserable people have the seeds of fever & disease in them before starting. In one sense this is not true—they have *nothing in them.* They are no doubt emaciated by long privation—but only need *reasonable* comfort & food and pure air to build them up—but on board many of these floating Laza[r] Houses—they find nothing—but loathsome dens to sleep in—if sleep they can—nothing to eat but what they can cook themselves in most inconvenient places on deck—where bad weather prevents cooking & they remain under closed Hatches festering in disease. Death comes to many of them in mercy—and strews the ocean with their bodies—and those who outlive the voyage (& they must be strong indeed to do so) land half dead & diseased & crowd our hospitals with infection and indescribable suffering.

This Bill provides a remedy. None of its requisitions are unreasonable—and no humane man who knows any thing of the matter w[oul]d countenance any alteration of the Bill (except to increase its requirements) or to permit its passage to a Law to be delay'd one hour.

That same cupidity and inhumanity which is evidenced by the present system may secretely strive to arrest this Bill or seek an alteration, but I hope ineffectually. The reason assign'd by some why the 4th Sec[tion] sh[oul]d be struck out—is because the Bill now before Parliament had such a section struck out—as it was opposed by agents engaged in sending off emigrants &c—but why sh[oul]d that guide us. England & all Europe may desire to get rid of a portion of their starving population on any terms. We are ready to receive them but "in mercy not in judgment." It is but right they sh[oul]d come to us measurably healthy. This bill will compass that end—not let them come as now—diseas'd & dying. I repeat that every hour[']s delay is full of human suffering—and in the name of common humanity I w[oul]d urge the passage of that Bill. Most resp[ect]f[ully] y[ou]r ob[edien]t Ser[vant], Ch: Aug. Davis.

ALS in ScCleA; variant PC in Boucher and Brooks, eds., *Correspondence*, pp. 434–435.

REMARKS IN DEBATE ON AN INTERNAL
IMPROVEMENTS BILL

[In the Senate, April 14, 1848]
[*Under consideration was a bill providing for the repair and improvement of a dam in the Ohio River. Arthur P. Bagby of Ala. opposed the bill on Constitutional grounds.*]

Mr. Calhoun. As the yeas and nays have been ordered, I desire,
before the question is put, to say a few words. If I understand this
case aright, there is an island in the Ohio, a little above the mouth
of the Cumberland, dividing the river into two parts, and rendering
the navigation difficult; and, in order to improve it, a dam was
thrown across from the Kentucky side to the island, and by the recent
freshets this dam has been destroyed. Now, although I hold to the
doctrine of strict construction, I have not the slightest doubt of the
right and duty of the Government to repair this dam; or to remove
the obstruction. It is the channel of one of the great navigable
rivers which belong to no particular State, but which serves as a
highway in which many States are interested; and if it be not done
by the General Government, it can be done by no power whatever.
The States are positively prohibited from entering into a work like
this. If the General Government cannot do it, it is clear that neither
Kentucky nor Indiana will make this improvement; for there is a
positive provision in the Constitution which prevents them from doing it. Under these circumstances, I hold it to be as clearly the right
of the General Government to repair this dam, under the provision
in the Constitution which gives the power to regulate commerce
among the States, as it is to repair light-houses or to replace buoys
that have been destroyed; and that the objection of the Senator from
Alabama [Bagby] is as applicable to the one as the other. I shall
give my vote most cheerfully for this bill.

Mr. Bagby. I do not understand that Congress is authorized to
do everything that the States are not authorized to do, or that the
States cannot do.

Mr. Calhoun. I did not say that. I say that the right exists, under
the provision of the Constitution which gives to this Government the
power to regulate commerce among the States.

[*Bagby replied at length.*]

Mr. Calhoun. I by no means rest this case on the fact, that
because the States have not the power, therefore the General Government has it. I place it on the fact, that the General Government
has the power to regulate commerce among the States, and that this

is a case which comes within that power. In confirmation of this conclusion, I stated, that the Constitution prohibited the States from entering into any treaty or agreement, by which those in the great valley of the Mississippi could unite and enter into an arrangement, by which the obstructions in that great river and its navigable branches could be removed. I also stated, that they were common highways for all those States, and not within the exclusive control of any one, as far as their navigation was concerned, and that it would be monstrous to conclude that a stream, on which we had as much or nearly as much commerce as on the ocean itself, was intended to be left by the Constitution without any power to supervise and improve its navigation. In reply, the Senator says, that this Government has the right to regulate commerce already in existence, not to create new channels for commerce. That may be admitted, without weakening my argument. The river itself forms the channel, and the commerce existed before the Government undertook to improve its navigation, just as in the case of the commerce on the ocean. Now, I put it to the Senator, has not this Government the right to establish light-houses, buoys, and beacons, under the power of regulating commerce? If so, I ask him to point out the distinction, and show on what principle it can exercise the power in the one case, and not in the other. The river, as well as the ocean, is the common highway of the commerce among the States, and its navigation is no more under the control of the States, separately, than that on the ocean. No just distinction can be made between the two cases; and the argument which can establish the rights of the Government to improve the navigation of the one, is equally strong to establish the right to improve the other. Both will have to be abandoned, or both admitted. To make the case, if possible, more parallel and close, I ask the Senator if the Government has not the right to establish light-houses, buoys, and beacons, over the [Great] lakes?

Mr. Bagby. Certainly—wherever your navy floats.

Mr. Calhoun. Then suppose a light-house is necessary to the navigation of the Mississippi, can we not erect one? Now suppose, instead of erecting a light-house, you guard against the obstruction in some other way, would you not have an equal right to do it in such a way as would be attended with the least expense?

[*Bagby argued that Congress's right to erect aids to navigation rested not upon the power to regulate interstate and foreign commerce but upon the power to maintain a navy. John J. Crittenden of Ky. pointed out that there were government vessels navigating the Mississippi River.*]

Mr. Calhoun. One word, if the Senator will allow me. There is a naval station in the Mississippi at Memphis, which is important to the Government; but what is more, this system of erecting lighthouses, buoys, &c., was established before there was a single Government vessel. It must then have been regarded as coming under the head of the power to regulate commerce.

[*Debate continued. Jefferson Davis of Miss. argued that, under strict construction, the power to regulate commerce was a power "to make rules, not to provide means." However, he felt, since the government had built the dam, the destruction of which had created great hazard, the government was obligated to deal with the situation; therefore he supported the bill.*]

Mr. Calhoun. As the Senator from Mississippi thought proper to attack the ground on which I rest my support of this bill, while he concurs with me in supporting it, I feel called on briefly to reply to his argument. He says the power to regulate commerce is restricted to the power to prescribe rules, and does not include the power to provide means for its safety and facility. And yet, while he takes this position, he admits the power of Congress to establish lighthouses, buoys, and beacons, to point the way into harbors, where duties are collected; and thus admits, to that extent, that the power of prescribing rules includes the power of providing for the safety and facility of commerce. And he thereby admits it to rest on the power to establish ports of entries and collection of duties. This admission concedes the whole right for which I contend, but places it on grounds far less safe and well-defined. The establishment of ports of entry and collection of duties are not confined to the seaboard. They extend on the Mississippi far up the stream, as high as St. Louis and Cincinnati; and on his own showing, Congress has the power, under the regulation of commerce, to provide for its safety and facility up to these points, by removing the obstructions in the channel of the river, which might endanger or impede its navigation. He will not, I feel confident, make a distinction between pointing out the danger, and removing the cause of it—between the power of establishing a light-house to point out snags and sawyers at night, and removing them. Nor can it be objected that the Mississippi is not navigable for sea-going vessels. Under the power of steam, it is navigated with almost the same facility that it would be, if, instead of a river, it was an arm of the ocean; while its great depth and volume of water admit vessels of as great a tonnage as most of the ports on the coast. Nor is it a sufficient objection to say that its navigation subjects it to great delay, in consequence of low water, or ice. Vessels are often delayed in consequence of adverse winds or calms off the ports on the coast; but that is not a good reason why they should not be made ports of entry, and have the entrance into them pointed out by light-houses, buoys, and beacons. If it were, the harbor at the mouth of Columbia river would forever remain without these facilities; for vessels have been known to lie before it for months, before they could enter; and, when they did, they entered with great hazard.

I do not wish to be understood by these remarks to give my countenance to the ground on which the Senator places the power. I regard it as utterly untenable and dangerous, as it would enable Congress to give any extension it pleased to the power. I pass without notice the other grounds on which he places the power "to provide and maintain a navy," as I have already replied to it in answer to the Senator from Alabama.

As to internal improvement—that is, improvement within a State— I am as much opposed to the exercise of the power by this Government as either the Senator from Mississippi or Alabama can be. I limit the power for which I contend to the great highways, common to all the States, and, of course, under the control and supervision of no one; to their exterior intercourse with each other, and not to the internal intercourse within their separate supervision and control. I feel assured that the ground on which I rest the power is the only one on which effectual resistance can be made to internal improvements, properly understood. To undertake to give a construction to the power which would include the seacoast, and exclude its afflux to the Mississippi and the [Great] Lakes, must end either in the entire abandonment of the power to establish light-houses, buoys, and beacons, or to give unlimited extension to the power of Congress to regulate commerce both within and without the States.

[*Davis replied, arguing that by Calhoun's interpretation, Congress's declaring of a port of entry on some interior river could justify expenditures for improvement of navigation at every point from the sea to that port. This would encourage a corrupt and profligate expenditure against the beliefs and interests of his constituents.*]

Mr. Calhoun. When the wind is adverse, the vessel may lay off for weeks without being able to enter a harbor. Buoys and beacons are necessary to point the way into harbors, and therefore they come under the regulation of commerce; and if we can provide these facilities on the seacoast, on what principle is it that we are prohibited from providing facilities on our great navigable rivers? Sir, I hold it to be as clear a power as any in the Constitution, demonstrably so, from the meaning which the phrase to regulate commerce had before the adoption of the Constitution. I have examined this subject with great care, and I have never examined any question upon which I have come to so decided a conclusion. Sir, it is monstrous to say that where the interests of so many States are concerned, we shall not exercise a power which is so clearly defined. How far it will extend to the smaller rivers I will not undertake to say; but as far as regards the Mississippi and the Ohio, the only result of setting up a narrow construction will be to make the power universal. You must give it the exercise it was intended to have originally, or there will be no limitation upon it whatever.

[*The vote was then taken and the bill passed 31 to 8.*]

From *Congressional Globe*, 30th Cong., 1st Sess., pp. 634–636. Also printed in Houston, ed., *Proceedings and Debates*, pp. 493–495. Variant in the Baltimore, Md., *Sun*, April 15, 1848, p. 4; the Charleston, S.C., *Courier*, April 18, 1848, p. 2; the Charleston, S.C., *Mercury*, April 19, 1848, p. 2.

To J[AMES] ED[WARD] COLHOUN, [Abbeville District, S.C.]

Washington, 15th April 1848

My dear Sir, Your letter indicates much & mature reflection on the character and tendency of the present great crisis of the civilized world. It is clear, that the old monarchies on the continent of Europe are about coming to an end. The intelligence & progress of the age have outgrown them; but it is by no means certain, that they are so advanced and enlightened on political science, as to substitute more suitable ["ones" *interlined*] in their place. I fear they are not. It seems to me, that what is called the progress party, both in this country & Europe, have not advanced in political knowledge beyond Dorrism; that is, the right of a mere majority to overturn law & constitution at its will & pleasure. They must be cured of this radical and most dangerous of all errors, before they can substitute in the place of those, that may be overthrown, better Governments. Nothing but wo[e]ful experience can apply a remedy; except, perhaps in Germany, where the advantage of an existing system of confederation of states, & the dread of France from the experience of the first revolution, may lead to establish a federal system some what like ours. I have far more hope of her, than of France, or any other of the continental Countries. Indeed, I look to her to save Europe, including France herself.

What I propose to publish on the subject of Government is not yet prepared for the press. I had hoped to have had it prepared last fall, but was so interrupted, as to fall far short of my calculation. I am, and fear will continue to be, too much occupied here during the session to do any thing towards its completion, but will resume it, as soon as I return home. I do not think any thing will be lost by the delay. I do not think the publick mind is yet fully prepared for the work, nor will be, until there has been such failure and embarrassment in the French experiment (which will be made under highly favourable circumstances) as will bring into distrust & doubt, Dorrism, so as to prepare the publick mind to have its errors & consequences pointed out, and to reflect seriously on the question; What are the elements, which are indispensable to constitute a constitutional popular Government?

I am obliged to you for the suggestions you have made, both in reference to the topicks to be discussed, & the precautions to be adopted in securing the copy right. My plan is to devide it into two parts; an elementary treatise on political science, ["&" *canceled*] to be follow[ed] by a treatise on the Constitution of the United States, not in the shape of commentaries, but a philosophical discussion on its character & construction in illustration of the elementary Treatise. To avoid details, as much as possible, I propose to annex the various speeches, Reports & letters, in which I have discussed Constitutional questions, & to refer to them in illustration of my opinion of the various parts of the Constitution, to which they relate. I hope I may have so far completed my labours, before I leave home next fall, as to enable me to submit the work to your perusal.

I wait the meeting of the Convention in France & the German Diet with deep interest. They will afford much light by which to judge of the future.

I see no reason to doubt, but we shall ["have" *interlined*] peace with Mexico. The administration intended to conquer & annex the country, but were defeated by ["my" *interlined*] speech on my resolutions, which ["so" *interlined*] effectually turned the tide of publick sentiment, ["&" *canceled and* "as to" *interlined*] compelled them to take Twist's [*sic*; Nicholas P. Trist's] treaty. Yours affectionately, J.C. Calhoun.

ALS in ScCleA; variant PC in Jameson, ed., *Correspondence*, pp. 749–751.

To A[NDREW] P[ICKENS] CALHOUN, [Marengo County, Ala.]

Washington, 16th April 1848

My dear Andrew, I am very happy to hear by yours of the 3d Inst., received by the last mail, that you are all well, & that the place is in such fine order & the crop so fairly started. I agree with you, that it is of vast importance, that we should make a good crop this year, and my impression is, that we shall, as there is every indication we shall have a dry summer. That, with our good start, ought without accident ensure a good crop.

I enclosed in my last, (which you could hardly have received, when you wrote that to which this is an answer) [Ker] Boyce's letter to me. I now enclose one since received.

I hope in a few days to get your answer to my letter enclosing his former, ["and" *canceled*] which will inform you, that the order to his agent was given with the understanding, that the interest, at least, will be paid on his debt. That must be done without failure.

I have not heard from Dr. [Ozey R.] Broyles since I wrote you, & conclude, he has experienced difficulty in collecting the money due to the estate [of Chester Kingsley], of which he has the management. We must make an effort, to raise funds to meet our engagements, and I hope the state of the money market will be favourable during the summer or fall, for the purpose. It is thought by many, that large amounts of funds will flow in from Europe for investment in our country, in consequence [of] the unsettled state of things there. Should that be the case, interest must fall, & we must seize the opportunity to fund our debt. In that event, we must visit New York and the other Northern cities, Philadelphia & Boston, for the purpose of making the negotiation. We shall probably not adjourn for 3 months yet. I will keep my eyes directed to the subject, and you advised of any opening which may present itself.

Every thing here is in a state of uncertainty, in reference to the Presidential election. The parties are more distracted than ever. [Henry] Clay's address has done him great injury with his party. It has in particular deeply offended the Southern portion. In the mean time, the address of the Barn burners, just come out, has weakened & distracted the Democratick party. They take strong grounds ag[ai]nst us on the Wilmot proviso, and proclaim that they must be received by the Baltimore Convention to the exclusion of the Hunker delegates from the State. That I take it will be impossible, and that a permanent split, with the loss of the State will be the result. I trust, out of all this confusion, a sufficient number of both parties will be found to be independent enough to make a rally to save ourselves & our institutions. As bad, as you suppose things to be here, it is not worse than the reality.

We are waiting with impatience for farther information from Europe. I have little hope from France, but a good deal of reliance on Germany. She has the materials for a good Govt. if they should be skilfully used. But we shall soon see.

My love to Margaret [Green Calhoun] & the children. Your affectionate father, J.C. Calhoun.

ALS in ScU-SC, John C. Calhoun Papers; PEx in Jameson, ed., *Correspondence,* pp. 751–752.

From R[OBERT] F. W. ALLSTON

Georgetown [S.C.,] 18th April 1848
Dear Sir, The foregoing memorandum I made this morning of what took place yesterday & I know of no one who should be sooner informed than yourself. You were nominated by resolution & I told the agitators that you would regard it as a mockery. Altho done in good faith, ["possibly" *interlined*] yet ill-advised. This Town (& Cheraw which will respond by concert) is made up of Yankees ["quiet, good citizens in their place" *interlined*] & jews in a great measure, who live by the negroe trade. They are becoming stronger every year. Col. [Donald L.] McKay is Pres[iden]t of the Bank here, a very clever man but often wrong-headed. He, together with one of the strongest of our men the only Planter present whom they elected Delegate, will do much to carry their point against the true policy of the State.* [*Marginal interpolation:* "Our immediate representative Mr. (Alexander D.) Sims too is of this way of thinking I believe."] This gentleman the Delegate I warned some days ago on the subject, but they have succeeded in drawing him in. Planters have their business to attend to in the country & public meetings are great bores to them. I attended (being known to be opposed to the objects of the gathering) as a public servant intent on being inform'd of what is going on, but determined not to interfere with the orderly assemblage of any portion of my constituents. Pray excuse this scrawl & interpret it honestly. Very Respectfully, R.F.W. Allston.

[Marginal P.S.] The Press, here & in Cheraw are both favorable to this purpose of attending the Baltimore convention.

[Enclosure]

"A meeting of those of the democratic party *in favor* of sending a Delegate to the Baltimore convention" was call'd by public notice, at first for "the 10th" afterwards for the 17th April. It took place on the day last mention'd. Capt. Leonard Dozier presided. It consisted of 54 persons besides the chairman. The planting community was represented by 1. ([*Two or three words canceled and* "there were" *interlined*] three planters in the lobby, who seem'd to attend as witnesses not as part of the meeting.) There were also three clergymen present, whether they intended to be consider'd as part of the meeting or not I am not aware. The medical faculty had 2 representatives I believe—but of the whole number, not more than 10 or 12 (one fifth) were free holders having a stake in the soil.

The proceedings of this meeting will be publish'd of course. I trust, however, it will not be represented as a meeting of the District. Although notice was given, it was held, designedly, ["on the Monday after court" *interlined and* "at" *canceled*] a time when every countryman was glad to be at home after his absence in attendance on the business of Court week. ["I attended as a public servant" *canceled.*] There was no discussion whatever.

Gen[era]l J[ames] M. Commander was appointed Delegate.

ALS with En in ScCleA.

To S[ETH] W. BENEDICT, [New York City]

Senate Chamber, 18th April 1848

D[ea]r Sir, I enclose $3 in payment of [William F.] Van Amringe's Natural history of man. Please acknowledge receipt of the same. Respectfully, J.C. Calhoun.

ALS in Long Island Historical Society, Brooklyn, N.Y.

From ANNA [MARIA CALHOUN] CLEMSON

Brussels, April 18th 1848

My dear father, Let me first of all reply to that part of your letter [of 3/7], in which you say you are actuated by higher motives, than I attribute to you, in your continued struggle against corruption. I do not now recollect what I said in my letter, which like all I write, or say, was done at the impulse of the moment, but I must have explained my real meaning very badly, if you thought I attributed to you any other than the highest motives, or the utmost disinterestedness & if you supposed [me] capable of doing otherwise, your indulgence was very great to reply to me so kindly as you do, but you ["too" *interlined*] well know my affection for you, not to be aware that I could never be guilty of wilful disrespect towards you.

Everything in Europe is still in the most unsettled state. What you say of the erroneous ideas entertained as to what is true liberty, never was more clearly proved than by what is at present going on in France. One cannot judge with any certainty of the course events are taking, unless on the spot, for the friends praise too much, & the ennemies blame too much, but from all I can put together, things are in a lamentable state & anarchy reigns for the moment. Mr. [Thomas G.] Clemson still insists that the Assembly will put all right, & that we must not judge from this state of transition, but for my part, I think the french too corrupt, & their ideas of a republic too wild, to have any confidence in the future. They say in France that they do not wish a republic as we have in America—that it is not *free enough* for them. That is rich is it not? But even if I thought the french nation advanced, & virtuous enough, for a republic, & her political ideas on that subject feasible, Paris seems to me & [*sic*] insuperable difficulty. According to my conception, (or rather, *yours* for of course my political opinions, are only a remembrance of your conversations,) no true republic can long exist with such immense centralization, as exists in Paris. *Paris is France*, & alone has made this revolution, & will always rule France, whatever may be the name of the government. It is to be hoped, however, that things may go better than I anticipate, for all agree that a republic in France is an inevitable experiment, & all desire to see it definitively established, even those who believe it will fail. It is also certain, (& there is the greatest evil,) that on the experiment France is making, depends the future government of Europe, & the more or less rapid advance of of [*sic*] true liberty & I confess it pains me to see such power over the happiness of millions, confided to those I think so incapable of solving the great problems of government. In the meanwhile all Europe is in agitation, & every one feels that we are on the eve of great events, & that it is impossible to say where things will be in six months. An article I read in an english paper this morning, makes me think that they begin at least to think the loss of Ireland very possible, & even in England herself, things are far from calm. All of which, with the necessity of maintaining the usual force in her colonies, renders it almost impossible that she should interfere in continental affairs. No nation on the continent, except Russia, can do more than maintain a doubtful peace at home, or defend her frontiers, & I think it more than probable, from the tone of their own official paper "The National," that the french will, at the earliest opportunity, take advantage of this state of things, to *annex* Belgium, which they has [*sic*] always considered as property unjustly wrested from them. This is dreaded very much here, yet they feel the impossibility of preventing it, unless aided by the other powers, who would seem to be prevented from moving, by the reasons I give above. If Belgium had proclaimed a republic, this danger *might* have been avoided but there is no telling. It is the old fable of the wolf & the lamb & a pretext is never wanting where the will exists. If the french come here we may be sent home shortly *for want of a place* but otherwise, as much as I desire to see you all, I see no possibility of my husband's deserting his place. To ask for a leave of absence, at such a time, would be ridiculous, & I must confess, I should urge him not to resign, (which would be the only means of returning,) even had he the intention of doing so, of which he has not the slightest idea. He still hopes things may calm, in time for him to ask for leave in June, but I see not the slightest chance of such being the case, & I fear, unless they *chase us off* as I said before, we cannot with common decency return home this year.

After a very warm spell we are again in winter & my hands are uncomfortably cold, even tho' I write not far from the fire. We are all notwithstanding very well, not even colds. [John] Calhoun [Clemson] will write you shortly. He asks me frequently to let him do so. I shall write to mother [Floride Colhoun Calhoun] next week, but as I do not write to any one at home by this mail, do let them know that all are well.

Mr. Clemsons [*sic*] joins me in love & the children send many kisses to grandfather. Ever your devoted daughter, Anna Clemson.

ALS in ScCleA.

From R[ICHARD] K. CRALLÉ

Lynchburg, April 19th, 1848

My dear Sir: I thank you for the copy of your Speech on the Ten Regiment Bill, accompanying your last letter. It has been repub-

lished here in two of the newspapers with the highest commendations. [William M.] Blackford says it is the ablest effort you ever
made. Indeed, before I had seen it, he pronounced in a company
collected together on the street, that it "*compressed in a few pages
more than would fill, if drawn out like other men, an octavo volume.*"
He was far more unqualified in his commendation than this. But
what has genius, talent, political foresight—moral elevation of sentiment, to do in times like the present? It does seem to me that the
Country is absolutely stu[l]tified, and labouring under a general and
ominous delusion. The Bill, I see, has passed and I believe without
Judge [Andrew P.] Butler's amendment. Nay, in addition to this
I perceive that another project is now before Congress to receive the
services of a large number of volunteers! And this, too, after a Treaty
of peace is absolutely ratified by the only *substantial Party.*

It is needless to enquire what the *People* think of these and other
matters. The *People*—the *masses*, have ceased to think for themselves. Yet there are amongst them very many of both Parties
seriously alarmed and disturbed. They perceive the existing evils—
apprehend those which are impending, but know not how to arrest
the one, or to forestall the other. This, I am sure, is true to a very
great extent; and the disturbance of the public mind consequent
upon it, is daily becoming deeper and more extended. I never witnessed as much Party apathy amongst the reflecting portion of the
people upon the eve of an election. No one seems satisfied with the
prospects before him. [Henry] Clay's late letter has produced deep
dissatisfaction with a large portion of his former friends in this section of the State; and I make no doubt the like feeling pervades
every other. Many think he is the evil genius of the Party—determined to rule or ruin. His letter, under the present aspect of affairs,
(should it lead to his nomination) destroys all hopes of the opposition in the State. Many of the Friends of [Zachary] Taylor will
allow the election rather to go by default, than vote for him; while
many others heretofore belonging to the Administration Party, will
return to the flesh-pots. The State is lost if Clay be the Candidate.

An article appeared in one of our Town[?] papers a few days
ago, calling upon the thinking portion of both Parties to rally around
you, and thus end at once the existing disturbances. It has elicited
general remarks on both sides, of a favourable character. It will be
followed up with another article on monday next, but there is only
a faint hope of rousing the public attention. The rabble are too
recklessly the slaves of Party, and the serious too intent on making
money. The one is positively—the other negatively the instruments

329

of their Country's disgrace and subversion. Still *your course* is the same—and I am glad to see that in a late vote, no friend, not even Butler or [Robert M.T.] Hunter, sustained you. It is better that it should be so. They are ["for" *canceled and* "of" *interlined*] the age and live *for the age. You* belong to no age—a truly great man—after the likeness of his Maker, looks upon time as a *punctum stans*—his ways are as direct as Truth, and his works are for all time.

How have Clay and [Daniel] Webster fallen! You once remarked to me that they might have *"impressed themselves on the age,"* had they faithfully applied the powers of their respective intellects. Now, the latter is almost universally regarded as a wretched and prostituted pensioner; while the other closes *"life last scenes"* with something worse than the *"tears of dotage"*—more pitiable than the antics of a *"driveller and a show."* For I hesitate not to say that his last letter is one of the most humiliating specimens of human weakness—one of the most sorrowful spectacles of a great mind distempered by ambition, that I have ever read. Lord Bacon's appeal, humble as it was, had more of virtue and dignity in it. It has deeply mortified some of his most devoted friends. Thank Heaven!—those who have *steadily* regarded *you* as the pole star of their political action—few though they may be—have nothing to regret in the past—nothing like *this* to apprehend in the future. As one of these I had far rather see you suffer the fate of Essex, so that some future Camden might say, *"he was a person not rightly calculated for a court, as being not easily brought to any mean compliances."*

The friends of Taylor regard this letter as equally selfish and *treacherous.* What will be the result? Will they finally be whipped in? or will there be an independent ticket? I take it for granted, Clay will be the nominee—and the Administration Party rejoice. It secures to them, they think, the public plunder for the next four years. We hear here daily, through members of Congress, that either [James K.] Polk or [Levi] Woodbury will be put on the course by the Baltimore Convention—*probably* the former—but this can scarcely be. Messrs. [James] Buchanan and [Lewis] Cass are both weak in the popular affection; and I am persuaded Woodbury is the strongest of the three.

I have just read your remarks on [William] Allen's Resolution. They are precisely such as I had anticipated. The next Steamer, I suppose, may furnish some more reliable data. I fear the French, under either of the Leaders, [Alphonse de] Lamartine or [Alexandre-Auguste Ledru-]Rollin, will adopt only the *worse features* of our institutions. *Mobocracy* is too generally regarded here and there as synonymous with Liberty.

Your remarks in reference to our old Friend (L.) [that is, Dixon H. Lewis] give me more concern than surprise. "Alas, poor human nature"! as Lord Chesterfield would word it. I am glad to learn, however, that his estrangement is, for the present, merely *political.*

I write in great haste, being compelled to attend to Mrs. [Elizabeth Morris] Crallé, in my hours of relief from business. She has been recently confined, having given birth to a *daughter* which we have determined to name after Mrs. [Floride Colhoun] Calhoun. She has been quite unwell, but is better today. Affectionately & truly yours, R.K. Crallé.

ALS in ScCleA; PEx in Boucher and Brooks, eds., *Correspondence,* pp. 435–436.

From J[ames] Hamilton, [Jr.]

Montgomery Ala., April 19[t]h 1848

My Dear friend, It is some times [*sic*] since I have heard from you and equally long since you have heard from me but on reaching this place this morning I met with the National Intelligencer which contained your Speech on the Resolutions tendering our congratulations to the French on their late ominous & I think scarcely *doubtful* revolution. I need scarcely tell you how entirely your remarks accord with that wisdom which belongs to the recorded opinions of your whole life. I entirely concur in your views & believe that the Revolution in ["France" *canceled*] must end in a bloody anarchy at home & a wide spread foreign War. To what extent the conflagration ["will go" *interlined*] no man can venture to predict.

I presume we may patch up a sort of Peace with Mexico to protect [ourselves; "the Govt." *interlined*] will have to come to your defensive line—at last.

As to our own politicks I have not a word to say. Since all hope has been abandoned of making you a Candidate for the Presidency[,] I have lost all interest in them. They are worse than insipid. They are absolutely disgusting.

You are aware that I own ["in part" *interlined and then canceled*] & represent ["a larger (*sic*) portion of" *interlined*] some $700,000 of Texian Bonds for which that Republic pledged her Revenues *arising*

331

from Customs for their payment. I have been waiting until the final settlement of the Mexican ["War" *interlined*] before I presented my memorial to the Congress asking one of two things[,] either that they pay our Bonds on the ground of a prior lien or give us Debentures on the Custom Houses in Texas for their payment.

I think the present moment an unpropitious one, for bringing forward such a Question. After all the expences annexation has entailed upon the Country Congress might feel little disposed to entertain the consideration of a topic involving the payment of some 5 millions of Dollars. Pray give me your opinion forthwith & direct to Savannah Geo. I will thank you likewise to send me Mr. Wescoats [*sic*; James D. Westcott, Jr., Senator from Fla.'s,] Report on Gen-[era]l [Leslie] Combs['s] Petition.

I shall be in Savannah about the 26[t]h of this month.

I met with a Gentleman in the Steamer in which I ascended the Alabama River who informed me that he was at your Son[']s [Andrew Pickens Calhoun's] place a few Days since & that he had the promise of making a splendid Crop. But what is the use of making Cotton [when] we cannot get any thing for it? I am concentrating on Sugar in Texas where my prospects are most auspicious. I left there a Sugar Crop of 600 Acres, one month in advance of the Loui-s[i]ana Crop. We can produce one 3d more in Texas at one third less expence.

Pray let me hear from you immediately directing to Savannah & believe me My Dear Sir faithfully Your devoted friend, J. Hamilton.

ALS in ScCleA.

From N[ATHAN] LORD, Pres[iden]t, Dart[mouth] Coll[ege]

Dartmo[uth] College [N.H.], April 19, 1848

My dear Sir, I have taken the liberty to send herewith a Eulogy lately spoken by me on Mr. [John Quincy] Adams, that I may ask your attention to that part of it which relates to the subject of Slavery. From the manner in which I have stated the issue of Slavery some of my friends have inferred that I lean to the Divine Right of that institution. I confess that leaning. But it is consequent upon comparatively recent & necessarily partial investigation, & I cannot yet fully justify to my own mind the impressions which are forcing themselves upon me. I wish to have a settled judgment. From my position in this Institution, particularly as a teacher of Moral & Political Philosophy, it is of consequence that I should have such a judgment, & that I should be always ready to give the reasons of it.

Therefore I take a liberty, which, though it ordinarily becomes not an absolute stranger, I shall rely on your known candor & generosity to excuse; namely of asking you to refer me to any authorities within your knowledge in which the argument for the Divine Right of Slavery in general, or Negro Slavery in particular is soundly & learnedly drawn out. And, if it be not too presumptuous I would also ask the favor of any suggestions from yourself which should seem to you useful in guiding an honest inquiry into this very difficult yet consequential subject.

If Slavery is of God the moral & religious people of the North ought to be convinced of it. Otherwise there will soon be no adequate restraint upon that levelling madness which is driving all things, the world over, as there is too much reason to fear, to a severe catastrophe; & not perhaps the least, though we least fear it, the people of our own country.

I am willing to believe any thing that is true, &, ["on proper occasions" *interlined*] to profess any ["on proper occasions, which" *canceled*] thing which I believe. But I would not give out presumptions for convictions, or put the interests which I represent in false or doubtful positions. I want light, which, at the North, it is difficult to obtain except on the surface of the whole matter. There is nothing in our Libraries or Journals that reaches directly the essential questions. There must be minds at the South which have been diligently set to work, in this respect; & I should esteem it a high favor to be put in the way of obtaining the results of their inquiries.

It has occurred to me that, if not now, yet in the recess of Congress, you might find a few moments of leisure, which you would willingly afford in giving me the benefit of your advice. I seek it only on my own personal account. Yet I have reference to those public interests to which your life has been so ably & honorably devoted. I should not thus venture to obtrude myself but for the profound respect with which I have been accustomed to regard your character, & your judgment upon questions which affect the most comprehensive & vital interests of the country. I am, dear Sir, With great respect, Your obed[ien]t Serv[an]t, N. Lord, Pres[iden]t, Dart[mouth] Coll[ege].

ALS in ScCleA; PC in Jameson, ed., *Correspondence*, pp. 1167–1169. NOTE: AEU's by Calhoun read, "N. Lord D.D." and "Estwick Evans[,] Phi[ladelphi]a Pa.[,] Crallé." During the 1850's Lord published a number of public letters on slavery.

From H[ENRY] BAILEY, [Attorney General of S.C.]

Charleston, 20th April, 1848

My dear Sir, This morning's mail has brought to me a printed copy of the President's [James K. Polk's] first [annual] message, with the accompanying documents, forming a large volume, for which I perceive by the frank I am indebted to you, and for which I write to return you my thanks. I feel indeed gratified, and flattered, by the source from which I acquire possession of this volume; but it is in itself more valuable to me than you perhaps imagine. I have very much desired to have it for the purposes both of information, & of reference. I have not time to be a diligent reader of newspapers, and the information derived from them in reference to public documents is ["always" *interlined*] imperfect, unsatisfactory, and of transient impression; and I often feel embar[r]assed, baulked, & worried, for want of convenient access to full & official records. As the volume you have sent me, is that which I should of all others have preferred, your present is of course very acceptable, & I beg to assure you it is on every account most highly appreciated. Its possession induces me to go further. I remember a female client whose understanding of the old adage that "one good turn deserves another" was, that the doing her one favor gave her a title to ask for another; and although I cannot say that this interpretation of the aphorism is certainly correct, I feel quite disposed to act upon it in the present instance. I will therefore take the liberty of asking, that whenever you have copies of public documents, especially such ["are on" *canceled and* "as relate to" *interlined*] important subjects, or ["are" *interlined*] of permanent character, ["which you have no better occasion for," *interlined*] you would oblige me by sending me one copy of them.

And this reminds me that I have not yet thanked you for another book which you sent me. I mean Mr. [William] Hickey's Constitution—which I duly received, and prize very highly. It is a valuable compend, & will prove a very useful *vade mecum*. It is quite a lucky idea; but the compiler has made a great mistake in omitting the

Articles of Confederation. The reason for the omission (page 129,) is fantastic & ridiculous. It *is* wanted, for comparison, & the better understanding of the new Constitution: and as it would not have sensibly enlarged the volume, the compiler ought not to have lost this fine opportunity of placing them in juxta position.

I was very much gratified by the course you took upon the French Revolution—you might indeed have gone further, but it was enough to clear your skirts of participating in the delusions to which ["this" *interlined*] great event has given birth, and it was not necessary, & would have been unwise, to incur the hazard of countenancing the absurd fal[l]acies of legitimacy & royal domination, by a marked condemnation of the Parisian emeute. In truth, ["however," *interlined*] the French revolution is an event which it seems to me ought to be regretted. What will be its issues, of course none can foresee; but I feel assured that it has retarded, rather than advanced the cause of liberty, which is inseparable from law & order, and put back the progress of human happiness. I would much rather, that they had done no more, than enlarged the elective franchise to an extent sufficient to have given the Institutions of France that democratic progression, which has attached to the British Constitution since the passing of the Reform bill. What that progression will end in, no one can divine, yet as the changes are gradual, and the progress is accompanied by the diffusion of knowledge, I cannot but hope for results grateful to humanity; but sudden changes, & violent attempts to establish republics, before the people are educated to conduct them, cannot in my judgment be otherwise than mischievous. In Europe they are looking to us, and yet none of them seem to understand our secret of securing liberty by dividing the powers of government between distinct, & incommunable departments: the central, invested with the concentrated power of the nation, and rendered mighty for conflict with foreign nations, but rendered powerless for domestic tyranny, by depriving it of internal jurisdiction; and the local governments rendered harmless, by depriving them of the material powers vested in the central government. But the grand balance wheel of our system—Nullification—the lawful power to obstruct the central government when it oversteps its jurisdiction—this great principle, without which even our system might fail—this is not even dreamed of by European statesmen. No part of Europe—I mean no great nation—(of course I except the Swiss cantons) is ripe for a genuine Republic. In Great Britain, & in Germany, there are habits of domestic local administrations, & of government by confederacies, which furnish elements, for educating the people to a capacity for a

Republic combining true liberty with law & order, and a successful national organization. In France every thing is to begin, and the whole of Rich[e]lieu's work has to be undone; for never was there a great country more thoroughly reduced to all the vices of centralization than France. If they were ["to" *interlined*] talk of reorganizing the old provinces, & giving them republican constitutions, with ample powers for domestic self-government, one might have hopes; but I see nothing to hope for in the present state of things—how long anarchy is to rule, & whether it is to be substituted by a military despostism [*sic*], or another Richelieu is to spread the net of legitimacy over the discordant materials—the results must be for a long time painful to contemplate.

You will perhaps be surprized at my writing you such an essay as this; but I trust you will pardon it when I add, that my only motive has been to hint that I desire very much to hear your views on this interesting subject, & to challenge your opinion by this crude expression of my own views. I don[']t mean that you shall be at the trouble of writing me a letter; but when in a speech, or in any other form, you express your views more precisely than you have done, I beg the favor of you to let me have a copy, or in some way have access to it. In the mean time I am Dear Sir, with sentiments of high regard & esteem Yours & & &c, H. Bailey.

P.S. By the way—what are we to do about the Presidential election? I trust we shall not go into any convention. I at least will have nothing to do with any of them. The situation of affairs, however, is interesting, for Mr. [Henry] Clay's letter must produce curious results. I do not regard it as evidence of dotage. It is perfectly characteristic of the man, & his course I have no doubt is adopted deliberately, & with a full apprehension of the consequences. It compels his party to nominate him, or dissolve. If nominated, he has hopes of being elected. But if he is not made President, whether that be because the Whigs won[']t nominate, or that the people won[']t elect—In either case I have no doubt he wishes the party broken up. His feeling is selfish. It is that of a reckless gambler, who has but half a chance of the game left, & this after a series of losses; & who if he can't win himself would just like to see his friends ruined with him. His mind is this, "I built & manned the ship. I built up whiggery. I embarked all my fortune in manning, equipping, navigating, & fighting her—& what have I got for it all[?] You made me give way again & again to others, & now you are again talking about 'availability.' It won[']t do. It won[']t avail with me. I must be captain now, or never; & if you can[']t make me so, you shan't make any body else. You must carry me in triumph or we shall all perish together. Give me my long promised reward—or I will fire the magazine, & make an end of all.["]

ALS in ScCleA. NOTE: William Hickey's "Constitution" is *The Constitution of the United States of America, with an Alphabetical Analysis; . . . with a Descriptive Account of the State Papers, Public Documents, . . . at the Seat of Government,* of which a third edition was published in Philadelphia in 1848. In a public letter dated 4/10, Clay had declared that he was reluctant to seek another Presidential nomination, but from fear that the party would dissolve if he did not run, he would allow himself to be considered a candidate at the Whig national convention.

To H[ENRY] W. CONNER, [Charleston]

Washington, 20th April 1848

My dear Sir, I am happy to learn that our friends in Charleston concur with the delegation in the opinion, that the State should not be represented in the [Baltimore] Convention.

On consultation, I find no difference in opinion, as far as I have been able to ascertain their views, in agreeing, that there should be combined action among the Southern States in reference to the great question, which involves their very existence, and the presidential question in connection therewith; but they cannot think, that the way suggested by Col. [Isaac W.] Hayne can contribute to that result.

It seems to assume, that there is a very marked distinction between the two parties in the non slave holding States, in reference to that question, and that the democratick is relative sound; and that by adopting the course he suggests, there is a prospect of controlling the nomination, or if we should fail ["in that" *interlined*], of rallying the delegation of Virginia, Alabama & some other Southern States in opposition to it. We do not think the assumption is well founded, and are of the opinion, that the actual state of things is very different from what he supposes. We cannot believe, that there is any marked distinction between the two great parties in those ["States" *interlined*] in reference to abolitionism. We can see no just reasons for thinking so.

It is true, that many of the leaders of the democratick party in them, have openly disavowed the Wilmot proviso; but there is not one of them, in so doing, who has not admitted principles, which will as effectually accomplish its objects, as the proviso itself. But this is

337

not the worst. It is manifest, their object in making the disavowals, is to secure our support in the presidential election; and that they have had very little effect in putting down the proviso among the people in those States; and no effect whatever, in arresting abolition, or its assaults on our institution. In proof of both assertions, many instances might be cited. I will mention only a few.

The very legislature, which nominated Gen[era]l [Lewis] Cass, in his own State [Mich.], after his disavowal of the proviso appeared, almost unanimously, shortly afterwards, adopted the proviso, and passed an act similar to that of Pennsylvania, to prevent the recovery of fugitive slaves. Again; notwithstanding the disavowal of the hunkers in New York, in their convention, to appoint delegates to ["the" *canceled*] Baltimore, the legislature of that State recently passed an act, of the same character, but which went still farther, and made it highly penal for a citizen of the State, to aid, even the federal officers, in carr[y]ing into execution the act of Congress & the provisions of the Constitution for delivering up fugitive slaves. All parties voted for it, hunkers, barnburners & whings; and it passed unanimously, with the exception of two votes. Other States have, during the last winter, passed the same discription of acts. Pennsylvania set the example the year before. The Democratick Convention of New Hampshire, which ["at" *canceled*] last met, adopted the proviso. Indeed it [is] remarkable, that the ["very" *canceled and then interlined*] States, to which the leaders belong, who have made these disavowals, ["and" *canceled*] have been the most forward in maint[ain]ing the proviso, or making these assaults on us. Two of them [James Buchanan and George M. Dallas], are from Pennsylvania; and yet, that State originated the former and took the lead in passing these hostile acts; and that too, under the auspices of democrats.

The truth is, that both parties court the abolitionists at our expense, & in total disregard of our rights or safety; & both are ready to sacrifice us, if ["it is" *canceled*] necessary, to elect their candidate to the Presidency, or to maintain their ascendancy in their own State. If the democrats defer more to us, it is because their party is stronger in proportion in the slave holding States. With the whigs, it is the reverse; and hence they defer less to us, and more to the abolitionists. This is the only difference between them as far as this vital question is concerned.

The South is kept ignorant of the actual state of things. The presses here are mere party organs. They live & fatten by party. They have but one object, to keep their respective parties together, in order to elect their candidate, & through him to get possession of the honors & emoluments of the Government. For this purpose, they studiously endeavour to keep the Slave holding States ignorant of the hostile acts of aggression of the other States, from ["the" *interlined*] fear, that a knowledge of them, would enfeeble & break up existing party connections, and they ["have" *interlined*] succeed[ed] to an extent that is truly surprising.

The effects of this is, to make an impression in the non slave holding States, that we are too timid, or too indifferent to make resistance to ["any" *canceled*] aggressions on their part, however great and outrageous; and hence, the rapidity & audacity with which they have increased of late. This will explain the recent occurrence in this district [of Columbia], of which you will see an account in the papers. If things go on, as they have been going much longer, we shall be assailled on all sides, & shall have to contend for our property at our doors, instead of contriving[?] to preserve our equality in the territories to be obtained from Mexico.

It must, I think, be appearant from this very brief statement, that, to the extent the course suggested by Col. Hayne, depends on the assumption, that there is an essential and marked distinction between the two parties in the non slave holding States in reference to this vital question, there is no foundation for it. Nor do, I think, there is any, in supposing, ["as he seems to do," *interlined*] that in taking the course he suggests, it would give us a control over the nomination, or, failing in that, of rallying any portion of the South with us.

The way the convention is constituted and the perfect subserv[i]-ency of more than five six[ths] of all the Slave holding States to party obligation, will render the few sound individual delegates insignificant, too much ["so as" *canceled*] to give them any control. If Virginia would stand fast, it would be different; but I learn from information, I cannot doubt, that there is no hope, that her delegation ["will" *interlined*] stand fast in good faith to her resolutions. I regard her, indeed, as one of the most subservient of all the slave holding states. I know the fact, that the resolutions were forced on the Convention by a few of our State rights friends, who will, on that account, not be appointed delegates. Whether the Alabama delegates will be more faithful to their resolutions, I have no information; but, if we may judge by their members of the House of Representatives, I think, there can be little hope they will. In this state of things, it would be in vain to expect we could do much to influence the action of the convention by adopting the course suggested; and would add few, or none to those, who would feel disposed to rally against the action of the convention, however adverse it might be to us. But, if in this, I mistake, if the Virginia delegates should faithfully adhere to the resolutions of their Convention, & be backed by Alabama, or should any portion of the delegates of the slave holding States, stand out against an obnoxious nomination, every member of our delegation in Congress, will be ready to back & support them to the utmost extent; and of this we shall not fail to apprise our friends, as they pass through here on their way to Baltimore. This would give our State all the weight, it could have, by our attendance in the manner suggested by Mr. Hayne; especially, as we are assured by your letter, that we would be backed by our constituents. As things stand, farther, I think, we ought not to go. Indeed, the composition of the Convention ought to make us cautious in connecting ourselves with it, or having any thing to do with it. No inconsiderable portion ["of its members" *interlined*] will be down right abolitionists, & a majority of the whole will consist of those, who have taken an active part, in hostile acts to us, or the representatives of those, who have, including the Wilmot proviso itself, and the object it is intended to effect. It will be difficult, if not impossible for ["a" *altered to* "the"] nominee of such a body, if elected President to be true to us, on the most vital of all questions to us. Of this the present incumbent [James K. Polk] affords an illustration. He was nominated by a Convention, which, as far as we know, had not a single abolitionists [*sic*]; and yet, notwithstanding he is a slave holder, he has not hesitated so far to defer to the abolitionists, as to appoint them to office. He has gone so far, this very session ["to appoint" *canceled and* "as to nominate" *interlined*] to a respectable & lucrative office [Collector of Customs at Philadelphia] the very man [Henry Horn], who moved the Wilmot proviso in the Legislature of Pennsylvania. He was rejected, not simply because he was an abolitionists [*sic*]; but because, there were serious charges against his honesty. If a Southern planter, elected as he was, could go so far, what can we expect from a northern man, nominated by ["a convention" *interlined*] like the one about to be held?

We, for these reasons, are decidedly of the opinion, the course suggested ought not to be adopted. We cannot think, there is the slightest danger, that our State will ["ever" *interlined*] slide into whiggery. We, as State rights Republicans ["Republicans" *canceled*] are far more opposed to the whigs, than the democrats. Indeed, my objection to the latter, as a party, is, that they approach too near the whigs. There is far greater danger, that the State will sink into hunkerism, than that she will ever become whig. Nor do we think

it would be right for our papers to denounce the whigs, for their errors & hostility to us, without also denouncing the democrats for
theirs. It would not be just, or fair. Besides, the errors of friends are
more dangerous than that of opponents, ["as" *interlined*] they are
much more apt to be contagious.

But, while we cannot approve of Col. Hayne's suggestions, we
are far from thinking the State ought idly look on. We ought, for the
present, stand fast, and be prepared to seize on every opportunity,
by which the South can be brought to unite, & to act together for its
salvation, to be a citadel & ["rallying" *canceled and* "a" *interlined*]
point for all ["in the South" *canceled and* "within her limits," *interlined*] that is sound, to rally on. As the danger increases, the ties
["of" *interlined*] the two parties in the South to the two in the north,
will daily become weaker. They have been greatly weakened since
the commencement of the session, & will, I think, be much more so
after the action of the two conventions. It will be impossible for the
Southern whigs to go for [Henry] Clay; and, it may be, for the
South[ern] democrats, or rather Republicans, to go for the Baltimore
nominee. If so, it may do much to break up the present old & corrupt
organization, and unite the sound of both parties, under the old State
rights Republican banner, & under the name of the Republican party.
If something of the kind be not done, we of the South may prepare
for the worst. The present organization is too rotten, ever to reform
or make anything of. The only course consistent with our principles,
interest, honor & safety is, as I most solemnly believe, ["is" *canceled*]
the one indicated, &, I hope, such will be the conclusion of our
Charleston friends when they come to see the whole ground.

If our papers have made no movement on the subject of the Convention, my advice would be to make none, unless there should be a
movement in its favour; and then to come out sufficiently strong to
put it down. It would give the advantage of acting on the defensive,
which is no small one. From all we can learn from our correspondence ["from" *canceled and* "with" *interlined*] the country, there is
no disposition to make any movement.

You are of course at liberty to show this to all friends. Yours truly,
J.C. Calhoun.

ALS in ScC; photostat of ALS in DLC, Henry Workman Conner Papers.

J[ohn] C. Calhoun and Others to President [JAMES K. POLK]

H[ouse] of Repr[esentative]s, April 20 1848

William B. Johnston Esq. of Camden S.C. is desirous to be appointed Consul at Belfast Ireland.

Mr. Johnston, has, for some time, been the Editor of the "Camden Journal" which will afford general assurance of his attainments. He has been engaged in the mercantile business, on a large scale, and, though unfortunate in business, he has great experience and skill.

Mr. Johnston is an upright and pious man, of the highest integrity. His mother lives in Belfast, and he desires to be with her during the remnant of her life; and it is for this reason, especially, that he desires the appointment.

All of which is respectfully submitted, A[lexander] D. Sims, A[rmistead] Burt, J[oseph] A. Woodward, J.C. Calhoun, R[ichar]d F. Simpson.

[P.S.] Mr. [Robert Barnwell] Rhett is sick at Georgetown, and cannot be consulted; but would doubtless be glad of an opportunity to cöoperate in this application.

LS in DNA, RG 59 (State Department), Letters of Application and Recommendation during the Administrations of James K. Polk, Zachary Taylor, and Millard Fillmore, 1845–1853, Johnston (M-873:46, frames 151–153). NOTE: The requested appointment was not made.

REMARKS ON THE DISTURBANCES IN THE DISTRICT OF COLUMBIA

[In the Senate, April 20, 1848]

[On April 15 a schooner had slipped away from a Washington landing carrying about eighty slaves belonging to citizens of D.C., bound down river for the open sea. The next day, thirty citizens in a steamboat overtook the fugitives, capturing the slaves and three white men. There followed several days of disturbances during which the abolitionist weekly press, the National Era, *was threatened. On 4/20 John P. Hale of N.H., who had recently been nominated for President by the Liberty Party, asked leave to introduce in the Senate a bill requiring the local governments of the District to pay compensation for any property damaged by "riotous assemblage." After some pre-*

*liminary discussion, in which Calhoun asked, "What is the bill?," the
presiding officer had the bill read.*]

Mr. Calhoun. I suppose no Senator can mistake the object of this
bill, and the occurrence which has led to its introduction. Now, sir,
I am amazed that even the Senator from New Hampshire should have
so little regard for the laws and the Constitution of the country, as to
introduce such a bill as this, without including in it the enactment of
the severest penalties against the atrocious act which has occasioned
this excitement. Sir, gentlemen, it would seem, have at last come to
believe that the southern people and southern members have lost all
sensibility or feeling upon this subject. I know to what this leads. I
have known for a dozen of years to what all this is tending. When
this subject was first agitated, I said to my friends, there is but one
question that can destroy this Union and our institutions, and that is
this very slave question, for I choose to speak of it directly. I said
further, that the only way by which such a result could be prevented
was by prompt and efficient action; that if the thing were permitted
to go on, and the Constitution to be trampled on; that if it were allowed to proceed to a certain point, it would be beyond the power of
any man, or any combination of men, to prevent the result. We are
approaching that crisis, and evidence of it is presented by the fact
that such a bill upon such an occurrence should be brought in to
repress the just indignation of our people from wreaking their ven-
geance upon the atrocious perpetrators of these crimes, or those who
contribute to them, without a denunciation of the cause that excited
that indignation. I cannot but trust that I do not stand alone in
these views.

I have for so many years raised my voice upon this subject that I
have been considered almost the exclusive defender of this great institution of the South, upon which not only its prosperity but its very
existence depends. I had hoped that younger members who have
come into this body, who represent portions of the country at least as
much interested as that from which I come, might have taken the
lead, and relieved me from the necessity of ever again speaking upon
this subject. I trust we will grant no leave to introduce this bill; that
we will reject it; and that if anything be referred to the Committee on
the Judiciary, it will be to make penal enactments to prevent these
atrocities, these piratical attempts, these wholesale captures, these
robberies of seventy-odd of our slaves at a single grasp. Delay is
dangerous on this question. The crisis has come, and we must meet
it, and meet it directly; and I will add, we have ample means to meet
it. We can put the issue to the North: if you continue to disregard

the provisions of the Constitution in our favor, we shall, on giving you due notice, retaliate by disregarding those in your favor. If you do not regard the stipulations of the Constitution in our favor, why should we regard those in your favor? If your vessels cannot come into our ports without the danger of such piratical acts; if you have caused this state of things by violating the provisions of the Constitution and the act of Congress for delivering up fugitive slaves, by passing laws to prevent it, and thus make it impossible to recover them when they are carried off by such acts, or seduced from us, we have the right, and are bound by the high obligation of safety to ourselves, to retaliate, by preventing any of your sea-going vessels from entering our ports. That would apply an effectual remedy, and make up the issue at once on this, the gravest and most vital of all questions to us and the whole Union. I do not intend to make a long speech on this occasion, but I would have felt myself to be lacking in my duty to the people of this District, to the people of the South, and to the people of the United States, had I not raised my voice against the introduction of such a bill on such an occasion.

Mr. [James D.] Westcott [Jr., of Fla.]. I am not going to make a speech on this bill, for the simple reason that I intend, after a few observations, to move to lay this motion for leave to introduce the bill upon the table, to stop debate, and ask for the yeas and nays.

Mr. Calhoun. The bill is not yet introduced.

Mr. Westcott. The Senator from New Hampshire asks leave to introduce the bill, and I move to lay it upon the table.

Mr. Calhoun. Better reject it. I trust we will meet it directly, and reject it.

Mr. Westcott. I did not understand the honorable Senator from South Carolina; but, now that I do, I am perfectly willing to adopt his suggestion.

Mr. Calhoun. I would greatly prefer to meet the motion directly, and reject it.

[*Westcott spoke at some length, pointing out that the disturbances had not been serious and that the abolitionist press had not been harmed, merely called upon by a party of peaceable citizens. Jefferson Davis of Miss. responded to Calhoun's mention of younger representatives of the South by commenting that he had refrained from speaking "from no want of accordance in feeling" with Calhoun, "but from deference to him who has so long and nobly stood foremost in defence of the institutions of the South." He spoke strongly against incendiaries who came among the people of the South, and was fol-*]

*lowed by Henry S. Foote of Miss., who spoke in even stronger terms.
There followed an interchange between Foote and Hale during which
Hale quoted at length from a statement of the editor of the* National
Era.]

Mr. Calhoun, (in his seat.) Does he make any denunciation of
the robbery?

Mr. Hale. He had quite enough to do in defending himself, and
it was no part of his duty to denounce others.

Mr. Calhoun, (in his seat.) I understand that!

[*There was further discussion between Foote and Hale. Then
Andrew P. Butler of S.C. asked Hale if he would support "a bill,
properly drawn, inflicting punishment on persons inveigling slaves
from the District of Columbia."*]

Mr. Hale. Certainly not, and why? Because I do not believe that
slavery should exist here.

Mr. Calhoun, (in his seat.) He wishes to arm the robbers, and
disarm the people of the District.

Mr. Hale. The honorable Senator is alarmed at my temerity—

Mr. Calhoun, (in his seat.) I did not use the word, but did not
think it worth while to correct the Senator.

Mr. Hale. The Senator did not use that term?

Mr. Calhoun. No. I said brazen, or something like that.

[*Hale declared that he would never be a party to "encroachment
upon rights guaranteed by the Constitution." He waged no war
against slavery except "a war of reason" and persuasion. He was
shocked to hear Calhoun denounce his bill as "calculated to repress
those citizens from the expression of their just indignation."*]

Mr. Calhoun. If the Senator will allow me, I will explain. I said
no such thing. But I will take this occasion to say, that I would just
as soon argue with a maniac from bedlam, as with the Senator from
New Hampshire, on this subject.

Several Senators. "Order, order."

Mr. Calhoun. I do not intend to correct his statements. A man
who says that the people of this District have no right in their slaves,
and that it is no robbery to take their property from them, is not entitled to be regarded as in possession of his reason.

[*A number of other Senators spoke, including Willie P. Mangum
of N.C., who deplored the "excitement" and moved that the motion
for leave to introduce the bill lie on the table.*]

Mr. Calhoun. Will the Senator be good enough to withdraw that
motion for a moment?

Mr. Mangum. Certainly.

Mr. Calhoun. If there is any responsibility in regard to this question, that responsibility is on me.

[*Mangum replied that the responsibility for the excitement was not on Calhoun but on the sponsor of the bill.*]

Mr. Calhoun. I am very happy to hear that such is the opinion of the honorable Senator; but I disagree with my worthy friend, the Senator from North Carolina, in several particulars. I do not look upon a state of excitement as a dangerous state. On the contrary, I look upon it as having often a most wholesome tendency. The state to be apprehended as dangerous in any community is this, that when there is a great and growing evil in existence, the community should be in a cold and apathetic state. Nations are much more apt to perish in consequence of such a state than through the existence of heat and excitement. Nor do I agree with the Senator from North Carolina in thinking that this is an analogous case to that of the question as to the reception of petitions on the subject of slavery; for we all know that in reference to the latter, the question was, whether the Senate was not bound to receive petitions in all cases and on all subjects. Now, here is a case in which there is no doubt whatever. All admit that the question of granting leave is a question depending upon the voice of the Senate, as a matter of discretion; there is no question of right whatever. Now, I submit to the Senator from North Carolina, whether, under the circumstances, a bill of this kind, introduced at such a moment, to subject the worthy citizens of this District to a high penalty, without containing a single clause for the punishment of those who commit outrages upon them, and deprive them of their property—without a single expression against such marauders, must not be considered a most extraordinary measure, let it come from whatsoever quarter it may? Can any man doubt, that, whether intended or not, the object of this bill is to disarm the worthy citizens of this District, so as to prevent them from defending their property, and to arm the robbers? That is the whole amount of it. The Congress of this Union is the legislature of the District of Columbia; and what is our duty on this occasion? It is, to protect these our constituents, who have no other protection but ours. It is our duty to stand forward in their behalf, when the extraordinary spectacle is presented to us of a vessel coming to our wharves under the color of commerce, and of the men belonging to that vessel silently seducing away our slaves, and getting nearly a hundred of them on board, and then moving off with them under cover of the night, in order to convey them beyond our reach. What is our duty under these circumstances? Is it not to take up the subject, as I trust the Committee on the Judiciary will do, and pass a bill containing the highest penalties known to the law against pirates who are guilty of acts like these?

I differ also from my honorable friend from North Carolina in this respect: he seems to think that the proper mode of meeting this great question of difference between the two sections of the Union is to let it go on silently, not to notice it at all, to have no excitement about it. I differ from him altogether. I have examined this subject certainly with as much care as my abilities would enable me; and if I am not greatly deceived, if I have any capacity to perceive what is coming, I give it as my most deliberate opinion, that if such course is pursued on our part, and the activity of those influences on the other side be permitted to go on, the result of the whole will be, that we shall have St. Domingo over again. Yes, and worse than that. Now, sir, we have been asleep; and so far from the thing being stationary, it is advancing rapidly from year to year. What has taken place within the last few weeks in the Legislature of New York? There is a provision in the Constitution protective of the rights of the South on this subject; and what is it? That the States shall deliver up fugitive slaves that are found within their limits. It is a stipulation in the nature of an extradition treaty—I mean a treaty for delivering up fugitives from justice. Now, what duty does this impose upon the States of this Union? It imposes upon them, upon the known principles of the law of nations, an active coöperation on the part of their Legislature, citizens, and magistrates, in seizing and delivering up slaves who have escaped from their owners. What has been done by the Legislature of the State of New York? I speak on the statements of newspapers, which have not been contradicted. They have passed a law almost unanimously—there being but two votes against it—making it penal for a citizen of that State even to aid the federal officers in seizing and delivering up slaves. They not only do not coöperate—they not only do not stand neutral, but they take positive and active measures to violate the Constitution, and to trample upon the laws of the Union; and yet we are told that things are going on very well, and will go on well if we only let them alone; that the evil will cure itself. This is what has been done in the State of New York. The only stipulation in the Constitution which confers any benefit upon us is, without the least regard to faith, trodden in the dust. And New York stands not alone in this matter; many other States have adopted similar measures. Pennsylvania, at the session before last, adopted one, not going to this extreme, but not falling greatly short of it. And what has taken place under that law? A most worthy citizen of Maryland, upon his attempting to recapture his slave, is murdered—that is the proper term—and the perpetrator of the act goes in great measure unpunished. There was a trial, and some one may have been found guilty, but little was done. I could go on and consume the whole day in tracing, step by step, the course by which every stipulation in favor of this description of property has been set at naught in the northern States. Now, if all this is the fact, I put it gravely and seriously to our brethren of the northern States, can this thing go on? Is it desirable that it should be passed without condemnation? Is it desirable that the South should be kept ignorant of all this? I put these questions. No, no. The very inaction of the South is construed into one of two things—indifference or timidity. And it is this construction which has produced this bold and rapid movement towards the ultimate consummation of all this. And why have we stood and done nothing? I will tell you why. Because the press of this Union, for some reason or other, does not choose to notice this thing. One section does not know what the other section is doing. The South does not know the hundredth part of all that has been done at the North. Now, since this occurrence has taken place, a suitable occasion is presented for gentlemen to rise here and tell the whole Union what is doing. It is for the interest of the North as well as the South. I do not stand here as a southern man. I stand here as a member of one of the branches of the Legislature of this Union— loving the whole, and desiring to save the whole. How are you to do it? It can be saved only by justice; and how is justice to be done? By the fulfillment of the stipulations of the Constitution. I ask no more—as I know myself, I would not ask a particle that did not belong to us, either in our individual or confederated character. But less than that I never will take. Sir, I hold equality among the confederated States to be the highest point, and any portion of the confederated States who shall permit themselves to sink to a point of inferiority—not defending what really belongs to them, as members, sign their own death warrant, and in signing that, sign the doom of the whole. Upon the just maintenance of our rights, not only our safety depends, but the existence and safety of this glorious Union of ours. And I hold that man responsible and that State responsible, who do not raise a voice against every known and clear infraction of the stipulations of the Constitution in their favor. This is a proper occasion, and I hope there will be a full expression of opinion upon it. I hope my friend from North Carolina will reconsider his motion, and not press it. Let us meet this question at once.

[*Stephen A. Douglas of Ill. stated that he had not been provoked to excitement by the debate, though other Senators had. He felt that Hale's bill had accomplished its purpose, which was to create such excitement.*]

Mr. Calhoun, (in his seat.) Not the bill—the occurrence.

[*Douglas congratulated Hale on his success. Thanks to Southern Senators his vote at the Presidential election will be double what it would have been. According to Douglas, Hale "with his principles," could "never have represented a free State of this Union on this floor but for the aid of southern speeches." Southern Senators, "breathing a fanaticism as wild and as reckless as that of the Senator from New Hampshire," were creating abolitionism in the North.*]

Mr. Calhoun. Does the gentleman pretend to say, that myself, and southern gentlemen who act with me upon this occasion, are fanatics? Have we done anything more than defend our rights, encroached upon at the North? Am I to understand the Senator that we make abolition votes by defending our rights? If so, I thank him for the information, and do not care how many such votes we make.

[*Douglas replied that he did not wish to create abolitionists in the North, but that such was the "inevitable effect" of the speeches of Southern Senators, whether intended or not.*]

Mr. Calhoun, (in his seat.) We are only defending ourselves.

[*There followed a discussion between Foote and Douglas. Douglas suggested that Southern Senators were fanning the flame of abolitionism because "It gives them strength at home."*]

Mr. Calhoun. I must really object to the remarks of the Senator. We are merely defending our rights. Suppose that we defend them in strong language; have we not a right to do so? Surely the Senator cannot mean to impute to us the motives of low ambition. He cannot realize our position. For myself, (and I presume I may speak for those who act with me,) we place this question upon high and exalted grounds. Long as he may have lived in the neighborhood of slaveholding States, he cannot have realized anything on the subject. I must object entirely to his course, and say that it is at least as offensive as that of the Senator from New Hampshire.

[*Debate continued among a number of Senators. Simon Cameron of Pa. deplored Hale's bill. His State was dedicated to the Constitution. The incident to which Calhoun had referred was an "occasional excitement" which "may for a moment have misled a few of her citizens." He predicted that a state of excitement, which had been caused by the Wilmot Proviso, was passing away and would soon be as "forgotten as a dream." He moved adjournment.*]

The motion being temporarily withdrawn—

Mr. Calhoun said: I rise simply to state upon what grounds I made the assertion that the act of Pennsylvania was similar to the act of New York, but did not go so far. The act of New York makes it penal even for the citizens of New York to aid the federal officers. The act of Pennsylvania does not; but makes it illegal for her magistrates and citizens to coöperate, except with the federal officers. Now, the provision of the Constitution of the United States requires an active coöperation on the part of the State, its citizens and magistrates, in the delivery of fugitive slaves; and anything short of that is a violation of the Constitution, and calculated to destroy the efficiency of the law of the United States in reference to that subject. To that extent the law of Pennsylvania, as well as that of New York, is unconstitutional.

[*After some more discussion, the Senate adjourned without any action. On 5/3 Hale asked the Senate to consider his motion for leave to introduce the "riotous assemblage" bill, but the Senate passed on to other business and never took up the matter again.*]

From *Congressional Globe*, 30th Cong., 1st Sess., Appendix, pp. 501–510. Also printed in the Washington, D.C., *Daily Union*, April 25, 1848, pp. 2–3, and April 26, 1848, p. 2; the Charleston, S.C., *Mercury*, May 1, 1848, p. 2, and May 2, 1848, p. 2; the Columbia, S.C., *South-Carolinian*, May 9, 1848, pp. 1–2, and May 12, 1848, pp. 1–2 (part); the Greenville, S.C., *Mountaineer*, May 19, 1848, p. 1 (part); Houston, ed., *Proceedings and Debates*, pp. 514–525. Variants in the Alexandria, Va., *Gazette and Virginia Advertiser*, April 21, 1848, p. 3; the Philadelphia, Pa., *Public Ledger*, April 21, 1848, p. 3; the New York, N.Y., *Herald*, April 21, 1848, p. 2, and April 23, 1848, p. 3; the New York, N.Y., *Morning Courier and New-York Enquirer*, April 24, 1848 (Supplement), p. 2; the Camden, S.C., *Journal*, May 10, 1848, p. 1.

To W[ILSON] LUMPKIN, [Athens, Ga.]

Washington, 21st April 1848

My dear Sir, You are right in supposing, that the existing party organization[s] look only to plunder. The sole object of strife is to elect a President, in order to obtain the control through him of the honors and the emoluments of the Government. The only material difference between the two parties is, that the democratick look more exclusively to plundering through the finances & the treasury, while the Whigs look more to plundering by whole sale, through partial legislation, Banks, Protection and other means of monopoly. The one rely for support on capital & the other on the masses; & the one tends more to aristocracy & the other to the power of a single man, or monarchy. Both have entirely forgot the principles, which originally gave rise to their existence; and are equally proscriptive & devoted to party machinery. To preserve party machinery & to keep up party union are paramount to all other considerations; to truth, justice & the constitution. Every thing is studiously surpressed by both sides calculated to destroy party harmony; & hence the South is kept in as great a state of ignorance of the aggressions of abolitionists, & the pandering to their appetite by both parties at the North, as if they belonged to a different community and had no interest, or concern, in reference to it. The abolitionists attribute our passiveness, not to ignorance ["of the actual state of things" *interlined*] but to timidity, or indifference, & are thereby emboldened to push on their aggressions, until at last, they have ventured to make a piratical descent on this District [of Columbia], and sweep off nearly 100 slaves at once. Fortunately the piratical vessel was captured. If this should not rouse the South, it is to be feared that she will sleep the sleep of death.

In the midest of this state of things, & while the Senate ["is engaged" *interlined*] in repelling the insult offered by [John P.] Hale of N.H. in asking leave to introduce a highly penal bill to protect the abolition press ["here" *interlined*] ag[ai]nst the indignation of the people of the District, an occur[r]ence took place, well calculated [to] raise the indignation of the whole South; Mr. [James K.] Polk sent in the renomination of an individual [Henry Horn] to a respectable & lucrative office [Collector of Customs at Philadelphia], who introduced the Wilmot proviso into the Pennsylvania ["legislature" *interlined*] & who for that, and other reasons had been rejected by the Senate. That he, a Southern man, elected by the South, should select such a moment to renominate such an individual, to conciliate our deadly enemies, is proof but too strong, how low the South has sunk, & what little dependence can be placed on even a Southern President, elected as Presidents now are, not by the people, but those who plunder them. Much excitement may be expected, when it comes to be acted on. I agree with you, that the hope of reforming the government is very faint. It will certainly be impossible, ["while" *canceled*] while the existing organization continues. If it should ever be done, the first step will be for the South to break up the present organization, by the union of the sound on both sides, and to rally on the old State rights principle, & under the name of the Republican party.

How wonderful are the occur[r]ences in Europe! They exceed

every thing that has ever occur[r]ed before, and there is no telling where they will end. You will see, that the news by the steamer just arrived, shows that ["they" *canceled and* "events" *interlined*] are still moving on with the violence of a tornado, and are sweeping every thing before ["it" *canceled and* "them" *interlined*]. God grant, that ["it" *canceled and* "the end" *interlined*] may ["be to" *interlined*] advance the cause of liberty & civilization. Your old friend, J.C. Calhoun.

ALS in ICHi, John C. Calhoun Papers; PEx in Wilson, ed., *The Essential Calhoun*, p. 341.

From I s a a c N. D a v i s

Clear Creek, Lafayette County Mi[ssissippi]
April 22d 1848

Mr. Calhoun, Having for years occationally written to you & received letters in reply, altho the longer portion of the time differing in politics, It would afford me much satisfaction, at this time, if you can fine time from the duties of your station, to hear from you.

I take it for granted the mexican war is closed, although the news of the ratification of the Treaty by Mexico, has not yet reached me. I feel, as an humble citizen, much gratified at such a "consum[m]ation so devoutly to be wished for" & you will pardon the liberty I take in tendering to you my hearty & unfeigned thanks for the support you gave that Treaty, objectionable as it might be & likely was in some of its features. I feel proud of an American statesman who can rise superior to & above party shackles or immaterial differences, & look to the interest & character of the whole nation. The country is safe while such spirits preside in our councils. I saw with trembling fearfulness & exulting[?] pride, the same thing take place on the Oregon Treaty.

I am as little disposed to indulge in idle compliments as you would be to receive them from such a source. Still I cannot say less to one who so eminantly deserves much more. The circumstances & history of this war is full of deep interest to the nation, not only on account of the immense flow of the best blood of the land & the accumulating drain of money expended but still more so on account of the extraordinary powers & principles attempted to be engrafted upon our institutions & people. These principles when once addopted, whether, with or without, constitutional sanction, become common law, & serve as precedents, alike astounding and dangerous. I allude to the exercise of Executive powers, not only at home but upon foreign & conquered provinces. I have observed, in my limited reading, that a time of war, under the blaze of military glory & stimulated patriotic zeal, that the most dangerous ag[g]ressions have been made by executive officers or rulers in all nations. This remark is doubly true, in this country, where from the nature of our institutions & the character of our people military feelings & glory never fail to excite us, not unfrequently, almost inordinately. Powers can be assumed & practized in such times with impunity that would cost a President his character if not his office in times of peace. We sleep upon a fearful Volcano—& save your self, no member of Congress, to my knowledge, has grappled with this Hidra monster of power, which has not only shown his paw, but boldly reared his Gorgon head, of late. I am not of that desponding temperament that leads me to think all is lost, but I believe there is a redeeming spirit in the land which will prevail even against aspirants & Demagog[u]es.

The "Willmot Proviso" too I think does & will, ere long, present a fearful "crisis." That too I doubt not, will be properly rebuked[?] in the good sense & moral tone of the nation.

These crude notions, will have but little of interest to you, still you will pardon one, who is in the western wilds, for hinting at them.

I am greatly in favor of the election of Gen[era]l [Zachary] Taylor to the Presidency, not because he is a military man, but because, among other things, I think he will endeavor to administer the government as it was done by our Fathers, & not making these crusades after new doctrines & powers. I fear any man however, in that office for power begets power, & it seems that as soon as a citizen is elected, he thinks too little of his former professions, & too much of the purple & scepter. Would it be asking too much of you to have your views as to the Gen[era]l[']s election prospects &C &C.

In fine I should be pleased to have any thing you please to give me & consider me your obe[dient] Serv[an]t, Isaac N. Davis.

[P.S.] Oxford, Lafayette Co. Mi[ssissippi], is my post office.

ALS in ScCleA.

To Ja[me]s Ed[ward] Calhoun, [Columbia, S.C.]

Washington, 23d April 1848

My dear James, Your apology is sufficient, for the tardiness of your correspondence. If you study as you ought, which I doubt not is the case, & take the exercise & relaxation necessary for health, you can have but little leisure.

The course you are pursuing relative to the election of the Valedictory orator of your Society, & the reasons you assign for it, are proper & creditable to your judgement & principles.

I infer from a statement in one of our papers yesterday, that there has been some disturbance in College. I hope you had no part in it.

The Revolution in Europe is truely wonderful, and cannot end without leaving that portion of the globe in a very change[d] condition, but I hope much for the better. My hopes are centred in Germany. She has the materials of forming a great confederacy, in which form only can popular institutions exist on an extended scale. I trust, she may have the wisdom & patr[i]otism to use them skilfully & successfully.

I transmit by the mail, that takes this, the President's [James K. Polk's] Message & Documents addressed to the Clairosophic [*sic*] Society & to your care. I wish you to present it in my name.

It is doubtfull when the session will terminate. I fear not till the last of July. Your affectionate father, J.C. Calhoun.

ALS in NcD, John C. Calhoun Papers.

From G[eorge] Robertson, "Private"

Lexington Ky., 24th April 1848

My dear Sir, About four years ago I presumed to ["write" *canceled*] address to you a very plain and candid communication concerning the Presidential election and your interests and proper position in regard to it. Whether you received it, or how you con[s]trued it's motives, or regarded it's suggestions, I never knew. I only know that you neither answered it nor indicated, by your subsequent course, approval of its sentiments. It was, however, the offering of disinterested patriotism and personal esteem—and, had it's presumptuous, though honest, counsels been followed, I am sure, as I have thought, that your own welfare and the honor of the country would have been greatly promoted. May I repeat the general sentiment? It is—*that no little questions of ephemeral policy can justify a truely good and great man in helping, into high places, unprincipled Demagogues, or politicians of inferior talents and doubtful character; and that the destinies of the Country are always safe in the hands of men of established good character and eminent abilities.*

These truths have been exemplified in the last four years. What perils and degradation have followed in the wake of triumphant [James K.] Polk & Co.? And how different would have been our condition and prospects had he been, as he ought to have been, beaten in the Presidential race?

Now—shall *he,* or any of *his sort,* be elected again? *You* will be as responsible for the answers as perhaps any American citizen: and *I* am confident that your own influence will be ["as" *canceled*] much ["affected" *canceled*] advanced by the election of such a man as Henry Clay, and will be greatly impaired, if not paralysed, by the triumph of Polk, [Lewis] Cass, Buckhannon [*sic*; James Buchanan], or [Levi] Woodbury. *I am satisfied* that Mr. C[lay] has no other feelings towards you than those of the kindest and most respectful character. And I am, moreover, satisfied that, should he be elected, you will approve the general spirit and tenor of his administration, and cooperate with it to save and restore our institutions, and national peace, and character. And, is not the election of such a man necessary, *just at this crisis?* Who else can meet it so well? Who, but he, can keep down, or *satisfactorily* give the *quietus* to, the slave agitation?

I neither desire nor have, perhaps, a right to expect any explicit answer. What I now venture to say to you, I say—without the knowledge of Mr. Clay—on my own responsibility, as your old and constant friend and the friend of my countries peace and glory. I count on your receiving it in the like spirit, and therefore pardoning this intrusion on your own clear vision and anxious contemplations. Y[ou]rs respectfully, G. Robertson.

ALS in ScCleA. NOTE: George Robertson (1790–1874) was a Ky. Congressman, jurist, author and lecturer in the Transylvania University Law School. He was a Representative in the State legislature in 1848.

To [WILLIAM W. CORCORAN & GEORGE W. RIGGS]

Washington, 25th April 1848

Dear Sirs, Below you have my name in blank, to be filled up with a sum sufficient to give me a check for $700 on New York as requested yesterday. I wish it for three months. Send the checky [*sic*] by the bearer, if you please. Yours truly, J.C. Calhoun.

ALS in DLC, Riggs Family Papers.

By [WILLIAM W.] CORCORAN & [GEORGE W.] RIGGS

Corcoran & Riggs
No. 2497 Washington 25 Ap[ri]l 1848
 $700
    Pay to Hon. J.C. Calhoun or order
Seven hundred ——————— %₁₀₀ Dollars
To Bank of America
    New York   Corcoran & Riggs.

PDS owned by W.G. Chisolm. NOTE: Calhoun's AES on the reverse side of the draft reads, "Pay to the order of Capt. Patrick Calhoun. J.C. Calhoun." An AES by Patrick Calhoun reads, "P. Calhoun, U.S. A[rmy]."

To A[NDREW] P[ICKENS] CALHOUN, [Marengo County, Ala.]

Washington, 26th April 1848

My dear Andrew, I have received your letter with the blanks ["with" *canceled and* "and" *interlined*] a statement of the probable amount of the sales of our cotton crop, with the balence after deducting payments. The last has, indeed, turned out a bad year for us, between a short crop & low prices; but we must not be discouraged, as bad as the prospect is. Regid economy in all things, & active & vigorous management of our affairs must be our motto. The boys, except Patrick [Calhoun], seem to be sensible of the necessity of economy, and exerting themselves; &, if I may infer from letters from your mother [Floride Colhoun Calhoun], she is exercising more than usual ["economy" *interlined*] for her. Patrick, I am sorry to say, has made another & quite a heavy call on me; but in terms expressive of great distress & deep mortification. I had to borrow money to meet it. I wrote him in kind, but strong terms, stating the great inconvenience to which it subjected me, & the injustice it was doing the rest of the family, accompanied by a strong expression of the absolute necessity of his living hereafter within the limits of his pay. I trust, and think, it will have the desired effect. I wish he was married to some good girl with property to live on, and was out of the army.

As to myself, I spend not a cent, I can help, & meet every thing with patience & fortitude.

I find it very difficult to raise money here. I had a free & full conversation, with [William W.] Corcoran, the wealthy banker of the House of Corcoran [&] Riggs, a few days since on the subject of negotiating a loan. He tells me, it is utterly impossible at present to obtain one for any considerable time, either from Banks, Brokers or individuals on any security at legal interest ["here or at the North" *interlined*], but thinks, that there will be a flow of money into the country after a while from Europe when loans can be had. I, however, doubt it. Acting on the safe side, I immediately wrote to [Ozey R.] Broyles, who informed me, that after examining into the condition of the estate, of which he has the charge, & consulting with the administrators, he thought, he could collect by fall $18,000, which, if it suited us, he would lend to us, that we would take that, or whatever sum would be at his disposal. Looking ahead, it seemed to me, we ought to omit no opportunity to secure any sum we could on long terms, as this will be. We can at least make out to meet interest, and hold out to weather the storm, if we can fund our debts on such loans, particularly as we have but one, or two more, instalments to pay on Cuba. Which is it?

As soon as I hear from you, as to the interest due [Ker] Boyce, I shall endeavour to make arrangements in reference to it, & the renewal of our notes in bank, as I see you have no means of meeting either.

Since I enclosed you Mrs. [Ann Mathewes] Ioor's note, I had another from her, informing me, that she had been informed, the money had been remitted. She says, the cause of her not knowing it, was the long time Mr. [John Ewing] Bonneau's letter, in answer to hers, was in reaching her. I hope hereafter, whenever you remit to her or, indeed, make any other remittance on our joint account, you would inform me forthwith to avoid trouble.

You say nothing about the crop in your last. I hope it continues promising, & has not been injured by the cold weather, we have had of late.

My love to Margaret [Green Calhoun] & the children. Your affectionate father, J.C. Calhoun.

ALS in NcD, John C. Calhoun Papers.

From [Thomas G. Clemson]

Brussels, April 26th 1848

My dear Sir, ["There are" *canceled and* "Among" *interlined*] the cogent reasons for my desiring to return to the United States, ["The first is, perhaps I may not be able to retain this situation" *canceled*] is The ar[r]angement of my pecuniary affairs, particularly the sale of my plantation & negroes, & ["lastly" *canceled*] my mother [Elizabeth Baker Clemson] is aged, very infirm & it is said will never recover from her present illness. Now however much appearances may be to the contrary I have great repugnance to trouble others with my feelings or my private affairs. Since receiving your last letter ["22nd March" *interlined*] the prospect is that I shall not be able to return to the United States & if so that my family must be left behind. I shall regret this on several accounts and among these it would grieve me, if my Mother lives to see me that she should be deprived the pleasure of seeing my children [John Calhoun Clemson and Floride Elizabeth Clemson]. I have told you in former letters that it required rigid economy for me to live on my salary, & if I came near it, it was by neglecting to do many things which I should have done for the respectability of the position I occupy. It has been as much as I could do to scrape along by drawing monthly for my pay, & should that fail me my family would want the necessaries of life if not bread, & at this time if my little outstanding debts were paid I should not have the sum of one hundred dollars. I have felt this to be a bad predicament for a long time & in the present state of affairs in Europe it ought not to be continued. If I obtain leave of abscence I have not the means to return for it will not require a less sum than twelve hundred dollars to return to the U.S. with my family & if I leave them behind me it will not cost much less, for I could not leave them here without means. In this state of things to apply for leave of abscence, (as I intended doing in June) might place me in a worse predicament for if it be true as I have understood that it is customary to retain the salary of diplomatic agents on leave of abscence to return to the U.S. I should deprive myself of all resources, & even if the salary be paid it is not paid in advance (& if I were to resign, which I have not the intention of doing without being assured that I can not retain the position or get another) my infit [*sic*] would only be paid after settling my accounts in Washington after my return. I have little or no property here which would give me means to raise money, for if I were to sell the little silver I have purchased and the other articles including even my wearing apparel, I could not raise an adequate sum to pay my expenses to the United States, for it will not take a less sum than six or seven hundred dollars for passage money from Europe to the America not counting the other expenses I must necessarily incur previous to embarking. When I received my outfit I paid more than one half of it to go against debts standing in the United States, & by the time I reached Brussels you may well suppose there could not be much left, for we came to Europe almost bare of clothes & all the necessaries of life. The furniture of my house has been hired & paid monthly. My plantation if it has sufficed its expenses, has yielded nothing; in fine so far as my private means have aided, I might have had none for I have yet to receive the first dollar. It ought not then to surprise you if I have desired to place a part of my means in a position to command money when I required it, & if I have been obliged to write you so frequently & urgently on a subject that no doubt is become disagre[e]able I can only regret it for it has not been a matter of mere convenience but of urgent necessity, stronger now than it has been. However I have made no request ["which" *interlined*] if made in the case of another you would not have been the first to blame me for neglecting. Besides there is a duty one owes his family & in the various contingencies of life I have desired to have my property arranged in a manner that will satisfy me that I have done my duty towards them. My plantation has yielded me nothing. I have been anxious & willing to turn it into a profitable investment[,] one that would yield me available income, but circumstances have prevented its being done. With regard to other moneys owed me by other parties I have been willing to give up two thirds of the money due if I could obtain one third in cash—but without avail. You & Andrew [Pickens Calhoun] have found it inconvenient to pay me the interest on the money you owe me & unavoidable circumstances have prevented the adjustment of our ["joint" *canceled*] accounts. I wrote you previous to the commencement of the present year that I was desirous to have the six hundred dollars you owed me on our joint account, it being a sum due for a carriage, harness & horses, which I stated when you took them you might have without interest. I presume the letter has miscarried, for I have not been informed whether the money would or has been paid. I have written Mr. [Francis W.] Pickens that I wished to sell my carpenter William, but that like every thing else connected with my affairs, remains dependent on eventualities. I have desired to act in accordance with your wishes and desires. I have endeavoured to place the matter before you in every business shape that my mind has suggested, without any apparent success & I confess that I fear a continuation of past delay. In your last letter you say that you find it impossible to pay me as I should have preferred & you don[']t know whether it will be possible to make a loan in the present state of the money market. Andrew Calhoun is as much liable for this debt as yourself, & yet so far as I can see he pays no kind of attention to the subject. You have thus far so stood between us, that he is utterly independent of my rights & wishes & if he has had the use of the money thus long it has been entirely on your account & if he keeps that portion for which he is liable any longer it will be because I can not prevent it. My necessities have been and continue to be as urgent as his can be & I have no inclination further to await his convenience either to raise the money or to come to South Carolina to make out accounts. I wish him to pay one half of the amount that is due & to prevent further difficulties I should be obliged to you if you would inform him of this ["my determination" *canceled*]. I can only repeat that in face of my wants a part of which I have detailed above that I have written thus with extreme reluctance. In order to avoid all further delay & to prevent further appeals from me to you & avoid giving you trouble in the matter I am willing to place the matter in the hands of any of your ["legal" *interlined*] friends in whom you may have confidence, living in Charleston, where the books of Mr. [John Ewing] Bonneau can be consulted and the matter of the account adjusted without any doubt. When the amount shall be ascertained, Andrew Calhoun to pay one half, & the remaining half to be continued to *you* ["in Carolina" *interlined*] according to law, the interest being annually paid until I shall require the principal to be paid on my giving six month's notice. If such a course should ["not" *canceled*] be ["unacceptable" *changed to* "acceptable"] to you[,] you can take the initiative & write the person you may select and on hearing from you I will forward ["him" *interlined*] a copy of the account I have sent you & write my desires.

In this settlement you will understand that the payment of one half the sum due is a necessity but I greatly prefer & insist indeed that this half should be paid by A. Calhoun & the other half become a debt from you to me, (in which he has no concern) & secured in Carolina. You may say that one half the sum is more than I require to return to the U.S. but you will agree with me that the state of things in which [I] can not command a hundred dol[lar]s in case of necessity should c[e]ase & I mention one half as a round sum & also as I before [sa]y[?] as a means of debarassing [*sic*] myself of any further connection with A. Calhoun. I should deeply regret if I was the cause either directly or indirectly of giving you trouble or embarrassment; on the contrary in wishing to avoid it I have placed myself in the position in which I am & in proposing the arrangement I have I can not imagine that you can be put to any difficulty for I should be much surprised to learn that A.C. could find[?] a difficulty in raising 5 or 30,000[?] dol[lar]s on his property in Alabama.

ALU (retained copy) in ScCleA, Thomas Green Clemson Papers.

To W[ILLIAM] G. CORDRAY, Brooklyn, N.Y.

Washington, 27th April, 1848
I thank you for the Print of the Washington Monument, designed by William Ross Wallace, Esq., which you were so kind as to send me. I do not profess to be a connoisseur in such things, but it strikes me as being original, bold and grand; and as requiring only execution and materials worthy of the design, to make a monument worthy of the Man! With great respect, Yours, &c., J.C. Calhoun.

PC in the Charleston, S.C., *Mercury*, July 25, 1860, p. 2 (a clipping of which is found in NNC, Ferris Papers).

REMARKS ON THE CALIFORNIA CLAIMS BILL

[In the Senate, April 27, 1848]
[*Under consideration was a bill authorizing Col. John C. Fremont and two of his officers to determine and pay claims for compensation resulting from the military campaign in California. James M. Mason of Virginia characterized the bill as unconstitutional because it made the three men officers of the government without Presidential appointment and Senate approval. He offered a substitute authorizing*

appointment by the President of a board of three commissioners. This provoked an extended discussion on the Constitutional point.]

Mr. Calhoun. Before the question is put, I desire to state the reasons upon which I shall feel myself compelled to vote for the amendment offered by the Senator from Virginia. I have bestowed upon this case that attention which the magnitude, both of the principle and the amount of money involved, seemed to me to demand; and after the best consideration that I have been able to give it, I have been brought to the conclusion that the original bill as reported by the committee [on Military Affairs], and the amendment which the committee now propose to substitute for it, are both unconstitutional. In order to understand whether this opinion of mine be correct or not, it will be necessary to understand what are actually the provisions contained in the bill and the amendment, and what is the object intended to be effected. We are told by two of the members of the committee that the object is, to prescribe the evidence on which the claims are to be allowed, and that the persons named are to act in the character of witnesses. If so, the bill and amendment are strangely drawn. I find not a word about evidence or witness, or having the least reference to either, and the language used excludes the possibility that the object was such as they allege. They are vested with the function to examine and allow, and not to testify. They act as a board of commissioners. The majority decides, and their decision is final. By what abuse of language, then, can individuals performing such functions be called witnesses; when they are of a character so wholly different? Two other members of the committee assign a very different object. They allege that it is intended to enable the three individuals named in the amendment to perform that which they would have performed at the time, had they had funds in their hands to meet the expenses incurred: that is, to enable Colonel Fremont to perform the functions of commander, and the other two those of paymaster and quartermaster, respectively. To judge of the correctness of this allegation, it will be necessary to ascertain what additional functions they would have had to perform if they had been in funds at the time. None whatever, but to pay as the expenses were incurred, instead of giving certificates for the amount. Colonel Fremont had performed all his functions as commander, as fully as if the ample funds had been furnished, and none but those of the paymaster and commissary [*sic*] had any left unperformed. Now, I ask, is it the object of this bill, or the amendment reported by the committee, to enable them to perform their unexecuted functions? Is it proposed that either of these disbursing officers shall perform the function of paymaster or commissary, or that Colonel Fremont should perform that of commander? There is not a provision to that effect. Their functions are to be entirely different. In the first place, instead of acting in their individual capacity and on their individual responsibility, as they would if the duties attached to each had been performed at the time, they are to act as a board of commissioners, to be governed by the votes of the majority, and be exempt from all responsibility. Their functions are as dissimilar as is their character. Instead of performing the duties of commander, paymaster, and commissary, they are to examine and allow the claims against the Government without being subject to any restriction, either as to rule or evidence. Indeed; in not a single particular does the provisions of the bill or amendment correspond with the object which the members of the committee allege was to be effected. But suppose they correspond in every particular: would it get clear of the constitutional objection, which the allegation is intended to avoid? How can Congress vest by law the functions to execute duties which appertained to these individuals in their official characters, now when they are no longer officers? That is the question. What are these functions? Do they partake of the character of office, or that of mere employment? The answer is to be found in the fact already stated, that they appertained to them in their official character, and could only be performed by them in that character; and we have just as much power to invest them with all their other functions as these—to appoint them to the full exercise of all as of a part. The one would not more clearly and directly usurp the rights of the Executive than the other.

But I regard the functions proposed to be conferred on these individuals as not only very difficult, but of a far higher character than those which they had to perform, had they been furnished with funds. They partake of those belonging to the highest order of the fiscal officers of the Government, to whom they would have had to account had the expenses been paid when incurred. To understand who those officers are, and to what extent these individuals would, in that case, have been held responsible, I will state the process to be gone through before their accounts would be allowed. They would, in the first place, have to present them to the proper bureaus of the War Department—the commissary to the Commissary General, and the paymaster to the Paymaster General. Then they would have undergone an administrative examination. What its nature is, can best be understood by giving the process. Take, for instance, the commissary: he would have had to exhibit the orders under which he made his purchases. They would have to state the number or amount of articles, and, where necessary, their description. These orders would have to be presented to the Secretary of War for his approval, if there should be any doubt of their propriety, judged of in reference to the number of troops or the nature of the service. He then would have to exhibit his vouchers, to show that the prices of the articles were reasonable, and would have to furnish evidence to that effect. If, on examination, all were found correct, the Commissary General would endorse his approval, and pass them over to the proper Auditor of the Treasury for his examination and audit. From him, they would pass to the Comptroller General of the Treasury, who would review the whole; and then, if approved, the account would be allowed and the officer credited. Such is the careful and refined process prescribed by law and regulation, for the settlement of military accounts, and such the process through which those now in question would have had to pass, if the officers had been in funds, and had paid them at the time. By the provisions of this bill and amendment, the whole process is all laid aside. The very officers who would thus have been held responsible to account for the proper application of every cent placed in their hands, are authorized to examine and allow their own accounts; and their certificates allowing them are made as conclusive of their justice and correctness as would have been their allowance on the final settlement of the Comptroller. They, in a word, are invested in effect with all the functions of these high and responsible officers. Indeed, they are invested with far higher. The latter are bound by law and established rules; but they are bound by neither. They act under their own unlimited discretion, and are bound to establish no rules and keep no record; nor has the paymaster, or whoever may hold the funds, any discretion as to payment. Their certificates are the only vouchers necessary to the settlement of his account, so that there is no responsibility anywhere. I venture to assert that there is no example in all our legislation of an act of the kind; and, to cap the climax, these individuals are to be appointed by an act of Congress to perform these high official functions, which otherwise would have to be performed by officers who hold stations among the highest under the Government—and all this on the ground that the functions they would have to discharge are mere employments, and not offices!

I do not oppose this monstrous measure on the ground of opposition to Colonel Fremont, or either of his associates in this high commission. Of the latter, I know nothing; but I have a slight acquaintance with the Colonel, and am so favorably impressed as to him, that I would as readily trust him as any other individual. But a regard for the Constitution, and the great fundamental principle, that no man shall be a judge in his own case, which embraces this, that no man should settle his own account, compels me to oppose it. It has been attempted to bolster it up by precedents, but without success. Not one has been cited that is applicable; and, if there were hundreds to the point, they could have no weight where the Constitution and the fundamental principles of justice are so palpably violated. This I believe to be the first time that the question of our power in like cases has been formally discussed. It is of great importance that our discussion, in so leading a case, should be right.

But, Mr. President, I hold that if there be any doubt in this case—if it be not clearly right—there are reasons of a delicate character why the measure should not be adopted. It would be indelicate for me more fully to explain myself; but I will be understood when I say, there are circumstances attending it which are calculated to induce the belief, should we adopt the measure, that we have been actuated more by the feeling of *esprit du corps* than we ought to be. We all know how liable we are to be influenced by those with whom we are associated in the discharge of our duties, and with whom we hold daily intercourse. We ought to allow for it, and guard against it, especially in a case like this, involving the Constitution and a fundamental principle of justice.

Having said so much upon the amendment reported by the committee, I must say that I have objections even to the amendment offered by the Senator from Virginia, although, as I prefer it to the amendment offered by the committee, I shall vote for it. My opinion is, that the simple way of adjusting all these claims, is to appoint two or three able officers belonging to the army, upon whom such duties appropriately devolve, and send them there to settle these expenses, as far as they can be legally settled.

From *Congressional Globe*, 30th Cong., 1st Sess., pp. 697–698. Also printed in Houston, ed., *Proceedings and Debates*, p. 544. Variants in the Washington, D.C., *Daily Union*, April 28, 1848, p. 3; the New York, N.Y., *Herald*, April 29, 1848, p. 4.

To Mrs. A[NNA] M[ARIA CALHOUN] CLEMSON, [Brussels]

Washington, 28th April 1848

My dear daughter, The Sarah Sands brought me a letter from Mr. [Thomas G.] Clemson and one from you to [Martha] Cornelia [Calhoun], but none was received by the Acadia from either of you.

I was happy to hear of the continued good health of yourself & Mr. Clemson and the children, & how much they grow and improve.

We all, on this side of the Atlantick, look with intense solicitude on the great events, transpiring in Europe, and no one more so than myself. As frequent as the arrivals of steamers now are, and as short as is the interval between their arrivals, there is no abatement ["of the anxiety" *interlined*] with which each succeeding one is looked for. If there be ["but" *canceled*] the interval of but a few days, as much and more exciting news is expected, than formerlly there was after one of a month.

I look, perhaps, with greater solicitude for the unfolding of the great events now in progress ["now" *canceled*] in Europe, as they afford me an opportunity to test the truth or error, of the principles, which I have laid down in my elementary discourse on Government. It is as yet in the rough draft, waiting the completion of the rough draft of the discourse on our system of Government. I cannot doubt the correctness of the principles, I have laid down, for they are drawn from facts in the moral world, just as certain, as any in the physical; but I am solicitious to see, how far they are subject to modification in their practical application to the present condition of the civilized world, which is so very different from any, ["which" *canceled and* "that" *interlined*] ever preceded it in many respects. There are powerful, long established, & widely extended errors now at work, which tend to universal disorder & anarchy throughout Christendom; while on the other hand there are ["other &" *canceled*] powerful causes in operation to counteract them, and which, I trust, and believe, in time, will overpower them, & give a fairer prospect, than has ever yet existed, to the cause of real liberty & civilization. But in the meane time, it is to be feared, there will be great disorders, conflicts & suffering. You will see, that I am still hopeful. Had such a revolution, so wide & so rapid, occurred 50 years ago, I would have dispaired, and regarded it, as the commencement of a great retrograde movement in the most advanced & civilized portion of the world. Even now, I regret—greatly regret its rapidity, extent, and too thorough & radical character, especially in France. It ought never be forgotten, that *the past is the parent of the present,* & that the past condition of Europe, which has given birth to a state of advance & civilization, far exceeding any heretofore known to the world, could not be a bad one. It may have, indeed, contained, within itself, causes calculated to retard, or prevent a farther progress; but these ought to have been removed cautiously, as experience pointed them out, ["without" *interlined*] overthrowing all at once the frame of Governments & ["the" *interlined*] social condition of communities, which led to such great & happy results; especially as such an overthrow must of necessity be accompanied ["with" *canceled and* "by" *interlined*] such universal embarrassment & distress, & run the hazard of a retrograde, instead of an advance movement, in the condition of the race.

I had, my dear daughter, no intention of writing you such a letter, when I took up my pen. I commenced, with the intention, to relate the ordinary occurrences of the day on this side of the Ocean; but the allusion to the far greater, taking place in Europe, has led me, insensibly, in the direction I have taken. You must take it, better for worse, as I have not time to write another, or space, more than breifly to touch on, what I intended to make the subject of my letter.

My health continues as usual. When I last heard from home (a few days since) all were well & doing well. Your mother [Floride Colhoun Calhoun] had turned to garadening & improving the yard, which Willey [William Lowndes Calhoun] writes, has kept her employed, cheerful & healthy.

With love to Mr. Clemson, & kisses for the children, Your affectionate father, J.C. Calhoun.

ALS in ScCleA; variant PC in Jameson, ed., *Correspondence,* pp. 752–753; PEx in Wilson, ed., *The Essential Calhoun,* p. 50.

Further Remarks on the California Claims Bill

[In the Senate, April 28, 1848]
[The previous day's consideration continued with a multisided and complicated debate about legalities and precedents in the procedures for settling claims against the government. Early in the debate, Calhoun interjected briefly into a speech by George E. Badger of N.C., to state that the procedures for settling claims in the Pension Office

of the War Department were different from procedures in U.S. courts that Badger was describing. Later:]

Mr. Calhoun. I rise, before the question is put, to make a very few remarks on the amendment of the Senator from Delaware [John M. Clayton] to the amendment reported by the committee, which will, I suppose, in point of order, be put first. That amendment provides that these officers, commissioners, or whatever they may be called, shall be sworn to perform their duties faithfully; secondly, that they shall not decide upon any claims in which any of them may be interested; and thirdly, that in cases where any claim has been transferred, the assignee shall receive no further compensation than the amount which they paid for the claim with legal interest. This amendment deserves a good deal of consideration. I am struck with the use of the word "appoint" in it. It says "the persons appointed to perform these duties." If you look to the amendment reported by the committee, you will find that the use of the word "appoint" is most carefully eschewed. You cannot find that word, nor any one of tantamount meaning, in the amendment, from beginning to end. I will not say that this avoidance of the use of that term was designed, but, certainly great care seems to have been taken to avoid the use of this word. Now, without going into verbal criticism, let me ask, what is the force of the word "appoint?" You do not "appoint" to an employment. That was never heard of. You "appoint" to office. It is the specific word which is always used in that connection; and, therefore, I have been struck at the occurrence of this word in the amendment of the Senator from Delaware. The human mind is a curious organ; and the force of habit will often lead to the use of terms of which the person may not be conscious. I take this to be a case of that description. The term "appoint" is legitimate in this connection, and has crept into the amendment, though carefully avoided in the original bill and amendment of the committee. Again: the amendment acknowledges that the exercise of the powers conferred upon these commissioners is liable to be very greatly abused. Without this amendment, the bill would allow the commissioners to decide upon claims in which they are personally interested. It is well to guard against that. Not that I suppose that these officers would abuse the power, but there is a liability to abuse. The amendment indicates another great abuse to which there is a liability under the original bill. These claims in the wilds of California are in the hands of persons who know nothing of their value; who are conversant only with Mexican faith, which is no faith at all; and, as they put very little value upon Mexican paper, they may estimate all other paper

equally low, and may have passed off these claims for a mere baga-
telle. Here is an obvious source of great abuse, against which the
original bill and the amendment of the committee do not make the
slightest provision. But, while attempting to guard against this
abuse, the Senator ought to have guarded against all other abuses;
and, from stem to stern, the whole of it is subject to abuse. What is
the whole amount of this thing? You withdraw from the regular
settlement to which all such claims in all other cases are subject—
claims against this Government to the amount of seven hundred
thousand dollars—and transfer their settlement to the three individuals named in this amendment.

There is not a particle of responsibility in the whole matter.
There is nothing comes before the Government but the certificate of
these gentlemen. The importance of the routine of examination
before all the regularly-constituted officers, can only be appreciated
by those who have had some practice in it. I claim the honor of in-
stituting this process of examination, and it has saved to the Government many thousands of dollars annually. When I became Secretary
of War, I found all the accounts were sent up to the treasury without
passing through the War Department at all. I found there were
great abuses. An act was passed, drawn up by myself, in which I
inserted the provision, that all accounts should pass through the several bureaus, and if all was found to be right after examination, they
should be endorsed by the heads of the bureaus, before presentation
at the treasury for payment. What was the effect of this? I found
the Medical department costing the Government a hundred thousand
dollars a year. I brought this expenditure down to twenty-five thousand dollars. Other expenditures were subjected to the same process.
The clothing accounts were reduced two-thirds; the quartermasters'
accounts one-half. The expenditures of the department were brought
down from four millions to two millions one hundred thousand.

From the heads of bureaus the accounts were sent to the Auditor,
an officer whose name indicates his duty, and then to the Comptroller, the highest officer of the treasury, before they were finally paid.
And you give to these gentlemen the same power that is confided to
all those officers. Can this be right? None of these officers have
equitable jurisdiction, yet these gentlemen are clothed by this bill
with unlimited powers. All this may be very safe in the present case.
That is not the question I make at all; but is it safe as a precedent?
I put it solemnly to gentlemen opposite.

Mr. [Thomas J.] Rusk [of Texas]. I simply wish to ask this question: If this expedition had been under the authority of the United

States, and Colonel Fremont had been commanding on detached service, would it not have been competent for him to have made the requisitions, and for the quartermaster to have supplied them on the spot, and for the paymaster to have paid the amount there, without going through these forms which the honorable Senator from South Carolina has been describing?

Mr. Calhoun. No question at all about that; but each officer would have acted, in that case, upon his individual responsibility.

Now, I put this important question: If you appoint this board of officers, where is the responsibility? What duty is to be performed by the officer who is to pay the claims allowed by this board? No other than that which the Secretary of the Treasury would have to do in regard to accounts which had regularly passed through all the forms of examination. The certificate of the board is his warrant for paying the money, and he is relieved from all responsibility. We have had precedent after precedent quoted which are not at all analogous. A very brief view will enable us to determine as to whether the duties assigned to these men are official duties or not; whether their functions are those of officers or not. Certainly they are official duties of the highest character. Is the Commissary General not an officer? They perform his duty, or ought to do it. Is the Auditor not an officer? They must perform all his duties, or ought to do it. Is the Comptroller of the Treasury not an officer? They are to perform all his duties, or ought to do it. And yet, performing all these duties, it is solemnly argued here, day after day, that they are not to discharge official duties—that they are not officers. If they are not, in the name of Heaven, what are they? Extend this case. It is not only in California that military operations have been carried on; we have had some in New Mexico, and some further south under General [Zachary] Taylor; others, on a larger scale, under General [Winfield] Scott. Are you willing to adopt the same process in these cases? Who would dream of such a thing? Who would be bold enough to come here, and propose that General Scott and his paymaster and his commissary should constitute a board to adjust all the accounts, and draw and pay away the money? Who would say that this would be a safe depository of power? Who would say, if they were authorized thus to act, that they would not be officers, to all intents and purposes, such as I have described? Can any man doubt it? There may be greater reason for deviating from the ordinary process in settling these claims, but the cases are in every respect analogous; and there are a thousand cases where the difficulty would be as great as in California. Why, the whole country would be startled, amazed, at the adoption of such a course of proceedings as this.

[*Debate continued. Lewis Cass of Mich. contended that the opponents of the bill would deprive the claimants of justice by requiring them to come to Washington for recovery.*]

Mr. Calhoun. No one supposes that these claimants are to come here to recover their claims. The question is, first, by whom will you allow them to be investigated and paid? by persons appointed by yourselves, and wholly irresponsible, or by persons appointed in conformity with the requisitions of the Constitution? The next question is, will you have them settled by the very men who incurred the expenses? There being a necessity for knowledge in regard to the claims, I should think it very desirable to appoint some officer who served in California to be a member of the board. My opinion is, that the true way is to send a quartermaster and commissary there, and, if necessary, to add a third person. Take any officer. I have no objection that it should be Colonel Fremont. He gave the orders, and very properly, I have no doubt; those orders must be presented to the commissary, and be fortified by his endorsement.

From *Congressional Globe*, 30th Cong., 1st Sess., pp. 704–707. Also printed in the Washington, D.C., *Daily National Intelligencer*, September 6, 1848, p. 1 (part); the Washington, D.C., *Daily Union*, September 9, 1848, p. 1 (part); Houston, ed., *Proceedings and Debates*, pp. 552–555.

REMARKS ON THE OCCUPATION OF YUCATAN

[In the Senate, April 29, 1848]

[*The Senate and House of Representatives received a message from the President (James K. Polk) drawing their attention to a war of extermination against the white race being carried out by the Indians in Yucatan. According to the President "our own security" requires that Congress take action "to prevent Yucatan from becoming a colony of any European power . . . and at the same time to rescue the white race from extermination or expulsion from the country." A motion was made to refer the message to the Committee on Foreign Relations.*]

Mr. Calhoun. Before that question is put, I rise to express my regret that the President should place this recommendation on any other ground than that of humanity. If I heard the message aright, he asserts the principle as deduced from Mr. [James] Monroe's declaration, that when the people of any portion of this continent is placed in the condition in which Yucatan is, and either party should be compelled to apply to us for protection, we should interpose and protect them, to prevent the interference of England, or some other foreign Power. A broad and dangerous principle, truly! It goes far beyond Mr. Monroe's declaration. It is difficult to say what limits can be fixed to it, or to what it would carry us, if reduced to practice. I take this early opportunity—for experience has brought me to strike at once on the introduction of an objectionable measure—to express my surprise and regret, that the President should seize such an occasion as this to recommend the occupation of Yucatan by our army, or a portion of it, if it could be spared, from Mexico. It is startling. Who can tell to what it will lead, and where it will end? How strange to recommend it at such a time, on the ground, if we did not occupy it, some other Power might! In the present condition of Europe, there is no more probability that England, or any other Power there, would seize on Yucatan, than that I, as an individual, would. Who can suppose, engrossed as she is, and all other Powers in that quarter of the globe are, with questions connected with their existence, that they could, for a moment, entertain an idea of the kind? England has enough to attend to at home. Who can tell what may be her condition? The supposition of the possibility of such a step on her part, seems to me strange and unaccountable. I did hope that the experience of the Mexican war—that precipitate and rash measure which has cost the country so dearly in blood and treasure—would have taught the Administration moderation and caution, and induced them to shun any course of policy calculated to plunge the country in a similar cost and sacrifice. Who can form an estimate of the expenditure, the sacrifice of life, and the difficulties to which the adoption of the President's recommendation in this case would lead? The condition of Europe ought to admonish us against taking it.

What are the causes which have lead to its present upheaving, and the reeling to and fro of all her governments? What are those which are assigned for the overthrow of the French monarchy, and the danger that threatens the British with the same fate? Among the prominent is the heavy burden imposed on the people, which has crushed them to the earth, and which has been continually increasing. It is charged that the onerous burden imposed on the people of France by the mighty wars of Napoleon, instead of being diminished, were actually increased, under the government of its late monarch [Louis Philippe], and that those imposed on the people of

England to resist his gigantic power, are as great as they were at the end of the mighty contest between the two Powers, allowance being made for the depreciation of the currency. Are we not fairly liable to the same charge? Has there been any alleviation of the burden imposed on our people by the payment of the debts of the Revolution, or the war of 1812? Are our expenses less than they were in the war of 1812, allowing for the depreciation of the currency during that conflict? Those who have not attended to the subject would be surprised, on comparing the expenses of the Government now with what it was during Mr. [James] Monroe's administration. It terminated in 1825, twenty-three years ago. The average expenditure of the administration did not exceed $10,000,000 annually, deducting the payment of the principal and interest of the public debt. It is difficult to say what it is now; it will probably be not less than $30,000,000. It is true, our population has increased, but it has probably not more than doubled, while our expenses have increased three-fold. And yet, heedless of consequences, it is proposed to adopt a course of policy before we have extricated ourselves from the burden and losses of the Mexican war, which may lead to expenses and sacrifices of which no one can form even a conjecture. I am willing, on the score of humanity, to go as far as we can with safety and propriety in this case. How far that is, I am not prepared to say; but I cannot possibly support the course of policy recommended by the President, as I understand the message. I am not certain as to what he intends; but be it such as I suppose or not, I cannot but regret that he should mix up what ought to be an appeal purely to our humanity, with the considerations he has. The case of Yucatan is indeed an awful one. In the midst of our sympathy we may derive instructions from it. The people of Yucatan, after they threw off the Spanish yoke, acting on the idea that all men are qualified to enjoy the blessing of liberty, and ought of right to possess it, liberated the large mass of their population, consisting of aborigines in a state of ignorance and subjection, and raised them to a level with themselves, by making them citizens. The result is such as we this day witness. They were too ignorant to appreciate liberty, or exercise the rights it conferred; and instead of gratitude, they have turned round and murdered those who conferred it on them, and laid waste and devastated the country. Such are the fruits of a misguided, misjudging philanthropy, combined with erroneous political notions, which is so prevalent at the present time, in more enlightened and civilized countries, but which, whenever reduced to practice, must lead to disastrous consequences.

From *Congressional Globe*, 30th Cong., 1st Sess., Appendix, pp. 590–591. Also printed in *Congressional Globe*, 30th Cong., 1st Sess., pp. 712–713; Houston, ed., *Proceedings and Debates*, p. 557; Benton, ed., *Abridgment of Debates*, 16:189–190. Variants in the Washington, D.C., *Daily Union*, April 30, 1848, p. 3; the Washington, D.C., *Daily National Intelligencer*, May 1, 1848, p. 1; the Alexandria, Va., *Gazette and Virginia Advertiser*, May 1, 1848, p. 3; the New York, N.Y., *Herald*, May 1, 1848, p. 3; the New York, N.Y., *Morning Courier and New-York Enquirer*, May 1, 1848 (Supplement), p. 1; the Philadelphia, Pa., *Public Ledger*, May 1, 1848, p. 3; the Charleston, S.C., *Courier*, May 3, 1848, p. 2.

From H[ENRY] W. CONNER

Charleston, April 30 1848

Your favour of the 20th was duly rec[eive]d & every opportunity has been taken to give the letter & its views an extensive circulation & I am happy to report that our friends here without exception as far as I know will conform themselves to your wishes by attempting no movement towards a convention. The disturbances in Europe & their distressing effect upon this section of country together with the late abolition movements at Washington will come much in aid to prevent any action of the people in other sections of the State I think just now in reference to the Baltimore convention. Your intention to confer with the Alabama & other delegates on their way to the Convention & the readiness of the So. Ca. delegation to repair to Baltimore if need be to cooperate in any combined movement of the South, has quieted every body here, & for the reason that it contemplates action & concert with the other slave States when necessary. This feeling is much stronger than the delegation at Washington are aware of ["at" *canceled*] & it will have to be watched & controuled in time or it may seek a wrong direction.

The Mercury will tomorrow & next day publish the debates upon the late ["slave" *canceled*] abolition movement at Washington & I think we will have an extra struck off & distribute a couple of thousand of them ["distributed" *canceled*] throughout the Southern States, addressing them to persons of influence—a large list of whom we obtained last summer during our movement against the Wilmot proviso & still have in hand.

The Georgetown resolutions appointing a delegate to the convention [James M. Commander] has barely been noticed by our papers & without comment. A meeting was spoken of at Walterboro but I have seen nothing of it. Our papers will remain on the defensive & say nothing if it can be avoided. Very Truly y[ou]rs &C, H.W. Conner.

ALS in ScCleA.

From JAMES WIRICK

Paw Paw Grove[,] Lee County Illinois [*ca.* May 1848] Sir, This present is one of the most important periods in the history of our government. Great and vital questions agitate the mind of the American People. These questions are soon to be settled. The manner in which they are to be settled is of the greatest importance as they will have a great influence upon the future happiness and prosperity of ["the" *interlined*] Union as well as the stabillity of Our Republican institutions. It is but little more that [*sic*] six months before we shall be called upon to cast our suffrage for a chief Magistrate and members of Congress. Under such sircumstances it becomes a matter of importance that a sutible man and one very very Quallified is selected as a Presidential Candidate in order to insure success. So unsettled are all Parties in this matter that the most sagacious Polititions do not venture to predict who the candidate will be with any degree of Certainty. Shall it be [Lewis] Cass[,] [James] Buchanon[,] [George M.] Dallas[,] [John A.] Dix[,] [Levi] Woodberry[,] [Thomas H.] Benton[,] [John C.] Calhoun or Gen. [William O.] Butler. It is inpocible to predict. One thing is certain if the two third[s] rule is dispenced with the Northern Democracy will hoist the name of a Willmot Proviso man. I am not prepared for such a cricis nor for the affect which it would have upon the harmony and stabillity of Our Federal Union, in fact you of the South must meet it at once or not at all, for it will certainly be upon you now, and will Conquer you if you don['']t Conquer it. The Presidential election of 1848 is the crisis. I see great danger in this new move and feel the necesity of meeting it promply. If the Abolition or Willmot Proviso party carry there points in the Baltimore Convention I shall consider the danger consumated and all Sothern interest sacrifised to Northern Abolition Fanaticism. Sir if you will have the goodness to transmit a communication with your Opinion of the Chances ["of Success," *interlined*] of the two Opposing parties of the North and South I will Ever Be Your most Obsequious Your Friend and fellow Citizen, James Wirick.

375

ALS in ScCleA. NOTE: This undated letter has been assigned an approximate date from internal evidence.

From AUGUSTUS MITCHELL

Portland [Maine,] May 3d 1848

My dear Sir, I have taken the liberty to enclose a few questions regarding the Ethiopian species. Some of them I have commented on at large. I dictated them myself—and then debated with the same honorable person—very much after the manner of Old Maj. Storm, on military tactics—when confined in a French prison. We are still here amidst ice-bergs, both locomotive, and floating. I am advocating with untiring vigilance the establishment of a *Sanitary retreat in East Florida for our invalids.* In this matter we ["are" interlined] strictly united with my esteemed Southern friends especially those of Charleston S.C. I think by dint of perseverance I shall succeed in this good work. I beg of you to do all you can for me in this enterprise. I am in want of friends. There are some in Congress who belong in this place—that could do a great deal for me, but I never had any friendship from these people here, how can I expect it? I anticipate with delight—my entire removal from here—and permanent residence in the South ["*if I can*" interlined]. My health has not been good since I last wrote you. Excuse all. With great esteem I am dear Sir your obed[ien]t Serv[an]t, Augustus Mitchell.

[Enclosure]

Portland Me., May 3d 1848

1st. Remote or ancient historical knowledge of the Ethiopian species.

2d. Peculiarity, and general character of that species originally as natives of Torrid Africa.

3d. The moral and physical developement of this species.

4th. Their comparative relations to the higher species of mankind.

5th. Have they had inherent powers of the mind naturally developed, which would have relieved them from that thraldom of ignorance, superstition, and indolence; which is, the predominant character of this unfortunate species of mankind.

6th. Are they capable of governing themselves, forming a social compact order of society, establishing a basis of government under their own chiefs, by which they may be regenerated without the aid of the whites.

7th. What are their phrenological developements, and can we safely

376

admit the doctrine of [Johann Gaspar] Spurzheim in supposing they can be placed on par of intellectual knowledge with the Caucasian species—should they be skilfully educated until the fifth generation.

8th. What are the principal evils which originate from the enslavement of the negro.

9th. How are we to remedy those evils in such a manner as the negro will be benefited by a removal from his native land under the jurisdiction of the whites.

10th. Does not comparative relations represent them as a distinct species of mankind.

11th. Why are there developed such a material difference in the Anatomical structure, conformation, and intellectual capacity of this species—as we observe in the Southern States of our Union.

12th. Are there not sufficient causes, to suppose, they were designed by our Creator, as servants to the superior order of mankind.

13th. What are the duties of the master towards the servant—and what are the proper duties of the servant towards the master.

14th. Would it be correct, judicious or safe for the our [*sic*] Southern brethren to attempt at the present day, a dissemination of education among their servants.

15th. Can they be educated by any possible means to bear the great change of freedom, which would render them safe and peaceable neighbors.

16th. What caused Great Britain to manumit her slaves in the West India Islands, and what was her policy in so doing.

17th. Will the late manumission of the negro, by the French, have a tendency to elevate their moral and intellectual character; preventing the deterioration and decay of their species.

18th. Has the want of physical education, and intellectual debasement of this species originated from passing too suddenly from under the control of their masters to one of unrestrained liberty.

19th. Has not the fate of ["this" *interlined*] peculiar species of mankind, been shrouded in darkness—by the mysterious designs of our Great Creator.

20th. Are not the pestilential shores of Africa, a designed hindrance to the introduction of light among them by the civilized world.

21st. Does not the numerous languages, and still more numerous dialects, spoken ["by" *interlined*] the various tribes, present an almost insuperable barrier against the dissemination of education, and the introduction of the Christian religion.

22d. Have they improved their condition beyond the rude-hut, and simple canoe, since the early dawn of literature by the Arabians, although in contact with civilized ["nations" *interlined*] for thousands of years.

23d. Can we successfully wage war against the eternal laws of nature.

24th. Is it not more correct to suppose that when the Omnipotent power of our Great Creator designs their liberation from stupidity and ignorance it will be done—and not until then. Augustus Mitchell M.D.

ALS with En in ScCleA. NOTE: An EU reads, "Aug. Mitchell[,] queries relating to Ethiopian race."

REMARKS ON THE ILLINOIS LAND GRANT BILL

[In the Senate, May 3, 1848]

[*Under consideration was Stephen A. Douglas's bill donating lands to the State of Illinois "for making a railroad" connecting Chicago and the Mississippi River.*]

Mr. Calhoun. The question in this case is a very simple one. We are authorized by the Constitution to dispose of the public lands. Here is a public improvement, projected either by the State or by individuals in the State through which it will pass, and by which the value of the public lands will be enhanced. If then, it will add to the value of our lands, ought we not to contribute to it? Would we not, as individuals, thus act? This is not a novel principle. It has been acted upon for more than twenty years. The case of the canal connecting the Illinois river with Lake Michigan is a striking one. There, alternate sections were given to make a canal, and I suppose I can appeal with confidence to the Senators from that State, whether the lands reserved to the United States were not disposed of afterwards readily?

Mr. [Sidney] Breese [of Ill.], (in his seat.) Thousands of acres were disposed of which would otherwise never have been sold.

Mr. Calhoun. I have seldom given a vote the result of which gratified me more, than the vote which I gave on that occasion. I then presided in that chair which you now occupy, and gave the casting vote. I take to myself, therefore, some share in the credit of that magnificent improvement. Indeed, I do not think that there is a principle more perfectly clear from doubt than this one is. It does not belong to the category of internal improvements at all. It is not a power claimed by the government as a government. It belongs to the government as a landed proprietor. And I will add, that it is not only a right but a duty, and an important duty. Now, what has been considered an equitable arrangement between the government and the State which may undertake an improvement passing through the public lands? Long since, it was agreed that the grant of ultimate [*sic*; alternate] sections was a fair contribution on the part of the United States considered as a proprietor; and from which the United States would be a very great gainer. It appears to me to be an equitable arrangement, and I doubt whether, in any case, either of a canal or a railroad passing through the public lands, the United States will not be a gainer. To that extent I am prepared to go, be the road long or short; if it be long, you gain the more; if it be short, you gain the less; and you contribute in proportion to your gain.

But while I approve of this principle, it seems to me upon a hasty examination of the bill, that it goes beyond the principle; and to that extent I cannot approve of it, for I put my views in this and in all similar cases upon principle, and not upon the ground of internal improvement at all, nor the power of the government to engage in such works. I observe that the bill provides that the State may locate the lands elsewhere in cases where lands adjacent to the line of the proposed road have been heretofore sold or otherwise disposed of. Now, it appears to me that that is going beyond the power of a proprietor. I think that the principle had better be adhered to strictly. I do not think six miles too great a breadth; but it appears to me to be ample—to be a very fair contribution on the part of the United States. There is also another difficulty which may be removed. I see that a period of fifteen years is allowed for the completion of the road. This is a very long period; but I do not object so much to it as to the absence of any restriction which will prohibit the State of Illinois from selling it out in the meantime. It is true the bill provides that if the road be not finished in fifteen years, the State shall refund the amount. Now, I object to the reestablishment of the relation of debtor and creditor, between the general government and the State; therefore, there ought to be a provision, that the sales should be proportioned, I do not say exactly proportioned—to the progress of the work. That can be easily managed. If the Senator who has charge of the bill, will upon due reflection accord to these suggestions, I shall most cheerfully vote for the bill, otherwise, I shall find great difficulty in doing so.

[*Douglas hoped the bill would pass as it stands. "We do not propose to sell the lands till the work be completed, when of course their value will be greatly enhanced."*]

Mr. Calhoun. Of course I do not wish to embarrass the bill. Let me suggest to the honorable Senator from Illinois, that if confidence be created in the successful completion of the work within a reasonable time, the attention of capitalists will be invited, and money may be borrowed on the lands.

[*Douglas remarked that a "work undertaken by Alabama failed in consequence of its being left to capitalists." Debate continued among several Senators. Arthur P. Bagby of Ala., after making reference to "inland seas" and ambitions for higher office on the part of some Senators, asked for assurance that the project would bring up the price of the remaining lands from the minimum to at least $2.50 an acre.*]

Mr. Calhoun. If the effect of the construction of the road be only to bring the lands more readily into market so as to sell for one dollar and twenty-five cents, it is, in point of fact, an increase of value. But, I believe that the remaining sections, after alternate sections have been sold, will sell more readily for two dollars and fifty cents an acre than for one dollar and twenty-five cents at present. It is for this reason that I am in favor of the measure. And yet the gentleman can see nothing in all this but impure motives, disguises of expression, as if every one who differed from him must be actuated by sinister and improper views. Sir, I wish to do justice to every one. No doubt the gentleman is influenced by honest views; and he has no right to doubt the honesty of mine. We are told that our system of improvement applied to inland seas is going to absorb all the means of the general government. This is a subject to which I have given some attention, and I lay it down as my deliberate opinion that two hundred thousand dollars annually supplied for the Mississippi and its great navigable branches will keep them in the most complete navigable order; whilst the losses which occur annually in the present condition of these rivers cannot be less than two millions of dollars. And yet gentlemen are willing that they should remain in their present condition. As far as the valley of the Mississippi is concerned, I will say that that portion of the country has received a smaller portion of the public money than any other section of the country. It will require a larger sum annually to keep up the light-house system on the coast, with the buoys and beacons, than it would to keep the Mississippi and its branches in a proper navigable condition. These are great inland seas. I hold it to be perfectly clear that Congress has a right under the constitution, to dispose of the public lands to the best advantage. And I shall cheerfully give my vote for any measure, by which they may be so disposed of as that the greatest pecuniary benefit will accrue to the treasury.

[*Several more Senators spoke, including Bagby, who referred again to "Presidential candidates" and "felicitous interpretations of the constitution."*]

Mr. Calhoun. The Senator will permit me to say that I did not make the remark in any such connection.

[*There was further exchange between Bagby and another Senator.*]

Mr. Calhoun. The Senator from Alabama, when speaking of the enhanced price of land, certainly alluded, though without intending any direct application probably, to disguised motives.

[*The bill passed its third reading by 24–11, both Calhoun and Bagby voting in the negative.*]

From Houston, ed., *Proceedings and Debates*, pp. 567–570. Partly printed in the Washington, D.C., *Daily Union*, May 6, 1848, p. 2; the Charleston, S.C., *Mercury*, May 10, 1848, p. 2; *Congressional Globe*, 30th Cong., 1st Sess., Appendix, p. 537. Variants in the Petersburg, Va., *Republican*, May 3, 1848, p. 2; the New York, N.Y., *Herald*, May 5, 1848, p. 4.

From W[ILLIAM] F. VAN AMRINGE

Montgomery[,] Orange Co[unty,] N.Y., May 3, 1848

Dear Sir, I am much afraid that you will think me troublesome by so often forcing my letters upon you; but think you will excuse me from a Knowledge of the fact that American authors, particularly on scientific subjects, are compelled to depend chiefly on distinguished names to introduce them to the public, as they can seldom hope for much, if any, assistance from publishers, whose interest is decidedly adverse to them. I have already some highly flattering & valuable letters, but shall think my list incomplete without the addition of your name, if you can, consistently with propriety, give it to me.

I very much regret the delay which occurred in delivering your copy, which most certainly would not have happened if my health had permitted me to attend to the business; but a person who, from any circumstances, is compelled to do business through others, is often subjected to inconveniences, if not to loss & mortification[.]

In the hope you will find the volume not unworthy of your patronage, I am, with great respect, Y[ou]r Mo[st] Ob[edien]t S[er]v[an]t, W.F. Van Amringe.

ALS in ScCleA. NOTE: This letter is addressed to "Hon[ora]ble J.C. Calhoun LLD." Van Amringe's book is described in his letter to Calhoun of 1/10/1848.

From O[ZEY] R. BROYLES

[Pendleton, S.C.,] 4th May 1848
My dear Sir, I have just recieved [*sic*] yours of the 25th April, communicating your acceptance of the loan, and your willingness to receive the sums as collected, giving promissary notes for each, to be consolidated by bond and mortgage [to the estate of Chester Kingsley] as soon as the whole is paid over &. This is in all respects acceptable and satisfactory, and believing we now have a clear and well defined understanding on all points of interest in the premises, I shall endeavour to consummate the arrangement with as much dispatch as possible. Very truly yours &, O.R. Broyles.

ALS in ScU-SC, John C. Calhoun Papers.

RESOLUTION REGARDING YUCATAN

[In the Senate, May 4, 1848]
Resolved, that the ["question" *canceled*] President ["of the U.S." *interlined*] be requested to communicate to the Senate all the correspondence between the Secretary of State [James Buchanan] & Don Justa Sierra the Representative of the Government of Yucatan, if not inconsistent with the public interest.

ADU in DNA, RG 46 (U.S. Senate), 30A-B6; PC in *Congressional Globe,* 30th Cong., 1st Sess., p. 727; PC in the Washington, D.C., *Daily National Intelligencer,* May 5, 1848, p. 1. NOTE: The resolution was agreed to. Calhoun was doubtless anticipating what happened a little later in the day's proceedings—the Committee on Foreign Relations reported out a bill to authorize the President "to take temporary military occupation of Yucatan."

REMARKS ON THE OCCUPATION
OF YUCATAN

[In the Senate, May 4, 1848]

[Edward A. Hannegan of Ind., for the Committee on Foreign Relations, guided the bill authorizing the President to occupy Yucatan through its second reading, and proposed that final consideration be taken the next day.]

Mr. Calhoun. I am in favor of deferring the consideration of the subject for a few days. The bill was only laid upon the table yesterday.

[George E. Badger of N.C. supported Calhoun.]

Mr. Calhoun. It seems to me there is a necessity for additional information. I hope the Senator will name another day.

[Hannegan contended that all information was available to the Senate and the case required quick action.]

Mr. Calhoun. It may be, and I presume it is the case, that this is a great exigency; but I do hope that this Senate is not to be forced, on every occasion, to act upon an emergency. From looking over the correspondence, very hastily, I perceive that even before the 7th of March last, the Administration was fully apprised of the state of affairs in Yucatan. They have taken their time to deliberate, and surely a few days may be allowed to the Senate. I have no disposition to occasion any unnecessary delay whatever. I am willing that Monday next [May 8] should be the day fixed for the consideration of the subject.

[Discussion continued among several Senators. Henry S. Foote of Miss. referred to "the attempt . . . to procrastinate our action."]

Mr. Calhoun. Does the Senator mean to charge me with a design to delay the action of the body?

[Foote delivered a long discourse to the effect that Calhoun always sought to delay proposals of the present administration.]

Mr. Calhoun. I did not know that the message had been printed and laid upon our desks till this morning. I have cast my eyes over it, however, and I see enough in it to induce, on the part of the Senate, the greatest degree of caution. If the peace and welfare of this country are of any value, the recommendations presented in this message call for the most deliberate and cautious consideration. There is, indeed, a great deal upon the score of humanity to excite our attention to this subject. I believe there is a wretched state of things in Yucatan; whether we can relieve it or not, is another question. The Executive has not been in any hurry in this business. If the Senator from Mississippi will look to the document which has been laid upon our desks, he will find that the letter from Mr. [Justa] Sierra of the 7th March complains that he had written previous notes to the Secretary of State [James Buchanan], to which he had received no answer; and these notes gave an account of the atrocities perpetrated in Yucatan, as forcibly and fully as any subsequent communication. Now, if the Executive took from the 7th of March till this day to consider the matter, surely we are entitled to one or two days in which to consider so grave a subject as this—for it will turn out to be one of the gravest subjects, full of complication and difficulty.

Now, I am not to be intimidated. I know how to discharge my duty here, whether alone or in company. My duty I know, and I cannot be driven from it. We were once urged into a war precipitately and hurriedly, for which we have paid dearly. I trust we shall not be driven into another war, and perhaps a more complicated one, in the same rash and precipitate manner. I desire delay, because it appears to me to be necessary, in order that we may obtain all the information. Many notes which have passed between Mr. Sierra and the Secretary of State have not been published, if we may credit that gentleman's statement. There is no communication here from the Commodore on that station, who could give us a great deal of information, no doubt, as regards both the origin and the character of the war, which should be known to us before we act. In my opinion, the document before us is very imperfect, and one day's delay is necessary before we make our decision.

[*Foote disavowed any attempt to "intimidate" anyone of such known fearlessness as Calhoun.*]

Mr. Calhoun. If the honorable Senator will give way for a moment, I will state, by way of explanation, that I expressed my regret that the President should mix up a question of pure humanity with high political considerations, connected with the general policy of the country.

[*According to Foote, in a lengthy and circumstantial discourse, Calhoun had complained about the Mexican War, and yet all its expense and suffering were "justly chargeable upon him more than upon any man in this nation." Calhoun had fathered internal improvements and the Mexican War and then turned against them and left others to defend.*]

Mr. Calhoun. I certainly had no expectation, when I asked further delay of a few days in relation to this subject, that it would give rise to so long a debate. I am sure the Senate will not expect me to undertake to repel the various charges of the Senator from Mississippi, old as well as new. I rise to make only a very few remarks upon a general subject, with which these charges have been connected. In the first place, I have given this Administration as full and complete support, upon all occasions, as my conscience would permit. There has not been a single measure of theirs, to which I could give my support, to which that support has not been given. I yielded to the Administration upon the question of the tariff, though the modification of it did not entirely suit me. I yielded upon the treaty, upon all the measures of preparation. I have dealt with this Administration as I have dealt with all Administrations from the time I first entered Congress. I have given no Administration, whether friendly or unfriendly to it, my support upon any measure that I thought to be wrong; and I have supported all measures that I thought right. I have acted irrespective of party upon all occasions. I think it proper, also, to make a few remarks relative to the annexation of Texas. I repel no charges against me for being the author of annexation. It is an act of which I never can repent. It was an act of necessity, indispensable at the time, and will be so considered hereafter. But we all took ground, Mr. Polk and the whole of us, that it was not a measure necessarily involving war; that we had recognized Texas; that we had a right to annex her; and that annexation was no just cause of war on the part of Mexico. We introduced the measure upon that ground, and in my opinion successfully. If anything has brought discredit upon that measure, it is this war with Mexico; and as far as I am concerned, or my reputation is concerned, I have a right to complain. I deny that the war was a necessary result of annexation.

[*Foote somewhat indirectly reiterated his contention that annexation led to the war.*]

Mr. Calhoun. The Senator must permit me to act upon my judgment: whether I owe a debt of gratitude to Mr. Polk or not; whether I am bound to support this war because the author of it, must be decided according to that judgment. I deny that the war necessarily grew out of annexation. On the contrary, I speak with the full knowledge of the circumstances connected with the subject, when I say, that in my opinion, the war could have been avoided by using ordinary discretion. I go further. In my opinion, it required a great deal of mismanagement to make the war. I was about to say, it required something like ingenuity, but that would be improper. I no [*sic*] not believe that the Administration intended war; it would be a serious charge to say they intended war. It would be an impeachable offense to say they intended war when they ordered General [Zachary] Taylor to the Rio Grande. But I ever believed that the movement could not be made without producing war. Can any man doubt it? They were told it would produce war. Amongst those with whom I conversed on this subject, there was very little difference of opinion; and that was known to be my opinion from the first. With the view of preventing war, I stated that opinion to the President. The gentleman entirely mistakes my course with regard to the Administration in speaking, not as an organ, but as one ardently attached to it, when he charges me with being its enemy, and as having come here to assail it. I took my seat here with great reluctance; and was rather compelled to come than otherwise; but believing I might be able to do something to avert a war with respect to Oregon, I came, with the most earnest desire to coöperate with the President; and no man knows it better than he does. I held frequent conversations with him in the kindest manner, and never spoke an unkind word with regard to the Administration, except when assailed in this body. So far from being the assailant, I appeal to the older Senators here, who have been much longer members in this body than the Senator from Mississippi, if I ever spoke an unkind word, except when compelled to do it. I believe the first instance in which I became the assailant was when this message was sent in, and then because I believed there is greater depth and danger in it than appears on the surface. It has upon the face of it the bearing of a question of humanity, but there is a complexion about it leading to consequences of which it is hard to foretell the termination. These, however, are topics which ought to be left for the discussion; and I regret exceedingly that the Senator from Mississippi has compelled me to say so much. I would be ashamed of myself, if I could permit myself in any case to be governed in my course, by enmity or friendship, for any Administration. I never have been so governed, and never shall. I look to the public interests in the discharge of my duty, and if I be mistaken, it is because I am honestly mistaken.

[*John P. Hale of N.H. entered the debate, declaring that the war had been caused by annexation and annexation had been for the extending of slavery. There was a long debate between Hale and Foote. Other Senators spoke. Lewis Cass of Mich. insisted that the bill be taken up tomorrow and attributed to Calhoun the argument for delay "that the Administration was apprised of the facts on the 7th of March."*]

Mr. Calhoun, (in his seat). Before that time.

[*Cass continued and said he had heard with regret Calhoun refer to "this wretched war."*]

Mr. Calhoun, (in his seat.) Rash and precipitate.

Mr. Cass. I am happy to hear the explanation. My impression was that the Senator had used the term "wretched."

Mr. Calhoun. I do not undertake to correct always. All who were here at the time will recollect what took place on the day previous to the declaration of war. The President's message was communicated to us, and on motion of the Senator from Missouri, (Mr. [Thomas H.] Benton,) that portion of it relating to the raising of an additional military force was referred to the Committee on Military Affairs, and the other portions of it to the Committee on Foreign Relations. My view in voting in favor of the motion was, that we might grant the military force at once to meet any emergency, and take time upon the declaration of war. But the two were united, and the very next day the whole was voted at a single dash. I was anxious for deliberation, because I did not believe that we should make a formal declaration of war at that period. My opinion was, that we should raise a provisional force, without adopting formal war measures, and then await the action of Mexico.

[*Cass declared that Calhoun's statement of his position at the time of the declaration was perfectly correct. However, Calhoun should now know that he had been in error and that the war had been inaugurated by the Mexicans.*]

Mr. Calhoun. It is very painful to me to be thus called upon so often in this irregular debate. I chose to say that this was a "rash and precipitate war," and gentlemen think it necessary to enter into a formal argument to show that it was not! Would it not have been enough if they had said that they thought differently? But there is always, it seems to me, a lurking suspicion in the minds of the gentlemen that their cause is not a good one; for I have never known a case in which there has been so much effort at all times to prove that the war was just and necessary. These frequent explanations, this argument at all times to prove the justice of this war, do not indicate a well-settled state of mind. I am at issue with the Senator from Michigan as to the fact that the Mexican Government authorized the war. [Mariano] Arista may have authorized it; [Mariano] Paredes may have authorized it. But that is not the question. It was the Congress alone that could have authorized the war. But the Congress was not in session, and therefore could not have made the war. The same mistake is made on our own side. The gentleman says that we had a right to order General Taylor to repel the attack. If he means that the Congress of the United States had the right to do so, I agree with him. Now, I put the argument to the Senator, and let him answer it if he can.

Mr. Cass, (in his seat.) I shall.

Mr. Calhoun. I am about to put the argument. The resolution of annexation admitted that there was a disputed boundary, because it expressly provided that it should be settled by the United States. Now, the utmost claim that Texas ever made was to the Rio Grande. I do not say that the Rio Grande was the boundary. That is another question. But Texas admitted that it was disputed. If there was any disputed territory, it must have been east of the Rio Grande. Now, I beg the attention of the gentleman to this question, to which I ask a specific answer. How are disputed boundaries to be settled? Is it not in one of two modes—by treaty or by war? If by treaty, the settlement is made by the President and Senate; if by war, the war power is exclusively with Congress. After the treaty power had exhausted itself, as the Senator and all have assumed, is it not perfectly clear that the settlement of the disputed boundary could be made only by the Congress of the United States? We had a right to order General Taylor to the Del Norte to repel invasion. It was not the President who had the right to issue that order, but Congress, who ought to have been called upon to do it. The same error, then, was made on both sides. It was only Congress who could make war on either side. The authority of Paredes, and the authority of the President of the United States, were no more than blank paper; therefore, the war was illegally and unconstitutionally made. I do not choose to argue this question, unless when assailed, and my views called in question. The gentleman says that annexation was a just cause of war.

[*Cass stated that he had said that annexation was the cause of Mexico going to war, but he had not said that it was a just cause.*]

Mr. Calhoun. The Senator said that Mexico threatened war, and went to war. Who does not know that she fumed and fretted; but was that any reason why we should take a high stand, and force a resort to arms? Not at all. Paredes showed a strong desire to terminate the controversy without war. It was he or his minister who made a proposition to Mr. [John] Black, looking to an accommodation of the difficulties between the two countries. True, it came to nothing; but it evinced the disposition of the Mexican authorities to settle the controversy without war. [José Joaquin] Herrera was turned out; but there were circumstances connected with his removal, aside from the proposition which he had made with this country. I have been informed, on good authority, that the gentleman afterwards appointed as secretary of legation [William S. Parrott?] was in Mexico at the time that this communication was made

388

by the Secretary of State to Mr. Black, our consul, late at night, at his own house, and under strong protestations of the absolute necessity of secrecy. I understand that the information was made public. Mr. Black is here; and if I am wrong, I can be corrected. But the fact has been stated, that the gentleman to whom I have referred, before he left Mexico, divulged it, and that the proposition that had been made thus came to the knowledge of the people of Mexico. These facts do not show that the Mexican authorities had a fixed and resolute desire to make war upon us. On the contrary, we are thus furnished with evidence that there was a desire to make peace; and I feel the deepest conviction that, having settled the Oregon question, the Mexican question would have settled itself, if General Taylor had not been ordered to the Rio Grande. I really regret that I have been obliged to take up the time of the Senate by these remarks in my own defence. I had not the slightest idea that any debate would have arisen. My sole object in asking for delay was to obtain an opportunity for examining the case.

[*Hannegan remarked that the Senate had lost sight of the question before it. However, he felt it necessary to repel charges he declared Calhoun had made that the administration had delayed communicating the Yucatan matter to Congress.*]

Mr. Calhoun. I only said, that the Administration did not regard the subject as one of so much urgency, inasmuch as they had full knowledge long ago of these calamitous occurrences in Yucatan. I by no means censured them for what they had done, but expressed the opinion, that as they had had an opportunity for deliberation, it was proper that the Senate should also have time to form their judgment.

Mr. Hannegan. The delay was occasioned in consequence of the endeavors of the Administration to collect information.

Mr. Calhoun. We have not a particle of that information.

[*Hannegan declared that the printed document had been presented to Senators on Monday (that is, May 1).*]

Mr. Calhoun, (in his seat.) I did not see the publication until to-day.

[*Several other Senators spoke. As time neared for a vote, Calhoun rose again.*]

Mr. Calhoun. One word in justification of the course which I shall pursue. It is important that we should have a knowledge as to the nature of this conflict in Yucatan. I have never seen the documents relating to the matter until this morning. I have had no information, except such as is contained in the public papers, and upon such information I never act. I desire to have the official information, for which the Executive department waited so long before they made up their minds to act in this matter, which calls so loudly upon their humanity. As soon as I get that information I shall be ready to act.

[*The Senate defeated motions to put the Yucatan bill on the calendar for May 6 and May 8 and agreed to Hannegan's motion to take it up tomorrow.*]

From *Congressional Globe,* 30th Cong., 1st Sess., Appendix, pp. 591–596. Also printed in Houston, ed., *Proceedings and Debates,* pp. 572–577. Variants in the Alexandria, Va., *Gazette and Virginia Advertiser,* May 5, 1848, p. 3; the Washington, D.C., *Daily National Intelligencer,* May 5, 1848, p. 1; the New York, N.Y., *Herald,* May 5, 1848, p. 2, and May 7, 1848, p. 4; the Philadelphia, Pa., *Public Ledger,* May 5, 1848, p. 3; the Charleston, S.C., *Mercury,* May 8, 1848, p. 2; the Charleston, S.C., *Courier,* May 8, 1848, p. 2, and May 9, 1848, p. 2; the Petersburg, Va., *Republican,* May 8, 1848, p. 2.

From FRANKLIN SMITH

Canton Mississippi, May 4th '48

Sir: Your letter, speech and the book which you sent me last winter arrived safely; as did more recently your overwhelming remarks on the powers of the president in disputed or conquered territory. If there had been wanting to any man's sagacity evidences that the republican ship was in danger of drifting away from the Constitutional tack upon which our fathers put her, they would be supplied by Col. [Jefferson] Davis' claim of right in the Executive to march the national forces on disputed territory—and General [Lewis] Cass' finishing blow that conquest ensuing the President can do any thing he pleases in the conquered territory not prohibited by the laws of nations! Col. Davis & Gen[era]l Cass! Not small men, but of the elite—the advance guard of intelligence and character in the country! I have not shewn your letter nor made known its contents to any one. I have still hoped that there would be a change in your determination and bright prospects as well as a sense of duty to demand such change. But if ["after" *interlined*] all the candidates for the Presidency shall have been presented and the issues upon which they are submitted made known, you should still consider it your duty not to be a candidate, I would be happy to have your views as to that person most fitting in your estimation to be voted for by a republican agreeing with you in sentiment. I abhor the blood stained tenet sought to be grafted on the republican creed of universal dominion and propagandism of our institutions by the bayonet—but I ["equally" *canceled*] abhor also Banks[,] tariffs and all the spawn of kindred quackeries.

Should you therefore—my first and only choise—decline to run, whom should I choose? Which would then be God and which Baal? Very respectfully your ob[edien]t S[ervan]t, Franklin Smith.

P.S. This correspondence is entirely of my seeking. Should therefore a compliance with my request conflict with your sense of propriety or duty or be deemed by you incompatible with good taste or your position, I hope you will regard this letter in either of those contingencies as simply an acknowledgment of the receipt of yours of Jan[ua]ry 25th and of the high honor which I am sensible that that letter conferred. F.S.

ALS in ScCleA. NOTE: An EU reads, "Judge F. Smith."

From R[ICHARD] HAWES

Paris Ky., May 5 1848

Dear Sir, I take the liberty founded on a most agreeable acquaintance formed in Washington, of addressing you on the subject of the Presidency. I have not the slightest intimation of your preference for any one of persons named for that office in the public prints, nor do know that ["you" *interlined*] will depart from the high & independent position you have occupied of testing every measure by its merits, irrespective of party. I have looked upon your conduct in Congress during this session with the highest gratification, and I assure you I with a sincerity free from all design, that I consider your bold & independent declaration of the soundest principles stated with great force & clearness have excited the highest admiration. I have differed most materially with you in some of your political opinions, yet I have been at all times so deeply embued with a sense of your sincerity & honesty, that I have ever wished to be of the same party with you, if it were possible.

I propose to state a few of my humble thoughts about the presidency, not with the ["wish" *canceled*] hope of any influence, or even wishing to draw a reply or disclosure, but to give my views of the matter, which I assure you are entertained to a very large extent in

Kentucky. ["By" *canceled*] It so chanced that I was made the president of the [Zachary] Taylor Convention of the 22 of February last, & that position has placed me in possession of a very accurate knowledge of the opinions of a large number of Whigs in this State.

I believe that Gen[era]l Taylor is an honest man, of excellent practical sense, of great decision & firmness of character, a good judge of human nature, free from unworthy ambition, unfettered by all personal or party engagements which would swerve him from his propriety, and who would probably administer the government to the satisfaction of a greater number of both of the great parties, than any other in the range of my knowledge. I am persuaded that he would do a great deal to correct what is considered a great evil in the working of our Government, I mean that tendency which makes the Executive every thing, & Congress comparatively nothing ["in our Government" *canceled*]. He would as I believe do much ["to" *interlined*] mitigate the proscriptive spirit of party, and to curtail the monstrous growth of Executive power & patronage. Upon the slavery question I think he is sound & immoveable, and if he could come into office with a large basis of popular support, I believe he could do much to arrest the daring assaults upon ["slave" *canceled*] the feelings & the rights of the slave States.

In view of our Mexican war, & the revolutions of Europe, it is important that we have a president of great prudence and that he be brought into power & be sustained by more than a mere party vote.

But for Mr. Clay there would have been a general union of both parties in Kentucky on Taylor, and altho the latter has been weakened by the attacks of the former he is still very strong. Mr. Clay cannot be elected president, & strange as it may seem to you, it is my firm belief that if he is the nominee of the Na[tiona]l Convention, he will not carry his own State. I am not sure that he could carry Kentucky if there were but two tickets, but if Clay is the nominee, there will be a triangular ticket which will defeat him.

It would give great force & solidity to Taylor[']s position if he had the countenance of your name, and I should be the more pleased, that it would have the effect of ensuring a participation on the part of your friends in the administration of the Government. There is certainly to be a new departure in the politicks of the nation, growing out of the questions about the Mexican war & its consequences, and the revolutions, & most probably the wars of Europe. Most of the old party issues have ceased to be practical. Mr. Clay may ruin his party for the next presidency, but he cannot be elected and many of the best whigs doubt if it be desirable that one embittered as he is with burning enmities, should be elected, in the present crisis. If as I expect, he will be defeated in convention, his next step will be to go to the Senate, and if he cannot dictate to Taylor, as he sought to do with [John] Tyler, will damn him. This Taylor will not submit to, & hence I have a strong wish that you should take a lead for him. You will pardon this intrusion on your time, & if I have crossed your views, let it pass. With high respect y[ou]rs, R. Hawes.

ALS in ScCleA. Note: An AEU by Calhoun reads, "Hon: Mr. Hawes[,] Sent Speech." Hawes (1797–1877) had been Representative from Ky. during 1837–1841 and would subsequently be the Confederate governor of Ky.

Remarks on the proposed occupation of Yucatan, 5/5. Edward A. Hannegan devoted a speech to replying to objections raised by Calhoun to the Yucatan occupation bill the previous day. Calhoun interjected brief comments from his seat. When Hannegan stated that Calhoun had been a member of [James] Monroe's cabinet for the "whole eight years," Calhoun said, "Yes, sir; nearly the whole." When Hannegan attributed to Calhoun the statement that the average annual expenditure during Monroe's administration was $10,000,000, Calhoun said: "The ordinary expenses of the Government." When Hannegan referred to "how far or to what extent the President ought to go," Calhoun interjected: "How far *we* ought to go." From *Congressional Globe*, 30th Cong., 1st Sess., Appendix, p. 597. Also printed in the Washington, D.C., *Daily National Intelligencer*, May 9, 1848, p. 2; the Washington, D.C., *Daily Union*, May 10, 1848, p. 1; Houston, ed., *Proceedings and Debates*, pp. 580–581.

Remarks in reply to Henry S. Foote, 5/8. Foote complained to the Senate of the newspaper reports of the debates of 5/4, in which Calhoun was reported as saying he did not think it necessary to correct a statement by Foote. "Mr. Calhoun took pleasure in saying that his remark had been misunderstood. It was a general remark and had no personal application to the Senator from Mississippi." From Alexandria, Va., *Gazette and Virginia Advertiser*, May 9, 1848, p. 3. Variant in *Congressional Globe*, 30th Cong., 1st Sess., p. 738.

Further Remarks on the Occupation of Yucatan

[In the Senate, May 8, 1848]
[Proponents of the bill for the occupation of Yucatan suggested that the territory would be occupied by Great Britain if the U.S. did not act.]

Mr. Calhoun. There are two questions involved in this matter. One is the danger of England taking possession of this country before we can; but, in my apprehension, there is no necessity for hurrying on that account. The other question is that of humanity. According to the provisions of this bill, we can render no aid for months to come. The only aid that can be furnished is in the hands of the President—I mean the naval forces—and I trust he will use them with the utmost effect. He has ample power to do so without the authority of Congress. I trust that the Senator from Connecticut [John M. Niles] will be permitted to have to-morrow for presenting his views to the Senate.

[Debate continued among several Senators.]

Mr. Calhoun. I think that the Senate must be satisfied, by this time, of the correctness of what I said when the message first came in—that there was a great deal in it to produce deliberation. When certain words are used in a message, I am always on the look out. Here comes a quiet message of but few lines, merely intimating that it is possible, and only possible, that Great Britain may take possession of Yucatan. But there is not a particle of information which leads us to apprehend such a result. The original basis of the recommendations of the President, however, is the question of humanity; but, connected with this, there is presented the supposition that there is actually danger of an English war for the possession of Yucatan. That I regard as the merest fiction. This is not, in my opinion, any such exigency as requires us to act at once, except as relates to the question of humanity.

[James D. Westcott, Jr., of Fla. made reference to a recent speech by Lord George Bentinck in the British Parliament which advocated British seizure of Cuba.]

Mr. Calhoun. I am very glad that the Senator has called my attention to the declaration of Lord George Bentinck, and I take this opportunity of exposing what I regard as a very fraudulent proceeding on the part of newspaper editors in this country. Lord George Bentinck is hostile to the present administration in England. When he made the declaration, the British Ministry, in the gravest manner, utterly disavowed it, and yet our editors have printed and published in every direction the remarks of Lord George Bentinck without publishing the contradiction. But the fact is as I have stated, that an express disavowal was made by the British Ministry in the strongest possible language.

From *Congressional Globe*, 30th Cong., 1st Sess., Appendix, pp. 606–608. Also printed in Houston, ed., *Proceedings and Debates*, pp. 590–591. Variant in the Washington, D.C., *Daily National Intelligencer*, May 10, 1848, p. 1; *Congressional Globe*, 30th Cong., 1st Sess., p. 738.

From H[ENRY] A. S. DEARBORN

Hawthorn Cottage
Roxbury [Mass.,] May 9, 1848

My Dear Sir, When the act passed authorizing the President to appoint additional Major & Brigadier Generals, I requested you to do me the favor of recommending me to Mr. [James K.] Polk for one of those offices; & as I retained no copy of the letter, I shall be very much obliged to you if you will do me the favor of returning it to me, for I am *"curious"* to have it, as we Yankees say.

I begin to have doubts, as to the ratification of the treaty [by Mexico]; & what is most astonishing, the indications are too apparent, that the President, [Lewis] Cass & [William L.] Marcy do not wish that it should be. What mad infatuation. I can not comprehend their motives. They are certainly most grossly deceived, if they think its rejection by Mexico & the renewal of the war will aid Mr. Polk in his *unwilling*, but *anxious*—& it would now seem, long plan[ne]d & secret supping & wining, to secure a nomination. Like Polonius, he was in hopes, by the giving out, that he would not, upon any condition, be a candidate a *second* time, that ["he could say when nominated" *interlined*] the people had *"wrung from him, his slow assent"* to listen to their *"sweet voices,"* from a high sense of patriotic duty. There are things deeper than wells; with this difference, that at the bottom of the latter truth ["truth" *canceled*] has her temple, while in the former, that meanest & basest of all qualities, *Cunning* hides her vile tricks, which put her disciples on the dead-low-water level of the pick-pocket; for cunning is never an eliment in great minds. It will make an adroit pilferer, but never a Red Rover. No distinguished statesman, no general, no man of preeminent genius & eminence, ever resorted to *cunning* to accomplish an object; they went boldly & fearlessly to work, like Lord Chatham, & [George] Washington.

Mr. [Thomas] Jefferson's prophetic remark has been mentioned, "The people in Europe will soon cease to venerate monarchs." Emperors & Kings have been at last treated like mere men, & as they are all either fools, or rascals, the people have kicked out of doors. With sincere respect, Your most ob[edien]t Serv[an]t, H.A.S. Dearborn.

ALS in ScCleA.

Further remarks on the bill for the occupation of Yucatan, 5/10. Several Senators urged the bill on the grounds of a British threat to Cuba with abolitionist intent. "Mr. Calhoun replied that he did not doubt that there was a disposition in the British Government to abolish slavery all over the world. But since the debate which had been referred to, a momentous change had taken place in the opinions of British statesmen on this subject, and there was nothing to be feared from the interference of England in our institutions." From *Congressional Globe*, 30th Cong., 1st Sess., p. 754. (A different report has Calhoun responding on this occasion to a Senator's reference to his letter [of 8/12/1844] to William R. King on British designs against slavery. "Mr. Calhoun defended his letter, and said that he might add, with an honest pride, that it had contributed to produce a change of sentiment in England, which had diminished her attachment to abolition to such an extent that she is now attempting to resuscitate a trade very much like the slave trade, with a view to the restoration of the prosperity of her West India colonies." This report also included a brief interchange between Calhoun and Lewis Cass as to whether the British disavowal of designs on Cuba could be trusted. From *Congressional Globe*, 30th Cong., 1st Sess., Appendix, p. 617. Variant in Houston, ed., *Proceedings and Debates*, pp. 605–606.)

From WYNDHAM ROBERTSON, JR.

Memphis Tenn., 10 May 1848

My D[ea]r Sir, Since the receipt of your very kind letter received several months ago, I have had occasion to observe from time to time the abolition movements which have been made in and out of Congress, and am more deeply impressed with the belief than ever, that if the Union is ever dissolved this same slave question will be at the bottom of it. I could however, but indulge the hope that the excitement incident to its agitation would have subsided, in a measure, upon the death of Mr. [John Quincy] Adams. But it appears not. The recent movement by [John P.] Hale & [Joshua R.] Giddings [Senator from N.H. and Representative from Ohio, respectively] evidently manifests a desire on their part and on that of their freinds, to make a decisive issue, so that the war may commence and the result be as it may. So far as the participation of Hale & Giddings in the attempt to *rob* the citizens of the District of Columbia of their property is concerned, and place it beyond their reach, there can be but one opinion entertained. The very fact of the introduction of a Bill, *tacitly* approving the course of the kidnappers and refusing, indirectly to make it a crime, is the strongest evidence of his having "aided and abetted" and encouraged them in their base purpose. My object in writing is to inform you that the people throughout the State are *grateful* for the course indicated by you and for the position assumed. A meeting of the citizens of this place will be held in a few days, the object of which will be to condemn in the strongest terms the action of the abolitionists in Congress, and to approve and applaud your magnanimous devotion to southern rights and institutions. This is nothing more than an act of Justice due to one who has so long and so consistently stood by us, throwing "oil upon the waters" when serious and alarming discussions have arisen. As I wrote you before, your popularity in Tennessee has greatly increased. At the late democratic State Convention held at Nashville, the leaders of our party by a large majority expressed themselves as favourable to your nomination for the Presidency—the delegate from this District is instructed *unconditionally* to go for you, and if I am not mistaken the whole west prefers you as the man of all others who is best entitled to our entire support. A *reform is needed*—there is obviously "something rotten in Denmark." The "Augean Stable" should be cleansed if it is not we may look for troubles which may destroy our Government and render us a *mockery* and not a *"model,"* in all time to come—if the machinery is once *deranged* it may be that it can be never righted—if it is we may be a deformity and we can never be a united and happy people. With Assurances of the warmest Regard I remain y[ou]r friend as ever, Wyndham Robertson, Jr.

ALS in ScCleA; PEx in Boucher and Brooks, eds., *Correspondence,* p. 436.

To T[homas] G. Clemson, [Brussels]

Washington, 13th May 1848

My dear Sir, I have been disappointed in not having received, either from you or Anna [Maria Calhoun Clemson], any letter by the last two steamers. It is at all times a source of pleasure to hear from you; but it is especially so at the present, when Europe is the scene of such extraordinary events. I know not how they may appear to you, who are in the midest of them; but to me, who look on at so great a distance, they appear to be without a parallel in the history of the world. They are, indeed, so much out of the ordinary course of events, that it is difficult to form an opinion, as to the results they will lead. My apprehension is, that the old system of things have been overthrown, before Europe had become prepared to establish a new & better; and that a long period of confusion and disorder, if not anarchy, may intervene before order can be restored, especially in France, where the impulse was first given. With this apprehension, I regard it of vast importance, that Great Britain, should resist the shock, that has overturned so many Governments; and, of course, was gratified to learn that she had passed successfully the crisis caused by the movements of the Chartists. If they had ended in a revolution, it would have greatly increased ["the force" *interlined*] & prolonged the period of the convulsion, through which Europe is now passing. ["It" *canceled and* "But as it is it," *interlined*] will contribute, I hope, not only to shorten it, but to guard thereby ["against" *interlined*] one of the greatest dangers to which she is at present exposed. I refer to that, which may be apprehended from Russia, in case Europe should be thrown into a state of distraction and disorder for any considerable period. In that event, her power might prove irresistible & her sway be extended over the greater part of the Continent.

As to ourselves, we are going on much as we did for the last few years. Every thing still remains in a state of uncertainty; the Mexican question, ["&" *canceled*] the Presidential election and all. It is just as uncertain, whether we shall have peace with Mexico, or not, and who will be nominated by the two conventions (although one meets in 9 days, & the other shortly after) & which of the two, who may be nominated, will be elected, as it was three months ago. In the meane time, another question has been started, which may involve us in as great difficulties, as the Mexican; I refer to the Yucatan. It is now under discussion. I expect to speak day after tomorrow, if I can get the floor, and shall discuss it fully.

I had a letter from home a few days since. All were well & the crop looking remarkable well. It has been remarkable cool for the season of the year for the last few days, but I hope not so much so, as to hurt the fruit, or crop materially.

My love to Anna & the children. I fear the state of things in Europe may prevent your intended visit, which I would greatly regret on yours & our own account. We anticipated much pleasure in seeing you all, and still hope we shall not be disappointed. Your affectionate father, J.C. Calhoun.

ALS in ScCleA; variant PC in Jameson, ed., *Correspondence*, pp. 754–755.

Petition of citizens of Charleston for uniform and cheap postage, presented by Calhoun to the Senate on 5/13. This undated document contains approximately 300 signatures, beginning with the mayor and other city officers. It requests that Congress "pass a Law to establish a uniform rate of Postage, not to exceed one cent on Newspapers, and two cents on each pre-paid Letter of half an ounce, for all distances . . . ." (The petition was referred to the Committee on the Post Office and Post Roads.) PDS in DNA, RG 46 (U.S. Senate), 30A-H14.1.

From H[ENRY] W. CONNER

Charleston, May 14, 1848

My Dear Sir, Your favour of the 10th is to hand.

It was an inference of my own that the So. Ca. delegation or a portion of them would repair to ["Washington" *canceled*] Baltimore in the event of any distinct organization of the Southern members of the convention. Others drew a similar inference but the terms of your letter of the 20th ult. were ["only" *interlined*] to the effect "if the Virginia delegates should faithfully adhere to the resolutions of their convention & be backed by Alabama, or should any portion of the delegates of the slave holding States stand out against an obnoxious nomination every member of our delegation in Congress will be ready to back & support them to the ut[t]ermost extent." We were led to the inference mainly from the belief that the Southern delegates or such of them as were sound would be forced into some seperate action of their own at the convention & that So. Ca. through her representatives (the members of both Houses of Congress) would be of necessity obliged to cooperate with them in some proper way.

The delegates to the democratic convention are daily passing through Charleston but make but little stop. Mr. [William L.] Yancey passed through yesterday. Col. [Isaac W.] Hayne & Col. [Franklin H.] Elmore saw him for a moment only. Senator [William R.] King from Ala. is now here on his way to Washington. Dr. [James G.M.] Ramsey a delegate from Tennessee goes on tomorrow or next day. He tells me [Lewis] Cass will be the first choice of Tennessee, but not his own I think. He is an old nullifier—an intimate personal friend of Mr. [James K.] Polk & very Southern in his notions & feelings. I will take the liberty of giving him a letter to you.

Gen[era]l [James M.] Commander from Georgetown will be the only delegate to the convention I believe from So. Ca.

The pressure of the times are keeping people very quiet in this State for the present. Very Truly y[ou]rs &C, H.W. Conner.

ALS in ScCleA.

To Gen[era]l H[ENRY A.] S. DEARBORN, [Roxbury, Mass.]

Senate Chamber, 14th May 1848

My dear Sir, I have not the correspondence of the last Session with me, and cannot, of course, comply with your request. I do not usually preserve letters of the kind, when the occasion is passed, & may not have preserved your's. But if I have, I will return it after my arrival at home. With great respect Yours truly, J.C. Calhoun.

ALS in CtY, Betts Autograph Collection.

From E. M. HOYT

New Haven Vt., May 15th 1848

Honoured Sir, The members of the "New Haven Library Association," entertaining an exalted sense of your high literary attainments, & patriotic devotion to the true principles of the Constitution of our beloved country, desire to obtain, your autograph signature, & if it will not be trespassing too much upon your time, & generosity, a copy of your life and speeches. This association is a large & highly intelligent one, and having long held your honoured name & public services, in esteem desire a visible remembrance, from your hand, to grace its collections, & enhance its interest for coming time.

Fearing to trespass farther upon your valuable time, I subscribe myself most respectfully your friend & Ob[edien]t Serv[an]t, E.M. Hoyt, Sec[re]t[ary].

[P.S.] Address E.M. Hoyt, New Haven, Vermont.

ALS in ScU-SC, John C. Calhoun Papers.

Speech on the Proposed Occupation of Yucatan

[In the Senate, May 15, 1848]
The Senate having under consideration the Bill to enable the President of the United States to take temporary military occupation of Yucatan—

Mr. Calhoun said: The President in his message recommends to Congress to adopt such measures as they may deem expedient to prevent, in the first place, Yucatan from becoming a colony of any European power; and, in the next place, to prevent the white inhabitants of that territory from being exterminated or expelled. In support of the latter, he informed the Senate that there is now raging a cruel and devastating war on the part of the Indians against the whites; and that, unless some foreign power should aid, they will be destroyed or driven from the country. In support of the other recommendation, he states that the Government of Yucatan has offered to the Governments of Great Britain, Spain, and the United States, the dominion over the country in order to obtain aid. The President also informs the Senate that, unless we grant aid, some other power will; and that, ultimately, it may assert its dominion and sovereignty over the territory—a result which, he informs us, would be in contravention of the declaration of Mr. [James] Monroe, and which must on no account be permitted. The Committee on Foreign Relations, in order to carry out these recommendations, have reported a bill which is now before us, the first section of which provides for taking military occupation of Yucatan, as recommended by the President.

Such are the recommendations of the President, and such the measure recommended by the committee. The subject is one of great magnitude. It is pregnant with consequences, both near and remote, which may deeply affect the peace and interests of this country.

It demands the most serious deliberation. I have bestowed upon it full attention, and have arrived at a conclusion adverse to the recommendations of the President and the report of the committee. I propose to show, in the first place, that the case of Yucatan, even as stated by the President himself, does not come within the declarations of Mr. Monroe; and that they do not furnish the slightest support to the measure reported by the committee.

In the message referred to, that of 1823, Mr. Monroe makes three distinct declarations. The first, and by far the most important, announces that the United States would regard any attempt on the part of the allied powers to extend their system to this country as dangerous to our peace and safety. To show that the case of Yucatan does not come within this declaration, all that will be necessary is to explain who were the allied powers—the object of their alliance—and the circumstances in which the declaration itself was made. The allied powers were the four great continental monarchies—Russia, Prussia, Austria, and France. Shortly after the overthrow of Bonaparte these powers entered into an alliance called the "Holy Alliance," the object of which was to sustain and extend monarchical principles as far as possible, and to oppress and put down popular institutions. England, in the early stages of the alliance, favored it. The members of the alliance held several Congresses, attended either by themselves or their ambassadors, and undertook to regulate the affairs of all Europe, and actually interfered in the affairs of Spain for the purpose of putting down popular doctrines. In its progress the alliance turned its eyes to this continent in order to aid Spain in regaining her sovereignty over her revolted provinces. At this stage England became alarmed. Mr. [George] Canning was then prime minister. He informed Mr. [Richard] Rush of the project, and gave to him, at the same time, the assurance that, if sustained by the United States, Great Britain would resist. Mr. Rush immediately communicated this to our Government. It was received here with joy; for so great was the power of the alliance that even we did not feel ourselves safe from its interpositions. Indeed, it was anticipated, almost as a certain result, that, if the interference took place with the Governments of South America, the alliance would ultimately extend its interference to ourselves. I remember the reception of the dispatch from Mr. Rush as distinctly as if all the circumstances had occurred yesterday. I well recollect the great satisfaction with which it was received by the cabinet. It came late in the year—not long before the meeting of Congress. As was usual with Mr. Monroe upon great occasions, the papers were sent round to each member of the cabinet, so that each might be duly apprised of all the circumstances, and be prepared to give his opinion. The cabinet met. It deliberated. There was long and careful consultation; and the result was the declaration which I have just announced. All this has passed away. That very movement on the part of England, sustained by this declaration, gave a blow to the celebrated alliance from which it never recovered. From that time forward it gradually decayed, till it utterly perished. The late revolutions in Europe have put an end to all its work, and nothing remains of all that it ever did. Now, by what ingenuity of argument, by what force of sophistry can it be shown that this declaration comprehends the case of Yucatan, when the events which called it forth have passed away for ever?

And yet the President has quoted that very declaration in support of his recommendation; but in a manner changing entirely its meaning, by separating it from the context as it stood in the message, and which referred it to the allied powers; and placing it in connection with a portion of his message which made it refer to Great Britain, Spain, or other European powers. The change has made the declaration so inconsistent and absurd that, had it been made by Mr. Monroe, as it stands in the President's message, it would have been the subject of the severest animadversion and ridicule, instead of receiving, as it did, the approbation and applause of the whole country. It would have placed England in the false position of acting against us and with the Holy Alliance in reference to the Spanish American republics; and it would also have placed us in the position of opposing Spain in her efforts to recover her dominion over those states; and, finally, it would have involved the absurdity of asserting that the attempt of any European state to extend its system of government to this continent, the smallest as well as the greatest, would endanger the peace and safety of our country.

The next declaration was, that we would regard the interposition of any European power to oppress the governments of this continent, which we had recently recognized as independent, or to control their destiny in any manner whatever, as manifesting an unfriendly disposition towards the United States. This declaration, also, belongs to the history of that day. It grew out of the same state of circumstances, and may be considered as an appendage to the declaration to which I have just alluded. By the governments on this continent, which we had recognized, were meant the republics which had grown up after having thrown off the yoke of Spain. They had just emerged from their protracted revolutionary struggles. They had hardly yet reached a point of solidity, and in that tender stage, the administration of Mr. Monroe thought it proper not only to make that general declaration in reference to the Holy Alliance, but to make a more specific one against the interference of any European power—in order to countenance and encourage these young republics as far as we could with propriety. This, like the other, belonging to the events of the time, has passed away with them. But suppose this not to be the case, I ask does the case of Yucatan come within this declaration? Has there been any interposition in the affairs of Yucatan on the part of any European power with the design of oppressing her or changing her destiny? If not, how can the case of Yucatan be comprehended in this declaration?

But, it may be said, although the case of Yucatan is not expressly comprehended in the declaration, yet it is so by implication, as it is meditated by England; for, after all, that is the government which is meant in the message, under the general term "European powers." The message indicates that England meditates such interference, and the Chairman of the Committee on Foreign Relations [Edward A. Hannegan] distinctly avows that opinion. Has England, then, manifested any disposition to interfere in order to oppress the people of Yucatan, or to change the character of their government from a republic to a monarchy? We have no evidence whatever on that point. It is true that the commissioner from Yucatan, Mr. [Justa] Sierra, would insinuate as much. He speaks of the Indians who are in hostility to the white people of Yucatan as having obtained arms from the British. He speaks with some degree of uncertainty, however, and is unable to say whether the arms were given or not, and cannot state how they were obtained by the Indians. He speaks also of the hostile temper of England, and gives several indications of that kind. But, in answer to all this, his own letter furnishes a conclusive reply. He tells us that the people of Yucatan could themselves have obtained an abundant and cheap supply of arms from the Balize—without stating why they were prevented, or why they did not obtain them. In my opinion the cause is different from that stated by the Senator from Massachusetts [John Davis]. It was owing to the fact that Yucatan was not considered as a neutral power, but as a part of Mexico, as far as the introduction of arms was concerned, and arms were in consequence made contraband; and, therefore, they were prevented from being introduced by our act, and not by that of the British Government, or its agent, or people at the Balize. One of the members of the committee goes a little further, and says that the settlement at Balize has sent arms and a military force along the coast of Yucatan, without stating any particulars. I do not find any evidence of this. I do not know whether it is a fact or not; but, if it be a fact, it still remains to be shown whether it was intended to relieve the people of Yucatan, or for the purpose of seizing and occupying the territory. The Chairman of that committee took higher ground, and, without assigning his proof, said boldly and distinctly that England meditated occupation of the country, and that we ought to pass this measure in order to prevent it. But the President himself does not put it upon this ground. He does not make this charge. He says, if we do not grant aid England may; and that, after granting it, she *may*—there is no stronger expression used—*may* ultimately assert her dominion and sovereignty over Yucatan. This is the utmost charge made by the President. Now, the question arises, suppose this contingency should happen, would it bring the case within the declaration just quoted? Not at all. England does not interpose as a hostile power. She does not come to oppress Yucatan. She comes at the request of Yucatan, and only to aid to rescue the people of Yucatan from extermination and expulsion by the Indians, according to the statement of the President himself. Again, suppose England should assert her sovereignty, would that bring the case within the declaration? Not at all; for the declaration is directed against interpositions to change the government and oppress the country. But, in this case, the tender of sovereignty is voluntarily made on the part of Yucatan. The acceptance of it may be objected to, and it may be contended that we ought not to allow it. I waive that subject for the present. I assert, however, without possibility of contradiction, that the case, even then, does not come within the declaration. The President himself gives strong indications that, in his opinion, it does not; for, although he refers to this declaration in the body of the message, he does not say a word in regard to it when he comes to make his recommendation. In this he calls upon Congress to prevent Yucatan from becoming a colony to some foreign power. That shows on which of the three declarations he rests his recommendation. It is upon the third and last, which refers to an entirely different subject. That declaration is, that the continents of America, by the free and independent condition which they have assumed and maintained, are not henceforth to be considered as subjects of colonization by any European power. It is upon this the President bases his recommendation. Is the case of Yucatan, then, comprehended in this declaration? I expect to show that it is not, with just as much certainty as it has been established that it does not come within the two former.

The word "colonization" has a specific meaning. It means the establishment of a settlement by emigrants from the parent country in a territory either uninhabited or from which the inhabitants have been partially or wholly expelled. This is not a case of that character. But here it may be proper, in order to understand the force of my argument, to go into a history also of this declaration of Mr. Monroe. It grew out of circumstances altogether different from the other two. At that time there was a question between Great Britain and the United States on one side, and Russia on the other. All three claimed settlements on the northwest portion of this continent. Great Britain and ourselves having common interest in keeping Russia as far north as possible, the former power applied to the United States for co-operation; and it was in reference to that matter that this additional declaration was made. It was said to be a proper opportunity to make it. It had reference specially to the subject of the northwestern settlement, and the other portions of the continent were thrown in, because all the rest of it, with the exception of some settlements in Surinam, Maracaibo, and thereabout, had passed into independent hands.

Now, having stated the history of these transactions, I contend that the word "colonization" does not apply to the case of Yucatan. That is the case of surrendered sovereignty over a people already there—a people who have tendered it, and, if accepted, freely accepted on the other side. Is that "colonization?" Can it be construed to be so by any forced interpretation? No; by accepting it Yucatan may become a province, or, to use the appropriate term that she employs, a "possession" of Great Britain, but not a colony.

When the Chairman of the Committee on Foreign Relations addressed the Senate a few days since, he related a conversation which he had with Mr. [John Quincy] Adams, in reference to this declaration; and, according to his statement, if I heard him aright, and he be correctly reported, Mr. Adams, in applying his observations to the whole of these declarations, stated that they all originated with himself, and were unknown to the other members of the cabinet until they appeared in Mr. Monroe's message. There certainly must be a mistake either on the part of Mr. Adams, or that of the Chairman of the Committee on Foreign Relations, as to the two first of these declarations. The history of the transaction, the Senator will perceive, if he examines the documents, shows distinctly that they came through Mr. Rush—originating, not with Mr. Adams, but Mr. Canning—and were first presented in the form of a proposition from England. I recollect, as distinctly as I do any event of my life, that all the papers in connection with this subject were submitted to the members before the cabinet met, and were duly considered. Mr. Adams, then, in speaking of the whole as one, must have reference to the declaration relative to colonization. As respects this his memory does not differ much from mine. My impression is, that it never became a subject of deliberation in the cabinet. I so stated when the Oregon question was before the Senate. I stated it in order that Mr. Adams might have an opportunity of denying it, or asserting the real state of the facts. He remained silent, and I presume that my statement is correct—that this declaration was inserted after the cabinet deliberation. It originated entirely with Mr. Adams, without being submitted to the cabinet, and it is, in my opinion, owing to this fact that it is not made with the precision and clearness with which the two former are. It declares, without qualification, that these continents have asserted and maintained their freedom and independence, and are no longer subject to colonization by any European power. This is not strictly accurate. Taken as a whole, these continents had not asserted and maintained their freedom and independence. At that period Great Britain had a larger portion of the continent in her possession than the United States. Russia had a considerable portion of it, and other powers possessed some portions on the southern parts of this continent. The declaration was broader than the fact, and exhibits precipitancy and want of due reflection. Besides, there was an impropriety in it when viewed in conjunction with the foregoing declarations. I speak not in the language of censure. We were, as to them, acting in concert with England, on a proposition coming from herself—a proposition of the utmost magnitude, and which we felt at the time to be essentially connected with our peace and safety; and of course it was due to propriety as well as policy that this declaration should be strictly in accordance with British feeling. Our power then was not what it is now, and we had to rely upon her co-operation to sustain the ground we had taken. We had then only about six or seven millions of people, scattered, and without such means of communication as we now possess to bring us together in a short period of time. The declaration accordingly, with respect to colonization, striking at England as well as Russia, gave offence to her, and that to such an extent that she refused to co-operate with us in settling the Russian question. Now, I will venture to say that if that declaration had come before that cautious cabinet—for Mr. Monroe was among the wisest and most cautious men I have ever known—it would have been modified, and expressed with a far greater degree of precision, and with much more delicacy in reference to the feelings of the British Government.

In stating the precise character of these declarations, and the manner in which they originated, I have discharged a double duty; a duty to my country, to whom it is important that these declarations should be correctly understood—and a duty to the cabinet of which I was a member, and am now the only survivor. I remove a false interpretation, which makes safe and proper declarations improper and dangerous.

But it is not only in these respects that these famous declarations are misunderstood by the Chief Magistrate of the country, as well as by others. They were but declarations—nothing more; declarations, announcing in a friendly manner to the powers of the world, that we should regard certain acts of interposition of the allied powers as dangerous to our peace and safety; interposition of European powers to oppress the republics which had just arisen upon this continent, as manifesting an unfriendly disposition, and that this continent having become free and independent, was no longer the subject of colonization by European powers. Not one word in any one of them in reference to resistance. There is nothing said of it; and with great propriety was it omitted. Resistance belonged to us—to Congress; it is for us to say whether we shall resist or not, and to what extent. But such is not the view taken by the present Chief Magistrate. He seems to hold these declarations as imposing a solemn duty on him as Chief Magistrate to resist on all occasions; and not only to resist, but to judge of the measure of that resistance. He tells us in this very message that it is not to be permitted, in any event, that any foreign power should occupy Yucatan. That is language for us to hold, not for the Chief Magistrate. And in conformity with that, he sends in a message without giving us one particle of evidence as to those great political considerations which influenced the cabinet decisions as stated on this floor, in declaring whether we shall occupy the country or not. I speak it not in the way of censure. I state it only as a matter of fact deducible from the message itself, and as evincing undoubtedly a great and dangerous misconception of these celebrated declarations. But this is not all. He tells you in the same message that these declarations have become the settled policy of this country. What, the declarations? Declarations are not policy, and cannot become settled policy. He must mean that it has become the settled policy of this country to resist what these declarations refer to; and to resist, if need be, by an appeal to arms. Is this the fact? Has there been one instance in which these declarations have been carried into effect by resistance? If there be, let it be pointed out. Have there not been innumerable instances in which they have not been applied? Certainly. Still stronger; these declarations, under this broad interpretation, were disavowed entirely three years afterwards by the vote of the Republican party, when the administration of Mr. Adams endeavored to carry them out practically, by sending ministers to the Congress at Panama, as will be seen by reading the debates and the proceedings on the subject. And let me say—for it is proper that I should make the declaration on this occasion—that there has been an entire revolution between the two parties in this country in reference to our foreign relations. At the commencement of our Government, and down to a late period—I will mark it—the commencement of [Andrew] Jackson's administration, the policy of the Republican party was to avoid war as long as war could be avoided, and to resort to every means to avert its calamities. The opposite party, without being a war party, had not so decided an aversion to war. The thing is now reversed; and hence I, who have endeavored to maintain the old ground of the party, have for years, on all questions connected with our foreign relations, been compelled to co-operate with gentlemen on the opposite side, and to resist those in the midst of whom I stand. No; it is not and never has been the established policy of the country. And if it should ever become so, to the wide extent to which these declarations have been interpreted to go, our peace would ever be disturbed; the gates of our Janus would ever stand open; wars would never cease.

What the President has asserted in this case is not a principle belonging to these declarations; it is a principle which, in his misconception, he attempts to engraft upon them, but which has an entirely different meaning and tendency. The principle which lies at the bottom of his recommendation is—that when any power on this continent becomes involved in internal warfare, and the weaker side chooses to make application to us for support, we are bound to give them support for fear the offer of the sovereignty of the country may be made to some other power and accepted. It goes infinitely and dangerously beyond Mr. Monroe's declaration. It puts it in the power of other countries on this continent to make us a party to all their wars; and hence I say, if this broad interpretation be given to these declarations, we shall for ever be involved in wars.

But, in disavowing a principle which will compel us to resist every case of interposition of European powers on this continent, I would not wish to be understood as defending the opposite, that we should never resist their interposition. This is a position which would be nearly as dangerous and absurd as the other. But no general rule can be laid down to guide us on such a question. Every case

409

must speak for itself—every case must be decided on its own merits. Whether you will resist or not, and the measure of your resistance—whether it shall be by negotiation, remonstrance, or some intermediate measure, or by a resort to arms; all this must be determined and decided on the merits of the question itself. This is the only wise course. We are not to have quoted on us, on every occasion, general declarations to which any and every meaning may be attached. There are cases of interposition where I would resort to the hazard of war with all its calamities. Am I asked for one? I will answer. I designate the case of Cuba. So long as Cuba remains in the hands of Spain—a friendly power—a power of which we have no dread—it should continue to be, as it has been the policy of all administrations ever since I have been connected with the Government, to let Cuba remain there; but with the fixed determination, which I hope never will be relinquished, that, if Cuba pass from her, it shall not be into any other hands but ours: this, not from a feeling of ambition, not from a desire for the extension of dominion, but because that island is indispensable to the safety of the United States; or rather, because it is indispensable to the safety of the United States that this island should not be in certain hands. If it were, our coasting trade between the gulf and the Atlantic would, in case of war, be cut in twain, to be followed by convulsive effects. In the same category, I will refer to a case in which we might most rightfully have resisted, had it been necessary, a foreign power; and that is the case of Texas. It has been greatly misunderstood. It sprung up in the midst of party excitement, when a large portion of both parties were opposed to annexation, and when it was difficult, if not impossible, to get a fair hearing. I never supposed, as has been stated on this floor, that Great Britain intended to subject Texas to her power. That was not my dread. What was dreaded was this: Texas being a small power, and Great Britain having a free and large commercial intercourse with her, and we almost none, although "bone of our bone and flesh of our flesh," she would gradually have been weaned of her affection for us. Kindness for England and aversion for us would have been the result. Such is the inevitable tendency between nations having conterminous limits. At that very time there were several questions between this country and Texas which, had it not been for the most amicable feelings which subsisted between us, would have ended in hostilities. A long line of more than a thousand miles illy defining the boundary between us and Texas, exposed us to the hazard of becoming involved constantly in war with her, supported by Great Britain and Mexico as her allies. I saw all this; I saw clearly that it was a case to resist interposition—and that there was no other mode by which effectual resistance could be made than by annexation; and therefore I was in favor of annexation, even at the hazard of war.

But I was asked by one of the members of the Committee on Foreign Relations, if I would be in favor of resisting Great Britain if she should assert sovereignty and dominion over Yucatan? I answer, I would not. And for irresistible reasons. I would not, because the country is, to a great extent, a most worthless one. Nearly one-half is destitute of a single stream—rocky and barren throughout the greater part; and it is only by means of the artificial reservoirs of water, that they are enabled to live through the dry season. I would not, because the possession of Yucatan would contribute nothing to the defense of the passage between it and Cuba, which is represented to be so important to our commerce. It is not without its importance—it is important to the inward trade, but not at all to the outward trade of the gulf. There is a constant current of wind and water setting in that direction, of which vessels going to New Orleans, or any other port on the gulf, may avail themselves. But on coming from those ports, they almost invariably take their way between Florida and Cuba, and thus the passage between Yucatan and Cuba is the inlet to a limited extent into the gulf, but not the outlet from it; while the passage between Cuba and Florida is the almost exclusive outlet and the principal inlet. I speak in reference to coasting vessels. In voyages from Europe they pass south of Cuba into the gulf.

But I take higher grounds. If it were ever so important, not only as an inlet, but an outlet, the occupation of Yucatan by England would add nothing to her power in cutting off our trade. Yucatan is very destitute of ports; there is not a frigate port laid down in the charts on the whole peninsula, unless that at the Balize be so. But with or without Yucatan, Great Britain possesses an uncontrollable power over the passage whenever she chooses to exert it. If ever we should be engaged in war with her, there is not a single vessel of ours, even if we were in possession of Yucatan, that could enter into the gulf by that passage, or depart out of it. The passage from the gulf between Yucatan and Cuba does not, as seems to be supposed, lead directly into the Atlantic, but into the Caribbean Sea—the portion of the Atlantic ocean, having on its north and west side Yucatan and Cuba; on the east the Windward Islands; and on the south all that portion of South America extending nearly from Oronoco to Yucatan. Great Britain has the complete command of that sea, the island of Jamaica being in the midst of it. Jamaica abounds with the

411

finest ports, and the most commodious naval stations. In addition to this, she has the Balize, which is nearer the point of Yucatan than Laguna or Carmen on the opposite side of the peninsula next the gulf, and which is the only port on that side into which even a sloop of war can enter, and of course the Balize is better calculated to command the passage. In addition, she possesses many of the Windward Islands to the east, and hence the complete command of the Caribbean Sea, and she will continue to possess it so long as she retains her ascendency on the ocean. It would be thus locked up effectually against us in time of war. In time of peace we do not need it. But I would not take military possession of Yucatan, if I were certain Great Britain would, for another reason. Not only because it is worthless, but because it would impose on us a very heavy cost of both men and money—first to take possession, and then to keep it. The extent to which our expenditures would go no man can estimate; we have no data on which we can act. The population is between five and six hundred thousand, of which only fifty thousand are said to be whites and mixed blood. The Indians, originally a very peaceful and quiet people, unaccustomed to arms, from being frequently called into the contest between the factions and the war with Mexico, have become accustomed to them, and possessed of some military knowledge. They are represented as very active, capable of marching rapidly, and in the habit of flying to the mountains to escape from their pursuers. In that climate, among the most arid upon earth, if these people fly before us, how or when will this war come to an end? It may prove another Seminole affair. Who can answer what will be the sacrifice of men and money?

But an Indian war would not be the greatest danger to which we would be exposed. To attempt to take military possession, with a view to prevent England from asserting sovereignty and dominion over the country—if that indeed be her intention—might bring us into conflict with her, and, it may be, with Spain, too. They, as well as we, are implored to accept the sovereignty, on condition of defending the existing Government against the Indians. Suppose they, as well as we, should accept the offer, and that we should find them with an armed force prepared to take possession. Must it not lead to a direct conflict of arms, unless one or the other give way? Would we be prepared, in such a case, to back out? And if not, what reason have we to suppose that others will not be as resolute to carry out their object as we are? Would not a conflict be inevitable? That such would be the result is anticipated by Mr. Sierra himself, who, speaking in reference to it, says that the condition of the country would be, in that case, "infinitely more unfortunate than it is now, because, in addition to all the evils of the present war, it would be exposed to become the theatre of another war." Are we prepared to occupy the country by military force, as recommended by the committee, at the risk of so great a hazard? I am not. I am in favor of peace, whenever it can be maintained consistently with the honor and the safety of the country. I can see no such necessity in this case, even on the supposition stated, as to induce me to incur such hazard, especially at a period like the present. Never was the future more uncertain. Events occur with electric rapidity. No man can tell what may come to-morrow; and never was there a time when caution was more necessary—when there was stronger inducement to husband our resources—to avoid quarrels and wars, or anything that can involve us in difficulty, in order to stand prepared to meet emergencies as they rise. He who looks abroad—he who looks at the eastern horizon, and does not see the necessity for caution, is blind to the future.

I would not take military possession, even under the contingency I have stated, for another reason. It would be a breach of good faith. Not long since we agreed upon the terms of a treaty with Mexico. That treaty, before this time, has been acted on, or is about to be acted on, by the Mexican Government; and until it is acted on we are bound in good faith to observe it. If it is acted on favorably, it becomes a permanent obligation. We have considered Yucatan as part of Mexico, as one of the States of the Mexican Republic. It is not comprehended within the line which is proposed to be drawn between us and her. We could not seize upon that State in conformity with good faith; nor could we in conformity with the armistice, for the same reason. The armistice makes some exceptions, but this is not one of them.

I have now stated my reasons against the measure reported by the committee to carry into effect the message of the President, recommending that we should adopt the measure to prevent Yucatan from becoming a colony of a foreign power. I now proceed to consider the next—to adopt measures to prevent the white population from being exterminated or expelled from Yucatan. And here let me express my regret that the President should, in the same message, unite two measures of such different characters—one an appeal to our humanity, which I would, as far as we could with propriety, act upon promptly, and at once; the other, involving the highest considerations of policy, and which requires much time and much deliberation. It is among the most complicated questions ever presented to this body, and by no means the least important. Why these different questions have been mingled I am not prepared to say. The emergency for the one seems to have existed long before the other. Danger to the white population has been known to exist since the middle of February, but the message has only been recently communicated to us. During this long interval, if the case appealing to our humanity had been brought forward, we might long ere this have rendered efficient aid. But, whatever may be the effects of the delay in reference to the Yucatanese, they are not chargeable to us. Higher considerations in reference to ourselves—considerations of policy—demand of us deliberation, and that deliberation, I trust, will be given, in despite of the charge of unnecessary delay. But I pass on to the question of humanity.

If this be a war of races in reality; if the white race be not responsible for this war; if they have used all manly exertions, and exhibited due courage in repelling the danger, strong indeed would be the appeal to my sympathies. I have no aversion to any race, red or black, but my sympathies are for the white race. I am not so much sophisticated by misguided philosophy or false philanthropy as to lose the natural feelings which belong to me. I go further. If this is a case of war between races; if the Indians have, without just cause, risen and threatened the massacre and extermination of the white race, who have acted so generously towards them as to raise them from the condition of slaves or serfs to that of citizens and freemen, this would present a strong case on the score of policy for interposition, connected with considerations belonging to progress, civilization, and liberty. It was the Spanish or white race—and in that we include the mixed races—who overthrew the Spanish power, and have throughout evinced the greatest attachment, under all circumstances, to republican government. They have all the wealth, and comprise nearly all the intelligence of the country; and on their ascendency, in my opinion, depends the future progress of civilization and liberty of Yucatan. It is true, they are not very elevated in their sentiments, nor very well informed on political subjects, but they are far better informed, and far more elevated in sentiment, than the Indian race can possibly be. If they can maintain themselves, there is some hope that Yucatan may go forward, that intelligence may increase, and that at some future day they may be prepared to take a higher position in civilization than at present. If the white race be overthrown and Indian ascendency established, there will be a directly opposite tendency to end in a despotic government, like that of Hayti. Perhaps a capable man may at first be elevated to power, and may govern tolerably well, but it will undoubtedly follow the course of Hayti. The tendency of power will be downwards, until it come down to the very bottom, and end in a savage state.

But if there are powerful considerations why we should interfere as far as we could with propriety for these reasons, there are very powerful ones why we should act with great caution. The case of Yucatan does not stand alone. All the causes operating there to produce the present state of things are operating in all the portions of this continent south of us, including Mexico, down on the eastern side of the Andes to Buenos Ayres, and on the western to Chili. All, all are in great danger of falling into the condition in which Yucatan is now placed. The history of all has been the same. The white and mixed races led in casting off the yoke of Spain. They, every where, elevated the Indian race to an equality with themselves. It was done most imprudently, and inculcates a solemn lesson. They conferred upon the Indians full political rights, subjecting them at the same time to unequal civil burdens. While they gave them the power of voting—the highest political power—they imposed a tax upon them exclusively of a most onerous character, so as to throw almost the whole burden of supporting the Government and the Church upon them. If the order had been reversed; if they had given them all civil rights, and dealt out to them more sparingly political rights, elevating the more intelligent, and extending the basis of suffrage as the intelligence of the Indian population increased, a very different result might have taken place. All these South American States consist of the same population—whites, mixed, and Indians. The African population is small. All will, I fear, be revolutionized in turn, and the whole of them be subjected to one melancholy fate, in spite of all that we can do. But I trust that it may be otherwise. The magnitude of this subject, however, should teach us caution. Whatever we do in this case, we set a precedent; we affirm a principle; and every one knows the force of precedents and asserted principles upon a population like that of our country. You will have to follow it in all other cases. Even now Venezuela is involved in a war every way similar. How it may end we know not. Guatimala has gone through the process. She is already under Indian authority. A man of remarkable character, it is said, is at the head of the Government. Things may go very well in his time, but how they will be managed afterwards who can tell? Look at the subject. Are we to declare now, by our acts, that in all those cases we are to interpose by force of arms, if need be, and thereby become involved in the fate of all these countries? Ought we to set such a precedent? No. The first duty of every nation is to itself—and such is the case preeminently with the United States. They owe a high duty to themselves—to pursue a line of policy which will secure their liberty. The success of their great political system will be of infinitely more service to mankind than the securing of the ascendency of the white race in the southern portion of this continent, however important that may be. But if, instead of pursuing this wise policy, such a course be entered upon as that recommended in the message of the President, I fear that, sooner or later, the ruins of our Government will be added to those which have fallen within the last few months. But, while I see the greatest reason for caution, I think that this Government, upon all occasions, ought to give encouragement and countenance, as far as it can with safety, to the ascendency of the white race—that it ought to be the guardian of the civilization, progress, and liberty of this continent, in reference to those portions of it where they are exposed to this danger. I will not say that in no case should we ever give them military aid, but for a case to justify this, it must be an extraordinary one, and to be judged of by its intrinsic merits, and not governed by a general rule.

I have said that if this be a case of war between races, if the white race be not responsible for it, if they have been patriotic and courageous in their own defence, it would present a strong appeal to my sympathy. But is it a war of races? I have examined the case with all the lights before me, and I shall now state the conclusion to which I have arrived.

It is now, I believe, substantially a war of races, but was not so at the beginning. It seems that, from the beginning of the Government of Yucatan, there have been violent factions, accompanied by a disposition on all sides to call in the aid of the Indians; and, in order to obtain their aid as voters, certain promises were made to them which have not been well fulfilled. It would seem that, in this case, one of the factions, to secure the Indian vote, promised the reduction of the capitation tax—an enormous burden which presses them to the earth. The conflict originated, it is said, in this wise. In the contest for power between Mendez and Barbachino, the partisans of the former, about Campeachy, made proposals to the Indians to reduce the capitation tax. Mendez, in consequence of these overtures, obtained the aid of the Indians, and was elected governor. But when he got into power he did not fulfil his promises. Instead of removing the taxes, he enforced their collection rigidly, which produced some disturbance. It seems further—for this is an inference rather than a statement—that the question of the war between the United States and Mexico entered into the quarrel, and that Barbachino leaned to the side of Mexico, while Mendez took the side of neutrality, which preponderated. It would also seem that the Indian resistance was at first feeble. In the midst of the conflicts of the contending factions it grew, and became at length so important and threatening as to occasion alarm and consternation. There has been almost no display whatever of courage on the part of the white population, and very little evidence of patriotism throughout the whole affair. All this tends very much to weaken my sympathies. Were the case confined to the male population I should have little or none. But there are helpless women and children, whose wretched condition, on the score of humanity, demands interference. I may add, that there is some information inducing the belief that it is not altogether even now a war of races. Barbachino is now in power; and such has been the violence of faction that a large portion of the forces of Mendez has withdrawn from the army on the change in the government. I will state, in this connection, what perhaps should have been said before, that the intelligence brought by a late arrival at New Orleans establishes beyond all controversy that England has not been implicated in the affair. It appears that even the British settlement at the Balize is threatened by Indians; that the city last captured is not more than one hundred miles distant from that settlement, and that a despatch had been sent for additional troops from Jamaica. This apprehension of an attack had resulted from the British settlement having sent down a few vessels to the coast of Yucatan to pick up the miserable fugitives. If there had been any suspicion as to the conduct of that settlement, or British subjects in that quarter, these facts ought to put an end to them for ever.

How far ought we to go, then, on the score of humanity? I am of the opinion that all the naval force which we can spare should be sent to relieve these helpless people, and that we should supply food and raiment for their present necessities, and convey them whereso-ever they desire—to Cuba or elsewhere. In a word, we should do all that humanity requires. But I cannot agree to carry out the pro-visions of a bill which authorizes the President to use the army and navy to take military occupation of the country. No considerations of humanity, or of the ascendency of the white race in Yucatan, justify, in my opinion, the adoption of such a course of policy. It is now clear that the white population, including the mixed race, is so prostrated and feeble, and the Indians so powerful, that not a hope remains of re-establishing the permanent ascendency of the former. We can, doubtless, by force, subject the Indians and reinstate the whites in power; but the moment we withdraw, the former state of things will recur. We will thus be perpetually engaged in this work. Now, I am not willing to incur the danger and the cost of maintaining the ascendency of the whites. I am not willing to have this task, which does not belong to us, assumed by our Government.

I come now to the amendment of the Senator from Mississippi (Mr. [Jefferson] Davis). As between the bill and the amendment, I prefer the bill. They both propose the same thing. It is true the amendment says only that the President shall have the power, without prescribing what he the President is to do with it. But the President has told us what he will do. He has told us as clearly as if it was put in the amendment. His object is to take military occupation of Yucatan—temporary to be sure, but it must end in permanent occupation. Now, I would rather do that with our own sanction directly which the President proposes to do, than under the cover of this amendment. Nor am I reconciled to the amendment by the preamble offered by the Senator from Alabama [Dixon H. Lewis]. I think the Senator had not seen all the documents when he offered that preamble. It does not reach the case. It presupposes an obligation on the part of the Government of the United States to defend the white race there because we had so crippled Mexico that she could not afford them protection. I believe I state the substance of the preamble correctly?

Mr. Lewis assented.

Mr. Calhoun. The case is very different from what the preamble supposes. Yucatan does not look to Mexico for protection. On the contrary, they are more alarmed at the danger they have to fear from Mexico than from the Indians. Unfortunately for themselves, they assumed a position of neutrality, or, as they say, of independence. They thereby became traitors in the eyes of Mexico; and, no doubt, they will be held responsible as such. Hence we see Mr. Sierra makes a strong remonstrance against the treaty with Mexico. Nay, he goes so far as to say that, as a matter of good faith, the United States should not permit Yucatan to be sacrificed. There has been, in my opinion, a good deal of mismanagement in reference to this whole affair. The people of Yucatan were recognized as neutrals or not, just as suited the pleasure of the President. So far as the collection of revenue was concerned, they were not neutral; as far as the importation of arms into the country was concerned, they were treated as belligerents, and the arms were made contraband of war, lest they should be transferred to Mexico. The effect has been this, and they complain of it: that they have been kept destitute of arms and means whereby to defend themselves in this contest. On reviewing the whole case, however, I think that the white population of Yucatan have, in a great measure, themselves to blame. The factious conflicts—fierce and maniacal—in which they have been engaged, to the last, have involved them in these frightful calamities. But the administration is not wholly irresponsible. They knew that Mendez had declared neutrality, if not independence, and approved of it. They beheld the progress of those Indians. They witnessed their devastations, and instead of interfering to defend those who had declared themselves to be our friends, stood by with arms folded, and they have incurred a very heavy responsibility. They ought to have given no countenance to their claim of neutrality and treated them as one of the Mexican States, or ought to have fully recognized their neutrality and independence. On the contrary, by regarding them as a Mexican State, or as a neutral and independent power, as best suited their convenience, they have placed the people of Yucatan in an awful condition, by leaving them unprotected from the fury of the Indians, and exposing them to be treated as traitors by Mexico; and we are now appealed to, at this late period, to remedy the evils resulting from this fluctuating and uncertain policy, when they are no longer curable but by incurring hazards and sacrifices we cannot be justified in making.

From Crallé, ed., *Works,* 4:454–479. Also printed in the Washington, D.C., *Daily National Intelligencer,* May 22, 1848, p. 3; the Richmond, Va., *Whig and Public Advertiser,* May 26, 1848, pp. 1–2; the Washington, D.C., *Daily Union,* May 31, 1848, p. 1; the Charleston, S.C., *Mercury,* June 21, 1848, p. 2, and June 22, 1848, p. 2; *Congressional Globe,* 30th Cong., 1st Sess., Appendix, pp. 630–633; Houston, ed., *Proceedings and Debates,* pp. 627–631; Wilson, ed., *Essential Calhoun,* pp. 133–152. Variant in *Congressional Globe,* 30th Cong., 1st Sess., p. 770; Benton, *Abridgment of Debates,* 16:202–203. Another variant in the Charleston, S.C., *Mercury,* May 19, 1848, p. 2, and the Richmond, Va., *Enquirer,* May 19, 1848, p. 4. Other variants in the Alexandria, Va., *Gazette and Virginia Advertiser,* May 16, 1848, p. 3; the Philadelphia, Pa., *Public Ledger,* May 16, 1848, p. 3; the New York, N.Y., *Herald,* May 16, 1848, p. 2, and May 17, 1848, p. 4; the Charleston, S.C., *Courier,* May 19, 1848, p. 2, and May 22, 1848, p. 2. Note: Crallé added a rare annotation to his publication of this speech: "The copy of this Speech in the editor's possession has endorsed on it, in the handwriting of Mr. Calhoun, the words *'It is badly reported.'"*

Remarks in Debate with Lewis Cass on the Proposed Occupation of Yucatan

[In the Senate, May 15, 1848]
[*At the conclusion of Calhoun's speech, Cass challenged Calhoun's assertion that Yucatan had no good harbor, referring to one reported by a Naval officer recently returned.*]

Mr. Calhoun. I have not spoken on this subject without taking pains to be thoroughly informed. That which the Senator represents as a port, is not a port; it is an open harbor. If I were to name the gentleman on whose authority I relied, I am sure it would satisfy the Senator. I may name him—Lieut. [Matthew F.] Maury. But this does not touch the question. Let the gentleman answer the reasons I have assigned for the position that, even with Yucatan in our hands, in case of a war with England that entrance to the gulf would be completely closed against us in consequence of her command of the Carribean sea.

[*Cass reiterated that there was a good harbor in Yucatan and asserted that steam power made it possible for the U.S. to contend with enemies in the channel between Cuba and Florida.*]

Mr. Calhoun in reply stated that Great Britain already possessed the command of the entrance to the gulf, and that in the event of war with her not a single vessel of ours could enter.

[*Cass argued that the U.S. should acquire naval ascendancy over Great Britain in the area.*]

Mr. Calhoun. The gentleman says that we must contend with the naval supremacy of Great Britain. Well, that is a great proposition. I do not deny it. But that is a different question altogether from the defence of this passage. If the gentleman aims at contending with the naval supremacy of Great Britain, let him do so in the proper mode. Let him avoid the expense of this Yucatan war. Let him put the navy into an efficient condition. If he aims at commanding the American seas, let him indulge no longer in his warlike enterprizes, which exhaust the means that ought to be applied to the support of the naval force.

Mr. Cass. The distinguished Senator will pardon me, but I do not precisely understand what his views are respecting the nature of re-colonization.

Mr. Calhoun. I said nothing about it. I spoke of colonization.

Mr. Cass. But I desired to ask what the Senator's views are. Will he allow me to ask him if he considers Jamaica a colony of England?

Mr. Calhoun. It is a "possession" of England.

Mr. Cass. I should like to know, then, the meaning of the word "colony."

Mr. Calhoun. How far Jamaica is a colony of England, it is not necessary to discuss. The expression in Mr. [James] Monroe's message is "colonization." Colonization is the act of colonizing, or sending out inhabitants to a country, to colonize, to settle peacefully in a country. I ask if the conquest of a country is colonization?

Mr. Cass. The act of conquest is not colonization, but the moment you conquer and reduce a country to subjection, you have a colony. The doctrine for which Mr. Monroe contended was, that European powers should not plant colonies on this continent.

Mr. Calhoun. Should not colonize.

[*Cass replied.*]

Mr. Calhoun. I shall restate the case and the gentleman may make as much as he pleases of it. The language of Mr. Polk is this: that obtaining aid from Great Britain, Yucatan may tender her her sovereignty, and Great Britain may assert dominion over the country; in one word, connecting this expression with the document itself, means that if Great Britain sends a force there, and obtains the sovereignty of Yucatan, it will be a case of "colonization." Would it be so? Not at all. It would be a case of tendered sovereignty, accepted by Great Britain.

From Houston, ed., *Proceedings and Debates,* p. 631. Variant in the Alexandria, Va., *Gazette and Virginia Advertiser,* May 17, 1848, p. 3.

From Geo[rge] Wood

Washington, May 15, 1848

My dear Sir: Thirty years since, through your kindness I was appointed a Clerk in the War Department, and during part of two years I had a desk which brought me into daily intercourse with yourself. I was a boy then, with some powers of observation and susceptibility of cultivation. The value of this brief official intercourse with a mind I then venerated as of the highest order (a sentiment which has deepened with the growth of years) has been of the greatest service to me—far more than may be conceivable to yourself.

Peter Schlemihl is the creation of vacant & solitary hours spent in the City of New York in the Winter of 1845–6, after having been displaced from Office on the coming in of Mr. [James K.] Polk's administration—a position of extreme hardship to one who has been trained to do but one thing. Casper Hanver released from his dungeon was not more unfit for active labor than is a Clerk of the Public Departments to take part in the pursuits of mercantile life. To save myself from *ennui* I took up *for the first time in my life* my pen to create a fiction—and so beguile the weary winter nights of the year '45–6. Of this labor you have in this Vol: the first fruits.

I beg you, my dear Sir, to accept it as the expression of my grateful recollections of your early friendship, and of my unceasing and unchanging admiration of your integrity and intellect. With all respect, I remain, the last of your "War Office Proper" Clerks. Geo: Wood.

ALS in AU, Amelia Gayle (Mrs. Josiah) Gorgas Scrapbook. NOTE: The accompanying book was *Peter Schlemihl in America* (Philadelphia: Carey and Hart, 1848). George Wood (1799–1870) became the author of three later works: *Modern Pilgrims: Showing the Improvements in Travel and the Newest Methods of Reaching the Celestial City* (1855), *Marrying Too Late, a Tale* (1857), and *Future Life; or Scenes in Another World* (1858).

From ——, [*ca.* 5/17/1848?]. All that remains of this letter is a cover addressed to Calhoun in Washington in an unknown hand with a barely legible postmark with no discernible place and a possible date of 5/17/1848. Calhoun's AEU on the cover reads: "Send autograph, and to send a volume of my speeches after my return home or return here." Manuscript owned by Bruce W. Ball.

To [ANDREW PICKENS CALHOUN, Marengo County, Ala.]

Washington, 18th May 1848

My dear Andrew, I write now in order to say, that I have not yet received a statement of the amount of interest due on the debt to Mr. [Ker] Boyce. It is desirable that I should be informed at an early date in order that I may make the necessary arrangement to meet it. There ought to be as little delay as practicable in doing so. If you have not got the amount, I wish you to obtain it without delay, & transmit it to me.

I wrote you some time since, and enclosed you a paper containing a list of sundry tracts of land lying in Marengo County, which had been bid off by a friend, and of which, if we desire it, we could take a part; and requested you to ascertain their location, & quality & give your opinion as to their value. I hope you have got my letter, & will give the subject your early attention. I have since learned that no. 18 is not included in the purchase, but I would be glad to have your opinion of its value for a friend. I think you told me, that absentees are double taxed in Alabama. Am I right in my impression?

I hope our prospect of a crop is good. The weather has been very cool here, but is now warm & favourable for the growth of vegetation. I learn from home that my crop looks finely, & that my business is going on well in my absence.

The members of the unconstitutional & fraudulent assemblage of Baltimore are in great numbers here. They seem to be much divided & distracted, & it is perfectly uncertain who will be nominated. I ["trust" *canceled and* "hope" *interlined*], that both it & the Philadelphia assemblage will break up in distraction, but I fear the cohesion of plunder is too strong for that.

I delivered my opinion at large a few days since on the Yucatan question to a very crow[d]ed House, and it is thought with great success. It will appear in the papers of tomorrow, or Monday. I am of the opinion that the movement has been effectually checked, & that it will be abandoned. So much for taking as I did, the ball at the first bounce ["as I did" *canceled*].

I hope to hear from you soon.

My love to Margaret [Green Calhoun] & the children.

ALU (signature clipped) in NcD, John C. Calhoun Papers. NOTE: An EU on the final page of this letter reads: "Autograph sent to Mr. Thomas, Columbia[,] S.C."

To A[ndrew] J. Donelson, [Berlin], 5/18. A two-page ALS to Donelson written in the Senate Chamber by Calhoun on this day was offered for sale as item 15 in *Catalogue of Autograph Letters, Play Bills, Books, [and] Signatures* (published by John Heise, Syracuse, N.Y.), No. 12 (1909), p. 2, and again in *The Collection of Autographs of James L. Foote, of Slatington, Pa.* (New York: Anderson Auction Co., 1911), item 164.

To ——, 5/18. Calhoun discusses the course to be pursued by Southern delegates who are passing through Washington on their way to the Democratic National Convention. "I am of the opinion one of them should to take [*sic*] decided stand against the admission of the Barnburners. They are our most implacable enemies, and are openly committed to the Wilmot proviso." Abs of 4-pp. ALS advertised for sale as item 227 in *A Catalogue of Autographs and Manuscripts, No. 69* (New York: Dodd, Mead & Co., 1903), p. 46.

From ELLWOOD FISHER

Cincinnati, 5 mo[nth] 19, 1848

Dear Friend, Until this morning I did not relinquish the expectation of being at Washington before the Convention at Baltimore. I have three times got ready and have been prevented by the illness of one or another of my family—this time by that of my second child. I shall not now be able to get there in less than three or four weeks as other engagements intervene.

I am under the impression that both party nominations this time will be failures. The anti slavery men of this State and I presume in others are making decided movements to defeat any nominee not fully pledged in their favour—and as it is I presume the policy—at least the intention of the Caucus men to evade the question, this will countervail them.

Perhaps it would be as well for both Caucuses to nominate non-committalists, and then for independent candidates ["on both" *canceled*] to be announced to oppose them. I should not be surprized if [Henry] Clay or [Zachary] Taylor is nominated at Phil[adelphi]a ["if" *canceled and* "that" *interlined*; John] McLean ["were to" *canceled and* "will" *interlined*] be brought forward separately. It is understood here that the recent call for an Anti slavery convention in the State signed by 3000 men has some such purpose.

The South may rest assured of the fact that hostility to their institutions is becoming more and more inveterate—and is extending. The Press is closed against any thing said on the other side, and filled with sarcasm and denunciation against her in every form of falsehood and virulence and folly.

This letter will probably reach thee on the eve of the Baltimore nomination. I have seen a number of the delegates from this section of the country and the South, and the indications are favourable to [Levi] Woodbury. The Kentucky men I think would go for him and some of the Indiana.

I do not see however that we can support any nominee of that body, pronouncing as it certainly will in favour of the War, and equivocating on the Wilmot proviso or evading it. Woodbury himself has fully endorsed the justice of the War in his letter to a New York Park meeting—and that with me is a serious objection.

I am highly gratified with thy position on Yucatan. When I come on to Washington I want to ascertain whether any thing is to be done ["south of" *canceled*] out of South Carolina for the true faith as I am determined that there shall be at least one paper more in the country not in base subserviency to party and to the worst passions of the community. With great regard thy friend, Ellwood Fisher.

ALS in ScCleA. NOTE: This letter was postmarked on 5/19 on the "Little Miami R.R."

To Col. JAMES ED[WARD] COLHOUN, [Abbeville District, S.C.]

Washington, 22d May 1848
My dear James, I am happy to have your approval of my remarks in reference to the French Revolution. I see they have attracted much attention in England, and drawn forth high compliments. I regard the failure of the Chartists in England as you do. It was the turning point of affairs in Europe. Had they succeeded, it would [have] been long—very long, before order & authority would be restored in Europe; but as it is, the revolutionary movements have gone, probably as far as it is destined to go, at least for the present.

I agree with you, that [Cadet William] Ransom [Colhoun] ought to resign & take the management of his father's [John Ewing Colhoun's] estate. I do not think it advisable for him to enter the army. The education he has already got at the [Military] Academy, will suffice to make him a good officer if ["the" *canceled and* "his" *interlined*] services ["of his" *canceled*] should be required to defend the country.

I will, with much pleasure, seize every opportunity to forward your desire to dispose of your landed estate, and ["will" *interlined*] adhere strictly to the prudential suggestions you have made, as to the course to be pursued. I hope you may succeed in getting a purchaser. It would enable you to contract your operations within more moderate limits, & requiring less fatigue & care to conduct them.

I fear, however, not much can be done through any of the diplomatick corps here[,] but if the derangement of business, and the state of uncertainty, as to the future, should continue in Europe, so as to make capitalists look to this country for investments, I may have an opportunity, through some of them, who would probably visit Washington[,] to render you efficient aid in carrying out your intention.

As to politicks, every thing still remains in a state of uncertainty. Although the Baltimore Convention is now in session, no one pretends to form an opinion, as to who will be the nominee. Report from Baltimore just received, says that [Lewis] Cass & [James] Buchanan will unite their forces, each having agreed to rally on the other, if ["the" *interlined*] strongest. If such should be the case, the former will probably be ["elected" *canceled and* "nominated" *interlined*]; but I put little faith in the rumour. I have no confidence in either.

It is now more doubtful than it has been, whether the Government of Mexico will ratify the treaty. The prospect would seem to be against it. Should it not be ratified, there will be a great effort made to take the Whole, but, I trust, I shall be able to defeat it, by taking ["my stand on" *interlined*] a defensive line—that of the treaty.

The Yucatan question is dropt for the present. Whether it will be revived will depend on circumstances. My speech ["against it" *interlined*] appeared in the [Washington Daily National] Intelligencer this morning. I will send you a copy, as soon as I can get some extra copies of the paper. It is thought it made a strong impression, and contributed principally to the dropping of the question for the present.

It was one of the wildest & most absurd measures ever proposed by the Executive. Congress will not adjourn probably before August.

My health continues good. I am sorry to learn by your sister's [Floride Colhoun Calhoun's] letter ["to me" *interlined*] that yours was delicate when you were at Fort Hill. I hope it is better. Yours truly & affectionately, J.C. Calhoun.

ALS in ScCleA; PEx in Jameson, ed., *Correspondence,* pp. 755–756.

From DANIEL PRATT

Prattville[,] Autauga Co[unty,] Ala.
May 22nd 1848

Sir, I have authorised Mr. G[eorge] Cooke an Artist from New Orleans to call on you and request of you to sit for a full length

Portrait should it comport with your many important duties to afford him the time.

I need not add proffessions of my high regard for your eminent talents and distinguished Services. Verry Respectfully Your Ob[edien]t Serv[an]t, Daniel Pratt.

ALS in ScCleA. NOTE: Pratt was a patron of Cooke (1793–1849) and built a gallery in Prattville, to house his paintings. An AEU by Calhoun reads, "Mr. Pratt. Set for portrait."

To H[ENRY] W. CONNER, [Charleston]

Washington, 23d May [1848]

My dear Sir, You will see by the proceedings at Baltimore, that Gen[era]l [James M.] Commander has been admitted to be a member of the Convention, and to cast 9 votes for the State, on his own allegation, that he was nominated by a meeting called for the whole State & felt himself authorised to represent the whole State! Nothing can [bet]ter ill[us]trate the [fr]audulent character of these conventions & the gross deception they practice on the Country. I trust our papers, one and all, will unite in denouncing as it deserves, the false statement of Commander & his audacious attempt to misrepresent the State. It is due to the State that the falsehood & fraud should be indignantly exposed. If it should pass with impunity, it may do much mischief.

That you may be [in] full possession of [all] the facts in reference to the number & composition of the meeting, I enclose, in confidence, a letter of Col. [Robert F.W.] Allston to me, which I will thank you to return after you are done with it.

The affair may be thought to be a small one, but it may lead to bad consequences, if not promptly and indignantly met. Truly, J.C. Calhoun.

ALS in ScC; photostat of ALS in DLC, Henry Workman Conner Papers. NOTE: James M. Commander was a Georgetown rice planter who had been sheriff, mayor, and brigadier general of militia. He was admitted to the Democratic National Convention to represent S.C., where he voted twice for Levi Woodbury and once for Lewis Cass for President.

To A[NDREW] J. DONELSON,
[U.S. Minister to Prussia]

Washington, 23d May 1848

My dear Sir, I am much obliged to you for enclosing me the note of Lord Westmoreland. I highly appreciate the good opinion of the intelligent & disinterested.

The views you take, and the opinions you express in reference to the present state of Europe, accord very much with my own. The moderation with which the revolution in France is thus far marked, and the non interference of the other powers of Europe with her affairs, constrasted [sic] with what occurred in the first, afford conclusive proof, that the lesson taught by the latter has not been lost, and gives hope, that the present may go through with far less sacrafice & miserary, and be terminated much more beneficially. But, we must not be too confident and sanguine. There is much to do, and many difficulties in the way to be removed before Europe ["can settle down" interlined] in a new, and stable state, better than that, which has been overthrown. Among the difficulties is that, to which you refer, I meane the financial. So long as the present revolutionary governments shall continue the heavy burthens ["of" canceled and "imposed by" interlined] those they have overthrown—so long, as they shall collect the present amount of revenue and continue the present extravagant disbursements, they will be exposed, not only to reaction, but convulsive movements, one after another, to be terminated in purely military governments. But great & difficult is the task of reducing taxes & disbursements. In old governments they cannot be reduced, to any great extent, without disturbing dangerously existing interests & where there exist heavy debts & large military establishments, as is the case all over Europe, without coming into conflict with the two most powerful interests, the stock holders & the army.

But as great as this difficulty is, it is by no means the most formidable. There are great political errors to correct, errors going to the they are instituted. Without going into them, which would carry me beyond the limits properly belonging to a letter, it is sufficient to say, that the prevailing opinion of the popular party, both in our country and Europe, that the *mere numerical* majority is the people, and have, as such, the indefeasible right to govern, is a great & radical error—so much so, that no government based on it can long endure. Such a government would be, but the absolute form of popular government, and not the constitutional form of such governments; and must, of necessity, soon degenerate, where the revenue and disbursements ["are" *interlined*] great, into absolute government of the monarchical form. Indeed, of all governments, that ["of" *interlined*] a popular constitutional government, is the most difficult ["by far" *interlined*] to constitute and maintain, in populous & wealthy communities, as the experiment now going on in France will in the end prove. Although it is making under the most favourable ["aspicious"(?) *canceled and* "circumstances" *interlined*] I have little, or no faith in its success.

Even we, I fear, with our happy start, and the most fortunate combination of circumstances, are destined to encounter great difficulty in maintaining & preserving ours. It has, in my opinion, long been working in the wrong direction, and with an increased force, I am sorry to state, under the present [James K. Polk] administration, which, while it has aimed in a right direction in reference to the internal concerns of the Union, has more than counteracted, whatever benefic[i]al effect that might have resulted therefrom, by the wrong direction given in reference to our exterior relations. The war with Mexico has reacted most unfortunately on our interior relations. It has added a heavy de[b]t, prevented thereby the reduction of duties & disbursements, & greatly increased the patronage of the government. I had hopes ["it" *canceled and* "the war" *interlined*] was coming to a close; but fear from the last intelligence, that the prospect is against the ratification of the treaty [by Mexico]. If it should not be ratified, it is to be feared, that a violent and successful effort will be made to conquer & hold in subjection the whole country.

In the meane time, another and dangerous question has sprung up in reference to Yucatan, more complicated ["than" *canceled*] even than that of Mexico. I enclose you a copy of my remarks on it, as printed in the Intelligencer, which ["will" *interlined*] give you my views in reference to it. It does not do me full justice. I simply corrected the reporter's notes, without writing out what I said from them. The ["speech" *interlined*] has not been printed in pamphlet, or I would send it in that form to you.

28th May. The Baltimore Convention has nominated [Lewis] Cass for Pres[iden]t & Gen[era]l [William O.] Butler for V. P[residen]t. The success of the ticket is very doubtful. Yours truly & sincerely, J.C. Calhoun.

ALS in DLC, Andrew Jackson Donelson Papers.

C[AVE] JOHNSON, [Postmaster General], to [John C.] Calhoun and [Armistead] Burt, [Representative from S.C.]

Post Office Department, 24 May 1848

Messrs. Calhoun & Burt: I have carefully examined the application transmitted through you, for an increase of the service on the route between Augusta & Greenville. There is no principle upon which the Department has acted since the passage of the Act of 3rd of March 1845, which would justify so great an increase of expenditure upon a route yielding so small a revenue to the Department—during the last year ending 30 of June 1847, the offices on the route yielded as follows:

Augusta	$4483		
Hamburg	573		
Edgefield C.H.	$489	Due West Corner	$ 98
Dentonville	22	Craytonsville	11
Longmire Store	60	Anderson C.H.	181
Winter Seat	55	Steeles	18
Fraziersville	67	Pendleton	198
Abbeville C.H.	210	Double Branches	17
	$903	Pickensville	28
		Greenville $583	
			551

making a revenue of only $1,454. The offices at the ends of the route receive their main supplies from other quarters; any reasonable sum added for the proportion of this route, of the proceeds of the offices at the ends, would be probably counterbalanced by the revenues properly belonging to other routes connecting with this at Abbeville C.H. Anderson C.H. & Pendleton. We now pay for tri-weekly service in 2 h. coaches on this line $3,575. It is difficult to conceive that the mails on a route yielding so little revenue and running tri-weekly cannot be transported in two horsepost coaches, as certified by the Postmasters.

It is very unusual to find the revenues so small on a route and the mails taken over them so large. An increase of the service, as proposed, can only be made with a view to the transportation of the mail as directed by the Act of 1845 and would add one thousand dollars annually to the expenses of the line, making the whole annual expenditure on it three times as much as the income.

That I may not be mistaken, however, in the size of the mails to be transported over it, I have directed the Postmasters to weigh the mails for a week passing over it, and the question will be left open for the returns. C. Johnson.

FC in DNA, RG 28 (Post Office Department), Letters Sent by the Postmaster General, S.2:8–9.

From D[AVID] J. McCORD

Fort Motte [S.C.], May 24, 1848

Dear Sir, I procured from France this winter a small volume, of great Merit, written by Mr. [Frederic] Bastiat one of the cleverest Free Trade writers of that country, and have had it translated, with the view to a publication in this country; as it is a small volume of about 170 pages and written in a style that renders it worthy of being a popular free trade manual. It is an admirable exposure of the Sophisms of the Protective system. Mr. John Russell, a very intelligent Bookseller of Charleston, an old nullifier, under[took] to have it published at the North, with a view to a more extensive circulation, and offered it to the Harpers and to [William H.] Appleton but they refused it, because it was opposed to their tariff principles, but it is now in the press of Mr. [George] Putnam of N.Y. and his and Mr. Russell's joint expense, and I have been requested by Mr. Russell to procure your countenance and approbation of the Volume, which he thinks will greatly assist its circulation. I will write to-day to Mr. Putnam to send you a copy by mail as soon as it is printed, and should it meet your approval, you will oblige us all, by a few lines to that effect, addressed either to myself or to Mr. Putnam and enclosed to Mr. Putnam to be published in such way as he may deem most beneficial.

Could you procure also the commendations of some distinguished northern & western free Trade man, for a similar purpose? I will direct a copy to be sent to Mr. [Robert J.] Walker, and if your intercourse with him, would allow of your asking a similar act from him, it would be desireable. I have no other interest in the matter than the good of our old cause. With great respect Your Ob[edien]t Serv[an]t, D.J. McCord.

[P.S.] I leave here for Pendleton 1st June, where I shall spend the summer.

431

ALS in ScCleA. NOTE: Louisa Cheves McCord, wife of David McCord, translated Bastiat's work. It was published in New York and Charleston in 1848 under the title *Sophisms of the Protective Policy.* An AEU by Calhoun reads, "Mr. McCord, Relates to Bastiat volume on free trade now in the press at N. York."

From J[ACOB] P. REED

Anderson C[ourt] H[ouse, S.C.], May 25/48

Sir, Altho, silent, I have no doubt but you were an interested looker on, from the first effort made by the Districts of Anderson & Abbeville to control the rout[e] of the Greenville & Columbia Rail Road, up to the location at Newberry; and Since that time I suppose the interest previously felt by you, has ripened into a fixed anxiety for the Success of the enterprize. You ha[v]e no doubt thought much as to its importance to the State—the section of country through which it will run and in which it terminates—the probabilities of its Success, value of the stock &c. &c. If so, now that there is no longer a sectional contest as to the rout[e], and all that remains to be done is to build the road, may I ask your views in refference to the work generally in some form for public use. It may be regarded as a fixed fact I think, that the road will be built, or rather that no other Connecting our section of the State with the Sea-board will ever be attempted. The graduation[,] Bridging[,] Tresseling &c from Columbia to Anderson C.H. will be put under contract in a short time, and the work pushed with all practicable speed to completion.

It is true the company have not sufficient funds to build the road, but we have no doubt they can be obtained. But to do so, it will be necessary we should bring every possible influence to bear and knowing the salutary effect the public expression of a favorable opinion from you would have upon our people from the Sea-board to the mountains has induced me to address you most respectfully asking the expression of that opinion. Whilst asking your opinions however, it may not be improper to suggest some of the more prominent points of view in which ["its" *interlined*] sanguine friends regard the enterprize.

We look upon the location, as decidedly the best that could have been made for a Rail Road of equal length, in South Carolina; for the following reasons.

Starting at Columbia the centre and Capital of the State, it runs up the east Bank of Broad River into the richest part of Fairfield

District, a distance of twenty two miles, where it crosses, and runs thence diagonally across more than half the upper part of the State a distance of 126 miles to Anderson C.H. a point within 12 miles of the Georgia & 40 of the North Carolina lines.

It runs through and contiguous to Nine of the largest and wealthiest Districts in the State, containing within its reach, somewhat in the form of a parallelogram, a population of 200,000 Souls. It cuts all the Rivers, market roads &c of more than one half the upper part of the State & at a point below most of the wealth and population, and hence the trade and travel of all that portion of the State & from beyond the mountains must come to the road naturally as water runs down stream. Its upper terminus is at a point where the trade and travel of 5 or 6 counties of Georgia and a number of North Carolina, can find a market nearer and better, than any other they can reach. In the districts of this State contiguous to, and that must trade to the road, is raised very nearly one half the cotton & more than half the corn[,] wheat[,] and other marketable products, raised in South Carolina.

Hence it will accommodate double the number of the inhabitants of the State with commercial facilities, than any other rout[e] could have done and avoids the necessity for another road.

It will carry to market double the amount of produce in, and from beyond the State, that any other rout[e] could have done & will return double the amount of merchandise, family supplies, &c. From the vast population hard by it, travel must also be greatly increased ["over" *interlined*] any other rout[e] attainable.

There is double the amount of population and wealth interested in its construction, that could have been interested in any other rout[e], and hence the chances of building it are doubled. It terminates as before remarked at one end, at Columbia, and by building up that place will add to the wealth and importance of the upper part of the State. At the other end, in a (comparatively) vast unoc[c]upied Country (Anderson & Pickens Districts) that only needs some stimulus of the sort, to increase its population, develope its resources, diversify its pursuits and render it one of the most interesting sections of the Southern States. It will convey to Charleston our own Sea-port, a very large trade from Georgia ["Tennessee" *interlined*] & North Carolina and the western Districts of this State, that has hitherto found its way to Savannah—promoting her Commercial importance, direct trade with other Countries & ["her" *interlined*] wealth—binding the State together as a unit—increasing her political & physical strength &c. &c. and in this connection its social,

433

political & military advantages might be looked to, and many enlarged views incident thereto taken.

Finally its friends are fully impressed from these and many other Considerations, that if economically built and Judiciously managed, its stock must pay exceedingly well.

These are some of the more general views, imperfectly & hurriedly expressed, entertained by the friends of the great enterprize in hand. They impress us fully with belief, laying all former predilections aside and looking ca[l]mly at the work, that no such location could elsewhere have been selected—that no such work in point of importance, has been, or could have been projected, within the State of South Carolina.

Will you do me the honor at your convenience, to give your opinions upon some or all the foregoing points & upon such others as you may be pleased, with permission to make them public.

Having been heretofore deeply identified with the work in hand—feeling unusual anxiety for its success—oc[c]upying the position of one of the Directors of the Company, and therefore officially bound to devote myself to it, I trust you will pardon the liberty I have taken in addressing you, and particularly the assumptions I have ventured in refference to your views and feelings as connected with the enterprize. My only object is to advance the interest of the work, and the expression of your opinions, I am sure will be of great importance to it.

The amount of available funds now on the Books of the Company exclusive of Greenville & North Carolina, supposing the road to stop at Anderson, is $623,000. The cost of constructing the road from Columbia to Anderson C.H. according to the Estimates of the Engineers with a light rail $742,000 and with the T. Rail $1,150,000. That it will be seen we have a sum very nearly sufficient to erect the road with a light Iron already subscribed, but whether or not, we have advanced too far to look back. If we let the present opportunity go & fail to b[u]ild the present road, I think it may be regarded as a final effort in the upper part of South Carolina. It must not be let go—the work is to[o] important to the State, and especially to our portion of it, to let it fail—the charactre of the Districts through which it runs and in which it terminates, and of the State of South Carolina are deeply implicated and their vindication demands that the work should be carried out. May I hear from you. I have the honor to remain with high regard, your most Ob[edien]t Servant, J.P. Reed.

ALS in ScCleA. NOTE: Jacob Pinckney Reed (1814–1880), was a well-known lawyer and had served in the S.C. House of Representatives. In 1868 he was one of the elected members of the U.S. House of Representatives refused their seats by the Reconstruction Congress.

To T[HOMAS] G. CLEMSON, [Brussels]

Washington, 26th May 1848

My dear Sir, Since my last I have received your's of the 26th April, with letters from Anna [Maria Calhoun Clemson] for her Mother [Floride Colhoun Calhoun] & [Martha] Cornelia [Calhoun].

I see by our last arrival, that France & Germany are begin[n]ing the work of reconstruction. That is the *task*; not but that they may ["form" *interlined*] new Governments for that is not difficult; but can they form such, as will stand and put an end to revolution? Germany, if wise, may; for she has the materials, but, I fear, that in France it will, at least for the present, prove impossible. She has it is evidently [*sic*] made great progress, since her first revolution, in political knowledge, which has thus far guarded her against those scenes of violence & blood shed which marked the first, but there are great difficulties before her. She is entering on an untrodden path; to reconstruct society, as well as Government, with materials not well suited to either ["purpose" *interlined*]. I shall watch the attempt with profound interest, but with little expectation of its success. I hope she will be permitted to have a fair opportunity, so that if she fails, it will be attributed to the intrinsick difficulty of the task, and not to interference and difficu[l]ties from without. If, under such circumstances, she should fail, I see no alternative for her, but an *imperial Government*.

Since I last wrote you, the prospect of the ratification of the ["treaty" *interlined*] by Mexico is more doubtful. The impression now is, that it will not be. In the meane time, we are threatened with a very ["trouble" *canceled and* "troublesome" *interlined*] question about Yucatan. I enclose herewith my remarks on the subject. It is not satisfactorily reported, although it passed under my revision. I simply corrected the report of the Stenographer, without writing ["it" *canceled and* "out" *interlined*] my speech. It will, however, give you a pretty correct & full view of my argument.

The Baltimore convention is now in session, but have not yet made a nomination. I will keep my letter open, until I hear the result. Among its proceedings, it has admitted a man of the name of [James M.] Commander, to cast the 9 votes of S. Carolina, although his au-

435

thority to act was derived solely from a small meeting in Georgetown of 54 persons, of whom the greater part were Yankee merchants & Jews doing business there, without having ["a" *canceled*] permanent residence. What a farce! And yet, as far as the party is concerned, the nomination of the body is the election of the President.

I greatly regret, that the state of things in Europe will, probably, deprive us of the happiness of seeing you, Anna & the children [John Calhoun Clemson and Floride Elizabeth Clemson] this summer, which we had so confidently anticipated at one time. I do not think, however, that you have much cause to regret it, as far as it relates to the business object you had in view. It would, I fear, be impossible for you to dispose of your place [in Edgefield District] & negroes & other property, if you were to make a visit, to advantage at this time. The reaction from the derangement of the commerce & business of Europe has so reduced the price of our great staples, & Cotton especially, and the same cause, with the war in Mexico, has so completely drained the specie circulation from the South, that property is not Saleable—not even negroes, but at a very reduced price. The pressure, in consequence, is greater than I have ever known in that quarter; so much so, that banks have ceased to discount. Unless there should be a great & favourable change between this & the end of the year, of which I fear there is no probability, you could not sell, but at a great sacrafice; I see no alternative, but to continue your present arrangement until the return of more favourable times. Such, at least, is my impression. I give it, leaving you to decide for yourself.

As to the money transactions between us, including Andrew [Pickens Calhoun], I certainly greatly regret to perceive your dissatisfaction, both because the accounts ["between us" *interlined*] have not been adjusted, and the interest has not been paid on what ["has been" *canceled and* "is" *interlined*] due to you. In reference to the former, you propose to leave it to any of my legal friends in Charleston, that I may select, ["who may" *canceled and* "to" *interlined*] adjust it, by reference to the books of Mr. [John Ewing] Bonneau. As to the latter, you propose, that after the account is adjusted, Andrew ["to" *canceled and* "should" *interlined*] pay one half & the other half to be continued in my hand, on certain conditions.

You must, I think, see on reflection, that our accounts cannot be adjusted in the manner proposed, as there are payments (for the land you bought) that did not pass through ["his" *canceled and* "Mr. Bonneau's" *interlined*] hands, & the vouchers of which are not at this time under my command, as they are at home, as I wrote you, among my papers. Besides, I see no necessity for adopting the mode you propose, as with your statement, received since I arrived here, and my own vouchers, which includes Mr. Bonneau[']s statement, there is not the slightest necessity to call in the aid of strangers, to settle a plain matter of account.

As to your other proposal, I cannot accept of it. I cannot agree to seperate my interest from ["Andrew(')s" *interlined*] in the noble estate in Alabama, created under his supervision & by his exertions; and which, if it has not yet yielded sufficient to discharge the debt contracted in purchasing the land & stocking the place, has been owing neither to his neglect, nor want of skill, or fidelity of management; but to the unprecedented depression of nine years in the price of cotton. I would rather make any sacrafice, than to take any step to shun any share of responsibility incurred in making the purchase, especially, as it was done with my full and deliberate consent & concurrence. You cannot be more desireous of an adjustment of our accounts, and of the final discharge of the debt due you, than I am. The former shall be done, among the first things, after my return home, and the latter, as soon as the money market will permit a loan to be made at legal interest, on bond & mortgage. At present, it cannot be done. I intended to have written to Andrew to come on for the purpose of making a negotiation in N. York, before we heard of the Revolution in Europe, the effects of which renders such a step impossible at present. It is due to the occasion to say, that, if our accounts have not been adjusted, the fault is not ours. The error made in your first letter, after you received our statement, made it impossible, until you could be heard from again, & your next, was not received, until after my arrival here, when I could not recur to my papers.

It is, also, due to the occasion to say, that, if we have not regularly paid the interest, we have nevertheless paid a large amount on the debt due you on our original settlement; and that, if the interest has not been paid on the balance, it has been owing to the fact, that we have been compelled to apply our surplus means to pay the instalments on the Cuba purchase, which, you know, was bought originally under an arrangement with you & for you, but which was accidentally left on our hands. I say this not in censure, but by way of explanation. As low as cotton has sold ["since we purchased" *interlined*], and short as the last two crops have been ["cut" *canceled*], we have been able to pay the instalments regularly, amounting in the aggregate to a sum equal to that due you. But one more instalment remains due. We have in the meane time kept down the interest on all our other debts, except that due Mr. [Ker] Boyce.

As to the carriage & Horses, they turned out to be a bad barg[a]in. The ["one" *canceled and* "horse" *interlined*] that baulked so badly, continued his bad habit, so as to render him useless as a carriage horse. One wheel of the carriage had the dished side turned inward, and the iron works proved bad from the brittle character of the metal. After offering to sell for a long time, without a purchaser, we had to part with it for $500 on credit and have not yet got the money. Your friend, under whose direction the carriage was built did not do you justice. But, I trust, before another year rolls round, that all our money transactions will be finally closed, and that you will have no farther vexation, or I trouble about them.

28th May. The Baltimore Convention nominated Gen[era]l [Lewis] Cass for the Presidency, & Gen[era]l [William O.] Butler of Kentucky for the V. Presidency, after much distraction and difficulty. I do not think the ticket will succeed.

Love to Anna & the children. Your affectionate father, J.C. Calhoun.

ALS in ScCleA; PEx's in Jameson, ed., *Correspondence*, pp. 756–757.

From [James L. Edwards]

Pension Office, May 26, 1848

Sir, I have the honor to return herewith Mr. Caradine[']s letter, and ["in reply to the same" *interlined*] to inform you that the papers transmitted to this Office by J[ames] F. Caradine, in support of the claim of Elizabeth Saunders widow of John Saunders have been examined and filed under the act of 7 July 1838.

Neither the service of claimant[']s husband nor the date of their marriage have been established in the manner required by the regulations.

The certificate of the Comptroller of North Carolina introduced as evidence of John Saunders[']s] service, exhibits a transcript of seven specia Certificates issued to ["the" *canceled and* "his" *interlined*] name ["of John" *interlined*] for service in the militia of North Carolina, amounting in the aggregate to £89-6 which would cover a period of service of nearly 2 years. Mrs. Saunders in her declaration states that her husband rendered but two terms of service of 3 months each making 6 mo[nths] only. If her statement ["of his service" *interlined*] be correct there must have been more than one John

Saunders engaged in that service. The proof now presented does not enable us to determine, which of these ["pay" *interlined*] certificates or whether any portion of them were issued to her husband. She will be required to show therefore by the testimony of those who were in service with him, that he fulfilled the full term under each engagement for which he was drafted, one day short of 6 months will be fatal to her claim.

Where no record evidence ["of" *canceled and* "as to" *interlined*] the marriage ["as to exis" *canceled*] can be produced, the testimony of Individuals may be received, provided, ["they can show by co" *canceled*] their statements are so corroborated by ascertained collateral fact, themselves ["matter" *canceled*] of record as to justify the department in fixing the date ["thereof" *canceled*] at which it took place with ["any" *canceled and* "some" *interlined*] degree of certainty. The affidavits of John Saunders and Mrs. Frances Lamb do not furnish satisfactory proof upon this point.

The additional evidence ["pre" *canceled*] in the case of Sarah Hays widow of George Hays does not remove any one of the objections urged in my communication to Mr. Caradine of the 28 October last. And ["the" *canceled*] her papers which were enclosed to him in order that the official character and the genuineness of the signature of the Clerk of the ["Clerk" *canceled*] Court of ["Ho" *canceled*] Jackson County Ga. ["might" *canceled and* "may" *interlined*] be certified by a member of Congress or the Secretary of State of that State, in conformity ["to" *canceled*] with the regulation in cases where the Clerk has no ["pub" *canceled*] seal of Office, have been returned with these defects still existing. The rules in this particular must be complied with before any evidence that may be presented can be considered.

We cannot admit either of these claims upon the proof now before the Department.

FC in DNA, RG 15 (Veterans Administration), Letters Sent, 1838–1866.

From T[HOMAS] EWING,
[former Senator from Ohio]

Lancaster [Ohio,] May 26th 1848
Dear Sir, I have read with very great satisfaction your excellant speech [of 5/15] on the Yucatan question published in the [Washing-

ton] Intelligencer of the 22nd. I accord entirely with your views as to the matter in question, but I more especially thank you for setting right, what no living man else could so well do, the true character, purpose & extent—indeed the actual history of the celebrated declaration of Mr. Munroe [*sic;* James Monroe] in his message of 1823. I am with high consideration & respect your Ob[edien]t Serv[an]t, T. Ewing.

FC in InND, Thomas Ewing Papers, Letterbooks, 2:91 (published microfilm, roll 4, frame 121).

From H[ENRY] W. CONNER

Charleston, May 27 1848

Yours of the 23rd with its enclosure is rec[eive]d & will have our immediate attention.

The Mercury noticed Gen[era]l [James M.] Commander & the Baltimore Convention yesterday. I hope to see it better done in Monday[']s paper.

The feeling of reprobation towards Gen[era]l Commander & the Convention for the monstrous outrage put upon us is universal & unmeasured. The first impulse was to call a public meeting to denounce it at once & solidly but our more considerate friends induced a delay for a day or two when a meeting would be held to respond to or reject the Baltimore nomination. It is agreed therefore to postpone the meeting until the receipt of that intelligence when it will take place & the whole proceeding be exposed & denounced in the proper manner. We expect of course to hear from you in full as to the course proper for us to pursue on the nomination by the same mail that brings the intelligence. We will wait to hear from you as long as we can but we cannot stay the proceedings but for a day or two. *The people will speak out & if we cannot stop the movement we must only try to give it a proper direction.*

If [Lewis] Cass is nominated the feeling will be to repudiate him in toto & to nominate Gen[era]l [Zachary] Taylor upon the spot with a declaration of our political principles & especially in reference to slavery & the rights of the South.

I hope most sincerely your views may come to us with the nomination.

The document enclosed me will be considered & used as confidential & be returned you in due time.

Tuesday or Wednesday next I think will be the day of public meeting. *I feel great anxiety to hear from you first.* Please say to Mr. [Armistead] Burt [Representative from S.C.] his letter is rec[eive]d. Y[ou]rs truly, H.W. Conner.

[P.S.] Let Mr. Burt telegraph me if necessary.

ALS in ScCleA.

From ROBERT HOGAN and Others

New York [City,] May 27th 1848

Sir, Your attendance is respectfully solicited at a meeting, to be held at the Broadway Tabernacle in this city, on the evening of Monday, the 5th prox[im]o for the purpose of extending to Ireland, in the present eventful crisis of her fate, that aid and sympathy, which, as Americans and lovers of Freedom, we should generously accord to any oppressed People, struggling for the achievement of social and political rights.

Hoping that the proposed demonstration will meet your approval, and be honoured by your personal participation, We are, Sir, with Sentiments of high respect, Your most obedient Servants, Robert Hogan, James K. Titus, Peter McLaughlin, W[illia]m F. White, J.C. Devereux, John T. Doyle, John A. McGlynn, Nelson J. Waterbury, Committee of arrang[emen]ts.

LS in ScCleA. NOTE: An AEU by Calhoun reads, "Invitation to attend a meeting in N. York for the relief of Ireland."

To Baron [FRIEDRICH] VON GEROLT, [Prussian Minister, Washington]

Washington, 28 May, 1848

I have examined with [as] much attention and care, as my engagements would permit, the fundamental law of the German Empire, proposed to the Diet by the Committee of seventeen; and agreeably to your request, I herewith communicate the suggestions, because I have not that full, accurate knowledge of the existing institutions of Germany, nor of the character, feelings and opinions of the German people, or the different interests of the communities of which they are composed, that is indispensable to form a constitution which would suit them, or to pronounce with any certainty, whether the proposed plan, or any other, would. Every constitution, to succeed, must be adapted to the community for which it is made, in all respects; and hence no one, in forming a constitution for itself, can derive much aid from that of others. With, then, the imperfect knowledge which I have, and which all must have, who have not long resided in the country, it seems to me, that the project errs in proposing to base the Constitution on *national unity* and to vest the union, or Empire, as it is called, with so vast an extent of power, as it does. It strikes me, that it would be impossible to induce the several communities, of which Germany is composed, to adopt it. To pass over all other difficulties, would the two great monarchies of Prussia and Austria agree to it? Would the sovereigns of either of them agree to be elected Emperor if his elevation to that high office would necessarily involve the relinquishment of his present crown? Or, if it would not, would either agree, that the other house add the imperial to his present crown? Or would either agree, that an inferior potentate, or any individual, however distinguished, should be elevated to a power and dignity greater than his own? It seems to me not; and that if there were no other difficulty in reconciling either of those powers to the project, this of itself would defeat it.

But, if it could be adopted, it strikes me, that it would not be advisable. A constitution based on national unity, and with such extreme powers, would, it seems to me, form too intimate and close a union, for a people divided into communities, with political institutions so very different and interests so very conflicting. The union would be much closer than that between the states of our union, and the powers possessed by the Empire would be much greater than those possessed by our federal government, although our State governments are far more homogeneous than the several German communities and the diversity of interest much less. And yet, experience has shown, that the tendency to concentrate all powers in the federal government is far stronger than that towards dissolution, contrary to the anticipation of many of the most experienced and wise of our statesmen, when the Government went into operation. Judged, then, by our experience, the constitution proposed for Germany, would end either in absorbing all the powers belonging to the Governments of the several communities and concentrate the whole in the Empire; or what is more probable, a conflict would occur between it and them, resulting from the Union being closer, than what interest and the sympathy of the parts would permit, which would end in the dissolution of the former.

With these impressions, I am inclined to think, that the existing confederation should be preserved, but improved and strengthened. What improvement should be made in the Diet, I am not prepared to say, but am of the opinion, that it would be advisable to vest it with powers, connected with the foreign relations of Germany and its defense against aggressions from abroad and with the interior relations of its several communities and the preservation of peace and harmony between them, but with no more, than may be indispensable for either purpose. I am also of the opinion, that no further change should be made in the formation of the Diet, than may be necessary to make it the safe depository of these and such other powers, as may be conferred on it. It would be safer, at first, to give too little rather than too much power. It would be easier to add, whatever power experience might show to be necessary, than to divest the Diet of such as may be found mischievous.

I look to Germany with deep interest. If France has taken the lead in pulling down the old Government it is reserved for Germany, if I do not mistake, to take the lead in the more glorious task of constructing the new on true principles. The character of the people is well suited to establish and maintain constitutional Governments, and has ample and excellent materials wherewith to construct them— far better than France, or any other country on the continent of Europe. On her success will depend, not only the successful consum[m]ation of what the recent revolutions aimed at in Germany, but in the rest of Europe. If she fails all others probably will. With great respect, Yours truly, J.C. Calhoun.

ALS in Geheimes Staatsarchiv, Nord Amerika, I C 10; PC in "John C. Calhoun and the Unification of Germany," in *The American Historical Review*, vol. XL, no. 3 (April, 1935), pp. 477–478; PC in Wilson, ed., *Essential Calhoun*, pp. 43– 45.

From DUFF GREEN

["Washing" *canceled*] New York [City,] Sunday [May 28, 1848] My dear Sir, I see in the nomination of Gen[era]l [Lewis] Cass, and the dissentions in the convention at Baltimore so much to encourage the partisans of Mr. [Henry] Clay ["that" *canceled*] and I have found his friends here so much resolved to force his nomination that I am convinced that we have no alternative but to choose between these rival demagogues or the nomination of a third candidate.

I fear that Gen[era]l [Zachary] Taylor is so much weakened by his letters and the imprudence of those who have acted in his name that we cannot make a successful rally on him as a third candidate, and I fear the more because he has not so defined his position as to inspire confidence in his position or his principles. I find that in this fearful crisis there are many eyes turned to you, and that a decided movement in Virginia or some of the Southern States would be ["respond" *canceled*] responded to here & elsewhere.

Consult your friends and prepare for the contingency of Mr. Clay's nomination. Yours truly, Duff Green.

ALS in ScCleA. NOTE: This letter was addressed to Calhoun in the Senate and was postmarked in New York City on May 29.

From J[AMES] K. PAULDING

Hyde Park
Duchess County [N.Y.,] May 30th 1848
My dear Sir, Many thanks for your admirable Speech on the Yucatan question and for the copy of Mr. [Henry A.] Wise's correspondence [as U.S. Minister to Brazil], the receipt of which I ought to have acknowledged before.

The facts stated by Mr. Wise, became known to me in substance, while in the Navy Department, being communicated by the commanding officer of the African Squadron, and by [Francis B. Ogden] the then Consul at Liverpool, who I requested to investigate the truth of certain reports I had heard. You may recollect a certain Mr. [Joseph John] Gurney, who was at Washington about that time, a great Philanthropist, in his way, like most Quakers. He called on me at the Department, to request I would appoint an officer to the command on the coast of Africa, zealous in the cause of suppression [of the transatlantic slave trade]; and I took the occasion civilly to advise him, while devoting his attention to the United States, to look a little into the conduct of his own countrymen. I then stated to him what I knew to be facts, in relation to the English capital and English manufactures which furnished the great basis of the Slave Trade as well as the extreme forbearance of the British Naval officers in respect to all measures for *preventing* the shipment of slaves.

Mr. Gurney expressed great surprize at this; thanked me in the most courteous terms; and assured me he would devote himself to a thorough enquiry into the subject on his return to England. Soon after his return, he made a great speech at a great public meeting, I think at Norwich, in which he spoke not only freely, but falsely of the Americans, but said not a word about his own countrymen. A few days since I met with a Naval officer who had lately been a collier on the coast of Africa, who stated to me that whenever a British cruiser captured a slaver she proceeded to Sierra Leone, where the best of the Negroes, were invariably selected for the use of the colony.

Your views on the subject of Yucatan, and indeed all South America, accord entirely with those I have long entertained. My opinion is that the dominions of the ancient possessors, will some day, perhaps not very distant, [*one word canceled*] be again resumed. The mongrel race of whitemen, or rather mulattos, is incapable, and unworthy of freedom, still less of exercising dominion over other races; and, I see nothing in perspective but perpetual struggles between a succession of rulers whose ambition to govern is only equalled by their incapacity for the task. I fear Europe is not much better off, and that the end of her struggles will be anarchy and barbarism. For ought I can see, she is destined to the fate of Asia.

The present condition and prospects of South America, strikingly exemplifies, the folly and danger of admitting a numerous race to all their civil rights, whose physical, or moral inferiority, [*one word canceled*] or whose natural incompatibility prevents them from enjoying any thing like social equality. They will be forever festering in the Body ["politick" *with the* "ti" *interlined*], and the end will inevitably be that the inferior race, must either exterminate the superior, or become their slaves. Equality is impossible, and a struggle inevitable sooner or later. The ascendancy of Mexicans & Peruvian Indians in these States, would be a subject of little regret to me, for any government, or none at all, is better than perpetual revolutions conducted by a succession of miserable Pettifoggers, whose folly takes away all dignity from distress, and makes even calamity radiculous [*sic*].

Your position in the minority, is a fine one. You can at least arrest bad measures, & this is almost equal to directing good ones. The great disadvantage however is, that you are frequently compelled to act with a party to whose fundamental principles you are so diametrically opposed. In this way you sometimes fall into bad company, and according to the old saying, The world judges of a man by the company he keeps.

Please to commend me to Mr. [John M.] Niles [Senator from Conn.], and thank him in my name for his last Speech [that of May 7, 1848, on the Yucatan question]. With the highest respect & regard Yours very truly, J.K. Paulding.

[P.S.] You will much oblige me by sending a copy of any future speeches.

ALS in ScCleA; PC in Aderman, ed., *The Letters of James Kirke Paulding,* pp. 482–484; PEx in Boucher and Brooks, eds., *Correspondence,* p. 437. NOTE: Paulding had been Secretary of the Navy, 1838–1841.

To L[EWIS] S. CORYELL, [New Hope, Pa.?]

[Washington, *ca.* May 31, 1848]
Dear Sir, My Yucatan speech has not been printed in pamphlet form; but you may find it in the Intelligencer of the 22d Inst.

South Carolina will not support the Baltimore nomination; but will not determine on her final course until she sees what the Philadelphia convention will do.

I have not yet heard from my son. Yours truly, J.C. Calhoun.

ALS in PHi, Coryell Papers. NOTE: By "my son," Calhoun apparently meant John C. Calhoun, Jr., who had gone to Philadelphia to study medicine.

To J[AMES] M. LEGARÉ, [Aiken, S.C.?]

Washington, 31st May 1848
My dear Sir, I am greatly indebted to you for your little volume of Poetry, which I doubt not, I shall read with pleasure after I am released from the drudgery of business here. Indeed, I have already glanced over a few of the poems with pleasure.

I regret, that you have been compelled to give up your projected literary enterprise and especially the cause which compelled you. I hope the restoration of your health will ere long enable you to resume it. Yours very truly, J.C. Calhoun.

ALS in the Episcopal Church Home for Children, York, S.C. (photocopy of ALS in ScU-SC, John C. Calhoun Papers). NOTE: The book by Legaré (1823–1859) that Calhoun was acknowledging was doubtless *Orta-Undis, and Other Poems* (Boston: William D. Tichnor & Company, 1848), an octavo volume of about 110 pages.

REMARKS ON THE BILL TO ESTABLISH A TERRITORIAL GOVERNMENT FOR OREGON

[In the Senate, May 31, 1848]

[John P. Hale of N.H. moved to amend the bill so as to prohibit slavery in the territory. Jesse D. Bright of Ind. hoped the amendment would not prevail, as immediate action on the bill was needed.]

Mr. Calhoun asked if it was the intention of the chairman of the committee to vote for the incorporation of this principle in the bill?

Mr. Bright said he should vote against it.

Mr. Calhoun said, if he could be assured that such was the general sentiment, he would not object to the immediate passage of the bill. But if this proposition was to be inserted, he desired that it might be met by a manly and full discussion. He was ready to meet the question; but if it was to be debated, he would go for fixing on some particular day.

[There was extended discussion among a number of Senators.]

Mr. Calhoun said he was not disposed to interpose any delay which his duty did not imperiously require. He wished to give a government to the Territory of Oregon immediately.

[After more discussion, the bill was postponed until the next day.]

From *Congressional Globe,* 30th Cong., 1st Sess., pp. 804–805. Variant in *Congressional Globe,* 30th Cong., 1st Sess., Appendix, pp. 685–689; Houston, ed., *Proceedings and Debates,* pp. 671–676. Other variants in the New York, N.Y., *Herald,* June 1, 1848, p. 4; the Baltimore, Md., *Sun,* June 1, 1848, p. 4; the Philadelphia, Pa., *Public Ledger,* June 1, 1848, p. 2; the Charleston, S.C., *Courier,* June 5, 1848, p. 2.

JUNE 1–30,
1848

Ⅲ

Much of Calhoun's correspondence concerned railroads and their potential for enhancing progress and prosperity. This was obviously a matter of widespread and increasing interest to large segments of American society.

The national convention of the Whigs met in Philadelphia. Henry Clay was set aside and General Zachary Taylor was put forth for President, with Millard Fillmore of New York as Vice-President. The effort of antislavery forces to affirm the power of Congress to forbid slavery in the territories was voted down and the platform was largely a recital of Taylor's virtues. For his part, Calhoun continued to recommend aloofness from the campaign, though many Southerners were enthusiastic, apparently, about Taylor.

By the end of June, with the end of the 1st session of the 30th Congress approaching, matters were coming to a head in regard to what was called by shorthand in the Congressional proceedings and in the press "the Oregon Bill." Shorthand for the whole question of control of the territories by the restrictions on slavery. For Calhoun the matter was simple. In a Union founded as a partnership among the States, the North, through a majority of both parties, intended to aggrandize all the benefits of common endeavor and sacrifice to itself.

Early in the session, a majority in the House of Representatives had passed a bill to provide a territorial government for Oregon, including in the bill a prohibition of slavery based upon the Northwest Ordinance. (The unauthorized territorial legislature had already enacted a prohibition.) The Senate declined to act on the bill but offered a substitute providing recognition of the existing laws of the territorial legislature. This the House rejected, repassing its original bill.

All were aware that something would soon have to be done in regard to governments for the territories of California and New Mexico as well as Oregon. Here matters stood when, on June 27, Jesse D. Bright, Democrat of Indiana and chairman of the Senate Committee on the Territories, offered an amendment to the House bill providing for the extension of the Missouri Compromise line to the Pacific.

On the same date Calhoun drew a line in the sand. He rejected the whole basis of antislavery and demanded for the South nothing less than equality within the Union. Unlike the other section, the South came asking no special favors from the government nor offering any interference to the North. "I have believed from the beginning that this was the only question sufficiently potent to dissolve the Union and subvert our system of government, and that the sooner it was met and settled the safer and better for all. I have never doubted but that, if permitted to progress beyond a certain point, its settlement would become impossible, and am under deep conviction that it is now approaching it, and that if it is ever to be averted, it must be done speedily."

Ⅲ

To J[ACOB] P. REED, [Anderson, S.C.]

Washington, June 1, 1848
Dear Sir:—I have read with interest your letter of the 25th May, on the subject of the Rail Road now in progress from Columbia to Anderson.

You do not err in supposing, I take much interest in its success. My predilection was, originally, in favor of the route from Greenville to Hamburg or Aiken, by Edgefield. I think still, that route has great advantages, but am decidedly of the opinion, that, if there be any one that can be fairly compared with it, it is the one adopted, and that it is beyond comparison, if not equal, the next best. I am, also, of the opinion, decidedly, that the choice between them is no longer an open question, and that the alternative now, is no road at all, or the completion of the one adopted. I entirely agree with you, if it be abandoned, the large and fertile portion of the State through which it will pass, and on which it will confer such great and permanent advantages, will have little hope of having another. With it, it would be one of the most flourishing portions of the State and the South; but without, one of the most depressed. With this impression, I trust, no one will think of abandoning it. There are ample means for its completion. Much of the work, the grading, the bridging, the getting of the timber, may be done by the stockholders; and at no time more advantageously than at present, when prices are so low, and money so scarce. A resolute spirit and strict economy in the expenditures, will carry the work through triumphantly.

I have not the time, or data to estimate the many great advantages of the route, or what profit the Stock would probably yield. But, I feel assured, you have not in your letter over estimated the former. The route is well laid out to command the trade and travel of the large, populous and fertile portion of the State through which it passes, and the contiguous portions of Georgia, Tennessee, and North Carolina. It has also great advantages for extending itself by prolongation and branches, with the growth of the extensive region, lying West and North of it, in population and wealth.

If these views be correct, and if the road can be completed within the sum estimated, and, if it should be economically managed, of which there cannot be much doubt, considering who are the stockholders, it will, after it gets fairly under way, in all probability, yield reasonable profits; with the prospect of very handsome, with the growth and increased prosperity of the country, and ultimately, large, when the road has attained its full extension.

But it would be taking a very narrow view, to look only to the profits on the stock, in estimating the gain of the region it would accommodate. The rise in the value of property; in the price of the various articles it produces; the enlargement of the number of such articles, by cheapening transportation and enlarging its market; the greater uniformity of price with the enlargement of the market; the growth of manufactures, for which the abundant water power, the health of the climate and cheapness of living afford so many advantages; and finally, the population and travelling, that would be attracted by the romantic and fine mountain region and the elevated plains that extend out from their eastern basis, must all be taken into account, in summing up its gain. These are so great, that the difference between what the region would be with the road and without the road, is that of a flourishing and prosperous country, and of a depressed, and at best, a stationary one—of one that retains its population and receives emigrants, and one that sends forth emigrants without receiving them. With great respect, I am, &c &c., J.C. CALHOUN.

PC (from the Anderson, S.C., *Gazette*) in the Columbia, S.C., *South-Carolinian*, June 19, 1848, p. 3; PC in the Charleston, S.C., *Courier*, June 22, 1848, p. 2; PC in the Edgefield, S.C., *Advertiser*, July 5, 1848, p. 2.

Remarks on the Oregon bill, 6/1. "Mr. Calhoun thought the striking out of the 12th section [which validated an existing restriction on slavery passed by the territorial government] would not remove the difficulty. There are three questions involved: 1st. The power of Congress to interfere with persons emigrating with their property into the State; 2d. The power of the Territorial Government to do so; and, 3d. The power of Congress to vest such a power in the Territory. The amendment moved by the Senator from Florida [James D. Westcott, Jr.] was the only course. He did not wish to delay the bill. But if the matter was to be gone into, it would be the best way to separate the military authority from the residue of the bill, and act on that at present." From *Congressional Globe*, 30th Cong., 1st Sess., p. 809. Also printed in Benton, *Abridgment of Debates*, 16:208. Variant in *Congressional Globe*, 30th Cong., 1st Sess., Appendix, p. 690; Houston, ed., *Proceedings and Debates*, p. 681. Another variant in the Charleston, S.C., *Courier*, June 6, 1848, p. 2. (The first variant cited, a somewhat fuller report, has Calhoun stating what would be a satisfactory solution to him: "precisely upon the constitutional compromises—that the territory is open to all the citizens of the United States; that it must remain open, and cannot be closed but by the people of the Territory when they come to form their own constitution, and then they can do as they please.")

From H[ENRY] BAILEY

Charleston, 2nd June, 1848

My dear Sir, I have just received your favor, relative to the nomination of the Baltimore Convention, to which I hasten to reply. I concur entirely in all your views, as well as to the impolicy, & even the impossibility of our supporting Mr. [Lewis] Cass, as to the necessity of suspending any action on our part, at least until the result of the Whig Convention is known. I regret to say, that on the latter point, however, there is a division of opinion among our friends; some of whom are so indignant at the course of Mr. [James M.] Commander, & his adoption by the Convention, that they insist upon our having a Public Meeting at once, to denounce the whole concern. Others of us think, the game rather small to meet for the purpose of denunciation merely; and that it would be dangerous to meet until we had determined upon some course to be taken for the campaign, inasmuch as a Public Meeting might plunge us against our will into a position, from which we could not retreat. We think that great caution & deliberation is required to determine our course wisely, & especially that we ought not to think of planning our campaign, until we have the benefit of the light to be thrown upon the field by the results of the Whig Convention. Still our young men are hot for immediate action, & some of our older heads, to wit, [Ker] Boyce, & [Henry W.] Conner, are just as unreasonable. [Franklin H.] Elmore & myself have succe[e]ded, ["with great difficulty," *interlined*], in postponing the meeting until tuesday next, but will have ["much greater" *interlined*] difficulty in further staving it off. I shall make use of your letter for that purpose; but if you were to drop a line to Boyce, or Conner, to urge upon them the evil of this precipitation it would be much more effectual.

I write in haste, in the hurry of our court business, & so must conclude. With sincere regard & esteem Your Ob[edien]t Servan[t,] H. Bailey.

ALS in ScCleA; variant PC in Boucher and Brooks, eds., *Correspondence*, p. 438.

From C[AVE] J[OHNSON, Postmaster General]

[Washington] June 2, 1848
I have examined the letter of W. Henry Calhoun, of Mississippi, in relation to the Post Office at Ashville, Miss. I find upon the 28 April last, the petition was acted on and the site of the office changed, and James W. Walker appointed. This was done upon the petition of 44 citizens and upon the recommendation of the Hon. Jacob Thompson [Representative from Miss.]. It was done upon the following grounds[:] 1st. The office was off the route from Pontotoc to Fulton about 2 miles; 2nd. That the new position is the most central to the neighborhood; 3rd. That the Fulton road has bridges & causeways across the creeks & swamps, making it passable at all seasons, and the old road has not the same advantages. I find upon examining the petition the names of Thomas H. Freeman & A. Mauldin.

I enclose the letter as requested of W. Henry Calhoun. [Signed,] C.J.

FC in DNA, RG 28 (Post Office Department), Letters Sent by the Postmaster General, S.2:23.

Petition of Charleston merchants, presented by Calhoun to the Senate on 6/2. This document, with 40 signers and dated 5/26, requests of Congress to approve a contract recently made by the Post Office Department for carrying mail between Charleston and Havana. (The petition was referred to the Committee on the Post Office and Post Roads.) DS in DNA, RG 46 (U.S. Senate), 30A-H14.2.

Remarks on the Oregon bill, 6/2. John M. Niles of Conn. argued that Congress had no authority to legislate about private property, such authority belonging entirely to the States. "Mr. Calhoun. I have great respect for the honorable Senator, and I depart from my usual rule in interrupting him. But we do not rest this question upon that foundation. I rest it upon the comity of the States of this Union. The territory of Oregon is the territory of the United States, and by the United States we mean the States in their federal capacity as members of this Union. I rest it upon the additional fact, that the States in their federal capacity are equal and coequal, and being so, no discrimination can exist between those who hold and those who do not hold slaves." Later in the proceedings, Samuel Houston of Tex. offered as amendment a simple declaration that the citizens of Oregon enjoyed all the rights of citizens of the U.S. Calhoun queried whether the provision would protect "the people of the South emigrating to that Territory" in their property rights. Houston replied, to which Calhoun responded that Houston's "object is to avoid any decision on this question" in the Senate. Calhoun suggested that a more direct way to effect that object, then, was simply to strike out the slavery section of the bill altogether. "All must desire to act in light rather than darkness." From *Congressional Globe*, 30th Cong., 1st Sess., Appendix, pp. 697–699. Also printed in Houston, ed., *Proceedings and Debates*, pp. 689, 694. Variants in the Baltimore, Md., *Sun*, June 3, 1848, p. 4; the Charleston, S.C., *Courier*, June 7, 1848, p. 2.

From R[OBERT] F. W. ALLSTON

Waccamaw Beach [S.C.,] 3d June 1848

Dear Sir, You were good enough to write to me in acknowledgment of my scrawl respecting the Georgetown meeting "in favor of appointing a Delegate to the Baltimore Convention." Until then I had begun to reproach myself ["for occupying your valuable time" *interlined*], & to apprehend that you might esteem it a want of personal respect (in which I would on no account be supposed by any gentleman ["to be" *interlined*] wanting) to send you a missive so unprepared. I was much relieved to find that you did not so construe it.

Your counsel would have been follow'd, I think, had we been sure of as large a meeting as the Conventionists had. But busy as all planters are necessarily at this season from April out, it would have been very unwise to attempt a counter-meeting. The only time ["to succeed" *interlined*] & ["the" *interlined*] best way would have been to have anticipated them, & have held a ["general" *interlined*] meeting in Court week & discuss'd the subject generally—but there was no concert among us, whom it took by surprise; and it (the scheme of delegation,) had been concocted and revised for 4 years by the Pres[iden]t of the Bank in G[eorge] T[own,] D[onald] L. McKay who did not broach it until late; after he had prepared a manufactory of public opinion—secured the Editor of the Georgetown paper by the expectation of getting the appointment of Delegate; & the Editor of the Cheraw Gazette [*Marginal interpolation*: * "These are the only two Papers publish'd in the 4th Congressional District."] in some way, and all the yankees & half the residents in the town to attend the meeting &c &c.

The habits of our substantial citizens are not favorable to public meetings—they are home-men & must be excited to it. Well generally the whole burthen & responsibility falls on one or two active men who having undertaken it have to do every thing—and then when an occasion offers for others to mislead ["to" *canceled*] individuals of the Mass, they are twitted with being led by the nose by —— and —— &c.

There were not wanting those ["among us" *interlined*] who thought Gen[era]l [James M.] Commander would not attend the Convention with so small a backing; and who were disinclined to shear[?] him of the honor he might derive from having been appointed for the purpose—the event has shown such how egregiously they were mistaken. Altho McKay himself beg[ge]d of some of us not to interrupt them, that they acknowledged themselves to be a minority, but desired simply the privilege to be heard as a minority, with a view to get the Congressional district [*one word canceled and* "sounded" *interlined.*] The Gen[era]l was demented enough to make the statement which he is reported to have made at Baltimore. It is humiliating to us of his acquaintance. He is a rising man of strong will & great energy & enterprise. It's not 8 years since he was an overseer, but his promotion seems to have been too rapid for his bal[l]ast in character. The "Hamburgh Republican" sustains them, & I doubt not they will make a strong contest in the 4th District if abused as I expect they will be, by the meeting in Charleston. A[lexander] D. Sims our representative, I think, more than sympathises with the movement. Tho' McKay is not his friend—Commander is. In a political contest here we the Planters cannot always do justice to ourselves. So ["a" *canceled*] great a number of proprietors are habitually absentees (out 108 in the District on ["the" *interlined*] rivers, 62 are absent 7 months in the year, 12 of that number have their residence abroad & are only here occasionally[)]! Well, the shop Keepers of Georgetown, all within sound of a bugle, muster as strong in number as the resident planters, who are scatter'd over 500 square miles with a negroe population of 17,000.

If a contest for the Baltimore Convention and its nomination should enter into the canvass to be decided in October, it will be justified & defended on the ground of the supposed intention or rather desire of many good Republicans to aid in the election of Gen[era]l [Zachary] Taylor, "who" they say "is a Whig, and would do us more harm if elected, than [William] Slade of Vermont or [David] Wilmot of Penn." If Gen[era]l Taylor should not be the nominee of the Whigs, I believe there will turn up for him a decided party in this State. At least, I thought so before his last letter [to J.S. Allison] about the "Veto." My own opinion is that he is better placed & more fittingly occupied, at the foot of the Sierra Madre.

You may deem me intrusive, my Dear Sir, engaged as you are but I wish'd to give you some idea of ["our" *interlined*] situation in this region. After reading, throw my letter in the fire & believe me to be with highest respect, R.F.W. Allston.

ALS in ScCleA.

From R[ICHARD] K. CRALLÉ

Lynchburg, June 3rd, 1848

My dear Sir: I thank you for the copies of your several Speeches on the California Bill and the Yucatan Message, the last of which reached me by the mail of Tuesday last. I had read Houston's report of it a day or two previously; and as a friend now attending the Superior Court here desired much to see it, I handed it to him on yesterday. He had heard from a brother lawyer of his acquaintance who had seen Houston's Report, that it was the ablest speech he had ever read. The questions involved are, indeed, presented with a force and clearness which surely must carry conviction to the minds of Congress, whatever cause their subserviency to the Executive may compell them to take.

I am very glad that an opportunity has been offered for you to explain the true meaning—the intended scope of Mr. [James] Monroe's famous cautionary protest in regard to European interference in the affairs of this Continent. It was high time to put the public right on so important a question; for as generally understood—as expounded by Mr. [James K.] Polk—as announced every where by demagogues, it certainly was made to assume higher grounds than foreign Powers would be disposed to grant. I have heard much of it before, and never could fully comprehend on what principle so sweeping a claim could be defended. The wonder is that, being so often and so needlessly dragged into notice, in the state papers of the last twenty years, England has not, before this, ["has not" *canceled*] inquired *by what authority we say these things*. I suppose no fit occasion has occurred to ask an explanation. But is it not likely that the recent Treaty, convention, or manifesto, which I see published to day, in which England claims the *protectorship* of the Mosquito Shoals, and, as such, dictates terms to the government of Nicaragua, will bring the question more fully before the world? I remember, while you were in the Department of State, that some question arose as to the course the British Government had adopted in order to get the control of the Country; and that you expressed some dissatisfaction at its proceedings. As well as I remember, some Indian of the Country, assumed to be of royal descent, was taken to Jamaica and educated and then placed in the formal possession of the Country; and who, in return for the favour, gave a sort of *political lien* on his territories. The particulars have, in some measure, escaped my memory; but these were the main points. You can ascertain them more in detail by calling on the Department, should Mr. Polk make further demonstrations of his belligerent propensities. By the bye, this subject seems to me to be of far more importance than that of Yucatan; for if the Treaty be in fact, *a veritable matter*, it warrants the inference that England, looking to our future acquisitions in the South, is determined to erect a barrier across the Isthmus of Darien, extending from the Atlantic to the Pacific, an[d] to secure the communication between the two by means of the Lake and the River San Juan. This communication I believe you thought impracticable on account of the extreme unhealthiness of the climate from the Lake to the Atlantic. But the movement, if it has been made or sanctioned by the Government, would seem to authorize a different conclusion.

The Baltimore nominations have been received here with a good deal of *sansfroid*. No exultation—no enthusiasm has been exhibited. The ticket is, in itself, a weak one; but by force of the Party machinery it will carry the State unless the Philadelphia Convention show some common sense, which I do not expect from them. I have published an article in the Paper which I enclose herewith, addressed to them, on the subject—but which I can hardly expect will have any the least [*sic*] influence. Numbers have been forwarded to many influential members of the Party—for the Proprietors of the Virginian, as well as the rank and file here would be very glad to see its recommendations carried out by the Convention. In my opinion there is no other prospect of success either in this State or the Union. Unless they select some man, *without Party pledges*, they will be signally defeated. [Zachary] Taylor *may*, but you *certainly* would carry the election. But, as I have observed, the Leaders of the Party will demand the previous promise of the spoils, which I know you will not give. But what will they do? As to Mr. [Daniel] Webster, Mr. [John J.] Crittenden, Mr. [Henry] Clay or Judge [John] McLean, I do not see how they can indulge the slightest hopes of success. And yet these present the only chances for a *strictly Party triumph*—and if they are forced to surrender that they must be forced to unite either on you or Gen[era]l Taylor; and such is the feeling existing between the friends of Clay and Taylor, that each, I suspect, would prefer you to the other. But a few days will determine.

I am very anxious to know what effect the nominations have produced on Messrs. [James] Buchanan, [Levi] Woodbury and their friends—and what part [Robert J.] Walker and [George M.] Dallas are playing. The two last, I doubt not, have kept the *first* pretty well hobbled for the last three years. [Thomas H.] Benton, I imagine, is thoroughly estranged. A gentleman lately in his company, informs me that he was become outrageous; and that, in speaking of you as likely to be brought before the Baltimore Convention, he broke out in his ordinary tone—*"No, Sir, no—Calhoun is too great a man— he is too pure a man ever to get the support of this miscalled Democratic Party."* These are strange sentiments, indeed, coming from such a quarter. He spoke freely of the Party and its Leaders—denouncing both vehemently. Verily, there is *nothing new under the Sun* if this be not.

I have not seen a detailed statement of the proceedings of the Baltimore Convention, and should be much obliged, if you should receive an extra copy, to have one for reference. I hear to day that in the latter end of the *feast*, there had nearly been the begin[n]ing of a *fray*—and that some resolutions affecting the subject of Slavery were very ominously *negatived* by the majority. And in this connection it occurs to me to call your attention to a late speech of Gen[era]l Bayley [*sic*; Thomas H. Bayly], which seems to me to assert some most dangerous doctrines; and Mr. [Robert Barnwell] Rhett or some other Southern man ought to answer him at length. Has he also gone over to *the enemy*? He sent me his Speech, and I intend at my first leasure to call the attention of the public to it, for it seems to me to grant nearly all that [Joshua R.] Giddings himself would ask.

I have lately received a long letter from [Dixon H.] Lewis in reference to the position he now occupies in relation to you. He seems anxious to escape *censure* as well as *misconception*. I know not how otherwise to account for so full an account of the matter, as my letter to which it was an answer did not call for it; in as much as I merely adverted to his votes on the Bills in reference to Mexico— and, incidentally, to your course—expressing a hope that there existed, at least, no want of kind feelings. He concludes his letter by assuring me that he admires ["you" *interlined*] as much, if not more than he ever did—and that, (to use his own words,) "*he would go up to the cannon's mouth for you.*" From the tenor of his letter, which is filled with unqualified expressions of kindness and admiration, I infer he is of opinion that some of *your friends* have endeavoured to excite you against him. He mentions no names; but refers to the subject in general terms. I am persuaded his feelings of regard have known no abatement. His chief fault is, perhaps, an innate love of majorities, coupled with a love of place. [William R.] King's opposition, no doubt, had a controlling influence on his recent course.

But I forget that I am taxing your patience by so long a letter. Mrs. Preston (known to you as Ann Saunders) has been with us for some days in a declining state of health, requests me to present her affectionate regards to you, as do all my household. She has been staying during a part of the past winter, with the family of her brother-in-Law, W[illia]m C. Preston, who, she tells me, speaks in the kindest and most respectful terms of you. Ever truly yours, R.K. Crallé.

ALS in ScCleA; PEx in Jameson, ed., *Correspondence*, pp. 1169–1172.

From H[ENRY] W. CONNER

Charleston, June 5, 1848

Your fav[our] of the 1st only came to hand this morning & I hasten to say that all is being done as you wish. Resolutions are prepared for the meeting tomorrow night that I think will be satisfactory to you. No nomination or preference of any candidate is intended for the present tho it is possible some person may introduce the nomination of Gen[era]l [Zachary] Taylor but it will be prevented if we can. I think it not unlike some of [Isaac E.] Holmes['s] friends may do something of the kind to endeavour to prop his falling fortunes up.

I am almost afraid there has been some designs in quarters little expected to cling to the party nomination of [Lewis] Cass, but nothing tangible or of a positive character has been presented & it is possible it may not be so.

Mr. [William L.] Yancey is here & I learn says we are car[r]ying out your views at Washington exactly.

My own opinion differed from many of our friends here & with yourselves at Washington but I yielded & am of course exerting my efforts to carry your views out to the full.

My opinion was & is that we *ought now even before this*[,] say immediately on receipt of Cass['s] nomination[,] to have come out promptly for Gen[era]l Taylor upon the broad ground of his being a slave holder & a Southern[er]—issues that are far above ["all" *interlined*] considerations of party distinction[—]& to have adopted at the same time the necessary measures for inviting a meeting of all the Southern States for the purpose of our common safety & common defence, the most effectual means of which would be to elect Gen[era]l Taylor. There are numerous objections to Gen[era]l T[aylor] on party grounds but the question will be shall we go for Cass[,] [Henry] Clay or Taylor & shall we go for him as democrats by nominating him now or following him as whigs or as identified with whigs after his nomination by their convention. In nominating him now we lead off & occupy a commanding position—if delayed, we loose [*sic*] all advantage of position. I feel that we have lost a great opportunity to take a leading & controuling position & to unite the whole South upon a principle of common safety but as I said before I yielded & am doing what I can to carry out the counsel of our friends here & at Washington. Very truly y[ou]rs, H.W. Conner.

ALS in ScCleA.

Remarks on printing a Patent Office report, 6/5. Under consideration was a resolution for printing 20,000 copies. "Mr. Calhoun. I do hope we shall know something about the size of the document before we order it. I believe the Senate two years ago ordered a somewhat similar document which cost them about ninety thousand dollars—a document made up of scraps for the most part. For my own part I am utterly opposed to the whole affair. I hope the resolution will not be taken up." From Houston, ed., *Proceedings and Debates*, p. 704.

From HAROLD SMYTH

Wytheville Va., June 5th 1848

Dear Sir, The Democratic Nominations for President and Vice President are before the world. The actings and doings of the convention at Baltimore are matters of history. The platform so called, or creed in the form of resolutions are published. All these things I have examined with care, and, permit me the question, *what is to be done?* Party is a horrible tyrant. Party trammels are iron chains that sink deep into the flesh. Is there no refuge from these conventions? Is there no more freedom at the ballot box? Are "chains and *slaverie*" the portion henceforth of the people of these States? A chained mind is more terrible to bear than a chained body. Shall a Caucus a Congressional Caucus transplanted from Washington, to Baltimore, or Philadelphia supplant the people in their right to select and elect their President? Who shall answer these questions? For myself I know not. But one thing I do know, or at least I think I know. And that one thing is—The Constitution must prohibit the corrupting hand and poisoning mind of the Executive from entering the Halls of Congress. Cannot an amendment be had, that will prohibit the President from appointing members of Congress to office during their term of service and for at least two years after they cease to serve in that capacity? Would not the present be a favorable time to secure such amendment? Would not the Whigs go for it? Dare the Democrats go against it?

From indications pending the Convention and since its adjournment may we not expect a third candidate before the country? Will not the Utica and Herkimer Delegates, and that portion of the Democracy of New York that they represent make war upon the Baltimore nomination? Will South Carolina submit to the degradation inflicted on her by her Gen[era]l [James M.] Commander? From indications I think neither will bow the neck. Then how is resistance to be made? It must be in the nomination of a third man, at least, by the New York Democracy. Who will that man be? Those who stand-forth the impersonation of the principles of Martin Van Buren, and of Silas Wright deceased, will not nominate an abolitionist—no never. They have chosen a point upon which to split—it is in fact a *technical* point, one not intended to be *enforced*. But, one from which to rally and build *for power*. I allude to the question of *free territory*—that is, that all Territory hereafter added to the domain of these States shall be prohibited to *slavery*.

I am now going to speak to this question in frankness. I I [*sic*] have uniformly denounced the Wilmot Proviso principle. Not that I apprehended the smallest diminution of rights (even if adopted) to Southern men. But, as a matter of *popular* policy. Mr. [Lewis] Cass, Mr. [James] Buchanan, and Mr. [Robert J.] Walker have said, in substance that *slavery* cannot go beyond the Rio Grande, or, into the California's. Because say they, slave-labor would not be profitable, and because these territories *have now* a free population, of every hue of color, that stand as equals in the social compact, and which would *inevitably* prevent the present toleration of slavery.

Mr. Walker pointed to the country beyond the Rio Grande as the outlet for slavery from these States. The question at this time presents itself after this form. The Territory composing New Mexico and California having been acquired in conquest, and by Treaty with a sister Republic under *duresse* of war, comes in suddenly, and not, as I am certain you would have preferred, by gradual acquisition, and peaceable annexation, and after our population had filled out, and begun to grow over upon these Territories. From this cause and under present circumstances, is it not impossible to introduce slavery *there*, until these States come into the Union, and the productions of the soil shall be found to demand slave-labor? No one will pretend that these territories when erected into States may not establish slavery.

The war has raised this free-territory question. Conquest has raised it. Precipitate acquisition has rendered nugatory for the time being, the idea that slavery will go along, and *grow up*, and shall be there at the formation of State Constitutions.

Then what should *policy* require at the hands of the South in the approaching Presidential election as regards the disaffection in New York? The disaffection is based ostensibly upon the Wilmot Proviso question. This in my opinion is not the point. The true policy is hostility to our wretched President and his miserable Cabinet. But to the Question. What does *policy* require at the hands of the South as it regards this disaffection in New York, and the insult to South Carolina, nay to the whole South? No one will pretend that Mr. Cass meets the resolutions of Alabama and of Virginia of last winter. No one will pretend that the 7th Resolution of the convention, as a platform, meets the Alabama and Virginia Resolutions. Then Mr. Cass is no better than a covert Wilmot Proviso-man. The Baltimore Convention 7th Resolution, is no better than a Wilmot-Proviso-provision sugar-coated. Will Southern men stand this? That is the first question. If not, what is left for them to do? Choose between evils? Certainly. Especially if in so doing they can prostrate these caucuses of Office-Holders and Office-seekers, and restore to the people a vote direct, and without dictation, for President and Vice President.

But as said before, would not this be a suitable time to strike away the corrupting hand of the Executive from tampering with and bribing the People's Representatives? Particularly after the nomination, if one shall be made, by the Utica & Herkimer Convention men of New York.

May I hope to hear from you (under any restriction you may impose) upon these topics?

I now turn to a smaller business. It is with regard to Postage on News-papers. I see Congress are revising the Post Office laws, and that the postage on Newspapers is to be altered. Papers going not more than 30 *miles* from the place where printed to be free. Cannot this distance be enlarged to 50 miles. Country papers in my humble opinion are more useful than City and Town papers—particularly the *Weekly's*—against these they have much of conflict. Ought not policy to build up the one and tax the other? Let village rivals control and build the politics of the country—Not Treasury fed city Journals. Fifty miles free by the *straightest line* would cover the circulation in a great degree of a country newspaper. I mark the word in a *straight line*, because our Post Master General [Cave Johnson] construed the former law by the route as travelled by the mail-Carrier, and thus papers were frequently taxed with postage when received thro the Post Office at a point not more than 12 or 15 miles from the printing Office. Ought not legislation to foster the country rather than the Cities? But I have done, a suggestion I make that you may consider it.

Will you send me a Pamphlet Copy of your speech on the Yucatan question? I have read it with great pleasure. Your friend, Harold Smyth.

ALS in ScCleA.

From J[OHN] TYLER

Sherwood Forest
Ch[arle]s City C[oun]ty Va., June 5, 1848
My Dear Sir, I thank you for the National Intelligencer containing your speech on the Yucatan question, which I have read with all the attention and [*one word canceled and* "interest" *interlined*] with which I invariably do whatever proceeds from you. This Yucatan affair is quite an awkward one in any aspect in which it can be regarded. If that Province is to be look[e]d upon as part and parcel of Mexico, then pending the war between that country and this, the insurrection which has arisen may be consider[e]d as actually favorable to us, while to take military possession would not only be useless, but would augment the difficulties of a final adjustment. If Yucatan claims to be an independant power and the U. States, upon *her* solicitation, moves in the matter, such movement is equivolent to a recognition of her independance, and furnishes new motives to hatred on the part of Mexico. Is that country in a condition to be thus recogniz[e]d? Is the Spaniard or the Indian in the mastery? You will remember that a somewhat similar case occur'd during our time in regard to St. Domingo. The Spanish portion of the Island claim[e]d to be independant of the black sway, and appeal[e]d to us to be recognized as an independant sovereignty, asking our favor and protection. I believe moreover that it was ready to make an unconditional transfer of itself to the U. States. Our sympathies were strongly enlisted in its behalf, but we did not feel ourselves call[e]d upon to obey those sympathies or to involve ourselves in the quarrell. I think the principle of policy which has been observ[e]d by the govt. through all time, not to interfere in the internal affairs of other countries, perfectly sound, and I should require a case of commanding character to induce its abandonment. I should certainly not wish to have G. Britain occupying any new position on this Continent which would give her any additional controul over our trade and commerce, but I apprehend on her part no such interference except upon the express request of Mexico. The surrender of the country

463

so soon as the disturbances should be quieted would seem to follow as a necessary consequence.

Your exposition of Mr. [James] Monroe's declaration is exceedingly valuable. It was necessary to the truth of history. I confess I never before fully understood it. The reasons set forth in your speech for your advocacy of Texas annexation are fully sufficient to justify the adoption of that measure, but I confess to the fact that the answer made by Sir Ro[bert] Peel to Mr. [Edward] Everett[']s enquiries as to the propositions made by certain persons [*one word canceled*] to G. Britain for pecuniary aid in order to procure the emancipation of slaves in Texas, decided me on the question as it did our lamented friend Mr. [Abel P.] Upshur. While the British Minister admitted that such proposals had been made, and declar[e]d that they had not been countenanc'd, he nevertheless took occasion *in substance*, also to say that the B. govt. would lose no opportunity which might arise, at any time or any where, to urge the subject of emancipation and would exert its best efforts to accomplish it. Seeing then the depressed condition of, not only Texas but Mexico, I could not but consider both the one and the other as accessable to her intrigues, and open to her policy. The considerations urg[e]d by you in your speech, were regarded by Mr. Upshur and myself as inconcievably augmented, in the event that this declaration of Sir Ro[bert] Peel should with zeal and industry be carried into effect, through the instrumentallity of a treaty of peace betwe[e]n Mexico and Texas. A constant border war would have prevail[e]d in the efforts on the one part to arrest persons flying from labor from Louisiana & Arkansas, and leading to open resistance on the other. And ultimately to war with Texas[,] Mexico & Great Britain on the one side and the U. States on the other. Such a treaty as I have alluded to would have given to G. Britain an absolute controul over the trade of Texas under the stipulations of a commercial treaty ["then easily(?) to be made," *interlined*] and in a short time have reliev[e]d her from all dependance upon us for the supply of cotton. Annexation secur[e]d us against these contingencies if it shall have done no more, and for one whatever of vituperation or abuse I may have suffer[e]d I am well content to bear, since the result cannot but be advantageous to the country at large. With sentiments of the highest respect and truest regard I am D[ea]r Sir Y[ou]rs &c, J. Tyler.

ALS in ScCleA; variant PC in Jameson, ed., *Correspondence*, pp. 1172–1174.
NOTE: An AEU by Calhoun reads, "Mr. Tyler[,] send speech."

From A. P. STINSON, "Private"

St. Joseph [Mich.,] June 6/48
My dear Sir, The Great Battle, in Convention, has been fought & my worst fears realised. "Whom the Gods design to destroy they first make mad" Seems to have been Literally fulfilled In Our party in that Convention. That we are a *Doomed Party* with Gen[era]l [Lewis] *Cass* as our Standard bearer, Is to my mind no Longer a problem. Now *Somebody is to be Cheated.* "*There is Cheating around the board*" Some where. Here the warmest Supporters of the Gen[era]l, & those in his Confidence are "*Wilmot Proviso*" Men! Our Legislature have on Two several occasions, with Great unanimity, Declared for the "*Proviso*," & with Equal unanimity Reccommended him ["(*Cass*)" *interlined*] as the Choice of Michigan to the office he has Just obtained!! I have been a voter Some 34 years, & Never did I See the Political Horizon more beclouded than Now. The *Whigs* are in *Extaies* [*sic*], they say & believe It too, "We can beat *Cass* with any man & not half try." Had *Judge* [Levi] *Woodbury* been Nominated he would have been Elected, as all who know him, feel Safe in him. If *Gen[era]l* [Zachary] *Taylor* Should get the Nomination or Run an Independent Ticket he will distance *Cass* Greatly in many States & might in the End be Elected. There are thousands in the *West* who will pair off, If there be any other Democratic, or Independent, Candidate Presented. The Conduct & the Result of the Baltimore Convention is but another Evidence of the *Corrupt* & Corrupting Influences of the *Caucus System* as Practised. I pray God It may be the Last.

What Shall we do? What Can we do? What ought we to do is in the mouths of many old & Long tried Republicans. I ask you Sir, (whose opinions I have ever Relied upon as *Sound*) what Is our Duty In this Emergency? I am, as you Know, No Proviso man, yet I have no Confidence that the *Gen[era]l* will Carry out the Sentiments Contained in his "Nicholson Letter." And If he would he will be Surrounded by Such a "Clique" of Political Demagogues, as would make him any thing but a Desirable Chief Magistrate. From the Tone of N.Y. Papers & others, there is Little Prospect of his obtain[in]g the Goal of his Ambition an Office all his Energies have been Directed to, Since his famous "*54°40′ or fight*" Speech in the Senate. If you have Leisure I desire your veiws & wishes on this matter. As Ever So I Remain yours faithfully, A.P. Stinson.

ALS in ScCleA.

To GEORGE BANCROFT,
[U.S. Minister to Great Britain]

Washington, 7th June 1848

My dear Sir, I take much pleasure in introducing to your acquaintance the gentleman, who will deliver you this, Joseph Allan [*sic*; Allen] Smith Izard E[squi]r[e]. He is [one] of the most respected of our citizens, and is connected on both sides, with the old and distinguished revolutionary families of Charleston. Ralph Izard, whose name is so familiar in our revolutionary history, was his grandfather; and William L[oughton] Smith, who took so distinguished a part in the debates of Congress in the early stages of our present Government, & who was afterwards a minister in Portugal, was his Uncle.

He is accompanied by his Lady, the daughter of our late Senator, the Hon: Daniel E. Huger, and Mrs. Emma H. Izard. I feel assured, that it would be needless to add more in order to recommend them to the Kind attentions of yourself & Mrs. [Elizabeth Davis Bliss] Bancroft. Yours Very truly, J.C. Calhoun.

ALS in NIC, George Bancroft Papers (published microfilm, reel 3, frames 2037–2038). NOTE: Joseph Allen Smith assumed the surname Izard to prevent the end of the Izard line. Smith was undoubtedly going to Europe to pursue his notable family interest in art and art collecting.

From JOHN H. HOWARD

Columbus [Ga.,] June 7th '48

Dear Sir, We have seen enough of political conventions to regard them in almost any other light than safe exponents of the public will. Neither of the great parties can justly claim for their representatives immaculacy in the announcement of the will of the party. Altho' I did not expect much from our convention I was still disappointed at the feeble support given to Mr. [Levi] Woodbury and really chagrined that he should have met with so little favor from the South. In this abandonment of Woodbury I feel certain our delegations from the South cannot justify themselves from the feelings of their constituents. I will not do injustice to Mr. [Lewis] Cass if I know it, but the estimate I have placed upon his political character forces me to the conclusion that he is an unsafe man. I fear he is a mere ["party" *interlined*] majority man, if his party upon a great question should be right, he would be right, and if the party should be wrong he might ["be" *interlined*] well expected to be wrong also. I dread the influence of the majority of his electors if elected at all. We may do better, possibly by looking around a little before we give way to the alternative of taking him on the one hand or submitting to a triumph of of [*sic*] the whigs on the other. The whig convention will have made their nomination before this reaches you; we can[']t of course sustain their candidate, because if elected by them, he will belong to them. If Mr. [Henry] Clay, [John J.] Crittenden, McClean [*sic*; John McLean], or [Winfield] Scott should be chosen, Gen[era]l [Zachary] Taylor being already in the field will be run and though he is unquestionably very deficient in qualification, his location connected with the circumstance of being rejected by the whigs makes him a safer candidate for the South, and the real constitutional party of the country than Gen[era]l Cass. I have therefore in such event determined to support him. But if the Southern whigs ["as I think they will" *interlined and then canceled*] should prevail in the convention ["as I think they will" *interlined*] and force Taylor on the whig party he will be in such bad hands that no democrat ought to trust him. Moreover if he receives the whig nomination and no other candidate is presented he will beat Mr. Cass & beat him badly. In this emergency I propose a bold and prompt movement. The chance of success is remote it is true, but not chimerical. It is to announce you as a candidate for President & Mr. Woodbury for vice president. We can have the ticket started in Georgia, not with the slightest prospect of success but for the purpose of saving Carolina & Newhampshire from taking the initiative. Our ticket of course would command a meagre support—very meagre—when both parties are pledged to their nominations, but Carolina and perhaps Newhampshire too would elect you and may we not from the stubborn opposition of all New England to Taylor expect some aid in that quarter, if no other[?] In all probability our example might bring out [Daniel] Webster—Clay being mortified at the choice of Taylor against a decided majority of the northern whigs would interpose no objection to his defeat and might also in this general breaking up of the party (which he says has been prophecied in the event that himself was not indicated as the head) consider himself justified in bringing the election into the house. If Taylor is nominated a large body even of Southern whigs who want Clay will consider themselves absolved from any obligation, because Gen[era]l Taylor has declared himself a candidate independant of their convention. The elements of discord will run high, and the true constitutional men may profit beyond their expectations by a bold and decisive movement.

If we move at all we should do it promptly, before parties settle down in submission to the dictation of their leaders. I remarked we would start the ticket in Georgia, but it would be better for your friends in Newyork to lead off, in this crisis; it would have more influence, but if they will not act promptly we though few in number can do it here. I know nothing of Mr. Woodbury[']s feelings since he has been spoken of for the Presidency; he might ["not" *interlined*] now be willing to run where I have placed him. You I presume though will be able to inform me and if he will not then let us take [John A.] Quitman, [Maj. Gen.] Persifor [F.] Smith, Buckhannan [*sic*; James Buchanan] if he will accept it or any other prominent man either civil or military who could bring proper aid to the ticket.

I repeat the position which I have laid down, that if Gen[era]l Taylor is nominated by the whigs that he will succeed over Mr. Cass if no other candidate is brought out, and the only way the country can escape a whig triumph in the event of *Taylor*[']s nomination is to bring the election into the house, by which my plan can certainly do no harm to the democratic party and may result in much good as I feel great confidence that if you were returned to the house even by a very low vote, that you would there be chosen in preference to Cass or Taylor. The free exercise of the elective franchise demands that these conventions should be broken down. I would greatly prefer seeing twenty candidates for President than one nominating convention, and the sound public voice of the country will approve of the independence of the man who puts his face against their partizan purposes, or more properly their purposes of *individual* and *selfish* preferment. If we break down the power of the conventions by supporting Taylor if the whigs should lay him aside, or yourself in the event Taylor should be nominated, we will in either case do essential service to the people of this government, by restoring to them their right of voting. Our preferences under the present odious system are smothered and we are not even allowed to give them utterance, all to avoid an ultimate choice by the house of representatives, which though to be avoided, if the will of the people could be as well expressed through another channel, still has the advantage of constitutional approbation and [is] in no way more objectionable than the present swindling system. If we act at all, we must act promptly. Yours Respectfully & friendly, Jno. H. Howard.

P.S. Please write me at once; you may rely upon your communication being treated *strictly confidential*. J.H.H.

[P.S.S.] If Taylor is the whig candidate I should not be surprized, at my ticket succeeding in Newyork.

ALS in ScCleA; variant PC in Jameson, ed., *Correspondence*, pp. 1174–1176.

To RICHARD RUSH,
[U.S. Minister to France]

Washington, 7th June 1848

My dear Sir, I take much pleasure in introducing to your acquaintance the gentleman, who will deliver you this, Joseph Allan [*sic*] Smith Izard E[squi]r[e]. He ranks among our most respected citizens, and is connected, on both sides, with the old and distinguished revolutionary families of Charleston. Ralph Izard, whose name is so well known in our revolutionary history, was his grand father; and William L[oughton] Smith, who took so distinguished a part in the debates of Congress, in the early stages of our present Government, and who was afterwards a minister in Portucal [*sic*], was his Uncle. He is accompanied by his Lady, the daughter of my predecessor in the Senate, the Hon: Daniel E. Huger, and Mrs. Emma H. Izard.

I feel assured, it would be needless to add more to ensure your kind attention to them. Yours very truly, J.C. Calhoun.

ALS in NHi (published microfilm of the Papers of Richard Rush, reel 22, item 11959.)

From E[DMUND] S. DARGAN

Montgomery [Ala.,] June 8th 1848

My Dear Sir, In Looking over the proceedings of the Democratic convention at Baltimore, I come to the conclusion, that the Seal is put to the bond. That the South with her institutions shall never have any inheritance, in the Territories ["of the" *canceled*] now owned or that may be acquired hereafter, by us. That is by the States of the union.

I do not attain this conclusion so much from the nomination, as from the action of that body in promulgating the Doctrines of the party. If this conclusion is correct then a vital threat is given not only to our institutions, but to our character and prosperity ["of" *canceled*] as a people.

I do not know all the causes ["that" *canceled*] or under currents that produced this result and see names connected with that body and approving of every thing done that I had some confidence in and therefore entertain a Lingering hope, that things may not be as bad as the result itself would indicate. Yet I cannot come to any other conclusion than the one stated.

I have therefore determined to write you and to request your opinion (if you can find time to answer this) of the consequences that will ultimately flow from the action of that convention and which I will be much obliged to receive, not however with any wish to communicate it to others, for that when necessary and proper, can be done better by others than by myself. But for the purpose of ["directing" *canceled and* "guiding" *interlined*] my own actions and taking the proper course in reference to the ["interest of the South" *canceled*] things as they are.

At this you will no doubt, Smile from a knowledge of the fact, that neither my opinion, or action can have any influence on the affairs of men. Yet there are but few who would more deeply regret than myself, the falling into an error—or being Lead[?] to chime in with those, who are opposed to the security of my own hearth stone.

I am now holding court at this place. I saw your son a few weeks ago in Mobile in good health. Your ob[edien]t Friend & Serv[an]t, E.S. Dargan.

ALS in ScCleA. NOTE: Dargan was an Associate Justice of the Ala. Supreme Court in 1848.

From W[ILLIAM] W. HARLLEE

Marion C[ourt] H[ouse, S.C.] 8 June 1848
Dear Sir, The nomination of Gen[era]l [Lewis] Cass, and proceedings of that clique of Ruckerites &c at Baltimore, are likely I think to place this State in an awkward position towards that party with which she has generally acted.

With the Northern wing of the Democratic party we have ever had but little sympathy, and with most of the politicians of that wing I have long since given up all hope of fraternizing. *Our democracy is talked* of merely, is recognised occasionally at democratic conventions, but is soon afterwards either deserted by those of the North who avow it, or laid aside until our votes are courted. I should have said this is what was formerly done, but the last meeting the disguises heretofore assumed, seem to have been only partially worn, and the refusal by the North & partly by the South & West to adopt Mr. [William L.] Yancey's resolutions, really looks as if ["the interests of" *interlined*] *party* are to be the only tests and guarrantees that we are hereafter to have.

This zeal for the success of party, and making it paramount to all other considerations, will soon settle its fate with us. Principles of course we cling to, but the blind adherence to party it seems to me we must at once repudiate. With respect to Gen[era]l [William O.] Butler should he accept I suppose there would be no particular objections as little of consequence is known of him except that he is a Kentuckian.

But as to Gen[era]l Cass a decided change will have to be made in the minds of our people on the subject of his opinions with respect to slavery & the Wilmot Proviso before he can muster a Corporal's Guard in So. Ca. The object of this communication is to request for my personal information if the opinion I have formed as to his position on that question be true, and I hope you will not regard it too great a liberty, or tax upon your time to ask your views.

1. Is not Gen[era]l Cass in favour of the Wilmot proviso upon principle? and has not this been the position recognised by him and his friends?

I am aware that when the question came up in the Senate he voted against it but in his speech he distinctly put his vote upon the ground that it was premature and uncalled for to make any regulations about Territory till we had a title to it. He seemed to have purposely avoided however a committal upon the question ultimately.

As there is a difference of opinion here, I should be extremely obliged to get your views as to his opinions upon this question at your leisure. Should the opinions of Gen[era]l Cass remain as now unsatisfactory to our people, It would seem to be useless to call the Legislature together to cast the presidential vote.

I once thought we might with propriety vote for Gen[era]l [Zachary] Taylor, but his [J.S.] Allison letter [of 4/22/1848] though it commits him but little, commits him too far for me, especially as to the exercise of the veto [*ms. torn*; power] with respect to the Tariff[,] Internal Improvements &c in which I think he clearly indicates that the majority of Congress is to Govern him. Besides this letter there is little known of his political opinions, and there seems to be little more propriety in voting in the dark, than in throwing our vote away altogether. I am Very Respectfully Your ob[edien]t Ser[van]t, W.W. Harllee.

ALS in ScCleA; PC in Boucher and Brooks, eds., *Correspondence*, pp. 438–440. NOTE: William Wallace Harllee (1812–1897) was a planter, railroad executive, State legislator, and militia general.

Petition of Maria Caldwell Robertson, presented by Calhoun to the Senate on 6/8. The petition, dated 2/20/1847 at New York City, asks payment of $587.31 for Revolutionary War loan certificates of James Caldwell. DS in DNA, RG 46 (U.S. Senate), 30A-H18.

From J[AMES] A. WILLIAMS

Baltimore, June the 8th 1848

Dear Sir, I have the happiness to acknowledge your note of the 31st ult. which owing to neglect of a clerk at the ["Post" *interlined*] office I did not receive, till the 8th inst.

Though much discouraged by your opinion in regard to the realization of my wishes expressed in my previous note, I am highly gratified by your very favourable opinion of my work.

I am indeed happy that "the larger portion of my views meet your hearty approbation," and from the fact that you have taken the pains to point out among them one particularly which you conceive to be erroneous, I flatter myself that you have given the work more than a hasty perusal.

In regard however to that error which is that, the Government is *partly national, and partly federal* I conceive you have misunderstood me.

You will upon examination perceive, that throughout the work I have observed the plain and real distinction between a State and a Government—between the U.S. and their Government. The expression then that the Government of the U.S. is partly *national* and *partly federal* has no necessary reffer[ence, nor] was any meant to the Character of the U.S.—its only aurthority. That indeed is purely and solely *federal*. The sov[e]reignty resides in ["in" *canceled*] the States—in each and all of them, for there is no other place where it can reside. Hence the General Government must be considered a part of the State government in each and all of them—responsible to each—ratified and enforced by each solely by its supremacy within its particular territory. This I conceive I have clearly exhibited in my article on the plan of the union.

My Remark then must be construed as applicable only and strictly to the Government—the Government alone—its *organization* and not its authority or responsibility. In a word I meant to be understood that, the agent of the States in the structure of all its branches except the Senate, ["recognizes" *interlined*] under various modifications, the influence of numbers. This influence I have denominated *national* in contradistinction to the egality of influence in the Senate which is *federal*. This latter is to the States a matter of original and un-alienated right while the influence of numbers is only perm[*ms. torn*]ted—the result of compromise and subject to alteration in the modes provided to the observance of which the ratification of each State—[*ms. torn; word missing*] has in good faith bound it. I have therefore[?] denominated our Government as partly national and partly federal.

In this view I am unable to perceive the slightest inconsistency on the contrary I regard this combination of the national and federal principles as one of the chief excellencies of our system. For; by this arrangement a more full and perfect expression of the deliberate will of the States is obtained—useful checks provided and also vari-ous politic combinations of interests securing to the Government harmony, stability and efficiency. With this explanation, I think you will agree with me and therefore omit any argument upon the point.

Politely soliciting a more particular examination of my work in regard to this subject and to be informed at your leisure of its result I present you Sir my respectful compliments and am Your most Ob[edien]t Serv[an]t, J.A. Williams.

ALS in ScCleA. NOTE: Williams published in Baltimore in 1847 *Plan of the American Union, and the Structure of its Government, Explained and Defended.* It was reprinted in Baltimore by Sherwood & Co. in 1848.

From W[illia]m Pickering

Albion[,] Edwards Co[unty] Illinois, June 10th 1848
Respected Sir, I learn with great pleasure that the Senate of the U.S. have passed an act appropriating alternate sections of public Lands in aid of the construction of the Cairo, Galena, Chicago and Central Cross Rail Roads of Illinois.

But regret the neglect of the *"Illinois Southern Cross Rail Road"* from *Alton on the Mississippi to Mount Carmel on the Wabash.*

To the History and design of this *Southern Cross Rail Road of Illinois* I respectfully request your valuable attention. Though a

stranger to you personally for which I ought to apologize for this intrusion, my only explanation which I suppose necessary at this time
arises from a belief that the Interests of Charleston, of South Carolina,
of Kentucky & of every portion of the U.S. directly or indirectly interested in the Charleston Atlantic and Mississippi Rail Road, are
identical with the *"Mt. Carmel and Alton, & the Mt. Carmel and New
Albany Rail Roads.* With this conviction rests my apology, which
I make known to you through my old acquaintance Judge [Sidney]
Breese, U.S. S[enator] from Illinois.

The *"Mount Carmel & New Albany Road,"* links Louisville to the
Wabash River, and the *"Mount Carmel and Alton"* Road continues
the connection by another link to the Mississippi at the last named
town, thus constituting a direct Rail Road from *"Louisville to St.
Louis."* And as the Citizens of Louisville have determined to finish
the Rail Road from *there to Lexington in Kentucky,* there only wants
one link more providing to unite Lexington with the Cumberland
Gap, or wherever the Charleston Road disgorges westward through
the Allegany Mountains, and then the line will be continuous from
Charleston to St. Louis, in the most *direct and eligible route practicable for Rail Road construction.*

I had expected to have remained silent on this subject until a
short time hence, when during this summer should circumstances
eventuate in our little rail road affairs as now appear promising, I
had hoped to have sought the pleasure of a personal interview for
the purpose of making this communication, and for the purpose of
soliciting information supposed necessary for the welfare of our
undertaking.

But this Senate Bill has taken us rather by surprise, it has come
["like" *interlined*] a sudden shower in parching dry weather, and is
equally grateful.

I have forwarded a Petition to the U.S. Senate to the care of
Judge Breese and Judge Douglass [*sic;* Stephen A. Douglas], praying
for a similar appropriation of public Lands to the *"Mount Carmel &
Alton"* Road ["with its branch to Shawneetown" *interlined*] which
is the *Illinois Southern Cross Road.*

And to the *Mt. Carmel and New Albany* Road, which is the *Indiana Southern Cross Road,* constituting together the continuous Rail
Road line from *Louisville to St. Louis,* praying for a similar grant of
Land to that already passed the Senate in favour of the *Cairo, Galena,
Chicago,* and *Central Cross Roads* of Illinois. And I pray your attention thereto and favourable consideration thereof: and further, of
the wants, & necessities, of a new Country requiring aid from the

fostering care of the General Government, to enable it ["to" *interlined*] become united to the Old thirteen Colonies on the Atlantic Coast, without which ["aid" *interlined*] it cannot effect so desirable an object. If these considerations come within the reach of the sympathies of your mind and feelings, then we should feel proud and grateful to receive your cooperation and support in favour of granting the prayer of our petition.

We think we have some further claims ["claims" *canceled*] than mere charity towards the needy, but I am afraid of being too troublesome, and cannot refrain again remarking I had hoped to have remained silent yet a little while longer, but without further apology must beg leave to state one thing more.

As a member of the House of Rep[resentative]s of Ill[inoi]s I have had ample opportunity for some time past of ["becoming convinced of" *interlined*] the anxiety nay determination of Boston, ["New York" *interlined*] Philadelphia, and Baltimore to become united with St. Louis by Rail Road lines through the *Northern Cross and the Central Cross Rail Roads* of Illinois, and the Bill which passed the Senate *will finish the immediate union of all those Atlantic Cities with St. Louis*; I speak *advisedly, knowingly*; then why not let *our Southern Cross Road* have the same favourable help? at the same instant of time? to enable *Southern Illinois to unite with Charleston?* If Congress should favourably pass this grant in favour of our Road, the Road would be begun right off from *St. Louis to Louisville*; then the weight and influence of the finished road from Lexington to St. Louis at this end; and the weight of influence of the finished portion at the Charleston end, would operate like the rushing of two mighty waters down a smooth valley for the purpose of forming a junction, which nothing could prevent. The short space between Lexington and the Cumberland Gap, from the force of circumstances would ["then" *interlined*] be made immediately, when ["the" *interlined and* "through" *canceled*] passengers ["fare" *interlined*] from Charleston to St. Louis and back again would make a profit to *both ends* and every portion of *the whole line*, which either end, or any portion of the middle taken separately, may seek in vain, without the entire thoroughfare—without this junction and continuation.

I hazard nothing in saying that the receipts for passengers fare upon the finished portion of the Charleston Road, would more than double, the moment a continuous line *was made to St. Louis*. And should not this Congress pass a grant in favour of our Southern Road, I am apprehensive for certain Reasons, no Congress hereafter ever will; Boston, New York, Phil[adelphi]a and Baltimore will ["then" *interlined*] enjoy their Rail Road lines to St. Louis; and Charleston will for all time remain without. Why was Southern Cross Road of Ill[inoi]s, left out? Yes Why? I have seen enough of partial Legislation in a small way to be a judge of its operation in Congress. With rightful apology I remain Respected Sir Yours resp[ec]tfully, Wm. Pickering, Pres[iden]t Mt. C[armel] & A[lton] R.R.

ALS in ScCleA. NOTE: William Pickering (1798–1873), a native of England and an 1820 graduate of Oxford University, immigrated to Edwards County, Ill. in 1824. He was a farmer, a civil engineer, and a Whig Representative in the Ill. legislature from 1842–1852. From 1862–1866 Pickering served as Governor of Washington Territory. An AEU by Calhoun reads, "Mr. Pickering[,] relates to the Mt. Carmel ["P" *canceled*] & New Albany rail road."

From LOUIS T. WIGFALL

Galveston, June 10, 1848

Dear Sir, I trust that you will excuse me for obtruding this letter upon your time and attention. The result of the Baltimore nomination connected with the critical position of the South, will I hope be considered by you as some, if not sufficient, excuse for the liberty I take. I have no means of knowing your views, much as I rely upon them, except by a direct application to you. I have the less hesitation in making this application, from your know[n] frankness & candor in, at all times, expressing your opinions, & giving your country the benefit of your judgment without a fear, or consideration, of the consequences that may result to yourself. I need hardly add, I trust, that any thing you may write will be regarded by me as entirely confidential and that a knowledge of your views is only sought for my own satisfaction and the government of my own course. It is for yourself to select your own time and manner of making public your position as to the next presidential election. Gen[era]l [Lewis] Cass's views as to the adjustment of the Slavery question in the territories we are about to acquire from Mexico are unsatisfactory to me as you will see by glancing at the paper which I take the liberty of sending you. In addition to these objections I consider him as unsafe, if not unfitted to be trusted with the direction of our foreign relations. He appears to be a propagandist & seems determined to hazard our own liberty from an insane hope of forcing it upon others who are neither capable nor willing to enjoy it. His fifty four forty and whole of Mexico notions make me apprehend much danger to our own government in the present troubled state of Europe should he be elevated to the Presidential chair. His sympathies for those struggling for liberty in other countries may make him forget that we have such a thing to lose in our own. The nomination by the whig convention will be known before ["you" *interlined*] receive this. Should Gen[era]l [Zachary] Taylor be the nominee have we any thing to hope from him? His views upon the veto power are certainly very objectionable and in the present state of affairs render him dangerous to be trusted. The [J.S.] Allison letter *I know* was concocted in Washington and ["written" *canceled and* "drafted" *interlined*] by Balie Peyton at Gen[era]l Taylor's house ["& brought down by him (Peyton) to N.O. for publication" *interlined*] for the purpose of securing his nomination by the Whig convention. I do not know Gen[era]l Taylor's views upon the Wilmot Proviso. His long devotion to Mr. [Henry] Clay however ["shews" *canceled*] would seem to raise the presumption that he is not very sensitive upon the subject of Northern aggression. *I think I may safely* ["say" *interlined*] that he will *not be run by his friends* should he *not be the nominee of the whigs.* Should he be nominated I am in doubt whether he can be trusted ["at this time" *canceled*] by the South since his entire identification with the whigs.

Upon these subjects I should be glad to have your views as fully as you may have leisure to write. I have removed to Nacogdoches and ["am"(?) *canceled and* "shall remain" *interlined*] here only for a few weeks. Should you have leisure to reply to this your letter will reach me ["at Naco" *canceled*] if directed to Nacogdoches.

Again apologising for this intrusion I remain, dear Sir Very Respectfully, Louis T. Wigfall.

ALS in ScCleA; PC in Boucher and Brooks, eds., *Correspondence*, pp. 440–441. NOTE: Wigfall had emigrated from S.C. and would be Senator from Tex. during 1859–1861.

Calhoun and 98 other Senators and Representatives, and 13 citizens of Washington, to John J. Crittenden, [Senator from Ky.], 6/12. They express regret at Crittenden's retirement from the Senate and invite him to a public dinner to be held at his convenience, "as a slight testimony of their confidence, respect and esteem" for his long public services. PC in the Richmond, Va., *Whig and Public Advertiser* (semi-weekly), June 20, 1848, p. 2.

J[ohn] J. Crittenden, Washington, to Calhoun and 98 other Senators and Representatives, and 13 citizens of Washington, 6/12. He accepts with pleasure their invitation to a public dinner in his honor, asking that it be held on 6/13 because of his impending departure. PC in the Richmond, Va., *Whig and Public Advertiser* (semi-weekly), June 20, 1848, p. 2.

REMARKS ON THE PATENT OFFICE REPORT

[In the Senate, June 12, 1848]
[*Under consideration was a motion to print 50,000 copies of this report* (*a compendium of national statistics*).]

Mr. Calhoun. The Commissioner of Patents [Edmund Burke], I believe, has already more duties than he can attend to. If gentlemen propose to divide the duties of the department, and have one individual to attend to the internal affairs, be it so. But I ask them to reflect before burthening the Commissioner with duties which he cannot perform. With regard to the merits of this work I will not express any opinion at present, but will content myself with asking for the yeas and nays upon the motion.

[*Debate continued.*]

Mr. Calhoun. It is said that the money that is to be appropriated for the printing of this book is to be taken from a fund that has been collected from inventors in payment for their patents, the cost of each patent, I believe, being about $30. This fund is set apart, and out of this we now propose to print this book for distribution. Now, I put the question, what right have we to take from the inventors this sum, and give it to any one portion of the country? If the expenses of the office do not require that the fees be so high, why not reduce them? Why should we sacrifice one class of people to benefit another class? It is said that this is for the benefit of the farmers and planters. How many will it benefit? Fifty thousand is but a small portion of the whole number of agriculturalists in this country. You propose to take the expenses out of a fund collected from one class of individuals in the community and bestow it upon a small portion of another class. You have just about as much right to do this as you have to take the money out of the Treasury. I put it solemnly to the Senator from North Carolina [George E. Badger], whether he can justify himself in taking it out of this fund?

[Debate continued among several Senators, during which it was asserted that Calhoun had been mistaken about the expense coming out of the Patent Office fund. Rather, it was to be paid out \of the contingent fund of the Senate.]

Mr. Calhoun. I do not know where this money is to come from, but I believe firmly that it is to be taken from that fund [of the Patent Office]. I ask the Senator to inform me what has become of that fund, if it is set apart by law and does not go into the common treasury? But be that as it may, we are not to take money out of the treasury to give it to one particular class of citizens, to make a mere donation to a particular class of individuals. Sir, the whole thing is wrong. It is unjust.

[Several Senators defended the printing of the report as supplying useful information to the people of the U.S.]

Mr. Calhoun. With regard to the California report, when that report was presented here by the honorable Senator fom Michigan [Lewis Cass], chairman of the Committee on Military Affairs, I objected to the printing of the large number proposed. Mr. Cass rose and stated that it was a most important document, and that it was necessary to the understanding of the claims, and the printing was accordingly ordered. But there is a vast distinction between a document which has a direct bearing upon the action of Congress, and one which has not. What act of legislation is ever expected to grow out of this report of the Commissioner of Patents? With regard to subjects connected with legislation, it is necessary that documents should be printed to enable our constituents—at least the intelligent portion of them—to understand how we perform our duty here. It is said that this document is sought for by the people, and that its publication will be popular. No doubt it will be popular with those who get the books, but will it be so with the people from whom the money comes with which the expense is to be paid. The tax-paying part of the people have a right to know what is going on here, but this is not the sort of document that will inform them.

From Houston, ed., *Proceedings and Debates*, pp. 707–708. Variant in *Congressional Globe*, 30th Cong., 1st Sess., pp. 827–828.

Memorial of citizens of Charleston, presented by Calhoun to the Senate on 6/13. This undated document, containing more than 200 signatures, requests the Congress to provide for erecting a new and larger Customs House at Charleston. (The memorial was referred to the Committee on Commerce.) DS in DNA, RG 46 (U.S. Senate), 30A-H3.2.

Remarks on Setting a Date for Adjournment

[In the Senate, June 13, 1848]

Mr. Calhoun said there was no Senator more anxious to return home than he was, but he could not reconcile it to his sense of duty to agree to an adjournment until they were enabled to dispose of the important measures that were to be acted upon. Every gentleman must perceive, upon a view of the calendar, that it was utterly impossible that the business could be completed within the time fixed by the resolution [7/17]. It was said that this was an embarrassing and inconvenient time for the transaction of business. He would admit it, and he lamented that it was so; but inconvenient as it was, it was not so inconvenient as it would be next session. Senators who had been here for a number of years would bear him out in saying, that the session that brought in a new President was a session in which little or no business could be done. So that the postponement of the business now was not a postponement to the next session, but a postponement to the session after the next. There never had been a session when there was greater urgency for the finishing up of the business. Many of the questions which they would have to discuss, would of course involve important considerations, bearing upon the Presidential election; but were they for that reason to shun them? There was the greater reason for discussing them, in order that the people might be fully informed of their true bearing. He thought the resolution was premature. It ought to be allowed to lie upon the table a few days until they ascertained what progress could be made. He regarded it as perfectly fallacious to hope that they could finish even the bills that required immediate action.

[*By a vote of 16 to 21 the Senate defeated a motion to take up the resolution for adjournment.*]

From Houston, ed., *Proceedings and Debates*, pp. 712–713. Variant in *Congressional Globe*, 30th Cong., 1st Sess., p. 835.

From J. F. G. Mittag

Chesterville [S.C.,] June 14th—48

Sir: The Candidates for the next Presidency are now fairly before the people nominated by their respective parties.

A grave question presents itself to ["the" *canceled*] your Constituents—shall they support Gen[era]l [Lewis] Cas[s] or Gen[era]l
[Zachary] Taylor[?] We are anxious to hear your views on this momentous subject. Yours Very Respectfully, J.F.G. Mittag.

ALS in ScCleA. NOTE: An AEU by Calhoun reads, "Mr. Mittag[,] wants my
opinion in reference to the Pres[identia]l election." John F.G. Mittag (1803–
1890) was a native of Md. who had moved to S.C. about 1827. He was a physician, lawyer, and innkeeper, and locally notable also as an artist and scholar.

REMARKS ON AN APPROPRIATION
FOR THE EASTERN CHEROKEE

[In the Senate, June 14, 1848]
[*Willie P. Mangum of N.C. was advocating an appropriation to compensate the Cherokee of that State in accordance with the Treaty of
New Echota. He appealed to Calhoun for support in recollection of
the ratification of that treaty in the Senate.*]

Mr. Calhoun. The Senator from North Carolina having made an
appeal to me, I will state that I very well remember the transaction
to which he has alluded—I mean the time and circumstances in which
this treaty came before the Senate. I was in toto opposed to it, because I considered it to be no treaty at all. My mind was directed to
that point mainly, and if I do not recollect the incident alluded to by
the Senator from North Carolina, I have no doubt of the accuracy
of his recollection. This treaty affords a remarkable example of the
danger of making a treaty with parties who have no power to make a
treaty. It came here and was ratified, Senators for one reason or
other, voting for it, although they knew it was no treaty at all. What
has been the consequence? We have already paid about ten millions
of dollars to twenty-five thousand Cherokees, because of this fraudulent transaction, and the account is not yet closed. As far as these
North Carolina Indians are concerned, I am inclined to think favorably of their claim after a hasty examination of the facts of the case.
One remarkable fact has occurred in the execution of this treaty.
The very parties who gave us all the trouble have received every
thing, and the parties who stood by us have received nothing. [Chief
John] Ross and his party have received all the benefits, while the
emigrating party and the North Carolina Indians, have fared very
badly. Ross, a man of decided talents, assumed the superiority, or
made the others subordinate, slaughtering them as he pleased, and

481

the government of the United States who had persuaded the people to go, stood by with folded arms. These poor Indians, living in the mountains of North Carolina, an ignorant and unoffending race, had, I suppose, very little agency or control in the business of the treaty, and have received very little, if any benefit.

From Houston, ed., *Proceedings and Debates*, p. 717. Variant in *Congressional Globe*, 30th Cong., 1st Sess., p. 840.

From [EDWARD GEOFFREY SMITH, Lord] STANLEY, [Earl of Derby]

St. James's Square [London,] June 14, 1848
Dear Sir, My eldest Son [Edward Henry Stanley] intends setting out tomorrow upon a twelvemonths Tour in the United States and in British North America, and is naturally desirous of being introduced to the acquaintance of the most distinguished men in the Country which he is about to visit; and having myself, as a young man, now four & twenty years ago, on a similar tour, had the pleasure of making your acquaintance, I hope I am not presuming too much upon that circumstance by seeking to obtain the same advantage for my Son, and requesting your kindness and good offices in furthering the objects he has in view. He will not, I believe, visit the Southern States before the winter; but he proceeds at once to Washington, where, as Congress will still be in session, he hopes to find most of its leading members, and yourself among the number. I need hardly add that I shall be most grateful for any attention you may be good enough to shew him. I have the Honor to be Dear Sir Your very faithful Serv[an]t, Stanley.

ALS in ScCleA.

From W[ILLIAM] L. YANCEY

Montgomery, Alabama, 14 June 1848
My dear Sir, I have reached home—and regret to say, that the public sentiment here is decidedly against taking any action against the nomination—and that nine-tenths, and I fear even a greater proportion, are determined to vote for the regular ticket. I find here not

more than half-a-dozen, who are ready even to pause and consider what should be done. I find also, however, great ignorance of the political character of [Lewis] Cass—and of his want of decision and consistency even as a Democrat. I find nearly all ready to award praise to me for my course—but not bold enough to face the storm.

I greatly fear that we cannot make even a start in Alabama, situated as we are without a single press—and all too poor to give their time to such an undertaking. If we had a press, we could do far better—and I honestly conceive that we would do well for our country, if by creating a third party, it would secure, in the event of our failure to grasp victory, success to the Whigs. Acquiescence in this nomination—or even silence & neutrality, will so corrupt public opinion at the South—by causing it to believe Cass['s] opinions to be good constitutional law, that hereafter when all may desire it—and it may be imperatively necessary to resist that arrogant & insulting action which our subserviency now must inevitably generate in the North, it will be impossible to rouse our people to resistance.

In this aspect, it is indeed all important to preserve—at least a neuclus around which to rally our countrymen—and if it is not preserved, I tremble for the result.

I have labored incessantly—but I begin to despair. I have hardly yet struck a spark from the flinty bosom of the party. Truly yours, W.L. Yancey.

ALS in ScCleA; PC in Boucher and Brooks, eds., *Correspondence*, p. 441.

To HENRY BAILEY, [Charleston]

Washington, June [*ca.* 15] 1848

My dear Sir, The whole of our delegation, with the exception of Mr. [Alexander D.] Sims, have received with much satisfaction, the proceedings of the meeting in Charleston [on 6/6]. They are, as they should be; & I hope, with the speech of Mr. [William L.] Yancey, will do much good.

Since their reception & the nomination at Philadelphia, the delegation has had another meeting, in which Mr. [Franklin H.] Elmore joined us, and we all concur, that the State ought to stand fast for the present, & wait farther developement, before she takes her final position, in reference to the presidential election. From present appearance, there will be many and important developements both in

& out of Congress, in the next two or three weeks, which will aid us much, in determin[in]g what position we ought to take. Within that period, there will be, probably, full discussion of the abolition question, under all its aspects, and a showing of hands on all sides in reference to it. There will be, also, a meeting of the Barnburners; and, ["also" *canceled*], probably, of the portion of the whigs, who may be dissatisfied with the nomination of General [Zachary] Taylor, which will enable us to see, what course both intend to take, and what effect, it will have on the election, & should have on us in taking our position. There are advantages, that belong to our present position, and ought not to be lost. Indeed, it may have much & beneficial influence, on the course of all parties, during this eventful period. At all events, the light it will cast on the future, will enable us to shape our course with more certainty, for accomplishing the great objects we have in view; the defence of our institution, & the salvation & prosperity of the South.

If Gen[era]l Taylor had been taken up as an independent candidate, our course would have been an open & clear one; but there is great difficulty in supporting him, as the nominee of the Whig convention. Indeed, I do not see, how it can be done consistently, or safely, unless events should take such a course on the abolition question, as to compel us to over look all other considerations, and vote for him, as a slave holder, & as such, identified with us, on that greatest of all questions. In the meane time, it seems to me impossible, or next to impossible, for us to vote for [Lewis] Cass. My relations with him, personally, are kind; but there are three or four objections to him, which I do not see, how they can be overcome. He is utterly unsafe on all questions connected with our foreign relations, as far as peace & war are concerned. He is excessively timid & fearful of responsibility, & will be surrounded by, & under the control of the 54,40 men, who, if possible, are less to be trusted than he is, on those questions. He has by his position on the slave question made concessions, which surrender every thing, as far as territories are concerned; and in which the South cannot acquiesce without endangering her safety. And, finally, by voting for him, we would sanction the acts of the convention, which nominated him; & thereby his position on the abolition question. It is a remarkable fact, that the late Convention, ["passed" *canceled and* "adopted" *interlined*], on the subject of abolition, the indentical [*sic*] resolution, ["they" *canceled*] adopted by the conventions of 1840 & 1844, without alluding to, or making the least reference to the Wilmot proviso, and the many ["other" *interlined*] agitating questions which have sprung up since; & thus, have admitted, by necessary implication, that in selecting, or supporting a nominee, they are to be laid entirely aside. How can we support a candidate, or act with a party, without an entire disregard of our safety, occupying, such a position on this the most vital of all questions to us?

If circumstances should not permit us to support Gen[era]l Taylor, then, in my opinion, we ["shall" *interlined*] have no alternative, ["but" *canceled*] but to rally on a third candidate, or to maintain our present position until the election and then to cast our vote for one or the other of the nominees, as our principles & safety may dictate. If our people can be kept out of the Canvass the latter would give us great weight and many advantages & would be greatly to be prefer[r]ed. But we shall have time, by waiting developements for the present, to reflect on the subjects and more ample means for forming a correct opinion, on these and other points. Yours truly & sincerely, J.C. Calhoun.

[P.S.] Show this to [Isaac W.] Hayne, [Henry W.] Conner, [Ker] Boyce & other friends.

ALS in NHi, McBean Collection.

From George Bancroft, [U.S. Minister to Great Britain]

90 Eaton Square London, 15 June 1848

My dear Mr. Calhoun, I ask the honor of introducing to your acquaintance and regard my young friend Mr. [Edward Henry] Stanley, eldest son of [Edward Geoffrey Smith,] Lord Stanley [Earl of Derby]. Your reputation on this side the Atlantic is so high, that every enlightened foreigner ["who visits our country" *interlined*] desires the honor of becoming known to you; and I am persuaded you will find in Mr. Stanley the ingenuousness & liberal curiosity, which will conciliate your esteem. He intends a wide tour in America, embracing the West Indies, & I have advised him on his return from the Havana to sail to Charleston.

Wishing you excellent health and long continuance of years of vigor and activity, I am ever my dear Sir Very faithfully yours, George Bancroft.

ALS in ScCleA.

From N[ATHANIEL] R. EAVES

Chesterville [S.C.,] June 15th 1848

Dear Sir, I see a Law of Congress was passed the 11 Feb[ruar]y 1847, giving a Soldier[']s land and back pay who died in the service in the war with Mexico, to dec[ease]d[']s] wife & children if he had such but if he left no wife & children then to his Father if he be dead then to his wife the parent to dec[ease]d. Here the provisions of the Law stop. Now as there was a young man by the name of Mr. [John] Guthrie who volunteered in the Palmetto Regiment So. Ca. volunteers. He was a brave and amiable young man who endured every toil & hardship incident to camp service and acted bravely at the taking Vera Cruz ["and endured" *canceled*] he arrived with the Regt. at Puebla and while there took sick & died; he left no wife[,] children[,] Father nor Mother, but left only three Sisters. A friend of mine got Mr. [William L.] Marcy[']s opinion who says they get none of the Soldier[']s land but may get his back pay: It cannot be possible that our Government will not give this small portion to dec[ease]d[']s] Sisters. There may be many like cases, hence is a sufficient appoligy for my directing your attention to this matter. It would afford me pleasure to have your views & support on this matter. If the Law is defective ought it not to be amended.

Sir I volunteered during the war with Mexico and was passed by Maj[o]r [Richard D.A.] Wade & Dr. [Charles] McCormick on the 22nd Dec[embe]r 1846 at Charleston. I conceive I done my duty as a soldier, having fought in all the battles from the taking Vera Cruz to the taking the city of Mexico except ["Cero" *canceled and* "Cerro" *interlined*] Gordo and Molina Del Ray in which battles the Palmetto Regt. did not take any part. They having been sent to take Alverado at & before the battle of the former and prepairing to attack Chapultepec on the 13th Sept. when the ["latter" *canceled*] battle was fought. And after the battle at the Garetta and the surrender of the city of Mexico some time in the latter part of Oct[obe]r 1847 Gen[era]l [Winfield] Scott (after we took possession of the city of Mexico) issued an order requiring all the captains of of [*sic*] companies to send him the names of any two of their company soldiers one to be a non commissioned officer and one to be a private soldier who had excelled in the various battles to the taking the city. I was attached to Captain R[obert] G.M. Dunovant's Company B of Chester District So. Ca., who has ["since" *interlined*] been elected Maj[o]r of said Regt.; he while Captain sent Gen[era]l Scott my name in obedience to said order ["as excelling in those battles" *interlined*]. I have never heard of what they have done in this matter since. I cannot believe but that Gen[era]l Scott done his duty in the premises to enable me to receive the benefit of that distinction for merited servises guarranteed by a late law of Congress for that purposes. I am remideless without ["your" *altered to* "I can"] enlist your kind aid and attention to this matter. I fought under Gen[era]l Scott in the various battles above set down and Colo[nel Pierce M.] Butler introduced me to him at Puebla when he became well acquainted with me and appeared well pleased with my servises as a soldier (for I would have no office in that service). From proceedings thus far I am informed I am entitled to a scrip of merit. Hence I ought to have it as it would be more highly prised by me than gold or silver. As the poore soldier got only nominal pay he ought to have what he is justly entitled too. From the commencement of the campaign to the death of Colo[nel] Butler on the 20th A[u]g[us]t [1847] Churubusco battle I messed with him & never drew any rasions. Ought not the Gover[n]ment to pay me what it would be worth in money it clearly is due me. Permit me to return you my heart warmed thanks for the various Congressional documents you have sent me. We are in extream excitement here about the two great parties who are now clearly before the public. The individuals who head those parties are Gen[era]l Cass and Gen[era]l Taylor. I am a candidate for the Senate and I am anxious to do that which is best to promote the interest and welfair of my beloved State and would ["be glad" *interlined*] to know (confidentially) your views on this subject. Although however much I may like Gen[era]l Taylor[']s military glory still as the modern whigs and the North has taken him up I feel that I should adhear to the man who is most likley to carry out the great democratic principles for I believe on the wise administration of our Gover[n]ment on those principles there will be safety to the South; hence Gen[era]l Cass appears to possess those principles which tend most to our safety. Hence I feel inclined to leave Gen[era]l Taylor with all his military glory and adhear to the man who will or is most likley to carry out our democratic principles. You was the great light which taught me those great political democratic doctrains and I hope we will be co workers in these doctrains for the future. Please do not consider me presumtious in asking your views on this momentious subject. With sentiments of high esteem & my best wishes for your health & hap-[p]iness [I] remain your ob[edien]t Serv[an]t, N.R. Eaves.

N.B. I send you a copy [*not found*] of my certificates of discharge for your amusement.

ALS in ScCleA. NOTE: Nathaniel Ridley Eaves (d. 1873) was a lawyer, planter, and entrepreneur who served a number of terms in both houses of the S.C. General Assembly. He enlisted as a private in the Palmetto Regiment while in his late forties, and later enlisted in the Confederate army in his sixties. Colonel was his militia title.

Remarks on the bill for the relief of John Devlin, 6/16. Under consideration was a bill to compensate a temporary Clerk who had apparently not been properly appointed or paid by the department which had employed him. "Mr. Calhoun briefly expressed his concurrence with the views already presented in opposition to the principle attempted to be established by the passage of this bill." From Houston, ed., *Proceedings and Debates*, p. 731.

[Martha] Cornelia [Calhoun], Fort Hill, to [John Calhoun Clemson, Brussels], 6/17. She acknowledges his recent letter and hopes that he and his family will soon come to Fort Hill again. She mentions various animals and amusements that he would enjoy and sends her love to his family. ALS in ScCleA, Thomas Green Clemson Papers.

From J[OHN] Y. MASON, [Secretary of the Navy]

Navy Department, June 17th 1848

Sir, I have the honor to acknowledge your reference to this Department of the application of Mr. Robert Lebby for the appointment of his son as a Midshipman in the Navy; and to inform you that the applicant is too old. The Regulations declare, that no one shall be appointed a Midshipman who is under thirteen or over seventeen years of age.

As requested, Mr. Lebby's letter is herewith returned to you. I am respectfully yours, J.Y. Mason.

FC in DNA, RG 45 (Naval Records), Miscellaneous Letters Sent by the Secretary of the Navy 1798–1886, 40:136 (M-209:15).

Remarks on "the bill for the relief of Phineas Capen, legal administrator of John Cox, deceased, of Boston," 6/17. Cox had apparently died at sea, and a pretended brother with forged documents had collected from the government sums owed to Cox, whose estate now asked compensation. "Mr. Calhoun wished the Senator [James D. Westcott, Jr.] would state the point precisely, whether the letters on which the department paid the money in this case were those in force and valid, and whether they had since been revoked?" Later Calhoun said that he "regarded the principle advanced in favor of the payment of this claim as an unsafe one. He believed it would leave the United States if carried out, without protection in the payment by the departments of similar claims in future. It would establish a dangerous precedent." From Houston, ed., *Proceedings and Debates*, p. 732.

From A. P. STINSON, "Private"

St. Joseph [Mich.,] June 17, 1848
My dear Sir, Immediately on the Receipt of the Nomination of *Gen-[era]l* [Lewis] *Cass* to the Presidency, I wrote you what were my fears. What then was matter of Prediction is now Litterally being fulfilled for since the Nomination of *Gen[era]l* [Zachary] *Taylor* the Democratic Ranks are fast thinning. Hundreds on Hundreds of those who heretofore have been "straight outers" are Leaving & uniting under the *Taylor flag* & among them are those who have wielded an Influence! It Looks to me as If *Taylor* was Destined to Sweep all before him. Had my old friend [Levi] *Woodbury* been the Nominee we Should have Seen a different state of things. *Gen[era]l Cass* Is not popular with the Masses & Hence the Desertion By Battalions. I feel Like going for "Old Rough & Ready" my self. And they Even Charge me with being "a Taylor man" & *threaten me with the* Loss of the Little Office I hold (that of *Keeper of the Lights* Here, with Some $500 p[e]r annum) & say "*Col.* [Thomas] *Fitzgerald the New Senator* appointed by the Gov. [Epaphroditus Ransom] will Procure[?] my Removal." That he will If he *dare*, & *Can*, I believe as he is my *bitter Enemy* & the only one I have in all the Country. He is *vindictive*, unprincipled as you may See, If you Chance to see Some of Our Papers. Now Sir, I desire that you will (If you are on terms which Justify It) See *Mr. Sec[re]t[ar]y* [of the Treasury, Robert J.] *Walker* under whom I hold my Office & see that I am not "Removed without Cause," unless Indeed it be deemed "*Cause*" In not giving in my adhesion to the *Baltimore Nomination* which I Look upon as you once said in a a [*sic*] Letter to me of Conventions "Corrupt & Corrupting." If that be the *Cause* of Removal of one, who has been a Republican

489

33 years then I Submit. Let me say Sir, the appointm[en]t of *Col. Fitzgerald Senator* of your Body will Loose *Cass* Hundreds If not thousands of votes in Michigan & In the West—as tis suspected ["He" *interlined*] (*Cass*) had a Hand in the appointment of this man—a Man whose Course has been more vasillating than any man I Know of. He is a *Rabid Cass man* Now, what he will be a month Hence no one Knows, nor do those who Know him best, Dare Hazard a "guess." If my dear Sir, you will See *Mr. Walker* (to whom I have written my self) I will be ["oblidged" *interlined and then canceled*] & see to him, If Changes are of any Kind Pressed, to allow me to Rebut I will feel under Renewed obligations to him & you. I do not think any will as none in truth Can be If I Except giving in my adhesion to Gen[era]l Cass' Nomination, that as at Present Advised, I cannot do & If that be made the "Sine qua Non" Just Let me Know It & I will at once, Resign & again be a *Freeman* & was my situation in Life so as to Justify It I would Resign Now *Instanter.* I am *poor* have had much sickness in my family & now have a Disabled wife, yet Poor as I am I have the Spirit of a man. I have seen *better days* as Gov. Woodbury can tell you. I hope to hear from you *soon* as I am *constantly annoyed* by *threats* of *Removal* by the *Sattelites* here of Col. *Fitzgerald.* I am as I Ever Have been Yours Devotedly, A.P. Stinson.

P.S. I desire you will Consider this as *strictly Confidential,* and If you think I will not Jeopardize my situation by *Coming out,* Please so say & Humble as I am I Can make tell. Please Remember that I Say Now, Gen[era]l Cass will not, Cannot get a party vote in his own State by thousands If Indeed he Carries at all. That he will if (as now seems to be the Prospect) a New Ticket gotten up, I have no belief nor will Carry a State in the west under such Circumstances. He is not, was not, the Choice of the People But a Packed Convention has thrust him upon us & we, the People, will thrust him off. A.P.S.

ALS in ScCleA.

From E[DMUND] W. HUBARD, [former Representative from Va.]

Saratoga [Buckingham County, Va.,] June 18th 1848
Dear Sir: A variety of causes have conspired to delay my acknowledging, the several valuable favors received from you, during the present session of the U.S. Senate. The new and corrected edition

of the Federal Constitution, is a Book which doubtless every man who receives it from *you*, will the more highly estimate, as coming not only from one who with [James] Madison, [John] Jay, & [Alexander] Hamilton, has fully mastered its principles, purport, & bearing, but in the clearest, most profound, and condensed manner explained its doctrines, meaning, & invaluable purposes. As an evidence of my high opinion, and that it might be known, that *you* gave me the corrected copy of our Federal Constitution, I clipped the envelop[e] containing the direction and your Frank, both in your own hand writing & pasted it on the inside of the Book. Thus I should like to see every copy printed by order of the Senate adorned, whether deposited in private or public Libraries. For no man has shed more light over that work than yourself. Your expositions of it will doubtless be most highly appreciated in all time to come. Great, varied, and incomparable as your mental powers are universally reputed to be, and therefore capable of accomplishing wonders in any direction you might see fit to direct your energies, yet I doubt whether you could well select a more noble or enlarged or useful field, than to devote your attention to elucidating & expounding the powers of the Federal Gover[n]ment. In this conviction, I am the more confirmed, because you possess the greatest purity & simplicity of character, environed by all the virtues that impart lustre & excellence to human life. This is illustrated by the fact, that the rancour of party madness, and the ruthless ferocity of political warfare, have so ["far" *interlined*] as my information extends, invariably respected your reputation, and vented their spleen upon simply what they characterise as your "abstractions." Had your principles as well as your convictions, been less exalted, you might have escaped even this censure, by yielding to popular feelings or temporary views of policy, what was due to your convictions of abstract right. Great merit and splendid abilities, are seldom united in one man, and whoever possesses them, need have no apprehension that sooner or later they will not command the homage they are entitled to. Those who *follow* are more generally the *temporary* favorites, because they cater for temporary ends, and are too sordid or short sighted to play the part of a pioneer, and open up new views, or combat popular prejudices. It is ["to" *interlined*] the great leaders in the empire of *mind*, that mankind eventually award the palm. Offices, the multitude may lavish upon their favorites, but *fame* they accord to the *great*.

Of all the men I have ever seen or heard of, I think you would most ably & fitly fill the office of Chief Magistrate. This has long been my deliberate opinion as well as my wish. But fortune seems to decide otherwise. I feel sure that the Country loses by this determination more than you can. I dare say those who may years after read the History of the present times will put the question, "why was *not* Jno. C. Calhoun of all other men of his day made President of the Republic"? This will convey a higher compliment, than some enjoy who have filled the office. I imagine nineteen out of every twenty reputable citizens if they had it in their power, would greatly prefer possessing *your* head and heart, to the empty honor or standing of our present President, or any of our Ex Presidents now living. You derive your greatness from God and your own ex[er]tions, and not from mortal breath or fortuitous circumstances.

I must add a few words about myself in closing. Having the good fortune to have a fine son & a lovely Wife, and great fondness for plantation matters, I think my lot is permanently cast amongst the yeomanry of the Land. My residence lies between my only Brother & my mother in Law's Mrs. [Martha Jones] Eppes. Having no Sister & very few relations, I hope to make up the deficiency by cultivating friendly relations all around me.

Pray accept assurances of my highest admiration & regard, & believe me sincerely y[ou]r Friend, E.W. Hubard.

ALS in ScCleA. Note: An AEU by Calhoun reads, "Curdsville, Va.," Hubard's postal address. Edmund Wilcox Hubard (1805–1878) had been Representative from Va. 1841–1847. He married Sarah Eppes, daughter of John W. Eppes, whose first wife had been Thomas Jefferson's daughter, and Martha Jones Eppes, daughter of the N.C. Revolutionary leader Willie Jones.

Remarks on the Naturalization Bill, 6/19. "Mr. Calhoun. It seems to me that some provision is necessary to be attached to this bill, to say how long the temporary absence may continue. There is another bill now before Congress on the subject of naturalization, and I would suggest that this bill be allowed to stand over, so that we may have the whole subject before us at once." From Houston, ed., *Proceedings and Debates*, p. 735. Variant in *Congressional Globe*, 30th Cong., 1st Sess., p. 854.

From M[ANSFIELD] TORRANCE

Columbus [Ga.,] 19th June 1848

Dear Sir, The annexation of a large portion of Mexican territory, has presented rather a new question to the people of the U. States. At first blush the doctrine laid down by Gen[era]l [Lewis] Cass, that the question of slavery was one for the people of the States & territories to decide, appears sound enough. I presume [it] would not be objected to by any one if the territory was *entirely* unsettled; but that not being the case, the question arises, "Shall the few ignorant Mexicans now in the country have the power of excluding the Southern people from settling amongst them with such property, as they choose to carry with them." Another question, equally grave, presents itself. "Shall we yield to Congress the power to decide the question?" A difficulty presents itself either way. If left to the *present occupants*, they will probably exclude our people, & would ["we" *interlined*] be in a better situation, by referring the question to a body in which we are in a minority? I have contended, that our (Southern) people should have permission to go there with their peculiar property & *risk* the decision of the majority when the territory forms a constitution & demands admission as a State; & that Congress should guarantee this privilege, but I have been met with this argument. "If you yield the settlement to Congress, will it not be surrendering our rights to the Wilmot Proviso men?"

If you have leisure I should like much to know your views on this subject. To me it appears surrounded with difficulties. It is a difficult matter for the South to get justice, in cases ["where" *canceled*] to us apparently very plain, how much more so, ["when" *altered to* "where"] there is a loop to hang a doubt upon.

I am glad to see that the [Charleston] Mercury, appears for the present disposed to remain neutral. Circumstances may render it wise for S. Carolina to take no part for the present at least, in the Presidential canvass.

Some of our whig friends are counting on So. Ca. going for Gen[era]l [Zachary] Taylor. I presume they are reckoning without their post. I have objections to Gen[era]l Cass. I think his course on the Oregon, Mexican & Yucatan questions ["have" *altered to* "has"] been unwise, but on most of the great questions he is much safer than any man can possibly be who will owe his election to the Whigs. Gen[era]l Taylor elected by the Democrats would ["have" *canceled and* "been" *altered to* "be"] a Democrat & if elected by the Whigs he must be a Whig. What then can we promise ourselves by supporting Gen[era]l Taylor. Maj. [John H.] Howard agrees with me as to the course of So. Ca. Cass is not our first choice, but we prefer him to Taylor. My respects to Mrs. C[alhoun]. Yours &c, M. Torrance.

ALS in ScCleA; PC in Boucher and Brooks, eds., *Correspondence*, p. 442. NOTE: Torrance (1798–1854) was a S.C. native and a lawyer.

From J[ohn] A. Campbell

Montgomery [Ala.,] 20 June '48

Dear Sir, I have for some time contemplated writing to you, to ascertain from you your views of the present aspects of public affairs.

The treaty with Mexico has been ratified. We have the promised "indemnity for the past & security for the future" in possession. Think you that any considerate Southern man feels either richer or safer for it?

We have the treaty of cession. There is no stipulation which abrogates the Mexican laws. We shall never obtain a law of Congress to embody the principle that the slave holder may carry his slaves into the territories. We shall never find a judiciary that will ["not" canceled] declare that the law of slavery prevails there. I consider the exclusion as completely established—the mischief as all done.

My impression is very strong that this has been a foreseen and a premeditated consequence ["of" canceled and "in" interlined] the action, of the advisers of this most unscrupulous & worthless administration.

The misfortune to us is that the Southern people have been active in all this. The name of [James K.] Polk in all the meetings of the ["democratic" interlined] party is the subject of eulogy. The people have been taught by the politicians that they cannot do too much for one who has fulfilled every pledge.

Thus with absolute & so far as I can see irremediable injuries received from him we are instructed that his administration is a triumph of Southern principles.

Our friends here now, see the wisdom of the counsel which warned them against the convention at Baltimore. They find they have been sacrificed & that they have no power at home to check the acceptance of the nominations made there. Those nominations will be ratified.

Notwithstanding however the prospect of certain defeat they are disposed to make a revolt—to form an independent party upon the ["platform" canceled] principles of the democratic party and to oppose the nominations of the Baltimore convention.

You will have an opportunity of seeing at Washington City whether it will have any encouragement from the public men there from the Southern States.

Will Mr. [Dixon H.] Lewis & Col. [Jefferson] Davis—will there be a public man from the South apart from South Carolina—who will be disposed to abandon General [Lewis] Cass in the face of the popular demonstrations at home.

Upon what person can we concentrate our votes for the Presidency? Will Mr. [Littleton W.] Tazewell of Virginia answer? Would he allow us the use of his name?

Would Col. Davis allow us to use his name for the Vice Presidency?

I write to you at the request of others. I am by no means satisfied that any good will come of this independent movement but I am willing to join in it if it is thought to be best.

Does Gen. Taylor's position forbid us to employ his name—my impression is that we cannot do so with consistency. I shall receive your letter at Mobile. Respectfully, J.A. Campbell.

ALS in ScCleA.

Remarks on the bill to prohibit the importation of adulterated drugs, 6/20. "Mr. Calhoun said, this attempt to remedy the evil would fail. The only remedy was to hold the vender [*sic*] liable. If we passed the bill, the public would use the spurious drugs with less caution than ever; and if we rejected it, the States and city corporations would take up the subject and provide a remedy." From the Washington, D.C., *Daily Union*, June 21, 1848, p. 2. Variants in *Congressional Globe*, 30th Cong., 1st Sess., p. 858; Houston, ed., *Proceedings and Debates*, p. 743.

From W[illiam] L. Yancey

Montgomery [Ala.], 21 June, 1848

Dear Sir, We have at last started. We have consulted sufficiently to effect a start. [Zachary] Taylor's position in the late Whig convention has thrown into ["our" *interlined*] arms all those Democrats who were for him heretofore. [James E.] Belser [former Representative from Ala.] resigns his place on the Taylor electoral ticket. [John A.] Campbell of Mobile quits his Taylor ground and is with us. Here, [George T.] Goldthwaite [later a Senator from Ala.], [John A.] Elmore, [Thomas S.] Mays, [Henry C.] Semple, [Sampson W.] Harris [Representative from Ala.], Belser, and kindred spirits are with us. We are raising funds to establish a press here. In that we need aid; but *we will* publish it, at all hazards. We will address the people in a manifesto very soon—this week. We will call a mass convention here, on the 12 July. At that convention we will nominate the ablest & purest electoral ticket ever put into the field in this State. But upon whom shall we rally for President? [Littleton W.] Tazewell [former Senator from Va.] & Jef[ferson] Davis [Senator from Miss.] are suggested here? Will they do? Will you write to Tazewell for us? And write me fully your opinions? The skies are brightening. I was despondent, a week ago. I am hopeful now. We are all so. We will move in force & effectively. Yours &—, W.L. Yancey.

ALS in ScCleA; variant PC in Jameson, ed., *Correspondence*, p. 1177.

REMARKS ON ADJOURNMENT

[In the Senate, June 22, 1848]
[It was proposed that Congress adjourn on 7/17 and reconvene in October (rather than December as it normally would have).]

Mr. Calhoun. It is my impression that the Senate can do more business in one month henceforward, than in two months after its next meeting. I believe this body has never permitted the business before it to go over to be revived at the next session. In every point of view, it is unparliamentary and dangerous. An adjournment now, without completing the business before us, will have the effect of postponing that business, not until the next session, but until the session after the next. At the next session we shall scarcely be able to do any thing at all [because of the transition of administrations]. The only chance for us is to continue where we are, and go on with as much dispatch as possible; and if we do this, I should think that within a month we might get through with the greater part of the business. I am as desirous to return home as any one; I feel as much inconvenience from remaining here; but I am willing to encounter that inconvenience, for the sake of accomplishing as much as possible of the public business, whilst we have it now in a partial state of preparation before us. With regard to meeting in October, a more inconvenient season could not be named for those of us who are planters. I do hope that the resolution will be laid upon the table for the present, and that we will proceed with the business before us with all possible dispatch.

From Houston, ed., *Proceedings and Debates*, p. 750. Variants in the Washington, D.C., *Daily Union*, June 23, 1848, p. 3; the New York, N.Y., *Herald*, June 24, 1848, p. 3; *Congressional Globe*, 30th Cong., 1st Sess., p. 865.

To A[NDREW] P[ICKENS] CALHOUN, [Marengo County, Ala.]

Washington, 23d June 1848

My dear Andrew, The enclosed note (copy) [*not found*] is from the agent of the trust Company, who was sent out some time since to see about the property. It states facts, which it may be important you [*ms. torn;* should(?)] know in determining on the question of the title to the property. The letter was written, in answer to one communicating the statement contained in your letter, in relation to it. I hope with the aid of the facts it discloses, that you will be able to ascertain with certainty, whether the tittle [*sic*] is good or not; and that you will be able to inform me, whether it be or not before I leave this[,] which will probably be abo[u]t the last week in July. It is important, I should know before I leave.

The Wheather [*sic*] here has been fine for the growth of crops; warm & rather inclined to be drey [*sic*]. I hope it is good with you and that our crop is, as promising as you could desire, and the health of the place good. William [Lowndes Calhoun] writes me, that mine at home is remarkably fine; and that all was[?] well. He has undergone a remarkable change. He is now very studio[us &] punctual, and seems to be possessed with much perseverance. I have very favourable accounts of the standing and good conduct of James [Edward Calhoun] in College, & John [C. Calhoun, Jr.] has been exerting himself much to acquire a knowledge of his profession; and, I understand, with good success.

My love to Margaret [Green Calhoun and] the children. Your affectionate father, J.C. Calhoun.

ALS in NcD, John C. Calhoun Papers.

To [ANNA MARIA CALHOUN CLEMSON, Brussels]

Washington, 23d June 1848

My dear daughter, If a long interval lies between the date of this and your last, you must attribute it to the fact, that my heavy correspondence, publick & private, and official duties, compel me to lengthen the period between my answers & the letters to which they reply, to a much greater extent than I desire in writing to you & the rest of the family. I correspond with all of ["them" *interlined*] which of itself occupies a good deal of my time.

The opinions you express in reference to the state of things in Europe are very sensible & just. There is no prospect of a successful termination of the efforts of France to establish a free popular Government; nor was there any from the beginning. She has no elements out of which such a government could be formed; & if she had, still she must fail from her total misconception of the principles, on which such a government, to succeed, must be constructed. Indeed, her conception of liberty is false throughout. Her standard of liberty is ideal; and belongs to that kind of liberty, which man has been supposed to possess, in what has been falsely called a state of nature—a state supposed to have preceded the social & political, & in which, of course, if it ever existed, he must have live[d] a part, as an isolated individual, without society, or government. In such a state, if it were possible for him to exist in it, he would have, indeed, had two of the elements of the French political creed; liberty & equality, but no fraternity. That can only exist in the social & political; and the attempt to unite the other two, as they would exist, in the supposed state of nature, ["with" *canceled and* "in" *interlined*] man, as he must exist in the former, must & ever will fail. The union is impossible, & the attempt to unite them absurd; and must lead, if persisted in, to distraction, anarchy and finally absolute power, in the hand of one man.

It is this false conception that is up heaving Europe, and which, if not corrected, will upset all her efforts to reform her social & political condition. It is at the same time threatening our institutions. Abolitionism originates in it, which every day becomes more formidable, & if not speedily arrested, must terminate in the dissolution of our Union, or in universal convulsion, & overthrow of our system of government. But enough of these general speculations.

We are in the midest of the presidential canvass. It will be one of great confusion. Neither party is satisfied, or united on its nominee; and there will probably be a third candidate, nominated by what are called the Barnburners, or Van Burenites. The prospect, I think is, that [Zachary] Taylor will succeed, tho' it is not certain.

The enclosed [*not found*] will give you all the home news.

It is still uncertain, when Congress will adjourn; but, I think it, probable it will about the 1st August.

My health continues good. I am happy to hear you are all well, & that the children [are] growing & doing so well. Kiss them for their Grandfather, and tell them how happy he is to hear, that they are such good children. Give my love to Mr. [Thomas G.] Clemson. Your affectionate father, J.C. Calhoun.

ALS in ScCleA; variant PC in Jameson, ed., *Correspondence*, pp. 757–759.

From H[ENRY] W. CONNER

Charleston, June 23, 1848

Your fav[our] of the —— Inst. was duly rec[eive]d & has been seen & read with much interest by most of your confidential friends in Charleston.

No public demonstration has been made by either party since my last tho a public meeting has & still is spoken of both by the friends of Gen[era]l [Zachary] Taylor & Gen[era]l [Lewis] Cass.

I apprehend a good deal of excitement during the summer but beyond voting for Gen[era]l Taylor as things stand at present I shall take no part.

I enclose you the private letter you sent me some time since which should have been done before.

Our news paper matter remains status quo, but it appears to me that it is due to the subscribers that something should be said to them. The paper I can well imagine cannot go on, & if so we should in some becoming manner announce it, keeping alive as much as possible the same spirit for some future occasion. I would be glad when you have sufficient leisure that you would advise ["me" *canceled*] us ["in" *interlined*] the matter. Very Truly y[ou]rs &C, H.W. Conner.

[P.S.] Strong efforts I think will be made for Cass, by the politicians but our people are decided for Gen[era]l Taylor.

ALS in ScCleA.

To A[NDREW] P[ICKENS] CALHOUN, [Marengo County, Ala.]

Washington, 24th June 1848

My dear A[ndrew,] Since I wrote you yesterday, I have been requested to state, that lot no. 18, containing 640 acres, & which, as I said in a former letter, was purchased by Mr. Mann[?], & forms, as it is believed, a part of the 2000 acres alluded to in your last, can be had for $2 per acre. I have also been requested to ask your opinion, whether if the title shou[ld pr]ove to be good, it would be advisable to take it at that price? Your affectionate father, J.C. Calhoun.

ALS in NcD, John C. Calhoun Papers.

From Geo[rge] Dennett, "Confidential"

Portsmouth, N.H., June 24th 1848

Dear Sir, I feel exceedingly anxious relative to the political movements going on between the two great parties in this country. Ever since I have taken an interest in the political affairs of the nation, I have always favored and acted with the democracy of the south as regards her institutions, and the doctrine that Congress has no right under the Constitution to legislate on the matter of Slavery in the District of Columbia by passing laws abolishing the same.

The controversy that now agitates the country in regard to new Territory is one of vital interest to the south. I do not hesitate to say that your friends in this quarter are equally strong with you on this point. They agree fully with you that there is nothing in the Constitution to prevent, in fact it gives to all the right of living and enjoying their property at the north or south as they please, or taking it from a State into a territory and there enjoy it as they please. Doctrines contrary to these are anti-democratic. Every lover of free principles and every lover of his country cannot consistantly take any other position. I have never been in a situation that enabled me to do any thing in behalf of those principles other than exert my feeble influence at the polls. [*Interpolation:* *"I have held the office of Naval office(r) in this district under Mr. Van Buren, and of Collector under Mr. Tyler, and was rejected by the Senate, in June 1844."] This I have always done, and still intend to do, if I can do so with effect. As matters now stand, I am at a loss to know how to act, and act efficiently with the South. Gen. [Lewis] Cass is the candidate of the democracy by nomination. He is not my choice. Of the three prominent candidates before the Baltimore Convention Judge [Levi] Woodbury had my preference. I know him well, and know him to be right on the southern policy—he is as strong for the south as any southern man.

I regret (as the south in that convention had no candidate of her own,) that Judge Woodbury was not nominated.

Gen. [William O.] Butler the nominee for Vice President. I suppose he will be far more acceptable to the south to preside over the Senate (in case of a tie vote) than the candidate of the Whigs, for the same office. I hardly see how the south can give the whig candidate for Vice [President] a single vote and be true to herself.

Gen. [Zachary] Taylor is the candidate of the Whig party, and can be relied on by the south with as much, if not more safety than Gen. Cass. At the same time Gen. Cass is sound on the Tariff, Internal improvements by the General Government, veto power, and Independant Treasury, and apparently so on the question of Slavery. Gen. Taylor has not, and probably will not make his views known to the public on these great questions.

It is in the power of your friends here to give the vote of this State to Gen. Cass or Gen. Taylor as will best serve the interests of the south, and they will do it, if they can understand what her interests are, or in other word which of these gentlemen will receive her support in the coming election. If we act in the dark we are likely to get into a false position—this we wish to avoid. We intend to vote, or not vote, as will best subserve the object in view.

The above has been written some days. I doubted the propriety of sending it to you, having had but a slight acquaintance with you. Having merely had letters of introduction to you some four years ago from Judge Woodbury & Hon. Lemuel Williams, then Collector of Boston. My attachment to your principles is the only excuse I have to offer for so doing.

Any reply you please to make to this letter, will be considered strictly confidential. Please send me a copy of your ["recent" *interlined*] speech on the territory question. With the highest respect, Your Obedient Servant, Geo. Dennett.

ALS in ScCleA; PC in Boucher and Brooks, eds., *Correspondence*, pp. 443–444.

From J[AMES] WISHART

St. Louis, June 24th, [18]48

My Dear Sir, Finding myself more frequently in the minority than the majority in politics, and often differing essentially from both sides Occupying a private position too, in which, while I could be of no benefit to others, I injured myself, I have so far withdrawn from politics as to side with neither. Although the principles of our republic are, like christianity, good in themselves, like it also, all that is good, is neutralised in the administration. Associations of all kinds embrace a majority who are far below mediocrity both in a moral and intellectual point of view. And of consequence when we attach ourselves to them we are compelled to descend below that graduation, to be on the same level, or be unpopular should we hold ourselves above it in either.

These considerations have led me to the conclusion that it is best to have as few associations of this kind as may be—No more than are requisite to the free and untrammelled exercise of our responsibilities as moral agents. Although I have seen principles at work which will ultimately effect great evil, my voice and efforts are impotent in arresting their progress, and therefore have resolved to confine myself to my own special and private relations.

I am not suited with either of the presidential candidates.

Gen. [Lewis] Cass is I believe a demagogue of a small size, and not reliable. Gen. [Zachary] Taylor is a tactician in military affairs, but I fear no statesman, but as my attention has been but little directed to this point for some time past, my opinion may be erroneous. Should you deem it a question worth your attention I shall be pleased to have your views on it.

Inclosed you will find a medical essay, embracing some new pathological views on idiopathic fevers. This has long been a controverted subject, without the prospect of the settlement of the question on either side. If I am not greatly mistaken, the devellopement of a law in physiology therein presented will bring this controversy to a close. This law has not been heretofore distinctly announced, or recognised by any pathologist, and when you see it, you will wonder how it could have been passed over so obvious does it appear. The reception of any communication from you, will alway[s] be greeted with pleasure, should you find time and inclination to favor me with your views. And if the important and responsible duties in which you have been engaged, have not driven me from your recollection, I hope you will indulge me with, at least, a short, if you cannot find time treat me to a long letter. With respectful regard, J. Wishart.

ALS in ScCleA. NOTE: Wishart's "medical essay" was probably his "An Inquiry into the Origin of Epidemics, and a Physical and Chemical Analysis of their Specific Cause, on a New Theory of Matter and Form," published in St. Louis in the *Medical and Surgical Journal* of June, 1848.

From Tho[ma]s J. Boyd

Wytheville Va., June 25th 1848

Dear Sir, I hope I shall be pardoned for troubling you with this note, and asking your opinion as to the propriety of sustaining Gen[era]l [Zachary] Taylor for the Presidency in preference to Gen[era]l [Lewis] Cass. You will, perhaps, recollect me, of the Wytheville Hotel. Your efforts to sustain the Constitution and true Honor of our Country, since I had the pleasure of seeing you in our village in Aug[us]t 1846, have received my unqualified approbation, & for which, as an American citizen I individually tender you my sincere thanks. I have not been able to approve the course of Mr. Cass. His views, if approved & sustained by the People, I fear will lead to the destruction of our Constitution & Government, virtually at least. I have thought it would be safer to take Gen[era]l Taylor. If you have a moment's leisure, will you favor me with your views on the subject? I believe there is no man living, who is more thoroughly in favor of *States rights Democratic principles*, if I understand them, than myself; and my desire is to support that man, of the two before the country, for the Presidency, who will do most, in all probability, to sustain those principles—in other words, who will do most to maintain the Constitution of the Country. The past spring I was elected a Delegate to the Legislature of this State, having declined, throughout the Canvass, to pledge myself to support the Baltimore nominee, and expressed a decided preference for Gen[era]l Taylor for the Presidency, over any one who was likely to be brought before the country for that station. There is another, who, I did not hesitate to say, was infinitely preferred by me, but whose bold, independent, and disinterested efforts in defence of the Const[it]ution would make him unacceptable to either of the leading parties.

A few lines from you will be very thankfully received. I need hardly say, that this note is strictly confidential, as will be considered your reply, unless you authorise me to use it as I may think proper. How is Gen[era]l Taylor, in regard to the Bank? The public debt will prevent much squabble between the Democrats & Whigs, for years to come, about other questions that have heretofore split them. Can Mr. [Millard] Fillmore be supported, under any circumstances, by a States rights man? With the highest consideration & respect, Your mo[st] Ob[edien]t Serv[an]t, Thos. J. Boyd.

ALS in ScCleA. Note: An AEU by Calhoun reads, "Col. Boyd of WytheVille Va."

From F[ITZ]W[ILLIAM] BYRDSALL

New York [City,] June 25th 1848

Dear Sir, I enclose you the Pronunciamiento of Mr. M[artin] Van Buren against the rights of the Southern people, together with the proceedings of the Barn Burners' Convention at Utica. Within the last twelve months there has been extending through the free States so called, a fanatical feeling for what the demagogues term free Soil and the non extension of Slavery. Be assured that if Mr. Van Buren had not ascertained the existence and spread of this feeling, he never would have come out so unequivocally and decidedly as he has.

When the nominations made at Baltimore & Philadelphia were promulgated I felt satisfied that in the success of either candidate, the rights of the South would be safe and consequently the Union. But it is known to me that the majority of people in both parties, as well as amongst the neutrals opposed to both, is in favor of the anti Southern Crusade. I find [Lewis] Cass men, [Zachary] Taylor men declaring against the "extension of slavery to territory now free." This war cry appeals to the prejudices of the Northern people as well as to their Sectional and selfish feelings; public opinion on this idea is accumulating and the South must do something to create a reaction in the popular mind. You have already advanced the right principles and the sound arguments as regards the rights of the Southern people but you have not been adequately sustained by Conventions, nor has the South, for its own sake, united upon you as the exponent of its cause, ["or" *interlined*] as the candidate of its choice. Neglect in this way, has had the effect of lessening the currency of those principles and of giving no force to those arguments. Hence it is that they have been called abstractions because the people whose rights and interests were involved, regarded them as theoretic and never united to give them "form and pressure."

The mighty torrent of public opinion in the Northern and middle States must be met and stemmed. The longer the conflict is pos[t]-poned the worse will it be when it comes. It is a poor shield to depend upon the veto of the Executive to defend the rights of the South. It is a great constitutional weapon but its exercise depends on the moral courage of one man.

I cannot help thinking that the Southern members of Congress should unite at the close of the Session in calling a great convention of the Southern States before the ensueing presidential Election. Surely twenty or thirty men from each ["slave" *interlined*] State could be found willing to assemble together in such a cause not only involving *all* their own rights but the preservation of the Union; I mean by the words "all their own rights," the Rights of the States—constitutional rights—Rights of person and of property. Resistance to the modern crusade includes every thing of any value to the State or the citizen.

The language of a great Southern Convention protesting against a violation of all rights dear to the Southern people—against a violation of the compromises of the Constitution and against measures whose success would inevitably dissolve the Union, would produce a reaction in the minds of the people, East[,] west[,] north & South of the very best tendency. I am Dear Sir yours Resp[ect]f[ull]y, F.W. Byrdsall.

ALS in ScCleA; PC in Boucher and Brooks, eds., *Correspondence*, pp. 444–445.

From JOHN HUMES GREENWAY

Philomathean Society [Charlottesville, Va.,] June 25th 1848
Sir, I have the *honor* to announce to you, that at a recent *meeting* of the Philomathean Society, of the University of Virginia, You were unanimously elected one of its Honorary members, and permit me *Sir* as the organ of communication, in behalf of the *Society*—to express a sincere and hearty *wish*, that this, may meet with your *entire approbation*, and that you *will* cooperate with us, in demolishing the *batteries* of *Ignorance*, and *cause* the burning and brilliant luminary of *learning*, which has thrown such a vivid light on other parts of the *world*, to shine as vividly and resplendently in our *own*. With sentiments of high respect I am Your most Ob[edien]t S[ervan]t, John Humes Greenway, Recorder.

ALS in ScCleA. NOTE: An AEU by Calhoun reads, "Honorary membership of the Philomathean Society."

Remarks on the Oregon Bill, 6/26. "Mr. Calhoun expressed an intention to address the Senate on the amendment proposed by Mr. Jefferson Davis. The object which the South desired to attain, he thought, would be best accomplished by this amendment, than by the indirect mode of striking out the 12th section." (Davis's amendment provided that no persons should be prohibited from taking slaves to Oregon.) On Calhoun's motion, the bill was postponed. From the Baltimore, Md., *Sun*, June 27, 1848, p. 4. Also printed in the Charleston, S.C., *Courier*, June 30, 1848, p. 2; the Charleston, S.C., *Mercury*, June 30, 1848, p. 2; the Camden, S.C., *Journal*, July 4, 1848, p. 2. Variant in *Congressional Globe*, 30th Cong., 1st Sess., p. 874; Benton, *Abridgment of Debates*, 16:214. Another variant in Houston, ed., *Proceedings and Debates*, p. 787.

From E[stwick] Evans

Philadelphia, June 27th 1848

Sir: I have several times, during the last few years, conferred upon myself the honour of writing you. The great questions of State rights; of slavery in general; of slavery as an institution of the South; of the extension of slavery to new States—embracing the Wilmot proviso; & slavery in the Dis[tric]t of Columbia, are now perhaps, more than ever important—& will become still more & more so. I feel strong, even on all these points. But the great thing needed is to let in light upon the public mind from the deep—["the elementary" *canceled*] the far-reaching elementary principles of man & of society. How few in this country even dream of the *Relative* in morals, liberty, society &c! How few have thought—(I have not yet announced it,) of the maxim that: all but God is complex, & consequently relative— embracing the law of circumstance—of charity!—that relative & that charity which often makes wrong right.

I want to publish, at once, the 2d No. on State Rights, making about 100–120 pages of document form. The 1st No. purposely discussed rather the general elements of the subject, with a suggestion or two on incidental topics, wishing it to stand, in some sense, as a whole, because I did not know whether I should be able to get out any further No.; but the 2 No., is made up of a close enquiry, wholly argumentative, into the terms, & spirit of the "Compact," the provisions of the Constitution, & the true principles of construction, as well as of the general distinctive difference between a government proper & our central system &c.

But on oneside[?]—as far removed as possible, in point of delicacy, I am desirous, as a mean of carrying out my plan of publishing my remaining numbers of Essays on State rights; & then, under a variety of anonymous signatures, in different presses, endeavouring to enlighten, & enlarge, the public mind, & neutralize the prevailing feeling of abolitionists on the questions before named in this letter: I am desirous of getting a location in Washington; somewhere in the

Capital. Perhaps you might deem it your *duty* to further this object. Perhaps you might mention it to Gen[era]l [Samuel] Houston [Senator from Texas] & *other friends* of the South. But *if* so, I should wish it to be, as you, of course, would do it, only as a matter of means & pecuniary convenience as to the means. I have *never* intimated this idea to Gen[era]l [Lewis] Cass; but he has been a personal friend of mine ever since 1818, & I have no doubt would be happy to serve me, as I certainly should him.

Leaving, Sir, the whole subject to your entire convenience, I have the honour to remain, with the highest consideration & respect, Your Obed[ien]t S[ervan]t, E. Evans.

ALS in ScCleA.

From GEO[RGE] G. HENRY

Mobile, June 27, 1848

Sir, Knowing you to be a Cotton planter, and that your practical information will enable you at once to perceive the demerits, or merits of a proposition, I beg to submit to you an idea, which has suggested itself to my mind, & which, could it in the present crippled condition of European trade & confidence be consum[m]ated, would have a very profitable effect on the Cotton planting interest, in anticipation too, of the *growing* crop of Cotton being larger *certainly* by 100 @ 150 M [that is, thousand] bales than our largest.

My engagement as a Cotton Factor & Corn merchant, has caused me to give a good deal of examination & reflection to what might be beneficial to the Cotton Interest.

The expression has often been used by planters, that if they had their way they would burn up half of the Cotton Crop—stating they would obtain more money for the other half. My suggestion would differ from that in this way. That a Leauge [*sic*] be formed by the Cotton planters throughout for their mutual advantage, and they should resolve that there should not be a bole of Cotton picked out after the *1st* day of *December next*, of this crop. Neighborhood meetings, at which they would resolve, as above provided it be general, and appoint from those delegates to County meetings, those County meetings confer and appoint State. The State appoint Delegates to attend a general convention of Cotton planters, confirming the compact. You are where there are many Cotton planters as Senators & Representatives, you could easily ascertain their views, and if they choose with you to take the matter energetically in hand by the 1st Monday in Sep[tembe]r, I believe a general convention might ["be" *interlined*] held. And I would suggest that the Leauge be permanent as by its concerted action much power and force could be attracted that is now entirely valueless. By an agre[e]ment of this character, you will perceive that a good propo[r]tion of the best hands might be hired to do Rail Road or Factory work from 1st Dec. to 1st M[ar]ch & perhaps from 1st May till Cotton picking time. As the hands on plantation properly worked can make more Cotton than the same can pick out.

A decided effort ought to be made to influence planters to direct a good deal of their force into manufacturing branches, & Slave labor, is vastly cheaper for those purposes than any other in this country, or I think in Europe.

Say a woman of 18 worth 450—Int[erest] @ 8% is	36.00
Insurance extra prm[?]. for life	12.10
The Int[erest] & Insurance per year is the hire per year	$48.10 and

no cotton planter certainly averages 8 per c[en]t. As to the value of the increase of negroes, their value in that respect[?] would be enormously augmented, as the business being lighter, the embryo, would rarely be destroyed as is the case on the farm under the average treatment. Hurriedly I throw together these suggestions, and submitting them to your consideration, believe me to be Most Respectfully Your Ob[edien]t Ser[van]t, Geo. G. Henry.

[P.S.] Should you desire to honor me with your views or to write me, please address me at Chunanugge [*sic*], Macon Co[unty], Ala., my summer retreat.

[Printed enclosure]

Geo[rge] G. Henry to ——

Mobile, July 20, 1847

Dear Sir—Reviewing my respects to you of a year ago, and that of 20th December last, the feelings of pleasure natural to one on realizing a much cherished hope, arises within me. The anticipations I so unequivocally expressed, were entertained, doubtless, by many others. Experience and a knowledge of mankind suggests, however, that to accomplish great enterprises, concert of feeling and action is required, and to produce which we must all know what each should do. If, to consummate this object, practical reasons are submitted, while they confirm and strengthen those whose interest it is to achieve it, it lessens the desire to oppose it of those whose interests have arrayed them on the other side. I have therefore thought it my duty, without reserve, to give to my friends such opinions as a close examination of the subject of their interests conduct me to.

The Cotton Planter now occupies a commanding position. Feeling for a number of years all the discouragements of low prices, he has been turning some of his industry into other channels: but other circumstances have come to his support and contribute much to it. The absence of any extensive lots of good public lands in the Cotton region is one; the flattering inducements to invest capital in many other branches of industry, another. The production of India and other countries too, to which I have frequently before drawn your attention, is failing. Without entering into detail, I will merely say that on the discussion, which was evidently not desired by the Ministers, of a petition to Parliament, from the citizens of Manchester, praying the Government to adopt measures for the promotion of the culture of Cotton in India, it was asserted that so far from its being consistent for the Government to act on it, that the culture there, even for domestic purposes was threatened with annihilation. As Cotton manufactures were taken there, and could be sold so low, there remained no inducement for the natives to cultivate it. In Egypt, the efforts of Mehemet Ali, commenced about 1822–3, and which at first seemed to flatter him, are resulting unprofitably, and competition from thence will be moderate. That from the West Indies and South America, is so reduced by resorting to other crops, that their production is also on the decline.

But advantageous as these all are, the moderation of your own crop of year before last, the scantiness of last year's, with certainly the precarious prospects of the growing one, with your ability now to hold your crops for your prices, will be found to constitute the most powerful causes for your present prospects, while the others secure their continuance.

Low prices was the result mainly of over-production, and does not the serious experience of the fact furnish us motives of the strongest personal as well as national considerations, for the pursuance of such a concerted system among Planters, as shall prevent its recurrence?

At this point I will introduce some figures, which I think will recommend themselves to your attention. The crop of 1844, the largest we ever made, was 2,400,000 bales, weighing on an average 440 lbs. each. It was sold at an average of 4¾ c[ents] per pound, which amounted to $50,160,000. The latter part of that and part of the following year was one of our most gloomy periods, as all our hopes of a check to production, were mere hopes. The crop of 1845, was 2,100,537 bales of 440 lbs. sold at 6¾ c[ents] per lb., amounted to $62,385,000. The crop of the past year in bales will be about 1,780,000, and allowing at each port the same weight of their bales for this as last year, their average is 428 lbs.; but if the proportionate falling off in weight elsewhere, equals what it appears to be at this port (13 lbs. a bale,) the average would only be about 416 lbs. But let us call it 420, and at 420 lbs. it would only make 1,697,722, (a few thousand less than my estimate of December last, which was 1,700,000,) and this crop sold at an average of 10 c[ents], produces you $74,760,000. Let me recapitulate.

*1844 . . . 2,400,000 bales at	4¾ c[ents]	. . .	$50,160,000
1845 . . . 2,100,537 "	6¾ c[ents]	. . .	62,385,000
*1846 . . . 1,697,722 "	10 c[ents]	. . .	74,760,000[.]

[*Marginal interpolation:* " **If the dif[ference] of the crop of 1844 from that of 1846—say 700,000 bales looses 25,000,000—how much will a crop of 850,000 bales larger than that of 1846 loose, thus 700,000 ["Bales" *interlined*]:25,000,000["$" *interlined*]::850,000 ["Bales" *interlined*]:$3,035,714 or for 2,550,000 bales 47,000,000$ only would be rec[eive]d."]

The result is amazing. And do these figures not address themselves to the minds of Planters, in unbounded force, and in the most urgent, as well as persuasive voice, entreat them to nurse and cherish, and not destroy their lands? For those lands and our climate are more precious than mines of gold. And do we not see that we have the strongest imaginable inducements to enter upon other enterprises? Throughout the South and especially Alabama, the best water power for Cotton Factories, and most valuable minerals abound. Several Railroads are projected that would be profitable, and the chartering of some good stock Banks is promised us by all parties. Strike out new modes of investment and take the lead yourselves in it, and your interest will be doubly promoted.

Let me here examine what the general profits on this seemingly fascinating pursuit have been for several years, and from that, those who wish to buy may be able to arrive at what would appear to be a fair remuneration due to the Planters for their Cotton; and Planters will see a good reason to follow the inclinations they have been exhibiting for several years, of investing in that which pays better.

If a company wish to establish a Manufactory, an Insurance Office, a Bank, a Railroad, or a Merchant to invest capital in some adventure, before they do so, they calculate what it will cost to manage that capital till the time for dividing profits or realizing; and what the chances of profit are on the average, over and above what is the usual interest on money lent on good security. If it is clear the enterprise will pay cost and interest, with perhaps a moderate margin for profit they enter upon it. If this be the case with those investments, should not one investing in planting require a similar calculation. Some will say certainly. I agree. I wish now to inquire what the average cost is of managing and doing, we may call it, the business of the capital alluded to in those various branches. If I were to say from 5 to 8 per cent. would be the cost for salaries of Presidents, Cashiers, Clerks, &c. I think I would be under the average. What are their profits? 8 to 12 per cent. is a low average. We will then say the gross product of their capital, charges and profits would average 15 per cent.

Now I come to a survey of the yield of the Cotton planting interest. I was forming estimates and averaging them, of what amount of capital was thus engaged, when I fell on that of the Secretary of the United States Treasury [Robert J. Walker]. He estimates the capital employed in Cotton planting at Nine Hundred Million of Dollars. I presume it will amount fully to that. Let us see the product of the crop of 1844, (say 2,400,000 bales,) on this capital. The crop you observe, as noted above, sold for $50,160,000 *gross*, which is a fraction *over 5½ per cent. gross*. The crop of this year yields $74,760,000, which is about 8¼ per cent. gross, and in either year falls immensely below what is considered the smallest yield on capital otherwise invested. Fifteen per cent. on $900,000,000, would be $135,000,000. The calculation is easy made that a crop of 2,000,000 bales of 420 pounds each, to bring $135,000,000 should sell at 16 c[en]ts per pound; or a crop of 2,200,000 bales of the same weight, at 14½ c[ents]. You must not understand it as my opinion that you will get such prices: I scarcely hope for such, but I present them to show how the account stands. I know that after this year there must arise in the aggregate an enormous sum of surplus money among the Cotton Planters, and I have ventured these remarks that they may begin to adopt measures for its employment, which will do the whole country good, and tend rather to increase their wealth and enhance prices than to reduce them to nothing again.

In approaching the subject of the prospects of the growing crop and its extent, I beg to make a remark about estimates. I have made them, that I might present to my friends that on which to base their calculations respecting the value of their crops. I have taken such pains as my mind and industry have given me the control of, to approximate to the truth. Something in the bounds of reason and probability, drawn from a careful consideration of all the information I acquire, is what I take pleasure in offering you. Thus feeling and intending, I say I do not think with one of our most favorable seasons from this out—warm dry fall and late frost—the crop can exceed 2,150,000 bales. If the rainy weather continues, cool nights prevail in September, the present appearance of the bore worm, rot and rust extend much further, or the caterpillar is extensively generated, this quantity will be lessened accordingly. The crops on the lands which produce about half the Cotton which comes to this Port, are very small, backward, and have very poor stands. Those on the other half, have better size, is backward, running to weed, and is pronounced by old Planters to be in a critical condition.

March, April and even May were the coldest spring months ever experienced in this climate, which prevented some Cotton from coming up regularly, killed some, generated the lice, causing bad stands, and replanting was continued till in June. A record has been kept in Georgia for many years, of the first appearance there of blooms, and this year they were one day later (15th June) than has ever before been recorded. From all former experience, the period of their appearance has shown itself a faithful index of what subsequently was the crop.

The consumption of Cotton generally has not been equal, for the past six months, to the corresponding time of last year, but its prospect of extension are more than equal to the prospect of supply. The Manufacturers seeing they would be compelled to stop for want of Cotton, closed some of their Factories and had others running only a limited number of hours, by which they have preserved the stock from complete exhaustion, and prevented prices from running up very high. The first four months of the year the weekly deliveries for consumption in Great Britain were only about 20,000 bales a week; since the commencement of May to 19th June it has been about 26,000 bales. They have undoubtedly worked their stocks down to the lowest verge. The cessation of manufacturers must result ere long in a scarcity of manufactures and yarns, as stocks everywhere are low and trade generally is good and increasing; so to supply their demand they will become actively engaged, and it will not be long before Cotton advances there.

Cotton, I consider, now assumes the attitude of money itself. Our exports of it in the raw and manufactured state together, pay five-eight[h]s to three-fourths of the amount of our imports. England buys it, adds to its cost 150 to 200 per cent. by manufacturing it, and with it pays a large amount of her debt, besides what she reserves for consumption. These are matters not unimportant, and understanding them, we must not allow ourselves to be forced from our position by any clamor they may choose to raise about capital directed towards rail-way shares, or insufficient harvests. The late accounts respecting the harvests in Europe are flattering, and fill all on the other side with gladness; and a check has been given to the progress of many railroads, by Parliament granting subscribers the privilege of withdrawing their subscriptions.

From the foregoing it is to be inferred, that if I were asked if prices would be pretty good next season, I should answer yes.

Were your crop to reach 2,200,000 bales, I should say a range of from 10 to 12½ c[ents] might be expected. If you make less you may get more, provided no false estimates of the crop are got up, such as some parties in Savannah made and promulgated, making the past crop 2,175,000. To these estimates and some made in Charleston, I attribute the cause of a large portion of the best Cotton of the Atlantic States, being early hurried to market, which was bought up at 7½ a 9 c[ents]. This, shipped to Liverpool, has had a serious influence on that market in prices, and from which I do not think they have fully recovered.

Although business has been laborious with Merchants, I think Planters have reason to feel pleased with the general course of prices at this Port, and submitting, in conclusion, my rather extended remarks to their judgment and discretion.

With a respectful tender of my services, I am, Your obedient servant, Geo. G. Henry.

ALS with En in ScCleA. NOTE: The enclosed printed letter has a marginal interpolation in Henry's hand. An AEU by Calhoun reads, "Mr. Henry, relating to Cotton."

SPEECH ON THE OREGON BILL

[In the Senate, June 27, 1848]

Mr. Calhoun. There is a very striking difference between the position in which the slaveholding and non-slaveholding States stand in reference to the subject under consideration. The former desire no action of the Government; demand no law to give them any advantage in the Territory about to be established; are willing to leave it, and other Territories belonging to the United States, open to all their citizens, so long as they continue to be Territories, and when they cease to be so, to leave it to their inhabitants to form such governments as may suit them, without restriction or condition, except that imposed by the Constitution, as a prerequisite for admission into the Union. In short, they are willing to leave the whole subject where the Constitution and the great and fundamental principles of self-government place it. On the contrary, the non-slaveholding States, instead of being willing to leave it on this broad and equal foundation, demand the interposition of the Government, and the passage of an act to exclude the citizens of the slaveholding States from emigrating with their property into the Territory, in order to give their citizens and those they may permit, the exclusive right of settling it, while it remains in that condition, preparatory to subjecting it to like restrictions and conditions when it becomes a State. The 12th section of this bill is intended to assert and maintain this demand of the non-slaveholding States, while it remains a Territory, not openly or directly, but indirectly, by extending the provisions of the bill for the establishment of the Iowa Territory to this, and by ratifying the acts of the informal and self-constituted government of Oregon, which, among others, contains one prohibiting the introduction of slavery. It thus, in reality, adopts what is called the Wilmot proviso, not only for Oregon, but, as the bill now stands, for New Mexico and California. The amendment, on the contrary, moved by the Senator from Mississippi near me, (Mr. [Jefferson] Davis,) is intended to assert and maintain the position of the slaveholding States. It leaves the Territory free and open to all the citizens of the United States, and would overrule, if adopted, the act of the self-constituted Territory of Oregon and the 12th section, as far as it relates to the subject under consideration. We have thus fairly presented the grounds taken by the non-slaveholding and the slaveholding States, or, as I shall call them for the sake of brevity, the northern and southern States, in their whole extent, for discussion.

The first question which offers itself for consideration is: Has the northern States the power which they claim, to exclude the southern from emigrating freely, with their property, into Territories belonging to the United States, and to monopolize them for their exclusive benefit?

It is, indeed, a great question. I propose to discuss it calmly and dispassionately. I shall claim nothing which does not fairly and clearly belong to the southern States, either as members of this Federal Union, or appertaining to them in their separate and individual character; nor shall I yield any which belong to them in either capacity. I am influenced neither by sectional nor party considerations. If I know myself, I would repel as promptly and decidedly any aggression of the South on the North, as I would any on the part of the latter on the former. And let me add, I hold the obligation to repel aggression to be not much less solemn than that of abstaining from making aggression; and that the party which submits to it when it can be resisted, to be not much less guilty and responsible for consequences than that which makes it. Nor do I stand on party grounds. What I shall say in reference to this subject, I shall say entirely without reference to the Presidential election. I hold it to be infinitely higher than that and all other questions of the day. I shall direct my efforts to ascertain what is constitutional, right, and just, under a thorough conviction that the best and only way of putting an end to this, the most dangerous of all questions to our Union and institutions, is to adhere rigidly to the Constitution and the dictates of justice.

With these preliminary remarks, I recur to the question: Has the North the power which it claims under the 12th section of this bill? I ask at the outset, where is the power to be found? Not, certainly, in the relation in which the northern and southern States stand to each other. They are the constituent parts or members of a common Federal Union; and, as such, are equals in all respects, both in dignity and rights, as is declared by all writers on governments founded on such union, and as may be inferred from arguments deduced from their nature and character. Instead, then, of affording any countenance or authority in favor of the power, the relation in which they stand to each other furnishes a strong presumption against it. Nor can it be found in the fact that the South holds property in slaves. That, too, fairly considered, instead of affording any authority for the power, furnishes a strong presumption against it. Slavery existed in the South when the Constitution was framed, fully to the extent in proportion to their population as it does at this time. It is the only property recognized by it; the only one that entered into its formation as a political element, both in the adjustment of the relative weight of the States in the Government, and the apportionment of direct taxes; and the only one that is put under the express guarantee of the Constitution. It is well known to all conversant with the history of the formation and adoption of the Constitution, that the South was very jealous in reference to this property; that it constituted one of the difficulties, both to its formation and adoption, and that it would not have assented to either, had the Convention refused to allow to it its due weight in the Government, or to place it under the guarantee of the Constitution. Nor can it be found in the way that the territories have been acquired. I will not go into particulars in this respect at this stage of the discussion. Suffice it to say, the whole was acquired either by purchase out of the common funds of all the States, the South as well as the North, or by arms and mutual sacrifice of men and money, which, instead of giving any countenance in favor of the power claimed by the North, on every principle of right and justice, furnishes strong additional presumption against it.

But if it cannot be found in either, if it exists at all, the power must be looked for in the constitutional compact, which binds these States together in a Federal Union; and I now ask, can it be found there? Does that instrument contain any provision which gives the North the power to exclude the South from a free admission into the Territories of the United States with its peculiar property, and to monopolize them for its own exclusive use? If it in fact contains such power, expressed or implied, it must be found in a specific grant, or be inferred by irresistible deduction, from some clear and acknowledged power. Nothing short of the one or the other can overcome the strong presumption against it.

That there is no such specific grant, may be inferred beyond doubt from the fact that no one has ever attempted to designate it. Instead of that, it has been assumed—taken for granted without a particle of proof—that Congress has the absolute right to govern the Territories. Now, I concede, if it does in reality possess such power, it may exclude from the Territories who or what they please, and admit into them who or what they please; and of course may exercise the power claimed by the North to exclude the South from them. But I again repeat, where is this absolute power to be found? All admit that there is no such specific grant of power. If, then, it exists at all, it must be inferred from some such power. I ask, where is that to be found? The Senator from New York, behind me, (Mr. [John A.] Dix,) points to the clause in the Constitution, which provides that "Congress shall have power to dispose of, and make all needful rules and regulations respecting, the territory or other property belonging to the United States." Now, I undertake to affirm and maintain, beyond the possibility of doubt, that so far from conferring absolute power to govern the Territories, it confers no governmental power whatever; no, not a particle. It refers exclusively to territory regarded simply as public lands. Every word relates to it in that character, and is wholly inapplicable to it considered in any other character but as property. Take the expression "dispose of," with which it begins. It is easily understood what it means when applied to lands, and is the proper and natural expression regarding the territory in that character, when the object is to confer the right to sell or make other disposition of it. But who ever heard the expression applied to government? And what possible meaning can it have when so applied? Take the next expression, "to make all needful rules and regulations." These regarded separately, might indeed be applicable to government in a loose sense; but they are never so applied in the Constitution. In every case where they are used in it, they refer to property, to things, or some process, such as the rules of court, or of the Houses of Congress for the government of their proceedings; but never to government, which always implies persons to be governed. But if there should be any doubt in this case, the words immediately following, which restricts them to making "rules and regulations respecting the territory or other property of the United States," must effectually expel it. They restrict their meaning, beyond the possibility of doubt, to territory regarded as property.

But if it were possible for doubt still to exist, another and conclusive argument still remains to show that the framers of the Constitution did not intend to confer by this clause governmental powers. I refer to the clause in the Constitution which delegates the power of exclusive legislation to Congress over this District, and "all places purchased by the consent of the Legislature of the State in which the same may be, for the erection of forts, magazines, arsenals, dockyards, and other needful buildings." The places therein referred to are clearly embraced by the expression, "other property belonging to the United States," contained in the clause I have just considered. But it is certain, that if it had been the intention of the framers of the Constitution to confer governmental powers over such places by that clause, they never would have delegated it by this. They were incapable of doing a thing so absurd. But it is equally certain, if they did not intend to confer such power over them, they could not have intended it over Territories. Whatever was conferred by the same words in reference to one, must have been intended to be conferred in reference to the other, and the reverse. The opposite supposition would be absurd. But, it may be asked, why the term territory was omitted in the delegation of exclusive legislation to Congress over the places enumerated? Very satisfactory reasons may, in my opinion, be assigned. The former were limited to places lying within the limits and jurisdiction of the States, and the latter to public land lying beyond both. The cession and purchase of the former, with the consent of the State within which they might be situated, did not oust the sovereignty or jurisdiction of the State. They still remained in the State, the United States acquiring only the title to the place. It therefore became necessary to confer on Congress, by express delegation, the exercise of exclusive power of legislation over this District, and such places, in order to carry out the object of the purchase and cession. It was simply intended to withdraw them from under the Legislatures of the respective States within which they might lie, and substitute that of Congress in its place, subject to the restrictions of the Constitution, and the objects for which the places were acquired, leaving, as I have said, the sovereignty still in the State in which they are situated, but in abeyance, as far as it extends to legislation. Thus, in the case of this District, since the retrocession to Virginia of the part beyond the Potomac, the sovereignty still continues in Maryland in the manner stated. But the case is very different in reference to Territories, lying, as they do, beyond the limits and jurisdiction of all the States. The United States possess not simply the right of ownership over them, but that of exclusive dominion and sovereignty; and hence it was not necessary to exclude the power of the States to legislate over them, by delegating the exercise of exclusive legislation to Congress. It would have been an act of supererogation. It may be proper to remark in this connection, that the power of exclusive legislation conferred in these cases must not be confounded with the power of absolute legislation. They are very different things. It is true, that absolute power of legislation is always exclusive, but it by no means follows that exclusive power of legislation or of government is likewise always absolute. Congress has the exclusive power of legislation as far as this Government is concerned, and the State Legislatures, as far as their respective Governments are concerned; but we all know that both are subject to many and important restrictions and conditions which the nature of absolute power excludes.

I have now made good the assertion I ventured to make, that the clause in the Constitution relied on by the Senator from New York, so far from conferring the absolute power of government over the territory claimed by him, and others who agree with him, confers not a particle of governmental power. Having conclusively established this, the long list of precedents cited by the Senator, to prop up the power which he sought in the clause, falls to the ground with the fabric which he raised; and I am thus exempted from the necessity of referring to them, and replying to them one by one.

But there is one precedent referred to by the Senator unconnected with the power, and on that account requires particular notice. I refer to the ordinance of 1787, which was adopted by the old Congress of the Confederation while the Convention that framed the Constitution was in session, and about one year before its adoption, and of course on the very eve of the expiration of the old Confederation. Against its introduction, I might object that the act of the Congress of the Confederation cannot rightfully form precedents for this Government; but I waive that. I waive also the objection that the act was consummated when that Government was *in extremis*, and could hardly be considered *compos mentis*. I waive also the fact that the ordinance assumed the form of a compact, and was adopted when only eight States were present, when the Articles of Confederation required nine to form compacts. I waive also the fact, that Mr. [James] Madison declared that the act was without shadow of constitutional authority, and shall proceed to show, from the history of its adoption, that it cannot justly be considered of any binding force.

Virginia made the cession of the territory north of the Ohio, and lying between it and the Mississippi and the lakes, in 1784. It now contains the States of Ohio, Indiana, Illinois, Michigan, Wisconsin, and a very considerable extent of territory lying north of the latter. Shortly after the cession, a committee of three was raised, of whom Mr. [Thomas] Jefferson was one. They reported an ordinance for the establishment of the Territory, containing, among other provisions, one, of which Mr. Jefferson was the author, excluding slavery from the Territory after the year 1800. It was reported to Congress, but this provision was struck out. On the question of striking out, every southern State present voted in favor of it; and, what is more striking, every southern delegate voted the same way, Mr. Jefferson alone excepted. The ordinance was adopted without the provision. At the next session, Rufus King, then a member of the old Congress, moved a proposition, very much in the same shape of the sixth article (that which excludes slavery) in the ordinance as it now stands, with the exception of its proviso. It was referred to a committee, but there was no action on it. A committee was moved the next or the subsequent year, which reported without including or noticing Mr. King's proposition. Mr. [Nathan] Dane [of Mass.] was a member of that committee, and proposed a provision the same as that in the ordinance as it passed, but the committee reported without including it. Finally, another committee was raised, at the head of which was Mr. [Edward] Carrington, of Virginia, and of which Mr. Dane was also a member. That committee reported without including the

519

amendment previously proposed by him. Mr. Dane moved his proposition, which was adopted, and the report of the committee thus amended became the ordinance of 1787.

It may be inferred from this brief historical sketch, that the ordinance was a compromise between the southern and northern States, of which the terms were, that slavery should be excluded from territory upon condition that fugitive slaves, who might take refuge in the Territory, should be delivered up to their owners, as stipulated in the proviso of the 6th article of the ordinance. It is manifest, from what has been stated, that the South was unitedly and obstinately opposed to the provision when first moved; that the proposition of Mr. King, without the proviso, was in like manner resisted by the South, as may be inferred from its entire want of success, and that it never could be brought to agree to it until the provision for the delivery up of fugitive slaves was incorporated in it. But it is well understood that a compromise involves not a surrender, but simply a waiver of the right or power; and hence, in the case of individuals, it is a well established legal principle, that an offer to settle by compromise a litigated claim, is no evidence against the justice of the claim on the side of the party making it. The South, to her honor, has observed with fidelity her engagements under this compromise; in proof of which, I appeal to the precedents cited by the Senator from New York, intended by him to establish the fact of her acquiescence in the ordinance. I admit that she has acquiesced in the several acts of Congress to carry it into effect; but the Senator is mistaken in supposing that it is proof of a surrender, on her part, of the power over the Territories which he claims for Congress. No, she never has, and I trust never will, make such a surrender. Instead of that, it is conclusive proof of her fidelity to her engagements. She has never attempted to set aside the ordinance, or to deprive the Territory, and the States erected within its limits, of any right or advantage it was intended to confer. But I regret that as much cannot be said in favor of the fidelity with which it has been observed on their part. With the single exception of the State of Illinois—be it said to her honor—every other State erected within its limits have pursued a course, and adopted measures, which have rendered the stipulations of the proviso to deliver up fugitive slaves nugatory. Wisconsin may also be an exception, as she has just entered the Union, and has hardly had time to act on the subject. They have gone further, and suffered individuals to form combinations, without an effort to suppress them, for the purpose of enticing and seducing the slaves to leave their masters, and to run them into Canada beyond the reach of our laws—in open violation, not only of the stipulations of the ordinance, but of the Constitution itself. If I express myself strongly, it is not for the purpose of producing excitement, but to draw the attention of the Senate forcibly to the subject. My object is to lay bare the subject under consideration just as a surgeon probes to the bottom and lays open a wound, not to cause pain to his patient, but for the purpose of healing it.

Mr. [Edward A.] Hannegan [of Ind.]. I am not aware that there is any such law in Indiana.

Mr. Calhoun. I spoke on the authority of a report of one of the committees of this body.

Mr. [Andrew P.] Butler [of S.C.]. In that report I alluded particularly to the northern and New England States; and Illinois, I believe, was the only exception.

Mr. [Thomas] Corwin [of Ohio]. Will the Senator allow me to inquire, what law on the statute-book of Ohio prevents the recapture of fugitive slaves?

Mr. Calhoun. My colleague can doubtless refer to the law. I made the statement on the authority of his report.

Mr. Corwin. There is no such law in Ohio.

Mr. Calhoun. I am very happy to find that it is so; and I should be equally happy if the Senator will make it out that there are no organized bodies of individuals there for the purpose of pilfering our slaves.

Mr. Corwin. Am I to understand the Senator, when he spoke of "incorporated individuals," as referring to the Legislature?

Mr. Calhoun. No; merely organized individuals—a very different thing from corporations.

Mr. Butler. On that point I refer the Senator to the documents on the files of the Senate. If the gentleman desires to call out explanations of that kind, he can be gratified.

Mr. Calhoun. I come now to another precedent of a similar character, but differing in this, that it took place under this Government, and not under that of the old Confederation; I refer to what is known as the Missouri compromise. It is more recent, and better known, and may be more readily despatched.

After an arduous struggle of more than a year, on the question whether Missouri should come into the Union, with or without restrictions prohibiting slavery, a compromise line was adopted between the North and the South; but it was done under circumstances which made it nowise obligatory on the latter. It is true, it was moved by one of her distinguished citizens, (Mr. [Henry] Clay,) but it is equally so, that it was carried by the almost united vote of the North against the almost united vote of the South; and was thus imposed on the latter by superior numbers, in opposition to her strenuous efforts. The South has never given her sanction to it, or assented to the power it asserted. She was voted down, and has simply acquiesced in an arrangement which she has not had the power to reverse, and which she could not attempt to do without disturbing the peace and harmony of the Union—to which she has ever been adverse. Acting on this principle, she permitted the Territory of Iowa to be formed, and the State to be admitted into the Union, under the compromise, without objection; and that is now quoted by the Senator from New York to prove her surrender of the power he claims for Congress.

To add to the strength of this claim, the advocates of the power hold up the name of Jefferson in its favor, and go so far as to call him the author of the so-called Wilmot proviso, which is but a general expression of a power of which the Missouri compromise is a case of its application. If we may judge by his opinion of that case, what his opinion was of the principle, instead of being the author of the proviso, or being in its favor, no one could be more deadly hostile to it. In a letter addressed to the elder [John] Adams, in 1819, in answer to one from him, he uses these remarkable expressions in reference to the Missouri question:

> "The banks, bankrupt law, manufactures, Spanish treaty, are nothing. These are occurrences which, like waves in a storm, will pass under the ship. But the Missouri question is a breaker on which we lose the Missouri country by revolt, and what more, God only knows."

To understand the full force of these expressions, it must be borne in mind, that the questions enumerated were the great and exciting political questions of the day on which parties divided. The banks and bankrupt law had long been so. Manufactures (or what has since been called the protective tariff) was at the time a subject of great excitement, as was the Spanish treaty; that is, the treaty by which Florida was ceded to the Union, and by which the western boundary between Mexico and the United States was settled, from the Gulf of Mexico to the Pacific Ocean. All these exciting party questions of the day Mr. Jefferson regarded as nothing compared to the Missouri question. He looked on all of them as, in their nature, fugitive; and, to use his own forcible expression, "would pass off under the ship of state like waves in a storm." Not so that fatal question. It was a breaker on which it was destined to be stranded; and yet, his name is quoted by the incendiaries of the present day in support of, and as the author of, a proviso which would give indefinite and universal extension of this fatal question to all the Territories. It was compromised the next year by the adoption of the line to which I have referred. Mr. [John] Holmes, of Maine, long a member of this body, who voted for the measure, addressed a letter to Mr. Jefferson, enclosing a copy of his speech on the occasion. It drew out an answer from him which ought to be treasured up in the heart of every man who loves the country and its institutions. It is brief: I will send it to the Secretary to be read. The time of the Senate cannot be better occupied than in listening to it:

> *To John Holmes*
> Monticello, *April* 22, 1820
> I thank you, dear sir, for the copy you have been so kind as to send me of the letter to your constituents on the Missouri question. It is a perfect justification to them. I had for a long time ceased to read newspapers, or pay any attention to public affairs, confident they were in good hands, and content to be a passenger in our bark to the shore from which I am not distant. But this momentous question, like a fire-bell in the night, awakened and filled me with terror. I considered it at once as the knell of the Union. It is hushed, indeed, for the moment; but this is a reprieve only, not a final sentence. A geographical line, coinciding with a marked principle, moral and political, once conceived and held up to the angry passions of men, will never be obliterated; and every new irritation will mark it deeper and deeper. I can say, with conscious truth, that there is not a man on earth who would sacrifice more than I would to relieve us from this heavy reproach, in any *practicable* way. The cession of that kind of property (for so it is misnamed) is a bagatelle, which would not cost me a second thought, if, in that way, a general emancipation and *expatriation* could be effected: and gradually, and with due sacrifices, I think it might be. But as it is, we have the wolf by the ears, and we can neither hold him, nor safely let him go. Justice is in one scale, and self-preservation in the other. Of one thing I am certain, that as the free passage of slaves from one State to another would not make a slave of a single human being who would not be so without it, so their diffusion over a greater surface would make them individually happier, and proportionally facilitate the accomplishment of their emancipation, by dividing the burden on a greater number of coadjutors. An abstinence, too, from this act of power, would remove the jealousy excited by the undertaking of Congress to regulate the condition of the different descriptions of men composing a State. This certainly is the exclusive right of every State, which nothing in the Constitution has taken from them, and given

to the General Government. Could Congress, for example, say that the non-freemen of Connecticut shall be freemen, or that they shall not emigrate into any other State?

I regret that I am now to die in the belief, that the useless sacrifice of themselves by the generation of 1776, to acquire self-government and happiness to their country, is to be thrown away by the unwise and unworthy passions of their sons, and that my only consolation is to be, that I live not to weep over it. If they would but dispassionately weigh the blessings they will throw away, against an abstract principle, more likely to be effected by union than by scission, they would pause before they would perpetrate this act of suicide on themselves, and of treason against the hopes of the world. To yourself, as the faithful advocate of the Union, I tender the offering of my high esteem and respect.

THOMAS JEFFERSON.

Mark his prophetic words! Mark his profound reasoning!

"It (the question) is hushed *for the moment.* But this is a *reprieve only,* not a *final sentence.* A geographical line coinciding with a marked principle, moral and political, *once conceived and held up to the angry passions of men, will never be obliterated, and every new irritation will mark it deeper and deeper."*

Twenty-eight years have passed since these remarkable words were penned, and there is not a thought which time has not thus far verified, and it is to be feared will continue to verify until the whole will be fulfilled. Certain it is, that he regarded the compromise line as utterly inadequate to arrest that fatal course of events which his keen sagacity anticipated from the question. It was but a "reprieve." Mark the deeply melancholy impression which it made on his mind:

"I regret that I am to die in the belief that the useless sacrifice of themselves by the generation of 1776, to acquire self-government and happiness for themselves, is to be thrown away by the unwise and unworthy passions of their sons, and that my only consolation is to be, that I shall live not to weep over it."

Can any one believe, after listening to this letter, that Jefferson is the author of the so-called Wilmot proviso, or ever favored it? And yet there are at this time strenuous efforts making in the North to form a purely sectional party on it, and that, too, under the sanction of those who profess the highest veneration for his character and principles! But I must speak the truth, while I vindicate the memory of Jefferson from so foul a charge. I hold he is not blameless in reference to this subject. He committed a great error in inserting the provision he did, in the plan he reported for the government of the Territory, as much modified as it was. It was the first blow—the first essay "to draw a geographical line coinciding with a marked principle, moral and political." It originated with him in philanthropic but mistaken views of the most dangerous character, as I shall show in the sequel. Others, with very different feelings and views, followed, and have given to it a direction and impetus, which, if not promptly and efficiently arrested, will end in the dissolution of the Union and the destruction of our political institutions.

I have, I trust, established beyond controversy, that neither the ordinance of 1787, nor the Missouri compromise, nor the precedents growing out of them, nor the authority of Mr. Jefferson, furnishes any evidence whatever to prove that Congress possesses the power over the Territory claimed by those who advocate the 12th section of this bill. But admit, for the sake of argument, that I am mistaken, and that the objections I have urged against them are groundless—give them all the force which can be claimed for precedents—and they would not have the weight of a feather against the strong presumption which I, at the outset of my remarks, showed to be opposed to the existence of the power. Precedents, even in a court of justice, can have but little weight, except where the law is doubtful, and should have little in a deliberative body in any case on a constitutional question, and none where the power to which it has been attempted to trace it does not exist, as I have shown, I trust, to be the case in this instance.

But while I deny that the clause relating to the territory and other property of the United States, confers any governmental, or that Congress possesses absolute, power over the Territories, I by no means deny that it has any power over them. Such a denial would be idle on any occasion, but much more so on this, when we are engaged in constituting a territorial government, without an objection being whispered from any quarter against our right to do so. If there be any Senator of that opinion, he ought at once to rise and move to lay the bill on the table, or to dispose of it in some other way, so as to prevent the waste of time on a subject upon which we have no right to act. Assuming, then, that we possess the power, the only questions that remain are, Whence is it derived? and, What is its extent?

As to its origin, I concur in the opinion expressed by Chief Justice [John] Marshall, in one of the cases read by the Senator from New York, that it is derived from the right of acquiring territory; and I am the more thoroughly confirmed in it from the fact, that I entertained the opinion long before I knew it to be his. As to the right of acquiring territory, I agree with the Senator from New York, that it is embraced, without going further, both in the war and treaty powers. Admitting, then—what has never been denied, and what it would be idle to do so in a discussion which relates to territories acquired both by war and treaties—that the United States have the right to acquire territories, it would seem to follow, by necessary consequence, that they have the right to govern them. As they possess the entire right of soil, dominion, and sovereignty over them, they must necessarily carry with them the right to govern. But this Government, as the sole agent and representative of the United States— that is, the States of the Union in their Federal character—must, as such, possess the sole right, if it exists at all. But if there be any one disposed to take a different view of the origin of the power, I shall make no points with him, for whatever may be its origin, the conclusion would be the same, as I shall presently show.

But it would be a great error to conclude that Congress has the absolute power of governing the Territories, because it has the sole or exclusive power. The reverse is the case. It is subject to many and important restrictions and conditions, of which some are expressed and others implied. Among the former may be classed all the general and absolute prohibitions of the Constitution; that is, all those which prohibit the exercise of certain powers under any circumstance. In this class is included the prohibition of granting titles of nobility; passing *ex post facto* laws and bills of attainder; the suspension of the writ of *habeas corpus*, except in certain cases; making laws respecting the establishment of religion, or prohibiting its free exercise; and every other of like description, which conclusively shows that the power of Congress over the Territories is not absolute. Indeed, it is a great error to suppose, that either this or the State governments possess in any case absolute power. Such power can belong only to the supreme ultimate power called sovereignty, and that, in our system, resides in the people of the several States of the Union. With us, governments, both Federal and State, are but agents, or, more properly, trustees, and, as such, possess, not absolute, but subordinate and limited powers; for all powers possessed by such governments must, from their nature, be trust powers, and subject to all the restrictions to which that class of powers are.

Among them, they are restricted to the nature and the objects of the trust; and hence no government under our system, Federal or State, has the right to do any thing inconsistent with the nature of the powers intrusted to it, or the objects for which it was intrusted, or, to express it in more usual language, for which it was delegated. To do either would be to pervert the power to purposes never intended, and would be a violation of the Constitution, and that in the most dangerous way it could be made, because more easily done and less easily detected. But there is another and important class of restrictions which more directly relate to the subject under discussion; I refer to those imposed on the trustees by the nature and character of the party who constituted the trustees, and invested them with the trust powers to be exercised for its benefit. In this case it is the United States, that is, the several States of the Union. It was they who constituted the Government as their representative or trustee, and intrusted it with powers to be exercised for their common and joint benefit. To them, in their united character, the territories belong, as is expressly declared by the Constitution. They are their joint and common owners, regarded as property or land; and in them, severally, reside the dominion and sovereignty over them. They are as much the territories of one State as another—of Virginia as of New York, of the southern as the Northern States. They are the territories of all, because they are the territories of each; and not of each, because they are the territories of the whole. Add to this the perfect equality of dignity, as well as rights, which appertain to them as members of a common Federal Union, which all writers on the subject admit to be a fundamental and essential relation between States so united; and it must be manifest that Congress, in governing the Territories, can give no preference or advantage to one State over another, or to one portion or section of the Union over another, without depriving the State or section over which the preference is given, or from which the advantage is withheld, of their clear and unquestionable right, and subverting the very foundation on which the Union and Government rest. It has no more power to do so than to subvert the Constitution itself. Indeed, the act itself would be its subversion. It would destroy the relation of equality on the part of the southern States, and sink them to mere dependents of the northern, to the total destruction of the Federal Union.

I have now shown, I trust, beyond controversy, that Congress has no power whatever to exclude the citizens of the southern States from emigrating with their property into the Territories of the United States, or to give an exclusive monopoly of them to the North. I now propose to go one step further, and show that neither the inhabitants of the Territories nor their Legislatures have any such right. A very few words will be sufficient for the purpose; for of all the positions ever taken, I hold that which claims the power for them to be the most absurd. If the Territories belong to the United States—if the ownership, dominion, and sovereignty over them be in the States of this Union, then neither the inhabitants of the Territories nor their

Legislatures can exercise any power but what is subordinate to them; but if the contrary could be shown, which I hold to be impossible, it would be subject to all the restrictions to which I have shown the power of Congress is, and for the same reason, whatever power they might hold, would, in the case supposed, be subordinate to the Constitution, and controlled by the nature and character of our political institutions. But if the reverse be true—if the dominion and sovereignty over the Territories be in their inhabitants, instead of the United States, they would, indeed, in that case, have the exclusive and absolute power of governing them, and might exclude whom they pleased, or what they pleased. But, in that case, they would cease to be the Territories of the United States the moment we acquired them and permit[ted] them to be inhabited. The first half-dozen of squatters would become the sovereigns, with full dominion and sovereignty over them; and the conquered people of New Mexico and California would become the sovereigns of the country as soon as they become the Territories of the United States, vested with the full right of excluding even their conquerors. There is no escaping from the alternative, but by resorting to the greatest of all absurdities, that of a divided sovereignty—a sovereignty, a part of which would reside in the United States, and a part in the inhabitants of the Territory. How can sovereignty—the ultimate and supreme power of a State—be divided? The exercise of the powers of sovereignty may be divided, but how can there be two supreme powers?

We are next told that the laws of Mexico preclude slavery; and assuming that they will remain in force until repealed, it is contended, that until Congress passes an act for their repeal, the citizens of the South cannot emigrate with their property into the territory acquired from her. I admit, the laws of Mexico prohibit, not slavery, but slavery in the form it exists with us. The Puros are as much slaves as our negroes, and are less intelligent and well treated. But I deny that the laws of Mexico can have the effect attributed to them. As soon as the treaty between the two countries is ratified, the sovereignty and authority of Mexico in the territory acquired by it becomes extinct, and that of the United States is substituted in its place, carrying with it the Constitution, with its overriding control over all the laws and institutions of Mexico inconsistent with it. It is true, the municipal laws of the territory not inconsistent with the condition and the nature of our political system would, according to the writers on the laws of nations, remain, until changed, not as a matter of right, but merely of sufferance, and as between the inhabitants of territory, in order to avoid a state of anarchy, before they can be

brought under our laws. This is the utmost limits to which sufferance goes. Under it, the peon system would continue; but not to
the exclusion of such of our citizens as may choose to emigrate with
their slaves or other property that may be excluded by the laws of
Mexico. The humane provisions of the laws of nations go no further
than to protect the inhabitants in their property and civil rights,
under their former laws, until others can be substituted. To extend
them further and give them the force of excluding emigrants from
the United States, because their property or religion are such as are
prohibited from being introduced by the laws of Mexico, would not
only exclude a great majority of the people of the United States from
emigrating into the acquired territory, but would be to give a higher
authority to the extinct authority of Mexico over the territory than to
our actual authority over it. I say the great majority, for the laws of
Mexico not only prohibit the introduction of slaves, but of many other
descriptions of property, and also the Protestant religion, which Congress itself cannot prohibit. To such absurdity would the supposition lead.

I have now concluded the discussion, so far as it relates to the
power; and have, I trust, established beyond controversy, that the
Territories are free and open to all of the citizens of the United
States, and that there is no power under any aspect the subject can be
viewed in by which the citizens of the South can be excluded from
emigrating with their property into any of them. I have advanced
no argument which I do not believe to be true, nor pushed any one
beyond what truth would strictly warrant. But, if mistaken; if my
arguments, instead of being sound and true, as I hold them beyond
controversy to be, should turn out to be a mere mass of sophisms,
and if, in consequence, the barrier opposed by the want of power,
should be surmounted, there is another still in the way, that cannot
be. The mere possession of power is not of itself sufficient to justify
its exercise. It must be in addition shown, that in the given case it
can be rightfully and justly exercised. Under our system, the first
inquiry is: Does the Constitution authorize the exercise of the power?
If that be decided in the affirmative, the next is: Can it be rightfully
and justly exercised under the circumstances? And it is not, until
that, too, is decided in the affirmative, that the question of the expediency of exercising it is presented for consideration.

Now, I put the question solemnly to the Senators from the North:
Can you rightly and justly exclude the South from territories of the
United States, and monopolize them for yourselves, even if, in your
opinion, you should have the power? It is this question I wish to

press on your attention, with all due solemnity and decorum. The North and the South stand in the relation of partners in a common Union, with equal dignity and equal rights. We of the South have contributed our full share of funds, and shed our full share of blood for the acquisition of our territories. Can you, then, on any principle of equity and justice, deprive us of our full share in their benefit and advantages? Are you ready to affirm that a majority of the partners in a joint concern have the right to monopolize its benefits to the exclusion of the minority, even in cases where they have contributed their full share to the concern? But to present the case more strongly and vividly, I shall descend from generals to particulars, and shall begin with the Oregon Territory. Our title to it is founded, first, and in my opinion mainly, on our purchase of Louisiana; that was strengthened by the Florida treaty, which transferred to us the title also of Spain; and both by the discovery of the mouth of Columbia river by Captain [Robert] Gray, and the exploration of the entire stream, from its source down to its mouth, by [Meriwether] Lewis and [William] Clark. The purchase of Louisiana cost fifteen millions of dollars; and we paid Spain five millions for the Florida treaty; making twenty in all. This large sum was advanced out of the common funds of the Union, the South, to say the least, contributing her full share. The discovery was made, it is true, by a citizen of Massachusetts; but he sailed under the flag and protection of the Union, and of course whatever title was derived from his discovery accrued to the benefit of the Union. The exploration of Lewis and Clark was at the expense of the Union. We are now about to form it into a Territory; the expense of governing which, while it remains so, must be met out of the common fund, and towards which the South must contribute her full share. The expense will not be small. Already there is an Indian war to be put down, and a regiment for that purpose and to protect the Territory has been ordered there. To what extent the expense may extend we know not, but will, not improbably, involve millions before the Territory becomes a State. I now ask, is it right, is it just, after having contributed our full share for the acquisition of the Territory, with the liability of contributing, in addition, our full share of the expense for its government, that we should be shut out of the Territory, and be excluded from participating in its benefits? What would be thought of such conduct in the case of individuals? And can that be right and just in Government which any right-minded man would cry out to be base and dishonest in private life? If it would be so pronounced in a partnership of thirty individuals, how can it be pronounced otherwise in one of thirty States?

The case of our recently acquired territory from Mexico, is, if possible, more marked. The events connected with the acquisition are too well known to require a long narrative. It was won by arms, and a great sacrifice of men and money. The South, in the contest, performed her full share of military duty, and earned a full share of military honor; has poured out her full share of blood freely, and has and will bear a full share of the expense; has evinced a full share of skill and bravery, and if I were to say even more than her full share of both, I would not go beyond the truth; to be attributed, however, to no superiority, in either respect, but to accidental circumstances, which gave both its officers and soldiers more favorable opportunities for their display. All have done their duty nobly, and high courage and gallantry are but common attributes of our people. Would it be right and just to close a territory thus won against the South, and leave it open exclusively to the North? Would it deserve the name of free soil, if one-half of the Union should be excluded, and the other half should monopolize it, when it was won by the joint expense and joint efforts of all? Is the great law to be reversed—that which is won by all should be equally enjoyed by all? These are questions which address themselves more to the heart than the head. Feeble must be the intellect which does not see what is right and just; and bad must be the heart, unless unconsciously under the control of deep and abiding prejudice, which hesitates in pronouncing on which side they are to be found. Now, I put the question to the Senators from the North, what are you prepared to do? Are you prepared to prostrate the barriers of the Constitution, and in open defiance of the dictates of equity and justice, to exclude the South from the territories, and monopolize them for the North? If so, vote against the amendment offered by the Senator from Mississippi, (Mr. Davis); and if that should fail, vote against striking out the 12th section. We shall then know what to expect. If not, place us on some ground where we can stand as equals in rights and dignity, and where we shall not be excluded from what has been acquired at the common expense, and won by common skill and gallantry. All we demand is, to stand on the same level with yourselves, and to participate equally in what belongs to all. Less we cannot take.

I turn now to my friends of the South, and ask, what are you prepared to do? If neither the barriers of the Constitution nor the high sense of right and justice should prove sufficient to protect you, are you prepared to sink down into a state of acknowledged inferiority; to be stripped of your dignity of equals among equals, and be deprived of your equality of rights in this federal partnership of

States? If so, you are wo[e]fully degenerated from your sires, and will well deserve to change condition with your slaves; but if not, prepare to meet the issue. The time is at hand, if the question should not be speedily settled, when the South must rise up, and bravely defend herself, or sink down into base and acknowledged inferiority; and it is because I clearly perceive that this period is favorable for settling it, if it is ever to be settled, that I am in favor of pressing the question now to a decision—not because I have any desire whatever to embarrass either party in reference to the Presidential election. At no other period could the two great parties into which the country is divided be made to see and feel so clearly and intensely the embarrassment and danger caused by the question. Indeed, they must be blind not to perceive that there is a power in action that must burst asunder the ties that bind them together, strong as they are, unless it should be speedily settled. Now is the time, if ever. Cast your eyes to the North, and mark what is going on there; reflect on the tendency of events for the last three years in reference to this the most vital of all questions, and you must see that no time should be lost. I am thus brought to the question, How can the question be settled? It can, in my opinion, be finally and permanently adjusted but one way, and that is, on the high principles of justice and the Constitution. Fear not to leave it to them. The less you do the better. If the North and South cannot stand together on their broad and solid foundation, there is none other on which they can. If the obligations of the Constitution and justice be too feeble to command the respect of the North, how can the South expect that she will regard the far more feeble obligations of an act of Congress? Nor should the North fear that by leaving it where justice and the Constitution leave it, she would be excluded from her full share of the territories. In my opinion, if it be left there, climate, soil, and other circumstances, would fix the line between the slaveholding and non-slaveholding States in about 36°30′. It may zigzag a little, to accommodate itself to circumstances; sometimes passing to the north and at others passing to the south of it; but that would matter little, and would be more satisfactory to all, and tend less to alienation between the two great sections than a rigid, straight, artificial line, prescribed by an act of Congress.

And here let me say to Senators from the North, you make a great mistake in supposing that the portion which might fall to the South, of whatever line might be drawn, if left to soil, and climate, and circumstances to determine, would be closed to the white labor of the North, because it could not mingle with slave labor without degradation. The fact is not so. There is no part of the world where agricultural, mechanical, and other descriptions of labor are more respected than in the South, with the exception of two descriptions of employment, that of menial and body servants. No southern man—not the poorest or the lowest—will, under any circumstance, submit to perform either of them. He has too much pride for that, and I rejoice that he has. They are unsuited to the spirit of a freeman. But the man who would spurn them feels not the least degradation to work in the same field with his slave, or to be employed to work with them in the same field, or in any mechanical operation; and, when so employed, they claim the right, and are admitted, in the country portion of the South, of sitting at the table of their employers. Can as much, on the score of equality, be said for the North? With us, the two great divisions of society are not the rich and poor, but white and black; and all the former, the poor as well as the rich, belong to the upper class, and are respected and treated as equals, if honest and industrious, and hence have a position and pride of character of which neither poverty nor misfortune can deprive them.

But I go further, and hold that justice and the Constitution are the easiest and safest guard on which the question can be settled, regarded in reference to party. It may be settled on that ground simply by non-action—by leaving the Territories free and open to the emigration of all the world, so long as they continue so; and when they become States, to adopt whatever constitution they please, with the single restriction, to be republican, in order to their admission into the Union. If a party cannot safely take this broad and solid position, and successfully maintain it, what other can it take and maintain? If it cannot maintain itself by an appeal to the great principles of justice, the Constitution, and self-government, to what other, sufficiently strong to uphold them in public opinion, can they appeal? I greatly mistake the character of the people of this Union, if such an appeal would not prove successful, if either party should have the magnanimity to step forward and boldly make it. It would, in my opinion, be received with shouts of approbation by the patriotic and intelligent in every quarter. There is a deep feeling prevailing the country that the Union and our political institutions are in danger, which such a course would dispel.

Now is the time to take the step, and bring about a result so devoutly to be wished. I have believed from the beginning that this was the only question sufficiently potent to dissolve the Union and subvert our system of government, and that the sooner it was met and settled the safer and better for all. I have never doubted but that, if permitted to progress beyond a certain point, its settlement would become impossible, and am under deep conviction that it is now rapidly approaching it, and that if it is ever to be averted, it must be done speedily. In uttering these opinions, I look to the whole. If I speak earnestly, it is to save and protect all. As deep as is the stake of the South in the Union and our political institutions, it is not deeper than that of the North. We shall be as well prepared and as capable of meeting whatever may come as you.

Now, let me say, Senators, if our Union and system of government are doomed to perish, and we to share the fate of so many great people who have gone before us, the historian, who, in some future day, may record the events tending to so calamitous a result, will devote his first chapter to the ordinance of 1787, as lauded as it and its authors have been, as the first in that series which led to it. His next chapter will be devoted to the Missouri compromise, and the next to the present agitation. Whether there will be another beyond, I know not. It will depend on what we may do.

If he should possess a philosophical turn of mind, and be disposed to look to more remote and recondite causes, he will trace it to a proposition which originated in a hypothetical truism, but which, as now expressed and now understood, is the most false and dangerous of all political error. The proposition to which I allude has become an axiom in the minds of a vast majority on both sides of the Atlantic, and is repeated daily, from tongue to tongue, as an established and incontrovertible truth; it is, that "all men are born free and equal." I am not afraid to attack error, however deeply it may be intrenched, or however widely extended, whenever it becomes my duty to do so, as I believe it to be on this subject and occasion.

Taking the proposition literally, (it is in that sense it is understood,) there is not a word of truth in it. It begins with "all men are born," which is utterly untrue. Men are not born. Infants are born. They grow to be men. And concludes with asserting that they are born "free and equal," which is not less false. They are not born free. While infants they are incapable of freedom, being destitute alike of the capacity of thinking and acting, without which there can be no freedom. Besides, they are necessarily born subject to their parents, and remain so among all people, savage and civilized, until the development of their intellect and physical capacity enables them to take care of themselves. They grow to all the freedom, of which the condition in which they were born permits, by growing to be men. Nor is it less false that they are born "equal." They are not so in any sense in which it can be regarded; and thus, as I have asserted, there is not a word of truth in the whole proposition, as expressed and generally understood.

If we trace it back, we shall find the proposition differently expressed in the Declaration of Independence. That asserts that "all men are created equal." The form of expression, though less dangerous, is not less erroneous. All men are not created. According to the Bible, only two, a man and a woman, ever were, and of these one was pronounced subordinate to the other. All others have come into the world by being born, and in no sense, as I have shown, either free or equal. But this form of expression, being less striking and popular, has given way to the present, and under the authority of a document put forth on so great an occasion, and leading to such important consequences, has spread far and wide, and fixed itself deeply in the public mind. It was inserted in our Declaration of Independence without any necessity. It made no necessary part of our justification in separating from the parent country, and declaring ourselves independent. Breach of our chartered privileges, and lawless encroachment on our acknowledged and well-established rights by the parent country, were the real causes, and of themselves sufficient, without resorting to any other, to justify the step. Nor had it any weight in constructing the governments which were substituted in the place of the colonial. They were formed of the old materials and on practical and well-established principles, borrowed for the most part from our own experience and that of the country from which we sprang.

If the proposition be traced still further back, it will be found to have been adopted from certain writers on government who had attained much celebrity in the early settlement of these States, and with whose writings all the prominent actors in our Revolution were familiar. Among these, [John] Locke and [Algernon] Sidney were prominent. But they expressed it very differently. According to their expression, "all men in the state of nature were free and equal." From this the others were derived; and it was this to which I referred when I called it a hypothetical truism. To understand why, will require some explanation.

Man, for the purpose of reasoning, may be regarded in three different states: in a state of individuality; that is, living by himself apart from the rest of his species. In the social; that is, living in society, associated with others of his species. And in the political; that is, being under government. We may reason as to what would be his rights and duties in either, without taking into consideration whether he could exist in it or not. It is certain that, in the first, the very supposition that he lived apart and separated from all others, would make him free and equal. No one in such a state could have the right to command or control another. Every man would be his own master, and might do just as he pleased. But it is equally clear, that man cannot exist in such a state; that he is by nature social, and that society is necessary, not only to the proper development of all his faculties, moral and intellectual, but to the very existence of his race. Such being the case, the state is a purely hypothetical one; and when we say all men are free and equal in it, we announce a mere hypothetical truism; that is, a truism resting on a mere supposition that cannot exist, and of course one of little or no practical value.

But to call it a state of nature was a great misnomer, and has led to dangerous errors; for that cannot justly be called a state of nature which is so opposed to the constitution of man as to be inconsistent with the existence of his race and the development of the high faculties, mental and moral, with which he is endowed by his Creator.

Nor is the social state of itself his natural state; for society can no more exist without government, in one form or another, than man without society. It is the political, then, which includes the social, that is his natural state. It is the one for which his Creator formed him, into which he is impelled irresistibly, and in which only his race can exist and all his faculties be fully developed.

Such being the case, it follows that any, the worst form of government, is better than anarchy; and that individual liberty, or freedom, must be subordinate to whatever power may be necessary to protect society against anarchy within or destruction from without; for the safety and well-being of society are as paramount to individual liberty as the safety and well-being of the race is to that of individuals; and in the same proportion, the power necessary for the safety of society is paramount to individual liberty. On the contrary, government has no right to control individual liberty beyond what is necessary to the safety and well-being of society. Such is the boundary which separates the power of government and the liberty of the citizen or subject in the political state, which, as I have shown, is the natural state of man—the only one in which his race can exist, and the one in which he is born, lives, and dies.

It follows from all this, that the quantum of power on the part of the government, and of liberty on that of individuals, instead of being equal in all cases, must necessarily be very unequal among different people, according to their different conditions. For just in proportion as a people are ignorant, stupid, debased, corrupt, exposed to violence within and danger from without, the power necessary for

536

government to possess in order to preserve society against anarchy and destruction, becomes greater and greater, and individual liberty less and less, until the lowest condition is reached, when absolute and despotic power becomes necessary on the part of the government, and individual liberty extinct. So, on the contrary, just as a people rise in the scale of intelligence, virtue, and patriotism, and the more perfectly they become acquainted with the nature of government, the ends for which it was ordered, and how it ought to be administered, and the less the tendency to violence and disorder within, and danger from abroad, the power necessary for government becomes less and less, and individual liberty greater and greater. Instead, then, of all men having the same right to liberty and equality, as is claimed by those who hold that they are all born free and equal, liberty is the noble and highest reward bestowed on mental and moral development, combined with favorable circumstances. Instead, then, of liberty and equality being born with man; instead of all men and all classes and descriptions being equally entitled to them, they are high prizes to be won, and are in their most perfect state, not only the highest reward that can be bestowed on our race, but the most difficult to be won, and when won, the most difficult to be preserved.

They have been made vastly more so, by the dangerous error I have attempted to expose, that all men are born free and equal, as if those high qualities belonged to man without effort to acquire them, and to all equally alike, regardless of their intellectual and moral condition. The attempt to carry into practice this the most dangerous of all political error, and to bestow on all, without regard to their fitness either to acquire or maintain liberty, that unbounded and individual liberty supposed to belong to man in the hypothetical and misnamed state of nature, has done more to retard the cause of liberty and civilization, and is doing more at present, than all other causes combined. While it is powerful to pull down governments, it is still more powerful to prevent their construction on proper principles. It is the leading cause among those which have placed Europe in its present anarchical condition, and which mainly stands in the way of reconstructing good governments in the place of those which have been overthrown, threatening thereby the quarter of the globe most advanced in progress and civilization with hopeless anarchy, to be followed by military despotism. Nor are we exempt from its disorganizing effects. We now begin to experience the danger of admitting so great an error to have a place in the Declaration of our Independence. For a long time it lay dormant; but in the process of time it began to germinate, and produce its poisonous fruits. It had strong hold on the mind of Mr. Jefferson, the author of that document, which caused him to take an utterly false view of the subordinate relation of the black to the white race in the South, and to hold, in consequence, that the latter, though utterly unqualified to possess liberty, were as fully entitled to both liberty and equality as the former, and that to deprive them of it was unjust and immoral. To this error his proposition to exclude slavery from the territory northwest of the Ohio may be traced, and to that the ordinance of '87, and through it the deep and dangerous agitation which now threatens to ingulf, and will certainly ingulf, if not speedily settled, our political institutions, and involve the country in countless woes.

From *Congressional Globe*, 30th Cong., 1st Sess., Appendix, pp. 868–873. Also printed in the Washington, D.C., *Daily National Intelligencer*, July 12, 1848, pp. 1–2; the Columbia, S.C., *Daily Telegraph*, July 17, 18, and 21, 1848; the Charleston, S.C., *Mercury*, July 17 and 18, 1848; the Charleston, S.C., *Courier*, July 18, 1848, p. 2; the Columbia, S.C., *South-Carolinian*, July 21, 1848, pp. 1–2; *Niles' National Register*, vol. LXXIV, no. 1904 (July 26, 1848), pp. 58–63; the Camden, S.C., *Journal*, July 26 and August 2, 1848; the Edgefield, S.C., *Advertiser*, July 26 and August 2, 1848; the Pendleton, S.C., *Messenger*, July 28 and August 4, 1848; the Greenville, S.C., *Mountaineer*, August 4, 1848, pp. 1, 4; the Washington, D.C., *Daily Union*, September 20, 1848, pp. 1–2; Houston, ed., *Proceedings and Debates*, pp. 779–785; *Speech of Mr. Calhoun, of South Carolina, on the Oregon Bill. Delivered in the Senate of the United States, June 27, 1848* ([Washington:] printed by [John T.] Towers, [1848]); Crallé, ed., *Works*, 4:479–512; Anderson, ed., *Calhoun: Basic Documents*, pp. 267–295; Lence, ed., *Union and Liberty*, pp. 541–570. Partly printed in *Congressional Globe*, 31st Cong., 1st Sess., Appendix, pp. 987–988, 993, 1389–1390; the Liverpool, England, *Chronicle*, August 18, 1848; *American Quarterly Register and Magazine*, vol. I, no. 2 (September, 1848), pp. 473–475; the New York, N.Y., *Journal of Commerce*, September 16, 1848, p. 1. Variants in the New York, N.Y., *Herald*, June 28, 1848, p. 2; the Baltimore, Md., *Sun*, June 28, 1848, p. 4; the Philadelphia, Pa., *Public Ledger*, June 29, 1848, p. 1; the Charleston, S.C., *Courier*, July 1, 1848, p. 2; the Charleston, S.C., *Mercury*, July 1, 1848, p. 2; *Congressional Globe*, 30th Cong., 1st Sess., pp. 875–876. NOTE: Most printings of this speech omitted the interchange with Hannegan and Corwin. At the conclusion of Calhoun's address, John P. Hale of N.H. arose to challenge Calhoun's assertion that Southerners had not approved the Missouri Compromise, citing the names of Southern representatives who had voted for the resolution containing the compromise. Calhoun, as reported only in Houston, *Proceedings and Debates*, p. 785, replied: "That was not the vote upon the compromise." He was supported by Reverdy Johnson of Md. who said: "That vote was taken after the compromise had been determined upon." The Charleston *Courier* report of 7/1 included the following commentary: "Mr. Calhoun's speech on the subject attracted the most profound attention. He spoke with an unusual degree of feeling, and with all his usual energy and felicity. . . . The crude reports every where spread, will convey erroneous or inadequate ideas of the argument." The Philadelphia *Public Ledger* report of 6/29 included these observations: "Mr. Calhoun made one of his best speeches in the Senate, on the subject of slavery, in reply to the bold attacks of Mr. Dix, of yesterday. For the first time, since the Conventions for the nominations of [Lewis] Cass and [Zachary] Taylor, the galleries were crowded, and the ladies, contrary to the rules of the Senate, filled the seats on the floor of that honorable body. While Calhoun spoke, there was no danger of their charms drawing the attention of Senators from the business before them." There was perhaps some interest added to this occasion by the fact that Senator Dix of N.Y., as a young ex-Army officer in his twenties, had been an intimate of Calhoun's and active in his 1824 Presidential campaign.

Remarks on the Charleston-Havana mail route, 6/27. John Macpherson Berrien of Ga. proposed to amend the bill establishing a mail route from Charleston to Havana by including Savannah as a stop on the route. "Mr. Calhoun. I have not the slightest indisposition to afford every accommodation to Savannah that may be reasonable and proper, but I hope the Senator from Ga. will not, in this instance, insist upon his amendment, as it may have the appearance, at all events, of interfering with the contract." From Houston, ed., *Proceedings and Debates*, p. 785.

From A[ndrew] W. Thomson

Unionville So. Ca., 27th June 1848

Dear Sir, I hope you will excuse me for writing to you at this time as I doubt not but you are and will be very much engaged for the remainder of the present session of Congress, but as I am now anxious to hear from you on a Subject of vital importance to all the southern people and especially the people of South-Carolina, I refer to the question who is to be our next president, and I admit to you most candidly it is at this time a question in which I am in doubt or at fault, as I have very serious objections to the only two candidates who are now before the people and I ["hope" *interlined*] soon to understand their positions better than I now do for I assure you if I were now compelled to give my vote for the one or the other it would be some what difficult for me to assign my reasons for voting for the one and rejecting the other, and all that I could do at this time would be to vote for Gen. [Zachary] Taylor and say that I did so on the ground of his being a Southern man and whose Interests are identical with the people of South Carolina, though I ["do" *canceled*] think it is at this time some what uncertain as how this State will vote in November, but if I were to give my own opinion as to what would be the vote of South-Carolina, I should say it is quite probable she will give her vote Mr. [Lewis] Cass, yet in this I may be mistaken but I think I am not. And here I will State to you ["or" *canceled*] Some of my objections to Mr. Cass. The first is that I am not fully satisfied as to his course on the Wilmot proviso and in the next place his course on the Oregon Question, in which our country was so near being invol[v]ed in a war with Great Britain—and in fact he does appear to me to be rather too pugnatious or bellicose in his habits and dispositions to suit entirely the tastes and habits of the American people, with others that might be urged. Nor am I wanting in objections to General Taylor and as you have a much better opportunity of being well informed as to the opinions the two candidates there than we can here will you be so good as say to me what you think our State ought to do in the matter if you have made up your own mind definitively on the matter.

I have ["one" *canceled and* "a" *interlined*] notion of my own which I do not remember to have seen any where expressed which I wish very much to see pressed at this time, when they are engaged in the Presidential contest as they will at this time regard our wishes and opinions.

The the [*sic*] point to which I refer is this. I wish congress to be compelled to express their opinion on the question as to our rights in the lands that are held as Territories of the United States. I think they ought to declare broadly & unqualifiedly that the citizens of all the States ["of" *canceled*] have equal rights to emigrate to and settle there with all such property as they may possess. Congress I think are the trustees having the possession of the territories in trust for all the people of the union. I have heard it urged that for congress to declare that they had no power under the Constitution to declare that they could not prohibit slavery in any of the Territories would be against us as that would be giving congress Jurisdiction of the Question and if they were to declare that they had not the power to exclude slaves they might at some other time declare they might declare [*sic*] that the slaves should be excluded and then we would be bound by that action of congress but I do not think that is the legitimate result. As what I contend for is that congress acts under a trust power under our Constitution holding and disposing of all the territories for the equal benefit of all the citizens and the declaration that they thus hold the Said Territories could never be tortured into a concession that they had the power to exclude slaves from the territories. What think of this hasty suggestion[?] Write me and say to me without reserve what you think our State ought to do as to the presidential Election. Hoping to hear from you soon as may suit your conveniance I am your friend and humble servant, A.W. Thomson.

P.S. I am a candidate for our next legislature and they suppose I will be elected and you know legislature will have to be called to vote for Electors. Will you do me the favor to look our State constitution and say who in your opinion ought be called the old or new members. A.W. Thomson.

ALS in ScCleA.

From THO[MA]S SMYTHE WILLSON

[Queenstown, Md.,] June 27th 1848

D[ea]r Sir, You may have observed, that on the 26th of April last a convention was held in Baltimore for the purpose of making an independent [Zachary] Taylor electoral ticket for the State of Maryland. That body was composed of the most respectable & talented portion of the two old parties, in this State, who were satisfied that neither of the parties as heretofore organized could or would meet the question of the Wilmot proviso, as it was necessary that it should be met in the slave States. We considered the issues between the Whigs and Democrats settled, *at least* for the next four years; and believed that no other question of importance could arise but that, presented by the "free soil men" of the north. With these views we made an electoral Ticket, composed of an equal number of Whigs & Democrats, to support Gen. Taylor as an independent candidate, put out an address to the people of the Union, and awaited the action of some of the other States with regard to the Vice Presidency. In the mean time, the Whigs, by a *fraud* upon their convention have nominated Gen[era]l Taylor as their party candidate and have associated with him for the Vice Presidency Millard Fillmore, a man deeply died in the worst principals of northern Politicians.

That man we will not take under any political expediency. We hold the ballance of power in this State and with an independent man as our candidate for the Vice Presidency, of high & pure character sound in the principals of the Constitution, we can carry the State against both the old political parties, by an overwhelming majority.

In your person is embodied every principal dear to our hearts. Is it too much to ask the use of your name and character in so good a cause? We should be better pleased did circumstances permit us to tender you our suffrages for the first, instead of the second office of this great nation and we shall hail the day with delight when we may do so. There is no man in this union that has the personal popularity on the Eastern Shore of Maryland that you have possessed for many years. We have found in you the great champion of our rights and the defender of all the compromises of the federal Constitution and South Carolina herself has never stood by your name & fame with more pride & pleasure than has the great majority of the Democrats of this shore & a very large portion of the Whig party. We can now unite upon one common platform, the Constitution—and do trust that you will allow us the use of your name ["in conjunction with that of Gen. Taylor" *interlined*] to break down the old party organizations and maintain the rights of the South.

The Whigs as a *party* can make no serious opposition to such a ticket, and it will give us thousands of Democrats who are reluctant to vote for [Lewis] Cass, and will not do so, if they can avoid it.

My Dear Sir be assured, I have no sinister object in thus addressing you. And tho' a Democrat from principal, party has no ties for me, when I see my country's welfare, and the compromises of the Constitution, about to be bartered away, for party aggrandizement. I hope you will consider this matter favourably and give me your vi[ews in] full. You will shortly receive a communication [*ms. torn; one or two words missing*] same subject from a committee of the Independent party in Queen Ann[e]s County—and I have written this partly to prepare you for that communication. Believe me Sir Your Sincere friend, Thos. Smythe Willson.

[P.S.] Address Dr. Thos. S. Willson, Queen's-town, Queen Ann[e]s County, E[astern] S[hore], Md.

ALS in ScCleA. NOTE: An AEU by Calhoun reads, "Mr. Wilson[,] ["relates" *canceled*] Asks to use my name for the Vice Presidency on Gen[era]l Taylor's ticket. Dr. Tho[mas] S. Wilson[,] Send speech."

From GEO[RGE] B. BUTLER

J[ournal of] Com[merce] off[ice] N.Y. [City]
1848 June 28

My Dear Sir, Messrs. [David] Hale & [Gerard] Hallock who have taken an important step in supporting the compromise line, desire to have your speech [of 6/27] as corrected, at the earliest moment, on the Territorial question, for publication in their paper.

Be good enough to send one to them or indicate in a letter to them, which of the several that may be printed, you most approve of publishing.

The outline of it that we have here has created a general desire to have the whole speech, and it will be generally read over the Country.

The compromise cuts under the miserable faction in this State who hope to get into power on their opposition to Slavery and strengthens Gen[era]l [Zachary] Taylor[']s chance for carrying the northern States.

Your kind letter and the speech were received, the latter will soon be published. Very truly Your servant & friend, Geo. B. Butler.

ALS in ScCleA. NOTE: An AEU by Calhoun reads, "Mr. Butler[,] Send Speech." David Hale and Gerard Hallock were the proprietors of the N.Y. *Journal of Commerce.*

From F[ITZ]W[ILLIAM] BYRDSALL

New York [City,] June 28th 1848
Dear Sir, I have just read a condensed report of your speech of yesterday in the Senate on the Oregon Bill. I must have that speech. For its principles, its arguments, its sentiments, I repeat I must have that speech if put up in pamphlet form. I beg you to forward one or more copies of it to me. I can treasure one for myself and make good use of others amongst my fellow citizens. By the way as regards your speeches of this Session, I have only had from you that of Jan[uar]y 4th 1848 and those of March 16 & 17. If you have any others of the present session by you in pamphlet form, I request one of each from you.

If the Southern States had been adequately true to themselves they would have rallied round you long ago. For their own sakes, they would have proclaimed you as their favorite in every meeting and convention and thus have given force[,] power and influence to the political doctrines you have taught—under which they alone can vindicate their rights. Had you been a citizen of the Northern States you would have been in the highest position in the Nation long ago, and we should have been saved from the false reasonings and pernicious influences of the Demagogues who have disgraced the country and demoralized both political parties.

The great men of the country are overlooked and men, not states-men are held up for the people to entrust their destinies with. The highest office is the game of political gamesters, who in order to win the game ["make" *canceled and* "of the public spoils" *interlined*] in-volve the existence of the federal Union itself, as a means to arrive at official elevation. It is awful that the Wilmot proviso should be the issue of a presidential election, and because two of the candi-dates are more or less against it, a third comes out in favor of it—shewing that his political life has been a lie—that his principles have always been subservient to his selfish ambition.

I think that your speech will set your countrymen to thinking in the right direction. When they think right and with due intelligence, they will easily see who should be their chief magistrate.

The [New York] Evening Post and Albany Atlas assures the pub-lic that [Martin] Van Buren will *not* decline the nomination. I can-not think he will carry a single State. I think it is in the power of your friends to send the Election to the House—the fourth candidate would be one of the three highest. I am Dear Sir Yours &c &c &c, F.W. Byrdsall.

ALS in ScCleA.

From H[ENRY] W. CONNER

Bank of Charleston S.C., June 28, 1848
Your fav[our] of the 24th is to hand & our Board agree to extend your note as desired.

You omitted to endorse the Blank enclosed us & we now return it filled up to your order at 6 mo[nths] for principal & Interest which return to us after endorsement.

The note is for	$5,493
Less ["Interest" *canceled*] Discount at 6 p.ct.	167.54
being the amt. of present note	$5,325.46

which will be charged when the new note is creditted. Very re-spectfully Y[ou]rs &C, H.W. Conner, Pre[siden]t.

P.S. I have nothing to add in reference to the state of things here since my last. There is an uneasy & discont[ent]ed feeling existing that promises no good.

As long since feared & expressed to you, there is now every pros-pect of the breaking up of parties here. The people are fixed in their determination not to remain neutral in the present election & shew great disposition to depose & set aside those whom heretofore ["have been" *interlined*] considered their local leaders. The feeling towards yourself I believe is as it always has been, but the wish I think is that you should continue to occupy the same high ground & to stand upon our true platform sustaining you un to [*sic*] the death but to let the members of the party as a party meet the enemy & fight in any form or with any weapons that he may care[?].

They still talk of public meetings, both the [Zachary] Taylor & [Lewis] Cass men, but the former has no leaders, but will not be long in making them. The Cass men seem not to be ready for a move yet, but are working[?].

I mention these things merely to give you an idea of how things are here.

ALS in ScCleA.

From Estwick Evans

Philadelphia, June 28, 1848
Sir: I, yesterday, did myself the honour to write you relative to State Rights, & certain great questions pertaining to the institutions of the South. Circumstances led me to write that letter somewhat in a hurry, & therefore beg leave now to add a few lines.

I originated, Sir, in Portsmouth New Hampshire; commenced my political career in that State in 1811; & after representing that town in the legislature for many successive years, & being what was called the legislative candidate for congress, left that State for Washington city, in 1829, & resided there until 1845; & then removed to this city. I am now a member of the Philadelphia Bar; & my practice immeasurably good & profitable for one so recently commencing. But I am desirous of having a more certain portion of my time which I can employ in the investigation of great questions concerning society, government, & the history & interests of this country. For about forty years I have watched the progress of things at the North, & at the South, & through all the mutations of parties; & I feel confident that I could do much for the truth—the union—the South—& much to neutralize the spirit of abolition.

In addition to my progressive work on State Rights, it would be my object to note the course of events as to the subject of Slavery, &

to present my views, under anonymous signatures, & through the press in various parts of the United States.

As to my politics, I think, Sir, they must be of the general character of your own: rigidly republican; but particular, cautious, & conservative.

With respect to the South, I wonder much that the unprejudiced & impartial public mind has tolerated certain movements at the North against the institutions of the former. It is too much even that a single individual at the North has presumed to interfere with the social condition of other & distinct Sover[e]ignties; especially so, when a solemn compact is superadded to the general duty of non-intervention.

Should I publish the 2d number of my Essays on State rights, which I am desirous of doing immediately, I wish, Sir, to dedicate it to you, (the liberty to do which I do not ask, lest I should be refused,) precisely in the following words, hoping that certain phrases in the first & last paragraph will make the step wholly unexceptionable. I have endeavoured to make the argument worthy of you, & not otherwise than creditable to myself.

Essay
on
State Rights
(No. 2)
by
Estwick Evans
Counsellor at Law
&
Member of the Philadelphia Bar.
With a dedication
July 1848.

To the Hon[orabl]e John C. Calhoun.

Sir: After waiting a while for the public to peruse my first Essay on State Rights, as far as they might be pleased so to do, I hasten, though wholly unauthorized, to dedicate the second to your very distinguished name.

As far back, Sir, as the eventful period of our last contest ["with Great Britain" *interlined*] I was impressed by your lofty patriotism, your unsurpassed talents, & the energy which you imparted to the legislative counsels of the nation, & afterwards to her administration as Secretary of War. And suffer me, Sir, to add, that nothing can lessen my regret that the course of events has so long prevented your receiving the first office in the gift of the country, but the consideration that this circumstance has elicited even stronger proofs of the purity & magnanimity of your nature, combined with a gubernative caution at once wise, conservative, & heroic.

Notwithstanding Sir, I have not the honour of the slightest personal acquaintance with you, I beg your acceptance, both for the past & future, of my respectful & friendly salutations. Estwick Evans.

ALS in ScCleA.

From G[AZAWAY] B. LAMAR

New York [City,] June 28 1848

D[ea]r Sir, I hope you will pardon me for the intrusion of this letter & for the suggestions I desire to make. I know you despise demagogism, yet I hope you will not look upon my suggestions as tending that way—but will be ready to view the matters calmly & dispassionately & if you can, as I trust you may, you will give them your aid as far as may be thought prudent & judicious.

We have now in the City Gov. [Joseph J.] Roberts & several colored missionaries from Liberia. I should have said *President* Roberts for that Colony has been declared independent & has put forth its claims to be considered & treated as one of the Nations of the Earth—and one object of their visit to this Country will be to attain its recognition on the part of this Government.

Another object will be to get some aid to enable them both to extend their Territory & to expel the Slave Factories, & Dealers from within their limits both as they now exist & as they progress in acquisition.

This latter object cannot be constitutionally granted except by & through a compromise of the Ashburton Treaty, whereby the annual expense incurred for the Naval squadron, *to prevent the Slave Trade,* might be given to them with the consent of Great Britain—& they would use it *to much more effect towards the object.*

At this juncture, when the colored race & the Institution of slavery stand so prominently forth on the politics of the whole country—a movement from you, on this behalf, would be like oil or balm poured upon a wound—it would remove prejudices which exist & would let the light so shine into the minds of some, that they would be willing to do justice to the South—despite of *political leaders.*

547

I beg to submit these to your consideration, and if you accord with me in opinion, I hope you will even before the parties arrive, make a move towards the object.

If you will take the trouble to examine a *Mr.* [Daniel A.] *Payne,* a colored man of the party, you will I think come to the conclusion, that the Colony will be rapidly & vastly extended there—& from its capacity will in a few years afford a refuge for all the free colored among us that can by themselves or the benevolence of others find their way to it.

I make these suggestions of my own accord, nobody knowing my views even, & I intend them merely as *suggestions*—if your opinion do not accord with mine you are the better qualified to judge & there will be no responsibility in giving them the go-bye. He says their emigrated population is 5000 & they have 70 to 75000 natives incorporated with them & every means, *except the pecuniary,* to extend their limits & influence to the interior to an almost unlimited extent—that the natives receive them kindly & ask them to instruct their children for them &c.

Please excuse the liberty I take, I am Very Resp[ectfull]y, G.B. Lamar.

ALS in ScCleA. NOTE: An AEU by Calhoun reads, "Mr. Lamar[,] relates to Liberia."

From F[RANKLIN] H. ELMORE

N. York [City,] June 29, 1848

My Dear Sir, I have this moment rec[eive]d the enclosed letters from Columbia, in answer to some I wrote to our friends. In my letters to [Robert H.] Goodwyn I desired him to show what I had written, explanatory of the course of action thought best by the Delegation, to [Adam G.] Summer & [Edward J.] Arthur (Ed[itor] of the [Columbia *Palmetto State*] Banner). I told Goodwyn of the injustice done you in the Banner & that I felt assured Arthur would regret it as soon as he knew his error.

The letter of Goodwyn is for yourself & any others you may please to show it to. Summer's you may show [Armistead] Burt [Representative from S.C.].

I send these, authentic evidences that all is going fairly at home. Summer is more easily moved, impulsive than Goodwyn & not quite so clear a judgement—but still his opinions in regard to you & in respect to the tendencies to commit to [Lewis] Cass are not to be disregarded. He & all that our friends can write to should be *frequently & decidedly written* to & *advised.* In that Summer is certainly right. You will remember at our consultation I gave the same advice. It seems to me that the Delegation is too fastidious & fearful of seeming to dictate. The truth is that you being where most of the movements originate, are earliest detected & most fully seen & comprehended, makes your opinions far more valuable to direct the judgement & action of the people at home than you appear to think.

I see no political men here and in the present exceedingly disturbed condition of things with all parties, one can hardly form an idea of the result. Mr. [Martin] V[an] Buren has mortified many of his oldest & warmest friends from all I can learn & has gained little credit by his course—but still I am not satisfied it will not prove a dangerous move for us in one sense & a happy one in another. It sets all opposed to him more near to us & the effect of a contest will be only to bring to a head under his lead & separate them from the masses, the humors most dangerous to us & more dangerous while unconcentrated in the system, than they will be when gathered where we can see & treat them as they deserve. At any rate, if the disease is to conquer us, we gain nothing by delay. While on the other hand we are every day growing weaker & therefore the sooner we come to issue the better.

I expect to be with you in a few days and am in haste Yours truly, F.H. Elmore.

[P.S.] Commercially matters are getting better & easier. Banks are not uneasy. Specie has ceased to go out & a better feeling prevails.

[Enclosure]
A[dam] G. Summer to Col. F[ranklin] H. Elmore
S. Carolinian Office, Columbia, 23d June 1848
My Dear Colonel, I am very thankful that you have intimated through Col. Goodwyn your whereabouts, for we had almost concluded you had been stolen somewhere North, and appropriated against the wishes of the good people of this bailwick. To give you a *resumé* of everything since I saw you would be more than my poor body would stand this hot afternoon—but I will say that in accordance with your note I did "jump on that whig Meeting" which *was never held,* and the servile admirers of [William C.] Preston made me sweat for a week or two—which led to some serious personal difficulties—through all of which I have passed triumphantly—elevating by my moderate action the, Democratic standard for consistency to

549

a high point. The respectable whigs cry *peccavi* & the nipping in the bud will retard the growth of the plant for years to come. You wish, no doubt, to hear from S.C. and to learn the state of feeling here. That is soon told. The State is as true as ever to the great principles of Republicanism—and is thoroughly democratic still. [Zachary] Taylor in one month will be repudiated by the few personal admirers who still cling to him. These few are among *the people—and the few Whigs* desirous of entering the next Legislature. The main body Guard of our Creed are as far from the *Single idea* of Taylor, as they would be from [David] Wilmot himself. The State is very [*one or two words illegible*] at this time and it is hard to prevail upon the people to wait for developments. They are anxious to hear the echoes of their own voices in praise of the man whom they may wish to elevate.

This, together with the onslaught of the Whigs of this town on me, has precipitated me fully two months in advance of my true wishes—hence my present position in regard to [Lewis] Cass—for I see no other chance for the South & South Carolina, but to vote for him. This is the feeling of the people. Such their expression. I am daily appealed to, from all quarters to know the probable course of our Congressional Representatives. I give the key signal "Go against Taylor—the Candidate of the Whigs." This does not satisfy them, and they cry out for some one to array against him—and they honestly take up Cass, & fill their mouths in his praise whilst we would wish to see them wait patiently. We are forced[?] to make the best of it and do our best to control the desire which they have to go ahead even of themselves.

I am glad to learn that Mr. Calhoun will give the people of the State a communication defining his position. It is much needed. Not that his old friends ever would desert him—but that there is a younger breed of actors, who from his having personally kept himself aloof from this people, have lost that magic influence inspired by communication. He has erred in not visiting the heart of S.C. for so many years. I appreciate his motive for so doing—but it is unfortunate for him—for the people are not satisfied in hearing of a great political light, *they must see it.* Many young men, who are now actors in an humble degree do not know him personally. I try to keep him in Spirit before me and recently have had [William H.] Scarborough to execute his "counterfeit presentment" for my sanctum, and as I write the keen piercing gaze of *the man* looks down upon me in that honesty of expression which speaks his [*one or two words canceled*] devotion to his country. However I might understand him. I never could be so heartless as to "give him a single sorrow" by rude and unguarded expressions of mine. I have carefully excluded such as have been written and presented to me for publication, as have been published else where, which whilst I know they have been given from no malice or *mal*-heartedness—have been in my opinion ill-timed and inapplicable. If Mr. Calhoun does publish a Letter induce him to send it to Columbia to be first published here, as the off an[d] on, course of the [Charleston] Mercury has I fear given that paper a backset which in the middle & upper country does not add to its usefulness. Besides its publication here would put it immediately into the hands of the small[?] politicians in the country.

What in the world is [Charles M.] Furman doing? The people are still knocking away at the Bank in various quarters and there is a general demand for a Reply to Anti Debt. Please hasten him on with the work. A commencement is all that is required and he then can easily go ahead.

I am half sick. Do write to me fully. You know where my heart is, even if my head goes wandering sometimes. So let me hear the signs of the times—if nothing else. Truly Yours, A.G. Summer.

[Enclosure]

R[obert] H. Goodwyn to F[ranklin] H. Elmore

Columbia So. Ca., 23rd June 1848

My Dear Elmore, I have this moment received your letter of the 18th (delayed as you will perceive in reaching me). I hasten to answer by return mail lest my letter may not meet you. I regret to learn that Mr. Calhoun has been at all mortified by the articles in the Banner of this place. [Edward J.] Arthur is an impetuous man, and wrote under an excitement produced by a Whig move, which you saw was made here about that time, and under suspicion from Whig authority that Mr. Calhoun and our whole delegation were going over to the whig party. I am sure that there are not six persons here who agree with him in the denunciation of Mr. Calhoun, and but few more who go with him in taking position at this time for Gen[era]l [Lewis] Cass. The general feeling not only here, but as far as I have heard all around us, is against Gen[era]l Cass, and that So. Ca. Should not commit herself in the Presidential question just now, but await further development. Our people ["here & in the back country" *interlined*] were, at one time generally in favor of [Zachary] Taylor; but ["his" *interlined*] Ingersol letter, & nomination by the Whigs have thrown them off, I think most decidedly from him. So far as I understand publick feelings here and about us, it is that we should await events before taking any decided position, as we can see no necessity for So. Ca. precipitately engaging in the contest, but much wisdom in delaying for a while. I regret much that Mr. Calhoun has been pained by the articles in the Banner, he has attached more importance ["to them" *interlined*] than they deserve for be assured that with the exception of Jos[eph] A. Black, [William M.] Myers, & [John C.] Thornton every body else about here felt indignation and disgust at them; and I believe Arthur is ashamed to repeat the denunciation. Mr. Calhoun and our Delegation still have the full confidence of the great body of our people, and I am sure that when the proper time arrives for them to take their position, they will find themselves sustained by the State, because we cannot but ["thin"(?) *canceled*] believe that they will be found contending for State rights & Southern rights as best they can under the circumstances which may present. Thornton the coach maker is the author of the article in the Banner you speak of. The Whigs here have become very quiet & still, & I think will keep so. Do say to Mr. Calhoun not to give himself any concern about what the Banner has said, for I have inquired from every where I could, and really do not believe that the feeling in that paper extends to beyond half a dozen persons here or elsewhere in the State. Do say to [Andrew P.] Butler and [Joseph A.] Woodward [Senator and Representative from S.C., respectively] I owe them an ["appol" *canceled*] apology for not answering their letters, but will pay my respects to them in a short time, so soon as I get a little better informed of how publick opinion is settling in our State on political matters. I have written in great haste and under frequent interruptions, and have not said all I would have said and as I should have said had I more time, but I am hurrying to save the next mail, and hope you may get enough out of this to give you some Idea of how publick opinion stands here. Do write me from Washington again as those letters enables me to remove doubts and misapprehensions from many. Our Delegation should write more than they do, the ["poli"(?) *canceled*] people complain much of the dark in which they are kept.

I[?] have sent in all about $90,000 Ninety thousand dollars of specie funds to the parent Bank. This is good help to them I have no doubt. I have heard nothing from them of late. Yours truly & Sincerely, R.H. Goodwyn.

ALS with Ens in ScCleA.

552

From E[stwick] Evans

Philadelphia, June 29, 1848

Sir: I *by no means* intended to write you again, having already written twice; but I am impelled to this step by seeing, in the paper of today, some remark upon the question in the Senate as to the extension of slavery, which I conceive to be extremely shallow & assuming. Allow me to say, Sir, that it is my nature to be for Truth; & that it is also my nature to feel for those who mean well, & are unfortunate, & hard pushed. The principle I advance in the early part of my first number on State Rights, that the States ought to be liberal & kindly disposed to each other, should be acted on as to Slavery. It seems hard that if a citizen of S. Carolina wishes to go on & settle in Oregon, he cannot carry, & keep there, his slaves. It is a question for his own conscience; & as long as his treatment of his slave is benevolent, the law of the land should not interfere. I do not believe that any individual citizen of State or Territory, nor any State government; nor the General government, has the slightest right, whatever, to interfere. If the Constitution of the U. States has any thing to do ["here" *interlined*] one way or the other, it favours the subject of slavery—favours it much; for compacts have often very extensive relations; & the relations here might easily be construed into tacit obligation on the part of the Free States. But it is important to go back to the elementary—the primary—the radical rights of man. He is an individual, & not a society; he has personal rights, *unless circumstances have justly deprived him of them before or after he comes into the world*; & when he enters into society, he relinquishes *only* what is *necessary* for the *legitimate* purposes of society. Some of his rights—natural rights, remain with him; & these rights constitute his personal *Sover[e]ignty*—yes, Sir, *personal* sover[e]ignty, that here ["he has" *interlined*] a right to contend with the whole community! The principle of Majority—so long boasted of, is an assumption & a mockery in morals, when it is based upon injustice. I have no space to spread out my ideas, in detail, here. There is an expanse of deep waters—with clouds of fire overhead! Were I of the South, Sir, I would not yield a hair's weight to the shallow assumptions of the North. Allow me to say that I have lived sixty years; (& although my hair is as white as snow, I have all the vigour of youth,) & I have all this time studied man, & things, & principles, & parties; & I say the North will never dissolve the Union, or co-erce the South. But if she should, let the Union go! The South can pursue her own glory alone.

I can say here but little more. Well, notwithstanding I am a Northern man; naturally against every thing the reverse of Freedom; & so educated—a very "Hebrew of the Hebrews" in democracy; yet I doubt much the standard of the past, or present, times, in judging of *races*, & society, & liberty, & government, & the so honoured principle & rights of *majority*. I am much disposed to say, among many other maxims in politics, (not in *morals*,) which I cannot set down here, 1st that there is *abstract* truth only in God. 2 that every thing other than *Him*[?] is, consequently, *Relative*; & that relative truth is ["often" *interlined*] very far from abstract truth in the relations of races, & individuals, & society.

I have not time to say much, or, perhaps, to do full justice to my opinions, & sentiments, & especially my motives. I would see the South, among other things, contend: 1 that the country cannot interfere, *at all*, (no individual or government,) with the slave institutions of the Southern States 2. A Southern man has a right to go into the Territories of the United States & carry his slaves with him, as of the nature of property, ["& continue to possess & enjoy them there" *interlined*]. 3. Congress has no right to require a Territory, when applying to be made a State, to relinquish slavery. 4 The Territory, in framing a constitution, has no right to prohibit slavery, as a private right. 5. The Territory, when it becomes a State, has no right to prohibit slavery. I have reasons & reasoning in abundance to sustain these positions. As to slavery in the District of Columbia: 1 Congress has nothing to do with the subject of slavery; they are *bound* to have nothing to do with it—excepting to prevent any body from doing any thing against it. 2 The spirit of the cession by Virginia & Maryland, by no means included the idea of free territory between them; it was no part of their meaning, because no part of their reason: the meaning of a law or contract is to be gathered from the reason of it. They would by no means have consented to such idea: it would be placing between them a Northern bull, to gore & destroy them: it would be a lodgment—a footing for fanatical abolitionism; & the whole South ought to war forever against it.

Pardon these obtrusions of my opinions, Sir, & accept the most respectful consideration, with which I have the honour to be, Your very Ob[edien]t Serv[an]t, E. Evans.

Addition: I am desirous of remarking further: 1st that it can be most easily maintained that the General government, although it operates in many things as a government *Proper*, is not *at all* so as it regards the reserved rights—reserved *Sover[e]ignty* of the States; that the States, as to *this*, are under a mere confederation—a mere league. Terms, especially *general* terms, mislead the mind: The term *government*, with us, is unfortunate. 2. As to slavery in ["the" *canceled*] itself, I profess nothing. I only take the ground of Philosophy in search for Truth. It cannot be shewn to be a crime, in morals or religion, & therefore none should interfere. There is, besides *caste*, races, [*one word canceled*] natural[?] scale of intellect, & the whole history of man, the complexness of things in this world; the need constantly of viewing things *Relatively*; the mysterious ways of Providence, the facts in scripture history; the difficulty of knowing what is, ultimately, good or evil; the continual eduction of good from seeming evil; the peculiar evils encountered by the black races in Africa; the vast ["advanges" *changed to* "advantages"], past & present, to them here; & the advance of the race, consequently, in morals, religion, & social improvement; & the benefits flowing to their native land, therefrom &c &c. Most Respectfully, E. Evans.

ALS in ScCleA.

From B. H. SHACKELFORD and Others

Warrenton Va., June 29: 1848
Sir, The undersigned beg leave to solicit your presence, at a mass meeting of the whigs of the 7th Electoral district of Va. favorable to the election of Gen: Z[achary] Taylor & Millard Fillmore, as President & Vice President of the United States, to be held on the 21st & 22d of July next, near the Fauquier white Sulphur Springs.

This invitation though given to attend a meeting of the whig party, with whom you have seldom acted is rendered appropriate from the fact, that the present condition of the country and the administrative policy which produced it, requires the active and patriotic intervention, of the eminent conservative statesmen of the land, (amongst whom we are proud to recognize you as chief,) in order to remedy the evils already produced, and arrest a policy so destructive of the balances of the constitution and the true interests of the people. The old issues of the whig party are measurably obscured, by the fatal tendencies of that policy, which inculcates a thirst for war and its glory, a desire for foreign Territory and its patronage. We have ever considered you, opposed, to the war & conquest policy of the present administration, an advocate of peace, the defender of the Constitution, and friend of the people. Holding the position you do, as one of the conservative Statesmen of the Union whose acts and opinions are looked to with anxiety by every true patriot, we cannot but indulge the hope that it will suit your pleasure & convenience, to attend our meeting & favor us and the country with your views upon the vitally important questions now for the first time to be discussed before the people, in this presidential canvass. Very Respectfully y[ou]r Ob[edien]t S[er]v[an]ts, B[enjamin] H. Shackelford, Ed. M. Spilman, R.W. Payne, Thos. M. Monroe, Ja[me]s V. Brooke, Samuel Chilton, John H. Skinner, Committee of invitation.

LS (with letter and all signatures in one handwriting) in ScCleA. NOTE: An AEU by Calhoun reads, "Invitation to attend a whig meeting at Warrenton."

From L[EWIS] H[ENRY] MORGAN

Rochester, Monroe Co[unty,] N. York, June 30, 1848
D[ea]r Sir, Will you send me a copy of your Speech in reply to Mr. [John A.] Dix [Senator from N.Y.] on the Oregon Bill. I have read it as given in the papers and wish it ["in" *interlined*] full for further study & to preserve. We are anxious in New York to hear all that may be said on both sides of this great question: and to do what justice requires in such ways as we may be able to act upon it. It absorbs the public mind, & will continue to do so more and more until it is settled. We are afraid of the indefinite propagation of the colored race, upon which the South seem determined. The feeling towards that race in the North is decidedly that of hostility. There is no respect for them, No wish for their elevation; but on the contrary a strong desire to prevent the multiplication of the race so far as it is possible to do so, by such legislation as shall be constitutional and just. The attachment to the Union is unceasing; and the Mass of the people have no disposition to encroach upon the Constitutional rights of the Southern States. But I think it must be regarded as certain, that if a conviction seizes the public mind, that Congress has power to make the territories of the Republic free without impinging the rights of any portion of the Country, this conviction will be persisted in to the last extremity. If the South gets the better of the argument, and it certainly will, if in the right, then the people of the North will be satisfied to see slavery spread. But if ["it" *interlined*] should be otherwise and the South should be unwilling to yield—we shall find our Republic in the greatest peril. The Unity of our race with the

same government & institutions, is of more consequence to the welfare of humanity at large, than the perpetual bondage of the whole African family. That Unity can only be perpetuated by concession and compromises.

I did not intend to write you a letter. I hope you will not consider my observations upon this great question in the least impertinent. It is a question upon which we cannot but feel the deepest interest. Yours very respectfully, L.H. Morgan.

ALS in ScCleA; PC in Boucher and Brooks, eds., *Correspondence*, pp. 445–446. NOTE: In 1848 Morgan (1818–1881) was an attorney. He began his notable career as "the father of American anthropology" in the 1850s. An AEU by Calhoun reads, "Morgan. Send Speech."

JULY 1–AUGUST 14, 1848

Ⅲ

As the first session of the 30th Congress entered its last weeks a Presidential campaign was going on. Calhoun wrote to Henry W. Conner on July 9 his customary advice: South Carolina should pursue its own interests and remain aloof from the "two miserable factions" that were demagogically contending for the spoils of the government.

There was much routine business but also the critical matter of the "Oregon Bill" as the session drew to a close. The Senate had to resort to unprecedented evening and night sessions.

On July 12 the Senate appointed a special committee to attempt to find a solution to the territorial slavery question. There were eight members, including Calhoun, equally divided among Democrats and Whigs and free and slave States. John M. Clayton, Whig of Delaware, was elected chairman. On July 27 the Senate adopted by a vote of 33 to 22 the recommendations of the "Clayton Compromise Committee": validation of the provisional laws of Oregon insofar as they were "compatible with the Constitution" and prohibition of territorial legislatures in California and New Mexico from passing any laws on slavery, with the suggestion that the Supreme Court could hear the question. Calhoun voted for the compromise. It was understood that, though he insisted on the lack of power of Congress or territorial governments to discriminate against slaveholders, he would accept the Missouri Compromise as a settlement, as long as the principle of the Wilmot Proviso, prohibition of slavery from all the territories, was not put into law.

The House tabled the Senate bill and sent over a bill providing for prohibition of slavery in Oregon. The Senate returned an amendment adding the Missouri Compromise. The House refused to concur. On the day before the session adjourned, the Senate accepted the House bill by a vote of 29 to 25. Calhoun urged upon President Polk a veto. He refused on the ground that the bill did not violate the Missouri Compromise and signed it on the last day of the session.

On August 10 Calhoun made his last speech of the session on the question. The Northern majority showed a fixed determination to rule the South. Every compromise was merely the staging ground for further aggressions, to which there was seemingly no end. As great as was its love of the Union, let there be no mistake that the South was prepared to defend itself. The speech was evidently aimed as much at the Southern reading public as at the Senate.

◫

From LOUIS MCLANE

Baltimore, July 1, 1848

My dear Sir, I am gratified, though not disappointed at hearing, from all quarters, of the power of your recent speech [of 6/27] upon the Oregon Bill; and I now write to ask that you would be so obliging as to send me a copy when correctly published.

It has long appeared to me quite clear that the power of Congress in the government of the Territories is subject to material limitations and restrictions that have been greatly exceeded in our past legislation; and that, in fact, over slavery the general government has no power whatever, except in the instances expressly referred to in the Constitution.

I am not without deep ["solictude" *canceled*] solicitude in regard to the agitation, at present prevailing in the north, upon this subject, which is not diminished by the extraordinary and unblushing treachery of some of the leaders. I do not forget however, that all the past assaults upon this institution and the rights of the South have proceeded from the party ["in its various guises," *interlined*] in opposition to the Democracy of the Country, and that in every instance real protection has been found in the power of the *Democratic Party*: and that I hope will be yet maintained, even at some sacrifice of individual feeling & preference. Even Southern men dependent upon northern federalism and modern Whiggery could afford no better security than "northern men" professing "southern principles." I remain, my dear Sir, with the highest esteem & regard, Your friend & obedient Servant, Louis McLane.

ALS in ScCleA; variant PC in Boucher and Brooks, eds., *Correspondence*, pp. 446–447.

From A[ugustus] B. Longstreet

Oxford [Ga.], 4 July 1848

Dear Sir, It was not until I seated myself to write to you, that I remembered this was the birthday of our independence. Perhaps it [is] ominous of good. Be that as it may I cannot resist the temptation to ["write to" *interlined*] you, for it seems to me that just at this time you hold the destiny of the South if not of the Union in your hands; though I confess I write more in dispair than in hope, for reasons that will be seen before we conclude. Let my views be submitted to you before I make the suggestion which grows out of them.

[Martin] Van Buren is forming a party upon the sole principle of the Wilmot Provison. This party as Van [Buren] very plainly sees will overpower any party which opposes it at the North. [Lewis] Cass with a strong party at his back is out in direct opposition to the Proviso. At last then we have a party which will carry our arguments upon this head to the doors of the Northern people; and whose political salvation is staked upon them. Now suppose the South *en masse* rallies to this party, and elects Cass; what must be the consequence[?] That party is forever ["alli"(?) *canceled*] detached from the abolitionists and the far West must unite with it. It will ["gr" *canceled and* "grow" *interlined*] stronger and stronger; for there is no sympathy between the east & the west. The only reason why the west is not with us now to a man, is, that it had no interest in the South, and would not uselessly hazard any thing in vindicating her rights. The Southwest will be every day growing stronger, and inspiring confidence in our northern auxiliaries. These powers united will in eight years' time from the 4 March next consign abolitionism to its merited contempt. Let Cass be elected ["by the vote of the South" *interlined*] and we shall have candidates enough at the north who will be ready to give any pledges that the South may demand upon the ["subject of" *interlined*] Slavery. And this they may do without any compromise of principle. In fact *principle* demands that they should do this now; and most of them know it; but hitherto they have been awed into silence and inactivity by the abolition clamor, which they could gain nothing by opposing. "But is Cass reliable? I know more about him ["a great deal" *canceled and* "than you do" *interlined*]." I answer "yes, perfectly reliable; if for no better reason, than that his interest and that of his party leave him no alternative but to do right.["] His pledge is given upon the delicate question and it is a rare thing that a man made President upon a a [*sic*] principle, abandons it during his term of office; and what

Cass may do when he gets out of office is of but little consequence. But I have no fears of him out of office—I should not fear Van Buren or Tom Corwin [Thomas Corwin, Senator from Ohio] in his situation. Withal all life is uncertain & suppose Cass should die [William O.] Butler is our President; a much safer man than [Zachary] Taylor; and he will strengthen the Union with our northern friends. Never have I seen, since the birth of abolitionism, a time so favorable to a final & complete triumph of the South as the present; but to avail herself of it, she must must [*sic*] renounce all claims upon the Presidency for two terms at least. After that she will probably a[l]ternate with the North & West. Set me down as no prophet, if every word of this does not prove true; and verily if all my prophecies had been recorded and remembered they would reflect no little credit upon my forecast.

Let us now look at the other side of the picture. Suppose we support Taylor, and elect him. He will ["probably" *canceled*] give us perfect security upon the slavery question for four years, and then, friendless at the north, and impotent at the South the whole northern power comes down upon us without mercy and without a disguise for injustice and oppression. I hardly think the Union will endure four years afterwards. Suppose Taylor should die; where then are we? Withal who knows any thing about General Taylor? I dread any man who comes into power under a whig nomination. [William H.] Harrison was any thing until he was elected; and then he was just a nose of wax in [Henry] Clay's hands. Let me remind you of your own arguments in 1836, which you had not concluded before I saw the force of them and adopted them; & time has verified them most fully. You said the Democratic principles, were the true principles for the South; and that she never could unite with the Whigs (federalists with a new name) without ruin to herself ["that" *canceled*]. That as a makeweight she could kick the beam as she pleased; and that in point of fact, she had her own way while she was almost powerless. I followed you instantly and I have never regretted ["it" *interlined*]. Where are the Southern whigs now? Just where you said they would be if they did not break from their whig alliances immediately. And ["how" *interlined*] is it now? The Democratic party are fighting with the old Jeffersonian creed upon their banner. Now this is not to be forgotten. Slavery is the main thing, but it is not every thing. If we must give up that, or every thing else, why let every thing else go; but if we can secure that and many things that we desire, ["besides" *interlined*] why all the better for us. When I say *Slavery* I mean the Constitutional rights of slaveholders of course.

561

Now Sir if you will come boldly out for Cass, upon these principles improved as you can improve ["them" *interlined*] Cass will get the South and be elected; and even if he is not, his party will remain firm, and we shall certainly prevail at the next election afterwards. To these views I could add many strong ones personal to yourself; but I would not have you, as I am sure I shall not have ["you" *interlined*] influenced by such motives. I pray you sir take these things into serious consideration; and remember that what you and I have to do for the country must be done quickly; for our time is nearly run out. We should try to make an impression which will last longer than four years. And this reminds me of a subject that I have long thought of addressing you upon. You must not die if God spares you two years longer without writing a commentary upon the Constitution. That [Joseph] Story's is lamentable faulty, I know; but if I could prove it the weight of his character would bear me down—at least ["till" *altered to* "for"] many long years. Not so with you. And even you have broached some doctrines that I never can subscribe to. Your old Bank notions for example. Congress has not the Constitutional power to establish a bank. The decision of the Supreme Court rest[s] upon the single principle that Congress may create an agency to accomplish a given power—and a bank is a suitable agent to manage its fiscal concerns. The difficulty with the argument is that a Bank is no agent of the Government, or it could not maintain an existence independent of it, as the old U.S. Bank did after [Andrew] Jackson removed the deposits [in 1833]. There was an *agent* that had no more connexion with the government than I had. But I am digressing. I fear your opposition to Cass is unconquerable. If so, mark the end of it. Your sincere friend, A.B. Longstreet.

ALS in ScCleA.

From CHESSELDEN ELLIS, "Private"

New York [City,] July 5, 1848

My dear Sir, Allow an old friend who feels as strongly as ever, his attachment to you personally and politically (tho' differing in some matters occurring since he saw you) to obtrude for a few moments.

I have devoted myself to *business, exclusively*, since the expiration of my Congressional term, so much so, that I have not read a message, or a document or a Speech in Congress or our Legislature, since that time; but always voting the regular nominations, satisfied that the party would get right in the main, notwithstanding its errors.

I observed in a Washington correspondent of some of our City papers a few days ago, that Senator [Jesse D.] Bright [of Ind.] had introduced the *Missouri Compromise* into the Oregon Bill & that it would extend to the newly acquired Mexican territory and it was stated that *you approved the measure* and *would be satisfied with it.* I have seen no contradiction of this Statement nor any analysis ["or outline" *interlined*] of your speech, and suppose therefore it is true.

If it be true, allow me to urge the importance of immediate and decisive action.

I should deeply regret to see [Martin] Van Buren whose friends *cut me down* in the election of '44 on account of my support of the *Annexation of Texas*, again come into power or even into important & gratifying prominence. But let me assure you, that unless this territorial slavery question be settled speedily, he will inevitably ride over both political parties in this State "rough shod." Our representatives would laugh at this prediction—but I assure you *they* are utterly incompetent to judge. The anti-slavery feeling in reference to this point, is deep and all-pervading at the north and the revolution which has begun will disappoint even its friends. I am *one* of the *people* mingling daily with *mere business men* and I am myself utterly astonished at what I see & hear on this subject, among them.

Unless this question be settled *now*, Van Buren will sweep this State and probably strong pluralities in some of the eastern States. Of the West I know but little.

If the question be now settled, [Zachary] *Taylor* will carry this State—without doubt. The breach is too wide in the democratic ranks to be healed, *ever*. [Lewis] *Cass* is utterly hopeless here in any event. Vast portions of the [Henry] Clay men will go over to Van Buren, if the question remains open. That question closed, they will, a great majority of the discontents, go into the *Taylor* ranks.

I should regret to see Van Buren go into the House, most severly[?]

Nothing but the definite Settlement of the question and the establishment of *territorial governments*, ["now" *interlined*] so as to leave all questions closed and determined, can in my opinion prevent the results I have predicted.

Do not imagine that I have abandoned *Catholic doctrines*. I am as firm and as open on the subject of the diffusion of Slavery as I was upon Texas Annexation and ever have been. I never get weary on those subjects. I even voted for the admission of Florida with *chains*

rivited by ["the" *canceled and* "her" *interlined*] *Constitution itself.*
My Van Buren Colleagues refused to do so. I have *detested* and
denounced the *Wilmot Proviso,* from the *outset* and now I would like
to see you lay *Van Buren once more, flat on his back.*

I write on my own motive entirely—have consulted no one, and
expect to have but little, if any thing, to do with politics, ever again.

I shall vote the Baltimore nomination—for I have never deviated
from *regular* nominations. But no one here doubts Taylor's election,
unless the Slavery question carries it into the House.

If I have mistaken your course, attribute it to the cause mentioned.

I have seen friends whom John Van Buren has approached and
I learn that his expectation is to carry the election into the House and
then take advantage of any thing available in the Chapter of acci-
dents. Failing in that object, they will aim to get up a northern "free
labor, free soil" party, as they call it, for future action, if the question is unsettled.

I would like a copy of your speech when the revised edition appears. With sentiments of sincere and high regard, believe me yours,
truly, Chesselden Ellis.

ALS in ScCleA; PC in Boucher and Brooks, eds., *Correspondence,* pp. 447–448.
NOTE: Ellis was a Democratic Representative from N.Y. in 1843–1845. An
AEU by Calhoun reads, "Ellis. Send Speech."

From J[OSEPH] W. LESESNE

Mobile, July 5th 1848
My dear Sir, I had commenced a letter to you a few days ago, dictated by the deep feeling of doubt and embarrassment with regard
to the approaching Presidential election which pervades to a greater
or less degree, all classes of conscientious and sober minded men at
the South. Before concluding my letter, Mr. [Martin] Van Buren's
manifesto, drawn forth by the nomination of the *Barnburners,* has
made its appearance, and so changed the aspect of affairs as to render
all previous enquiries and speculations almost out of place. Still, so
far as I am concerned, the difficulty does not appear to be diminished,
but rather augmented by this startling phenomenon; and I am as
much at a loss what course I ought as an individual to pursue as
before this extraordinary document made its appearance.

I have concluded, from various indications in So. Ca. that so far, your own judgment is in favor of entire inactivity at the South in regard to the Presidency and of employing all our energies in producing union and concert of action among ourselves. Hitherto, I have been strongly inclined to regard this as our true policy; altho' not without some misgivings as to its soundness for practical purposes. Nearly the entire Democratic party of the South who may vote for Gen[era]l [Lewis] Cass, will do so reluctantly, and only because they consider that the South will be safer in his hands than in those of Gen[era]l [Zachary] Taylor. Of course I speak of those who do really reason on the subject; for here, as elsewhere, the mandates of party are still sovereign over a large number who do not reason at all, except upon the chances of the spoils of political victory.

For my own part, I have no faith in Gen[era]l Taylor, or rather none in our attaining under his auspices any better position on the great question of *the Territorial rights of the South.* Like Gen. [Andrew] Jackson, there are ten chances to one, that he will fall into the hands of the worst men of his party—because these are the first and most successful to assail an unexperienced man with the sort of sycophancy, and to yield to him that sort of unmanly subserviency so grateful to, and so potent with, military men, even the most disinterested and sagacious of them. Southern Statesmen are wholly unequal to the task of contending with the unscrupulous host who will surround Gen. Taylor as soon as he is elected. Therefore I can see nothing to be gained by throwing our influence in his favor, with the calculation of rendering the course of his administration subservient to our policy and rights. The Whig party already possess him, and will retain their hold; and the mere fact that he is a slaveholder, is in the view I take of the question of slavery in the Territories, a most insufficient and slender dependance.

With regard to Gen. Cass, he is to me, the most obnoxious of all the candidates whose names were before the Convention—the most objectionable *sectionally* and *nationally.* He is of the *progressive democracy* in the worst sense of that phrase; a phrase in this country, of very questionable propriety in the mouth of any one—for *stability, conservatism,* are the social elements we most need, and *progress* (which with the class to whom this idea is addressed, means *agitation, experiment,* and *mob-supremacy*) is ["ought" canceled] what we ought most to dread. With Gen. Cass, "*progress*" means Territorial acquisition by fair means or foul indifferently. He is the representative, to my mind at least, of the worst elements in the country— *North western* ignorance and vulgarity, popular violence and ambition—an uneducated demagogue, (the most dangerous ["of the" *interlined*] species,) in principle and by nature; and under his guidance, if his past course foreshadow his future, we shall be launched into an endless career of ambition and insolence; and be involved in wars of plunder with every friendly power that owns an inch of tempting soil in ["the" *canceled and* "our" *interlined*] neighbourhood. On his advocacy of such a war, his claims rest: and his election would be esteemed by him and his friends the popular [*one word canceled and* "vox Dei" *interlined*] approving the past and proclaiming the path of his future glory. His views too, with regard to the right of Territorial legislation on the subject of slavery, are as objectionable as it is possible for them to be. To confer the right of legislating on this subject upon the people of the Territories, is to give away in advance the rights of the South to an equal participation in the benefits of all past and future Territorial acquisition—a concession which I am amazed that so many at the South are found willing to make by giving him their support.

Such are my feelings with regard to the two men; and I am satisfied that they are shared by a larger number at the South who are reckoned upon by Gen. Cass and his friends than is generally supposed.

What effect is the movement in N. York destined to produce, which ought to modify the course it behooves the South to pursue in the coming contest? What change has been wrought in the existing elements of party strife by the startling appearance at the head of that movement of so cool and crafty a man as Mr. Van Buren? To me I confess, he presents himself in quite a new character; that of a bold, unscrupulous and vindictive demagogue. His letter is marked by most decided ability. It is precisely suited to the purpose for which it was written, and is conceived and was manifestly designed, as the fierce war-cry of a new and formidable party. With regard to the want of all conscience and principle it manifests, it does not at all surprise me. My earliest conceptions of him were of a shrewd and unprincipled political huckster—the subservient tool of his party, capable, when it suited his purposes, of soaring with it to a certain height of patriotism, and equally ready to wallow with it in the gutter, to mingle in its worst debauches, and to defend its most atrocious acts. But I confess I had no idea that he could, unaided and alone, rise to the dignity of revenge; and in pursuit of it, hazard the ruin at once, of himself, his friends and his ["party" *canceled and* "country" *interlined*].

But aside from this, I regard his letter as a development deserving the most anxious and sober consideration at the hands of the Southern people. A new party is to be formed at the North—to us, the most formidable that has ever yet existed—a party founded upon avowed hostility to the South, and whose professed purpose is to proscribe us to our present limits, and to bring its whole moral influence and that of civilized Europe in its new movement towards freedom, in its new state of unrest, and volcanic eruption, to bear against us. And the present agitated condition of the universal mind of man is seized upon as the auspicious moment for this most terrible and atrocious purpose. Our *condition* was never more dangerous—our *duty* never more solemn: both call for a degree of calmness and sobriety always more desirable than we have ever evinced on this question, but now absolutely necessary to our safety. The time is near at hand when our fate is to be decided. In a few years we must be prepared to say whether we will withdraw from the Union, or purchase a farther fraternity in it by giving up our slaves and consenting to social ruin and disgrace. We have no longer vulgar abolition to contend with. The Party now forming occupies a higher position, and operates on an infinitely wider basis.

On this point God grant that we may be united. But whether we shall or not, is by no means certain, and will depend perhaps altogether upon the wisdom or folly of the course we pursue in the approaching election.

It appears to me that if the friends of Mr. Van Buren succeed in bringing out respectable nominees at their approaching convention with a prospect of rallying a strong party to their support, the Southern States ought to meet in Convention without distinction of party, and take counsel what they shall do. But this suggestion which in time past has been so often made, and would have benefitted us so much had it been adopted, is not I fear, likely to meet with much favor. Nothing appears to be sufficient to rouse the South to a sense of her danger. The circle of the conflagration has for years past been rapidly contracting around us. But until the magazine is on fire, and it is too late, we shall I fear, remain practically blind and indifferent. Very truly &c, J.W. Lesesne.

P.S. I do not see under existing circumstances how you can withhold the public expression of your views with regard to the duty of the South in the present emergency. But of this you are of course best able to judge. I should personally feel much obliged by hearing from you on the subject, if you determine to withhold a more public expression. Since my recent change of pursuits I have been able to give but a very limited attention to passing events, and I have taken no public part whatever in politics. Your lamp has ever thrown a broad and cheering light on my path—and would be most grateful to me now, and useful, if only to aid ["me" *canceled*] in guiding my own humble footsteps. You must be aware how very various and conflicting the opinions of even good and able men at the South are with regard to the question of slavery in the territories. All profess to be agreed that the Southern people are entitled to occupy them with their slaves as much as the Northern people with their goods and chattels. But how is this right to be enjoyed? how is it to be endangered? and if assailed, how is it to be protected? whether the question is not a purely legal or a political one? These are points upon which no two persons are entirely agreed, and are full of intrinsic difficulty.

Since writing the above the news of your speech has reached us—but I have seen only a sketch of it. Mr. Van Buren[']s acceptance of the nomination comes also by Telegraph. J.W.L.

ALS in ScCleA; PC in Boucher and Brooks, eds., *Correspondence*, pp. 450–453.

From Eustis Prescott

Boston, 5th July 1848

My Dear Sir, I have been spending a few weeks in this City and State with the hope of further recruiting my strength—having been much debilitated during my long illness—but now I am happy to say nearly restored.

During this period of idleness I have not been an inattentive observer of political movements, and as I am extremely anxious to know your views as to the probable results of this singular *triangular* warfare, intrude upon you my own observations.

John Van Beuren is a man of more talents than his Father—a ready stump Orator, calculated to entrap the masses, and has devised this platform of *free soil* on which to advance himself hereafter as its head. Principle—they have none, and the leaders care not a rush about the extension of slavery, it is however a good trap to gull the Fanatics.

I have little doubt that [Martin] Van Buren will be nominated by the Buffalo convention, and if so, it is very possible—nay probable, that he will get the votes of Maine, New Hampshire, and Ohio &

barely possible New York & Massachusetts. This would beyond doubt take the election into the House, of the result there you may be enabled to judge ere the session closes.

The Democratic convention committed a great blunder in nominating Gen[era]l [Lewis] Cass—a trimming politician of moderate talents—little personal popularity, and open to attacks from every quarter, and sure to have the decided hostility of Van Buren and his friends—for to him they have always attributed V[an] B[uren]'s want of success in the convention of 1844.

Judge [Levi] Woodbury ought to have been the candidate, and with him, success would have been almost certain, even against Gen[era]l [Zachary] Taylor, this I urged strenuously upon my friends in the convention.

Gen[era]l Taylor I consider a very unsafe man, he is already in the hands of designing *Whig* politicians—mere Office-seekers of very inferior talents, and has himself declared he will be a mere Executive officer. [Millard] Fil[1]more is much more objectionable, and his defeat—if possible, is I think of paramount importance for the protection of southern interests and southern democratic principles. Gen[era]l Cass I think cannot be elected—how then can [William O.] Butler be separated from him—he I believe to be a very safe man altho of moderate talents.

The Nine votes of South Carolina may decide the election, and she may again have the honor of sacrificing herself for her principles—glorious little State how I honor you!

Can a State vote only for Vice President? if not, she can vote for one of her own sons as Pres[i]d[en]t and Wm. O. Butler for Vice. Two or three States might I think in this manner elect the Vice Pres[iden]t.

The election of Free trade and State rights men to Congress becomes at the present juncture of paramount importance, and I have, and shall, urge it very strongly on my friends. I hope to be in New Orleans (altho at present out of business) in Dec[embe]r next.

I am very desirous of receiving copies of your speeches at this session, as also the report of the Commiss[ione]r of Patents, if you can conveniently favor me with them please address ["me" *canceled*] care of C.N.S. Rowland 55 Water St., New York if subsequent to the 12th Inst. up to which date I shall be in this city at No. 1 Fremont Place.

I had yesterday the pleasure of seeing my Father [Joseph Prescott] (now 87) preside at the meeting of the Society of the Cincinnati—the only Medical Officer I believe now alive, of the Revolutionary Army. He was the only *original* member of the society present, and *three* only are alive out of near 400 at the close of the war.

There is a claim before the Judiciary Committee of the Senate in which I am the only person now interested—altho it is in the name of *E.P. Calkin & Co.* of Galveston for damages on goods seized after the acts of annexation &c were complete. Gen[era]l [Chester] Ashley [Senator from Ark.] had it in charge I think as Chairman, since his death I know not who is Chairman, will you oblige me by an enquiry of the Chairman & urge a report in favor. Very truly & respectfully your friend, Eustis Prescott.

ALS in ScCleA; PEx in Boucher and Brooks, eds., *Correspondence*, pp. 448–449.

Remarks on a point of order, 7/5. A discussion of setting a date for adjournment turned into an argument among a number of Senators about motivations. It was said that the friends of Zachary Taylor wanted to adjourn early to avoid a vote on the Oregon bill. The Chair ruled the discussion out of order, which provoked further debate. "Mr. Calhoun said that, although he would have desired to see this debate arrested earlier, he thought it could not now be stopped without injustice to those Senators who were entitled to reply." From *Congressional Globe*, 30th Cong., 1st Sess., p. 897. Variants in the Washington, D.C., *Daily National Intelligencer*, July 6, 1848, p. 3; the Charleston, S.C., *Courier*, July 10, 1848, p. 2; Houston, ed., *Proceedings and Debates*, p. 822.

To George Bancroft, [U.S. Minister to Great Britain]

Washington, 6th July 1848

My dear Sir, I take pleasure in presenting to your acquaintance, John Perkins Jun[io]r E[s]q[uir]e a young gentleman of Mississippi of good education, & highly respectable talents & standing. He visits Europe, with the view of travelling & improving his health. Your attention to him will place me under obligation to you. Very truly Yours & &, J.C. Calhoun.

ALS in DLC, George Bancroft Papers. NOTE: Perkins (1819–1885) was subsequently U.S. Representative and Confederate Senator from Texas.

A[ndrew] P. Butler and J[ohn] C. Calhoun to President [JAMES K. POLK]

Senate Chamber, 6th July 1848

Sir, Having learned that the case of Lieut. L[ucius] B. Northrop late of the 1st Reg[imen]t of Dragoons, is before you, for restoration to his command we beg leave to ask for him your favorable consideration.

Mr. Northrop bore a high reputation in the army and was wounded when in the discharge of a difficult and hazardous duty— from this wound his present disability resulted. Other officers we are informed have been permitted to remain in the army when permanently disabled, and we hope no inviduous distinction will be made against this gallant, honorable, and unfortunate officer. Very Respectfully y[ou]rs, A.P. Butler, J.C. Calhoun.

LS in DNA, RG 94 (Adjutant General's Office), Letters Received (Main Series), 1822–1889, N-88 (M-567:628, frames 359–361); PC in James T. McIntosh and others, eds., *The Papers of Jefferson Davis,* 3:331–332. NOTE: Polk appended an AEI reading: "Referred to the Secretary of War: July 14th 1848." This document is signed by Butler and Calhoun, but the text is written in the hand of Senator Jefferson Davis whose name does not appear on the document. Northrop was later to be the controversial Commissary General of the Confederate Army.

To R[ICHARD] RUSH, [U.S. Minister to France]

Washington, 6th July 1848

My dear Sir, I take pleasure in presenting to your acquaintance John Perkins E[s]q[uir]e Jun[io]r of Mississippi. He comes recommended to me from a high quarter, as a young gentleman liberally educated & of highly respectable standing & character. He travels for the improvement of his health.

I commend him to your kind attention. Very truly Yours & &, J.C. Calhoun.

ALS in NHi, Richard Rush Papers (published microfilm, reel 21, item 11583).

From A[NDREW] J. DONELSON, [U.S. Minister to Prussia]

Berlin, July 8th 1848

My dear Sir, I was much honored by your letter of the 23d of May. Since then I see that the Whigs have thrown aw[a]y Mr. [Henry] Clay and taken Gen[era]l [Zachary] Taylor. I am too far off from the scene of action to express an opinion upon the result of the contest, but think that I can be scarc[e]ly mistaken in supposing that the canvass will be very exciting. It looks to me as though it would turn less upon the ["real" *interlined*] policy of either Whigs or Democrats, than upon the patronage in the gift of the President, and in this point of view that there is reason to anticipate bad effects from it.

Here as in all the portions of Europe except Russia, the agitation still continues, and with less menacing features, so far as the general peace is concerned, than at the breaking out of the French Revolution. Germany is about to try our Federal system and to see whether it will not do to apply it to states governed by Kings, as well as to those governed by Presidents & Congresses. In this spirit the Arch duke John of Austria has been chosen *vicaire* of the new Government at Frankfort, who will without doubt accept the office. But he will ["he" *canceled*] go into a Government that will have originated from no definite views of its powers. He will soon see that it is no easy matter to harmonize the prejudices and interests of 30 or 40 independent states.

It is to the Zoll verien [*sic*] that is to be attributed the reform now proposed in Germany. That association has opened to the eyes of the people the advantages of a system which would so far nationalise Germany as to make her one people in foreign negotiations and in the regulations of her customs fronteir [*sic*]. In the pursuit of this object other considerations now enter, until it may be said that there is nothing either local or national, that is not the subject of popular discussion and legislative inquiry throughout every German state.

Stump speakers are now daily heard advocating the dethronement of monarchs, the abolition of all titles of nobility, and the adoption of institutions as democratic as those of any of our States. All that the monarchs can do is to bend to the storm, and to avail themselves of the good will of their subjects in making the best bargain they can for the preservation of their personal property, and in maintaining a position which will enable ["them" *interlined*] to interpose their weight, if the crisis produces anarchy instead of Governments.

You will remark that these constituent assemblies all exercise legislative powers. They not only supersede ancient Governments but they regard each of their decrees as a Law. The incompatibility of such a pretention with the true sovereignty of the people, is already illustrated by the act creating the *vicaire* and defining his functions. The state Governments perceiving that such a claim of power was inconsistent with their sovereignty, have thought to guard against such an influence by notifying the Arch duke that they concurred with the Assembly in inviting him to that office. It is evident however from the debates at Frankfort that that assembly considers itself competent to put into operation a new Government without the consent of the states. Here then is a source of trouble which sooner or later must end in a serious conflict.

A difficulty of the same nature remains to be solved by each particular state when settling the constitutional basis of its Government. The local Assemblies declare that the sovereignty possessed by them is supreme because it was confer[r]ed by the people, and that all their acts are binding as laws without further reference to the people. What then becomes of the Kings who as parts of the existing system may or may not accept what is done by the Assemblies? Or if they do accept what guaranty have the people that the assembly will have adhered to their instructions? The Assembly may by compact with a King ["may" *canceled*] make a very bad Government, one as oppressive as that which it supersedes.

Such are some of the difficulties resulting from the prevalent ideas of the omnipotence of the existing Assemblies in Germany. They will satisfy you that the revolution is but in its beginning, and that it is not yet entirely certain that its objects will be attained without civil war.

But however ["some" *canceled*] discouraging are some of these considerations, we cannot doubt that the German states will settle down finally upon a system resembling ours. The attempt at Frankfort will have the good effect of enlightening the public mind, and preparing monarchs to abdicate positions which the changes of society make no longer necessary. Some of them I believe would now do so if they could be sure of the queit [*sic*] possession of their personal estates.

Very few probably of those who have taken the lead in the creation of a new Federal Government, are aware of the consequences which will follow. Even if a monarch or an Emperor be made the Executive head it is incompatible with the preservation of this feature in the state Governments. No people will consent to be taxed ["to keep up" *interlined*] two sets of Kings: and if they submit to the one created at Frankfort it may be expected that after he shall have assisted them in dethroning the local monarches, these last will unite in depriving him in his turn of this privilege: and then there will remain nothing but republics united as ours by a limited constitution, but possessing more centralising powers.

This King has just got out of the difficulty in which he was placed by the Danish war—there being an armistice of three months. He is also doing what he can to satisfy his Polish subjects, there being a commission now instituted to examine that whole subject, and see what Government will suit them.

It is said that the Emperor Nicholas has sent some troops across the Turkish line into Maldavia [*sic*]—but the minister of the Sultan at this court told me to day that if the fact were so it would be on the invitation of the Sultan. He says *the only two conservative Governments in the world ought to help each other.* The sooner Russia extends her dominion in that quarter the better it will be for civilization, which will soon react upon her and force her to adopt a more free system of Government.

In looking over my letter I find that I have not thanked you for your Yucatan speech. I certainly would not encumber the United States with such a possession. All our strength should be reserved for Cuba, which belongs to us by nature, and is becoming more and more necessary to enable the holders of slave property in the U. States to preserve it.

I hold that the institution of slavery if abandoned in the Tropical regions will leave the Anglo Saxon as incapable there of maintaining his true character as it has left the Spaniard in Mexico. The only inquiry is whether it is better for humanity that that portion of the world should relapse into a savage negro & Indian state, or be gradually improved by permitting the white man to continue the civilization which he is capable of enforcing as the legitimate superior of the negroe or Indian. I am with great respect y[ou]r ob[edien]t ser[van]t, A.J. Donelson.

[P.S.] Pardon so rough a scrawl—which I intended to rewrite—but official duty has not left me the time. A.J.D.

ALS in ScCleA; PEx in Boucher and Brooks, eds., *Correspondence*, pp. 454–456.

REMARKS ON THE OREGON BILL

[In the Senate, July 8, 1848]
[*John Davis of Mass. was speaking on the restriction of slavery from the Territories.*]

Mr. Calhoun. I am very unwilling to interrupt the Senator, whom I have heard with a great deal of pleasure, however much I disagree with several of his sentiments. I rise now only for the purpose of correcting one of his statements, in order that it may not go uncontradicted. The Senator has said, that after the formation of the Constitution, the free States and the slaveholding stood eight to six; but the Senator will recollect that Vermont came in after the formation of the Constitution, and that Delaware, being regarded as a doubtful State, which I am sure every one will acknowledge, the free and slaveholding States then stood exactly in the same proportion. The Senate will also recollect that there was three times as much territory north of the Missouri line as there was south of it.

[*Davis continued, arguing that the territory north and west of Missouri was largely unsuited for settlement.*]

Mr. Calhoun. The Senator has been misinformed. The greater part of that territory is well watered. It is very far from being an arid region. It abounds with streams and innumerable lakes, and, if my information be correct, a very large portion of the country has a soil exceedingly fertile. If the Senator will look at the map, he will find that there is a beautiful valley of upwards of two hundred miles in length, containing some of the best land in all those regions. But the decisive fact is the large Indian population which has found sustenance there.

[*Davis continued, later remarking that party politicians tended to forget the interests of the country in seeking "to effect certain objects."*]

Mr. Calhoun. The Senator entirely misapprehended the tenor of my remarks. I should scorn to restort to arts of that description.

From *Congressional Globe*, 30th Cong., 1st Sess., Appendix, pp. 896–897. Also printed in the Washington, D.C., *Daily National Intelligencer*, August 10, 1848, p. 2; Houston, ed., *Proceedings and Debates*, pp. 858–859. Variants in *Congressional Globe*, 30th Cong., 1st Sess., p. 910; the Baltimore, Md., *Sun*, July 10, 1848, p. 4; the Charleston, S.C., *Courier*, July 13, 1848, p. 2.

From E[phraim] M. Seabrook

Edisto Island [S.C.], July 8th 1848

My Dear Sir, Although I have the honour of but a slight personal acquaintance with you, yet I trust you will pardon me the liberty of writing you, when I assure you, that I am influenced by no other motive than that of the profoundest respect for your opinions.

The Presidential contest presents a political crisis which calls for the greatest deliberation, caution, and wisdom; and I feel in common with my fellow citizens, the greatest solicitude that our State should occupy her true position. The objections which exist against both ["parties" *canceled*] candidates and parties render a choice difficult, and at best but an alternative of evils. The position of General [Lewis] Cass on the Slavery question, his unsoundness on the "Internal Improvement System" and his unsafeness on the foreign policy of the country, as evidenced by his course on the Oregon and Mexican questions, render him exceedingly obnoxious to a So: Ca: republican; and especially so, when considered as the representative of the radical democracy of the North.

On the other hand, there are strong objections to General [Zachary] Taylor, although sound on the Slavery Question. His elevation to the Presidency, would be that of simply a successful General and over statesmen grown grey in the service of their country—his ignorance of politics (from his own mouth) and therefore his liability to be made the tool of bad and designing men. His views as expressed in his [J.S.] Al[l]ison letter [of 4/22/1848], and his liability to be taken possession of by the Whig party when once in power, and the establishment of all their party measures. These are certainly strong objections to him.

These considerations have occupied my own mind and not without great embarrassment. If you could find time and inclination, I ["would" *interlined*] feel myself honoured and instructed by any light or counsel from you. The privacy of your communication will depend entirely upon your *will*. If it meets with your *approbation*, it will be shown to a *few* of the leading gentlemen of the Parish (St. Johns Colleton) which I have the honour to represent—if otherwise it will be strictly *confidential*. With considerations of profound esteem your humble Serv[an]t, E.M. Seabrook.

[P.S.] Please direct to care of John Fraser & Co., Charleston.

ALS in ScCleA; PEx in Boucher and Brooks, eds., *Correspondence*, pp. 453–454.

To "Col." Ja[me]s Ed[ward] Colhoun, [Abbeville District, S.C.]

Washington, 9th July 1848

My dear James, I forwarded by the first opportunity through the Prussian Minister the two letters you enclosed to Bremen; and have since received the Platt [*sic*] of your fine estate, with the accompan[y]ing note, but have had no opportunity of exhibiting it to advantage. There have been very few foreigners here, and none that I have heard of that would probably take any interest in an enterprise, such as your estate offers. There are but few European ["foreign" *canceled*] Ministers here. There is none from France, England, or Belgium, & the Prussian Minister will probably soon leave for Madrid. I think your best chance would be through Mr. [John S.] Skinner[?] or some friend in New York [City], which is the great centre of emigration [*sic*] and ["where" *interlined*] no doubt agencies ["are" *interlined*] established to give them information where to purchase and locate to advantage.

I do hope you may succeed in making an advantageous sale, & in that case, fix yourself some where in our vicinity. Your mountain estate must one day or another become valuable.

The Senate is engaged in a debate on the Oregon territorial bill. It has been very able & high toned on the part of the South, with a great concurrence of views between the Whigs & democratick members of the South. I do hope our present danger will bring about union among ourselves on the most vital to us of all questions. All other questions ought to be dropt. In union lies our safety. I opened the debate on our side. My speech will be printed in pamphlet form in a few days when I will send you one. Most of my friends think it the best I ever m[ade] and if I may judge from the number of applications I have received for copies from the North, will be in great demand there. It is difficult to say, what will be done. The present appearance is against the prospect of doing any thing. I would not be surprise[d], if Congress should adjourn & leave things just as they are. It will not probably be in session more than a month longer. Yours affectionately, J.C. Calhoun.

ALS in ScCleA; PEx in Jameson, ed., *Correspondence*, p. 759.

To H[ENRY] W. CONNER, [Charleston]

Washington, 9th July 1848

My dear Sir, I can well conceive how difficult it is for the mass of the people to occupy a neutral position in a presidential contest; and, however advisable, I think it in this case, I should dispair in the attempt to prevent it, were it not for the difficulty in the way of our people, consistently with their principles, to enter into a canvass in favour of either ["nominee" *interlined*]. I would not advise neutrality, when the time to cast our votes arrive[s]. It is the debasing & distracting effects of the canvass in favour of ["those" *canceled and* "candidates" *interlined*], who fall far short of our political standard, that I dread. Each party would have to vindicate its nominee in all things, & condemn that of its opponents, and the whole State would sink into two miserable factions, one a [Lewis] Cass & the other a [Zachary] Taylor faction, without any fixed principle or rule of policy. It is that I dread, & that I desire to avoid. By waiting quietly to the time of voting, if nothing in the mean time should justify us in taking sides, we may avoid so great an evil, & cast our vote without loss of character, and union among ourselves; where it can best be done for our safety. But, if the community should become too impatient to take so wise a course, which you all on the spot can best judge, it would only remain to yield to what cannot be resisted, and make the most of it.

The debate on the Oregon territorial bill has been conducted on the part of the South with great ability & sperit, both by the whigs & democratick Senators of the South. [John M.] Berrien [of Ga.] has made and [*sic*] able & well toned speech, & [Reverdy] Johnson of Maryland is to speak tomorrow, & will, from what I hear, take high grounds. [James M.] Mason of Virginia & [Herschel V.] Johnson of Georgia have made excellent speeches on the Democratick side. I hope we may at last open our eyes to the danger and forgetting all things else, join heart & hand for the defence of the South.

My speech has been reported by the Reporters of the Senate. I sent last evening to the ["post" *interlined*] office a copy for each of our city papers, with a few verbal corrections. I hope it may appear in each, with proper notice, & receive a wide circulation. The demand for it at the North, I understand is large. It is doubtful what, or whether any thing will be done. There will be many disclosures made, as to real opinions of both whigs & democrats at the North &

West before the discussion & voting are closed. Yours truly, J.C. Calhoun.

ALS in ScC; photostat of ALS in DLC, Henry Workman Conner Papers.

To Col. N[ATHANIEL] R. EAVES, [Chester District, S.C.]

Washington, 9th July 1848
Dear Sir, When I received your letter, I was preparing to discuss the Oregon territorial bill, and since its delivery, I have been so much engaged with my official duties ["the" *canceled*] as to be compelled to suspend my correspondence, which I hope, will satisfactorily explain the delay of my answer.

A bill has passed the Senate, and, I understand the House too, extending the provision of the existing law, as to lands & back pay, to the brothers & sisters of the deceased, which will remedy the evil to which you refer. As to the case of rations, the law is express, against allowing commutation, so that you cannot receive pay for your's, during the period to which you refer.

I have not had an opportunity to see Gen[era]l [Winfield] Scott (who has been absent or sick since his return) and to ascertain, what has been done, under his order, after taking possession of the City of Mexico, to which you refer. He is now at his residence in New Jersey, but I have applied to the A[d]jutant General to get the information for me, and will send it to you as soon as received. I have made enquiry of Col. [Jefferson] Davis of Miss[issipp]i, who commanded a regiment of the Miss[issipp]i Volunteers & who is now a Senator & a member of the Military Committee, in reference to the "Script of merit." He says there is no authority for giving one; & that, he presumes, that the mistake originated in confounding it, with an order to transmit the names of highly meritorious soldiers to the War Department, for the purpose of selecting the most deserving for promotion.

You inform me, that two parties are forming in the State; one for Gen[era]l [Lewis] Cass & the other for Gen[era]l [Zachary] Taylor, and ask my opinion, as to what ought to be done?

I have had the same question propounded to me by several of my constituents, and will give you the answer, which I have given to all. In my opinion, neither of the nominees comes up to our stand of the true principles & policy of the Republican party, & that we cannot enter into a canvass in favour of either, without lowering our Standard, & distracting & dividing of the State, greatly to her injury every way. I object to Gen[era]l Cass, on the ground, that he is not sound on the Slave question. I have examined his letter [of 12/24/- 1847] to Mr. [Alfred O.P.] Nicholson with great care, and I can give it no interpretation, which does not give to the laws of Mexico the power of excluding Slaves from the Territory acquired from her; and if they should be annulled by Congress, which does admit, that the inhabitants of the Territory may exclude us. I regard this, but the Wilmot proviso in its worst form. That requires Congress to pass an act to exclude us; but this requires one to admit us. I will not attempt to state what I regard to be the true view in reference to this vital subject here, as I have fully expressed them in a speech which will appear in pamphlet form, in two or three days, when I will send you a copy.

I object, also, to him on the ground, that he is unsound on the question of internal improvement. He voted for the abomindable bill, which Mr. [James K.] Polk vetoed, and also against his veto.

I, again, object, because he is not safe on the question of peace & war; and that, if he should be made President, there would be danger of his getting the Country into war. There are others & strong objections to him, which I pass over, deeming them sufficient to show, that he does not come up to the true republican standard.

I object to Gen[era]l Taylor on the ground of his not being sound on the veto ["question" *canceled and* "power" *interlined*], which I regard as important at this time. I also object to him on the ground, that his opinions are not sufficiently well known on the question of free trade, subtreasury, and others; & that as far as they are known, they do not appear to be favourable to us. We do not know ["his opinion" *interlined and then canceled*] even on the Slave question, what are his opinions; but we may, I think, safely conclude, that he is sound on that, as he is a cotton planter and the owner of several hundred slaves.

Such being the objections to [e]ach, I am of the opinion, our true course is to stand fast for the present on our principles, & wait & see what is to come, before we take our final stand, in reference to the two nominees. Before the end of the Session, we shall have a much clearer view of the course that will be taken by the Northern wing of both parties; and what ["course" *interlined*] we ought to take in reference to the most vital of all questions to us. I hold *that*, as Mr. [Thomas] Jefferson did, as far above any and all other questions, and on it, in my opinion, the South should unite, regardless of all others, if we wish to save ourselves & our posterity from the greatest of calamities. If nothing should occur to enable us ["in the meane time" *interlined*] to decide, on satisfactory grounds, what side we ought to take, we ought, in my opinion, [to] avoid the canvass altogether, & cast our votes when the time comes, where our safety, & that of the South, and a regard to our principles, may demand.

I do not intend what I have said for the publick, but have no objection, that you should make them known to such as may desire to know my opinion. I wish to conceal nothing, but desire to avoid any thing like dictation, or interference with the free choice of the State, in deciding, who shall be the next President.

I enclose in a package, which will go in the same mail with this, the forms of proceedings to be observed, to obtain land, or scrip, or back pay. With great respect yours truly, J.C. Calhoun.

[P.S.] There is, I think, no chart of the land yet made intended as bounty to the soldiers, but will see & send you one if there is.

ALS in ScU-SC, John C. Calhoun Papers.

From D. Macaulay

Office of "The New Orleans Miscellany"
New Orleans, 9th July 1848

Dear Sir, Every thing you advance in the Senate, particularly referring to slavery, or the "Wilmot proviso," I read with the greatest interest; and presuming the speech you delivered lately connected with these subjects has been published in full, you would do me a particular favor if you would take the trouble of addressing a copy to me, as Editor of the New Orleans Miscellany.

Some years ago I had the pleasure of meeting with you at Washington: & you will remember me at once from the fact that you recommended a little work I published [at Washington in 1843] entitled the "Patriot's Catechism: or the Duties of Rulers and Ruled." This seems to me to be a very portentous period in the history of our country; and I am much gratified with the views you entertain on those great points with which the South should feel an intense interest. I would have addressed copies of my periodical to you but I know you have more of such sent you than ["your" *altered to* "you"] have leisure to read. Trusting you will excuse this liberty I have the honor of remaining with every sentiment of respect, Your most Obliged, D. Macaulay.

ALS in ScCleA. NOTE: An AEU by Calhoun reads, "McCauley. Send Speech."

From E[STWICK] EVANS

Philadelphia, July 11, 1848
Dear Sir: I have this moment had the distinguished honour to receive your letter of the 10th & crave the privilege of tendering you my acknowledgements. I am happy, Sir, that you entertain favourable views of my ideas on the great subject now before the nation, & that you appreciate my motives. I did fear that you might from the extreme principles that I advanced, apprehend that I might, in zeal for strong & clear belief of right, overleap the suggestions of discretion. No Sir, discretion is most strong a duty & sometimes a deeply solemn one. I only ["spoke" *interlined*] of extreme right, as a tenable ground, & a position to do glorious battle for, if the worst should ever come to the worst. I know of no subject involving so much depth & richness as that of the rights of the citizen slave holder in the territories of the U. States, &, believe me, when I say that there is such a beauty in *right*, as a moral subject, especially when blended with deep & generous ratiocination—&, more still, when directed against prejudice, & power, & tyranny ["that one is happy, without any other reward, in sustaining it" *interlined*]. Why, Sir, which is worst, for a good man—a kind man, to take care of his slave, whom he does not know what to do with, else, consistent with the welfare of that slave, or his own safety—or the Despotic pretentions of the cold & self-inflated Northerner against the Natural & Constitutional right of the citizens of neighbouring Sovereignties?

But I really beg you to excuse my writing you so much *again.* I only intended a line or two of acknowledgement. I shall feel honoured by your transmission of the pamphlet, & shall read it with great pleasure & attention.

I trust the South, whilst she plays her part of the game—if I may so speak—(it *is* a Game) with great prudence, & tact—keeping back, as far as not needed, ulterior[?] ground, that might prejudice—I do hope that she will see every thing annihilated, even, rather than relinquish *Right.* Right, Sir, is a glory, & what are all perishable things worth, in comparison with this, relation of our *Moral* being?

582

I have the great honor to subscribe myself Your obliged & ob[edien]t,
E. Evans.

ALS in ScCleA.

REMARKS ON THE TEXAS NAVY BILL

[In the Senate, July 11, 1848]
*[The bill would authorize the President to increase the U.S. Navy
by incorporating the ships and navy officers of the Texas Republic.
Several Senators objected, arguing that the President would be appointing officers unconstitutionally without submitting nominations
to the Senate.]*
Mr. Calhoun said, that although the meaning of the word navy
was ambiguous, yet the usual construction embraced officers as well
as ships. He was therefore disposed to give it that construction,
which was the one unanimously put on the resolution annexing
Texas. He thought that as Texas was now one of the States of the
Union, deprived of her potential voice, she ought to be treated with
kindness and liberality. He thought the bill might be so modified
as to do away with any objection of a constitutional character. No
injustice could be done to our own officers, nor need the feelings of
any one of them be wounded by the admission of these officers. He
added a few words in defence of Commodore [Edwin W.] Moore,
whose conduct in leaving the service of the United States in a time
of peace, and entering the Texan service, was not only free from reproach, but deserving of praise.

From *Congressional Globe,* 30th Cong., 1st Sess., p. 922. Variants in the Washington, D.C., *Daily Union,* July 12, 1848, p. 2; the Baltimore, Md., *Sun,* July 12,
1848, p. 4; the Charleston, S.C., *Courier,* July 15, 1848, p. 2; Houston, ed., *Proceedings and Debates,* p. 868.

REMARKS ON THE FUGITIVE SLAVE QUESTION

[In the Senate, July 12, 1848]
*[During lengthy debate on the Oregon territorial bill, Thomas Fitz-
gerald of Mich. said Calhoun had wrongly accused that State of interfering with the recovery of fugitives. No laws could be found on
the books of the State for that purpose.]*

Mr. Calhoun. I respond very cheerfully to the appeal made by the Senator from Michigan, but I am very sorry to say that the answer will not be satisfactory. The amount of my remark was, that the ordinance of 1787 was a compromise between the North and the South; that the South yielded up to the northern States the exclusive right of settling the Northwest Territory, and that the North entered into a solemn stipulation with the South that they would deliver up fugitive slaves; and the point of my charge was, not that any specific laws had been passed, but that the northern States had pursued a course which has rendered utterly null and void that stipulation. I am sorry to say that Michigan is one of those States; and if the Senator wants proof of that, I refer him to a memorial from the Legislature of Kentucky, presented this very session, which has been referred to a committee who have examined all the facts, and ascertained that citizens of Kentucky, in endeavoring to reclaim fugitive slaves found in Michigan, were overpowered and prevented from recovering their property. Now, the stipulation into which these States entered was not simply that they would not pass laws rendering that stipulation nugatory, but that they should pass laws to protect us, and use their whole power and authority for the purpose of delivering up these fugitive slaves. If Michigan have passed no law against us, she has either omitted to pass laws to fulfill that stipulation, or neglected to enforce them within her limits.

[*Fitzgerald regretted that there were in Michigan a few individuals who had caused trouble, but the great body of the people and the legislature did not approve of them and should not be blamed.*]

Mr. Calhoun. Michigan was bound to pass laws to carry out that ordinance. I wish I could place my hands upon the report in reference to the facts presented in the memorial from the Legislature of Kentucky. A greater outrage never was committed by one people upon another than in that case. Insult was heaped upon injury; and I ask, was the State justified in remaining a passive spectator? Again, is it not known, that for years, there have been organized individuals in Michigan, who have run our slaves through her territory into Canada? Has she taken any steps to prevent that? I do not say these things willingly, but with great reluctance. Would it were otherwise! I would rejoice if the stipulations of the Constitution were fulfilled on all sides; but I must say, that there have been most flagrant violations of these stipulations; not on the part of Michigan alone, but on that of almost every one of the free States.

Mr. [Thomas] Corwin [of Ohio]. I wish to inquire whether the

Supreme Court has not expressly decided that the States can pass no such laws whatever?

Mr. Calhoun. My colleague [Andrew P. Butler of S.C.], who has been investigating that subject, will answer the Senator.

[*Butler discussed at length the case of Pennsylvania vs. Prigg.*]

Mr. Calhoun. I would state, in addition to the explanation of my colleague, that at the time [1842] I regarded that decision as the most extraordinary one ever made. It had been the practice of the non-slaveholding States to pass such laws, and their constitutional power to do so had never been questioned. The provision of the Constitution for the recovery of fugitive slaves, is connected with another immediately in juxtaposition with it—the provision for the delivering of fugitives from justice. Both come under what is called extradition treaties, perfectly familiar to every public man, and as well interpreted as any treaties in the world can be interpreted. Every State in the Union takes an efficient part in the delivery of fugitives from justice. That is the case, also, with respect to England. I appeal to every man who has ever been in the State Department, whether the States do not take efficient steps in the delivery of fugitives from justice? And shall another provision, standing in the Constitution, worded in the same manner, receive a different and most absurd interpretation? For, if the States are to stand by themselves, and make no efforts whatever, who does not see that the power of the United States will not be competent to fulfill the law, if the power of the United States is so very remote that it can never be exercised? The committee has reported a bill with a view to carry into effect the powers of the United States; and we shall see how the gentleman will act on that bill.

[*Corwin said that a majority of the bench had made their decision.*]

Mr. Calhoun. I do not recognize the decision.

[*There was a long discussion between Corwin and Butler.*]

Mr. Calhoun. I cannot permit the Senator [Corwin] to escape even under a decision of the Supreme Court. By express contract between the rest of the States and the people inhabiting these Territories, which are now States, the latter bound themselves to deliver up our fugitive slaves. They are the parties to that contract, under the ordinance, and it has not been superseded by the Constitution.

Mr. Corwin. Have not the Supreme Court, to which reference has been made, interpreted our rights, duties, and powers, under that compact?

Mr. Calhoun. Simply and only under the Constitution of the United States. They could not put aside a contract. It stands upon higher principles. It stands entirely on different ground from the case in Pennsylvania. The decision has not been confirmed, and I trust never will be. I have always considered it as the most extraordinary decision ever made. But I put that aside, and present the positive contract between these parties. There was no United States Government then to fulfill it. The old Congress had no such power. There stands the contract, and will ever stand, around which it is impossible to go.

[*Corwin argued that the obligations of the Northwestern States to the South were identical under the Northwest Ordinance and the Constitution, and that the Supreme Court had defined what those were.*]

Mr. Calhoun. I cannot permit even that view of the case to pass. The Constitution expressly provides for the continuance of this contract between the United States and the people that inhabited the Northwest territory. The 6th article of the Constitution contains an express permission that "all debts contracted and engagements entered into before the adoption of this Constitution shall be as valid against the United States under this Constitution as under the Confederation." Now, is it not manifest that the ordinance of 1787 looked to its fulfillment under the present Government, and not the old Confederation, which had no machinery, no capacity to execute it? If the words of the ordinance and those in the Constitution are precisely the same—and I have not compared them—it is one of the strongest arguments to show that the decision of the court was wrong, and that the words of the Constitution ought to have received the interpretation of the prior words, instead of the prior words receiving the interpretation of the latter.

Mr. Corwin. I do not intend to controvert the right of the gentleman to take an appeal from the decision of the Supreme Court, but I do not know where he can find any revisory power at present.

Mr. Calhoun. That being admitted, everything is admitted. These States, if they have not violated the stipulation, have permitted it to be violated incessantly. It is of that we complain.

[*There followed lengthy debate in which many Senators took part. William L. Dayton of N.J. felt that the question of slavery in Oregon, California, and New Mexico was not a "practical question" but a political "excitement."*]

Mr. Calhoun. I am very glad to hear the Senator from New Jersey say that this is not a practical question; and I hope, therefore, that he will leave it open. We are in favor of free territory, and opposed to monopoly. We wish to leave the soil open to every American citizen, so long as it remains a territory, leaving the people to form their own government when it becomes a State.

Mr. Dayton. The Senator goes for free territory; so do I. The question is in reference to free territory in Oregon, and the people of Oregon want the territory to continue free; and all that the Senator asks is, that the restrictions may be removed, so that he can go there with his slaves.

Mr. Calhoun. The Senator says that it is an abstract question; why not leave it open? We got Oregon from France and Spain—both slaveholding communities. We got New Mexico and California also from a slaveholding community. Strike out the 12th section of the bill, and leave the territory as you find it.

Mr. Dayton. I am for leaving the territories as we found them, and I trust the Senator will join with me. I would leave it as it now is with great pleasure, exactly as you find it—free from slavery.

Mr. Calhoun. It is slave territory. Did we not get it from slaveholding countries?

Mr. Dayton. Not at all. I hold that we did not get Oregon through the purchase of Louisiana. I hold that the discussion proved, if it proved anything, that Oregon did not come from that source; and certainly we did not get New Mexico from that source.

Mr. Calhoun. Certainly. Slavery existed throughout the dominions of Spain on this continent. We got Oregon partly from Spain and partly from France—both slaveholding communities.

[*Dayton asked if Calhoun believed that slavery could ever exist in Oregon, and if not, why he desired "to change the existing law which has been adopted by the people."*]

Mr. Calhoun. Whatever territory we purchase from any community, if slaveholding at the time of the purchase, the territory must follow that law. Every one who remembers the discussion knows that more reliance was placed upon our title through France than on any other. One of the ablest gentlemen on that side of the Chamber (Mr. [George] Evans [former Senator from Maine]) declared that that was our strongest title. All the possessions of Spain were open to slavery. Now, I put it to the Senator, that he is bound to unite with us, and make it free territory—open to every American citizen.

[*Discussion continued until the Senate voted 31 to 14 to appoint a select committee on the issue.*]

From *Congressional Globe*, 30th Cong., 1st Sess., Appendix, pp. 914–919. Also printed in Houston, ed., *Proceedings and Debates*, pp. 879–884. Variant in *Congressional Globe*, 30th Cong., 1st Sess., pp. 927–928; Benton, *Abridgment of Debates*, 16:221–222. Another variant in the Baltimore, Md., *Sun*, July 13, 1848, p. 4; the Charleston, S.C., *Mercury*, July 17, 1848, p. 3. Another variant in the New York, N.Y., *Herald*, July 15, 1848, p. 3.

From JOHN L. MANNING and P[ETER] DELLA TORRE

[Charleston?,] July 13th 1848

My dear Sir, The indications are very strong every where that this State will cast its vote for Mr. [Lewis] Cass in the coming presidential election. There has been we fear, too long hesitation between the respective nominees of the Whig and Democratic Conventions and by default Mr. Cass seems to be the favourite.

There are some of us who have conscientiously awaited the course of events, under the hope that we might be able openly to support Gen[era]l [Zachary] Taylor as being a slave holder and a Southern man in feeling; and we are unwilling to sustain Mr. Cass because he is an expediency man, & would not act, in his administration, from settled conviction and principle, in any course which he might take upon the slavery question, in its various aspects. He is not a man, moreover, if we rightly appreciate him, who will take responsibility in any emergency of the government, and lead, instead of being ["lead" *altered to* "led"] by his party.

What are we to do then in this posture of affairs? I should be unwilling to believe that this State is ["willing" *canceled and* "ready" *interlined*] to support for President a man who is willing that we should hold our property thro' the mercy or moderation of the North without regarding our rights under the Constitution? And yet without some decided and energetic course of action and that both prompt & immediate the State will do it. Without this decided course, to support Gen[era]l Taylor would be to create a division in the State which would lead to bad political results. The Mercury is the only popular press that still keeps aloof. The others in the State have declared their preference for the nominee of the Baltimore convention.

Many of the Parishes are willing & ready to support Gen[era]l Taylor but the large and more populous districts are disposed to take the opposite course.

Under these circumstances we venture to address you, and to beg some information from you. We do not know but that circumstances have arisen to warrant a change in the policy of the State as indicated in your letter to Mr. [Henry W.] Conner, of the 12th June. If you will will [*sic*] be kind enough to give us your views upon the matter as it now stands you will be doing us a service, but what is of infinite more consequence you will be of service to the State and to the Union; for a confidence is expressed and entertained on every side in your wisdom which will now as ["the" *canceled*] has always been the case give tone and direction to public sentiment ["here" *interlined*]. We write as individuals merely, and of course your letter will be confined strictly to ourselves, unless it may be compatible with your wishes that its contents shall be made known to your warm friends of this place as hitherto.

Pardon us, Sir, if we take a liberty with you. But what seems to us to be a critical position in ["the" *interlined*] State, with regard to its future influence and usefulness, will with you, we are sure, be deemed a sufficient excuse. Always with profound respect and consideration Your friends, Jno. L. Manning, P. Della Torre.

[P.S.] Direct to Mr. ["Torre" *canceled and* "P.D. Torre" *interlined*] in Charleston who will ["f" *canceled*] read & forward your letter to me.

LS in ScCleA. NOTE: John Laurence Manning (1816–1889) was at this time a member of the S.C. Senate from Clarendon District and Torre a member of the S.C. House of Representatives from Charleston. Manning became governor 1852–1854.

Remarks on the bill for settlement of the Cherokee claims, 7/13. "Mr. Calhoun expressed some doubt as to the manner in which he should give his vote. He could not give the reasons by which he was actuated, as he was not aware that the injunction of secrecy had been removed, in relation to the matters connected with the subject." (In response to Calhoun's point, the Senate went into executive session.) From *Congressional Globe*, 30th Cong., 1st Sess., p. 932.

Remarks on a bill to establish a Branch Mint in New York City, 7/14. Andrew P. Butler of S.C. offered an amendment to establish a similar Mint in Charleston. "Mr. Calhoun remarked that he hoped the amendment would prevail. Charleston had now an extensive trade with the West Indies, and that trade was continually increasing in consequence of the extension of the railroad from Charleston to the West. No small amount of coin coming from the West Indies to Charleston would be the result of this trade; and a branch mint at that place would be of immense advantage, not only to Charleston, but to a large region of country." (The amendment passed but the bill was defeated.) From Houston, ed., *Proceedings and Debates*, p. 890. Variant in *Congressional Globe*, 30th Cong., 1st Sess., p. 937.

To J[OSEPH] W. LESESNE, [Mobile]

Washington, 15th July 1848

My dear Sir, I send by the mail, that takes this a copy of my late speech. It has been well received here on all sides, and, my friends think, has made a strong impression.

You have well expressed all my views on all the subjects on which your communication [of 7/5] touches. I think, as you do, in reference to Gen[era]l [Zachary] Taylor, [Lewis] Cass, & [Martin] Van Buren & their positions & associations. As between the two first, I can take no part; and I had hope our State would occupy a neutral position between them, until the time of election arrived, and then cast its votes, where her safety & that of the South might require. But I apprehend from indications there, my hope will not be realized; and that a warm and debasing canvass will take place between candidates neither of whom represent either our principles, or policy. It appears to me the best course for our friends, is to take little or no part in the Canvass, but to cast their votes when the time arrives, where, in their opinion, it can be done with their views, most in conformity with the considerations I have stated.

In my opinion, the best result, that can take place, is the defeat of Gen[era]l Cass, without our being responsible for it. His election would place [Thomas H.] Benton, [William] Allen & the most dangerous men of the party at its head; & Would expose the Country to war; & would perpetuate the Caucus system. His defeat on the contrary, would throw off that portion of the party, & compel it— the party—to take our grounds & save us from the Hazard of war; for Gen[era]l Taylor & the whigs are for peace. If he (T[aylor]) should be elected, I have no doubt his would be a whig administration, but they could not do much mischief. The bank is obsolete; the Tariff can undergo no great change, as it now stands not far from the maximum revenue point, and all that can [be] raised from imposts will be required for the use of the government. Nor will the subtreasury be repealed, in my opinion, without the establishment of the bank. On the contrary, if He should be defeated, the Northern whigs will go off in a body, if they find they can not support themselves by selecting a Southern man, & join the Van Buren move, & thus unite the North against us, but if he should they will look to the South to keep a majority. Now, as strange as it may be thought, I am of the impression, we have more ultimately to hope from the whigs, than the democrats, in reference to the Slave question; for reasons, which, I think, will readily occur to you on reflection. Certain it is, that thus far, the hostile movements have come from the latter. Witness [David] Wilmot & Van Buren's and other movements I might cite. Yours very truly, J.C. Calhoun.

Transcript in NcU, Southern Historical Collection, Joseph W. Lesesne Papers.

To [SARAH MYTTON MAURY, Liverpool]

[Washington, *ca.* July 15, 1848]
We have been looking with deep solicitude on the great events on your side of the Atlantic. My fears have greatly preponderated over my hopes, and continue to do so. There cannot be a more fearful spectacle than the overthrow of an old and established government over a wealthy and populous community, without any certainty of establishing in its place one capable of protecting it against anarchy.

I am among those who were not without apprehension as to the fate of your government, and who rejoice that it has been able to maintain itself. Had it yielded to the storm, it is impossible to say what would have been the consequences.

You will receive herewith a copy of a speech delivered by me [on 6/27] on the most exciting and dangerous question that ever agitated our union. An attempt is making by a special committee, of which I am a member; to adjust it; but it is quite uncertain whether it can be done.

PEx (from the Liverpool, England, *Chronicle* of 8/19) in the New York, N.Y., *Journal of Commerce*, September 6, 1848, p. 1. NOTE: The above excerpt of Calhoun's letter was published under the head "Mr. Calhoun on Slavery &c. Communicated by Mrs. Maury."

To Eustis Prescott, [New York City]

Washington, 15th July 1848

My dear Sir, I transmit by the mail, that takes this, a copy of my speech & of the Patent office report.

As far as my observation extends, it very much concurs in the opinion you express of the state of things at the North, relative to abolition, and also, as to what you say, in reference to the acts of the Baltimore Convention, and the nominees of both conventions.

I had hope that S.C. would abstain from entering into the Canvass, & cast her vote quietly, where she might think it ought to be, when the time for voting came, ["but from," *canceled*] but from present indications, I fear, I am mistaken. Yours truly, J.C. Calhoun.

ALS in ScU-SC, John C. Calhoun Papers.

From F[itz]w[illiam] Byrdsall

New York [City,] July 16th 1848

Dear Sir, I have read the corrected publication of your speech on the Oregon Bill—to my great instruction and delight. The Report of it which was given in the New York Herald was imperfect and greatly mutilated. I am also much pleased to find that it has been published in full in the N.Y. Express and N.Y. Journal of Commerce, as this will tend to the general diffusion of an intellectual effort so so [*sic*] well calculated to make men think upon the subject it elucidates.

I fervently hope that Congress will not adjourn until this question so imminent to the safety of the Union is settled. The present Session presents the best oppertunity we ever can have for a definite settlement, and thereby keep it out of the presidential contest. Both parties should be desirous of this, that is, the Whig & Democratic parties. The Senate should not consent to adjourn untill the ["House" *interlined*] comes to a deciding vote. The cry of "free territory" is becoming as potent, as that of "Protection to American Industry" used to be.

When General [Lewis] Cass was in this city, a Gentleman directed his attention to a clause in the Constitution, which by a forced interpretation of one word, is held to imply that Congress has the power to prohibit the introduction of Slaves into the territories, and

592

even their migration from State to State. Section 9 of Article 1 says "the *migration* or importation of such persons as any of the States" &c&c. As the Dictionaries give the meaning of the word migration, "the act of changing residence or place;" "to go—pass or travel"; accordingly, it is insisted upon that Congress can constitutionally prohibit the migration of slaves, the changing of residence from State to State, or State to territory. In vain do we urge here that the accepted meaning of the word has no such import—that changing of residence within the United States, is neither migration[,] emigration nor immigration—and that migration means the going out from one Empire or National Dominion to another.

The placing of [Millard] Fillmore on the Ticket with Gen[era]l [Zachary] Taylor I like not, for he is politically one of the most ultra Whigs. It might prove dangerous for such a man to have the casting vote in the Senate. Every Northern Whig is either for a Protective Tariff, or the Wilmot proviso or both; but there are many, very many Democrats of the North who are opposed to the latter, and almost all to the former. I am beginning to think that the Election of Cass & [William O.] Butler would be safer for the South than the success of Taylor and Fillmore. The success of Cass will drive the Van Burenites out of the Democratic party, while if the South contributes largely towards his defeat, the anti Wilmot proviso Democrats of the north finding themselves not sustained by the South, will in chagrin give up and be forced to follow the [Martin] Van Buren lead. Would not this result in the formation of a Northern party composed of Wilmot proviso Democrats—Wilmot proviso Whigs and the remains of the Cass party?

The Van Burenites of the Evening Post Squad will do their utmost to procure the nomination of Van Buren by the Buffalo Convention of the 9th August. They propose also to have Judge [John] McLean put on the ticket with the Sage of Kinderhook.

Please accept my thanks for the Copy of your Speech. I am with deep Sentiments of Respect Yours &c &c &c, F.W. Byrdsall.

[P.S.] I enclose you a graphic article from [Mordecai M.] Noah's paper [Noah's Times and Weekly Messenger] of to day—characteristically describing Van Buren. I know of no *better* act of patriotism than to put down Van Buren and his gang—I hold him to be the vilest traitor and the worst man the country ever was cursed with. Certainly it appears to me from the bitter hostility which he and his manifest toward Cass, that the success of the latter would be the most complete overthrow of the former.

Gen[era]l Taylor does not take well with the intelligent Northern

Whigs—and he is losing ground with the Northern Democrats. His late letters are subverting the good effects of the former ones.

It might turn out that the Electoral vote of So. C. may decide the contest. I should like to see you one of three candidates before the House.

ALS in ScCleA. Note: *An AEU by Calhoun reads, "Mr. Byrdsall."*

From JAMES SHEPPERD and Others

Edgefield C[ourt] H[ouse] So. Ca., 16th July 1848
Dear Sir, The undersigned Committee request the pleasure of Your Company on the 27th instant, at a Barbacue, to be given near this place, by the Citizens of the District to the "96 Boys" a Company of the Palmetto Regiment just returned from the Mexican War. Very Respectfully, James Shepperd, A[llen] B. Addison, George Boswell, Leroy H. Mundy, Rob[er]t Meriwether, Committee.

LS (with all signatures in one handwriting) in ScCleA. Note: *An AEU by Calhoun reads, "Invitation to Edgefield."*

From BENJ[AMIN] F. PORTER

Cave Spring, Geo., 17 July 1848
My dear Sir, You are no doubt so frequently solicited to a correspondence by men who have no other motive than to draw out, for the purpose of exposing your opinions, that it is a delicate task even for a frank man to communicate with you. But I trust you have learned enough of me to know that however our opinions have differed as to men, I have always felt the value of your great services for the Country, and have always been content to trust its destiny to your hands. It is so rare to see eminent statesmanship united to unsullied private virtue, and to unstained independence that, a slight breach of conventional propriety may be excused in those, who feeling the value of such instances, would guide their own course, by the judgment of such a man as you are.

What, my dear Sir, are we of the South, to do in the present alarming juncture? Up to the present time I had suffered myself to hope, that the love for the Union which I had hoped was strong over the northern States, if not their interests, would have stifled the various efforts being made, to interfere with the rights of the South. I am forced now to believe that nothing will stay the hand of abolition; the more especially, as I find, all over the South, men, who are now openly contending for the right of the people of territories to prohibit the emigration of slave holders. This from slave holders strikes me as a very alarming feature in events; and yet the supporters of Gen[era]l [Lewis] Cass in Alabama, are very generally yielding this point. This course appears to me so inexcusable that, I can neither pardon it, nor see any thing but utter ruin in its tendency. Now, though for some time acting with the Whig party, I could support no man or measure ["at" *interlined*] all equivocal on this point; and I had expected as much from Southern Democrats. At this time it seems to me that those not blind by the fanaticism of party, should be acting together; and take some decided steps to save the South. I look upon this topic, as one of higher importance than all others. The Tariff, banks, internal improvements, &c. are in a measure but matters of government practice—the regulation of its machinery: but this affects the soul of the Constitution. The effects of the first may pass away, or be bad, or good, as times and ["ch" *canceled*] circumstances change, but *this* must last forever in the destruction of the Union and of the Constitution; and in the reestablishment of the worst of tyrannies. Would it not be best for us, at once to establish a paper in the South, devoted exclusively to our protection in this matter? This is my impression; and I am willing to give up my energies wholly to it. I have already corresponded with many on this matter, and all admit the necessity, but ["do" *interlined*] not act. Now my plan is to act promptly, the very moment the necessity arises, for nothing great or meritorious can be effected without energy and firmness. Do not suppose that I write you as a politician. Not so. There is too much of Machiavelliism in politics for me. I am in this matter in downright earnest; and too much is at stake with us, to trifle now. I shall therefore be gratified to know your opinions, expressed with the frankness which induces me to ask for them, and without a fear that they are committed to unworthy hands. Whatever you say to me shall be kept with the confidence which an honorable ["man" *interlined*] owes to himself, as well as to others.

I shall spend a month or so at this place. With the sincerest regards Your admirer and friend, Benj. F. Porter.

ALS in ScCleA; PC in Boucher and Brooks, eds., *Correspondence*, pp. 456–457. NOTE: An AEU by Calhoun reads, "Judge Porter."

From E[stwick] Evans

Philadelphia, July 18, 1848

Dear Sir: Pardon me in *yielding* to the desire to acknowledge the receipt of your speech on the Oregon Bill, which you did me the honour, & favour, to transmit. That very hour, I read, with avidity & close attention, this impress of your mind—your intellectual & moral being; & permit me to say that I joy in such exhibitions of intellectual superiority & grandeur; & to add, that I do not know that you have advanced a single idea that my judgment does not accord with. This circumstance does honour to myself.

Allow me, as I *am* writing again, to say that even Philosophy itself does not look far enough ahead. Preventive philosophy, like preventive justice, is the best sort; & it is important to look broad & wide on the subject of slavery—in relation, not to its supposed evil or possible continuance for a long series of years, but with respect to *Conflict* between the South & the North, with its endless animosities & woes.

Men look on the surface of things, especially when ["it is favoured by" *interlined*] their pride of piety, (no man estimates piety higher than I do,) & their ready prejudice. There should be a new face put upon this whole matter. Its *elementary* relations, both as it regards the laws of nature, religion, & society, & also the *spirit* of the constitutional compact, which involves the broad grounds of that very Sovereignty & Liberty which is the basis of the States & their citizens, ["should be fully presented" *interlined*]. The citizens of the South, have an equal—a full right to go where they please, as it regards the Territorial regions of the country; & to carry what they please—seeing that there is no crime in all this, & nothing but a mere difference of opinion; & I gravely raise the question, too, whether, on the principle of the constitution, & a fair parity of reasoning, the slaves, in Oregon for example, should not have the weight prescribed in the constitution of the General Government in the formation of a constitution for admission. And if *this* constitution declares for slavery or says nothing about it, what right has the North, in Congress, to interfere? I love the North—her rivers & mountains, & the well-remembered sun beams & sweet rains that greeted my infancy. But I love not her coldness of heart, her prejudices, her egotistical Despotism—& her narrow cunning! I love Truth & Justice more than all—infinitely; & wherever they dwell, even if with my enemy, I embrace them—& him!

As it regards the little matter of position in the retired & quiet

Capitol—at least a part of the year, I seek only more certain leisure after office hours & means more certain to publish. I finished a full work on Slavery, five years ago; & a work on Power—its moral elements & abuses; & last fall I had finished a full work on Govern-[men]t, covering completely, your correct & beautifully expressed & wonderfully condensed ideas contained in the last few paragraphs of your speech on ["the" *interlined*] Oregon bill lately delivered. My wish was to present this bearing of the subject on the *Relative*—the great talisman of morals in Government, & legislation, & law, & indeed all the institutions & proceedings of society, & of private life also. My wish was to go to Europe & circulate it far & wide, in the *hope* to check that too ardent & too progressive spirit of Democracy, arising, as you illustrate it, from those general, false, & illusive phrases "all men are born free & equal" &c; ["but I had not the means" *interlined*]. Mankind, Sir, want a new starting point—to make new observations, & take a new departure; they have taken the course of a tangent instead of a circle. Alas for Europe! I entertain a *holy* hope for free government every where as far as *practicable*; but I cannot express my deep & soul-sick grief at what is taking place in France &c.

The position of which I spoke, I would take but for a little while; & my sacrifices would be great, because my family are here. I seek, surely, no such humble *honour*. I have always been accused of inordinate ambition. Such is my nature; but I thank Heaven that I never saw the moment when I wanted Power, nor the moment when I would have bartered principle for popular applause. Oh, Sir, what would be our condition if not sustained by, (infirmaty as it may be,) self-esteem!

If I should take a position in one of the bureaus of the Capitol, I should wish it to be quietly accomplished through some chief Clerk, who would regard the influence of Gentlemen in the House & Senate, & the coming Power after the 4th of March. I am a Democrat, & am a personal friend of Gen[era]l [Lewis] Cass. I am also, or have been, a conservative. General [Samuel] Houston probably knows me only through my first No. of State Rights, which he received last winter. I opposed Mr. [James K.] Polk; but as this is now a dying dynasty, I suppose it is not of much consequence to any body. Some other distinguished men, I am well known to—particularly to Mr. [Daniel] Webster, who was at the Bar with me in New Hampshire. The Rev[eren]d Mr. [Ralph R.] Gurley, chaplain of the *House* I think, knows me fully.

Had I not felt that I ought to acknowledge the receipt of your speech, I should deeply regret having troubled you with another letter—& *I shall* as it is. With the highest consideration, & perfect esteem, Your most Ob[edien]t Serv[an]t, E. Evans.

P.S. I love not boasting, Sir, nor esteem it; but I think if I had the position I have suggested, I could quiet the subject & leave it wholly Free—wholly to itself. I have a high opinion of mind—of moral influence—of the pen. I should write over the signature of the "North," & I should privately consult you.

ALS in ScCleA.

From Lewis F. Allen

Black Rock [N.Y.,] July 19, 1848

Dear Sir, The New York ["State" *interlined*] Agricultural Society will hold its Annual Cattle Show and Fair on the 5th 6th & 7th days of September next at Buffalo. The ["N.Y." *interlined*] State Exhibitions have now become objects somewhat allied to National importance in the Estimation of the public, and from the preparations making in various parts of this, as well as some neighboring States, ["individuals of" *interlined*] which purpose joining in our Exhibition, we anticipate a festival of uncommon interest this year. An attendance of at least 50,000 Strangers is confidently Expected.

It has been the rule of the ["former" *canceled*] presidents of the Society (and which position I now fill,) to invite some distinguished gentleman from abroad to deliver the annual address which is always the closing part of our labors—and as this duty now devolves on me, in behalf of the Society, I most respectfully and cordially invite you to discharge that office. Mr. [Daniel] Webster, of the Senate, Mr. [Martin] Van Buren, Gov. [William H.] Seward, Gov. [Silas] Wright, Mr. [George] Bancroft of Mass.—now minister at St. James, & other distinguished gentlemen have favored the Society thus in former years, and it would now give us the greatest pleasure to have so distinguished an agriculturist as well as so renowned a statesman as yourself discourse to our Society and the multitude ["to be" *interlined*] assembled on that occasion, as we know you can do—on the ["absorbing" *canceled and then interlined*] subject ["of agriculture" *interlined*] *and its Collateral* interests.

Several gentlemen of your State, whom I have had the pleasure of personally knowing, have favored us in previous years with their attendance. Among them was Col. [Robert F.W.] Alston, President, I believe, of your State Senate—and it is partially owing to a conversation I had with him last fall at Saratoga, in which, replying to a direct question of mine, ["he believed" *interlined*] that you would probably (if within the limits of your commune[?]) accept an invitation to address our Society, that I have ventured to ask this duty at your hands.

You are a frank man, Mr. Calhoun, as well as a sincere and an honest man—and I only say this now—which might otherwise appear mere flattery & commonplace ["elsewhere" *interlined*]—to preface what follows, which is, that from the political position which you hold in relation to this section of the United States you may feel that the prevailing sentiments of the people here would be prejudicial to your presence. Let me assure you, my dear Sir, that nothing would give us greater pleasure, than to welcome you into this quarter of the Union, and to take an "Honest Nullifier" by the hand, and to give you a free and hospitable reception at the hands of the *New York State Agricultural Society*. Rely on it, your presence among us will do good, all round. Many of our best men will be here. It will be *neutral ground*, when we all meet on a common footing and to discuss one great pervading and absorbing subject—the improvement of our agriculture. I have deemed it necessary to say thus much that you might be aware of our feeling towards you, should you, as I trust you may, come among us—and to put aside all bias in the matter, I will remark that I am myself a whig and opposed to your party in politics—but whig as I am, and having a most profound respect for your personal character and exalted patriotism, I should feel particularly honored in your acceptance of this invitation.

As I am an entire stranger to you personally, I beg to refer you, to either Messers. Senators [John A.] Dix, or [Daniel S.] Dickinson, or Gov. [John] Davis of Massachusetts, also of the Senate—Mr. N[athan] K. Hall of the H. Representatives or to Gen[era]l [Winfield] Scott of the army, to all of whom I am known.

Will you oblige me with an early reply, as in case of your refusal, which I trust will *not* be, I must apply to some other gentleman. The address will be delivered on the last day of the show 7th September. Very truly & respectfully Your friend & ob[edien]t Ser[van]t, Lewis F. Allen, Pres[iden]t, N.Y. State Ag[ricultural] Society.

P.S. I need hardly add that while with us you will be the guest of the Society—and in case you do come, an *early* arrival will be most welcome to us—L.F.A.

ALS in ScCleA; PEx in Boucher and Brooks, eds., *Correspondence*, pp. 458–459. NOTE: An AEU by Calhoun reads, "Invitation to deliver an ag[ricultura]l address."

To R[OBERT] H. GOODWYN and Others of the Committee, [Columbia, S.C.]

Washington, 19th July, 1848

Gentlemen; I greatly regret that my official duties here prevent me from accepting your invitation to be present at the festival to be given in honor of the Palmetto Regiment on the 26th inst. I, in common with the whole State, feel deeply indebted to our Regiment for the lofty bearing and heroic valor displayed by it on all occasions during the whole term of its service. Both officers and men, by their skill and bravery, have nobly sustained our flag, and by their achievements, reflected lasting honor on themselves and the State. They have fulfilled our expectations to the utmost, as high as it was. Beyond, it was impossible for them to go.

With these impressions, I heartily mingle my voice with that of the whole State, in a cordial welcome to the Gallant Palmetto Regiment on its return home. With great respect, I am, &c. &c., J.C. Calhoun.

PC in the Columbia, S.C., *South-Carolinian*, August 4, 1848, p. 1.

From R[OGER] JONES

A[djutant] G[eneral's] O[ffice,] Washington, July 19 1848

Dear Sir: In returning herewith the letter [of 6/15] of *Mr.* [Nathaniel R.] *Eaves* I respectfully inform you that, not a single recommendation in favor of volunteers for Certificates of merit under the 17th section of the act of March 3, 1847, has been received at this office. The Orders of Maj. Gen[era]l [Winfield] Scott, alluded to by Mr. E[aves] have been referred to, and are such as he represents; but what action, if any, was taken under them, I regret my inability to say.

The law referred to, I had supposed, did not embrace the volunteer service, for if otherwise it would present the incongruity of *one of the subalterns*, in a Company of volunteers receiving ["his commission" *interlined*] from the *President* of the United States, while the others, with the Captain and fixed officers derive their Commission, from the Governor of the State &c. Very resp[ectfull]y, R. Jones, Adj[utan]t Gen[era]l.

FC (No. 1471) in DNA, RG 94 (Adjutant General's Office), Letters Sent (Main Series), 1800–1890, 25:245 (M-565:16, frame 155).

R[OGER] JONES to A[ndrew] P. Butler and J[ohn] C. Calhoun

W[ar] D[epartment,] A[djutant] G[eneral's] O[ffice]
Washington, July 19, 1848

Gent.: Your letter of the 6th inst. to the President [James K. Polk] applying for the restoration of L[ucius] B. Northrop, late a Lieutenant in the 1st Dragoons, has been referred thro' the War Department to this Office, and in reply I respectfully inform you that on the 26th ult[im]o instructions were received from the Secretary of War [William L. Marcy] to re-appoint Lieut. Northrop in his regiment, which will be done accordingly on the happening of the first vacancy. I am Gent. &c, R. Jones, Adj[utan]t Gen[era]l.

FC (No. 1470) in DNA, RG 94 (Adjutant General's Office), Letters Sent (Main Series), 1800–1890, 25:245 (M-565:16, frame 155).

REMARKS ON THE COMPROMISE BILL

[In the Senate, July 19, 1848]

[John M. Clayton of Del., speaking for the select committee on Oregon, described and defended the bill. It provided for recognition of the slavery restriction already passed by the Oregon provisional territorial government insofar as it was not incompatible with the Constitution; and at the same time forbade territorial governments of California and New Mexico from legislating on the subject of slavery, thus indirectly affirming the Missouri Compromise. Clayton hoped the bill would provide a permanent adjustment of tension between the North and South. He added that he spoke only for himself and not formally for the committee, and that the bill spoke for itself.]

Mr. Calhoun. I am exceedingly gratified by the explanation of the Senator from Delaware. Had it not been made, it might have been supposed in some quarters that the whole committee had concurred in all the particular views which he for himself had expressed. I agree with him in testifying that it was the unanimous understanding of the committee that the bill should speak for itself; and I may add, that it was also understood by me that this was to be a permanent and not a temporary settlement of the whole question.

From *Congressional Globe*, 30th Cong., 1st Sess., p. 953. Also printed in the Washington, D.C., *Daily National Intelligencer*, July 20, 1848, p. 3; *Congressional Globe*, 30th Cong., 1st Sess., Appendix, p. 1140; Houston, ed., *Proceedings and Debates*, p. 898; Benton, *Abridgment of Debates*, 16:224. Variants in the Baltimore, Md., *Sun*, July 20, 1848, p. 4; the New York, N.Y., *Herald*, July 21, 1848, p. 4; the Charleston, S.C., *Courier*, July 24, 1848, p. 2.

From LEWIS F. ALLEN

New-York State Agricultural Society.
Agricultural Rooms,
Buffalo ["Albany" *canceled*] July 20 1848
Dear Sir, The N.Y. State Agricultural Society will hold its Annual Cattle Show and Fair in this city on the 5th 6th & 7th days of September next.

You are most respectfully and cordially invited to deliver the annual address before the Society on that occasion. The address will be delivered at the great tent of the Society on the show grounds in the afternoon of the 7th.

Should we be favored with your Services on this occasion we shall consider it a high honor conferred upon our Society and welcome you as one of the most distinguished Agriculturists of South Carolina, through whom New York will cordially extend the right hand of fellowship in that noble interest which is engrossing the highest talent and the acutest intelligence to promote in the greatest degree.

The annual address delivered before the Society is published with the Transactions of the Society for the year by order of the Legislature of New York Several thousand copies (bound) of which are distributed in this and other States and sent to the several Agricultural Societies of Europe and I need hardly add that it would exceedingly gratify the Society to be able to add an address from one who has been so long identified with the most absorbing questions in our national councils as well as highly distinguished as a practical and successful agriculturist.

An early answer will most oblige D[ea]r Sir your friend & ob[edien]t Serv[an]t, Lewis F. Allen, Pres[iden]t.

P.S. This should have accompanied [the s]emi-official letter which I forwarded [yes]terday as partially explanatory. I now send [yo]u two newspapers which will give you some [ide]a of the extent of our shows and the patronage they receive. I most ardently hope you will be enabled to comply with my request. Most respectfully y[ou]r ob[edien]t Serv[an]t, L.F. Allen.

Please direct to Black Rock P.O.

ALS in ScCleA. Note: An AEU by Calhoun reads, "Invitation to deliver the annual address before the New York Ag[ricultura]l Society."

From WILLIAM BIGGS

Vicksburg Miss., July 20 1848

D[ea]r Sir, Pardon the liberty I take in addressing you, (an entire stranger) but my great respect for you as a gentleman and statesman prompts me. Your recent great effort in the Senate, placing the South in her proper attitude has been in this region of country, grossly misrepresented and as I am, so great an admirer of you, and desirous of placing you in a proper position, must request a correct copy of your speech delivered on that subject. If not published in pamphlet form please refer me to a paper giving a correct report of it. The political horizon I look upon as dark and lowering, and I look to you as my polar star, my great hope, in the present emergency. You have on more than one occasion, relieved us from impending danger, and I fondly hope you may be able to do so again, but I must say I have great fears for the future. If however, a severance is forced upon us, as much as we may regret it, it becomes our duty to prepare for the result. At your convenience I should be glad to be favored with your views, from time to time, on the course persued by our northern breathren, and the imperative duty we owe to ourselves in preparing and defending as best we can. I am and always have been one of those so much abused thorough going States rights men, and consequently have admired your course more than any other man living, and hope yet to see the day when the people will not be so wedded to party, that justice and patriotism, cannot have its reward, and that you may be elevated to that position which I so much desire, "The chief magistracy of this nation."

I am the Brother of [Asa Biggs,] the former member of Congress from the first Dist. of No. Ca., now represented by Hon[ora]ble

D[avid] Outlaw, and must refer you to the Hon[ora]ble P[atrick] W. Tompkins [Representative from Miss.] as to who I am. Very Truly yours, William Biggs.

ALS in ScCleA. NOTE: An AEU by Calhoun reads, "Mr. Biggs. Send Speech."

From W[ILLIAM] W. HARLLEE

Marion C[ourt] H[ouse, S.C.,] 20 July 1848

Dear Sir, I have been for some time in receipt of your esteemed and valued favour in reply to mine, for which I hope you will accept my sincere thanks. It satisfies me more conclusively of the necessity of an independent position and a fearless adhesion to Southern interests in the game for the Presidency now playing by the partisans of the day. It is a contemptible game for power on both sides for which truth[,] consistency and principle would be willingly surrendered by each for success. Neither of the candidates have to my mind that manliness of purpose which could enlist the sympathies or call forth the energies of the patriotic advocates of *principle* in their behalf.

To Gen[era]l Cass my objections from the first were instinctive, as I felt that his associations, character and conduct were ["identified" *interlined*] with a class which would make it appear treasonable in *us* to fraternise with. His course at home and abroad has been ["that" *interlined*] of a time serving cringing sicophant who will swim with the tide if he can, without that stability of character which could be relied upon in an emergency.

Towards Gen[era]l Taylor my sympathies have tended as he is identified in interest with us and as his [J.S. Allison] letters *at first,* shewed the honesty, bluntness and integrity of an upright and ingenuous soldier, but recent developements I fear have exhibited an overweening desire for civil place and station which instead of elevating his character would go very far to wither the laurels he was [*sic*] won as a gallant soldier. His repudiation of the veto in that Allison letter, and his quiet acquiescence in the claims set up by the Abolitionists thus far convince me that we have little to hope for if we join the Whigs and the anomalous factions who will rally to his support. I can regard neither of the men as the honest representative of ["any" *changed to* "the"] principles I have chosen for my guide, neither of them approximate sufficiently to them to make me as yet forsake my identity as a southern man, and an adherent to the principles of my faith, and I feel therefore that there is at *this time* at least

604

no obligation on me to be the supporter or partisan of either. There is however an augury which has appeared since the speech delivered by you on the Wilmot Proviso that gives some hope of the Union of the South. If the South will take a position on this subject we shall be relieved from much difficulty. The Presidential election is a mere speck in comparison to what we have at stake, and all that we have to hope for can be gained by union amongst ourselves. Both parties at the North must yield to the justice of our position. It will not take long for one of them to see who is to gain most by *yielding first*; and if our own interest and safety can ["for awhile" *interlined*] give place for party speculations, I could feel much confidence in an early settlement of our troubles. "To this complexion it must come at last" if we make our *constitutional rights* the "sine qua non," of our recognition to either party and on this ground I for one at least am determined to stand.

I should not have troubled you with any reply on the subject of your letter, but ["for the" *interlined*] very kind and flattering manner in which you pleased to notice ["the" *altered to* "my"] importance personally in your confidential note.

It would afford me much satisfaction to yield to the desires of my friends on that point if I could be of any advantage in giving position to our own State and I should have done so ere this, but for the necessity of devoting this part of my life at least, to the preparations necessary to rear up and educate my children, and to provide for the future. The necessity of some action towards our immediate representative has struck me for some time past and I should have moved before this but for the fact, that being considered by many as the most available to supplant him if I commenced the opposition I should be called upon to take his place, which would involve a sacrifice of private interests that I do not think justified by the emergency, as there are others who could make them, and are willing to do so, who could perhaps ["as" *canceled*] give as much satisfaction to his constituency and could represent their interests as creditably, if not more so than myself. Gen[era]l [John] McQueen a sound, dignified and respectable gentleman, with better native talent than he has is now in the field, and was at the receipt of your letter, against him. I think his chances good for success. Whatever I can do consistent with the interests of my brother Dr. [Robert] H[arllee] who is a candidate for Senator from this District with opposition I shall do. So far as I am individually concerned for the present, I shall keep aloof & not even return to the Legislature, as I have accepted a position in the Wilmington & Manchester Rail R. Co. which is now going to work, & which if I can effect any thing in, I should regard of greater service to this section of the country than I could else-where[?] accomplish. With sentiments of the highest Respect, I am y[ou]r obed[ien]t S[ervan]t, W.W. Harllee.

ALS in ScCleA. NOTE: "Our immediate representative" is perhaps a reference to Representative Alexander D. Sims.

From J. MCNAUGHTON

Ogdensburgh, N.Y.
St. Lawrence County, July 20, 1848

Sir, Please send me a copy of your speech, in which—not distrusting the soundness & health of our governmental fabric—you had the boldness & the justice—which ignorance & fanaticism wonders at as "Sublime audacity"—to apply the pruning knife to error which lay too near the vitals of our liberty.

In this corner, far north, where, from appearances, disrespect to good faith & the Constitution is universally prevalent, there are not-withstanding firm friends of both, & they congratulate the lovers of liberty, that there is wisdom in the great Carolinian which prompts his exertions in her behalf, to maintaining the *equality* & *sovreignty* of the States, which alone can preserve the Union. Yours Respect-fully, J. McNaughton.

ALS in ScCleA.

REMARKS ON THE NAVAL APPROPRIATIONS BILL

[In the Senate, July 20, 1848]
[John M. Niles of Conn. proposed an amendment to withhold certain advances of funds to be made to contractors for mail transportation by ocean steamers.]

Mr. Calhoun said that when the bill first came before Congress he opposed its passage; but as it had become a law, and as he main-tained the principle that encouragement should be extended to con-tractors in the faithful performance of their contracts, he felt dis-posed to vote in favor of the proposition now before the Senate. In this determination he was strengthened by the fact that the proposition had met with the approbation of the head of the department [Secretary of the Navy John Y. Mason]. He would, therefore, vote in favor of giving this advance to the contractors.

[*There was extended debate among a number of Senators.*]

Mr. Calhoun. I can assure gentlemen that I had no idea of perverting or misconstruing the tone of the debate. The whole object of my remarks was, to bring out the true state of the case, inasmuch as my understanding of it heretofore was picked up informally. I now understand this subject before us to involve three contracts. For one, sir, I must say that I am altogether opposed to making the advances asked for. If the credit of the individuals asking for advances is good in ordinary times, they will have no difficulty in having the money they require loaned them. The application for these advances has been based mainly upon the ground of the tightness of the money market. That state of things has passed away.

[*John M. Clayton of Del. disputed Calhoun's contention that the money market had eased.*]

Mr. Calhoun. I do not think at any rate that the state of the money market should be the great consideration in this matter. Nothing is a good consideration but what is a *quid pro quo*. As to this whole affair my impressions from the beginning have been against it. I believe now, as I have ever believed, that it would be better to leave the matter open to private enterprise. I shall vote in favor of the motion made by the Senator from Connecticut.

From Houston, ed., *Proceedings and Debates*, pp. 906–907. Variant in the Baltimore, Md., *Sun*, July 21, 1848, p. 4; the Charleston, S.C., *Mercury*, July 24, 1848, p. 2; the Charleston, S.C., *Courier*, July 24, 1848, p. 2. Another variant in *Congressional Globe*, 30th Cong., 1st Sess., p. 964.

From ELLWOOD FISHER

Cincinnati, 7 mo[nth] 21, 1848

Dear Friend, It was not until the first of this month that the health of my family was sufficiently restored to make it prudent for me to leave home. And a few days ["afterwards" *interlined*] I was myself attacked with the same malady, influenza, with which they had been visited and I am but just getting well. My affairs have suffered so much by so much sickness that I am afraid they will prevent me from visiting Washington the present Session.

I have read with great satisfaction thy speech on the Oregon bill. It will probably produce a deeper effect on public opinion than any other even of thy speeches. The doctrine of natural equality as entertained by the mass of men seems to have been based in ancient times on the tradition or dream of a primitive golden age ["of equality," *interlined*], and among the Romans at least on the prophecy of its restoration which Virgil describes in his Pollio [*sic*]. Since the Christian dispensation a millenium has been expected. Hence the sects of Protestant reformers as they have successively arisen have announced their approximation to that era, and have insisted on a greater degree of equality among their own members, and when they obtained political power have as in New England and Pennsylvania ["insisted on" *canceled and* "established" *interlined*] greater equality of political condition. This sentiment has operated as a strong auxiliary to the political theories of [John] Locke and [Algernon] Sydney in this country. And in attempting to maintain this doctrine against the existence of African slavery and against the effects of accumulated capital as the country advances in wealth, we behold the rise of abolition and ["agrag" *canceled*] agrarian parties. The conflict rapidly approaches. The South has been much influenced by northern literature and the press on the subject and has been much misled. But such is the magnitude and prominence of its interest in maintaining its existing condition that I do not see much danger immediately from without or within. In the North on the contrary the struggle between capital and labour is more serious and with universal suffrage I don't see how property will be able to sustain itself.

Much distraction and confusion prevail here among the several parties and much discontent with all. I believe if the election were to occur immediately not more than three fourths of the voters would attend the polls. In Kentucky the coolness of many friends of [Henry] Clay towards [John J.] Crittenden and the actual opposition of some, will render his majority small perhaps not over two thousand. In this State extensive disaffection exists among the Whigs and not a little among the Democrats and I regard the vote of Ohio as very uncertain.

I was dissappointed in the nomination of [Zachary] Taylor. A Telegraphic despatch was received at Louisville by W[illiam] J. Graves [former Representative from Ky.] from [Josiah] Randall of Philadelphia both leading friends of Taylor, a little before the Whig Caucus met, announcing that Taylor was given up. And it was on that circumstance I wrote what I did in my last letter. How it came about that the Ohio Whig delegation threw off their vote on [Winfield] Scott who never had in this State a tythe of Clay[']s strength I have never understood nor does Clay. He is sore, and refuses to ratify publicly the nomination of Taylor although he declares that he will vote for him.

I believe that the adoption of the Miss[ouri] Compromise substantially, would satisfy the mass of both parties here: although a large number would pronounce for repeal: and might ultimately agitate a majority in its favour. Among the mass of the people *as yet* a good deal of apathy prevails on the subject—but the talkers and scribblers of both parties oppose the rights of the South to any portion of the acquired territory. One good effect of the nomination of Taylor has been to compel the Whig leaders to desist from anti slavery doctrines.

For my own part although I thought it would be difficult for circumstances to arise which would prevent me from taking some part in the canvass yet I find myself compelled now to adopt a masterly inactivity. The election of [Lewis] Cass I would consider as the adoption by the country of the policy of making War with every nation with whom a quarrel could be provoked: that of Taylor I regard as a final exclusion of civilians from the Presidency. Between evils both of such magnitude I cannot consider it the duty of a citizen to choose—he had better assume the responsibility of neither.

I have seen some evidence of a purpose to establish in the South a party of its own with a candidate of its own. This I think the proper course and the only hesitation I have as to its expediency is the unaccountably [*sic*] apathy of the South on such an occasion as this. Perhaps events are at hand to change this state of things. At all events I hope our friends will not permit themselves to be submerged in either of the existing parties. With greatest regard thy friend, Ellwood Fisher.

ALS in ScCleA.

From JAMES L. GOULD

Yale College, July 21st/48
Linonian Society

Dear Sir, Being requested by the above Society to address you I do it in their language and for them & would respectfully ask of you answers to the following questions inasmuch as it has been asserted that you never belonged to our Society while in College and never signed your name to the Constitution where it stands written. And in proof of this assertion they claim that they have in their possession a letter from you signifying the same which we deny and to clear up these points of controversy I have in the name of Linonia addressed you. Did you ever belong to the Linonian Society of Yale College? Did you ever belong to any Society in College? Did you sign your name to the Constitution of the Linonian Society? By answering soon as convenient these queries you will greatly oblige your humble Servants, the Members of Linonia ["and" *canceled*] who are unwilling to admit that you was not an active member of their Society. With high considerations of Respect and Honor your Humble Servant, James L. Gould, Yale College, N. Haven Ct.

ALS in ScCleA.

From S[ylvester] Graham

Northampton Mass., July 21, 1848
Dear Sir, Two years ago, I took the liberty to address you on the subject of the Presidency, and asked you to consider the importance of compromise on the part of our leading statesmen, in selecting and supporting presidential candidates. I expressed and [*sic*] ardent desire to see both Mr. [Henry] Clay and yourself elected to that high office; and entreated you to favor the election of Mr. Clay on the highest and noblest grounds of patriotism, and as the surest and most honorable means of securing your own succession. I know not whether you found time to read my letter, or regarded it as worth your time to read it. However it may be, it has not been my honor to receive any acknowledgement of the letter from you.

I have just this moment closed the reading of your Senatorial speech on the Oregon Bill, delivered on the 27th ult.: as presented to me in the New York Tribune. I had heard some of our most learned men—members of the Bar and of the Bench—speak of it as highly sophistical and fallacious; and declare that, in their opinion, you could not have been honest and sincere in uttering it. But the impression which I have received from the perusal of it, is totally different. I have read it with great interest and—pardon me for adding—not a little pride. Fifteen years ago—in the autumn of

610

1833—I was invited to address the Lyceum of New Bedford. I took for my tex[t] or subject on the occasion, the words in the opening of the Declaration of Independence—"All men are created equal;" and made a speech of about forty five minutes length; in which I advanced exactly the same views that you have, on the same subject, in the Senatorial speech before me. I said—as you say—that, however plausible and acceptable the sentiment of this proposition, a great fallacy lay at the bottom of it—that all men were not created: only the first pair were created, and the rest were born, not men, but infants; not equal, but in physical, mental and moral constitution and capabilities greatly unequal—in very unequal circumstances, and under very unequal influences; and almost everything in the circumstances, events and influences surrounding and acting upon us, as individuals, from birth to death, served to increase the inequalities between us—making us greatly unequal in bodily health, strength, ability to labor, power of endurance, &c; greatly unequal in intellectual education, scope, energy, sagacity &c; greatly unequal as to [*one word altered to* "virtue and vice"]; greatly unequal as to independence or servility of spirit; greatly unequal as to enterprize and indolence; greatly unequal as to wealth and poverty: in short, greatly unequal in every respect. It was regarded as great temerity in me to dare to controvert the "sublime doctrine" of Thomas Jefferson, But I never had so much reverence for human authority as for ["the" *erased*] truth; albeit it is gratifying to me to find one of the best analytical minds in our political world, according so perfectly with my own.

Six years ago—in the autumn of 1842—the question came up in one of our political meetings—Is it expedient to form a third political party, or a party of political abolitionists? I took the negative of this question, and entered into an extensive and scrutinizing inquiry as to the legitimate authority and power of Congress in relation to Slavery. This inquiry led me into a summary review and analysis of all human Governments—contemplating man in his individual, social and political capacities, states, relations &c; the primary source of political power and sovereignty; the distribution, adjustment and economy of political power in the several forms of human Government, the origin, character and purposes of our own State & Federal Governments, &c, &c. I spoke without interruption, and with great earnestness for four hours and a quarter; and presented exactly the same views on the subject that you have in the Speech before me. I showed, by precisely the same course of reasoning, that Congress has no constitutional, no legitimate right nor power to abolish slavery in the several States, nor in the District of Columbia (except as the special legislature of the District, and then only as the true representatives of the people of the District, acting in accordance with their will) nor to abolish nor prohibit Slavery in the territories; nor any legitimate authority to prohibit the introduction of slavery into any of the free States in the Union; that Massachusetts, if she chose to do so, could, at any time, become a Slave State, and Congress has no authority, no constitutional power to prevent it, and no right to meddle with it; except so far as the institution affected the relations and reciprocities ["of" *erased*] between the State of Massachusetts and other States; and so far, only to regulate it so as to secure the equal rights, and preserve the peace and harmony, and promote the common prosperity of the several co-ordinate States of the Federal Union: and that the ordinance of 1787 prohibiting Slavery in the northwestern territories was the result of the exercise of purely usurped power. These views were shockingly surprising and almost astounding to the good citizens of Massachusetts who listened to me; and the next evening, two of the ablest lawyers of the place (one of whom now sits high upon the Bench of the Supreme Court of Massachusetts) came out against me, and did their best to refute my argument and demolish my positions. I replied to them on the third evening; and there the debate ended. No man seemed disposed to prolong ["it" *interlined*].

I think, therefore, you will not consider it unbecoming in me to say that I have read your speech which so fully sustains me—which is so nearly identical, in views and reasonings, with my own, with great interest and no little pride. And Sir, a principal object in my addressing you on this occasion, is to ask you to send me a copy of your Speech in pamphlet form, as revised by yourself, that I may preserve it.

I cannot close this letter with entire self respect, however, without ingenuously avowing to you, that, I cannot regard the institution of slavery in the same light that you do. That most men, in your situation should regard it as you do, would not surprise me. But that you—and I speak not in flattery, but in solemn honesty—that you who possess a mind of such extensive information, of such keenly analytical and rigorously philosophical power, should so regard it, is a matter both of great surprise and deep regret to me. For to my mind, it is a clear philosophical certainty that the institution of Slavery is a very great evil—greater, perhaps to the master than to the Slave—greater to our nation than to the colored race. And because I sincerely wish to see you in all respects, an illustrious specimen of manhood, I wish that you regarded Slavery as Mr. Jefferson professed to regard it. Yours with profound respect, S. Graham.

ALS in ScCleA. Note: An AEU by Calhoun reads, "Mr. Graham. Send Speech."

From Dr. J[AMES] B. DAVIS

Constantinople, July 22nd 1848
My D[ea]r Sir, Since I have witnessed the hostile feeling of Europe, particularly of England towards the institution of slavery, I have looked with much anxiety to the future in my own country. Our destiny must abide Public opinion. The tide of public opinion has been setting against us all over Europe, and we have never made an effort to check or aid its ultimate formation. While the Northern fanatic disseminates his falsehoods over the whole world, we have not a Journal that reaches beyond the limits of the United States to contradict and convict him. I made a slow tour through Europe to this place two years ago, and conversed with a great many English & French. Since I have been here, my opportunities have been no less frequent; and I have never conversed with one individual who had any idea of the relative position of master & slave, of their treatment &c; and I have seldom left a man whose opinions & feelings were not entirely changed, or who was not brought to doubt whether the institution of slavery was not a blessing. The subject has been invariably introduced, & the information sought after, by them.

The deplorable condition of agriculture in the hot climates of Europe[,] Asia[,] Africa & America, where black slave labour is not employed, illustrates one fact, that no *white* man can labour in the *hot* sun of the South, and the *free black man will not.* The West Indies, at the present moment, is a lesson to the world if they will read it.

The experience I have had in the cultivation of Cotton in Turkey satisfies me that Cotton cannot be made without loss, if *control-*[*l*]*able* labour is not used—and that is the extent of slavery in America.

The whole of Europe has ever demonstrated the fact that inasmuch as the white labouring population cannot be educated—and, even in the most degraded state of ignorance ever sensible that they are born equal, and not destined by the Creator to be *always* menial, they are ever on the look out for change, at any hazard. The conse-

613

quence is easily seen, that in all *warm* climates, where the poor are always indolent, ignorant[,] vicious & miserable there has been & will be revolution after revolution to the end of time. Temporarily they have & can be kept down by despotic Governments, but this seems[?] now [*two or three words canceled*] has passed. The *negro* knows, acts & feels that God has put a mark of inferiority upon him & this of itself secures his individual satisfaction & happiness.

Such facts with the comparative exemption from riot and disorder, and the acknowledged superiority of the educated class in slave compared with other countries, have never failed to produce a strong impression on those I have met with, in favour of the institution of slavery.

We have had in Constantinople for sometime past Mr. C[harles] M[a]cfarlane of England, of literary reputation, a man alike distinguished for his general information, for his good sense, & his English politics. He is a thorough Englishman, and will sustain English institutions in England while he admires America, and would never wish to see her government & institutions changed. He has ever held the same opinions as yourself on the subject of slavery. And for the sake of drawing England and America nearer together, & perpetuating by mutual interests and combined power their great & liberal institutions, he is determined to wage war against all fanaticism—to oppose Abbolitionism [*sic*] in the north, as he has ever condem[n]ed emancipation in the West Indies. I have suggested to him and my Brother N.H. Davis now here, an enterprise certainly of no small importance to our country, and one which demands your cordial support viz. to establish an Anglo American paper in London, which is to be the organ of the South on this great subject, as well as of Agriculture, Politics, Commerce & Literature.

I am well assured a more suitable person than Mr. Mcfarlane could not be found on the English side. My Brother if he is not himself equal to the task will secure equal abilities from America: but he is of the Carolina school, & looking upon it as a project of great magnitude, he will abide a conference of persons entirely co-operating in this ["magnitude" *canceled and* "enterprise" *interlined*]. I therefore beg your plan of its organization sent here as soon as possible.

My Brother has written by this mail, to F[ranklin] H. Elmore & others of his friends. I trust it will meet with your hearty cooperation and that we shall have a well digested plan, which will be entered into as soon as arrangements can be made.

Mr. Mcfarlane thinks that when once started by the People of the ["Southern" *changed to* "South"], Merchants & Planters, & recognized as *authority*, it will become a mighty engine in Europe & that a large number of persons of influence are now staggered by the condition of Europe & the West Indies. They consider this apprenticeship a "specious pretext" and are willing to listen to reason. Very resp[ectfull]y your &, J.B. Davis, M.D.

P.S. Pardon the omission [that is, the blankness] of this page as I must write other letters this mail & can't write it over—my eyes are bad, & painful to write.

ALS in ScCleA; PEx in Jameson, ed., *Correspondence*, pp. 1177–1179.

From J[OHN] H. HOWARD

Columbus [Ga.,] July 22nd '48
My D[ea]r Sir, I have read your speech upon the Oregon bill with a great deal of pleasure. Fanaticism in the plenitude of its wildness cannot be insensible to the justice of its rebuke, while Northern intelligence & Northern virtue must acknowledge the triumphant refutation of the doctrines which they have too long maintained. I wish the speech were in every house from, the Mexican to the Canada line. I have such reliance upon truth that I believe your speech so clear & incontrovertible will have the effect to settle the question if it can but receive a general circulation through the length & breadth of our glorious union. Your friends, & the real friends of the Constitution & the Union every where would do much for the stability of the government & the rights of every section, to lay this speech upon the table of every reader. It *must* and *will* have a powerful influence in all circles, and cannot fail to moderate the violent & convince the thinking.

Col. [James S.] Calhoun, late from Mexico proposes to raise a regiment of *Georgians* to settle in California upon your policy of defending the lines of our territory from Mexican aggression. I approve his plan though it is not yet matured. He will go to Washington ["in a day or two" *interlined*] for the purpose of getting the authority from the President [James K. Polk] or from congress. I have advised him to confer with you and I hope you will be able to concoct some plan to effect his object. We want a fair start in the territory & should throw into it all the Southern influence, which we may be able to do. Calhoun's purpose is to carry with him men of

615

superior character to the common soldier picked[?] up about the towns & cities, who will go there for the purpose of identifying themselves permanently with the country. I hope his views may meet your approbation, as they have my fullest confidence, and while you are serving him you will serve the country more. Yours with much respect, J.H. Howard.

ALS in ScCleA.

FURTHER REMARKS ON THE TERRITORIAL COMPROMISE BILL

[In the Senate, July 22, 1848]
[*John M. Niles of Conn. made a reference to the bill as accepting the claims of "the advocates of slavery here."*]

Mr. Calhoun. Will the Senator yield for a moment? I beg that the Senator will not represent me as an advocate of slavery. That is not the attitude which we maintain. We stand here only as claiming the rights which belong to us as confederated members of this Union, and we are willing to rest our rights upon the high ground on which the Senator from Delaware [John M. Clayton] has placed them, where our forefathers placed them, and where we place them. That is all. We claim nothing for slavery—nothing at all. We wish to see this Union preserved, and its harmony preserved with it; for it is worthy to be preserved only upon the principles of harmony.

[*There was extended debate. Roger S. Baldwin of Conn. presented an amendment which would eliminate the provisions of the bill regarding New Mexico and California, leaving only Oregon with the tacit slavery restriction.*]

Mr. Calhoun. I rise to make but a single remark. Every Senator must know that the decision on this amendment will determine the fate of the bill.

[*The amendment was defeated 17 to 37.*]

From *Congressional Globe*, 30th Cong., 1st Sess., Appendix, pp. 1141, 1145. Also printed in Houston, ed., *Proceedings and Debates*, pp. 919, 923. Variant in *Congressional Globe*, 30th Cong., 1st Sess., p. 988. Another variant in the Baltimore, Md., *Sun*, July 24, 1848, p. 4; the Charleston, S.C., *Mercury*, July 27, 1848, p. 2. Other variants in the New York, N.Y., *Herald*, July 24, 1848, p. 2; the Charleston, S.C., *Courier*, July 27, 1848, p. 2. NOTE: This debate was evidently imperfectly reported. In the first variant cited, Calhoun is reported as interjecting brief remarks into a discussion between Samuel S. Phelps of Vt. and James D.

Westcott, Jr., of Fla. as to whether the bill would prevent the territorial legislature of Oregon from legislating regulations for slaves and free blacks. "Mr.
Calhoun said the committee did not pretend to settle the question. It was left
where the Constitution placed it." And in the second variant cited, Calhoun was
reported as concurring with Daniel S. Dickinson of N.Y. on the power of the
territorial legislatures to make domestic regulations: "Mr. Calhoun made a few
remarks of a similar character as to this power of punishing black criminals in
these territories, about which he conceived there would be no difficulty."

J[ohn] C. Calhoun and Others to ROBERT J. WALKER, [Secretary of the Treasury]

[Washington] July 22nd 1848

Sir, we beg leave to recommend to you for ["appraiser" *canceled*] In-
spector for the Port of Charleston South Carolina, of adulterated
Drugs John M. Clapp, a Gentleman of high literary and scientific
attainments. J.C. Calhoun, A[ndrew] P. Butler, R[obert] B[arn-
well] Rhett, R[ichard] F. Simpson, D[aniel] Wallace, A[rmistead]
Burt, J[oseph] A. Woodward.

LS (in Rhett's handwriting) in DNA, RG 56 (General Records of the Department of the Treasury), Applications for Appointment as Customs Service Officers,
1833–1910, box 19, John Clapp. NOTE: An EU reads, "App[oin]t Mr. Clapp &
so inform Mr. Rhett."

From JOHN CARROLL WALSH

The Mound, Harford Co[unty] Md.
near Jerusalem Mills P.O., 22d July 1848

My dear Sir, You are no doubt aware that the course Gen[era]l
[Zachary] Taylor has pursued, directly, himself, since the Whig Convention, and indirectly through the Louisiana delegation, in that
Convention, has entirely dissevered the connection between him and
his independent friends throughout the Country. As one of those
who espoused his cause in the State, I feel myself free to say I have
been deceived in the man, and what I mistook for a high, honorable,
and independent course appears to have been one of consummate
fraud, and deceit. I can also say, that in common with other of your
friends, in this State, one great inducement with us to join the independent movement in behalf of Gen[era]l Taylor, was, the belief at

the time you were favorably disposed towards him. Our Independent State Convention, meets on the 27th (Thursday next) in Baltimore, when from the enclosed communication [*not found*] you will see I suggest the maintenance of an independent organization under your leadership.

Not wishing to act precipitately, or without your consent, I would be pleased to hear if it meets your approbation that your name should be brought before our Convention for the purpose indicated. There is no manner of doubt, that many of our best citizens, now attached to both parties, would far prefer seeing you in the Presidential Chair to any one living, and who would if they were allowed an opportunity gladly prove it by their suffrages.

If you reply to this immediately you will direct to me Jerusalem Mills, Harford Co[unty] Md. and I will receive your letter on Tuesday, if you should delay replying until after Monday night, you will direct to me, Baltimore, as I shall leave home for B[altimore] on Wednesday so as to be there by Thursday morning.

The mail which leaves Washington on Monday night reaches here on Tuesday evening, and then we get no mail until Thursday, it being a tri weekly one.

I presume it is scarcely necessary to mention, that any communication which you may be pleased to make, shall, unless otherwise desired, be considered by me as sacredly confidential. With true regards Very faithfully Yours, Jno. Carroll Walsh.

ALS in ScCleA.

To THO[MAS] G. CLEMSON, [Brussels]

Washington, 23d July 1848

My dear Sir, I received in the regular course of the steamer yours of the 27th of June, and Anna's [Anna Maria Calhoun Clemson's] to her mother [Floride Colhoun Calhoun] of the same date. I would have answered ["it" *canceled and* "yours" *interlined*], immediately, but was prevented by the pressure of my official engagements, as a member of the Committee, raised to settle the question of slavery, as it relates to our recently acquired territory. After a laborious effort of more than a week, the Committee, consisting of 8 members, 4 from each party, & 2 from each division of the party, North & South, selected by their respective sections, agreed on a bill, with scarcely a division, which is now under discussion in the Senate, with a fair prospect of passing by a large majority; & which I hope will permanently settle this vexed & dangerous question. The settlement is based on the principle of non interference, as laid down in my speech on the Oregon territorial bill, of which I send you a copy, accompanying this. It was found, after trying every other, that it was the only one, on which there was the least chance of adjusting it. It is regarded here, as a great triumph on my part. A trial vote in the Senate yesterday, stood 37 in favour of the bill against 17 opposed. The opposition is mainly composed of the supporters of Mr. [Martin] Van Beuren [*sic*].

As to the Presidential election, it is very doubtful, & will probably remain so, to the last. There is no enthusiasm about it. There are great objections to both candidates.

The progress of events in Europe is very much such as I anticipated. There are too much error and misconception of a deep & dangerous character at the bottom of the movement to hope for much good. I have briefly touched one of the leading in the speech, that goes with this, at its close. There are others not less dangerous.

I had a letter from your overseer not long since. He writes, that the crop was promising.

I read with pain the part of your letter relating to our private affairs. I certainly must have been very unfortunate in my expressions, if they be such, as to justify you in the long train of remarks, in which you have indulged. I shall abstain from any comments on them. They have satisfied me, that we ought never to have any pecuniary transactions between us, and I shall be as anxious to terminate ["of" *canceled*] all of the kind, when we meet, as you possibly can be; when I hope all possibility of any difference between ["us" *interlined*] will cease.

I am happy to learn that you have obtained leave of absence; and, as I learn from Anna's letter to her mother, that she & the children will accompany you, provided your means will admit, I have made arrangement to remit to you $600 in order to remove any possible difficulty on that score. The remittance will be made in the course of three or four days, & I will apprise you of it as soon as the arrangement is closed. If you had apprised me earlier of your determination to ask for leave, it would have been remitted sooner but I hope it will be in time. It would be a great disappointment and a loss of much happiness ["both on" *canceled*] should she & the children not accompany you.

Congress will probably adjourn about the 20th next month.

With love to Anna & the children I remain Your affectionate father, J.C. Calhoun.

ALS in ScCleA; PEx in Jameson, ed., *Correspondence*, pp. 759–760.

From R[ICHARD] K. CRALLÉ

Lynchburg, July 23rd 1848

My dear Sir: I received, some days ago, your favour of the 10th inst.; and by the mail before the last a pamphlet copy of your speech on the Oregon Question. I had, however, read it before as published in the National Intelligencer—the Paper having been handed to me for that purpose. Both Paper and Pamphlet have since passed from my hands, for great is the interest it has excited, especially amongst the grave and thinking portion of the Community. My attention was first called to it by Mr. [Chiswell] Dabney, the President of the Bank of Virginia here, and a leading member of the Bar, who pronounced it the ablest argument he ever read. Though a leading Whig, and hitherto by no means a political friend, it has so affected him that he hesitates not to say that he would prefer to see your name before the Country above all other men for the Presidency. He cannot, he says, vote for either of the Candidates now before the People. His feelings and opinions have an echo in the bosoms of thousands of others, if they would give them expression.

As far as my own opinion may go, I concur with those to whom you refer in your letter, that it is the ablest, the most philosophical I have ever read. As to its *arguments* there can be no answer—and its philosophical reflections near the close deserve to be read as a morning and evening lesson in every man's family. I have read it this morning aloud to some company, and though it was the Sabbath, it has furnished a topic of conversation for most of the time spent with me. It furnishes material for a volume, and it would be well if some competent hand would review it *seriatim* in one of our established literary Reviews.

I have compared the grounds it covers—the views and arguments contained in it, with those heretofore occupied and urged by Messrs. [Charles] Pinckney, [William L.] Brent, [John] Sergeant [Representative from Pa.] and others in 1820, when the Missouri Compromise was before Congress, and, saving in some points, none even approach it except the speech of Mr. Pinckney—and his only as to facts in

620

reference to the ordinance of 1787. He states ["only" *canceled*] that only 17 or 18 members were present, and that the Congress—the Convention then being in session, had dwindled into utter insignificance. His arguments however are tame and common place. As to the tone, character, force and effect of this speech, I declare to you, I had rather be the author of it than to be the possessor of any earthly office. It will live when our institutions are only matters of history.

But what is to be the end? I rejoiced to see that you were one of the Committee, but I fear you will not be sustained. To run a direct line would be but an extension of the Compromise; and while it might give *temporary quiet,* I fear it would but strengthen a precedent which has already produced bitter fruits. It would seem to yield up forever the Constitutional question, and this will sooner or later draw after it all the powers now claimed by the Abolitionists. It would be better, *for the future* to leave the question open as you suggest, but I much fear you cannot do this even without danger. For, unless guarded against, it might bring up Bayley's [*sic*; Thomas H. Bayly, Representative from Va.] notion of the right of the Judiciary to act finally on the question of slave *property*, during the existence of the Territorial Government. But you will, I am sure, guard all these points as well as you can. The question *will unite the South*—of this I have no doubt—and you can safely occupy the strongest grounds. [Lewis] Cass is not strong enough to stagger the South on the question. *If there be peace,* he may, perhaps, unite the Party to a considerable extent; but if his friends take a wrong position on the subject he will lose every State. His hold on the Party is already slight and daily weakening. I think it highly probable, if Whiggery do not, as usual run mad, that he will lose Virginia in despite of [Thomas] Ritchie and the organization. The defection of [Martin] Van Buren has shaken men's confidence in the integrity of Norththron [*sic*] aspirants for favour. Both Parties, I verily believe, would this day gladly compromise on you. Situated as I am it is impossible to see far on the horizon; but if the Buffalo Convention should much further disturb the political elements, it may yet become necessary to look beyond the present candidates. [Zachary] Taylor, I dare say, preserves his hold, but the tenure is by no means strong *as yet.* I have been *forced* out twice before the people, but the result, as I designed, has been to disturb the leaders on both sides. I have on good authority, that arrangements are being made to invite me to Richmond and to Charlotte C[ourt] H[ouse] and to several other places. With my present information I am unwilling to answer the call. I prefer Taylor as the only means, *as things at present stand,* to get rid of that infernal dynasty which has so long corrupted the Country—but I designed not to take any part in the canvass. Your last letter gives me no clue to your own views. If you wish that they should be unknown for the present, do not, I beseech you, say a word in reply on this head. You ought not, and I am sure *will not* take any *active part* in the canvass. Neither your principles, standing, position or character will allow this. The grounds you occupy are too high, and the responsibilities of your position too momentous to admit of it. The remarks of Mr. [Isaac E.] Holmes [Representative from S.C.] leaves the public to think that you will favour Taylor, and even my own course has, *I am told,* been mentioned in the newspapers as "ominous" of this. I can relieve you of the suspicion if you desire it—and, indeed, have discussed the matter with myself whether I ought not to do so. A *word* from you will answer on the subject.

It may be proper in this connection to state that, in what I have said to the public, I have steadily avoided committing even myself. The grounds I have taken are the [*sic*] Gen. Taylor is the safer candidate *so far as the slave question is concerned,* but that, if he acknowledged himself to be *the candidate of the Whig Party,* in the ordinary acceptation of the term, I could not support him. The time is come, I think, when the mastery of these two factions is in your own hands. The divisions in their respective *cliques* have so weakened both, (if the Buffalo Convention act as I suppose it will) that you can, in a measure, dictate terms. You are yet *young in Constitution—vigorous in intellect,* and we who have looked to you for so many years, with warm, and honest and hopeful hearts, fondly cling to the patriot's, the *Christian's* trust that God will spare you either *in person* to retrieve the lost honor of the country, or to leave things in such a condition that weaker and humbler men may do it, should Providence call you from the theater of action. This is my trust—it has been my *hope* for many years. Parties must be organized on different grounds, or the worst consequences must follow. You have a high and independent position. There is no Senator in your body who is a *free man,* except yourself. Your State alone can be surely relied on. You can look to the *Country*—others must look to *their places.* In this there is high *moral sublimity*—as well as vast *political power.* How they shall be employed, I leave, with the most perfect confidence, without even a *thought of care,* to yourself. As to the *Country,* I know it will be the wisest and the best—as *to yourself,* I regard the future as already written, and feel not the least misgiving that he whom I and others have loved and trusted, as *first* in mind and morals, will be *first* in the estimation of posterity.

I write in great haste—and have not time to overlook what is written. If Mrs. [Floride Colhoun] Calhoun and Miss [Martha] Cornelia [Calhoun] be with you, (as I infer from your letter,) present to them both our joint and affectionate salutations. With high regard and esteem I am truly yours, R.K. Crallé.

P.S. As I am extremely anxious to know what course the Committee has adopted, I would thank you for a copy of their Report as soon as it appears.

ALS in ScCleA; PEx's in Boucher and Brooks, eds., *Correspondence*, pp. 459–460.

From B[ARTHOLOMEW] R. CARROLL

Charleston, July 24[t]h 1848
My dear Sir, There are gentlemen in this city said to be in correspondence with you, who are circulating the report that they have your authority for saying, that Gen. [Lewis] Cass'[s] letter [of 12/-29/1847] to Mr. [Alfred O.P.] Nicholson, does not sustain the positions of the South as expressed and insisted upon in your late speech on the Oregon Bill. Will you be kind enough to say whether their inference is correct[?] And if the views in the Nicholson letter differ from your own—in what particulars?

A large portion of your friends in this city are of opinion that Gen. [Zachary] Taylor is too latitudinarian in his opinions—and therefore, unsafe to be supported by South Carolina; and while at present they are disposed to hold back, they desire to prepare for the event of having to sustain Gen. Cass. A reply to the above, at your earliest leisure, will, in behalf of many of your friends oblige Y[ou]r ob[edien]t Ser[van]t &c, B.R. Carroll.

ALS in ScCleA.

Further remarks on the compromise territorial bill, 7/24. Thomas Corwin of Ohio attributed to Calhoun the position "that we were under obligations to preserve forever" equal numbers between the free and slave states. "Mr. Calhoun. I said nothing of the kind." From *Congressional Globe*, 30th Cong., 1st Sess., Appendix, p. 1163.

Also printed in the Washington, D.C., *Daily Union*, December 5, 1848, p. 2; Houston, ed., *Proceedings and Debates*, p. 944. Variant in the New York, N.Y., *Herald*, July 26, 1848, p. 4.

John C. Calhoun and Others to Maj. Gen. WINFIELD SCOTT

WASHINGTON, JULY 24, 1848

SIR: It affords us great pleasure to hand to you the enclosed invitation to a public dinner, at such time as may suit your convenience.

The desire of all is to manifest, not only their admiration for your distinguished services during the whole of your military career, but no less their personal regard and friendship for yourself.

Will you oblige us by naming such early time for the dinner as may suit your convenience. Very respectfully, your obedient servants, John M. Clayton, John C. Calhoun, Rob[er]t C. Winthrop, John A. Rockwell, Moses Hampton.

[Appended:] The Invitation.

The UNDERSIGNED wish to tender to Gen. SCOTT the honor of a public dinner, at such time as may suit his convenience. Deeply impressed with the great services he has rendered the country in the war with Mexico, just closed with the important agency he has had in consummating an early and honorable peace, and, most of all, desiring to show our respect for the patriotism, humanity, skill, and bravery of a man whose whole life has been one of ardent devotion to the public good, alike in war and peace, we desire personally to tender him this mark of our common regard for his services as a soldier, and his virtues as a man. [Signed by 108 persons, including "a large number of Senators and Representatives," and "other Citizens."]

PC in the Washington, D.C., *Daily National Intelligencer*, August 14, 1848, p. 3; PC in the Richmond, Va., *Whig and Public Advertiser* (semi-weekly), August 18, 1848, p. 4.

To LEWIS F. ALLEN, "Pres[iden]t N.Y. A[gricultural] S[ociety]," [Black Rock, N.Y.]

Washington, 25th July 1848

Dear Sir, I am in the receipt of [your] communication of the 19th Inst., informing me, that I have been selected to deliver the annual

Ad[d]ress before the New York State Agricultural Society, which will hold its annual Cattle show & fair on the 5, 6, & 7th of September next, at Buffalo.

I feel greatly honored by the selection and would be happy to meet the wishes of the Society, but it is entirely out of my power. My private and domestick engagements and duties, will compel me to return home as soon as I am released from my official duties here, which I fear will not be much before the time assigned for the delivery of the Address.

I am under obligations to you for the very kind terms, in which you have made known the wishes of the Society. Be assured, nothing of a political character could have induced the least hesitancy in meeting its wishes, if circumstances had been such, as to permit me to accept the honor tendered me, for so I consider it. I freely accord to all the right I claim for myself on all occasions, of a full & free expression of opinion. As a devoted friend of agriculture, I do not permit political, or party difference to have any influence with me in whatever is calculated to advance its interest, or promote its prosperity. With great respect I am & &, J.C. Calhoun.

ALS in NcD, John C. Calhoun Papers.

From J[OHN] C. C. BLACKBURN

Barnesville Ga., July 25th, 1848

Respected Sir: Having ever looked upon you as the guiding star of my political course, I would most respectfully solicit your views upon the next Presidential issue: Do you think Gen. Lewis Cass sound upon the "Wilmot Proviso"? and if not do you think a "South Carolina nul[l]ifier" would be acting consistently to support Gen. [Zachary] Taylor, knowing at the same time that he is the nominee of the Whig Party. Your answer to this ["letter" *interlined*] is most respectfully solicited by one, who, though a stranger to you personally, feels proud to bear your name, as well as to recognize in you a strong supporter of the rights of Southerners. Very Respectfully, J.C.C. Blackburn, M.D.

ALS in ScCleA.

Remarks on the Missouri Compromise, 7/25. In the course of a long speech on the slavery and territories question, James D. Westcott, Jr., of Fla., stated that Calhoun, the only surviving member of James Monroe's cabinet, had no recollection of certain discussions referred to in a memorandum that were supposed to have taken place in 3/1820. "Mr. Calhoun. I have no recollection of any written opinions being asked for or given; but I have a distinct remembrance of the apprehensions existing in all quarters of the consequences that might ensue from the difficulty not being adjusted, and which constrained the South, after resisting the restrictions attempted to be imposed for two sessions, to acquiesce finally in the bill proposed as a compromise." From the Washington, D.C., *Daily Union,* December 3, 1848, p. 1. Also printed in *Congressional Globe,* 30th Cong., 2nd Sess., Appendix, p. 58.

From JAMES B. REYNOLDS, [former Representative from Tenn.]

Clarksville (Tennessee), July 25, 1848
My dear Sir, I read with great pleasure, on yesterday, your Speech on the Oregon Bill, for which noble effort, I hasten to present you my profound thanks.

This subject (Slavery) has agitated the country too long. I hope it will now be finally settled. I can hardly perceive, how honourable gentlemen from the North can resist your arguments. They must prevail triumphantly.

I am glad you exposed Mr. [Thomas] Jefferson's truism which he improperly placed in the Declaration of Independence", "that all men are born free and equal." There never was a greater absurdity since the days of Adam: And had it not the sanction of his great name, it would have been laugh'd to scorn years ago. You know that many of those gentleman's opinions, were grafted on French notions, erroneously call'd Phylosophy. They were imbibed on the eve of that abominable Revolution in France. As to the most foolish of all of them, is the one under consideration. You have given it the death blow now. Indeed, was it not a very grave subject, and addressing a grave and very dignified Senator, I would insist, that "Madam Sal" had too much influence over the mind & body of the Sage of Monticello! Whatever may have been the cause, you well know, that many of his dictums have done vast injury to this great Republic.

You are under a promise to visit Nashville. I think you might extend this visit, and say that Clarksville shall be included, having an old friend there. It is only 50 or 60 miles below, and on the same river.

I hope you will excuse this scrawl and allow me soon ["the" *canceled*] to improve the opportunity.

Have the goodness to present me most respectfully to Mrs. [Floride Colhoun] Calhoun, and I pray you, that I may continue favourably in her recollection, untill I again have the pleasure of paying you a visit. I have the honor to remain my dear Sir Ever yours most Truly & Sincerely, James B. Reynolds.

[P.S.] There ought to be 50,000 copies of your admirable Speech distributed. Mr. [John M.] Berrien[']s [Senator from Ga.] ought also to have a great circulation, &c.

ALS in ScCleA.

To F[LORIDE COLHOUN] CALHOUN, [Pendleton]

Washington, 26th July 1848

My dear wife, I have been prevented from answering your last letter for more than 10 days, by incessant engagements, which has left me me [*sic*] no time to attend to my correspondence. You have seen by the papers, that a Committee of 8 was raised, to whom was referred the subject of the territories. I was placed on it contrary to my wishes; but being placed there, I had to devote my mind to the subject. It proved to be one of great difficulty. The Committee finally succeed[ed] in agreeing to a plan for the adjustment of the subject, which is now under discussion in the Senate Senate [*sic*] &, I think, will be adopted by a large majority of the body. Whether it will pass the House is doubtful.

The time for adjournment is not yet fixed, nor will it be, in my opinion, until, the fate of the measure is known in the House. It will probably be sent there tomorrow, when its fate will soon be known, and the adjournment fixed. I do not, however, think that we can possibly adjourn before the mid[d]le of next month.

I received a letter last Sunday from Willie [William Lowndes Calhoun] & the preceeding from James [Edward Calhoun]; and am happy to learn that all are well; and every thing doing well at home.

I wrote to John [Ewing] Bonneau some time since to send you the sugar & hope you have got it. I ["shall" *canceled*] shall write him in my next to send the wine.

The weather is very hot at this time, which makes our laborious sittings very exhausting. I rise every morning shortly after sunrise and am employed from the time I am dressed almost incessantly in attending to my official duties, writing letters, ["or" *interlined*] reading the current news until 4 o[']clock, and often latter [*sic*]. Our regular dining hour is 4 o[']clock. The warm weather and the want of relaxation have reduced me some what, but my health is as good as usual.

Mr. [Thomas G.] Clemson has obtained leave of absence & will return this fall if not necessarily detained by the disturbed state of Europe, which, I think, not probable from present appearance. In anticipation, I have made arrangement to remit him $600, in order to place him in ample funds to bring his family with him. It would have been remitted sooner, but he had not obtained leave to return, & it was uncertain, whether he would. All difficulties now being removed I hope we shall have the pleasure of seeing them all by October.

Your friends here are all well as far as I know. They always inquire about you affectionately. Mrs. [Mary Hopkins] Pleasonton still looks badly, but says she is better.

Mr. & Mrs. [Armistead and Martha Calhoun] Burt unite in love to you all. Remember me to Mrs. [Margaret Hunter] Rion & James [Rion].

I enclose a receipt for preserving fruit in their natural state & an account of a new mode of Churning. The first is worth a trial, & if I can get a churn of the kind I will send it on. You may certainly get one by writing to Edward [*sic*; James Edward Boisseau] & sending him the account enclosed. Your affectionate husband, J.C. Calhoun.

[P.S.] I send a letter from Anna [Maria Calhoun Clemson] to you. Tell James [Edward Calhoun] I will write him shortly.

ALS in ScCleA.

To James Ed[ward] Colhoun, [Abbeville District, S.C.]

Washington, 26th July 1848

My dear James, I informed you in my last, that I had received your letter including a plat of your home tract. A few days since, I received your last enclosing a plat of your mountain domain. I shall omit no opportunity, which holds out any prospect of meeting the object of your desire; but, as I wrote you before, I fear nothing can be done here. Few foreigners of business visit this place, and the ministers are not of a character, that would take any interest in the subject.

Your mountain domain is certainly a fine one; and will, no doubt, in time be very valuable. I hold it to be almost certain, that the Anderson rail road, will terminate on the Tugalo[o] at the foot of the mountains. From Anderson to AndersonVille there is one continuous ridge; and from thence ["to" *canceled*] the valley of the Tugalo[o] affords a fine route to the foot of the mountains. The distance from Anderson thence cannot exceed, I suppose, 60 miles.

In the meane time, if you should continue disposed to make sales of your tract there, I am of the impression that it could be sold in Vermont to better advantage, than ["at" *canceled*] any where else. The people there are accustomed to sheep raising & a mountainous country, & can readily form a corrept [*sic*] conception of the advantages of your domain. If you should think with me, I will show your plat to some of the delegates from that State, to whom I could give my impression of the country.

The Senate have under discussion the Territorial bill. It will probably be voted on today; and will, I think, pass the body by a large vote. Its fate is more doubtful in the House.

We shall not be able to adjourn I fear before the 15 or 20th Next month. Yours affectionately, J.C. Calhoun.

ALS in ScCleA.

From Junius Hall

Boston, July 26th 1848

Dear Sir, I notice that a letter in favor of the "Granville & Columbia Railroad" has recently been written by you. Having charge of a rail-road Journal which is published in this city, & in which it is our desire to publish whatever is of importance, as connected with the railway interest of the country, I would solicit, a copy of this letter for publication, if you have no objections thereto. I have directed a few No.'s of our paper to be sent you, from which you'll be able to judge somewhat of its objects & the manner in which it is conducted. We should be glad to receive from you any communication on the subject of Rail-roads in your own State or any information respecting them, which it may be desirable to publish. Trusting that you will excuse the liberty I have taken I am, Yours Respectfully, Junius Hall.

ALS in ScCleA. NOTE: An AEU by Calhoun reads, "Junius Hall, relates to rail Road."

Remarks in exchange with George E. Badger of N.C., 7/26. In citing authorities on the power of Congress over the territories, Badger mentioned the opinion of [William] Pinkney [during the Missouri Compromise deliberations when Pinkney was Senator from Md.]. "Mr. Calhoun said he had always the impression that Mr. Pinkney . . . was an abolitionist. He had addressed a meeting in Hagerstown in favor of abolitionism." Badger disputed Calhoun's statement. From *Congressional Globe*, 30th Cong., 1st Sess., p. 1001. Also printed in Benton, ed., *Abridgment of Debates*, 16:234. Variant in *Congressional Globe*, 30th Cong., 1st Sess., Appendix, p. 1175; Houston, ed., *Proceedings and Debates*, p. 957. Another variant in the New York, N.Y., *Herald*, July 28, 1848, pp. 3–4.

REMARKS ON THE MISSOURI COMPROMISE

[In the Senate, July 26, 1848]
[*The Senate was nearing the end of protracted debate on the territorial government bill. John A. Dix of N.Y. quoted an alleged memorandum and letter of James Monroe stating that he and his Cabinet unanimously had accepted the Constitutionality of Congressional restriction of slavery from the Territories.*]
Mr. Calhoun. If the Senator will give way, it will be perhaps better that I make a statement at once respecting this subject, as far as my recollection will serve me. During the whole period of Mr. Monroe's administration, I remember no occasion on which the

members of his administration gave written opinions. I have an impression—though not a very distinct one—that on one occasion they were required to give written opinions; but for some reason, not now recollected, the request was not carried into effect. He [Monroe] was decidedly opposed to the imposition of any restriction on the admission of Missouri into the Union, and I am strongly of the impression that he was opposed in feeling to what was called the Missouri compromise.

[*Reverdy Johnson of Md. disputed whether the letter was authentic. In further discussion Dix stated the letter to be a copy, and quoted from John Quincy Adams's diary passages which had been supplied to him concerning Cabinet opinions on the Missouri Compromise.*]

Mr. Calhoun. Has any search been made in the State Department for these written opinions?

[*Dix and James D. Westcott of Fla. both stated they had looked for such documents and could not find them.*]

Mr. Calhoun. If any written opinion was ever given by me, it has entirely escaped my memory; and I feel satisfied, if ever given, it was very little more than an assent or dissent to the course adopted by the administration. Mr. Adams had the advantage of keeping a diary, which no doubt may be relied upon, as far as he is individually concerned; but which, of course, is liable to mistakes, as far as it represents the views and acts of others. In this case there may be some explanation, if all the facts were known, which would reconcile his statement with my recollection. But of one thing I feel perfectly sure, that I could never have directed my attention and formed an opinion on so important a subject, as a member of his cabinet, and reduced it to writing, for the purpose of being preserved, without recollecting it.

[*Johnson argued that the documents did not support the position Dix was maintaining and that Monroe had erased the word "unanimous" in the letter.*]

Mr. Calhoun. I feel justified in saying, from all the circumstances of this case, including the facts stated by the Senator from Maryland, and the absence of any written opinion on the file of the State Department, that notwithstanding the certificate from Mr. Adam's diary, no such opinions were given as it states. There is some mistake about it, but how it originated I am at a loss to conceive. Perhaps it may be explained by the vague impression, as I have stated, on my mind, that the opinions were called for, but never formally given in writing, at least not beyond a mere assent or dissent as to the course ultimately adopted. I know well all about the compromise; the cause which led to it, and the reason why, that the northern men who voted against it were universally sacrificed for so doing. It is quite a mistake, as some suppose, that they were sacrificed for voting for the compromise. The very reverse is the case. The cause I will proceed to state: During the session of the compromise, Mr. [William] Lowndes and myself resided together. He was a member of the House of Representatives, and I was Secretary of War. We both felt the magnitude of the subject. Missouri, at the preceding session, had presented herself for admission as a member of the Union. She had formed a constitution and government, in accordance with an act of Congress. Her admission was refused on the ground that her constitution admitted of slavery; and she was remanded back to have the objectionable provision expunged. She refused to comply with the requisition, and at the next session again knocked at the door of Congress for admission, with her constitution as it originally stood. This gave rise to one of the most agitating discussions that ever occurred in Congress. The subject was one of repeated conversation between Mr. Lowndes and myself. The question was, what was to be done, and what would be the consequence if she was not admitted? After full reflection, we both agreed that Missouri was a State made so by a regular process of law, and never could be remanded back to the territorial condition. Such being the case, we also agreed that the only question was, whether she should be a State in or out of the Union? and it was for Congress to decide which position she should occupy. My friend made one of his able and lucid speeches on the occasion; but whether it has been preserved or not, I am not able to say. It carried conviction to the minds of all, and in fact settled the question. The question was narrowed down to a single point. All saw that if Missouri was not admitted, she would remain an independent State on the west bank of the Mississippi, and would become the nucleus of a new confederation of States extending over the whole of Louisiana. None were willing to contribute to such a result; and the only question that remained with the northern members who had opposed her admission was, to devise some means of escaping from the awkward dilemma in which they found themselves. To back out or compromise, were the only alternatives left; and the latter was eagerly seized to avoid the disgrace of the former—so eagerly, that all who opposed it at the North were considered traitors to that section of the Union, and sacrificed for their votes.

[*Dix continued his speech, stating that "we are engaged in a struggle to enlarge the area of slavery."*]

Mr. Calhoun. I must beg the Senator from New York to state me more correctly. We are not contending for the extension of the area of slavery; and if he places us upon that ground, he places us in a very false position. What we do contend for is, that the southern States, as members of our Union, are entitled to equal rights and equal dignity, in every respect, with the northern; and that there is nothing in the constitution to deprive us of this equality in consequence of being slaveholders.

From Houston, ed., *Proceedings and Debates*, pp. 960–962. Also printed in *Congressional Globe*, 30th Cong., 1st Sess., Appendix, p. 1179. Partly printed in the Washington, D.C., *Daily National Intelligencer*, August 23, 1848, p. 4. Variants in the New York, N.Y., *Herald*, July 27, 1848, p. 2, and July 28, 1848, p. 4; the Charleston, S.C., *Courier*, July 31, 1848, p. 3.

Remarks on the Select Committee on Oregon

[In the Senate, July 26, 1848]

[*John M. Clayton of Del. was describing the committee's work on the Senate compromise bill.*]

Mr. Calhoun said that the committee were brought to a dead stand. The impression was that they could do nothing more. No man was prepared to state anything. If his memory served him, the Senator from New York, Mr. [Daniel S.] Dickinson said, "Can't we do something?" and suggested non-interference. He could not say what gentleman made the bill. It grew out of an emergency; it grew out of pure necessity. It was this or nothing at all.

Mr. [John] Bell [of Tenn.]. It came by chance.

Mr. Calhoun. Every part was deliberated upon.

Mr. Bell. I meant that this was a thought that flashed on the committee.

Mr. Calhoun. It was made precisely as the Constitution was made.

[*Bell said the question now was, was it expedient to adopt the bill.*]

Mr. Calhoun. That is the question.

From the New York, N.Y., *Herald*, July 28, 1848, p. 4.

REMARKS IN DEBATE WITH WILLIAM L. DAYTON ON THE COMPROMISE BILL

[In the Senate, July 26, 1848]

[*Dayton of N.J. avowed that the Select Committee on Oregon had accepted the principle of exclusion of slavery from the Territories by accepting, for three months, the existing act of the Oregon territorial legislature to that effect.*]

Mr. Calhoun. Not at all. The committee did not decide the question of constitutionality.

[*Daniel S. Dickinson of N.Y. supported Calhoun. Dayton repeated that by accepting the laws of the territory Congress had decided that they were constitutional.*]

Mr. Calhoun. We did not decide whether they were constitutional or not.

Mr. Dayton. Then the Senator from South Carolina and those who go with him are just in this position. They vote for extending a law now in existence in the territory of Oregon which they believe to be unconstitutional.

Mr. Calhoun. We inserted the words if not inconsistent with the constitution.

[*There was further discussion. Dayton asked if "southern gentlemen" intended to support the restriction of slavery from Oregon as a part of the compromise.*]

Mr. Calhoun. Southern gentlemen are perfectly indifferent on the subject.

[*Dayton asked if the territorial law came again before Congress for approval, would Calhoun support it.*]

Mr. Calhoun. I do not. I believe it to be unconstitutional.

From Houston, ed., *Proceedings and Debates*, p. 966. Also printed in the Washington, D.C., *Daily National Intelligencer*, October 11, 1848, pp. 1–2; *Congressional Globe*, 30th Cong., 1st Sess., Appendix, pp. 1183–1184.

From [JOHN R. MATHEWES]

[Charleston?] July 27, [18]48

My Dear Sir, On my return to the Mountains I rec[eive]d your public Documents relative to the Mex[ica]n War & feel myself obligated for the attention as it contains so much authentic & interesting matter as we seldom get from Washington City. I have conversed with both parties in our neighbouring State[;] there never was so little *party* zeal since my knowledge of its workings in that State. The intelligent of *both* parties however rally upon one truth. Praise to the merits of John C. Calhoun.

I heard a hunker from the Baltimore convention surrounded by a group of his gaping constituents swallowing every word of his ridiculous relations of what happened there & what was to happen hereafter. He was an acclimatized yankee & his whole wallet of political information consisted of the ridicule of So. Ca. & her Senator. We had a redeeming feature & that was his praise of Mr. [Francis W.] Pickens who alone had the temerity to be indipendent in So. Ca. & oppose the opinion of one individual &c and a great deal more of such trash. Your course however seems to excite the anxiety & respect of those who are not seeking office—beyond the limits of Carol[in]a. I believe at last that the Southern Public are diverting at last their gaze from the Presidency to their own salvation. We are here in the midst of a depopulated City—Gone to ["Savannah" *canceled and* "Columbia" *interlined*] & to meet at the Charleston Depot those returning and tomorrow is the Grand day at Home. Crops of every discription, are unexceptionable & such Seasons I have never seen from the mountains to the Seaboard and those who have sped the plough will reap the Harvest.

My Son rec[eive]d from N. York a letter from a friend nearly related to some of the respectable politicians of that State. I consulted with some of my political friends here who for their talents & purity merited the confidence that the circumstance required & they came to the conclusion that whilst you were occupying ["throughout the union" *interlined*] a position far above any or the Highest office it would be an intrusion upon ["your" *interlined*] pursuit to give one idea ["publication" *interlined*] for the diversion of the insincere & selfish portion of Congress & thereby enable them to recede from the Honest position they have been brought to and now hold. Extract—"[Zachary] Taylor will most probably receive the vote of N. York. If not him why then [Martin] V[an] Buren—but [Lewis] Cass stands no chance indeed from what I hear I am induced to believe that Cass will only receive the vote of Main[e] & Wisconsin certain among the North[er]n & Eastern States. I have it from sources deserving of credit that had Mr. Calhoun been nominated immediately after the Baltimore convention he would have completely distanced Cass at the North and no more wo[ul]d have been heard of the Free Soil Party. This is only the result of ambitious politicians taking advantage of a popular prejudice for their own advancement

& for the destruction of Cass, than whom no man enjoys a greater contempt among the Northern people. It w[oul]d both surprise & please you to see how great a regard is felt here for our great Statesman Mr. Calhoun & how constantly the wish is express[e]d that he could be the President. It appears to me a great mistake that he was not nominated in opposition to Cass. You must not confound the Free Soil party with the Aboliti[oni]sts—they are entirely different & entertain no friendship for each other, tho' I am not sure but that the first is the most dangerous to us." I have much to say to you—business inter[r]upts, but I hope to see you here before I leave for the mountains about the last of August. ever y[ou]rs [John R. Mathewes.]

ALU in ScCleA.

From F[itz]w[illiam] Byrdsall

New York [City,] July 28th 1848
Dear Sir, I enclose a public call for a meeting in the Park this afternoon in opposition to the territorial Bill just passed by the Senate of the U.S. This is the first appearance of the call in form.

To this call we find—F[rancis] W. Edmonds (brother of John W.)[,] George H. Purser ex ald[erman] 4th Ward—Saul Alley—Jonathan J. Coddington—B[enjamin] F. Butler—James McCullough—W[illia]m C. Bryant—Azariah C. Flagg—Myndert Van Schaick—Sam[ue]l J. Tilden[,] Ex. Ald[erman Daniel C.] Pentz—Sol[omon] Townsend ex member assembly—Jesse Oakley, (brother Judge [Thomas J.] Oakley)[,] Park[e] Godwin son in Law of W.C. Bryant—all prominent Democrats; And, Joseph Hoxie—Horace Greel[e]y—Mat[t]hew L. Davis—Willis Hall—David Graham[,] W[illia]m D. Murphy—Freeman Hund [*sic*; Hunt] Editor of the Merchants Magazine leading and prominent Whigs. With regard to the rank and file of names to the call, the Whigs and abolitionists number about three to one of those who have belonged to the Democratic party.

I hope and trust the Bill will also pass the House. The Whigs as a party have never liked the South and do not now, and a large portion of the Democracy are malevolent because of the Offices and ["this" *interlined*] is the sum total principle of Van Burenism.

After Gen[era]l Cass left this City the Van Burenites reported that Thomas H. Benton had expressed himself that if he had been aware there was so much opposition to Cass in New York, he would not have accompanied him hither. Some friends of Cass believing this to be a fabrication, addressed a letter to the Senator stating their belief, requesting an answer on this point, but none has yet arrived. There were nine signatures to the letter all highly respectable and none of them an office holder. It is therefore highly probable the great Missourian said so.

After the present territorial Bill is settled—a southern Demonstration should be made to set forth among other things the amounts in shoes, hats, clothing and piece goods of northern manufacture, annually consumed by the South. Also the amounts derived from the South by the north in profits on manufactures—Insurance—freights—Commissions[,] brokerages and the other numerous rills which unite and carry to this part of the Union the whole surplus production of the south over and above a bare support. It is the Ocean of these abstractions from the South that builds up northern towns, improvements &c. and leads shallow people to conclude that slavery is hurtful to southern prosperity. Labor is labor whether slave or free, and any country that retains its proceeds, or derives them from another country, must prosper. A proper shewing up of these facts—by figures and clear calculations shewing forth the prosperity that would accrue to the South by going into manufactures[,] owning ships &c and training slaves to other labor besides plantation industry, would touch the north where it is sensitive in the pocket. It is *not* by means of slavery per se, that the South is behind the north for the fact is that the products of the South and manifold profits derived therefrom, have built northern towns, Railroads—steam boats—ships &c. All this ought to be exhibitted. For years I have never ceased to insist that the north derives more of the profits of slavery than the owners of slaves, and the northern people are more interested in that institution than the Southern people. I am Dear Sir Yours with deep Respect, F.W. Byrdsall.

ALS in ScCleA; PEx in Boucher and Brooks, eds., *Correspondence*, pp. 460–461.

From J[oseph] W. Lesesne

Mobile, July 28th 1848
My Dear Sir, A thousand thanks for the copy of your speech. And, indeed, I must not only thank you but tender you the unfeigned homage which every good man must feel for this noble offering to the Country and to mankind. If you had never uttered another this

would secure you that attention and affectionate audience with posterity to which the wise and the good must chiefly look for that infinite sphere of usefulness which providence has assigned them. I see nothing to add and nothing to take away. In its matter [it is] exactly what was wanted, and in manner at once suited to the occasion, and fulfilling in its severe and subdued taste the highest conditions of art, without appearing, and doubtless, without being so designed.

If this seem to be the language of flattery you are wholly to blame for it; for you have left no choice between silence and these expressions. I am truly glad that you have so effectually dessected the mischi[e]vous fallacy of universal equality that *deforms* our Declaration of Independence—if one can say so of a document the extravegance, and ["numerous" *interlined*] inaccuracies of which are only to be palliated by the excitement from which they sprang. Mr. [Thomas] Jefferson brought this disorganizing paradox with him from the tempestuous atmosphere of France, and derived his convictions (for such they were) of its truth from that insane philosophy which still agitates that unhappy country with its debasing errors. It was from Helvetius, of whom he was a great admirer, that he derived ["them" *canceled and* "many of these," *interlined*] and whose demoralizing work "*On Man*" laid in a subtle and refined logic the foundations for all the impracticable schemes of Socialism which have seized upon the minds of the laboring classes in almost every part of Europe. It is truely singular that a mind like Mr. Jefferson[']s, of such striking penetration and forecast, should have afforded a congenial soil for such hideous errors. He has, however, always appeared to me, to have had an anfirmity [*sic*] for paradox quite equal to his love for the true—and his mind distinguished as much if not more for its keenness and sagacity than for its generalizing and constructive power.

I regret very much to see the recent movement in Charleston. It can do no good and may do much harm. It is impossible for us to link our fortunes permanently with the Whigs. Their conservative feelings rest on such false principles, and are directed to such unsound, unjust and impolitic measures, that a union with them must be always painful and short-lived. It is a party over whose counsels, neither wisdom, moderation, nor forbearance preside. Hence altho' its moral elements are at present infinitely better than those of their opponents, they can never serve any just cause effectually. To me, it appears, that the geographical line between parties will in a short time be so effectually drawn, that we shall find soon enough and by a much better test than now exists who are our friends and who our enemies on either side, without entangling ourselves with an uncertain alliance which we may have to dissolve. Our true course is clearly what you indicate in your last letter—to wait events without attaching ourselves prematurely and unbidden to either party. We can do justice to ourselves and to both sections of our opponents best in this way.

I have always feared the dangerous elements in the Democratic party. Their threatening prominence towards the close of Mr. [Martin] Van Buren's administration alarmed the whole country, and his defeat was a signal rebuke by the thoughtful and responsible classes administered by the election of a candidate in whose ["capacity" *interlined*] no one reposed entire confidence. The lesson is about to be repeated still more loudly and emphatically. But the bad spirit existing in the democratic party has been steadily growing for years past, and under its guidance the ship of state, notwithstanding these adverse winds, is making steady and dangerous progress towards the rocks upon which, some day or other, I fear, we are destined to split. Europe is adding a bloody and mournful page to history for the instruction of mankind. May *we* read it with attention and profit, and with increased and increasing reliance upon that Great Being who thus permits[?] the insolence of opinion, the contempt for past experience, and of all existing institutions, ["to inflict upon themselves" *interlined*] such awful chastisement. Very truly your f[rien]d &c, J.W. Lesesne.

ALS in ScCleA.

Remarks on adjournment, 7/28. There was discussion of whether 8/7 or 8/14 should be set for adjournment. "Mr. [Edward A.] Hannegan [of Ind.] and Mr. Calhoun thought the business could all be done by the 7th. There was now nothing to be gained by sitting longer." From *Congressional Globe*, 30th Cong., 1st Sess., p. 1009. Also printed in Houston, ed., *Proceedings and Debates*, p. 981. Variant in the Baltimore, Md., *Sun*, July 29, 1848, p. 4; the Charleston, S.C., *Mercury*, August 1, 1848, p. 2.

From G E O [R G E] B. B U T L E R, "(Private)"

New York [City,] July 29 1848

My dear Sir, The free soil &c meeting here yesterday, was a decided failure, notwithstanding great efforts to produce an impression by it. The names published for the call shew that our substantial Citizens are not in the movement. The Journal of Commerce has met ["the movement" *canceled and* "it" *interlined*] with manliness and decided effect, and will continue its course until the excitement has cooled down. The meeting yesterday will do much towards withdrawing those from it, who go into these questions for the purpose of being with the strong side. I have written on the subject every day when not engaged in a Rail Road cause, and was urgent with Mr. [Gerard] Hallock of the Journal of Commerce, to devote his paper to the side of the question, which since, it has so ably sustained. I do not doubt that the patriotism of the Country, wil[l] finally triumph over those who endeavor to break up the compromises of the Constitution. The tone of the South in its present freedom from all violence, in its willingness to accede to compromise, in its moderation will be a great help in the final settlement of the question. This should be impressed on the South. A few who stood almost alone here at the outset, are constantly strengthened by the support of men of moderation and patriotism.

We have this moment received the news of the defeat of the bill in the house. Its passage would have strengthened the Barnburners, and I am inclined to think it wise not to pass any measure this Session. They will have less force in pressing an affirmative measure against the interests of the South, then in attacking one passed before the north has had time to mature its views and settle down into a truly patriotic ground.

I have been in favor of a line 36°30′ instead of the measure which passed the Senate, although it would have been satisfactory to me as an adjustment of the question. Let all the violence and invective come from the north. The South ought to assume no other attitude than that of decided firmness, and true patriotism. All will then be well. Very truly, Geo. B. Butler.

ALS in ScCleA; PC in Boucher and Brooks, eds., *Correspondence*, pp. 461–462.

To A[nna] M[aria Calhoun] Clemson, [Brussels]

Washington, 30th July 1848

My dear daughter, Although I wrote to Mr. [Thomas G.] Clemson a few days since by the steamer, I cannot permit so favourable an opportunity to pass, as the return of Mr. [Napoleon Alcindor] Beaulieu, without writing to you; especially as I expect to be too much occupied for the residue of the session to write again before my return home.

I learned by your letter to your mother [Floride Colhoun Calhoun], that Mr. Clemson had applied for leave of absence, and that you apprehended, that you would not be able to accompany him on account of his want of funds. I wrote him immediately, that I would remit him ["immediately" *canceled and* "without delay" *interlined*] the $600, required for the purpose. I have made arrangement to do so through the Bankers (Corc[o]ran & Riggs) of this place, and am only waiting the return of Mr. Corc[o]ran from a visit to New York to make the remittance, which will reach in time, as I understand at the Dept. of State, that Mr. Clemson will not leave until the 1st Oct[obe]r. His return without you & the children would have been a cause of great greif [*sic*] to us all. Had the sum required been ten times greater, it would be remitted to prevent it.

Since I wrote Mr. Clemson, the territorial bill, reported by the Special Committee of 8, passed the Senate by a vote of 33 to 22, but was laid on the table in the house by a vote of 112 to 97. It is very doubtful whether any bill can pass. The excitement is great, and no one can say what is to be the result. Many suppose the Union is in danger. Congress will probably adjourn on the 14th of next month, so that if any thing is to be done it must be done quickly.

John [C. Calhoun, Jr.] is with us, on his return from the Philadelphia medical school, with his ["degree" *canceled and* "diploma" *interlined*] in his pocket; so that he is now Dr. Calhoun. He passed, I learn, a highly satisfactory examination. About a third of the class failed to pass. He leaves tomorrow for Fort Hill, where I hope the whole family may meet again when you arrive.

I had ["a" *canceled*] letters from both James [Edward Calhoun] & William [Lowndes Calhoun] a short time since. All were well, with the prospects of a ["of" *canceled*] very good crop.

I am much gratified to hear, that you are all well, & that the children [John Calhoun Clemson and Floride Elizabeth Clemson] are growing & improving so fast. I shall be very happy to see them, and do not doubt, that they are all you describe them to be.

Kiss them for their grandfather, & tell them how much I wish to see them. With love to Mr. Clemson. Your affectionate father, J.C. Calhoun.

ALS in ScCleA.

From J. H. Alexander

Baltimore, 31 July 1848

Sir, I hope that the liberty I take of addressing you now with such a slight personal acquaintance as I have the honor to lay claim to with you, will find excuse in the goodness of my intention and the obvious respect which to my address itself manifests. The topic, upon which I desire to make the suggestions following—i.e. slavery under the Territorial Govern[men]ts of our new acquisitions, Oregon, California &c—is besides one of great general interest and even more; for it does not require great sagacity to perceive that the main question, to which recent and present discussions are only collateral, will become at no very distant day a turning point in the permanence of our Union itself. And if upon a topic of such acknowledged moment, I prefer to address you rather than one of my own representatives, it is because (and I do not say this merely to turn a compliment) you may be justly regarded in all the aspects and stages of this question as the great exponent and bulwark of the South.

It is quite unnecessary that I should dwell ["upon" *interlined*] or even allude to any of the generalities of the Institution of Slavery whose existence from the earliest times—semper et ubique—all ethnography teaches, physiological considerations justify and Revelation itself sanctions, nor need I say more than that I have no doubt of the *in*ability of Congress under our Constitution to legislate definitively upon this or any other subject so as in any wise to embarrass the future sovereign legislation of the States that may be expected to grow up out of these Territories. My object is only, after the recent failure of the method of adjusting the difficulty proposed by the Senate, to suggest another method which I have not heard spoken of yet, which I would not therefore be surprised to find objected to on the ground of novelty but which reposing, as it seems to me, upon firm ground in abstract essential equity I hope will recommend itself still farther by presenting itself in the aspect of a reasonable and not too costly compromise.

Such compromise must in all matters of business, and still more in the workings and collisions of a Government like ours, be frequently admitted: but I may be excused for saying that in this matter the tender consciences of Northern gentlemen have led them to confound the distinction between *compromise* and *surrender.* No one would be more ready than myself, on the principle that things lawful are not always expedient and that the greatest of National blessings is Peace in both action and council—to admit in all cases the former: in a question of the latter I should partake most likely of the sentiment of the French guard at Waterloo.

I assume then that we of the South are ["willing" *canceled*] no ways desirous of extending and perpetuating Slavery *per se* and for its own sake; and that we are even ready and willing to do away with the whole Institution *if we could afford it.* That we cannot afford it, however, is proved in our own consciousness and w[oul]d be proved overtly in the resistance that we should certainly meet if we were to undertake a crusade against the Factory-labor and consequent degradation of Caucasian blood in the North. All that we can do, then, is to compromise by the north's coming in and bearing its fair share of the cost of the sacrifice they desire us to make.

This compromise is what I desire to suggest; and which would occur by the introduction, into any Bill for Establishing Governments in the Territories, of a clause providing for the salvation of all slaves brought into these territories by actual settlers, *their purchase with the funds of the United States* and their *transfer after such purchase to the American Colonization Society to be conveyed to and settled in Africa* with all convenient speed.

Your rapid and acute perception, Sir, will recognize in a moment the equity of this procedure, and your judicious discrimination will not fail to distinguish between objections that however plausible at first sight are only against the *form* and those against the substance of the measure. As for the executive details, they flow I think naturally and easily upon the recognition of the principle. At least I w[oul]d not presume to trouble you with them until I had your permission.

However a proposition ["might" *canceled*] of this kind might succeed or not i.e. however (in modern phrase) *available* it might be, it at least seems to me calculated to answer one end; that is to test the earnestness of the conscientious opponents of slavery. If the outlay of a few thousands of dollars should be the objection to a plan for diminishing the area of that calamity and helping on their benevolent design—both the calamity and the benevolence would be placed in a position for being measured by a new and juster standard.

Again excusing myself as far as may be necessary for the freedom I have taken in this communication, I have the honor to remain, Sir, Very respectfully y[ou]rs, J.H. Alexander.

ALS in ScCleA.

From F[ITZ]W[ILLIAM] BYRDSALL

New York [City,] July 31st 1848
Dear Sir, I perceive with great mortification that the defeat of the Senate Territorial Bill in the house, was accomplished by 8 votes from the Slave States. That any 8 members of any party from that section of the Union could be found to vote against a measure so essential at this crisis, not only astonishes, but shocks all those feelings connected with the preservation of the co-equality of the States. If those 8 men only knew the state of fanatical sentiment in this section of the country, they would rather suffer any odium than have voted to give not only a fresh impetus, but an increase to a movement of the most fearful portent to the Southern States. When any of those 8 men meet [Samuel S.] Phelps of Vermont, or [Auburn] Birdsall of this State, they should feel shame enough to wish the ground to sink and cover them up. Surely, surely they cannot be aware of the crusade that is now increasing against the institution of Slavery to a most fearful magnitude in the free States. Even in the New York Custom house there is a strong majority of the Officials Clerks &c. in favor of the Wilmot proviso. Among the citizens too, it is a common objection that Slaves enter into the Representative basis of the lower house of Congress. This is continually dinned in my ears, both by zealots and moderate men. I meet this objection by the correct remark that as in the north and free States, men, women, aliens, free negroes, and all persons count equally in apportionment for members of Congress—so in the South should all persons whether slaves or free be equally counted in the representative basis, and that the three fifths arrangement instead of being a concession to the Slave States, was in fact a concession to the north. But what is truth against prejudice?

If the South cannot maintain its equal rights to the territory of the United States—here then we have the beginning of the end. There is no constitutional right of the Southern people clearer than their right to go with their property of any kind into the territories of the Union. A man from the North, or from the East, the West or the South, carries with him to the new territories, all the rights of person and of property which he had in the State he left, so far in extent as the same rights are not contrary to the Constitution of the United States. When the territory becomes sufficiently populous to form a State then the people will have the Sovereignty of State Rights and not before. In the mean time the General Government is bound to protect the settlers from the north or the South in all their rights of person and of property. But Congress has no authority to give the right of voting in conquered territory to Indians, negroes, or mixed breeds, in making constitutions or laws to Govern. This appears to me to be common sense view of the Subject.

If the Southern people cannot maintain their equal rights as to their settling in new territory, what other rights under the Constitution can they maintain? If defeated on the Wilmot proviso principle, will the crusade began against them stop at that point? They are self deluded who imagine an affirmative. The ground against the Proviso is as strong a fortification as they can stand upon. The Statements of those Whigs and democrats who are now uniting with the Abolitionists, that they mean not to interfere with the Slavery existing in the Slave States are all hollow. The only way to make such statements prove true is to take a stand untill the proviso is defeated. A victory here will preserve all the rest. Accept the heart-felt respect of, F.W. Byrdsall.

ALS in ScCleA; PC in Jameson, ed., *Correspondence*, pp. 1180–1181.

Remarks on the Naval appropriations bill, 7/31. Both Senators from S.C. objected to a provision requiring authorized mail steamers to stop at Charleston "if practicable." "Mr. Calhoun said Charleston and Savannah, it is known, are neighboring ports. A line of steamers has been established from Charleston to Cuba, to touch at Savannah. In the contract with Mr. [Albert G.] Sloo, there is also a provision that his steamers shall touch at Charleston and Savannah, and there is no reason why the words 'if practicable' should be inserted in regard to one more than the other. There was no reason why Charleston should not have an equal advantage with Savannah, in regard to these vessels." Later Calhoun "explained, that the Senators from

South Carolina had yielded their assent to strike out the words 'if practicable' as applicable to Savannah, and he could see no reason why the objectionable words should be retained in regard to Charleston." From the Baltimore, Md., *Sun*, August 1, 1848, p. 4. Also printed in the Charleston, S.C., *Courier*, August 4, 1848, p. 2. Variant in *Congressional Globe*, 30th Cong., 1st Sess., p. 1016; Houston, ed., *Proceedings and Debates*, p. 984.

Remarks on an amendment to the civil and diplomatic appropriations bill, 7/31. Under consideration was a provision to prevent any member of Congress from receiving more than $1,000 in mileage payments. "Mr. Calhoun contended that members of Congress were worse paid than any other portion of the government. It would have been wiser if, in the first instance, a specified allowance had been made for them. He knew of no better mode of making the compensation just than this system of mileage, which he did not regard as fixed too high. He concurred in the views of the Senator from North Carolina, (Mr. [George E.] Badger,) that a difference ought to [be] made between the member who is two thousand miles from his family and his business, and him who is within two hundred miles of both. He also regarded it as a point worthy of consideration that this mileage had its effect in discouraging any attempt to remove the seat of government to a more central position, and referred to the situation of the principal capitals of the European nations, which were always located near the most assailable points, and not in the centre of the kingdoms to which they belonged." From Houston, ed., *Proceedings and Debates*, p. 985. Also printed in *Congressional Globe*, 30th Cong., 1st Sess., p. 1017.

From J[ohn] Y. Mason, [Secretary of the Navy]

Navy Department, August 1st 1848

Sir, I have the honor to acknowledge the receipt of yours of the 30th ult[im]o in relation to young [Edward R.] Shubrick. By the Act of Congress of the 3d March 1845, South Carolina is entitled to thirteen Midshipmen. She now has in the service eleven. Assurances have been given to the Hon's [*sic*] Messrs. [Joseph A.] Woodward & [Armistead] Burt that an appointment would be given to a youth from each of their Districts, which will fill the number to which the State is entitled. I have deemed it my duty in conformity with the spirit of the law to diffuse the appointments through the States. Heretofore, the city of Charleston has had a very large proportion of the Midshipmen from South Carolina. After the appointments from the Districts of Messrs. Woodward and Burt I understand there will be two Congressional Districts in the State without a Midshipman. I am respec[tfull]y yours, J.Y. Mason.

FC in DNA, RG 45 (Naval Records), Miscellaneous Letters Sent by the Secretary of the Navy, 1798–1886, 40:245 (M-209:15).

Remarks on an amendment to the civil and diplomatic appropriations bill, 8/1. The amendment would eliminate an appropriation for the Commissioner of Patents to compile and publish agricultural statistics. "Mr. Calhoun was in favor of the amendment, as he thought the mania for purchasing books and book-making required to be checked. He thought, too, that the Commissioner had enough to do without meddling with these matters, and with which the government ought not to connect itself." From Houston, ed., *Proceedings and Debates*, p. 987. Also printed in *Congressional Globe*, 30th Cong., 1st Sess., p. 1024.

From JOHN CARROLL WALSH

The Mound, Harford Co[unty,] Md.
near Jerusalem Mills P.O. 1st August 1848
My dear Sir, Your favor of 25 ult. was received by me, at Baltimore, in due time, but I deferred acknowledging it until my return here.

You will have seen by the papers that our Independent State Convention met on the day appointed, and dissolved the independent organization, so far as Gen[era]l [Zachary] Taylor was concerned. A majority of your friends deemed it best, as it was found that no unanimous action could be had, to quietly seperate, leaving each member of the Convention at liberty to act as he pleased, and "bide the time" when your friends could act without having their movements trammelled by a connection with any other individual, or his friends.

You may rest assured, my dear Sir, that your friends in this State would be proud to join in a movement with those in other portions of the confederacy which would have for its object your election to the Presidency, and you will find, if your standard is raised, that the number and character of those who will rally round it, will prove to the world the estimation in which your public life is held by the people of this country.

You no doubt recollect the remarks made in Congress, years ago, by Mr. [Thomas P.] Grosvenor [former Representative from N.Y.], in reference to yourself, your friends wish to see his predictions verified. He said "Let the honorable gentleman continue with the same independence, aloof from party views and local prejudices, to pursue the great interests of his country and fulfil the high destiny for which he was born. The buzz of popular applause may not cheer him on the way, but he will inevitably arrive at a high and happy elevation in the view of his country and the world."

"The buzz of popular applause" you are well aware, has not sounded in your ears when engaged in some of the great acts of your life, yet many of those, who from different motives, were at the time either silent, or abusive, have since acknowledged their having wronged you, and would gladly avail themselves of an opportunity to render you that justice so eminently your due. With high regard Very faithfully Your friend &c, Jno. Carroll Walsh.

ALS in ScCleA.

From J[OHN] D. WILSON

Society Hill [S.C.,] 4th Aug[us]t [18]48

Dear Sir: From the unsettled state of public sentiment in regard to the approaching Presidential Election, I am induced to request your views in regard to the political merits of the two gentlemen who have been nominated by their respective parties. I need not say, that unless permitted, these views shall be regarded as private.

My own position before the people of Darlington [District, S.C.], as a candidate for a seat in the State Senate, will compel me sooner or later to declare my opinions; and with the information now in my possession, I cannot take any step, that will lead to a committal. To you sir, I in common with the old States Rights Party of So. Ca., look for ["council" *altered to* "counsel"], in a matter, in which, I believe the rights of the South are involved.

Some months ago, my personal preference was for Gen[era]l [Zachary] Taylor. But first, his letter [of 4/22] to Mr. Alison [*sic*; John S. Allison], particularly that paragraph in reference to the Veto

Power; and subsequently his nomination by the Whig Convention, with the qualified abandonment of his independent position by ["the" *altered to* "his"] Louisiana friends in that Convention, caused me to look with some distrust. And now his acceptance of the nomination of that Convention, without the slightest declaration of principle, particularly in reference to the absorbing question before the country, induced me to conclude that he may be regarded as the candidate of that party, with the understanding that he will, if elected, carry out their principles and policy.

To Gen[era]l [Lewis] Cass, my objections are strong. His course in the Senate on the Oregon question, and the Mexican War, prove that he is ultra; and but for wiser counsel, the country would have been involved in calamity. Yet there is one redeeming virtue. Whilst Minister at the French Court, he took a bold and decided stand, that seems to me, must meet the approbation of every American.

And now sir, having briefly expressed my own opinion in regard to Gen[era]l Taylor and Mr. Cass, will you permit me to ask you for information. Your opinion is frequently asked for, and would go far to settle public sentiment with reference to this vexed matter.

I now carry out, a long cherished desire, and have been urged to it, from seeing the report of the proceedings of Congress in regard to the ["Oregon" *canceled and* "'Compromise'" *interlined*] Bill.' From the report ["of" *altered to* "in"] the [Charleston] Mercury, the bill was carried in the Senate by Southern Democrats aided by northern and western democrats; and defeated in the House by the votes of 15 Southern Whigs. The result of this effort at compromise, has made the matter more complicated. If left to pursue my own course, I would support neither of the gentlemen nominated. But this I suspect, would be distasteful to the majority.

It is probable, that my name is unknown to you; But I am a South Carolinian, whose highest effort is to promote the interest of his State, and looks to her most experienced statesman for information. I cannot go to my own immediate representative (Mr. [Alexander D.] Sims), because I believe his opinions would be partial, and not as effective.

For the sincerity of my interest in the information asked, I refer you to Mr. [Armistead] Burt, Mr. [Joseph A.] Woodward or Gen[era]l [Daniel] Wallace [Representatives from S.C.], with whom I have had the pleasure of an acquaintance in the Legislature of our State.

And now Sir, will you allow me to ask a reply at your earliest convenience? I am with sentiments of high regard, Y[ou]r obedient servant, J.D. Wilson.

ALS in ScCleA; PEx in Boucher and Brooks, eds., *Correspondence*, pp. 462–463.

From Ch[arle]s Edmondston, "Chamber of Commerce," Charleston, 8/5. He encloses a memorial of this date from citizens of Charleston requesting restoration of former mail arrangements. The new arrangements are detrimental to commerce. (Calhoun presented the memorial to the Senate on 8/8.) ALS with En in DNA, RG 46 (U.S. Senate), 30A-H14.2.

Remarks on the bill to grant certain public lands to the State of Arkansas which were unsold because subject to flooding, 8/5. "Mr. Calhoun thought that the general government ought to do something for the purpose of reclaiming this immense mass of unsaleable and useless lands. He had reported [on 6/26/1846] a bill for the purpose, and he hoped this matter would not be pressed until he could call up his bill, which he would do next session." (The bill was tabled.) From Houston, ed., *Proceedings and Debates*, p. 1002. Also printed in *Congressional Globe*, 30th Cong., 1st Sess., p. 1043. Variant in the Washington, D.C., *Daily National Intelligencer*, August 8, 1848, p. 3.

From ANNA [MARIA CALHOUN] CLEMSON

Brussels, Aug. 7th 1848

My dear father, Like you I have so many to write to, that I am forced to make the intervals between each, longer than I could wish, but we are too well assured of each other[']s affection, to require that it should be manifested by frequent letters, or in any other way.

We are in the midst of preparations for our departure, which as you may suppose keep me much occupied in mind & body. The voyage is a long one & requires many arrangements, especially as we go by sailing vessel, which by rendering the time longer & uncertain, renders more clothing necessary, than if we went by steamer. I must confess, I dread the long voyage, & should have greatly preferred the steamer, but we literally shall not have money enough to pay our passage in that way, so we are forced to take the other. We shall leave Havre between the 25th of Sept: & the 1st of October, so

I shall return without seeing England at all, which I regret, but the same all powerful reason, want of money, prevents our traversing England, as that way is much more expensive than through France, & we must look at every cent in order to make ends meet. In this, as in every thing else, when we cannot do as we like, we must content ourselves to do as we can so I try not to think of all the suffering & fear, I must endure, & try only to remember the pleasure of once more seeing my family. I should like much not to be forced to take the children [John Calhoun Clemson and Floride Elizabeth Clemson] to Carolina, if I could help it—indeed it seems almost impossible I should do so. To the plantation, where our business calls us, they certainly cannot go at the commencement of winter. To take them to Pendleton, & leave them there for a short time, & then bring them back again, when the roads are at the worst, seems an unnecessary & disagreeable trip, for I cannot spend the winter in Pendleton. Being only at home for a short time, I want to be near you as much as possible. Whereas, if mother [Floride Colhoun Calhoun,] sister [Martha Cornelia Calhoun] & yourself would meet us either at Washington, Philadelphia, or New York, (which last would be best of all,) I would leave the children with mother, & Mr. [Thomas G.] C[lemson] & myself could go south with little or no baggage, or trouble, see to our affairs, & when I had done I could return to Washington, & pass the winter between there & Philadelphia, in the midst of my family & that of Mr. C[lemson]. This plan seems to me delightful, & would only require mother to come on a few weeks before the session commenced. If *you* could not leave so soon, we could meet in Pendleton or Edgefield, & go on & rejoin the others when you went to Washington. Do try & arrange this for me, I entreat you. I do not know how I could lug about with me the children, my fat Belgian nurse, & all the additional baggage they would require, besides, being a stranger, I fear she ["(the nurse)" *interlined*] would get homesick & discontented, if I took her immediately, in the winter, into the country, & left her there, alone among strangers, as I must do if they went to Pendleton, & she is such an excellent person, & such a treasure to me, that I am anxious to make her like the country well enough to remain there if I do. For all these good reasons, I do hope you will persuade mother, & sister, to meet me as I said before, even if you cannot, in which case they could pass their time very pleasantly at Philadelphia, till we returned. Mother would have no trouble with the children, for their nurse is perfectly trustworthy & more careful of them than I am myself & they are dear good little things & very obedient & affectionate. If mother came, she should try & be there

651

the middle of October, for they tell me that at that season, the westerly winds prevail, & we may have a short passage, which Heaven grant we may!

If I can only take the children looking so well & so gay as they do now, I shall be very happy. They are full of the idea of going home, & talk of nothing else. I am sure you will be content with them. They are backward in their learning, it is true, but you will not blame me for *that*, for I only follow your ideas of which I heartily approve with regard to youthful prodigies—but tho' backward in their studies, they are beyond their age in every thing else, & tho' very wild & full of life, they are affectionate, reasonable, & obedient, & have excellent principles. At first you will laugh to hear how drolly the[y] mix french & english in speaking but that is only from habit & when they find they are not understood they will lose it in a week.

For politics, they are really not worth writing about. Every thing is in confusion & there is such a want of fixed ideas & principles & so much egotism that I don[']t know what is to come of it all. France is for the moment quiet but why? Paris is in a state of siege which they are afraid to raise & under the name of republic they have a military despotism with the commanding general for President. Even those who sincerely desire liberty are so discouraged & disgusted by all the intrigues & difficulties by which they are surrounded & see so little hopes of ultimate success that they fold their arms & look on. Lamartine is no more heard of than if he never existed. In the meantime in spite of the good harvest this winter must be one of misery & horrors & no one can say what a month or even a day may bring forth.

I must stop & write to Willy [William Lowndes Calhoun] from whom I received a charming letter the other day.

All send love. Your devoted daughter, Anna Clemson.

ALS in ScCleA.

From HENRY O'RIELLY

Albany [N.Y.], Aug. 7, 1848
Dear Sir, In arranging the papers of President [James] Monroe, I am authorized by Mr. [Samuel L.] Gouverneur to address the friends and correspondents of that statesman respecting such papers and

information as they may choose to communicate for elucidation historically or biographically.

It is of course needless to say a word to you concerning the momentous affairs embraced in Mr. Monroe's long public history. Your connexion with many of those matters, and your knowledge of all, together with your personal relations to the Ex-President, induce me to address you first in the correspondence which I am now commencing for the purpose of *completing* the collection by eliciting such documents or information as it may be agreeable to supply. The recent Oregon (or territorial) discussion, in its references to the opinions of Mr. Monroe's Cabinet, illustrates the necessity for *thorough* inquiry, when we compare the Journal of Mr. [John Quincy] Adams with the obvious meaning of the *erasures* in Mr. Monroe's letter, and with your own recollections. I may add that, in a trust so important, so intimately connected with the Public History of Events & of Statesmen in the Career of this Confederacy—I could not allow myself to pursue the task without invoking the Judgment and aid of a gentleman whose own history is so intimately interwoven with that of the Ex-President and of the United States.

Any papers or information which you may choose to communicate, will be held in the same sanctity as those of the Ex-President; and I have not permitted a line to be used in any way, save with the consent of the family and for the elucidation of truth under appeals made to the "Monroe Papers."

It was at the request of Mr. [James D.] Westcott [Jr., Senator from Fla.], and by the consent of Mr. Gouverneur which I requested Mr. Westcott to obtain, that I furnished the extracts referred to in the recent Oregon Discussion; and, with similar purpose, I will take pleasure in furnishing you with the "authenticated copies" of certain documents (not with me, just now) which you desire for "preservation among your papers."

In the unaffected diffidence with which I undertook the arrangement of the papers committed to my charge by the representatives of the Ex-President, I am encouraged by the thought that singleness of purpose in the cause of truth will measurably extenuate the deficiencies of literary execution. The "Memoir," which may be termed an Autobiography arranged chiefly or in great part by Mr. Gouverneur from the notes of the Ex-President, is referred to by John Quincy Adams, as the "precious papers of the Ex-President," in the letters (now before me) with which Mr. A[dams] acknowledged the perusal as a fitting preliminary to the Discourse which he pronounced in Boston on the Death of Mr. Monroe.

It would afford me great pleasure, personally, as it certainly would promote historical accuracy, to be favored with your Judgment on doubtful & important points in the prosecution of the task; and I would endeavour to avoid trespassing too largely on your attention.

Hoping that the subject will excuse the liberty I take in addressing you thus, Respectfully yours, Henry O'Rielly.

ALS in ScCleA. NOTE: Henry O'Rielly (1806–1886) was a noted editor, author, and early advocate of the construction of telegraph lines.

Remarks on a donation of public lands to the State of Alabama for railroad construction, 8/8. "Mr. Calhoun thought the policy of these appropriations of the public lands was beneficial in increasing the value of the public domain. As to internal improvement, he denied in toto the power of the general government to carry it on." Calhoun made later unreported remarks in the same debate. From Houston, ed., *Proceedings and Debates*, p. 1009. Also printed in *Congressional Globe*, 30th Cong., 1st Sess., p. 1051. Variant in the New York, N.Y., *Herald*, August 10, 1848, p. 4.

[Maj. Gen.] WINFIELD SCOTT to John C. Calhoun and Others

ELIZABETHTOWN, (N.J.,) Aug. 9, 1848

GENTLEMEN: Returning, prematurely, from the sea shore, I have the honor to find here your communication tendering me, on the part of a large number of the Members of the two Houses of Congress, a public dinner on any day that I may name—an invitation the most flattering, but which, on account of continued physical debility, I am obliged to decline.

I had, earlier, the happiness to receive from every member of the present Congress, in the form of certain resolutions, the highest distinction that could be bestowed upon a citizen-soldier. The present invitation, expressing the private consideration of so many of the most distinguished Representatives of the States and People of the Union, without regard to party, superadds every obligation of personal thanks and gratitude, on, gentlemen, Your fellow-citizen and friend, Winfield Scott.

PC in the Washington, D.C., *Daily National Intelligencer,* August 14, 1848, p. 3; PC in the Richmond, Va., *Whig and Public Advertiser* (semi-weekly), August 18, 1848, p. 4. NOTE: This letter was addressed to J[ohn] M. Clayton, J.C. Calhoun, Rob[er]t C. Winthrop, J[ohn] A. Rockwell, and M[oses] Hampton, members of the committee of invitation.

SPEECH ON THE PROPOSAL TO EXTEND THE MISSOURI COMPROMISE LINE TO THE PACIFIC

[In the Senate, August 10, 1848]

Mr. Calhoun's Speech on the amendment offered to the bill from the House for establishing a Territorial Government for Oregon, proposing to extend the Missouri Compromise line to the Pacific Ocean.

He said: I shall vote against this amendment, but for reasons very different from those assigned by the Senator from Mass. (Mr. [Daniel] Webster.) I shall vote against it, because, in the first place, I regard it as ambiguous. In proposing to extend the Missouri Compromise line westward to the Pacific, it makes no provision whatever to protect the rights of the South to the portions of New Mexico and California South of latitude 36 30, while it surrenders to the exclusive occupancy of the North all that lies North of it. Whether it gives us any security or not to the portion lying South, is left entirely to construction. The most zealous advocate of the Wilmot Proviso may vote for it on the construction that it surrenders to the North all lying north of the line and leaves open to contest all south of it, while on the opposite construction, that it secures by implication the rights of the South to all lying south of the line, a zealous opponent of that proviso may vote for it. As to myself, I am for plain dealing on all questions, and especially on this, in reference to which, we have already experienced so much bad faith on the part of the North; and cannot therefore vote for any measure susceptible of such opposite construction. It is time, that all ambiguity should cease on this question, and that every portion of the Union shall distinctly understand, what to expect in reference to it. Should this amendment be adopted, it is certain one side or the other will be deceived, nor can there be much doubt, as to which it will be. It may be laid down as an established rule, that where the stronger party refuses to be explicit, as in this case, the weaker if it yields its assent will in the end be deceived and defrauded.

I shall, in the next place, vote against this amendment for another reason not less conclusive with me. The Senator from Massachusetts (Mr. Webster) and others, who act with him on this occasion, oppose it, because they are resolved to pass the bill as it came from the House without amendment or modification in order to assert the absolute and unconditional power of Congress over the territories, and then to establish a precedent in this case, to exclude the South from all other territories of the United States now possessed or hereafter to be acquired. It is that, and not the exclusion of slavery from Oregon, where they well know there is no probability of its introduction, which makes them so unyielding and intent on passing this bill, as it came from the House, but they cannot be more intent on asserting the power than I am against its assertion, and in maintaining our rights and equality in reference to all the territories belonging to the Union. I for one shall not yield an inch, nor give a vote which can by implication be construed to surrender our full right and equality as members of the Union. The North cannot have a deeper interest in asserting absolute power over the territories, than the South has in resisting it. If it be important to her, as the means of extending her power and ascendency over this government, it is still more so to the South to resist it, not only as indispensable to the preservation of her rights and equality but her safety itself; thus thinking, I can neither vote for the amendment, nor the bill with the amendment, if it should be adopted.

I go further, I would not vote for the bill, even with the amendment proposed on a former occasion by the Senator from Kentucky, (Mr. [Joseph R.] Underwood,) as effectually as that would protect us in the portion of New Mexico and California lying South of 36 30. I would not because it might be construed to admit by implication the absolute power over the territories for which the North is so strenuously and obstinately contending. But, although I would not vote for it, I would acquiesce should the proposition come from the North, provided it should be offered in the spirit of harmony, and should receive her support, in the same way, that we acquiesced in the Missouri Compromise, and from the same motive, a cherished regard for the Union. But while I would acquiesce in a compromise thus offered and supported, I cannot imagine a course more humiliating and dangerous, than for the South, or the feebler party to propose such a compromise, or to adopt it by her votes, united with a small portion of the votes of the North, against the votes and the bold and arrogant claims of the rest to the absolute power to exclude us at pleasure from all the territories. Instead of a compromise, it would be a surrender on our part, with a pistol at the breast. Its impolicy would not be less than its infamy; for what possible assurance would there be, that such a compromise would be respected? The evidence it would afford of our want of spirit would but tend to unite and animate the North. In a short time the few, who voted with us from that section, would be discarded, as in the case of the Missouri Compromise, and others hostile to us would take their place; when the united North would regard our proposition and vote as a surrender of the power, and treat with merited scorn our humiliating and base surrender.

Having now announced the course I intend to take in reference to this amendment & bill, I propose before I conclude to avail myself of this, as a fit occasion to state what I believe to be the present state of this question, and in what it must end, unless it should be speedily and effectually arrested. In executing what I propose, I deem it to be a duty to my constituents and the country to be perfectly explicit and unreserved in my remarks. To understand the nature of a disease, and the laws by which its progress is governed, and the stage at which it has arrived, is the first and indispensable step preparatory to applying a remedy.

There are diseases of the body politic, as well as our natural bodies, that never will stop of themselves. Abolition is one of them. If left to itself, it will pass through all its stages, from the first agitation, until it ends in emancipation and destruction of the government. The cause is to be found in the nature of the disease, connected with the character of our political institutions, as I shall proceed to show.

If traced to its source, it will be found to originate in the belief of not a small portion of the people of the North, that slavery is sinful, notwithstanding the authority of the Bible to the contrary. It is not necessary, with the object in view, to ascertain the cause of this belief. It is sufficient for my purpose, that such is the fact, and that the conviction is deep and sincere, with not a few. But certain it is, that the belief is of recent origin. There was a period and that not long ago, when it did not exist, when the Northern States were slave-holding communities, and extensively and profitably engaged in importing slaves into the South. It would be, not a little curious and interesting to trace the causes, which have led, in so short a time, to so great a change; but I forbear the attempt, because it would give a greater range, than what I propose to my remarks. But it is pertinent to state, that an increased attachment and devotion to liberty cannot be enumerated among them. On the contrary, the standard of liberty, instead of being raised, has been greatly lowered, with the progress of abolitionism. Before it took its rise, no people were regarded as free, who did not live under constitutional governments. With us the standard was so high, that we regarded no people as free, who did not live under popular, or as it was then called Republican Governments. Even within my recollection, it was a subject of dispute whether the English people were free as they were governed in part by a king and an aristocracy. But now, every people are called free, however despotic the government. Even if conquered and subject to the unlimited control of a foreign government, they are regarded, not as slaves, but free. Indeed serfs are scarcely regarded as slaves, and have little of the sympathy of the abolitionists. The term slave is now restricted almost exclusively to African slavery, as it exists on this continent, and its Islands; and it is only in that form, that it excites the sympathy, or claims the attention of abolitionists. In none other do they regard it as sinful, if they are to be judged by their acts. In their eyes, sugar, coffee, cotton, or any other article made by the conquered and enslaved Hindoos or serfs of Russia, is free made, and that only made by enslaved Africans on this continent, or its Islands is slave made. To so low a standard has freedom or liberty sunk; and yet those who have so degraded it, claim to be its exclusive friends, and in their delusion, regard all other forms of slavery, as innocent, except that in which it exists with us! To abolish African slavery in that form, is to extinguish slavery, according to their conception, every where, and introduce universal liberty!

It is not at all surprising, with this impression, there should spring up a strong fanatical feeling in the North, in favor of abolition, which needs nothing but some exciting cause to rouse it into action. The abolition of African slavery in its old form in the British West India Islands and the long and violent agitation, which preceded it, did much to arouse the feelings at the North, and confirm the impression that it was sinful. But something more was necessary to excite it into action, and that was a belief, on the part of those, who thought it sinful, that they were responsible for its continuance.

It was a considerable time before such a belief was created, except to a very limited extent. In the early stages of this government, while it was yet called and regarded to be, a federal Government, slavery was believed to be a local institution, and under the exclusive control of the Government of the several States. So long as this impression remained, little or no responsibility was felt on the part of any portion of the North, for its continuance. But with the growth of the power and influence of the government, and its tendency, to consolidation, when it became usual to call the people of these States a nation, and this government national, the States came to be regarded by a large portion of the North, as bearing the same relation to it, as the counties do to the States, and as much under the control of this government, as the counties are under that of their representative State governments. The increase of this belief was accompanied by a corresponding increase of the feeling of responsibility, for the continuance of slavery, on the part of those in the North, who considered it so. At this stage it was strengthened into conviction by the Proclamation of Gen. [Andrew] Jackson, and the act of Congress authorizing him to employ the entire force of the union against the government and people of South Carolina. Both were based on the assumption, that this government had the unlimited right, in the last resort, to determine the extent of its powers, and to enforce obedience on the part of the States, on all questions, in which the extent of the powers delegated to the United States, and those reserved to the States and the people might be involved, an assumption, which in fact, confers on this government absolute and unlimited control over the States, and all their institutions, and makes it in practice a consolidated government.

Such assumption could not but have a powerfull effect in rousing into action the heretofore dormant feeling of abolitionism. It was accordingly roused into action for the first time in 1835, two years thereafter. It commenced with a simultaneous and widespread circulation of incendiary publications all over the South, and has continued increasing ever since, without the least indication of abatement.

Having traced abolitionism to its source and explained the cause, which roused it into action, I shall next proceed to explain, the cause why the agitation has continued to advance, with increased violence without any symptom of abatement.

The cause certainly is not to be found in the nature of that, in which it has been shown to originate. Fanaticism from its nature breaks out into violent movements, and soon exhausts itself by its extravagance and folly; unless it comes to be combined with some more steady and permanent cause of action. The reason is to be found in the fact, that fanaticks as a class have far more zeal, than intellect, and are fanaticks only because they have. There can be no fanaticism, but where there is more passion than reason; and hence in the nature of things, movements originating in it, run down in a short time by their folly and extravagance. This instance would have formed no exception. The fanaticks with whom the agitation commenced were of no standing, or weight, while they possessed in a high degree the ardent zeal, and the feeble intellect belonging to that description of persons. If left to themselves, the agitation would long since have ceased.

Nor is it less certain, that the continuance of its increase without the least tendency to abatement, is not to be found in any interest the North has in abolishing slavery. Her interest is the very reverse. It has often been assigned, as a reason for abolishing it that it is hostile to the prosperity of the South, and that it is the real cause of its relative poverty compared with the North. Be that as it may, no one can have the assurance to assert, that slavery with us has been or is hostile to the prosperity of the North. If the South does not profit by it, the North beyond question has and is profiting by it and that to a vast extent. Strike out the product of slave labor, and with it the great staples of cotton, rice, tobacco, and sugar, and what would become of the commerce, the shipping, the navigation, and the manufactures of the North and the revenue of the Government? What would become of her great commercial and manufacturing towns, and her vast tonnage and shipping, crowding every harbor and afloat on every sea?

But, if the cause of the continued increase of the abolition agitation is not to be found in the nature of fanaticism, in which it originated, nor the interest of the North, where is it to be found, except in its connection with the party movements of the day, for which our political institutions afford such remarkable facilities? To realise the extent of these facilities, it must be borne in mind, that our system of Government throughout, both State and Federal, is based on elections; that the distribution of all the honors, and vast patronage of both depends on them, and that the people every where are divided into two parties, nearly equally divided, in most of the States, and are ever engaged in ardent struggles to obtain, or retain a majority, and thereby the control of Government, and with it the distribution of its honors and emoluments. The consequence of this state of things is, that, if a party held together by some cohesive force, stronger than the ties, which hold together the two political parties, should spring up each of the two in their ardent struggle for the mastery, would court it, and, if necessary to obtain its support, profess a regard and attachment to its cause. Such is the abolition party; or, at least, such was [it] in its origin. In their fanatical zeal, they believed slavery to be sinful, and that, in their efforts to put it down, they were serving the cause both of God and man. Now if we add, that at the North, where it originated, the two political parties are usually more equally divided, and the struggle between them still more ardent than at the South, not only because their own local patronage is generally larger, and that they are to a far greater extent, the recipient of the emoluments of the Federal Government, but also because the tendency to conflict between the democratical and aristocratical elements of society is far stronger there than at the South. Such being the case, it was next to impossible to prevent abolitionism from connecting and combining its movements with the party movements in that quarter of the Union. Each party there, and especially the weaker for the time, would be sure to bid for the votes of the abolitionists; and for that purpose countenance favor and support them and their movements, however averse in reality they might be to them, or however mischievous they might regard their movements. They thus became the object of courtship by both parties, and it is not at all wonderful, that they should increase in number and influence under the joint patronage of the two, until their weight became so considerable, as to be sufficient to turn the scales in favor of either in several of the Northern States. At that stage it began to be sensibly felt in the action of the Federal Government, and especially in the election of the President and Vice President, the common center of the struggle of the two great parties throughout the Union. This influence extended to elections even with us, and thereby gave a powerful impulse to the cause of abolition in the North and at the same time has divided, distracted, and debased the South.

It is not necessary, with the object I have in view, to enter into a minute investigation to show how this has been effected. It is sufficient to state the leaders of the two parties soon perceived, that this new element, which had infused itself into the political movements of the North, had a strong tendency to separation of the Northern and Southern wings of the respective parties, and that to preserve their unity it was indispensable to adopt efficient measures to counteract it. Each perceived that its success over the other in the Presidential election, and of course to obtain or retain the power to distribute the honors and emoluments of the Government among themselves, depended on it. For this purpose, the leaders of the parties both at the South and North, including their respected organs, adopted the policy to observe silence and to keep out of sight as far as possible, the movements and progress of the Abolitionists and the countenance and support they received from their respective parties at the North; and when compelled to notice any act or movement, too marked to be passed in silence, to denounce in a feeble tone as possible, and at the same time to throw, whatever blame they attach to it, on the opposite party, and to excuse their own. This policy has been observed with such success by the party leaders and organs as to keep the people of the South, to a great extent, ignorant of the movement of the Abolitionists, and the actual progress they have made towards accomplishing their object. It has done more, and worse. It has kept the South divided, distracted and engrossed in Presidential struggles, in which it has comparatively little interest, and indifferent to that which vitally concerns her safety. It has not stopped there, it has so blunted her feelings as to render her almost indifferent to the greatest insult and the most flagrant aggressions on her right, so much so that when the support of the Abolitionists and their movements by both parties at the North became at length, too glaring to be any longer concealed, instead of uniting, in a bold and manly stand in opposition to both, the leaders and organs of the two parties at the South have entered into a pitiful contest to prove, that their respective candidate and party at the North are less hostile to us, than are their opponents, as if nothing was left us, but to choose the least hostile for our protector! Can degradation go further?

Under the debasing influence of this policy, both parties at the South have permitted their northern associates to court the abolitionists, and receive their votes without losing ours, in the election of the President and Vice President. Is it then wonderful, that they should increase in strength and influence, while we in the same degree should become weak and insignificant? Under the same debasing influence, we have yielded step by step; made concession after concession; permitted aggression after aggression, and submitted to insult after insult, until the North has lost all respect for us, and come to believe, that we cannot be kicked into resistance. That such has been the consequence, I appeal for proof to the history of the progress of abolition, from its first outbreak in 1835, to this time. The whole consists of concessions on our part, and aggressions on theirs; concessions made and aggressions submitted to by both parties at the South, in order to preserve their connection with their respective parties at the North, and each followed by an increase of strength on the part of the abolitionists & decrease on that of ours, until they have attained sufficient power and influence to form a political party of their own, with sanguine hopes of electing their presidential candidate, and to obtain the control of the federal Government, if not now, in a few years. Nor will they be deceived, if things be permitted to progress, as they have heretofore done. If we continue to pursue the same policy we have thus formed, the same causes which have raised them to their present height, and sunk us to our present depression,

will continue to operate with increased energy, until we shall cease
to have the spirit and power, to resist, and shall be compelled to submit, without effort, when emancipation, the great object of agitation,
will be consecrated.   Nothing short of some efficient remedy speedily
applied can prevent the catastrophe; to so dangerous a stage has the
disease already reached.

The first step towards applying such a remedy is to cease to look
for it to the old party associations, and the presidential election.
They have been tried, fully tried, and have utterly failed.   Instead of
remedy, they have acted as the wind to the flame, increased its fury
and extended it far and wide.   Without them, it would long since
have cleared of itself, and that without reaching our borders or endangering our safety.   To find the remedy, we must then cease to
look to them, and to look to ourselves.   There it may be found but
even then only in our Union, and fixed resolve to arrest the disease,
be the consequences what they may.   We have still the power to
protect ourselves, if we have not lost the spirit and patriotism to put
it forth.   We must prove by our acts, that we still have the blood of
our patriotic and heroic ancestors running in our veins, and that our
long submission to insult and aggressions has been caused, not from
a want of spirit to defend our rights, but from a regard for the union.
If we evince by our acts, fixed determination to hold no political connection with any party at the North, which is not prepared to enforce
the guaranties of the Constitution in our favor and respect our rights,
a host of true and faithful allies, would soon rally to our support
there; unless indeed the disease has already made such progress, that
the North is willing to sacrifice the Union on the altar of abolition.
If such should prove to be the case, it would only prove the imperious
necessity of looking to ourselves, and ceasing to look to either party
at the North for the protection of our liberty and safety.   In that
event, he among us, would be a traitor to the South, who would not
spurn old political party associations, when they stood in the way of
Union among ourselves.

But as greatly as the north is already tainted by abolitionism, I
do not believe it is so much so yet, as to be ready to sacrifice the
Union for its sake.   That it has made rapid progress within the last
two or three years is certain.   No stronger proof of the fact need be
furnished than what is doing at this time, at Buffalo, in New York,
where there is now collected a numerous assembly from every portion of the North, consisting of abolitionists of every shape and description, combined with no inconsiderable number of men of influence belonging to both of the two great political parties and under

the lead of one [Martin Van Buren], who a few years since stood at the head of the Democratic party, and filled the highest office in the Union. The avowed motive for assembling is to form a distinct and separate political party, sectional in its object and character, and having for the main element of its union the entire exclusion of the South from all the territories belonging to the United States acquired, or to be acquired. For this purpose, they propose to nominate candidates for the Presidency and Vice-Presidency at the approaching election, in the hope of throwing the present election into the House of Representatives, and carrying the next succeeding by a popular vote. And who can tell, if we permit the state of things, that has raised abolitionism from its humble start to so great an elevation, to be continued, what may occur in the next four years? If under its influence, it has attained sufficient strength already to aspire to the Presidency, what is there to prevent its success at the end of the next 4 years, if its operation is permitted to be continued? Or who can tell even if that should not be the case, whether within the same period, alienation and hostility between the two sections may not be so increased and the South so divided, distracted and weakened, that it will be then too late to save the Union, if not, also, too late to save ourselves? Already the occurrences of the last few months are calculated to destroy all confidence in the support of either party at the North. Less than a month since, there was a fair prospect of the adjustment of the territorial question on the compromise of the Constitution itself, without a surrender of a particle of constitutional right on either side. Since then, so strong has been the demonstration at the North against that or any other adjustment, or even against the acceptance of any concession on our part short of a formal surrender of all rights under the Constitution to the whole that the members of both parties from that section, united almost to a man, against every measure which did not contain the assertion of the absolute right in Congress to exclude us at its pleasure from all the territories. I have great respect and sincere feelings of kindness for many of the members from the North who have in so short a period changed their position, and voted against us. It was done no doubt in deference to what they believed to be the wish of their constituents, and not from any change of opinion on their part, but that is no cause of consolation to us, nor is it calculated to increase our reliance on them hereafter. It only proves, that they are sounder than their constituents, and that we cannot rely on them when their opinion on this question differs from theirs and that instead of looking to them, or their professions, or promises, we must look to the opinions and acts of those they represent.

With such irresistible evidence before us of the great and rapid progress of abolitionism without the slightest indication of abatement, he is blind who does not see if the state of things, which have caused it should be permitted to continue that it will speedily be too late, if not to save our selves, to save the Union. It is clear beyond dispute that a great majority of both parties at the North are resolved to maintain and carry out the principles of the Wilmot Proviso; or what is the same thing in effect, the doctrine of free soil. The argument is exhausted and the decree pronounced, never to be reversed, unless by the united and fixed resolve of the South, that it shall not be carried into execution. Congress may indeed possibly agree to extend the Missouri Compromise at the next session to the Pacific, but if it should it would be not on the ground of right, but as a mere matter of concession and grace on their part, to keep us quiet, and not, as heretofore, to adjust disputed claims by compromise, or to have any force as a precedent in our favour, in case of any future acquisition of Territory, even if it should be Cuba.

But suppose in this I should be mistaken, and that the extension of the line should put at rest the territorial question, and with it the Wilmot Proviso, which no one, who knows the unanimous sentiment of the North in reference to what they call free soil, can believe, that would not stop abolitionism. As bad as the Proviso is, it is not the worst or most dangerous form of its assaults; and the only effect of arresting it, would be to concentrate and give increased vigor to its attacks on more vulnerable and vital points. Movements have already been made in the other House, during the session by both parties of the North, towards abolishing slavery in this District, to be followed, no doubt, in time, by like movements to abolish it in all the forts, arsenals, Navy yards and other places, over which Congress has exclusive power of legislation. The same argument, which would apply to abolishing it in this District, would equally apply to all such places; and let me add, the same argument, that would establish the absolute power of Congress over the territories, would establish with almost equal force, its absolute power over this District, and all such places. And hence, among others, the reason, why the North has contended so pertinaciously, and obstinately for the power over the territories. Now when it is added, that this District and many of the forts, arsenals, Navy yards, and other places of the same discription, are situated in the midst of the South, and that the

North holds almost unanimously, that slavery can only exist, where it is established positively by law, and that the moment a slave puts his foot where it is not so established, he ceases to be a slave, who can doubt but that the abolition of slavery in them, would be far more dangerous to us, than the application of the Wilmot Proviso to all the territories? It would open every where, throughout the entire South, asylums to receive our fugitive slaves, who would, as soon as they entered, cease to be so. How long could slavery continue in the other portions of the south under such a state of things? And what would we gain by turning the attacks of the North from the territories, to these more vulnerable points?

But these are not the only vulnerable points. There are others not much, if any, less vital. It is not only through Congress, but also through the legislation of the Northern States, and the acts of their public functionaries, that we have been assailed. It is well known, that one of the strong objections which the South had to entering into a more intimate Union with the North, was the danger to which we would be thereby exposed in reference to our slaves. To guard against it, and to reconcile us to the Constitution, the Northern States entered into a solemn guaranty, to deliver up fugitive slaves on the demand of their owners. Instead of complying with this solemn stipulation, by passing laws to carry it in execution and make it the duty of their public functionaries and citizens to co-operate in seizing and delivering them up as they were in duty bound to do, there is scarcely a single Northern State, that has not passed laws, which in effect have annulled the stipulation. They, indeed have practically expunged it from the Constitution. And we on our part have permitted this flagrant violation of the Constitution and our rights under it to be perpetrated without effort to resist rather than party associations should be disturbed. They have gone farther. They have permitted societies to be organized, not only to assault and disturb the relation between master and slave, but to seduce them from their masters, and pass them secretly and rapidly into Canada, and there to place them beyond the reach of recovery, and the stipulations of the Constitution. Such outrages would between independent states, be sufficient cause to justify war; and will, if we permit them to be continued, end in abolitionism, by rendering slave property worthless, without the aid of the Wilmot Proviso, or any other measure of aggression.

There still remains another mode of attack, that of itself, if permitted to go on, will be followed by the same result. I allude to the continual and incessant agitation of the subject, both in and out of

Congress. It is of itself a great and dangerous outrage on our ac- knowledged rights and property. No one doubts, but we have the right to hold slaves, and all admit that neither this Government, nor any State government, has the right to abolish slavery in the States where they exist. But, if we have the right to hold them as property, we have also the right to hold them in peace and quiet; and all at- tempts to disturb, or question our rights with the view to its sub- version, are direct and dangerous outrages. If permitted to continue, the incessant agitation and denunciation of ourselves, and of the relation existing between the two races with us, which has so long been carried on through Congress, the press, and every other way, must in the end destroy that relation. It would not only dispirit and debase us, but create hope and expectations on the part of our slaves incompatible with their position and relation to us.

It is, then, manifest that the extension of the Missouri compro- mise line to the Pacific, even if it should put at rest the Proviso, would not stop abolitionism, or prevent it from accomplishing its end. Its agitation and attacks would still continue directed against points at least as vulnerable, and some of them of a description beyond the power of the federal Government to interfere in order to arrest, even if disposed to do so, of which however there is no probability.

I have now stated my reasons for believing that the abolition agitation will never stop of itself, or ever will be through the Presi- dential election, or the action of this Government, and that nothing short of the united and fixed determination of the South to maintain her rights, at every hazard, can stop it. Without that, the end must be emancipation in the worst possible form, far worse than, if done by own own voluntary act, instead of being compelled to adopt it, at the bidding of a dominant section, whose interest and sympathy for them and hostility to us, would combine to reverse the present re- lation between the two races in the South by raising the inferior to be the favored and superior, and sinking the superior to the inferior and despised.

I have now freely and explicitly expressed my conviction of what must be the result, if the causes, which have led to the present state of things should be permitted to continue; and also how only that result can be prevented. In doing so I have but performed what I believe to be a solemn duty, not only to my own constituents, and the section, where Providence has cast my lot, but to the whole Union. My conviction is strong, that all, the South and North—the Union, and the institutions of the country are in imminent danger, and that it cannot be averted, unless the causes which have led to it, and the

667

only means by which they can be counteracted, should be clearly seen and promptly resorted to. My object has been to point them out. If I am right the South is under solemn obligation both to herself and to the rest of the Union, to rally and take the remedy in her own hands, and that speedily as the only possible mode to bring the North to pause and reflect on consequences, if indeed, it be not already too late for that; and if, unfortunately it should prove to be so, to save herself.

I know that very different motives may be attributed to me. There are those who can see no danger to the Union, from aggressions injustice, or violation of the Constitution, while they are ever ready to cry out disunion, against every attempt to repel them. I have so often been the subject of their assaults, that I have learned to contemn them, and to leave it to the whole tenour of my life to repel them. Nearly forty years of my life have been devoted to the service of the Union. If I shall have any place in the memory of posterity, it will be in consequence of my deep attachment to it and our federal system of Government, and earnest and honest efforts to uphold and perpetuate them. But as strong as is my attachment to the Union, my attachment to liberty and the safety of the section where Providence has cast my lot, is still stronger; not that I am sectional in my feelings, for I have ever looked with deep interest to the good of the whole, and rejoiced in the prosperity of every portion. Nor have I ever in any instance supported the interest of my section, at the expense of any other. If I have stood up for it on many and important questions it has been defensively—to repel aggressions on its rights, to which, as the weaker section, it has often been subject. In doing so, I have ever regarded myself, not only as performing a duty I owed to it, but to the whole Union; for I hold it to be true, in a federal system, like ours, that the section or portion of the Union, which permits encroachment on its constitutional rights, when it can prevent it, to be not much less guilty than that which perpetrated the wrong. Our Union, and political institutions can only be preserved, by preserving the rights and equality established among its members by the Constitution, and these can only be preserved, by the stronger portion of the Union abstaining from encroaching on the weaker, or if it should not, by the weaker States placing themselves on their reserved rights and repelling the encroachments. Such are the impressions under which I now act, and have ever acted, in resisting aggressions on the right[s] of the South. I aim not at change or revolution. My object is to preserve. I am thoroughly conservative in my politics. I wish to maintain things as I found them established. I am satisfied with them and am of the opinion that they cannot be changed for the better. I hold it to be difficult to get a good Government, and still more difficult to preserve it; and as I believe a good Government to be the greatest of earthly blessings, I would be adverse to the overthrow of ours even, if I thought it greatly inferior to what I do, in the hope of establishing a better.

Thus thinking, my sincere desire is to preserve the Union; and let what will come I shall take care, that my course shall be such as to free me from all responsibility should it be destroyed. I shall place myself immoveably where duty commands, on the defensive—against aggressions, and injustice and encroachments, and in support of right, justice and the Constitution, be the consequences what they may. If the result should be severance of the Union, and the overthrow of our system of Government, the responsibility will fall not on the assailed, but the assailants—not on those whose aim is to defend rights, but those whose aim is to violate them—not on those who struggle to maintain the Constitution, but those who struggle to invade it. It is not for us, who are assaulted, but for those who assail us, to count the value of the Union. To us, without the observance of the guaranties of the Constitution, the Union would be a curse instead of a blessing—a sword to assault and not a shield to defend. It is for our assailants to count whether the Union with the observance of its guaranties on their part, is of sufficient value to them to be preserved or not. If in their estimate it would be so small as to put its safety at stake, rather than to be restricted to the observance of its guaranties: How could they expect us to cease resistance to their aggressions, when the Union, if they should succeed, would be to us the greatest of curses, instead of being one of the greatest blessings, as it would be, with strict adherence to the Constitution?

But great as its blessings would be to us, in that case, it would be in every view far more so still to the North. It would even be more necessary to their safety than to ours. The very institution, which is the object of their incessant denunciation and assaults would be the Palladium of our safety. The danger to which it is exposed and the necessity of defending it for the common safety of the whole South would constitute a central point of interest, that would unite us with links of iron within, which no force could dissever, while it would present without an unbroken and impenetrable front. It would do more. From the conservative character of the institution, it would prevent that conflict between labour and capital, which must ever exist in populous and crowded communities, where wages are the regulator between them, and thereby secure and preserve with us a settled and quiet condition of things within, which can never be experienced in such communities. The North on the contrary would have no central point of union to bind its various and conflicting interests together; and would with the increase of its population and wealth be subject to all the agitation and conflicts growing out of the divisions of wealth and poverty, and their concomitants, capital and labour, of which already there are so many and so serious.

But it is not in reference to safety only, that we would be the least sufferers. We would be far less so in a pecuniary point of view. Indeed, in that respect, we would be great gainers, instead of being losers. The first effect would be to establish direct trade between us and the rest of the world. Our imports, in consequence, would at once rise from their present depression to be equal in value to our exports, in conformity to the established principle that imports and exports of a country must in a series of years balance each other or nearly so, when fairly valued. On the same principle, their imports would fall off and sink to the level of their exports. The consequence would be, that with the same rates of duties, our revenue from imports, would more than double theirs, and what is of great importance, all of its proceeds would be expended among ourselves, instead of the far greater part being expended as it is at the North, to the great increase of their wealth and diminution of ours. With this great increase of imports and of revenue and expenditure with us, and falling off with them, there would be with us, a corresponding increase of commerce, navigation, ship-building, tonnage, seamen, and general prosperity and increase of wealth, and a corresponding falling off with the North!

Nor would we be less capable of defending and protecting ourselves than they. We would have the advantages of closer unity, a greater exemption from agitation and discord within, with a much greater revenue from imports. These are great and commanding advantages, in estimating the relative strength of communities. Nor would we be weakened, as it is generally supposed by the possession of slaves. The most powerful people that ever existed, in proportion to numbers, the Romans, were far greater slave-holders, than we are, while slavery exists with us in a form much less calculated to weaken, and more calculated to strengthen, than with them. That our people possess equal courage, skill and capacity to endure the fatigues and exposure of military life, the recent war with Mexico abundantly prove[s]. They have at least equalled in all these respects, troops from the North.

But notwithstanding we have so much less to fear from disunion, we are profoundly anxious to preserve the Union, if it can be done consistently with our liberty and safety. It is for you to say by your acts: whether it can be preserved on these conditions, or not. I say by your acts; for we have been too often deceived to rely on promises or pledges. The only proof we can accept, is for you to desist from your agitation and assaults on our rights and to respect the compromises of the Constitution. Until that is done, there can be no security for either our liberty or safety in the Union; and until we are secure in them, we are bound by the highest obligation of duty to ourselves, and our posterity, to continue our resistance to your assaults and to adopt whatever measures may be necessary to make it successful.

From the Pendleton, S.C., *Messenger*, October 20, 1848, pp. 1–2. Also printed in the Charleston, S.C., *Mercury*, October 26, 1848, p. 2; the Charleston, S.C., *Courier*, October 25, 1848, p. 2; the Washington, D.C., *Daily National Intelligencer*, November 1, 1848, pp. 1–2; the Washington, D.C., *Daily Union*, November 9, 1848, p. 2; the Greenville, S.C., *Mountaineer*, November 10, 1848, pp. 1, 4; Crallé, ed., *Works*, 4:513–535 (misdated 8/12/1849). Partly printed in Wilson, ed., *The Essential Calhoun*, pp. 389–390. Variant in the Baltimore, Md., *Sun*, August 12, 1848, p. 4; the Charleston, S.C., *Courier*, August 14, 1848, p. 2; the Charleston, S.C., *Mercury*, August 14, 1848, p. 2; the Richmond, Va., *Enquirer*, August 15, 1848, p. 1. Another variant in the New York, N.Y., *Herald*, August 12, 1848, p. 3; the Richmond, Va., *Whig and Public Advertiser*, August 25, 1848, p. 1. Another variant in *Congressional Globe*, 30th Cong., 1st Sess., p. 1060; Houston, ed., *Proceedings and Debates*, p. 1015. NOTE: Charles M. Wiltse comments rightly (*John C. Calhoun*, 3:354) that this was one of Calhoun's "greatest speeches, as profound, as solemn and foreboding in its tone as any words he had ever uttered." Wiltse also recognized (p. 537) that the speech presents more than usually challenging textual and contextual problems. The Senate proceedings on the Oregon bill in the last week of the session were hectic (with night sessions), complicated by amendment and maneuver, and sketchily recorded. The speech given on August 10 could not have had much advance preparation. Ordinarily, Calhoun would have looked over a reporter's notes within a few days after the speech was given and prepared a version for publication. That was not possible on this occasion. According to the Pendleton *Messenger*, Calhoun brought the notes home with him, and when time allowed, prepared a version for publication in the *Messenger*, which he knew would be reprinted elsewhere. Whether the "notes" were Calhoun's own or those of a reporter is not clear, but we would surmise the latter. This speech may be more of a studied literary composition after the fact than was generally true of Calhoun's speeches. By the time the session was over, of course, Calhoun's purpose was not to create a verbatim transcript of the hectic debates but to give his sentiments to the public in the most effective form.

From Geo[rge] H. Thatcher

Ballston Centre [N.Y.,] August 10th 1848

Hon. Sir, Your polite note in acknowledgement of my letter was duly received. I should have written again long ere this, but I held back for the purpose of seeing the effect of the Treaty upon the North, & also for the nominations—particularly that of the Buffalo Convention. It is with a sad heart that I now write you. Sad from its forebodings. I hope you will not deem it presumption in me if I address you in a tone of familiar confidence though I have not the honor of an intimate acquaintance. And I do so because I entertain for your character both as a man of integrity & as a patriot the profoundest respect; & also because I believe you will use the information & the facts I lay before you for the good of the *whole* country.

When I wrote you before, the prospects of peace were dark; & the eventual subjugation & annexation of Mexico began to be seriously entertained as a project by no small portion of our Northern politicians. Attempts were made to reconcile the North to this on the ground that the *effect* would be ultimately to overthrow slavery. *How* I endeavoured to explain to you in my former communication. But the Treat thwarted this project at its inception. For a time the opponnents of slavery were much perplexed as to the *precise form* of opposition it would be best to adopt; but have now settled down on the platform of the Buffalo Convention. A crisis is now indeed at hand, & if not averted by the action of the present Congress, it will put the strength of our Union to a severer test than it has ever before encountered; & even, if Congress adopt the Missouri Compromise, extending the line through to the Pacific, it will not wholly take the wind out of the sails of that great Northern organization that is fast forming under the auspices of Mr. [Martin] Van Buren. You will of course perceive at a glance that my apprehensions are all associated with this pregnant movement. Should Congress adjourn without settling the question of slavery extension, you need not be surprised if this party sweep ["all" *interlined*] the Northern & perhaps the entire free States. Whatever the leading presses of the two great parties may say, this movement is not a trifling matter; & the result will verify what I assert. Many things concur to give this organization a formidable character & to precipitate the great crisis which the anxious eyes of our sagacious statesmen have long anticipated. 1st The division in the Democratic party. Those known as Barnburners, beyond a doubt, constitute the largest portion of the party in this State, & they have sympathizers in other States that, in point of numbers are not to be despised. 2nd The *masses* of the Democratic party have but little confidence in the political integrity & *stability* of Gen. [Lewis] Cass. His *former* course on the Proviso & his *present* position appear to them too glaringly inconsistent to be reconciled with strict purity of motive. Hence in innumerable instances, those who, in former years, have been known as the staunchest adherents of the party have come out in open opposition, while thousands of others—the rank & file are in a state of utter indifference, or rather in a transition state. They are going over to Van Buren by thousands.

3d The *masses* of the Whig party at the North are disgusted with the nomination of Gen. [Zachary] Taylor. Their political attachments to Mr. [Henry] Clay had assumed so much the character of personal friendship that they feel most deeply wounded. Added to this is a *distrust* of Gen. T[aylor]'s political orthodoxy. They feel that in his nomination there was a virtual abandonment of the great *issues* of the party. Hence, say they, we are under *no obligation* to support him. But when they associate with this the idea, which they almost invariably do, that the nomination was a *Southern* movement, their resentment rises to exasperation. "What!" say they, "is there to be no end of this? Have the South a perpetual right to the presidency? Are they not satisfied with having the presidency more than three fourths of the time since the foundation of the government? And a corresponding proportion of the offices of the government? Are ["we" *interlined*] to be continually subject to the dictation of a *minority* of the population of this country? Must we who pay the great burthen of the taxes be continually cheated out of ["their" *changed to* "our"] rights? Will the South eternally presume upon our forbearance? No—give us a leader, no matter who, & we will resist. We will bear it no longer." Such is the *spirit* of their language. But as they have no *Whig* candidate of their own besides Gen. T[aylor] they too are coming out for Van Buren—regarding him as the only resource left.

4th There is a remarkable increase of hostility to slavery among *all* classes of our population within the last four years. Besides the constant efforts of ecclesiastical bodies, lecturers, anti-slavery politicians, presses &c &c, this feeling has been greatly increased by the Mexican war. Religious men look upon that war as both unjust & needless, & the impression is very general that it was waged for the benefit of slavery. Hence they ask Is it not time something was done to arrest the aggressions of slavery? Here let me remark, that had your Southern brethren listened more to your advice on the subject of the Mexican war, all classes would have been better off. Besides other disasters, it has only added fuel to the flame of sectional discord. After the admission ["of" *interlined*] Texas, they ought to have been content, or, at least, to have obtained by negociation what they have sought by war & blood. Since all is over & they can see your predictions *all* verified by the result, I hope they will now do you justice for saving the country from a war with England. That laurel, had you no other, were enough for one man to live for. If among your countrymen there be a single heart that does not warm with gratitude towards you for that act of your life, I can only say, there are baser specimens of humanity on earth than I had supposed. But to return. It is not the least deplorable consequence of the war that it has aroused to an alarming degree the sectional prejudices of the North. 5th Our old political leaders here feel chagrined that for a long series of years the South have had the Lion's share of the spoils, & are exceedingly anxious to take their revenge. "Now," say they, "we have the opportunity. We will go for Van Buren." 6th Another thing favourable to Mr. Van Buren is the position of the Catholics. He was always popular with them. He almost invariably received their vote. Then they are to a man opposed to slavery. The Irish portion of them were made Abolitionists by [Daniel] O'Connel[l] before they came here. Besides they have the impression that the Mexican war was not entirely free from the machinations of Protestants, & that the Irish soldiers were ill *used* by our generals. I might enumerate other things that tend to the same result, but it is needless. You may rest assured that Mr. Van Buren will receive a vote that will astonish the old politicians. The party presses do not *fairly* reflect the sentiments of the masses on this subject. Gen. T[aylor]'s prospects at the North are any thing but encouraging, while Cass is out of the reckoning. Van Buren, I think, will get enough to carry the election into the House, & then, as parties will be so nearly divided, the balance of power will lie very much in your own hands. For the eleven votes of South Carolina may then be cast by *one man* (i.e. in effect) on a more important theatre than it was a few weeks ago in Baltimore. I place these facts before you that you may use them if you deem them of any importance. Great events are in store. You cannot be too well prepared for them. When the decisive hour arrives I hope there will be a conciliatory disposition on all sides.

It would gratify me to hear again from you. If you wish to propose any questions in regard to movements at the North, I will endeavour to answer them to the best of my ability. I presume I might ["not" *interlined*] agree with you altogether on questions of policy; but I will answer you in all candour & fairness. Meantime I subscribe myself, & shall remain Yours truly, Geo. H. Thatcher.

ALS in ScCleA.

From W[illia]m Willis

Farrsville Virginia, Aug. 10th 1848

Dear Sir, Owing to the long lapse of time no Doubt you may have forgotten me and even at this late Hour I fear I shall be trespassing on your Patience. It is now about 26 years since I was in your Presence at Washington. My Business there at that time was to get some Patent Rights and in order to aid me in the Despatch of such I Procured A Letter from Friend [Eldred] Simkins of South Carolina asking your assistance. I shall have to trouble you once more Wishing to learn from the Dead Letter Office if there is any ["Thing" *interlined*] Remaining there for me. It may be necessary to add that I was Bred & Born in Charlestown South Carolina. And now I am done with the Present and shall Interest you with something else. I noticed in one of the Public News Papers that the Shade Trees on Avanue Walk was threaten[e]d by A small Worm that was about to prove Fatal to the Foliage of the Same and that theay were About to Send North for Birds in order to Rid them of Such A Pest. I have this Season Hit upon A Plan which completely expels every thing of the kind and shall Inform you of the Result In order that you may test the Same. Respectfully Your, Wm. Willis.

[Enclosure]

Remedy for Fruit and Shade Trees

I have Around my House Several Shade Trees and which have been moore or less Attacked every Summer by the Catterpillers. This Summer as the Catterpiller Season came on I took pieces of Woolen Cloth and Greased them well Then took Sulpher and Sprinkled over the Same Rubbing it in at the Same ["time" *canceled*] time. Those I fastened in the Crotch of the Trees with Nails. The Result was that in A Short time theay Disappeared and might be Seen Retreating down the Tree and what ["to"(?) *canceled*] proves this more fully the Fly or Miller has entered the House at Night and Deposited its Eggs on the Window Curt[a]ins and have witnessed their Hatching of Young ones.

I wish you to Communicate this to the Proprietor of the Patent Office Considering this as one of the best modes of using Sulpher in this manner. Numer[o]us has been the Experiments to expell this Curculio I think this will have the Desired Effect. And here the Cotton Planter may make good use of the Same in Expelling the Catterpiller from his Fields and the gard[e]ner may Profit by It Likewise. The Atmosphere is so Pregnant with Sulpher where this Application is made use of that the Fly Cannot approach near enough to Deposite its Eggs. I have Just answered to a Call I noticed In the Dollar News Paper from North Carolina. I have considered this matter for years, cannot something be done to expel from our Orchards and our Fields Such a Pest so Ruinous[?] I think I have hit upon one which will have the Desired Effect in so doing. Wm. Willis.

[P.S.] This ["is" *interlined*] all written without the use of Glasses as I have no use for them at all and now ["being" *canceled*] am uppords of Fifty years of Age having overcome the Same by Perseverance. Wm. Willis.

ALS with En in ScCleA. NOTE: An AEU by Calhoun reads, "Preserving fruit Trees & & &c from catterpillars."

TO THO[MAS] G. CLEMSON, [Brussels]

Washington, 11th Aug[us]t 1848

My dear Sir, I herewith enclose the first of the duplicate of a bill of exchange for £130 drawn by the firm of Co[r]c[o]ran & Riggs on George Peabody of London.

Congress will adjourn on the 14th Inst., & I shall leave immediately after for home.

Nothing very material has occurred since my last. The Oregon territorial bill from the House was passed last evening by the Senate with an amendment attaching the Missouri Compromise to it. It is doubtful whether the House will agree to it, or not. If it should not the bill will be lost.

The Buffalo Convention is in session, & has, it is said, nominated [Martin] Van Buren. It is uncertain to what it will lead. If the movement should not run out with the election, it will lead to the formation of two great sectional parties, & that to results, which may lead to great changes.

The election thus far, judging from indications, is more favourable to [Lewis] Cass, than [Zachary] Taylor. I retain & intend to retain my independent position.

We shall anxiously wait to see you all. With love to Anna [Maria Calhoun Clemson] & the children, I am your affectionate father, J.C. Calhoun.

ALS in ScCleA; PEx in Jameson, ed., *Correspondence*, pp. 760–761.

REMARKS ON THE PAYMENT OF MEXICAN CLAIMS

[In the Senate, August 11, 1848]

[*Under consideration was a bill to carry out provisions of the Mexican peace treaty in regard to U.S. claimants against Mexico, and particularly a proposal to appropriate funds out of the Treasury to pay off a certain group of claimants.*]

Mr. Calhoun said there was no stipulation of the *treaty* which provided for the payment of this $900,000 out of any other fund than the $3,250,000—the government did not owe it, and it could not be exacted of them—and if it were to be taken from the $3,250,000, it would be an act of gross injustice to the other claimants to pay it full, with interest.

[*There was further discussion.*]

Mr. Calhoun still objected that a discrimination was made between the unliquidated claims. Part were thus to be paid *in full*, from the treasury, and others pro rata from the $3,250,000. He should vote against the amendment, and then against the section itself.

From the Baltimore, Md., *Sun*, August 14, 1848, p. 4. Also printed in the Charleston, S.C., *Courier*, August 17, 1848, p. 2. Variant in *Congressional Globe*, 30th Cong., 1st Sess., p. 1067; Houston, ed., *Proceedings and Debates*, p. 1021.

Amendment to the Mexican claims bill, 8/11. Calhoun offered the following amendment: "*Provided*, That this section shall be construed to provide for the payment only of such awards or parts of awards, without interest, as were concurred in by both the American commissioners on the part of the United States [in a convention of 1839]: *And provided further*, That the payments provided for by this section, shall be made out of any money in the treasury not otherwise appropriated, or in stock of the United States, bearing interest at six per cent. per annum, as the President may direct." (The amendment was adopted 31 to 7.) PC in *Senate Journal*, 30th Cong., 1st Sess., pp. 573–574; Ms. draft in DNA, RG 46 (U.S. Senate), 30A-B2.

Remarks on a measure to exempt newspapers from postage, 8/11. "Mr. Calhoun suggested that the Senate should be very careful not to embarrass the whole machinery of the Post Office Department. These provisions exempting newspapers from postage, might seriously affect the revenue." From Houston, ed., *Proceedings and Debates*, p. 1022. Also printed in *Congressional Globe*, 30th Cong., 1st Sess., p. 1068.

From Mrs. E[STHER] M. SHUBRICK

Charleston, August 11th [18]48

Sir, Precious as your time is I must beg a moment to express the gratitude felt by myself and son [Edward R. Shubrick] for the kindness you have testified towards us. Aware of the many pressing demands upon your attention at present, the friends who take an interest in my family fully appreciate the prompt & energetic efforts you have made in his behalf.

As to myself I fear to give words to the sentiments ["with which" *canceled*] they have inspired, least to one of so calm and cool a judgment as yourself, they appear exag[g]erated. I shall therefore only allow myself to say that you have made me a bankrupt & I must call upon Heaven to pay the debt, and if the prayer of the widow & orphan is heard not a thorn of the many knit with the flowers which compose the wreath of civic fame shall ever be allowed to pierce your brows and—I was about to add, the wish of Moore for his friend viz. That while treading the path of life the side that the sun's upon may be yours. But the wish is only a poet's dream; in a life which by the will of God many dark shadows must lie in the path of every man, our prayer shall be that the recollection of the good you have done while toiling on the rough road of political distinction may dispell the shadows ["ere their gloom is felt" *interlined*] and that the State's Right oak may be spared to afford its protection in the storms which are gathering over our Southern States. Believe me Sir with the highest respect and admiration one of your most grateful constituents, E.M. Shubrick.

ALS in ScCleA. NOTE: An AEU by Calhoun reads "Mrs. Shubrick." Edward Rutledge Shubrick was a Midshipman in the Navy from 2/9/1849 until he resigned on 4/26/1853. His father, Capt. Edward Rutledge Shubrick, was one of four brothers who served as Naval officers; he died at sea on 3/12/1844.

FURTHER REMARKS ON THE OREGON BILL

[In the Senate, August 12, 1848]
[*The majority in the House of Representatives had refused the compromise amendments the Senate had made and continued to adhere to the absolute prohibition of slavery from the territories. This left the Senate with only a few choices. Defeat the bill and leave Oregon without a legal government; ask for a committee of conference; or acquiesce in the House version.*]

Mr. Calhoun expressed his apprehension that there was a fixed majority in this Senate and in the House opposed to any further trial at conciliation. Still he hoped the Senate would preserve a correct position, and vote for the appointment of a committee of conference. He might say, without any self-flattery, that he had all along foreseen this result. Let those who opposed the views of the South lay their cause before the country, and defend it as they could. The great strife between the North and South is ended. The North is determined to exclude the property of the slaveholder, and of course the slaveholder himself, from its territory. On this point there seems to be no division in the North. In the South, he regretted to say, there was some division of sentiment. The effect of this determination of the North was to convert all the southern population into slaves; and he would never consent to entail that disgrace on his posterity. He denounced any southern man who would not take the same course. Gentlemen were greatly mistaken if they supposed the Presidential question in the South would override this more important one. The separation of the North and the South is completed. The South has now a most solemn obligation to perform—to herself—to the Constitution—to the Union. She is bound to come to a decision not to permit this to go on any further, but to show that, dearly as she prizes the Union, there are questions which she regards as of greater importance than the Union. She is bound to fulfill her obligations as she may best understand them. This is not a question of territorial government, but a question involving the continuance of the Union. Perhaps it was better that this question should come to an end, in order that some new point should be taken.

He had given what he deemed a clear constitutional vote on the compromise bill. He had also voted for the introduction of the Missouri compromise into this bill; although he could not constitutionally vote for the bill, which he regarded as artificial. Gentlemen may do with this bill as they please. If they will not give now what the South asks as a compromise, she will, at the next session, demand all, and will not be satisfied with anything less.

[*Debate continued. Samuel Houston of Texas "regretted" that Calhoun had used "menacing language against the Union."*]

Mr. Calhoun explained that he used no menace. He spoke of his own position.

[*There was more debate, and a difference of opinion over whether the bill could be referred back to the Committee on the Territories at this stage of proceedings.*]

Mr. Calhoun said the reference would be in conformity with parliamentary rule. The committee might propose to retain some, and recede from other amendments.

From *Congressional Globe*, 30th Cong., 1st Sess., pp. 1074–1076. Also printed in the Washington, D.C., *Daily Union*, August 13, 1848, p. 2; the Washington, D.C., *Daily National Intelligencer*, August 14, 1848, p. 1; Houston, ed., *Proceedings and Debates*, pp. 1024–1025; Benton, *Abridgment of Debates*, 16:250–251. Variant in the Baltimore, Md., *Sun*, August 14, 1848, p. 4; the Charleston, S.C., *Courier*, August 17, 1848, p. 2; the Charleston, S.C., *Mercury*, August 17, 1848, p. 2. Variant in the New York, N.Y., *Herald*, August 14, 1848, p. 4; the Richmond, Va., *Whig and Public Advertiser*, August 29, 1848, p. 1. Another variant in the New York, N.Y., *Herald*, August 15, 1848, p. 4; the Richmond, Va., *Whig and Public Advertiser*, September 1, 1848, p. 1. NOTE: The first cited New York *Herald* report of this day's proceedings describes Calhoun as sharply and successfully calling Thomas H. Benton to order for digressing from the question on the floor.

FINAL REMARKS ON THE OREGON BILL

[In the Senate, August 14, 1848]

[*On the last day of the session, an effort was underway to pass the House version of the bill and send it to the President before adjournment, which required suspension of a longstanding joint rule.*]

Mr. Calhoun said, if there was any responsibility, it was on the majority, and not on the minority. By the rules of the Senate, the Oregon bill was lost, and the majority well knew that. They felt conscious of the fact, and therefore they had added all the other bills to it in this resolution; and thereby they had assumed the responsibility of all the consequences. The existing rule on their Journal was a convincing proof that the Senate was of opinion that it was improper to send bills to the President on the last day of a session, as he could not sign them off-hand. There might be great constitutional questions involved, requiring great consideration, and the Constitution allows him ten days to decide upon bills. But they proposed to send this bill to him on the last day of the session; and if there ever was a bill that ought not to be pressed on the President to decide instanter, this was one. How long had it been before them? Some five or six weeks; and they had even violated the day of rest, which was not regarded as a legal day; and yet they would send it to the President one hour and a half before the adjournment of Congress. That was all the time they proposed to allow him. He understood what was the great point of contest between parties in that House. The opposite party wanted to have the absolute, despotic control over the Territories. They knew there was not such an example to be found in all the legislation of this country. They all knew that the Missouri compromise would not have passed, but that the North were anxious to protect themselves by the adoption of the line of 36°30'. And how was it on the admission of Texas?

Mr. [Reverdy] Johnson, of Maryland, suggested to the Senator from South Carolina to make a motion.

Mr. Calhoun said he would. After some other observations, he said this was the first time the Wilmot proviso had ever been attempted to be carried into effect. He concluded by moving to strike out from the resolution all that part of it which relates to the Oregon bill, and on that motion he called for the yeas and nays.

[*Calhoun's motion was defeated 20 to 37, and after further proceedings the resolution from the House of Representatives was adopted.*]

From *Congressional Globe*, 30th Cong., 1st Sess., p. 1084. Also printed in the Washington, D.C., *Daily National Intelligencer*, August 15, 1848, p. 2; Houston, ed., *Proceedings and Debates*, p. 1030. Variant in the Washington, D.C., *Union*, August 15, 1848, p. 2. Another variant in the Baltimore, Md., *Sun*, August 15, 1848, p. 4; the Charleston, S.C., *Courier*, August 18, 1848, p. 2; the Charleston, S.C., *Mercury*, August 18, 1848, p. 2; the Richmond, Va., *Enquirer*, August 18, 1848, p. 4; the Columbia, S.C., *South-Carolinian*, August 22, 1848, p. 2. NOTE: Most of the sources cited reported brief remarks earlier in this day's debate in which Calhoun had defended Hopkins L. Turney of Tenn. against Daniel Webster's effort to call him out of order.

SYMBOLS

◫

The following symbols have been used in this volume as abbreviations for the forms in which documents of John C. Calhoun have been found and for the repositories in which they are preserved. (Full citations to printed sources of documents can be found in the Bibliography.)

Abs	—abstract (a summary)
ADS	—autograph document, signed
ADU	—autograph document, unsigned
AES	—autograph endorsement, signed
AEU	—autograph endorsement, unsigned
ALS	—autograph letter, signed
ALU	—autograph letter, unsigned
AU	—University of Alabama, Tuscaloosa
CSmH	—Huntington Library, San Marino, Cal.
CtY	—Yale University, New Haven, Conn.
DLC	—Library of Congress, Washington
DNA	—National Archives, Washington
DS	—document, signed
En	—enclosure
Ens	—enclosures
EU	—endorsement, unsigned
FC	—file copy (usually a letterbook copy retained by the sender)
GU	—University of Georgia, Athens
ICHi	—Chicago Historical Society, Chicago, Ill.
InND	—University of Notre Dame, South Bend, Ind.
LS	—letter, signed
M-	—(followed by a number) published microcopy of the National Archives
NcD	—Duke University, Durham, N.C.
NcU	—Southern Historical Collection, University of North Carolina, Chapel Hill
NHi	—New-York Historical Society, New York City
NIC	—Cornell University, Ithaca, N.Y.
NjP	—Princeton University, Princeton, N.J.
NNC	—Columbia University, New York City
PC	—printed copy
PDS	—printed document, signed
PEx	—printed extract
PHi	—Historical Society of Pennsylvania, Philadelphia

RG	—Record Group in the National Archives
ScC	—Charleston Library Society, Charleston, S.C.
ScCleA	—Clemson University, Clemson, S.C.
ScU-SC	—South Caroliniana Library, University of South Carolina, Columbia
ViLxW	—Washington and Lee University, Lexington, Va.

BIBLIOGRAPHY

〖〗

This Bibliography is limited to sources of and previous printings of documents published in this volume.

Aderman, Ralph M., ed., *Letters of James Kirke Paulding*. Madison: University of Wisconsin Press, 1962.

Alexandria, Va., *Gazette*, 1808–.

American Quarterly Register and Magazine. Philadelphia: 1848–1851.

American Review. New York City: 1845–1852.

Anderson, John M., ed., *Calhoun: Basic Documents*. State College, Pa.: Bald Eagle Press, 1952.

Anderson, S.C., *Gazette*, 1843–1855.

Athens, Ga., *Southern Banner*, 1831–?.

Baltimore, Md., *Sun*, 1837–.

Benton, Thomas H., ed., *Abridgment of the Debates of Congress*. 16 vols. New York: D. Appleton & Co., 1854–1861.

Boucher, Chauncey S., and Robert P. Brooks, eds., *Correspondence Addressed to John C. Calhoun, 1837–1849*, in the *American Historical Association Annual Report* for 1929. Washington: U.S. Government Printing Office, 1930.

Camden, S.C., *Journal*, 1826–1891?.

Catalogue of Autograph Letters, Play Bills, Books, Signatures. Syracuse, N.Y.: published by John Heise, 1909.

Catalogue of Autographs and Manuscripts, No. 69. New York: Dodd, Mead & Co., 1903.

Charleston, S.C., *Courier*, 1803–1852.

Charleston, S.C., *Mercury*, 1822–1868.

Charleston, S.C., *Southern Baptist*, 1846–1860.

Charleston, S.C., *Southern Patriot*, 1814–1848.

Collection of Autographs of James L. Foote, of Slatington, Pa. New York: Anderson Auction Co., 1911.

Columbia, S.C., *South-Carolinian*, 1838–1849?.

Columbia, S.C., *Telegraph*, 1847–1851.

Congressional Globe . . . 1833–1873 . . . . 46 vols. Washington: Blair & Rives and others, 1834–1873.

Crallé, Richard K., ed., *The Works of John C. Calhoun*. 6 vols. Columbia, S.C.: A.S. Johnston, 1851, and New York: D. Appleton & Co., 1853–1857.

De Bow's Review. New Orleans: 1846–1880.

Edgefield, S.C., *Advertiser*, 1836–.

Georgetown, S.C., *Winyah Observer*, 1841–1852.

Greenville, S.C., *Mountaineer*, 1829–1901.

Houston, James A., ed., *Proceedings and Debates of the United States Senate. First Session—Thirtieth Congress.* Washington: 1848.

Huntsville, Ala., *Democrat,* 1823–1853?.

Jameson, J. Franklin, ed., *Correspondence of John C. Calhoun,* in the *American Historical Association Annual Report* for 1899, 2 vols. Washington: U.S. Government Printing Office, 1900, vol. II.

"John C. Calhoun and the Unification of Germany," in the *American Historical Review,* vol. XL, no. 3 (April, 1935), pp. 477–478.

Lence, Ross M., ed., *Union and Liberty: The Political Philosophy of John C. Calhoun.* Indianapolis: Liberty Press, 1992.

Liverpool, England, *Chronicle,* 1828–1868.

Louisville, Ky., *Courier,* 1843–1868.

McIntosh, James T., et al., eds., *The Papers of Jefferson Davis.* 9 vols to date. Baton Rouge: Louisiana State University Press, 1971–.

Memphis, Tenn., *Daily Appeal,* 1847–1890.

Merchant's Magazine and Commercial Review, The. New York: 1839–1870.

Nashville, Tenn., *Whig,* 1838–1855.

New York, N.Y., *Courier and Enquirer,* 1827–1861.

New York, N.Y., *Herald,* 1835–1924.

New York, N.Y., *Journal of Commerce,* 1827–1892?.

Niles' Register. Baltimore: 1811–1849.

Pendleton, S.C., *Messenger,* 1807–?.

Philadelphia, Pa., *Pennsylvania Freeman,* 1843–1850.

Philadelphia, Pa., *Public Ledger,* 1836–1934.

Richmond, Va., *Enquirer,* 1804–1877.

Richmond, Va., *Whig,* 1824–1888.

Speeches of Mr. Calhoun, of South Carolina, on the Ten Regiment Bill; and in Reply to Mr. Davis, of Mississippi, and Mr. Cass. Delivered in the Senate of the United States, March 16 and 17, 1848. Washington: printed by John T. Towers, 1848.

Speech of Mr. Calhoun, of South Carolina, on His Resolutions in Reference to the War with Mexico. Delivered in the Senate of the United States, January 4, 1848. Washington: printed by John T. Towers, 1848.

Speech of Mr. Calhoun, of South Carolina, on the Oregon Bill. Delivered in the Senate of the United States, June 27, 1848. [Washington:] printed by [John T.] Towers, [1848].

Tallahassee, Fla., *Floridian,* 1828–1898.

Tuscaloosa, Ala., *Independent Monitor,* 1837–1872.

U.S. Senate, *Senate Documents,* 30th Congress.

U.S. Senate, *Senate Journal,* 30th Congress.

Washington, D.C., *Daily National Intelligencer,* 1800–1870.

Washington, D.C., *Union,* 1845–1859.

Wilson, Clyde N., ed., *The Essential Calhoun: Selections from Writings, Speeches, and Letters.* New Brunswick, N.J., and London: Transaction Publishers, 1992.

INDEX

Ⅱ

Abbeville District, S.C.: 54, 430, 432–
435, 577, 629.
Abd-ul-Mejid: mentioned, 574.
Abolition: xv–xvii, 10, 18, 35, 98–102,
105, 112, 137, 149, 155, 161–163,
170, 202–203, 213, 221, 267, 289,
292–294, 298, 307, 310–312, 333,
337–338, 340, 342–351, 374–375,
377–378, 386, 396–397, 410, 414–
415, 424, 444–445, 448–449, 458,
461, 464, 484, 498, 506, 521, 523–
524, 532–535, 537–538, 545–546,
560–561, 563, 566–568, 583–584,
592, 595, 606, 608–609, 611–615,
621, 630, 635–636, 644–645, 657–
674.
Abridgment of Debates: documents in,
371, 401, 451, 505, 583, 601, 630,
679.
Abstractions: xiv, xvii.
Acadia (ship): 366.
Adams, John: mentioned, 522.
Adams, John Quincy: from, 171;
mentioned, 161, 206, 262, 332, 397,
406–407, 409, 631, 653.
Adams-Onís Treaty: 155, 522, 530.
Adams, W.: mentioned, 10.
Addison, Allen B.: from, 594.
"Address of the Southern Delegates
in Congress": anticipated, 136, 291.
Africa: 162–163, 271–272, 277, 376–
378, 444–445, 547–548, 555, 613,
643.
Agnew, E. and J.W.: from, 305;
mentioned, 54.
Agriculture: in Calhoun-Clemson
family, 9, 13–14, 41, 151, 196, 199,
231, 234, 258, 262–263, 295, 298–
299, 305–307, 313, 324, 332, 356–
361, 399, 422–423, 425–426, 436–

438, 497, 499–500, 619, 628, 641,
651; mentioned, 21–22, 44, 58, 78,
111, 145–146, 148, 257, 261, 297–
298, 433, 478, 492, 575, 598–599,
602–603, 613–614, 624–625, 629,
647, 652; Southern, 34, 43, 257,
286, 288, 325–326, 454–455, 464,
507–513, 533, 580, 614–615, 635,
637, 660, 670, 675–676.
Aiken, S.C.: 9, 263, 289, 446, 449.
Alabama: xix, 13, 22–25, 43, 149, 156–
158, 167, 176–177, 187–188, 191–
192, 197, 205, 213–217, 257–258,
315, 324, 331–332, 337, 339–340,
356, 374, 380, 399–400, 422–423,
426–427, 437, 458, 462, 469–470,
482–483, 494–497, 499–500, 507–
513, 564–568, 590, 595, 637–639,
654; Senators from (*see* Bagby,
Arthur P.; Lewis, Dixon H.).
Alabama River: 332.
Alaska: 276, 278, 406–407.
Albany, N.Y.: 273, 311, 602, 652.
Albany, N.Y., *Atlas*: mentioned, 544.
Albion, Ill.: 473.
Aleutian Islands: 278.
Alexander, J.H.: from, 642.
Alexandria, Va.: 163, 174–175.
Alexandria, Va., *Gazette and Virginia
Advertiser*: documents in, 28, 48,
53, 54, 235, 259, 282, 342, 371, 383,
393, 401, 420.
Allen, Lewis F.: from, 598, 602; to,
624.
Allen, William: mentioned, 28–31, 50–
52, 201, 282–283, 290, 330, 590.
Alley, Saul: mentioned, 636.
Allison, J.S.: mentioned, 455, 471,
477, 576, 604, 648.

687